JOHN GAY

JOHN GAY

A Profession of Friendship

David Nokes

OXFORD UNIVERSITY PRESS

1995

Oxford University Press, Walton Street, Oxford OX2 6DP
Oxford New York
Athens Auckland Bangkok Bombay
Calcutta Cape Town Dar es Salaam Delhi
Florence Hong Kong Istanbul Karachi
Kuala Lumpur Madras Madrid Melbourne
Mexico City Nairobi Paris Singapore
Taipei Tokyo Toronto
and associated companies in
Berlin Ibadan

Oxford is a trade mark of Oxford University Press

Published in the United States
by Oxford University Press Inc., New York

British Library Cataloguing in Publication Data
Data available

Library of Congress Cataloging in Publication Data
Nokes, David.
John Gay, a profession of friendship / David Nokes.
Includes bibliographical references and index.
1. Gay, John, 1685–1732. 2. Authors, English – 18th century –
Biography. I. Title.
PR3474.N64 1995   82'.5–dc20   [B]   94–5384
ISBN 0–19–812971–8

1 3 5 7 9 10 8 6 4 2

Typeset by Datix International Limited
Bungay, Suffolk
Printed in Great Britain
on acid-free paper by
Biddles Ltd.,
Guildford and King's Lynn

For Janet

All this we must do, to comply with the
taste of the town.

(*The Beggar's Opera*, III. xvi)

PREFACE

IT is over fifty years since the last full-length biography of John Gay appeared. In that time, although *The Beggar's Opera* has successfully maintained its reputation as a favourite of the theatrical repertoire, its author has been chiefly honoured by a respectful silence. During the past half-century Gay's life and works have attracted a steady trickle of academic monographs; but successive revolutions in post-war critical taste, which have done so much to revitalize the reputations of his contemporaries Pope and Swift, have left Gay virtually untouched. Like his Beggar, Gay endures an awkward in-between status; deemed too marginal and plebeian in his literary offerings to command the attention of the Eng. Lit. critical heavyweights, yet too patrician in his social aspirations to enlist the sympathies of those eager to champion the unheard voices of the eighteenth century's literary underclass, women, servants, and the provincial poor.

My own fascination with the lives of the great Augustan satirists dates back some twenty-five years, to the time when I began my Cambridge doctoral research study of the Scriblerus Club. Ten years ago I published a biography of Swift entitled *Jonathan Swift: A Hypocrite Reversed*. The writing of that book was a bewitching task; the engagement with such a formidable personality was full of unexpected pleasures, as well as uncomfortable moments of self-examination. Yet, even as I wrote it, I never lost my curiosity for the career of Swift's less-celebrated Scriblerian companion; indeed, writing the life of Swift enabled me to gain a much clearer understanding of the essential similarities and differences between the characters of these two satirists and friends.

The chief inspiration for beginning serious work on this book came from my participation in the 1985 John Gay Tercentenary Conference held at Durham University's Collingwood College. The organizers of that conference, Peter Lewis and Nigel Wood, subsequently edited a collection of several of these conference papers in a volume entitled *John Gay and the Scriblerians* (London, 1988). As will become obvious throughout this biography, I am heavily indebted to the insights generated by these contributions, and I wish to offer my thanks to the conference organizers and to the various participants including Stephen Copley, Alan Downie, Brean Hammond, Ian Haywood, Yvonne Noble, Claude Rawson, Carolyn Williams, and Tom Woodman. One other participant, Pat Rogers, requires special thanks for having been a constant source of information and inspiration for my own work on eighteenth-century literature over the past twenty years. Other friends and colleagues who have helped me with informal advice include Gerald Baker, Ian Bell, Tom Deveson, Paul Fussell, Jocelyn Harris, Adam Phillips, and Angus Ross. Bill Speck drew my attention to Gay's unpublished letter to Burlington among the Chatsworth MSS, and Howard Erskine-Hill, with his unrivalled knowledge of Pope's life and works, has provided much invaluable advice.

My search for new documentary records of Gay's life was assisted by the staffs of numerous libraries and archives. I should like to acknowledge the help I received at Barnstaple, Gay's birthplace, from J. M. Rowe, Head Librarian, and the staff of the North Devon Record Office, from Peter Boyd, Museums Officer of the North Devon Athenaeum, from M. C. Taylor, Barnstaple Town Clerk, from Dr Alison Grant, and from Professor Joyce Youings, former President of the Devonshire Association. Mr Anthony Pretor-Pinney kindly gave me permission to study and make quotations from his family manuscripts, the 'Pinney Papers', currently lodged in Bristol University Library. Mr Richard Williams, Librarian of Birkbeck College and Curator of the Mapledurham Papers, allowed me to study and make quotations from the unpublished Mapledurham MSS. My thanks are due to the Trustees of the Chatsworth Settlement for permission to include Gay's letter to Burlington, and, in particular, to Mr Peter Day, Keeper of the Devonshire Collections at Chatsworth, for his help in my researches there. I should also like to acknowledge the assistance of Miss J. Coburn, Head Archivist of the Greater London Record Office, of Miss J. Swarbrick, Chief Archivist of the City of Westminster, and of the staff of the Victoria Library, of Dr G. A. Knight, Principal Archivist of Lincolnshire County Council, and of Norman Leveritt, Honorary Curator of the Gentlemen's Society of Spalding. Above all, my thanks are due to the staffs of the Public Record Office in Chancery Lane, of London University's Institute of Historical Research, of the Library of the Victoria and Albert Museum, and of the Department of Manuscripts of the British Library.

Fortunately, the general critical neglect of Gay's writings has not inhibited the enthusiasm of editors, who have produced handsome modern editions of all his works. I am indebted to C. F. Burgess for his edition of *The Letters of John Gay* (Oxford, 1966), to Vinton A. Dearing for *John Gay: Poetry and Prose* (Oxford, 1974), and to John Fuller for *John Gay: Dramatic Works* (Oxford, 1983). My own practice in this biography has been to modernize all quotations (except when quoting from a previously unpublished manuscript); but my work has been enormously assisted by the scholarly labours of Gay's Oxford editors in establishing texts of his writings.

It has always been Gay's fate to be the victim of his own ambivalence; too often he appears as a courtier *manqué*, a deferential literary aide-de-camp, and accidental satirist, dutifully imitating the idioms of his more celebrated friends. In this biography it is precisely that ambivalence which I endeavour to explore; that fatal lack of self-belief which can undermine the most accomplished literary talent, and that self-deprecating search for affection and acceptance which places friendship before fame, and domestic comfort before the uncertain rewards of literary notoriety. Part of the intention in writing this book was to explore the inner life of a man whose literary career so poignantly exemplifies the enduring realities of social and personal compromise that frequently, and intimately, affect a writer's work. If Gay's life contains fewer moments of sublime literary inspiration than the careers of those whose biographies more habitually claim our attention, it will, I hope, strike a chord with many who recognize within it some unheroic and uncomfortable truths about the life of writing. Although sheltered by the possession of a tenured academic post, my understanding of the precarious vicissitudes of Gay's literary career has undoubtedly been enhanced by my own occasional participation in the hectic and volatile world of television writing. And I should like to offer thanks to those whose friendship and example have helped me to find my way through this modern Grub Street: they include Robert Bierman, Ruth Caleb, Hanif Kureishi, Kevin Loader, Tristram Powell, and David Profumo.

Finally, my research for this book was greatly assisted by a grant from the Leverhulme Trust. I wish to express my thanks for that, and to my Head of Department, Professor Janet Bately, for allowing me sabbatical leave from my teaching and administrative duties. I was also helped by two part-time research assistants, Jeremy Tagg and Janet Barron. My indebtedness to Janet Barron is easily the greatest of all. Not only did she assist me in searching through the archives of Barnstaple and Chatsworth, but, as my partner throughout the years that I have been working on this book, she has provided constant encouragement, sympathy, and support. Appropriately, this book is dedicated to her.

London   D.N.

1994

CONTENTS

PART III. A Free Man (1728–1732)

LIST OF ILLUSTRATIONS

ABBREVIATIONS

Arbuthnot, *Works*	*The Miscellaneous Works of Dr. Arbuthnot* (2 vols., Glasgow, 1750–1)
Ault	Norman Ault, *New Light on Pope* (London, 1949)
Baratier	*Lettres inédites de Bolingbroke à Lord Stair 1716–1720*, ed. Paul Baratier, Paris, 1939)
Calamy	Edmund Calamy, *The Nonconformist's Memorial*, abridged and corrected by Samuel Palmer (2 vols., London, 1775)
Dearing	John Gay, *Poetry and Prose*, ed. Vinton A. Dearing, with the assistance of Charles E. Beckwith (2 vols., Oxford, 1974)
Deutsch	Otto Erich Deutsch, *Handel: A Documentary Biography* (London, 1955)
Faber	*The Poetical Works of John Gay*, ed. G. C. Faber (London, 1926)
Fontaine	*A Tale of the Huguenots; or, Memoirs of a French Refugee Family* (from the original manuscripts of James Fontaine), ed. F. L. Hawkes (New York, 1838)
Fuller	John Gay, *Dramatic Works*, ed. John Fuller (2 vols., Oxford, 1983)
Gribble	Joseph Besley Gribble, *Memoirs of Barnstaple* (Barnstaple, 1830)
Halsband	Robert Halsband, *The Life of Lady Mary Wortley Montagu* (Oxford, 1956; repr. 1961)
Hume	Robert D. Hume, *Henry Fielding and the London Theatre, 1728–1737* (Oxford, 1988)
Irving	W. H. Irving, *John Gay: Favorite of the Wits* (Durham, NC, 1940)
Johnson, 'Gay'	Samuel Johnson, 'Gay' in *The Lives of the English Poets* (1st pub. 1779 and 1781; Oxford University Press edn., 2 vols., Oxford, 1906, repr. 1964)
Journal	Jonathan Swift, *Journal to Stella*, ed. Harold Williams (2 vols., Oxford, 1948)
Lang	Paul Henry Lang, *George Frederic Handel* (New York, 1966)
Lees-Milne	James Lees-Milne, *Earls of Creation: Five Great Patrons of Eighteenth-Century Art* (London, 1962)

Letters	*The Letters of John Gay*, ed. C. F. Burgess (Oxford, 1966)
Lewis and Wood	Peter Lewis and Nigel Wood (eds.), *John Gay and the Scriblerians* (London, 1988)
Mack	Maynard Mack, *Alexander Pope: A Life* (New Haven, Conn., 1985)
Macklin, *Memoirs*	*Memoirs of Charles Macklin Comedian with the Dramatic Characters, Manners, Anecdotes, &c., of the Age in which he Lived*, ed. William Cooke (London, 1804)
Nicoll	Allardyce Nicoll, *A History of English Drama 1660–1900*, ii: *Early Eighteenth-Century Drama* (3rd edn., Cambridge, 1952)
Nokes	David Nokes, *Jonathan Swift: A Hypocrite Reversed* (Oxford, 1985)
Pope, *Corr.*	*The Correspondence of Alexander Pope*, ed. George Sherburn (5 vols., Oxford, 1956)
Prose Works	*The Prose Works of Jonathan Swift*, ed. Herbert Davis *et al.* (14 vols., Oxford, 1939–68)
Schultz	William Eben Schultz, *Gay's 'Beggar's Opera': Its Content, History and Influence* (New Haven, Conn., 1923)
Spence	Joseph Spence, *Observations, Anecdotes, and Characters of Books and Men*, ed. J. M. Osborn (2 vols., Oxford, 1966)
Stephens	*The Guardian*, ed. J. C. Stephens (Lexington, Ky., 1982)
Swift, *Corr.*	*The Correspondence of Jonathan Swift*, ed. Harold Williams (5 vols., Oxford, 1963–5)
Swift, *Poems*	*The Poems of Jonathan Swift*, ed. Harold Williams (3 vols., Oxford, 1937)
Winton	Calhoun Winton, *John Gay and the London Theatre* (Lexington, Ky., 1993)

I hope to bring you proof that my
friendship was not merely profession.
(Lord Courtlove, *The Distressed Wife*, I. iv)

I hope I have no occasion to make any
professions of friendship to you . . .
(Gay to Brigadier Dormer, 1725)

Introduction

> Mr Pope brought some of *The What D'Ye Call It* in his
> own handwriting to Cibber ... When it was read to the
> players, Mr Pope read it though Gay was by. Gay always
> used to read his own plays. Cibber after this, seeing a knife
> with the name of J. Gay upon it, [asked,] 'What, does Mr
> Pope make knives, too?'
>
> (Colley Cibber, 1748)

AUTHORS are out of fashion. In pronouncing the death of the
author, modern critical theory has done its best to end the personality
cult of the godlike autonomous creator of his own fictional world.[1]
Texts are not singular, but plural; they exist in a state not of being
but of becoming. Infinitely indefinite, their meanings are not fixed
immutably by some original authorial *fiat* but evolve and change
continually within a collaborative discourse of writer and readers
alike. The author does not stand outside his (or her) work, but is
subsumed within it; identity becomes text and an author's name on
a title-page has only the status of another fictive sign, within the
text's free play of signifiers.

Given the prevalence of this view, it is surprising that John Gay
has not attracted more critical attention. For Gay is the invisible
author, a kind of human pseudonym, not so much a ghost-writer as
a ghost that is written. Hostile witnesses, like Cibber, chose to
regard him as little more than a cipher, dismissing his name on a
title-page as a mere Popeian subterfuge. Gay was frequently repre-

---

[1] Roland Barthes, 'The Death of the Author' (1968), repr. in David Lodge (ed.),
Modern Critism and Theory: A Reader (London, 1988), 167–72.

sented not merely as Pope's ally, but as his alias, his willing
scapegoat, or, in a favourite well-worn simile, as a burly Ajax
shielding a malevolent and diminutive Teucer. In his verse farce
The Confederates (1717), J. D. Breval (who spiced his satire by
himself adopting the pseudonym 'J. Gay') pictured Pope gloating
secretly over his skill in making Gay take responsibility for the
'failure' of their play *Three Hours after Marriage.*

> Safe from the cudgel, [I] stand secure of praise;
> Mine is the credit, be the danger Gay's.

With monotonous regularity Gay was, and still is, denied responsibility for his 'own' works. In 1730 the *Universal Spectator* confidently
assured its readers that 'Mr Gay was not the sole author of *The
Beggar's Opera*', ascribing some of its best-known airs to either Pope
or Swift. Other songs were attributed variously to Lord Chesterfield
and Sir Charles Hanbury Williams; while the idea of having music
in the opera was ascribed not to Gay at all, but to John Rich, the
Duchess of Queensberry, and a 'junto of wits'.[2] Similarly, in 1733,
the *Daily Courant* asserted that Gay's posthumous play *Achilles* was
in fact the product of an unlikely theatrical collaboration between
Bolingbroke, Pulteney, Sir William Wyndham, the Duke of Queensberry, Arbuthnot, and Pope. 'Mr Gay', it pronounced, 'could not
deviate into so much dulness', offering insult in the guise of praise.
Like the *Tatler*'s 'Isaac Bickerstaff' or the *Guardian*'s 'Nestor
Ironside', the name 'John Gay' seemed to identify not an individual
but a clubland institution.

Time and inadvertency merely compounded this expropriating
habit. In his *Dictionary* Johnson found a lexicographical niche for
Gay under 'motion', citing these lines from the ballad ''Twas when
the seas were roaring.'

> Cease, cease thou cruel ocean,
> And let my lover rest:
> For what's thy troubled motion
> To that within my breast?

But when Noah Webster took over the same quotation for his

---

[2] Macklin, *Memoirs*, 60. See Pope's comments to Spence: 'Dr Arbuthnot was the sole
writer of *John Bull*, and so was Gay of the *Beggar's Opera*'; and 'we now and then gave a
correction or a word or two of advice, but 'twas wholly of his own writing'. Spence, items
137 and 244; i. 57, 107.

Dictionary, he attributed it to Gray, not Gay. The lines themselves were ones which William Cowper particularly liked, but he too found it difficult to believe that Gay had written them unaided; he was 'well informed', he claimed, that 'the most celebrated association of clever fellows this country ever saw', namely Swift, Arbuthnot, Pope, and Gay, had all contributed to their composition.[3] The tradition of condescending to Gay's own literary achievements is obvious in Johnson's 'Life of Gay'.

Gay was the general favourite of the whole association of wits; but they regarded him as a playfellow rather than a partner, and treated him with more fondness than respect.[4]

Undoubtedly Gay was largely responsible for perpetuating this image of himself as a genial literary nonentity. Authorship implies authority; yet Gay's most characteristic literary persona is both self-effacing and self-mocking. A man who gives his works titles like *Trivia* and *The What D' Ye Call It* seems determined to subvert his own claims to serious literary recognition. Moreover, Gay was a natural collaborator, and several of his best-known works were both inspired in their inception and polished before publication by his fellow Scriblerians, Pope, Arbuthnot, and Swift. Where other authors seek to stamp the mark of their individual identity indelibly on every page, Gay chose the anonymity of a composite literary persona. Throughout his life he played the role of unassuming friend, a man so instinctively deferential in his tastes and opinions that he seemed almost to surrender his own identity. 'What will become of me I know not', he once confessed to a friend, 'for I have not and fear never shall have a will of my own.'[5] Naturally submissive, he would present himself in the role of aide-de-camp or acolyte. 'Gay they would call one of my élèves,' Pope liked to boast, ignoring the fact that he was actually three years younger than his 'pupil'.[6] Early on in their relationship Pope assumed the habit of deploying Gay as a willing literary lieutenant, happy to fight his battles (physical, as well as verbal) by proxy. In the dedication to *The Mohocks* Gay delivered a gratuitous snub to the critic John Dennis for no other

---

[3] Letter to Revd W. Unwin, 4 Aug. 1783; *The Correspondence of William Cowper*, ed. Thomas Wright (London, 1904), ii. 92.

[4] Johnson, 'Gay'.

[5] *Letters*, 47.

[6] Spence, item 150; i. 62.

reason than that Pope was feuding with him at the time. Three years later it was Ambrose Philips that Pope was feuding with, and Gay cheerfully chipped in with his mock-pastoral burlesque *The Shepherd's Week*. 'It is to this management of Philips that the world owes Mr. Gay's pastorals,' Pope declared, as if showing off his clever pupil's work.[7]

Gay's response to such charges was itself typically self-effacing. In the advertisement to *Trivia* (1716) he wrote: 'The world, I believe, will take so little notice of me, that I need not take much of it.' He even affected to regard such gibes as a form of back-handed compliment. The critics, he suggested, had 'allowed me an honour hitherto only shown to better writers: that of denying me to be the author of my own works'. If anything, he seemed almost to encourage, rather than prevent, such misattributions. In the advertisement to *Three Hours after Marriage* he boasted of 'the assistance I have received in this piece from two of my friends' (i.e. Pope and Arbuthnot); but when, in the event, the honour of having their names joined with Gay's turned to disgrace, he promptly volunteered for the scapegoat role. 'I will (if any shame there be)', he told Pope, 'take it all to myself.'[8]

Even in a period when anonymous and pseudonymous publication was the norm, Gay's authorial diffidence is unusual. Submerged in 'Scriblerus', 'Barnivelt', and 'Baker', manipulated by Pope, hijacked by Breval, and transliterated into Gray, his 'own' literary identity seems at best a rhetorical fiction. Though Swift's name seldom appeared on a title-page, his distinctive *voice*, however disguised in the assumed persona of a Bickerstaff, Draper, or Gulliver, was its own authoritative signature. Gay's name actually appears on more title-pages than Swift's; yet his authorial identity is far less strongly defined. Throughout his life Gay experienced an acute social diffidence, a lack of confidence which inhibited him from laying a direct claim to the dignity and status of a distinctive public identity. His treatment of his letters is indicative. Pope's *Correspondence*, like Swift's, fills five fat scholarly volumes; both men (but Pope especially) took care to marshal an official version of their letters as a public monument to their literary careers. But Gay's *Letters* (even with the inclusion of some new items published for the first time in this biography) barely fill one slim volume. Pope assembled his letters

---

[7] Pope, *Corr.* i. 229.
[8] *Letters*, 32.

both as exhibitions of epistolary art and, judiciously edited, as a form of self-justifying autobiography. But Gay, whose personal letters are themselves often collaborative compositions, made no attempt to create a public memorial from these private professions of friendship.

Just eighteen months before his death, Gay made a strange assertion to Swift:

You and I are alike in one particular, (I wish to be so in many), I mean that we hate to write upon other folk's hints. I love to have my own scheme and to treat it in my own way.[9]

Since Swift himself had provided Gay with the 'hint' for *The Beggar's Opera*, he was more than a little surprised by this claim. He wrote back to suggest that while it was 'past doubt that everyone can best find hints for himself . . . it is possible that sometimes a friend may give you a lucky one just suited to your own imagination'.[10] But the irony of Gay's claim lies in the subconscious way its style contradicts its sentiments. Even this apparent declaration of literary independence is expressed in the form of a deferential compliment, not as an assertion of selfhood, but as a wish to be *like Swift*.

In death, as in life, it was Gay's friends who took responsibility for supervising Gay's public reputation. Pope quickly determined on a policy of careful censorship. 'Our poor friend's papers are partly in my hands', he told Swift, 'and for as much as is so, I will take care to suppress things unworthy of him.'[11] Swift wholeheartedly concurred in this policy of censorship. 'I think it is incumbent upon you to see that nothing more be published of his that will lessen his reputation,' he wrote, adding: 'I would be glad to see his valuable works printed by themselves, those which ought not to be seen burned immediately.'[12] Not only Gay's writings, but also the details of his early career, were subject to the same rigorous policy of selective disclosure. In 1736 Pope did all he could to dissuade Richard Savage from publishing information about Gay's early career. 'As to that of his being apprenticed to one Willet, etc', he protested, 'what are such things to the public? Authors are to be remembered by the works and merits, not accidents of their lives.'[13] Instead of inconvenient facts Pope preferred the sublimity of symbols;

[9] Ibid. 113.
[10] Swift, *Corr.* iii. 495.
[11] Pope, *Corr.* iii. 365.
[12] Swift, *Corr.* iv. 133, 153.

witness his epitaph for Gay's monument in Westminster Abbey:

> Of manners gentle, of affections mild;
> In wit, a man; simplicity a child: . . .
> A safe companion, and an easy friend,
> Unblam'd through life, lamented in thy end.

This depiction of Gay as a personification of childlike innocence has had a lasting influence on his posthumous reputation; less than fifty years ago a leading scholar could describe him, quite unselfconsciously, as an 'Augustan Peter Pan'.[14] Such infantilizing images have confirmed the tendency to deny Gay's authorship of his 'own' works; as a child he could not, clearly, be credited with full responsibility for such complex works as *The Shepherd's Week* or *The Beggar's Opera*, which must naturally have been supervised and finished by a mature adult. In his *Epistle to Dr Arbuthnot* (1735) Pope established another honorific myth, casting Gay in the role of neglected genius.

> Blest be the Great! for those they take away,
> And those they left me—for they left me Gay,
> Left me to see neglected genius bloom,
> Neglected die! and tell it on his tomb;
> Of all thy blameless life the sole return
> My verse, and Queensb'ry weeping o'er thy urn.   (ll. 255–60)

As one recent scholar notes, Pope's verses 'create an impression of the great man perishing in Mozartian poverty'.[15] But the facts tell a rather different story. At his death Gay left an estate worth more than £6,000 (somewhere near £200,000 at current values); and, far from being buried in a pauper's grave, his funeral was something of a grand occasion. After lying in state at Exeter Change in the Strand, his coffin was carried in a magnificent hearse 'trimmed with plumes of black and white feathers, attended with three mourning coaches and six horses' for burial in Westminster Abbey. His pallbearers included two lords and a general and the funeral service was

---

[13] Pope, *Corr.* iv. 38.

[14] James Sutherland, 'John Gay', in *Pope and his Contemporaries: Essays Presented to George Sherburn* (Oxford, 1949), 201–14. Even Edmund Curll, in a hurriedly assembled *Life of Gay* (1733), colluded in the process of elevating Gay to a status of amiable puerility. 'His personal character', Curll declared, 'was perfectly amicable; he was one of the most natural, inoffensive and disinterested of men.'

[15] Brean Hammond, '"A Poet and a Painter, and Ten Pound": John Gay and Patronage', in Lewis and Wood, 25.

conducted by the Bishop of Rochester. He died, as Arbuthnot noted, 'as if he had been a peer of the realm'.[16]

The more one examines Gay's career, the more such contradictions proliferate. In his letters Gay complains constantly at his failure to gain a suitable court employment; but in fact he benefited handsomely from both public and private patronage. His writings proclaim the virtues of independence, yet he chose to live his life as a perpetual dependant in the stately residences of his aristocratic patrons. His satires rail bitterly against the insincerity of court friends, yet he constantly sought the acquaintance of those whose false promises he despised. He glorified in the label of 'honest John Gay', yet his own career was a pattern of political opportunism, frequently switching allegiance in the quest for wealthy patrons. His friends habitually portrayed him as a rakish ladies' man, yet there is no record of any lady who actually succumbed to his charms. He assumed a persona of childlike innocence, yet this inoffensive child was responsible for the most successful and subversive theatrical satire of his generation. As Arbuthnot reported with gleeful incredulity to Swift after the government's banning of *Polly*: 'The inoffensive John Gay is now become . . . the terror of ministers.'

In an influential article published almost twenty years ago, Arthur Sherbo debated whether Gay should be classed as a literary heavyweight or lightweight, as an effective social critic or an innocuous pastoralist.[17] In this biography I shall attempt to explore, if not resolve, the contradictions that give rise to such a question. The picture of Gay which emerges is not of a 'neglected genius', an 'Augustan Peter Pan', or 'honest John' but of a man whose struggles for literary and social recognition led him, paradoxically, to project a personality whose most distinguishing characteristic is its lack of distinction. Questions of attribution must necessarily bulk large in this study of an author who so instinctively blurred the distinctions between individual and collaborative composition. Yet I have sought, as far as possible, not to perplex the reader with protracted discussions of verbal parallels and disputed lines. Where I have fresh evidence, or new attributions to propose, I do so in the notes; where I am silent on such matters, I accept the judgements of Gay's most recent editors.

More importantly, I seek to explore the reasons which led Gay so

---

[16] Swift, *Corr.* iv. 101.
[17] *Scriblerian*, 8/1 (1975), 4–8.

often to diminish his own claims to authorial independence. Inured from early years to a subservient role as shop assistant, domestic servant, and Grub Street hack, Gay never overcame the habit of submission. Much of his adult life was spent in an often futile, and increasingly obsessive, quest for aristocratic patronage, producing an occupational tone of inoffensive servility. Yet it is in these ostensibly self-deprecating professions of obligation and friendship that Gay's satire has its origins. His satiric writings have none of the lofty Horatian independence of Pope, nor the snarling Juvenalian moral indignation of Swift. What they disclose is the supplicant's professional smile of ingratiation which curls, almost imperceptibly, into a mocking grin. As a writer, Gay found his voice in the ironic reverberations of courteous allusions and received ideas. His satire is a kind of unacknowledged rebellion against the pose of inoffensive deference which he felt obliged to maintain; it is a subtle and deceptive art, often at its most ironic when it appears most ingenuous. Even his most dutiful literary allusions and *hommages* to honoured friends like Pope and Steele are not without subconscious hints of parody. In some ways, too, Gay's lack of authorial definition is subsumed within a larger literary ambiguity. The characteristic form of Gay's writing is a generic hybrid, a literary burlesque, mingling together high and low, classic and demotic idioms to produce a heterogeneous work which defies generic categorization. And just as his satiric style subverts the notion of fixed taxonomy of literary forms, so his diffidence in projecting a distinct authorial identity represents an implicit challenge to the notion of authority which authorship implies.

The study of John Gay's life is a study of a world of cultural exchange in which an author's public identity is just one form of currency in the hectic trade of court places, political offices, subscription lists, South Sea bubbles, and Grub Street feuds. The author's life is a text, written by circumstances, edited by accidents, and canonized by the conscious endeavours of well-wishers and critics to produce an image of consistency from the randomness of contingencies. I have sought to defamiliarize John Gay, resisting those legends that have tended to inscribe his life within the safe, conventional genres of children's fable, comedy of manners, or social polemic. Rather, I wish to suggest that Gay's life, like his writings, defies the textual determinacy of strict generic categories; or, in other words, that the author lives.

PART I

Trading Places
(1685–1714)

ONE

In Paternal Land

ON the night of 11 June 1685 the Duke of Monmouth, illegitimate son of the late Charles II, landed at Lyme Bay to begin his Protestant rebellion against the newly consecrated monarch, James II. A week later he reached Taunton, by which time his original force of eighty-two men had swollen to an army of 3,000. Every day brought fresh recruits. Economic hardship as much as Protestant loyalty helped to increase his ranks with unemployed cloth-workers and miners from the Mendips. Reinforcements came from London and from all across the West Country, including volunteers from the north Devon ports Barnstaple and Bideford with their strong Dissenting traditions. When Monmouth set out from Taunton on 21 June, he rode at the head of an army of some 7,000 men marching confidently towards Bristol. But then his luck began to change. First the weather turned against him and torrents of rain lashed down on his bedraggled forces. Then Monmouth himself fell victim to a fatal indecisiveness. Having marched his troops to Keynsham, within five miles of Bristol, he wheeled them about and marched them back towards Bridgwater. Tired and dispirited, soaked through and poorly fed, his followers began to drop away. Within a week their numbers had dwindled back to some 3,000. But, relying on the element of surprise, on 5 July Monmouth chose to launch a night attack on the King's forces, camped at Sedgemoor. His troops were deployed late in the evening, marching silently in a heavy mist. Suddenly, whether 'by accident or treachery', a single shot rang out which alerted the enemy.[1] For two hours Monmouth's forces withstood the onslaught

---

[1] According to Defoe, himself a rebel volunteer. See Daniel Defoe, *A Tour through England and Wales*, ed. G. D. H. Cole (2 vols., London 1928), i. 269. See also W. R. Emerson's account in *Monmouth's Rebellion*, (Oxford 1951).

of two battalions and several cannon, but failed to advance, mistakenly believing a stream in front of them was too deep to ford. Eventually the rebel army broke up, retreating in disarray, pursued by the King's cavalry, which hacked and shot down stragglers as they struggled through the boggy ground. About 2,000 men escaped from the battlefield alive, hiding in ditches, fields, and outhouses. But a policy of high rewards for arrests, coupled with ruthless penalties for harbouring fugitives, resulted in the capture of some 1,500 former rebels within a fortnight.

On 30 June, just one week before the battle of Sedgemoor, John Gay was born in Barnstaple, north Devon.[2] In the months that followed, Judge Jeffreys's 'Bloody Assizes' toured the West Country from Salisbury and Dorchester to Exeter, Taunton, Wells, and Bristol, exacting a terrible revenge on supporters of the rebellion. The cells of Barnstaple castle, like many others throughout the region, were used to hold prisoners awaiting trial and execution. Over 300 people were executed and many hundreds more were either tortured or sent for transportation to the West Indies. As one member of the House of Commons later remarked: 'Those in the west did see such a shambles as made them think they had a Turk rather than a Christian for their King.'[3] The beheading of Monmouth himself in London on 15 July was a particularly gory business. John Evelyn was there to witness the axe-man's incompetence: 'the wretch made five chops before he had his head off, which so incensed the people that had he not been guarded and got away they would have torn him in pieces.'[4]

These events were of considerable concern to members of Gay's family, many of whom were prominent in the local Dissenting community. Gay's grandfather Jonathan Hanmer was already subject to government surveillance as the leader of an illegal Nonconformist congregation. Gay's headstrong cousin Azariah Pinney had taken part in Monmouth's rebellion, been quickly arrested, and was now awaiting trial and execution. Also named among the list of 'rebels to be transported' was one 'John Gay', although his relationship with the poet's family cannot be firmly established.

This strong commitment to the Protestant cause was entirely in

---

[2] He was baptized in Barnstaple parish church on 16 Aug. 1685.

[3] Sir Robert Cotton, speaking in the House of Commons, 14 May 1689; quoted by David Ogg in *England in the Reigns of James II and William III* (Oxford, 1955), 153.

[4] John Evelyn, *Diary*, ed. E. S. De Beer (6 vols., Oxford, 1955), iv. 456.

keeping with the twin traditions of mercantile endeavour and puritan faith which characterized the north Devon ports of Bideford and Barnstaple throughout the seventeenth century. During the Civil War the vast majority of Barnstaple's citizens, following their mercantile interests, had adopted the cause of parliament. All but three of the town's burgesses were parliament men, and the corporation raised several levies to fortify the town against royalist incursions.[5] Yet, despite these heavy fortifications, the town was twice forced to yield to the King's forces, and after the defeat of the parliamentary army at Torrington in August 1644 was occupied by royalist troops. A year later Barnstaple was even considered safe enough for the Prince of Wales to choose it as his summer headquarters. 'No place was thought so convenient for his residence as Barnstaple, a pleasant town in the North part of Devonshire, well fortified, and a good garrison in it.'[6] Not all the Gay family were hostile to the monarchy. Charles's hostess during his stay in Barnstaple in June 1645 was Grace Beaple, widow of one of the town's wealthiest merchants and herself a Gay by birth. But this royalist occupation merely represented a brief and unwelcome interruption of Barnstaple's traditional allegiances. The town gave an enthusiastic welcome to the Commonwealth forces under General Fairfax which came to its rescue in the last year of the war and Grace Beaple suffered the usual fate of collaborators, with puritan reprisals against her mansion in Southgate Street. An inventory of goods and chattels taken at her death in 1650 estimated a value of '£25. 9s 0d for ye goods in ye Star Chamber' where Charles had slept; while Grace's personal jewellery was valued at no more than £62. After the Restoration her granddaughter petitioned Charles for £2,000 as compensation for loss and damages. The new monarch, always more liberal with compliments than cash, assured her of his gratitude, and made her a grant of just £200.[7]

The town's burgesses proved equally resistant to royalist demands throughout the 1680s. Served with a writ of *Quo warranto* in 1684 as

---

[5] See R. W. Cotton, *Barnstaple during the Great Civil War 1642–46* (London, 1889), and Gribble, 37.

[6] Earl of Clarendon, *The History of the Rebellion and Civil Wars in England*, bk. ix, para. 43; ed. W. Dunn Macray (Oxford, 1888), iv. 47.

[7] See Revd J. F. Chanter, 'Charles, Prince of Wales at Barnstaple and his Hostess', *Transactions of the Devonshire Association*, 49: 389 (read at Barnstaple, 26 July 1917); details of the inventory of Grace Beaple's goods are preserved among the uncatalogued muniments of Exeter Cathedral.

part of Charles's policy of raising revenue by bringing recalcitrant boroughs to heel, the corporation reluctantly surrendered their charter to the crown in September. It was restored to them the following month, but, as the town's historian comments, 'A heavy fine was doubtless exacted as the price of its restoration by the despotic Charles.'[8] Yet, whatever their secret sympathies with Monmouth's ill-fated rebellion in 1685, the aldermen were sufficiently prudent to guard against any explicit demonstrations of support. The borough accounts for the politically turbulent year of Gay's birth testify that 'the city fathers nourished the healthy wish to be reckoned on the winning side'.[9] Among payments recorded, we find the following items:

Paid several persons for riding scout, each 6s 8d.
Paid for fetching the great guns and drawing them to their several posts, £3.4s.
Paid for bringing back horses and other things, when the prisoners were carried to Exon, 16s.
Spent when news came that King Charles was recovered, £2. 10s.
Item for ringers and sending messengers to Justice Lovett and Colonel Bassett, 13s.
Item spent at the news of the taking of the Duke of Monmouth, £1.os od.
Item spent when King James was proclaimed, in wine and beer, £9.19s.6d.
Item spent at the news of the routing of the rebels, £2.
Paid for ale for the ringers, the 6th February, 1s.
Spent in a treat for Sir John Rolls and other gentlemen, and Sir Arthur Chichester, £4.18s.
And for several barrels of strong beer for the country soldiers, £3.12s.
Paid expenses for the reception of the Duke of Albemarle, £1.10s.[10]

Sadly, the corporation's attempt to buy off James's displeasure by toasting his coronation in wine and beer proved unsuccessful. In January 1687 he issued an Order in Council removing from office two aldermen, the deputy recorder, the town clerk, and eight other members of the corporation. A year later he went further, disbanding the entire corporation as a consequence of 'their perverse temper in

[8] Gribble, 303
[9] Irving, 18.
[10] *Reprint of the Barnstaple Records*, ed. J. R. Chanter and Thomas Wainwright (Barnstaple, 1900), ii. 163.

disputing his Majesty's mandate'.[11] Yet, despite such affronts to their civic dignity, the citizens of Barnstaple were understandably cautious at the news of Prince William's landing at Torbay in November 1688.

When, after the landing of the Prince of Orange in Torbay, his proclamation was brought to Barnstaple, a number of the inhabitants assembled for the purpose of learning its contents at a house, now the Fortescue Arms; but so great and so general was the dread which the recent executions of Monmouth and his adherents had inspired, that for some time no-one could be found bold enough to publish the contents of the instrument of the meeting; at length one of the company took courage, and jumping on a table, read the proclamation aloud.[12]

The Gays had been established among Barnstaple's leading families for several generations. Richard Gay was the town's mayor in 1533 and again in 1542 and the poet's great-grandfather Anthony Gay was mayor of Barnstaple in 1638. Through his marriage to Elizabeth Beaple, daughter of Barnstaple's richest merchant, Anthony Gay also substantially increased the family's wealth and property, purchasing the estate of Frithelstock, near Torrington, which remained their country seat until 1823.[13]

Throughout the seventeenth century the Gays possessed substantial houses in several of Barnstaple's main streets, as well as many outlying properties. They were prominent in trade, as well as civic and religious affairs, and enjoyed an enviable reputation throughout the county of Devon. However, the Gays were not only wealthy but prolific, and the value of their substantial holdings was gradually diminished by being parcelled out among a numerous progeny. Anthony and Elizabeth Gay had nine children; the poet's grandfather, John Gay, had eight; and the poet himself was the last of a family of five children. As the youngest son of a younger son, John Gay's patrimony was hardly great, and in his poem *Rural Sports* he describes himself as one 'who ne'er was bless'd from Fortune's hand | Nor brighten'd plough-shares in paternal land'. Such feelings of impoverishment were no doubt intensified by the sense of being a poor relation in a family whose fortunes, until recently, had been secure.

---

[11] Gribble, 302–3.
[12] Ibid. 303.
[13] Irving, 6.

Nevertheless, Gay's immediate family enjoyed a fairly comfortable existence. His mother was a Hanmer and could boast kinship with the family of that name in Hanmer, Flintshire, and with Lord Hanmer of Bettisfield. Sir Thomas Hanmer, later Speaker of the House of Commons and editor of Shakespeare, was one of Gay's relations. According to the parish records for 1694, his father William Gay, who occupied a house in the High Street, paid a weekly poor-rate of 5*d*. on this property, which was the highest rate in the street and among the highest in the town. By comparison, Gay's uncles Thomas Gay and John Hanmer paid weekly poor-rates of 2½*d*. and 2*d*. respectively for their houses in Joy Street and the High Street. These parish records raise a question about the traditional identification of Gay's birthplace. It has customarily been asserted that Gay was born in Joy Street; but the surviving rate-books show that it was actually Gay's uncle Thomas who, from the 1670s until his death in 1706, occupied the house, known as the Red Cross 'in Joy Street at the corner next High Street', which now bears a blue plaque indicating the poet's birthplace. Since it seems most improbable that Gay was born in his uncle's rather than his parents' house this is almost certainly a mistake. Winsome myths and legends surrounding this 'Augustan Peter Pan' have played a part in perpetuating this error. For those with a sentimental attachment to the talismanic influence of names, the pleasing notion that the boy called Gay should have been born in Joy and tutored by Luck has had an irresistible appeal. Sadly, the realities of Gay's life do little to sustain such an allegorical fairy-tale.[14]

Another cherished myth concerning Gay's childhood presents the landscape of his native Devonshire as the source and inspiration for his later fascination with pastoral themes. In her impressionistic book *John Gay* Phoebe Fenwick Gaye offers this lyrical account of his childhood world.

The young Gays were being brought up in a county where snow never fell and ice never formed and where, on the hottest day, sea-winds invigorated; a county of red sandstone and soft marl, whose pastures were grazed by sheep as ruddy as the earth on which they trod, in a town with a quiet wide river with green banks, fringed with the tongues of ferns, planted with elms

---

[14] See the Barnstaple Rate 1649–94 (ref. 3985) in the North Devon Public Records Office, Barnstaple Library. Gay's schoolmaster at Barnstaple grammar school was Robert Luck. Some readers may feel that I have been similarly influenced by the associations of Gay's own name in my conjectures about his sexual orientation.

and crossed by a stone bridge, ancient even then . . . Even in December the farmers' wives, bringing their fowls and cream to Barnstaple market, could decorate their wares with violets and primroses. The warmth and mildness which in Devon and Cornwall could draw out the crumpled buds so far in advance of England's other counties, was also kind to young animal and human life. If there was not joyfulness in Joy Street in those early days, when the children were young and the parents ignorant of coming tragedy, then joy indeed is far to seek.[15]

Even in its meteorological details this account is woefully mistaken. Devon in the seventeenth century was no more sheltered from inclement weather than it is now. In December 1676 Barnstaple suffered its worst winter in living memory, causing the river Taw to freeze over. John Sloly, the town clerk, noted: 'It was so hard frozen that many were fain for to roast their meat for to eat it because they could not get water for to boil the pot.'[16] More importantly, such bucolic fantasies ignore the importance of Barnstaple as a trading centre. John Gay was brought up not in a pastoral Arcadia but in a busy trading port, and the river Taw was anything but 'quiet'. Throughout the seventeenth and eighteenth centuries Barnstaple was the principal landing place for Irish wool and yarn, which was carried overland to the manufacturing towns of east and mid-Devon. As late as 1739 it was named as one of the eight ports in England to which the importation of woollen goods from Ireland was limited by statute.[17] Tobacco was another principal import, although Bideford, with its deeper harbour, was gradually usurping the trade in this commodity. One Barnstaple merchant complained bitterly in 1674, 'Bideford hath stolen it all away,'[18] and Customs House records confirm this general trend. In 1683 Barnstaple imported some 150,000 lb. of tobacco, but Bideford imported almost four times that amount.[19] Sixty years later Defoe was still describing the two neighbouring north Devon ports as keen trading rivals. 'If Bideford has a greater number of merchants, Barnstaple has a greater com-

---

[15] Phoebe Fenwick Gaye, *John Gay* (London, 1938), 15.

[16] Quoted by Gribble in his 'Transcripts of Town Records'.

[17] Statute of 12 Geo. II.

[18] See Daniel Defoe, *A Tour through the Whole Island of Great Britain, 1724–6*, abridged and ed. Pat Rogers (Harmondsworth, 1971), 245–6.

[19] The exact figures are 155,572 lb. for Barnstaple and 566,718 lb. for Bideford (Exeter PRO, 961/1). I am indebted for this information to Dr Alison Grant; see also Jacob M. Price, *France and the Chesapeake: A History of the French Tobacco Monopoly 1674–1791* (Ann Arbor, Mich., 1973).

merce within land, by its great market for Irish wool and yarn etc.
with the serge-makers of Tiverton and Exeter who come hither to
buy.' Both towns, Defoe noted, 'have a large share in the trade to
Ireland, and in the herring fishery, and in a trade to the British
colonies in America. If Bideford cures more fish, Barnstaple imports
more wine and other merchandises.'[20] Customs House returns for
1727 and 1728 record imports of tobacco into Barnstaple worth
£54,700 and throughout the years of John Gay's childhood the town
enjoyed a flourishing trade in corn, wine, wool, pottery, and other
goods with France, Spain, Ireland, Italy, Portugal, Norway, Newfoundland, North and South America, and the West Indies. Gay's
own family were intimately involved with all this commercial activity,
particularly with the West Indian trade. As a boy he was brought up
with first-hand knowledge of business methods and acquired an
early insight into the competitive instincts necessary for survival in a
ruthless commercial world. His uncle Matthew, youngest of his
father's brothers, died while trading in the West Indies. His aunt
Martha in Bristol suffered a more ignominious fate. During the late
1670s she had impulsively ventured her whole fortune in various
West Indian enterprises. Her letters contain lists of cargoes compris-
ing several hundred pounds' worth of laced shirts, gloves, and
other fancy goods, dispatched to Jamaica and Barbados. But she had
misjudged her market. The business failed; she fell bankrupt and
suffered the humiliation of a two-year imprisonment for debt in
Newgate gaol from 1681 till 1683. The family, or part of it, rallied
round to help her, paying the weekly sum of 3s. 6d. to the Keeper of
Newgate, Isaac Dennis, to maintain her in tolerable prison quarters.
Meanwhile her disgruntled son-in-law Thomas Walden began a
protracted lawsuit to seize her household goods in fulfilment of his
marriage settlement with her daughter. Thereafter, until her death
in 1700, Martha's account-books make depressing reading, a sorry
catalogue of lawyers' bills and apothecaries' accounts for lenitives
and quieting draughts.[21]

The ruin of his aunt Martha's trade had a disastrous effect upon
the future prospects of the infant John Gay. Although we have no
conclusive information about his father's occupation, there is evi-

---

[20] Defoe, *A Tour through the Whole Island*, 247.
[21] See the Pinney family papers, held at Bristol University Library: box 1, DM 58 1/
45; DM 58 2/2–2/4.

dence to suggest that he had been employed as Martha's commercial agent in Barnstaple. Among the numerous detailed statements of accounts between Martha Gay and Thomas Walden are some which name William Gay as her intermediary. One reads: 'To money remitted by William Gay and paid you by various people, one in London as by your own account, £115.' Elsewhere, in Martha's cash-book for 1686, we find the item: '£15 by cousin Will Gay.'[22] When, many years later, Gay hit on Newgate prison as the setting for *The Beggar's Opera*, he was choosing not merely some arbitrary low-life topos for his satire on political corruption; he was revisiting in his imagination the place where his own prospects of fortune died.

Born at a time of civil strife, Gay was brought up in a household where the language of trade and the dutiful observances of Nonconformist worship provided his earliest moral code. Another of Martha Gay's daughters, Naomi, married Nathaniel Pinney, son of a wealthy merchant family with extensive trading interests in the West Indies. Familiar letters between Nathaniel and his enterprising sister Hester are penned with the prudential deliberation of financial accounts. Every year the punctilious Nathaniel would draw up a detailed 'Statement of Account', setting out in two neat columns the extent of their mutual obligations in terms headed 'debitor contra creditor'.[23] Nathaniel's brother Azariah was of a completely different character; where Nathaniel was sober, prudent, and calculating, Azariah was rash, impulsive, and cavalier. While Nathaniel buried himself in business matters, Azariah spent the summer months of 1684 aiding his sister Sarah in a runaway marriage. Together the pair of them were 'every day on horseback' running and hiding from their father's angry pursuit. A year later, after his reckless gamble of joining Monmouth's rebellion, Azariah was again on the run, hiding this time from the King's troops. Nathaniel wrote angrily to Hester of their brother's 'unpardonable acts of disobedience'. He complained that Azariah and Sarah had brought the family into disrepute by their 'mischievous deeds' and sternly counselled Hester against any similar acts of foolhardiness, especially in the matter of matrimony. Azariah though was confident that his charm would be

---

[22] Pinney Papers, DM 1/54.
[23] Pinney Papers, red box 2, 'Hester Pinney', folder iii.

sufficient to frustrate Nathaniel's efforts to turn the family against
him: 'because not one of my sisters has any kindness for my brother,
but I find they all have for me.'[24] His faith in the kindness of his
sisters proved well founded. Following his arrest, Azariah Pinney
was saved from execution when Hester, who kept a lace-shop in the
New Exchange, paid a fine of £65 to commute his death penalty to
transportation, and set him up in business in the West Indies. Such
transactions were very common: 'There was a great trade in selling
pardons to delinquents, in which Jeffreys shared large sums with
James.' Some 800 former rebels were transported to the West
Indies, providing a considerable profit to the royal family. 'Whatever
doubts there may be regarding the economic motives of Monmouth's
rebellion, there can be no doubt regarding the economic motives of
those who stamped it out.'[25]

Stories of the two Pinney brothers were among the favourite
family anecdotes of Gay's childhood and it is tempting to find, in
the opposition of their characters, an early prefigurement of the
antithesis between Peachum and Macheath. Like the cavalier
Macheath, the young Azariah, after his career of rebellious escapades,
was sent to the West Indies while his calculating brother confirmed
his Peachum-like credentials by becoming a government agent.[26]

Monmouth's rebellion was not the only significant political event
in the West Country in the year of Gay's birth. The fears of
Catholic bigotry which largely motivated Monmouth's supporters
received a powerful reinforcement from the observation of events
across the channel. In 1681 Louis XIV embarked upon a policy of
persecuting Huguenot families by instituting the dragonnades. Regiments of cavalry were sent into the provinces to be billeted on
Huguenot families, who could only secure exemption from this
brutal imposition by converting to the Catholic faith. For those who
clung to their Protestantism, torture and the destruction of their
property were the usual penalties. The inhabitants of Barnstaple
received first-hand information about the ordeals of their co-religion-
ists as Huguenot refugees began arriving in north Devon. Even

---

[24] Pinney Papers, red box 3, folder ii; red box 1, DM 58 1/53.
[25] Ogg, *England in the Reigns of James II and William III*, 153.
[26] During the Jacobite uprising of 1715 Nathaniel Pinney received a warrant from
James Stanhope, Secretary of State, for the arrest of a suspected rebel sympathizer: 'He is
a Roman Catholic and his trade is either to make or to scour and clean arms ... His
Majesty's service is very much concerned in this.' (Pinney Papers, box 1, 2/49.)

before Louis XIV took the final step, in 1685, of expelling all Huguenot families from France with his Revocation of the Edict of Nantes, Protestant boat-people had been arriving there 'in shoals'. In 1681 the *Current Intelligence* reported:

Plymouth, Septem 6. This day came in hither a small bark from Rochelle with thirty-nine poor Protestants who are fled for their religion. They report that five or six boats more full of these poor distressed creatures parted from those parts at the same time; and we hear that one of them is already put into Dartmouth.[27]

By 1685 the waves of refugees had turned into a flood and many boats crammed full of penniless and famished Huguenots landed at the north Devon ports of Appledore, Bideford, and Barnstaple. Jacques Fontaine's memoir *A Tale of the Huguenots* contains a graphic account of the terrors of such an escape.[28] Though the French authorities had forbidden all vessels to leave harbour, Fontaine contrived to hire a 'little shallop' to get them from the coast and arranged to transfer to an English ship further out at sea. Under the cover of darkness he, together with his fiancée and ten others, passed in their small boat beneath the bows of the pinnaces keeping guard at the harbour mouth. They had a prearranged signal, raising and lowering their sail three times, by which the English ship would recognize them. However, once out at sea, they were distraught to see their rescue vessel challenged and turned away by a French frigate which then bore down on them. 'Our situation was dreadful,' writes Fontaine. 'We were in perfect despair and knew not what to do.' Yet, with characteristic ingenuity, Fontaine persuaded the boatman and his son to counterfeit drunkenness so they could 'as if by accident let the sail fall three time' to inform the English ship, just visible in the distance, of their identity. Their little pantomime worked and they slid past 'within pistol-shot of the frigate'. The only challenge came when the boatman began beating his 'drunken' son with a rope's end. 'The people in the frigate threatened that if the father would not have more patience with his son, they would come and treat him the same way.' Their voyage on the *Industry* of

---

[27] Quoted by Dr Alison Grant in 'The Huguenots of Devon', published jointly with Dr Robin Gwynn in *Transactions of the Devonshire Association*, 117 (Dec. 1985), 163.

[28] *A Tale of the Huguenots; or, Memoirs of a French Refugee Family*, 'translated and compiled from the original manuscripts of James Fontaine by one of his descendants' (New York, 1838), 105–20.

Barnstaple, returning home with a cargo of wine, brandy, walnuts, and salt, took eleven days because of contrary winds and the refugees, overcrowded and short of food, were often seasick. They were also practically penniless as the master of the vessel extorted a huge fee for transporting them to safety. But when they reached Barnstaple they were pleasantly surprised by the warmth of their reception.

God, who had not brought us to a safe country to have us die of starvation, touched the hearts of the principal inhabitants of Barnstaple, who, having sent to find us, all twelve, each took one of us into his house and treated us with unbelievable kindness and friendship . . . that we might have been their own children or their brothers.[29]

In his final years, and much to the surprise of literary friends, John Gay chose 'industry' as his watchword. It is tempting to imagine that, in thus signalling his return to Barnstaple values, he recalled to mind that proud vessel, the *Industry*, which had transported so many Huguenots from tyranny in France to the Nonconformist liberties of England.

However, the auguries in the Huguenots' new home were not all so favourable. Fontaine was shocked at the savage punishments inflicted on Monmouth's supporters. The gibbeted remains of heads and limbs still hanging from several of the town's main buildings were ominously reminiscent of the brutalities from which he had just escaped.

I was told by the Presbyterians that the unfortunate people who had been executed after the Duke of Monmouth's rebellion a few days before our arrival, and whose heads and quarters I saw exposed on all the towers, gates and cross-roads, looking absolutely like butchers' shambles, had many of them been guilty of no crime but that of being Presbyterians.

Otherwise, the Huguenots found in Barnstaple a congenial atmosphere for their own entrepreneurial instincts. The first thing that struck Fontaine upon landing, destitute and starving, in the town was 'the extreme cheapness of bread'. With his last halfpenny he had sent a child to fetch some bread; the child returned with a huge loaf, and Fontaine describes himself 'feasting' on it. Immediately his mind was filled with the commercial opportunities revealed by this

---

[29] Fontaine, 115; quoted by Grant, 'The Huguenots of Devon', 163.

chance encounter. 'It instantly occurred to me that if I had only some money at command to lay out in grain to send to France, I should realize a large profit.' Before long Fontaine was involved in new business ventures, and the details of his trade offer a grisly insight into the cut-throat realities of the world in which Gay was raised. Having dispatched a cargo of grain to France, Fontaine ordered a return shipment of salt, unaware that the ship's captain was secretly involved in the darker side of the trade in refugees. In addition to the salt, the captain took on a human cargo of some eight or ten Huguenots. Once out at sea he demanded that all their money should be placed in his safe-keeping, but then made sail for Spain, not England, claiming an unfavourable wind. Between Bilbao and San Sebastián, the crew deliberately ran the ship aground, leaving it a complete wreck. 'Here was an end of my cargo of salt,' comments Fontaine; 'it returned to the sea from whence it came.' But, he adds, 'the most horrible part of the story is yet to come'.

The captain and crew went ashore in the boat with the money, leaving the passengers to be drowned, every wave going completely over the wreck. One of their number, a lady of quality, who owned the largest part of the treasure, wore a quilted petticoat which buoyed her up so entirely that she might have floated ashore, had not the captain seized her. He put off in his boat as though he would have assisted her, and when he got within reach he plunged her under water and held her down for a length of time, so that the petticoat, which had in the first instance resisted the water, becoming saturated, prevented her rising.[30]

There is no evidence that the Gays themselves took part in the lucrative trade in refugees but undoubtedly they had business dealings with those who did, and were familiar with the ruthless privateers who, under the guise of Protestant principle, grew rich from this commerce in human misery.

Though the status of the Gay family among Barnstaple's mercantile and civic élite had declined somewhat in the years immediately preceding the poet's birth, it still occupied a prominent role in the town's Dissenting community. In *The Nonconformist's Memorial*, Edmund Calamy's roll-call of religious martyrs 'ejected or silenced' by the Act of Uniformity, 'that fatal Bartholomew', enacted on 24 August 1662, we find these names: Mr John Gay: 'left the university [Oxford] because he could not submit to the terms imposed. He

---

[30] Fontaine, 119.

lived afterwards at Barnstaple in Devonshire and was useful there.'
Mr Robert Pinney: 'He was well-beloved by his parishioners. He
continued a preacher among the Nonconformists till his death,
about the year 1698. He was often in trouble in Charles the
Second's reign and was forced to leave his family for a considerable
time.' John Pinney: 'an eloquent, charming preacher . . . After his
ejectment he had many troubles by excommunications and fines. He
was twice imprisoned, once in England and once in Ireland.'[31]
Undoubtedly the most influential religious figure in Gay's family
background was his grandfather Jonathan Hanmer. Forsaking the
comfortable existence provided by his family's wealth and powerful
connections, Hanmer had broken with the Established Church and
formed his own Dissenting congregation in Barnstaple, known as
the Castle Meeting.

He had a wonderful talent in composing sermons and a way of delivering
them which few attain to . . . His lectures in Barnstaple were greatly
thronged, many attending who lived many miles distant; and some of them
persons of character and distinction.[32]

These illegal gatherings of Hanmer's followers, which were frequently subjected to surveillance and disruption by officials of the
Church and State, soon took on the clandestine excitement of a
subversive cult. Sometimes they 'assembled in a private malt-house,
or warehouse, for fear of spies and informers'. At other times they
held their crowded meetings in the open air, posting sentries to
guard against discovery. 'In their hole-and-corner meetings . . . they
hung their harps upon the willows, and to prevent observation,
singing of psalms was studiously avoided, and they had two or more
confidential friends on the look out to give the signal of alarm.'[33]

Jonathan Hanmer died in 1687 when Gay was only 2 years old,
but he was succeeded as leader of the Castle Meeting by his son,
Gay's uncle John Hanmer, who soon attained an equally distinguished reputation. Calamy refers to him as 'a star of the first
magnitude' in the Dissenting community. John Hanmer was a
generous and kindly man, respected for 'the sweetness of his temper,
his learning, the judgement and exactness of his composures, and

---

[31] Calamy, i. 180, 354, 444.
[32] Ibid. i. 340.
[33] H. W. Gardiner, *A Cursory View of the Lives of the Rev. Jonathan Hanmer, A. M.
and the Rev. John Hanmer A. M.* (Barnstaple, 1828), 28–9.

the gravity and seriousness with which they were delivered'.[34] From the early 1680s until his death, aged 65, in 1707, he maintained a life of regular habits and strict religious principle. 'His custom was to rise about four or five in the morning, and to remain in his study till the time of family prayer; soon after which, he went to his study again, till about noon ... His work was his delight.' One further aspect of Hanmer's character is worthy of specific notice. We are told that 'he took a particular delight in instructing younger persons'.[35] Without doubt he would have found a special pleasure in instructing the children of his sister Katherine, ensuring they received a sound moral education according to Dissenting principles, and endeavouring to inculcate in them his own disciplined habits of study and meditation.[36] Apart from such formal religious instruction, Hanmer may also have entertained his young nephews and nieces with anecdotes of recent local controversies. Several stories concerned the former vicar John Trender, who once had the temerity to attack the town's aldermen for not attending church. Trender compared them to 'two fat oxen, that they would not hear when Christ called unto them but drew backwards and drew others from Christ'. Unfortunately for Trender the aldermen were lurking unseen at the back of the church, and promptly had him arrested for this 'indecent behaviour'. On another occasion Trender was gaoled for playing on a pipe and tabor after nine o'clock at night, and it took the combined efforts of the Bishop of Exeter and the Earl of Bath to free him. But Trender was determined to have his revenge. The following Sunday, a freezing cold day, he preached for a full *eleven* hours, and, as the town clerk records with some understatement, 'wearied his audience'.[37] More serious stories concerned the persecution endured by Hanmer's own father in the cause of his faith. For several years before establishing the Castle Meeting congregation, Jonathan Hanmer, still an ordained minister of the Church, had been at odds with some of his most influential parishioners. For long periods his salary was withheld while his religious

[34] Quoted by Irving, 21–2.

[35] Gardiner, *A Cursory View*, 36–7.

[36] In 1687, when Hanmer assumed leadership of the Castle Meeting congregation, Gay's sisters Katherine and Joanna were aged 11 and 5 respectively and his brother Jonathan was 8. Gay's eldest sister Elizabeth had died in 1685.

[37] These stories are contained in the diary of the town clerk, Philip Wyot, and published in J. R. Chanter, *Sketches of the Literary History of Barnstaple* (Barnstaple, 1865), 104.

views were subject to ecclesiastical scrutiny. Thereafter, as the
leader of an illegal sect, Hanmer's life and liberty were often in
jeopardy, and he 'was frequently compelled to leave them, in order
to avoid prison'.[38]

Inevitably then John Gay was brought up on a strong diet of
stories of religious persecution; stories of his grandfather fleeing
from arrest and summoning his loyal congregation to secret worship
in the open fields; stories of the followers of the Protestant Duke of
Monmouth, including his cousin Azariah Pinney, executed and
gibbeted, or else fined and transported for daring to fight for their
faith; stories of other devout kinsmen, John Gay, John and Robert
Pinney, ejected from their livings by the Act of Uniformity; stories
of the Huguenot refugees, forced into exile in peril of their lives for
clinging to their Protestant faith. The Huguenots in particular
would have provided an ever-present reminder of the realities of
religious persecution since the little former chapel housing the
Barnstaple grammar school which Gay attended was used by Huguenot groups as their Sunday meeting-house. All round him Gay
would have found powerful reminders of the strong Dissenting
traditions which helped form the character of his native town. His
daily walk to school took him past the Almshouse, founded and
endowed by Thomas Horwood, former mayor and merchant of the
town in 1659, and, adjoining it, the Free School, endowed by his
widow Alice Horwood for the education of '20 poor maids'. Yet
curiously, although his family were deeply involved and highly
respected in the Dissenting community, Gay never seems to draw
upon this strong Nonconformist tradition in his writings. The social
satire in his work has its sources not in English puritanism but in
the classical humanism of Horace, Juvenal, and Virgil. When *The
Pilgrim's Progress* is mentioned in his burlesque play *The What
D'Ye Call It*, it is placed, as an object of comic parody, in the hands
of a semi-literate yokel who is so moved by the title-page that he can
read no further.[39]

In fact there is a striking contrast between Gay's reticence about
his family's religious persecution and the way Swift fashioned a
similar pedigree into a heroic model for his own satiric principles.
Swift's grandfather Thomas Swift, vicar of Goodrich in Hereford-

[38] Gardiner, *A Cursory View*, 28.
[39] *The What D'Ye Call It* (1715), II. i.

shire, remained fiercely loyal to Charles I throughout the Civil Wars and was 'plundered by the roundheads six and thirty times'. In his brief 'Fragment of Autobiography' Swift proudly boasts how this heroic grandfather sewed all his money into a quilted waistcoat, rode to a town that was held for the King, and presented the waistcoat to the governor,

who, ordering it to be unripped found it lined with three hundred broad pieces of gold, which as it proved a seasonable relief must be allowed an extraordinary supply from a private clergyman with ten children of a small estate, so often plundered and soon after turned out of his livings in the church.

Some years later Swift went even further in recalling the sufferings of this revered ancestor, telling Pope that he had been 'persecuted and plundered two and fifty times by the barbarity of Cromwell's hellish crew'.[40] Gay might equally well have cited the case of his own grandfather Jonathan Hanmer as just such another symbol of fierce independence of spirit. He too had suffered persecution for his faith. He too had been deprived of his salary and living; he too, though the father of nine children, had bravely endured threats of imprisonment rather than compromise his conscience and, cast out from his meeting-house, had braved spies and informers to preach in the open fields. But, while Swift was proud to identify with this first hero as a valiant opponent of tyranny, Gay made no mention of the equally heroic strain of Protestant militancy in his own family background. Even when he too suffered government persecution, with the banning of his play *Polly*, he made no reference, in his repeated protestations of honesty and integrity, of this honourable precedent of principled dissent.

This contrast casts an illuminating light on the two men's characters and on their instinctive styles as satirists. Both Swift and Gay experienced powerfully ambiguous feelings of displacement in the fashionable milieu of literary London. A posthumous child, Swift felt distanced from his family, of whom he gives only the most grudging and selective account. Admitting the misfortune of having been 'dropped' (i.e. born) in Dublin, Swift nevertheless insisted on his Englishness, and spent much of his career in search of surrogate

[40] Jonathan Swift, 'A Fragment of Autobiography', in *Prose Works*, v. 189; Swift, *Corr.* v. 150.

fathers, like Sir William Temple and Lord Oxford, whose aristocratic patronage, though never matching his demands, went some way to acknowledge his need for dignity and status. Gay too, orphaned at an early age, spent much of his life rejecting and concealing his family background in Nonconformity and trade, fashioning instead a new 'polite' social identity, under the protection of such wealthy patrons as Lord Burlington, William Pulteney, and the Duke of Queensberry. But whereas in Swift these feelings of displacement and inferiority led to an arrogant assertion of independence and the creation of an imperious public persona, in Gay they had the opposite effect. Gay's instinctive pose is apologetic; his characteristic role is as a dependant, modest, deferential, and inoffensive.

In June 1694, when Gay was not quite 9 years old, his mother Katherine died. Her brother Hanmer preached the funeral sermon, which he dedicated to Gay's father with these consoling words:

Dear Brother . . . Oh let the remembrance of her holy conversation be ever powerful to quicken you and yours to be followers of her as she was of Jesus Christ, that it may be seen that you have not forgotten that you were once favoured with such a wife, nor your children that they were once blessed with such a mother.[41]

Barely a year later William Gay did indeed follow his wife; he died on Gay's tenth birthday, leaving four orphaned children. Gay's eldest sister Katherine lost no time in securing her own future. An attractive woman of 19, she shortly afterwards married Anthony Baller, son of Joseph Baller, a prosperous merchant in the town.[42] The remaining children, Jonathan aged 16, Joanna 13, and John 10, were supported by their uncles, lodging either with Thomas Gay in

[41] Hanmer took his text from Col. 1: 27: 'To whom God would make known what is the riches of the glory of this mystery among the Gentiles; which is Christ in you, the hope of glory.'

[42] The fortunes of the Baller family within the trading community of Barnstaple seem to have risen just as those of the Gays went into decline. Benjamin Baller was the town's mayor in 1704 and he, together with his relations Joseph and Nathaniel Baller, were among those petitioning the Queen in 1709 to protect the fishing fleet of Barnstaple against French harassment in the seas around Newfoundland. The family had a shop under the town's Guildhall, and in his will, dated 3 Mar. 1711, Joseph Baller left an annuity of £10 for the benefit of the Meeting-House for Dissenters. See BL Add. MSS 61620, fos. 57–8; Barnstaple Castle Record, vol. 185; Irving, n. 7.

Joy Street, or, more probably, with John Hanmer in his modest dwelling further down the High Street.[43]

By this time Gay had begun attending Barnstaple grammar school, which was housed in a small angular building called St Anne's Chantry, just behind the parish church and a short walk from his home. Originally a chapel built over the parish charnel-house, the school was cramped and gloomy, with its narrow windows looking out across a graveyard. But however inauspicious the school's physical appearance, Gay was fortunate in both his teachers and his fellow pupils. His school contemporaries included William Fortescue, a lifelong friend and later a successful lawyer who rose to become Master of the Rolls; and Aaron Hill, who was to prove an indefatigable literary entrepreneur. Gay's first schoolmaster, William Rayner, was a model of sober, traditional schoolmasterly virtues: 'highly skilled in languages, attentive and consistent in the performance of his duties, and remarkable for strict discipline.'[44] An excellent classical scholar, it was he who awakened Gay's early interest in Homer, Virgil, and Horace. When in 1698 Rayner moved to Tiverton, he was succeeded by Robert Luck, an altogether more charismatic figure. Educated at Westminster and Christ Church and lately entered into holy orders, Luck was clever, young, and consumed with vanity concerning his own abilities as a poet. In later years Luck liked to boast that it was he who had first fostered Gay's early literary talents. His poetical *Miscellany*, published four years after Gay's death, included a poem dedicated to Gay's former patron, the Duke of Queensberry, which took the opportunity to remind his Grace of their shared endeavours to promote the career of their favourite protégé.

> O Queensberry! could happy Gay
> This off'ring to thee bring,
> ''Tis his, my lord', (he'd smiling say)
> 'Who taught your Gay to sing.'[45]

---

[43] Irving writes: 'Uncle Thomas Gay took over the big house [i.e. the Red Cross in Joy Street] and the children with it' (Irving, 7). But this assertion is based on a misreading of the parish rate-book. Thomas Gay had already been occupying the Joy Street house for over twenty years and it was Hanmer who showed the greater concern for the moral welfare of the young.

[44] *Reprint of the Barnstaple Records*, 194.

[45] R. Luck, AM, Master of Barnstaple School, *A Miscellany of New Poems on Several Occasions* (1736).

Elsewhere in the same poem, 'The Female Phaeton', Luck shame-lessly flattered the Duchess of Queensberry, imagining her borrow-ing the sun's chariot for a day to 'set the world on fire'. Yet what is most shameless of all about this sycophantic exercise is the fact that Luck plagiarized the whole poem, without acknowledgement, from Prior's work of the same name published almost twenty years earlier.[46] Luck's poetry reveals him as a compulsive flatterer, system-atically capitalizing upon the reputations of his more distinguished former pupils. Interwoven among his own verses are juvenile poetic exercises by former 'members of my little family'. Presenting himself as 'an humble servant of the Muses for almost half a century' he addresses himself with 'candour' to 'those gentlemen whom I have had the honour to educate'.

They ought (I think) to read my performances as favourably as I examined theirs. One of that number, now a great, and (what is more valuable) a very good man, will forgive the liberty I take to print his translation of the 15th Ode of Hor. Epod. done by him when young under my care. I read it then with too much pleasure ever to forget it. 'Tis to gratify his modesty I conceal his name.

This heavy-handed compliment to Fortescue is typical of the name-dropping style of a volume which also includes poetic genuflections towards Gay's friends Pope, Swift, and Handel. While contrasting his own minor talents with their lofty achievements, Luck evidently sought a certain reflected glory from association with such influential 'friends'.

> Small thanks attend on a superfluous gift.
> Fables to Gay? Satires to Pope or Swift?
> Who verses writes to his poetic friends,
> To Handel music, flowers to Miller, sends?[47]

Yet, as the subscription list to Luck's *Miscellany* reveals, even such bare-faced flattery paid dividends. Fortescue subscribed for seven copies and Pope for two.

However mediocre Luck's own poetic gifts, this does not diminish his importance as an influence on Gay's developing literary sensibil-ity. What is most evident from all Luck's writings is his enormous

---

[46] Luck 'borrows' the whole structure and language of Prior's poem, merely adding his own stanzas on Gay in an attempt to justify this extravagant eulogy of a lady he had presumably never met.

[47] Luck, *Miscellany*, 61.

and infectious enthusiasm for the arts in all their forms. His love of literature, his delight in music and drama, and his irreverent taste for witty, topical satire certainly helped to fire Gay's youthful imagination. Most importantly, this vain, energetic, cavalier figure represented a very different perspective on the world from the dutiful, industrious Nonconformist and mercantile values of Gay's home life with Hanmer. Politically, Luck and Hanmer were poles apart; Hanmer a conscientious puritan, Luck an ardent royalist. Many years later, on 30 January 1735, Luck marked the anniversary of Charles I's execution with a celebratory poem on the theme of Charles the martyr.

> Blest martyr! for whose fate
> And our forefathers' crimes, we weep . . .[48]

As was common in poems and sermons on this theme, Luck drew a direct parallel between the death of 'God's vice-regent' Charles and the martyrdom of Christ.

> Like thee, by his own subjects tried,
> A crown of thorns thy master bore . . .

The parliamentary cause, which Gay's grandfather Jonathan Hanmer had served so faithfully, is represented in Luck's poem as the 'viper's hiss' of traitors and fanatics.

But it was Luck's enthusiasm for drama which made the most lasting impression on his pupil Gay. Soon after his appointment Luck inaugurated a tradition of school plays, usually performed in Latin. The plays chosen were adapted from Terence and Plautus, though Luck had a habit of interpolating his own musical verses into the text, to be sung by a schoolboy ensemble. His *Miscellany* includes the English version of one such piece, entitled *Scena Barumensi* ('A Barnstaple Scene'), introduced in these words: 'The Latin of the following Song was sung when the gentlemen of Barum school acted Terence's comedy called *The Self-Tormentor*.' Luck composed his own prologues and epilogues for the plays performed, giving them a local and topical application. The prologue to *The Adelphi*, which appears to have been performed in English as *The Brothers*, takes up the cause of schoolboys, reluctantly compelled to toil through the Latin accidence.

---

[48] Ibid. 186.

When Britain's senate wisely did decree
To set the bar from learned jargon free
Had we but interest, we'd have begged a clause
In favour of poor boys, as well as laws.
Were *hic, haec, hoc* dismissed, with *qui, quae, quod,*
Truants and dunces would not fear the rod.

The prologue concludes with an appeal for vernacular drama.

Terence henceforth be banished from our scenes;
Not all who hear him know what Terence means.[49]

Thirty years later it was Gay's *Beggar's Opera* which effectively banished another form of foreign entertainment 'from our scenes' and it is interesting to speculate on the influence of this schoolboy manifesto on Gay's own later burlesque of non-English theatrical forms.

Irving suggests that the interest in drama which Luck inspired among his pupils was widely shared by Barnstaple's citizens. 'The town had always been liberal in its support of such things,' he declares, 'whether it was the King's Players who arrived, or mere strollers.'[50] In fact this is the reverse of the truth. Recent research has been unable to trace any theatrical activity in Barnstaple from 1630 until the 1760s apart from the school plays which Luck himself produced.[51] On the contrary, regular entries in the borough accounts make clear the stern official disapproval of such licentious diversions. In several places we find items like the following: 'Given to the Earl of Worcester's players, being in town, to depart the town *without playing here*, xs [ten shillings].' Another entry reads: 'and of xxs [twenty shillings] more paid to players *to rid the town of them.*'[52] The industrious puritans who dominated the town's corporation regarded the theatre with open hostility and treated travelling players as idle vagabonds who needed to be sent packing. Other items in the borough records confirm the atmosphere of civic rectitude in which Gay grew up. An 'Order in Council' of the corporation in 1698 resolved that 'no buns be given away by the mayor' while a recent

---

[49] Luck, *Miscellany*, 143.
[50] Irving, 11.
[51] See S. L. Reader's unpublished study of theatre in Barnstaple, compiled 1970: North Devon Athenaeum D:792.
[52] North Devon Athenaeum 3792 no. 229/5. My italics.

by-law, aimed at transforming Barnstaple into a model of urban hygiene, might have amused the future author of *Trivia*. 'Item 33: Also it is ordained that no inhabitant of this town do suffer his hogs, pigs or ducks to go at large in the streets, upon pain of losing 1d for every foot for every time.'[53]

Undoubtedly John Hanmer, who played such a leading part in the town's religious community, would have shared this official distaste for theatrical entertainments. And this issue would have further sharpened the contrast in Gay's mind between the sober puritanism of his uncle and the high-spirited literary enthusiasm of his schoolmaster. For all his love of theatre and song, Robert Luck was no mere dilettante or pied piper, but a clergyman whose blend of High Church Christianity with patrician classical tastes presented Gay with an attractive alternative to his family's mercantile values. Luck took his responsibilities seriously, as both a clergyman and a schoolmaster; his sermon on 'The Orphan's Legacy' preached in Barnstaple parish church in May 1734 reveals a conscientious concern with pastoral duties and the responsibilities of parenthood.

The surest and most effectual provision parents can make for the welfare of their children is to lead a godly, righteous and sober life. 'Tis this will derive a blessing upon them, and leave them a lasting inheritance ... A child's best legacy is his parents' virtue.[54]

These are sentiments from which John Hanmer himself, charged with the care of his sister's orphaned children, could hardly have dissented.

Throughout Gay's teenage years these two men, Luck and Hanmer, represented two contrasting perspectives on the world. And, if the evidence of Gay's name carved on a pew in Barnstaple church is to be believed, he idled more boyhood hours away in the parish church than at his uncle's meeting-house, though the authenticity of this 'relic' is not beyond doubt.[55] It would seem possible,

---

[53] Statutes of the Corporation of Barnstaple, 1689; see Gribble, 303, 360–4.

[54] Luck's text is taken from Ps. 112: 2: 'the generation of the upright shall be blessed.'

[55] The carving of the name 'John Gay' on an old pew of Barnstaple parish church takes us back into the realm of myth and legend. Above the name is a date, 1695, and above that again another name, Phin: Pet. Of these Phoebe Fenwick Gaye comments: 'It came about that the ten-year-old John Gay and a school companion, one Phineas Flett [*sic*], were kicking their heels idly during sermon in the parish church one day, and that they chose to occupy the time by cutting their names on the oak pew in front of them.

though this is merely speculation, that Hanmer, seeing his nephew's intelligence and gift for words, might have entertained hopes that he would follow his own vocation as a Dissenting preacher. But for Gay the world of theatre, song, and classical literature held a more seductive appeal. For a young adolescent, recently orphaned and chafing at the almost penitential discipline of his uncle's strict regime, Luck offered an irresistible role-model of rebellion and escape.

Gay's father's early death, and the collapse of his aunt Martha's trade, banished any hopes Gay might have cherished of an easy entrance into genteel literary life. In more favourable circumstances he might have expected to follow several other members of his family up to Exeter College, Oxford.[56] Luck liked to boast of his success in training up his 'little family' for university, and proudly reserved a special section of his *Miscellany* subscription list for university men.[57] But present financial exigencies prohibited any such opportunity for Gay. Whatever money there was went to purchase a commission for his brother Jonathan, who had opted for an army career. His sister Joanna followed their elder sister Katherine's example in making an advantageous match, marrying William Fortescue's brother. For Gay, the best prospect that his family could offer was a respectable career in trade. Reluctantly he accepted

Phineas, by virtue possibly of superior age and pushfulness, cut his first, in large bold characters—PHIN FLETT, 1695. Underneath, in a smaller and much neater hand, John Gay cut his.' Apart from the inaccuracy of the transcription—the name is clearly Phin Pet—this impressionistic account ignores several details which cast doubt on the authenticity of this 'relic', still preserved in Barnstaple's North Devon Athenaeum. The date, 1695, is clearly carved by the same hand that carved the name Phin Pet. The Petts were a Devonshire family associated for some 200 years with the Royal Navy. Yet the only known Phineas Pett was vicar of Totnes from 1669 till his death in 1674. The name 'John Gay' is carved by a different hand, but there is no reason to link it with the carving of Pett's name, nor with the date 1695. Many things about it invite suspicion. The carving is stiff and formal, without any sense of individuality. Moreover, just a few inches to the side another name has been carved, Rich, the name of the producer of Gay's *Beggar's Opera*. It is difficult to resist the suspicion that these carvings are the work of a later hand, supplying a convenient autograph of the town's most famous literary son. As with so many other 'facts' about Gay's life, this most 'solid' piece of evidence may be another well-meaning fabrication.

[56] William Gay of Barnstaple (1633), John Gay of Barton, Devon (1634), and John Gay of Frithelstock, Devon (1661), had all matriculated at Exeter College. Other members of the family matriculated at Trinity College (1688) and Merton College (1699); Joseph Foster (ed.), *Alumni Oxonienses 1500–1714* (Liechtenstein, 1968).

[57] At Cambridge Luck lists 46 subscribers, 31 of them at Gonville and Caius; at Oxford, 13 subscribers, 8 of them at Exeter College.

this, but with the proviso that he must at least be permitted to leave provincial Barnstaple and try his fortune in London. His cousin Hester Pinney still kept her lace-shop in Exchange Court off the Strand, and it seems probable that it was she who introduced him to a neighbouring silk-mercer, John Willet, who was in search of an industrious apprentice. Some time before his eighteenth birthday Gay left Devon and came to London as an apprentice in Willet's drapery shop above the New Exchange.[58]

[58] Some of these details are conjectural. It is Pope who mentions the name Willet in a letter to Savage concerning the proposed biographical entry on Gay to be published in *The General Dictionary* (2 Dec. 1736). As usual Pope is concerned to insist on the dignity of Gay's career, and to obscure vulgar or demeaning details: 'as to that of his being apprenticed to one Willet, &c, what are such things to the public? (Pope, *Corr.* iv. 38). The Drapers' Company records mention several Willets, including Thomas, Caleb, and John, who entered their apprenticeships in 1663, 1678, and 1727 respectively (*Roll of the Drapers' Company of London*, ed. Percival Boyd (Croydon, 1934)). The rate-books for the Westminster parish of St Martin-in-the-Fields include the name of a 'mercer' John Willett trading in the 'Outward Walk above New Exchange' from 1702 to 1705, which would include the initial period of Gay's apprenticeship. From 1705 to 1706 these same premises appear under the names of Ann and Sarah Willett, while a James Willett is listed paying rates on a property in the Strand from 1705 to 1709. All this would suggest a family business with more than one outlet within the area. As late as 1815 a James Willett, described as a 'mercer' of St Clement Dane's parish, is included among a number of ratepayers complaining against misappropriation of funds by the Holborn Estates Charity (Westminster Public Records, 10/338a).

TWO

The London Apprentice

> On the first step of a young fellow depends his character for
> life.
>
> (*Achilles*, 1.i)

VERY little is known about Gay's early years in London. A single
business letter, sent from Willet's shop to a distant cousin in
Barnstaple, is the only solid piece of evidence we have from those
formative years during which he accomplished the transition from
draper's apprentice to literary neophyte. Never given to acts of
public retrospection, Gay chose to draw a veil over the details of a
decade during which, it seems, he was variously employed as shop
assistant, Grub Street hack, and domestic secretary. Pope co-oper-
ated in this cover-up, deliberately suppressing information about
Gay's early career. By this amnesiac process an unedifying period in
Gay's life was effectively erased from the official record. The Gay
whom Pope met in 1711 could thus be represented as an innocent
tabula rasa ready to receive the keen impressions of his friend's
literary genius, rather than a man of 26, whose character was already
deeply etched with ten years' toughening experience of the compro-
mises and expedients of London life.

We are left to draw what inferences we can from Gay's silence,
Pope's evasiveness, and the innuendoes of frequently hostile witnesses. The task though is not impossible. Silence can be eloquent;
Pope's sensitivity on certain points is itself highly revealing and a
careful reading of Gay's poetry throws up many tantalizing clues to
the early experiences which stimulated his imagination and helped
to form his character. In reconstructing the 'events' of this period it
is not possible to pretend to strict factual accuracy. But at least, in
deconstructing one mythic version of Gay's life, we can explore the

cultural preconceptions upon which such myths are based, and the social subterfuges which they conveniently conceal.

Irving also passes quickly over this formative period of Gay's life, finding nothing either surprising or demeaning in his employment as a draper's apprentice. 'This arrangement was normal enough at that time', he asserts: 'Younger sons of county families often got their start in life his way.' He insists that those early biographers who pictured Gay resenting this menial occupation 'merely transfer a share of their own snobbery to the poet' and takes it as an article of faith that Gay harboured no such snobbish prejudices himself.[1] This view, however, must be questioned. Throughout his life Gay demonstrated an acute class-consciousness; and, even as a youth of 19, he would have been painfully aware of the vast gulf in social status which separated a London boy apprentice from a university graduate or army officer. In August 1704, just as Gay was beginning his period of indenture to Willet, his brother Jonathan gained his commission as a lieutenant in Lord North and Grey's regiment of foot on the battlefield of Blenheim. A year later Jonathan was promoted to captain in Colonel Owen Wynne's newly raised regiment of foot and served with the regiment in Ireland.[2] It would be surprising if Gay did not reflect bitterly on the contrast between his brother's military honours, his schoolfellows' Oxford opportunities, and his own terms of menial employment.

Apprenticeships at the time took many forms, but the most common type, particularly in London, was the parish apprenticeship. This was a kind of cheap labour whereby foundlings and workhouse children were compulsorily bound to a master craftsman, trader, or journeyman for a term of years for a fee of £5 or so. The London apprentices whose ranks Gay joined in 1704 were not, in the main, the 'younger sons of county families' but parish children, orphans, and foundlings, contracted to a form of virtual slave labour. A report in 1700 declared:

Apprentices put out by a parish are frequently placed with poor, ill-natured or unskilful masters, who either force them out from them by a bad

---

[1] Irving, 24–5.

[2] The Blenheim Roll records that Lieutenant Gay was paid £14 bounty money. He received his Captain's commission on 25 Mar. 1705. The regiment was sent to Ireland in 1706, and served at the siege of Douai, in Flanders, in 1710; Charles Dalton, *English Army Lists and Commission Registers, 1661–1714* (6 vols., London, 1892–1904), v (pt. i), 64, 184; (pt. ii), 45. See also BL Add. MSS 9762, fo. 143.

maintenance or severity before their times are out, or when they are out, send them from them but bunglers in their trade, or masters of such a one as will turn to no account.

A later report was even more damning in its findings:

The greater part of those who now take poor apprentices are the most indigent and dishonest, in a word, the very dregs of the poor of England, by whom it is the fate of many a poor child not only to be half-starved and sometimes bred up to no trade, but to be forced to thieve and steal for his master, and so is brought up for the gallows into the bargain.[3]

The records of the Old Bailey and Quarter Sessions reveal a dismal tale of ill-treatment and starvation. In 1686 Thomas Browne was released from his apprenticeship to John Leake, a glover of St. Margaret's Westminster, as his master had absconded, leaving Browne almost starved, naked, 'eaten up' with vermin, and 'crippled by beatings'. In 1710 the Middlesex Sessions released Daniel Lee from his indentures to Robert St John, a barber and wig-maker of St Martin-in-the-Fields, declaring that 'the said Robert, by reason of his bad circumstances had for three months absconded . . . and gone into the Mint in Southwark for shelter, leaving his said apprentice in a starving condition, almost naked and wholly unprovided for'. St John's wife had advised the youth 'to pilfer and steal for his livelihood'.[4] Even those apprentices not bound by parish regulations were confined by the terms of their indentures to a form of strict domestic servitude. Advertisements appearing in the London papers made it clear that a runaway apprentice was regarded as lost property, just as much as a lost dog or stolen watch.

Whereas Charles Vandersman, about 16 years of age, wearing a brown greatcoat, his own light brown hair, went away from his master, Mr Ellis, joiner in Heathcock Court in the Strand, on Monday the 4th instant. This is to warn all people from entertaining the lad at their peril; and whoever brings him to his said master shall receive 5s reward and reasonable charges.[5]

Gay was not a parish apprentice, and the terms of his employment

[3] *Some Thoughts Concerning the Maintenance of the Poor* (1700), 12; *Enquiry into the Cause of the Increase of the Poor* (1738), 43; quoted in M. Dorothy George, *London Life in the Eighteenth Century* (1925; Penguin edn., Harmondsworth, 1965), 224–5.

[4] *Middlesex Records*, Jan. 1683–6 and Oct. 1710; quoted by Dorothy George, *London Life*, 226.

[5] *Weekly Journal or Saturday Post*, 16 July 1720.

were no doubt far superior to those endured by Browne and Lee. His letter, sent to his kinsman Nicholas Dennis, a wealthy Barnstaple businessman, in January 1705, indicates that the Willets maintained a regular trade with his friends and relations in Devon, and suggests that Gay himself was treated more as part of the family than as an unpaid servant.

London Jan 10 1705

Coz: Dennis, I sent your bed away last Thursday seven-night, the carriage paid to Exon, directed to Mr Athey's as you ordered. The bed comes to £16, and with it I sent you an easy chair of the same as the bed, which my mistress advised me, being very useful, and fashionable he hath made the best sort; it comes to £3, I hope they will please you. I am at present much out of order; I have not heard as yet what the frames that the bed and chair is put up in comes to, but I will not fail of giving an account of everything in a post or two. I have sent you herein the carrier's note for the carriage. Pray tell coz. Richard Parminter that Mr Rolles hath paid me for his neck-cloths. My service to all friends. I am your loving friend and humble servant, John Gay.

Address: To Mr Nicholas Dennis, merchant in Barnstaple, Devon.[6]

Yet, however amiable his master, Gay would have found himself subject, through his articles of indenture, to a whole range of petty rules and regulations governing his daily conduct, both within his place of employment and outside. Former London apprentices made good, like Samuel Richardson and William Hogarth, liked to paint a rosy picture of the prospects for the keen and industrious apprentice who avoided the snares of idleness and dissipation and applied himself with diligence to his chosen trade. For them, the strict rules and prohibitions invariably enshrined in the formal articles of indenture represented not merely a sound code of business practice but a moral basis for life. In *The Apprentice's Vade Mecum* (1734) Richardson set down commandments to be observed by every dutiful

---

[6] *Letters*, 1; Nicholas Dennis (1679–1760) was a leading merchant in Barnstaple and a subscriber to the laying out of the town square in 1715. The exact relationship between Gay and Dennis is unclear, though the friendship between their two families went back for several generations. The parish rate-book for 1683 records Richard Gay living in the house formerly occupied by an earlier Nicholas Dennis, deputy recorder of Barnstaple 1662–4 (Barnstaple Public Records, 3971). The two men also had a mutual connection with the Fortescue family. Nicholas Dennis's mother Jane was a Parminter.

apprentice. He must not 'commit fornication or contract marriage'; he must not 'play at cards, dice, tables, or any other unlawful games'; he must not 'haunt taverns' and must at all costs 'avoid loitering or idleness, that terrible bane of youth'. His dress must be sober and respectable, but without any hint of foppishness or ostentation: 'Pride in dress', Richardson declared, 'is an evil big with terrible consequences, and lifts up the young man's mind far above his condition.' The dutiful apprentice must shun lewd jokes and lewd women and keep the sabbath sacred. But above all he must avoid playhouses. Richardson devoted ten pages of his homiletic pamphlet to the 'shameful depravity' of the stage, and the 'pernicious consequences' of spending time there. Playhouses, he complained, were not only 'the great resort of lewd women', but the plays themselves were calculated to have an equally corrupting effect 'on young and unguarded minds'. Most plays, he protested, especially those written in the 'late licentious age' of Charles II, took a malicious delight in ridiculing sober citizens and conscientious men of trade.

To make a cuckold of a rich citizen is a masterly part of the plot; and such persons are always introduced under the meanest and most contemptible characters. All manner of cheats and frauds and villainies committed against such are encouraged, and inculcated upon an audience; the genteeler part of which are too ready to take the hint, as the men of trade throughout the kingdom every day find to their cost. And this in a kingdom which owes its support, and the figure it makes abroad, entirely to trade; the followers of which are infinitely of more consequence, and deserve more to be encouraged, than any other degree or rank of people in it. Can it then be prudent, or even decent, for a tradesman to encourage by his presence, or support by the effects of his industry, diversions so abusive of the profession by which he lives, and by which not only these caterpillars themselves, but the whole nation is supported.[7]

But Gay was only too familiar with such pious homilies on the dignity of trade. For him the only compensation of his new employment was the opportunity it afforded to sample a metropolitan life, excitingly different in its diversions and allurements from the narrow rectitudes of Barnstaple. Indeed, from the evidence of his own plays, Gay was an avid theatre-goer. During his first year in London

[7] *The Apprentice's Vade Mecum* (1734), pt. i, pp. 3–12; pt. ii, p. 25.

he would have had opportunities to see several Shakespeare plays; the theatre season of 1704–5 included productions of *Hamlet*, *Titus Andronicus*, *Timon of Athens*, and *Macbeth* at Drury Lane, while *Othello* and *1 Henry IV* were performed at Lincoln's Inn Fields. There were productions of *Volpone* both at Drury Lane and at Vanbrugh's handsome new Queen's theatre in the Haymarket, a *Bartholomew Fair* at Drury Lane, and a comedy entitled *A Match in Newgate* which was successful enough to be revived the following year. In April 1706 he almost certainly saw Farquhar's *The Recruiting Officer* at Drury Lane, opposed by D'Urfey's surreal comedy *Wonders in the Sun* at the Queen's theatre; both plays were to have an important influence on his own later writings.[8]

Other distractions of a more sensual nature were close at hand. The New Exchange, where Gay worked, had acquired a particularly *louche* reputation. In his popular gazeteer, *The London Spy*, first published in 1700, Ned Ward described its galleries, shops, and alley-ways as 'a seraglio of fair ladies', the haunt of 'cherubimical lasses who, I suppose, had dressed themselves up for sale to the best advantage, as well as the fopperies and toys they dealt in'. The main customers of these teenage vamps, Ward noted, were beaux, 'who, I imagined, were paying a double-price for linen, gloves or sword-knots to the prettiest of the women, that they might go from thence and boast among their fellow fops what singular favours and great encouragements they had received from the fair ladies that sold 'em'. Gay was equally intrigued by the enticements of this 'jilt's academy' where girls were 'admitted at nine years old, and taught by eleven to out-chatter a magpie'. In setting himself to learn the tricks of the mercery trade, he, like Ward, was fascinated by the beguiling sales-patter of these street-wise shop-girls, some of which Ward arranged in the form of a ditty.

> Fine lace or linen, sir?
> Good gloves or ribbons here;
> What is't you please to buy, sir?

[8] Farquhar was greatly amused by D'Urfey's curious hybrid work at the rival house: 'He brought down a huge flight of frightful birds upon me, when (Heaven knows) I had not a feathered fowl in my play, except one single Kite. But I presently made Plume a bird, because of his name, and Brazen another, because of the feather in his hat; and with these three I engaged his whole empire, which I think was as great a wonder as any in the sun' (*The Recruiting Officer*, ed. Michael Shugrue, Regents Restoration Drama Series (Lincoln, Nebr., 1965), 4).

Pray, what d'ye ask for this?
Ten shillings is the price;
It cost me, sir, no less,
I scorn to tell a lie, sir.

Madam, what is't you want,
Rich fans of India paint?
Fine hoods or scarfs, my lady?
Silk stocks will you buy,
In grain or other dye?
Pray madam, please you eye:
I've as good as e'er was made-ye.[9]

Ten years later the area had acquired an even more disreputable character, and there were dark rumours about the sort of clientele that frequented its shops and taverns. In his poem 'The He-Strumpets' John Dunton identified the New Exchange as the favourite haunt of a club of sodomites, 'Men worse than goats | Who dress themselves in petticoats . . . These doat on men, and some on boys, | And quite abandon female joys.'[10] After the strict puritan morality of Barnstaple, the hedonistic and transvestite atmosphere of this haunt of 'cherub-imical lasses', 'jilts', 'he-whores', and 'he-concubines' must have come as something of an eye-opener. And the evidence suggests that Gay, like Hogarth's idle apprentice, was all too easily tempted from the narrow path of righteousness and industry. One of his earliest bio-graphers writes:

The trade which he chose to be put apprentice to was a mercer, but he grew so fond of reading and study that he frequently neglected to exert himself in putting off silks and velvets to the ladies, and suffered them (by reason of his wanting to finish the sale in too few words) to go to other shops, where they might be kept longer in play. This way of gossiping about among the silk mercers is said to be practised among young ladies, often for amusement or to cure the vapours, when in reality they want to purchase nothing. Not being able to go through this slavery, and doing what he did in the shop with a mind quite bent another way, his master seldom put him forward to serve, but some other, who had the business more at heart. By degrees Mr Gay became entirely to absent himself from

---

[9] Ned Ward, *The London Spy* (1700), ed. Ralph Strauss (London, 1924), 214–16.
[10] John Dunton, *Athenianism; or, The New Projects of Mr John Dunton* (1710), pt. ii, project iv, pp. 93–9.

the shop, and at last, by agreement with his master, to withdraw from it and retire into the country.[11]

There is no evidence to contradict this claim that Gay's release from his indentures was obtained 'by agreement with his master'; yet the decision to abandon his apprenticeship midway through, and with, apparently, no immediate prospect of alternative employment, was still a bold one. Nothing in Gay's subsequent career suggests a man given to impulsive or independent gestures; on the contrary, his career was largely shaped and guided by the influence of friends, without whose promptings he often found himself in a state of paralysing indecision. And, however uncongenial he may have found his role as a draper's apprentice, it seems unlikely he would have thrown it up without the hint, at least, of something better and the encouragement of some influential friend. The career of William Kent, his exact contemporary and friend, offers an instructive parallel. Like Gay, Kent was born in 1685 in a provincial seaside town, Bridlington in Yorkshire. His family, like Gay's, were of modest social standing and clearly believed a trade apprenticeship was the best means of securing their son's future prospects. Accordingly, as Horace Walpole wrote, Kent was

put apprentice to a coach-painter, but feeling the emotions of genius, he left his master without leave and repaired to London, where he studied a little, and gave indications enough of abilities to excite a generous patronage in some gentlemen of his own county, who raised a contribution sufficient to send him to Rome, whither he accompanied Mr Talman in 1710.[12]

For both Kent and Gay, patronage was the essential prerequisite for an artistic career. A crucial turning-point in both their lives came with their inclusion among the artistic entourage of the young Earl of Burlington after his return from Italy in 1715. In the years that followed, Burlington House became a hothouse for the artistic avant-garde. Painters and poets, architects and interior decorators, composers and opera-singers, all enjoyed the Earl's bountiful patronage. However, recent scholarship, examining the prevailing atmosphere of the Burlington House milieu, has discerned a distinct

---

[11] William Ayre, *Memoirs of the Life and Writings of Alexander Pope, Esq.* (1745), ii. 97.

[12] Horace Walpole, *Anecdotes of Painting in England*, ed. R. L. Wornum (London, 1849), iii. 777.

homo-erotic undertone within this cultural coterie, raising a suggestion which is worth exploring further.[13] Traditional studies of
eighteenth-century patronage have tended to concentrate on political
affiliations, without sufficiently regarding the personal compliancy
that was no less necessary in successful aspirants to patronage.
William Kent was well aware that personal charm was just as
important as artistic genius or political acquiescence in securing the
financial assistance he needed. And the insistent preoccupations of
Gay's later satires suggest that he too had learnt early on in his
career that private ingratiation as much as public flattery was vital to
maintaining a patron's favour. The intensity of his later attacks on
the fawning, cringing, sycophancy of those dependent on great
men's favours suggests that something more intimate than simple
political integrity had been compromised in his own early efforts at
self-promotion. Likewise, the urgent attempts of Pope and Swift to
suppress and sanitize the details of Gay's early private life would
seem to confirm a suspicion that there was something they wished to
conceal more shameful than a mere background in trade.

It seems quite probable that the guilty secret which they wished
to hide was homosexuality. Such an assertion must of course be
made with caution. Although this suggestion has been raised before,
it has never been explored in detail, and the evidence upon which it
rests is, necessarily, inferential.[14] Moreover, in recent years, the
disclosure of secret homosexual tendencies has become something of
a biographical cliché, an almost routine exercise in posthumous
'outing'. And, in dealing with an eighteenth-century subject, clear
evidence is particularly difficult to establish. The Sodomy Acts of

[13] 'All his life Kent lived with Burlington; his place in the Burlington household was a
very special one, and there is no reason not to presume a close homosexual relationship.'
John Harris, *The Palladians* (London, 1981), 18. In private correspondence John Harris
has confirmed this view. 'I was the first to suggest an homoerotic relationship between
Burlington and Kent, and I got flak for it! . . . Kent was extremely feminine, giggly, fun,
whereas Burlington was clinical and aloof. I think it is legitimate to explore this . . . Kent
possessed a face like a woman's, very soft.' Private letter to me, 12 Dec. 1989.

[14] G. S. Rousseau finds a 'frequently homoerotic' tone in the correspondence of the
Scriblerians, 'especially [of] John Gay, who never married and whose psychological
attachment to the older, if occasionally paternal, Pope merits more attention than it has
received.' G. S. Rousseau, 'The Pursuit of Homosexuality in the Eighteenth Century', in
R. P. Maccubbin (ed.), *'Tis Nature's Fault: Unauthorized Sexuality during the Enlightenment* (Cambridge, 1987), 134. Rousseau's arguments must be treated with some caution;
he discerns homo-erotic tendencies in almost all the major writers of the period, and fails
to notice that Gay is actually three years *older* than the 'paternal' Pope.

1533, which remained in force throughout the seventeenth and eighteenth centuries, made homosexuality a capital offence and, although rarely enforced, ensured that this 'unnamable practice' was surrounded with the utmost secrecy. To the extent that it was acknowledged to exist at all, it was a matter of private gossip and innuendo, and customarily associated with a debauched and decadent court.

The homosexual liaisons of James I—possibly unknown outside the court—relaxed the sense of oppression in England because the court was, and remained well into the seventeenth century, the center of homosexual activity. But opinion turned when the second Earl of Castelhaven was exposed. His 'sodomitical compulsion' with men *and* women resulted in a set of trials in the 1630s that called attention to the acts of 1533 and 'to all those practising the unnamable'.[15]

Rochester's closet drama *Sodom; or, The Quintessence of Debauchery*, and the persistent rumours concerning William III's unnatural fondness for his alleged 'catamite' the Earl of Albemarle, confirmed a general tendency to regard such liaisons as the peculiar depravities of court and aristocratic life. Pope shared the conventional horror at this vice. His uncorroborated assertion 'Addison and Steele [were] a couple of h——s' (hermaphrodites) was clearly intended to wound their reputations, while his savage attack on that 'amphibious thing' the 'hermaphroditical' Lord Hervey is full of homophobic rage.[16]

Gay's writings though are characterized by an ambiguous sexuality with distinct hermaphroditic tendencies, while his private life is notable for a conspicuous silence concerning any emotional or sexual ties. His friends always liked to picture him as a thoroughgoing rake. Pope's letter welcoming Gay home from Hanover in September 1714 is typical.

Hast thou passed through many countries, and not tasted the delights thereof? Hast thou not left thy issue in divers lands, that German Gays and Dutch Gays may arise, to write pastorals and sing their songs in strange countries?[17]

Gay did his best to maintain this pose, often striving to affect the

---

[15] Ibid. 137.
[16] Spence, item 188; i. 80.
[17] Pope, *Corr.* i. 255.

jaunty, rakish air of an experienced ladies' man. In cheerfully lubricious ballads he would celebrate the carnal delights of 'Molly Mog' or 'Nelly Bennet'. An apocryphal anecdote describes Cibber 'breaking in upon Mr Gay's privacies, found him engaged with his own daughter, and therefore pulled him off'.[18] But in reality there is no evidence of his sexual involvement with any women at all, and his half-hearted courtship, late in life, of Anne Drelincourt, was decidedly unenthusiastic. By contrast his letters to male patrons are characterized by intense professions of affection. One early friend and patron was the young Earl of Warwick, a youth thirteen years Gay's junior. Warwick was a self-styled connoisseur of debauchery, and a devotee of every kind of sexual prank. It was he, aged only 18, who 'slily seduced' Pope and Cibber into a 'house of carnal recreation, near the Haymarket' intent on setting Pope up with 'a girl of the game'.[19] This was a kind of aristocratic libertinism which fascinated Gay. He sent Warwick regular salacious accounts of his own Continental jaunts, though sadly none of these has survived. ''Tis impossible to owe you more love and gratitude than I do already,' he told Warwick in 1720.[20] The following year Warwick's dissolute life-style took its toll, and he died, still aged only 23, 'killed ... with his debauchery'.[21] Gay was devastated by the news. 'I loved him,' he told Francis Colman, 'and cannot help feeling concern whenever I think of him.'[22] The Earl of Burlington was another youthful nobleman whose patronage of Gay was characterized by hints of homo-erotic affection. Although never identified as a sexual libertine, Burlington's enthusiasm for all things Italian, and in particular for Italian castrati, provoked accusations of cultural, if not personal, decadence. Burlington House was frequently represented as fostering an 'unmanly' atmosphere of artistic depravity. Commenting on the homo-erotic intimacy of Burlington and Kent,

[18] Spence, item 253; i. 111.

[19] Cibber told the story in his *Letter from Mr Cibber to Mr Pope* (1742), where he claimed that he himself had interrupted this sexual encounter, out of concern for Pope's *Homer*, which might have been 'cut short by laying up our little gentleman of a malady which his thin body might never have been cured of' (pp. 44, 47, 49). Pope repudiated Cibber's account of the incident, but did acknowledge that Lord Warwick had 'carried me and Cibber in his coach to a bawdy-house' (Spence, item 251; i. 110).

[20] *Letters*, 6. On the misdating of the letter, see Dearing, 601.

[21] G. E. Cokayne (ed.), XII. *The Complete Peerage of England, Scotland, Ireland* (rev. and enlarged edn., 12 vols., London, 1910–59), ii. 418.

[22] *Letters*, 39.

John Harris argues: 'The *frisson* that such suggestions evoke is often caused by a picture of hard homosexuality, whereas it was, and is, often playful and not necessarily deeply sexual.'[23] A previously unpublished letter, which Gay sent to Burlington in 1722, is revealing in its professions of lover-like devotion.

I hope your lordship knows me; if you do, you must know that I love you . . . If you knew how often I think upon your lordship you would now then think of me [*sic*] I hope you will not forget me, for I know my heart so well that it will always be sensible of your favours, though I must own I love you more for what I see in yourself than for what you have done for me, which is much more than I can ever deserve.[24]

Such evidence must be treated with circumspection. Expressions of love in the male correspondence of this period are quite common, and need not convey any implication of homosexuality. Yet there is an unusual emotional intensity in the way Gay addresses himself to Warwick and Burlington which is quite different from the style of his correspondence with Pope and Swift. The tone he adopts is one almost of infatuation, presenting himself as a suitor, desperate to please the object of his affections. Though there is no clear evidence of a homosexual relationship with either patron, the lover-like eagerness of Gay's efforts at ingratiation hints at such a possibility. The abruptness and intensity of the sudden rift between Burlington and Gay following the success of *The Beggar's Opera* has some savour of a jealous lovers' spat. In parodying Italian opera, Gay was ridiculing the Earl's darling project, and his gesture of artistic independence seems to have struck Burlington as a form of emotional betrayal.

So, was Gay gay? And if so, did he use his sexuality as a means of recommending himself to patrons? If the suggestion seems preposterous, it is worth remembering that one of his closest friends was Mrs Howard, who owed her own advancement to her position as the king's mistress. The two of them met at Hanover in 1714, both sharing an intention to ingratiate themselves with the incoming royal dynasty. Mrs Howard was determined to escape the grinding poverty which had driven her, the previous year, to sell not only her meagre household furniture, but also her hair. She found a means of

---

[23] Private letter to me, 12 Dec. 1989.
[24] Gay to Burlington, 3 Oct. 1722; Chatsworth MSS 173.

doing so by exploiting her sexuality and becoming the mistress of
the Electoral Prince George. For all his seeming innocence, Gay was
equally intent upon freeing himself from a life of poverty and menial
employments. In 1706, still bound by the terms of his apprenticeship, he was determined to escape the drudgery of the drapery trade
and launch himself on a literary career. What he most needed was
the protection of some wealthy nobleman, and the atmosphere of the
New Exchange was one in which such contacts could easily be
made. The tone of Gay's later letters and poetry suggest that he may
have quickly learnt, in that 'jilt's academy', the appropriate beguiling
patter. Dunton attacked the transvestite fetishism of fashionable
sodomites ('Men worse than goats | Who dress themselves in
petticoats), but Gay's poems frequently betray a transvestite fascination with women's clothing which seems to go beyond the necessary
expertise of a silk-mercer's apprentice. In his *Epistle to the Earl of
Burlington* (1720) he describes a delicious state of erotic excitement
occasioned by wearing a chambermaid's smock:

> If women's gear such pleasing dreams incite,
> Lend us your smocks, ye damsels, ev'ry night!   (ll. 107–8)

In his posthumously produced play *Achilles*, the Homeric hero is
dressed in women's clothes throughout, leading the *Daily Courant*
to denounce the play as an exhibition of 'so much obscenity and
scurrility that it raised a general abhorrence in the audience'.[25] But
the most intriguing example of this transvestite tendency occurs as
the climax of the first book of Gay's early poem *The Fan*.

> How shall I soar, and on unweary wing
> Trace varying habits upward to their spring!
> What force of thought, what numbers can express,
> Th'inconstant equipage of female dress?
> How the strait stays the slender waist constrain,
> How to adjust the manteau's sweeping train?
> What fancy can the petticoat surround,
> With the capacious hoop of whalebone bound?
> But stay, presumptuous muse, nor boldly dare,
> The *toilette's* sacred mysteries declare;
> Let a just distance be to beauty paid,

---

[25] *Daily Courant*, 12 Feb. 1733.

None here must enter but the trusty maid.
Should you the wardrobe's magazine rehearse,
And glossy manteaus rustle in thy verse;
Should you the rich brocaded suit unfold,
Where rising flow'rs grow stiff with frosted gold;
The dazzled muse would from her subject stray,
And in a maze of fashions lose her way.   (ll. 227–44)

These lines recall Gay's recent experience in the rag-trade. Like the
'trusty maid', the silk-mercer's assistant is initiated into all the
intimate female mysteries of hoops, stays, and petticoats. Gay's
fetishistic fascination with the details of feminine underwear simultaneously conveys a thrill of voyeuristic excitement and a sense of
personal indignity. There is, he acknowledges, something unbecom-
ing to the heroic muse in the intimate familiarity with which he
rehearses 'the wardrobe's magazine'. Yet, while directing his 'presumptuous muse' to soar above such effeminate preoccupations,
Gay nevertheless allows his lines, and his imagination, to linger
among them. Relegated to the role of silk-mercer's apprentice, Gay
no doubt felt that he too had lost his way in a 'maze of fashions'; yet
the sensuous delight with which he itemizes each garment suggests a
sexual excitement beneath the pose of literary condescension. Gay
approaches the traditional satiric subject of female fashions not with
the patronizing tone of the masculine moralist, but with the sly,
indiscreet knowledge of the lady's outfitter and transvestite spy.
Often, in his mock-heroic satires, Gay puts this expertise to use,
suggesting a corsetry of whalebone and linen beneath the heroic
Roman postures of great men. Thus he begins the second book of
The Fan with lofty evocations of both Homer and Milton:

Olympus' gates unfold; in Heav'ns high tow'rs
Appear in council all th'immortal pow'rs;
Great Jove above the rest exalted sat . . .   (ii. 1–3)

This sudden change of tone to literary grandiloquence contains an
ironic backward glance towards the wardrobe crammed with hoops
and stays from which the muse has just emerged; the unfolding of
Olympus's gate reminds us irresistibly of the unfolding of a brocaded
suit just four lines earlier. Gay's early familiarity with 'th'inconstant
equipage of female dress' gave him a yardstick for measuring all
subsequent manifestations of human vanity. But it also seems to

have satisfied a deeper, but related, psychological instinct. The 'rising flow'rs' which 'grow stiff' at the manteau's rustle and the rich brocade hint at a form of sexual arousal associated with female dress; and the sense of delirium that follows, as the 'dazzled muse' strays from her subject and is lost 'in a maze of fashions', reinforces an impression of fetishistic ecstasy.

Clues like these may seem an insubstantial basis for deciding on the nature of Gay's sexuality, a subject which must inevitably remain a matter for conjecture. But if Gay was, as I believe, at least a latent homosexual, it would provide a partial answer to several unresolved questions in his career. It is perfectly possible that simple disaffection with his duties at Willet's shop led to an increased sense of boredom and frustration which culminated in a decision to break the terms of his indentures. In his letter to Nicholas Dennis he describes himself as 'much out of order' and clearly, whatever secret pleasure he derived from the rustle of manteaus and brocades, he found the business side of the mercer's trade irksome and undignified. In my view, it is more likely that this decision was prompted by the advice of an unknown friend or would-be patron encouraging Gay to develop his literary talents. And, in the *louche* atmosphere of the New Exchange, any patron thus promoting the interests of a provincial youth might expect to be repaid with more than literary favours. But, in offering this hypothesis, it is important to resist presenting an updated version of Pope's 'ruling passion' theory: 'This clue once found, unravels all the rest.' Whether Gay was homosexual, celibate, or, as his friends liked to pretend, a promiscuous heterosexual, he encountered problems in seeking to establish his literary career which no early patron was willing, or able, to overcome. One thing is clear. In the later months of 1706 Gay's affairs reached some kind of crisis and he finally resolved to abandon his career in trade. At that point he returned to Barnstaple to reassess his prospects.

THREE

Grub Street Apollo

. . . I find I have quite forgot The British Apollo . . .
(J. G., *The Present State of Wit*, 1711)

GAY did not remain long in Barnstaple. In July the following year his uncle Hanmer died, and Gay set out once more for London. Now a young man of 22, his future prospects were still unclear. He had turned his back on the trading and commercial worlds in which so many of his family and acquaintances were employed, but lacked the money and the social connections necessary to promote him into a more sophisticated milieu. His only known contact in the literary world was his former school-friend Aaron Hill, and it was Hill he turned to on his return to London. Thirty years later, when writing his *Life of Gay*, Richard Savage was advised to contact Hill for information about Gay's early career. By that time, though, Hill's recollections were distinctly hazy.

I would willingly satisfy the curiosity of your friend in relation to Mr Gay, if it were not easy to get much fuller information than I am able to give from Mr Budgell or Mr Pope; to the first of whom the beginning of his life was best known, and to the last, its afternoon and evening. That poem you speak of, called *Wine*, he printed in the year 1710, as I remember: I am sure I have one among my pamphlets, but they lie (like ideas in an unlogical head) so oppressively numerous, and obstructively mixed, that to distinguish any one of them, out of the heap, is a task of more labour than consequence. Yet I will look for it, and send it to you, if 'twill be of use, or satisfaction, to any gentleman of your acquaintance. As to your question, whether Mr Gay was ever a domestic of the duchess of Monmouth, I can answer it in the affirmative. He was her secretary about the year 1713, and continued so till he went over to Hanover, in the beginning of the following year, with Lord Clarendon, who was sent thither by Queen Anne. At his return, upon the death of that queen, all his hopes became withered, 'till Mr Pope, (who, you know, is an excellent planter) revived and invigorated his bays; and indeed very generously supported him, in some more solid improvements; for I remember a letter, wherein he invited him to partake of his fortune, (at that time but a small one) assuring him, with a very un-poetical warmth, that as long as himself had a shilling, Mr Gay should be welcome to sixpence of it; nay to eightpence, if he could contrive but to live on a groat. So much for Mr Gay.[1]

Savage promptly applied to Pope for fuller details, only to find this 'excellent planter' was equally evasive in his reply. Like Hill, who thought it a task 'of more labour than consequence' to hunt out a lost poem, Pope found himself 'in so much hurry' that he was unable to supply further particulars.

I answer yours by the first post, since I find they are in so much haste about Mr Gay's Life. It is not possible for me to do his memory the justice I wish in so much hurry, therefore I would by no means have my name made use of, where I cannot have the account such as it ought. I only recommend to your friendship that nothing be said of any particular obligations that worthy and ingenious man had to me, further than a sincere esteem and the natural effect of it. I am sure they will do him injustice if they say more on that article. And as to that of his being apprenticed to one Willett, etc., what are such things to the public? Authors are to be remembered by the works and merits, not accidents of their lives. But if they will speak of his condition of life, let them remember to say he was born of an ancient family, and secretary, not servant, to the duchess of Monmouth. As to that, which would be most material, his true character, it was every way amiable; and none of his school-fellows could draw that, which was manifested in the future course of his life to those of the nobility and first geniuses of his time, who loved him, and with whom he conversed entirely. I take Mr Hill's zeal very kindly, and it is agreeable to that spirit and warmth which he always shows for virtue and learning. I am only afraid of his exceeding in what he says concerning me. I do own I wish, since I cannot now contribute (upon the foot the work stands) any additions, that I might have the power of some expunctions, and could see the proofs to that end. Otherwise it will be better I should not be privy to the least of the matter.[2]

---

[1] Hill to Savage, 23 June 1736: *The Works of Aaron Hill, Esq., in Four Volumes* (1753), i. 338

[2] Pope to Savage, 17 Oct. 1736; Pope, *Corr.* iv. 37–8.

What is most noticeable about Pope's response is the clear desire to dignify Gay's memory by suppressing all suggestions of lowly origins or menial employments. Pope prefers to dismiss Gay's apprenticeship as a thing of no consequence, and is careful to raise Gay's status in the Duchess of Monmouth's household from that of servant to the more respectable role of secretary. He is also clearly concerned lest Gay's former schoolfellows should supply Savage with indiscreet anecdotes of Gay's early years which might detract from the sanitized accounts furnished by 'those of the nobility and first geniuses of his time, who loved him'. And, characteristically, while Pope found it impossible to supply Savage with additions to his biography, he nevertheless requested the right to make tactful 'expunctions' from the drafts. Pope is notorious for having thoroughly revised and re-edited the published version of his corres-pondence, carefully expunging *risqué* letters to such disreputable early friends as Henry Cromwell. Doubtless part of his reluctance to expatiate on Gay's early career was due to a desire not to expose some less than glorious episodes in his own past history, since, almost certainly, it was the *louche boulevardier* Cromwell who had first brought them together. Similarly, too much emphasis on Gay's poverty, or on the broken terms of his apprenticeship, might cast an unwelcome ironic reflection on the high-minded pose that Pope now adopted towards his Grub Street foes. In the 'Letter to the Publisher' included among the Prolegomena to the *Dunciad Variorum* (1729) Pope defended himself against the charge of unfairly attacking impoverished authors. 'I question not but such authors are poor', he wrote; 'but poverty itself becomes a just subject of satire when it is the consequence of vice, prodigality, or neglect of one's lawful calling.'[3] Charges of prodigality, and of neglecting his 'lawful call-ing', could equally be levelled against Gay, and even the hint of secret 'vice' could not be entirely discounted.

For a more objective account of this period of Gay's life we must look not to his over-protective friends, but to an enemy, the pseu-donymous E. Parker, 'Philomath', who, in his scurrilous *Key* to *Three Hours after Marriage* (1717), offered this mocking summary of Gay's early career.

He was born of honest tho' mean parentage, who by their thrift and industry made a shift to save wherewithal to apprentice him out to a stuff

---

[3] *The* Dunciad *Variorum*, 'A Letter to the Publisher' (1729).

man, but at the expiration of his time, being taken from that employ, he became amanuensis to Aaron Hill Esq., when that gentleman set on foot the project of answering questions in a weekly paper called *The British Apollo*.[4]

Aaron Hill was Gay's exact contemporary, but had already enjoyed a far more glamorous and cosmopolitan career than his provincial school-friend. Born in Beaufort Buildings in the Strand, he was sent to Barnstaple when only 9 years old, following the death of his father, who had made an illegal sale of the estate entailed on his infant son. However, Hill completed his education in greater style at Westminster, and, shortly after his fifteenth birthday, sailed to Constantinople, where Lord Paget, a distant relation, was ambassador. Returning three years later he set about compiling a volume of Turkish memoirs; but this work, intended as a prestige publication to boost his literary reputation, needed careful preparation. In the mean time Hill busied himself with dull but lucrative hack-work on the *British Apollo*, a 'question-and-answer' journal designed to cater for the tastes of London's self-improving middle classes. Published at first twice weekly, in February 1708, the *British Apollo* was soon appearing three times a week as subscriptions flowed in, and Hill gathered a team of willing friends to help him satisfy his readership's demands for esoteric information. The *Apollo*'s success was largely founded on the eclecticism of its interests. In response to an apparently insatiable public curiosity for strange facts, its columns were filled with ostensibly authoritative information on all manner of topics—arts and sciences, morality, theology, medicine, and manners. No subject was too recherché for Hill's self-styled 'society of gentlemen' to tackle, and they pronounced with equal apparent confidence on queries concerning the virtues of tobacco, the blackness of negroes, on why venereal disease affects the bridge of the nose, and on whether the water that Christ turned into wine was red or white.

The idea for such a periodical was not new. Back in 1691 John Dunton had launched his own omniscient question-and-answer paper called the *Athenian Gazette*, later renamed the *Athenian Mercury*. The circulation and reputation of this journal remained high for several years, attracting support and contributions from such distinguished figures as Lord Halifax and Swift's patron, Sir

---

[4] E. Parker, 'Philomath', *A Complete Key to . . . Three Hours after Marriage* (1717).

William Temple. Even Swift himself had honoured Dunton's contributors in an early eulogistic ode as 'ye great unknown and far-
exalted men'.[5] The *Athenian Mercury* had ceased publication some
ten years before the appearance of the *British Apollo*, but Dunton
fiercely resented Hill's attempt to copy his original formula. Denouncing Hill's 'piracy' as 'the greatest arrogance that I ever saw in a
hackney writer', Dunton reacted by publishing a rival paper called
Dunton's Apollo, a name chosen, he assured readers, not 'out of
ostentation' but 'purely to show how sordidly Mr H—— has acted
to interlope with my question project, and to continue it several
months under the title of *British Apollo*'.[6]

Gay had more than just the fact of former school acquaintanceship
to recommend him to Hill's notice. His first poem *Wine*, published,
perhaps with Hill's assistance, in May 1708, was a virtuoso performance, consciously designed to attract both literary and political
attention. In this it was at least partially successful; the pirate
publisher Henry Hills considered the poem sufficiently appealing to
rush out another edition later that summer.[7] *Wine* is a highly
characteristic piece; a brief but nevertheless ambitious *jeu d'esprit*;
deliberately ephemeral, yet still revelling in a multi-layered literary
allusiveness. What appears at first sight as a Miltonic parody is in
fact a kind of double jest, a parody of a parody, imitating the mock-
Miltonic burlesque of John Philips's poem *The Splendid Shilling*
(1701). Johnson was not much taken with this kind of derivative
humour. He said of Philips's poem: 'To degrade the sounding words
and stately constructions of Milton by an application to the lowest
and most trivial things, gratifies the mind with a momentary triumph
over that grandeur which hitherto held its captives in admiration.'
But he denied Gay even this 'momentary triumph'.

The merit of such performances begins and ends with the first author. He
that should again adapt Milton's phrase to the gross incidents of common
life, and even adapt it with more art, which would not be difficult, must yet
expect but a small part of the praise which Philips has obtained; he can
only hope to be considered as the repeater of a jest.[8]

Gay though does more than merely repeat Philips's jest. He com-

[5] 'Ode to the Athenian Society' (1691), in Swift, *Poems*, i. 13–25.
[6] *Athenian News; or, Dunton's Oracle*, 11–14 Mar. 1710.
[7] The poem was advertised as 'just published' in the *Daily Courant* for 22 May 1708.
[8] Samuel Johnson, *The Lives of the English Poets* (Oxford, 1964), 'J. Philips', i. 22–3.

bines an affectionate burlesque of Milton with a knowing parody of some of Philips's own works.[9] The opening is typical:

> Of happiness terrestrial, and the source
> Whence human pleasures flow, sing heavenly muse,
> Of sparkling juices, of th'enliv'ning grape
> Whose quick'ning taste adds vigour to the soul . . .
>
> (*Wine*, ll. 1–4)

This is an obvious parody of the opening of *Paradise Lost*:

> Of Man's first disobedience, and the fruit
> Of that forbidden tree, whose mortal taste
> Brought death into the world, and all our woe,
> With loss of Eden, till one greater man
> Restore us, and regain the blissful seat,
> Sing heav'nly muse . . .
>
> (*Paradise Lost*, i. 1–6)

In this cavalier gesture Gay pokes fun at the sober pieties of his puritan background, transforming the 'mortal taste' which 'brought death into the world' into the 'enliv'ning grape, | Whose quickening taste adds vigour to the soul'. Gay's emphasis is on life, not death, as he teasingly decants spiritual causes into spirituous effects. In his poem *Cyder* (January 1708) Philips had similarly fermented Milton's forbidden fruit into a wholesome rustic beverage which still retained some savour of pre-lapsarian joys.

> Thy gift, Pomona, in Miltonian verse
> Advent'rous I presume to sing . . .
>
> (*Cyder*, ll. 3–4)

Celebrating this native drink, Philips claimed that Hereford cider

> far surmounts
> Gallic, or Latin grapes, or those that see
> The setting sun near Calpe's towering height.
>
> (*Cyder*, i. 535–7)

Devon, like Herefordshire, was a cider-growing county, but in this, his first London poem, Gay was as keen to distance himself from

---

[9] For a detailed commentary on Gay's parodic allusions throughout this poem to Milton's and Philips's works, see Dearing, ii. 474–85.

home-brew tastes as from home-town morality. Assuming a patrician air he mocks the descent of Philips's muse from the martial grandeur of his poem *Blenheim* (1705) to lie 'inglorious, flound'ring' in this provincial brew:

> Languid and faint, and on damp wing immerg'd
> In acid juice, in vain attempts to rise.
>
> (*Wine*, ll. 125–6)

By contrast Gay adopts the pose of a sophisticated wine connoisseur:

> Name, sirs, the wine that most invites your taste,
> Champagne or burgundy, or Florence pure,
> Or hock antique, or Lisbon new or old,
> Bordeaux, or neat French White, or Alicant . . .
>
> (*Wine*, ll. 197–200)

Wine is a highly self-conscious poem, with more than a hint of adolescent bravado in the way it perverts sober Miltonic sentiments into bacchanalian pranks. There is a conscious dare-devil air in the way the antics of Gay's tavern-companions parody the ambitions of Satan's fallen angels. 'Jocund and boon', like Eve after eating the forbidden fruit,[10] these 'rais'd souls . . . hie to [the] Devil' (tavern), where the companionable code of Ben Jonson's *leges conviviales* defies any higher moral authority. The resulting ambiguity of tone is most evident in an uneasy sexist posturing. Women are specifically excluded from this Dionysiac fraternity, and wine is presented not as the prelude to sexual pleasure, but as the antidote to insatiable marital demands.

> Whether inveigling Hymen has trappan'd
> Th'unwary youth, and tied the Gordian knot
> Of jangling wedlock, indissoluble;
> Worried all day by loud Xantippe's din,
> And when the gentle dew of sleep inclines
> With slumb'rous weight his eye-lids, she inflam'd
> With uncloy'd lust, and itch insatiable,
> His stock exhausted, still yells on for *more* . . .   (ll. 22–9)[11]

---

[10] *Paradise Lost*, ix. 793.

[11] These last three lines were omitted from Bell's edition of Gay's poems (1773), which also excluded this piece of schoolboyish priapic parody: 'O thou, that first my

Several of the poem's more crudely misogynistic lines were later
omitted by Gay's over-protective editors, who thereby suppressed
much of its psychological interest. In introducing himself in this
mock-satanic guise, Gay toys with a sense of transgression. Not only
the sober pieties of Barnstaple are mocked in this stylish burlesque,
but also the sexual pleasures of ordinary domestic life.

Politically, the poem walks a tightrope. Consciously designing it
as an exercise in literary self-promotion, Gay displays a dexterity in
political compliment without risking commitment to a clear party
line. Ostensibly it suggests Whiggish sympathies, parodying Philips's
Blenheim, a poem designed to put a Tory gloss on Marlborough's
victory and written, Johnson suggests, 'at the house of Mr St John'.
Amid their drunken revels, Gay's companions offer loyal toasts to
Queen Anne, her royal consort Prince George, and five leading
figures of the Whig political establishment.

> The hero Marlboro' next, whose vast exploits
> Fame's clarion sounds, fresh laurels, triumphs new
> We wish, like those he won at Hockstet's field.
> Next Devonshire illustrious, who from race
> Of noblest patriots sprung, whose soul endow'd,
> And is with ev'ry virtuous gift adorn'd
> That shone in his most worthy ancestors,
> For then distinct in sep'rate breasts were seen
> Virtues distinct, but all in him unite.
> Prudent Godolphin, of the nation's weal
> Frugal, but free and gen'rous of his own
> Next crowns the bowl, with faithful Sunderland,
> And Halifax, the muses' darling son,
> In whom conspicuous, with full lustre shine
> The surest judgment, and the brightest wit,
> Himself Maecenas and a Flaccus too . . .

>   (*Wine*, ll. 232–47)

But the political significance of these lines is far from clear.[12] The
statesmen mentioned were all prominent Whigs, yet the tone of
Gay's praise has that characteristic hint of exaggeration that teeters

---

quicken'd soul engaged, | Still with thy aid assist me, what is dark | Illumine, what is low,
raise and support . . . | (ll. 113–15; cf. *Paradise Lost*, i. 22–4).

[12] 'The politics behind these five toasts is curious and confused,' Dearing, ii. 483.

on the brink of parody. '*Wine* is a burlesque,' one recent scholar reminds us: 'Why then should it be automatically assumed that the toasts at the end of the poem are to be read unambiguously?' In terms of the poem's burlesque strategy, 'it is far from clear whether this is a list of faithful or fallen angels . . .'

It is distinctly unusual, in the literature of the period, to find Lord Treasurer Godolphin described as 'free and gen'rous of his own' resources; he was not a notably altruistic man. Worse, to call Sunderland 'Faithful' borders on the perverse, as he was notoriously irreligious![13]

In his *Directions for a Birth-Day Song* (written 1729) Swift pre-scribed an ironic strategy for disguising satire as panegyric:

> Thus your encomiums, to be strong,
> Must be applied directly wrong:
> A tyrant for his mercy praise,
> And crown a royal dunce with bays:
> A squinting monkey load with charms;
> And paint a coward fierce in arms.
> Is he to avarice inclin'd?
> Extol him for his gen'rous mind.   (ll. 117–24)

Was Gay's praise of the 'free and gen'rous' Godolphin likewise intended as an ironic accusation of avarice? Two years before the publication of *Wine*, Dr Joseph Browne was pilloried for his poem *The Country Parson's Honest Advice to that . . . Worthy Minister of State, My Lord Keeper*, which consisted entirely of the names of Whig politicians ironically praised for virtues which they lacked.

> Be wise as Somerset, as Somers brave,
> As Pembroke airy, and as Richmond grave;
> Humble as Orford be; and Wharton's zeal
> For church and loyalty would fit thee well.

As Professor Downie notes: 'There seems little distance between this ironic praise of Wharton's religious zeal, and Gay's extolling of "Faithful Sunderland".'[14] What Gay has contrived in this poem is

---

[13] J. A. Downie, 'Gay's Politics', in Lewis and Wood, 45–8. I am indebted to Professor Downie's comments in this analysis of Gay's poem.

[14] Interestingly, *The Country Parson's Honest Advice* concludes with a mock roll-call of Whig virtues, including 'Devonshire's chastity', 'Godolphin's probity', and 'Halifax his modesty', which bears a striking resemblance to the terms of Gay's toasts.

an equivocal and highly characteristic double bluff. On one level, these toasts, with their ostensible pledges of Whig loyalty, were no doubt intended as an exercise in political ingratiation. No aspiring young author of the time would omit flattering the literary judgement of that patron of the arts Lord Halifax. It was likewise a shrewd hint to praise the 'gen'rous' nature of the Lord Treasurer, who controlled the purse-strings of court patronage. But, read another way, Gay could explain these sycophantic lines away as cunning ironic gibes. Throughout his life two competing ambitions dominated Gay's mental outlook; the first, a compulsion to achieve social and literary respectability through the protection of a wealthy and influential patron; the second, a determination to retain a sense of his own integrity and honesty. At times the struggle between these two conflicting drives produced a kind of schizophrenia, resulting in listlessness, illness, and a debilitating uncertainty about his own identity and values. While his social ambitions drove him to flatter those whom he despised, his conscience forced him to tinge each sycophantic phrase with satire. In literary terms he found a constant refuge in irony; and *Wine* shows him, at the outset of his career, already well skilled in the deceptive political art of double-edged praise.

Wine is a youthful exercise, ostentatious and sometimes uncertain in its parodic effects, and ambiguous in both its literary and political affiliations. It is the self-consciously irreverent and daring work of a young man who knows that, from his uncle's point of view, he has already gone to the devil, but who, from his own perspective, has yet to find which fallen angel to serve. In the short term at least, he chose to serve Aaron Hill.

The *British Apollo* was Gay's university. Hill's 'society of gentlemen' comprised a lively and eccentric group of self-styled polymaths, quacks, and dilettantes. A few were men of genuine learning, many with a medical background. Dr James Mauclerc, son of a Huguenot doctor from Montpellier, was admitted to the College of Physicians *in forma pauperis* in 1689. His copy of the first two volumes of the *British Apollo* can still be seen in Harvard University Library, with marginal notes to indicate that he answered some seventy questions during that period.[15] Dr William Coward combined a taste for religious polemic with some dogmatic theories on poetry, while Dr

---

[15] In later years Mauclerc collaborated with Samuel Richardson in compiling *The Christian Magazine, or Treasure: Containing a Choice Collection of many Remarkable*

Roger Grant found fame and fortune as a miracle-working oculist. From time to time the columns of the journal were enlivened by verses supplied by more distinguished literary names. The Poet Laureate, Nahum Tate, who had collaborated with Hill in some translations from Ovid's *Metamorphoses*, made some occasional contributions.[16] And the future Poet Laureate Nicholas Rowe, currently preoccupied with his edition of Shakespeare, also found time to celebrate his friendship with the *Apollo* circle in some verses *To the Gentlemen Concerned in the British Apollo, upon their Design of Introducing Music into their Quarterly and Monthly Papers.*[17] Rowe and Gay remained firm friends until Rowe's early death in 1719 and it seems reasonable to assume that Gay may have helped to cement their friendship by offering assistance with his work on Shakespeare in the early months of their acquaintance.

Much of the day-to-day running of the *British Apollo* was undertaken by Hill's friend, the would-be poet Marshall Smith, a man whom Dunton singled out for special vilification. Continuing his vendetta against the 'dull, ignorant, false and impertinent scribblers' of this 'pirate' project, Dunton jeered at Smith's snobbish pretensions and taste for gaudy waistcoats, mocking him as 'a proud, whimsical, blundering, conceited fop, a British jest, a walking farce'.[18] Apart from managing the journal, Smith specialized in answering questions on art and aesthetics, which allowed him ample opportunity to promote his own book *The Art of Painting* (1692), thus:

Q. Who was the best author that ever treated of painting?
A. Signior Paulinus, an Italian, writ the best treatise on that art which

Passages upon Several Important Religious Subjects, Taken out of the Writings of Some of the Most Eminent Modern Divines (1748).

[16] Nahum Tate (1652–1715), Poet Laureate since 1692, had collaborated with Hill in translating *The Celebrated Speeches of Ajax and Ulysses* from book 13 of Ovid's *Metamorphoses* (May 1708). Later, Tate also assisted Marshall Smith, Hill's deputy on the *British Apollo*, when he was imprisoned for debt in the Queen's Bench prison. Tate did all he could to raise subscriptions for Smith's series of religious *Monitors* (1713), and also helped him revive the question-and-answer format of the *British Apollo* in a new journal, the *Oracle*. Subscribers to this new periodical were informed: 'Whereas M. Smith, Gent. has had an extraordinary sucess on the presenting his poems called the *Monitors*, insomuch that above twelve hundred of the best families in England have made him generous returns, and also have encouraged him to publish a weekly paper of such kind as may both improve and delight; and the rather because formerly he was the undertaker of the paper called the *British Apollo* . . .' (*Daily Oracle*, first issue, 1 Aug. 1715).

[17] *British Apollo*, 10 Aug. 1709; Rowe's library, sold on 26 Aug. 1719, included a copy of Gay's *Trivia*.

[18] *Athenian News; or, Dunton's Oracle*, 11–14 Mar. 1710.

hath come to our knowledge, but 'tis a very scarce book. In English a gentleman of our society writ one some years since. All we can say of it is that had he seen one before it in English, which discovered that the author so well understood the art, he had not writ his.

Self-advertisement of this kind was a hallmark of the *British Apollo* style. Mutual admiration flourished, and contributors to the *Apollo* shamelessly exploited its columns to promote their own works. In 1710 Smith supplied some typically sycophantic verses for the second edition of Hill's *The Present State of the Ottoman Empire*:

> Thou, whose fresh youth, with sense of years, is crown'd,
> And in whose early springs such ripe autumnal fruits are found . . .

A year earlier, when William Coward published a pedantic treatise on poetic style, it was Gay's turn to do the prefatory honours. His lines 'To the learned ingenious Author of *Licentia Poetica discuss'd*' make depressing reading.

> Through your perspective we can plainly see,
> The new discover'd road of poetry;
> To steep Parnassus you direct the way
> So smooth, that vent'rous travellers cannot stray,
> But with unerring steps, rough ways disdain,
> And by you led, the beauteous summit gain . . . (ll. 6–13)

Coward himself was more modest about his talents, declaring:

> Thus Reader, here you see th'abortive piece,
> Seeming the product of a long disease,
> Or rather brat of some convulsive fit . . .

As usual, the columns of the *British Apollo* were filled with shameless puffs for Coward's abortive 'brat'.

Q. What book would you advise me to buy, to give me a true taste of poetry?
A. Dr Coward's *Licentia Poetica* by all means.

Fortunately, Gay's own poetry offers reassuring proof that he was never remotely tempted to follow Coward's plodding footsteps to Parnassus. Even his dutiful eulogy contains a tiny hint of rebellion, concluding as it does with an alexandrine, an extravagance of which Coward disapproved. His praise of Coward, like his praise of Godolphin, has the kind of exaggeration that hints at ridicule.

Licentia Poetica Discuss'd is a determinedly patriotic work. Coward's own poetic output, heroic in both form and proportions, was consciously inspired by the lofty style of Sir Richard Blackmore's mighty religious epics.[19] Accordingly, his poetic treatise is full of praise for Blackmore's English epics, interspersed with attacks on the many 'botches' and 'blunders' of those incompetent foreigners Horace and Virgil. Coward even includes a commendatory letter from the Duke of Marlborough, written, allegedly, from the battle-field of Blenheim, to support his jingoistic comments on the stirring virtues of English heroic verse. By contrast, Coward had nothing but contempt for the kind of hybrid comic forms in which Gay was later to excel, reserving his strongest strictures for 'clownish' pastorals, filled with 'local idioms'. 'He that writes so', Coward declared, 'may as well insert *Scotch proverbs*, and the *Yorkshire dialect*, as embellishments of poetry.' Five years later Gay did just that, deliberately flouting the solemn precepts of this 'learned and ingenious author'. The verses of *The Shepherd's Week* are filled with an ostentatious display of archaic and dialect terms ('scant', 'eftsoons', 'welkyn', 'ween', 'dight', 'sheen', 'deft', 'meed', 'shent', 'rear', 'kee', and 'glee') in glorious contravention of Coward's rules. Even Chaucer fell foul of Coward's prim linguistic prohibitions.

> Old Chaucer's language, tho' good nervous sense,
> None now can imitate without offence.
> For like a suit unfashionably made,
> His words by time and custom are decay'd.

But Chaucer was always a firm favourite with Gay. And, as if in deliberate defiance of Coward, he chose to invoke Chaucer at his most offensive in 'Monday' of *The Shepherd's Week*, by flaunting his borrowing of the word 'queinte' from *The Miller's Tale*, an obscene term for the female genitals which in modern English has only four letters. In fact, Coward's prohibitions seem to have served Gay as a satiric prescription. By identifying all those literary blemishes which, in his view, failed the 'true test of poetry', Coward provided Gay with the ready-made ingredients for his own mock-pastoral burlesque.

Coward was equally outspoken, though less respectable, in his

---

[19] Coward's own devotional poem *Abramides; or, The Faithful Patriarch* (1705?) is a monumental work, modelled on Blackmore's epics and filling over 300 pages.

religious views. His *Second Thoughts Concerning Human Soul* (1702), denounced as a seditious heresy, had been publicly burnt by order of the House of Commons.[20] But if heresy was Coward's speciality, miracles were the preserve of another of Hill's team, the oculist Roger Grant. Evidently a man with a flair for self-promotion, Grant first came to public notice following an operation he performed on a blind boy, William Jones of Newington, in June 1709.[21] The *Tatler* carried this heart-warming account of the boy's miraculous cure.

The work was performed with great skill and dexterity. When the patient first received the dawn of light, there appeared such an ecstasy in his action, that he seemed ready to swoon away in the surprise of joy and wonder. The surgeon stood before him with his instruments in his hands. The young man observed him from head to foot; after which he surveyed himself as carefully, and seemed to compare him to himself; and, observing both their hands, seemed to think they were exactly alike, except the instruments, which he took for parts of his hands. When he had continued in this amazement for some time, his mother could not longer bear the agitations of so many passions as thronged upon her; but fell upon his neck, crying out, 'My son! my son!' The youth knew her voice, and could speak no more than 'Oh me! Are you my mother?'[22]

Three years later, in a letter to the *Spectator*, 'Philanthropus' recalled this 'famous instance' of the miraculous cure of Jones, asserting that 'several hundreds' had been restored to sight by Dr Grant's 'happy hand'. 'I myself', Philanthropus declared, 'have been cured by him of a weakness in my eyes next to blindness, and am ready to believe anything that is reported of his ability this way.'[23] By this time Grant had been appointed oculist and operator-in-extraordinary to Queen Anne, and boasted a distinguished clientele of society patients. Not everyone, however, was so convinced of his talents. An anonymous pamphlet entitled *A Full and True Account of a Miraculous Cure of a Young Man in Newington, that was Born Blind, and was in Five Minutes Brought to Perfect Sight* (1709) presented Grant as a shameless fraud. His miracles, it snobbishly declared, were 'the more wonderful' since Grant himself was 'an illiterate and unlearned man, and had the disadvantage to be

[20] See marginal annotations to the British Library copy of *Second Thoughts Concerning Human Soul*, shelf-mark 8467.bbb.29.

[21] Grant's advertisements appeared regularly in the *British Apollo*.

[22] *Tatler*, 55 (16 Aug. 1709).

[23] *Spectator* (1 Sept. 1712).

bred up in the mean profession of a cobbler'. The *Female Tatler* too took a more sceptical view of Grant than its male counterpart. Artfully linking Coward's heresy with Grant's miracles it merged them into one identity as the *British Apollo*'s house-surgeon, 'Dr Pusillanimous who, upon *Second Thoughts* is set up for a great scruple-salver as well as oculist'.[24]

On one topic the *British Apollo* was surprisingly evasive. Readers curious to discover the identities of Hill's sagacious 'society of gentlemen' were soundly rebuked for their presumption. 'It must suffice to say the number of the society is large enough, and all of them of sufficient age, to answer far more pertinent questions than yours.' And, although the membership of the *Apollo* team can be established with relative confidence, it remains impossible to identify their individual contributions. Thus we have no way of knowing the nature or extent of Gay's own writings for the journal. In retrospect he regarded his time on the *Apollo* as a period of ignominious hack-work, and never attempted to reprint any of these early essays. However, some guesses at his handiwork may be attempted. The columns of the *Apollo* are littered with initials, ostensibly of corres-pondents who submitted questions, though this was almost certainly a convenient fiction. In all likelihood the majority of questions, like the answers, were concocted by the journalists themselves. The initials which recur most often (namely A.B., J.B., T.C., S.R., J.S.) fail to correspond with the names of the *Apollo's* known contributors, suggesting a deliberate policy of mystification. But there is one exception to this rule. The initials J.G. are found in several places, usually associated with the more light-hearted queries. In the *Apollo* for 30 December 1709 we find the following exchange.

Q. Gentlemen, I asked a young woman whether she would have me, and she said yes, and as soon as she had said the words, my nose dropped several drops of blood. I desire to know of you whether you think my life may attend with sorrow. J.G.

A. Indeed a very dismal omen, for we suppose your nose might drop these drops (the exact number of the words you used in courtship), which seems to forebode that when you have married her, what from the tempta-tions from the wits abroad, and provocations from a nizey at home, your spouse will lead you such a wretched life as will make your heart bleed as long as you live together.[25]

[24] *Female Tatler* (12 Sept. 1709).
[25] *British Apollo*, 30 Dec. 1709.

J. G.'s other queries include a request for a cure for freckles and an urgent demand for a strict definition of incest. Two years later, Gay's first prose pamphlet *The Present State of Wit* was also signed 'J. G.', and, although it cannot be proved that the *Apollo's* 'J. G.' was Gay, the nature of these contributions is quite consistent with the mock-serious tone of his later writings. Probably Gay also had a hand in the *Apollo's* extensive commentary on the Hungarian twin girls who were put on public exhibition at a house in Cornhill in the summer of 1708. These girls, joined Siamese-fashion at the genitals, were widely advertised as one of the fashionable freak-shows of the London season.

At Mr John Pratt's, at the Angel in Cornhill . . . are to be seen two girls who are one of the greatest wonders in Nature that ever was seen, being born with their backs fastened to each other, and the passages of their bodies are both one way. These children are very handsome and lusty and talk three different languages; they are going into the 7th year of their age. Those who see them may very well say they have seen a miracle, which may pass for the 8th wonder of the world.[26]

Sharing common genital and rectal orifices, these girls provoked considerable salacious curiosity, usually disguised as scientific inquiry. As Swift wrote to a friend in Ireland: 'Here is a sight of two girls joined together at the back, which, in the news-monger's phrase, causes a great many speculations; and raises abundance of questions in divinity, law and physic.'[27] The fact that they were also highly accomplished for their years, able to read, write, sing 'very prettily', and converse in several languages, only added to the girls' newsworthy appeal. They were the topic of much learned debate at the Royal Society; their private parts were subjected to manual exploration by eminent doctors of science and religion; and their public exhibition provoked an avalanche of queries to the *Apollo*, throughout the summer months.[28]

---

[26] Reprinted in John Ashton, *Social Life in the Reign of Queen Anne* (London, 1882), i. 279.

[27] Swift, *Corr.* i. 82; 10 June 1708.

[28] They were first mentioned in the supernumerary issue of the *Apollo* for Nov. 1707, and were subsequently discussed in issues 37, 38, 39, 42, and 46 (June–July 1708) and in issue 69 for 6 Oct. 1708. For the Royal Society's discussions of the twins see *Philosophical Transactions*, 50/1 (1757), 311–17. Charles Kerby-Miller includes an extensive discussion of public reactions to the twins in his edition of *The Memoirs of Martinus Scriblerus* (New York, 1966), 294–6.

Several years later these twins also provided the model for the 'Double Mistress' episode in the Scriblerians' collaborative satire *The Memoirs of Martin Scriblerus*. This has prompted the suggestion that Arbuthnot, in whose hand the surviving draft of the 'Double Mistress' chapter is written, may also have supplied the entries on them for the *Apollo*. However, this suggestion, made in ignorance of Gay's association with the *Apollo*, is a typical example of the tendency to underestimate Gay's own authorial contributions.[29] *The Memoirs of Scriblerus* grew out of Pope's proposals for a satirical monthly, to be entitled *The Works of the Unlearned*, which would parody the polymathic pretensions of such Grub Street encyclope-dias as the *British Apollo* itself.[30] Gay was well equipped with hints for both the substance and the pseudo-learned style of such a work. Among the subjects of Martin Scriblerus's philosophical studies are an inquiry into the nature of the animal spirits, an experiment to discover whether venomous bites could be cured by soothing music, and an exploration of the anatomy of the Hungarian twins, all topics formerly discussed in the columns of the *British Apollo*.[31]

Throughout the first eighteen months of its existence the *British Apollo* was a flourishing and profitable venture, although its frequent boast of having several thousand subscribers was probably a wild exaggeration. However, with the appearance of Steele's *Tatler* in April 1709, the *Apollo*'s circulation began to dwindle. By now, anyway, Hill's first enthusiasm for the venture had been largely overtaken by other, more glamorous literary projects. His Turkish memoirs were eventually published in 1709 under the title *A Full and Just Account of the Present State of the Ottoman Empire*. Lavishly produced, dedicated to Queen Anne, and published by subscription, this handsome, illustrated volume has for its frontispiece a dashing portrait of Hill, aged 24, a rakish-looking man-about-town, with long flowing wig, ruffle shirt, and full, pouting lips. The subscription list, headed by Queen Anne, makes a conspicuous display of Hill's

---

[29] The suggestion is first made in G. W. Niven's brief work *Selections from the 'British Apollo': A Study in the Evolution of Periodical Literature* (Paisley, 1903). Niven appears to have been unaware of Gay's link with the *Apollo*, noting only the passing reference to the journal made by 'John Gray [*sic*], the author of the *Fables and Beggar's Opera*' in his pamphlet *The Present State of Wit* (1711), 40. Both Irving and Kerby-Miller treat the suggestion of Arbuthnot's authorship of the *Apollo* articles with scepticism.

[30] Pope's proposals were first outlined in the *Spectator*, 457 (Aug. 1712).

[31] *British Apollo*, 16 June 1708; 24 Mar. 1710.

aristocratic connections, including the names of the Earl of Peterborough, the Duke of Queensborough, and Lord Paget. Yet for the most part its columns are filled with the humbler trades and professions, descending to woollen-drapers and cheese-mongers. Hill's Devonshire friends also make a respectable showing with Gay, Fortescue, and Azariah Pinney all subscribing for a copy. In style as well as subject-matter, Hill's *Ottoman Empire* strikes a pose of worldly sophistication. Much of the book's unspoken appeal lay in its titillating voyeuristic descriptions of Turkish sexual customs, the secrets of the seraglio, and the enticements of the slave-market. The Turkish ladies, Hill assured his readers, were 'lasciviously inclined . . . receiving promiscuously all such as chance or assurance throws in their way'. Hill promises he will

not only trace the Sultan in his amorous pastimes with the virgins of his pleasure, but admit the reader to the close apartment of the seraglio ladies, nay and into the retired magnificence of their bedchambers, but shew him all the various scenes of love and courtship which are practised daily by their Lord and them, even to the consummation of their utmost wishes; and if the British ladies are desirous of further information, will advance a step or two beyond it.[32]

Filling his pages with arousing descriptions of aphrodisiac wines and perfumes, baths and unguents, Hill portrays 'the poor female victim, who is trembling all this while with dreadful apprehensions', escorted at last by eunuchs to the bagnio, undressed and adorned before the nuptial rite. He reveals the secret practices of the slave-market, where prospective purchasers 'feel their breasts, hands, cheeks . . .'[33] Intermingled with these erotic descriptions are anecdotes, like episodes from *The Arabian Nights*, in which unwary strangers, merchants or sailors, unwittingly stray into the harem of some Turkish potentate, and then are called upon to perform Herculean feats of sexual prowess to satisfy the amorous appetites of the enslaved and beautiful inmates.

This exotic work of up-market erotica was clearly intended to launch Hill as a major literary figure. And, in the short term at least, it yielded handsome dividends. In November 1709, while the theatre at Drury Lane was dark, William Collier, a courtier MP, made a

---

[32] *The Present State of the Ottoman Empire*, 149.
[33] Ibid. 103.

surreptitious bid to oust the current licence-holder, Christopher Rich, by agreeing to pay a higher licence-fee of £4, rather than £3, per day. To facilitate this take-over bid he secretly enlisted the support of the company's seven leading actors by promising to appoint them all as joint managers of the theatre. However, once the licence was granted, Collier promptly reneged on this promise and appointed Hill as general manager instead. Not surprisingly, this sleight of hand was fiercely resented by the actors. As Hill told Collier: 'that unexpected blow was a great surprise to 'em; resented warmly by all.'[34] As a result the ensuing theatrical season was one of the most turbulent in the long history of Drury Lane. In a gesture of conciliation, Hill invited Booth, one of the leading actors, to become manager of rehearsals; but he, 'with an insolence peculiar to his nature, refused it, unless they might, all seven, be restored to their management'. So Hill appointed his own brother to take charge of rehearsals, while taking the opportunity to fill the stage with his own plays. In January he produced his tragedy *Elfrid; or, the Fair Inconstant*, which he had hurriedly dashed off in the fortnight before Christmas. In February he drew upon his experience of the Orient to devise a spectacular accompaniment to the Dryden–Davenant adaptation of Shakespeare's *The Tempest*, consisting of 'a surprising entertainment, after the Turkish manner, as it was performed in the seraglio at Constantinople by the Kister Aga and a great number of his eunuchs'. In April he produced his one-act farce *The Walking Statue; or, The Devil in the Wine Cellar*, followed later the same month by his comedy *Squire Brainless*.

Hill was now increasingly anxious to appear as Steele's ally, rather than his rival. In the advertisement for the benefit night of his play *Elfrid* on 5 January 1710 he went out of his way to insist that he could not 'omit doing justice to the ingenious author of the *Tender Husband* [i.e. Steele], who endeavoured, as much as possible, to persuade the manager of the new house to put off that play, and the interest that was made for it, to another night'. In an adroit and timely move he quickly sold the *Apollo* to Marshall Smith. Two months later, reacting to yet another of Dunton's attacks, Smith implicitly acknowledged the *Apollo*'s shrinking market by admitting that the journal, which had once supported a staff of eight, was now

[34] Hill to Collier, 5 June 1710; quoted in *Vice Chamberlain Coke's Theatrical Papers 1706–1715*, ed. Judith Milhous and Robert D. Hume (Carbondale, Ill., 1982), 142.

his sole responsibility:

> I considered that the charge of a whole sheet and fine paper, would render the profit divided not worth the while for eight gentlemen to be concerned about it, therefore I have for some time bought off the interest of everyone concerned with me.[35]

But in buying out his fellow shareholders in the *Apollo* Smith made a poor bargain. By the end of 1709 not only had the popularity of the *Tatler* badly affected sales, but attacks on the *Apollo* were becoming more numerous and ill-natured. It is some measure of Smith's foolhardy confidence, or possibly his shortage of copy, that he was prepared to find space in his columns for this sour comment.

> You bastards of Apollo, I have sent you several letters but your ignorance has made you keep silence, for I see in every paper you *ansur* nothing but some *redicolous* silly stuff of your *oun* inventing and as I have heard in sundry coffee-houses, I shall give a little of your *charector* to the *Tatler*, I will write you no more but *redicule* you on all occasions. Your paper deserves the name of the *Brutish Apollo*, rather than *British Apollo*. I am, with disrespect, R.S.[36]

In a somewhat desperate effort at damage-limitation, Smith opted to flatter his up-market rival. In March 1710 he published the following innocent query.

> Q. 'Tis allowed your paper was the first in these times published under the notion of an amusement, and very probably the success of it gave birth to a thought of the author of the *Tatler* under the name of Esq. Bickerstaff, to proceed in another way of amusement, so that in some sense he may be said to invade your property. I doubt not but by this time, you are sensible, the encouragement he has met with hath tended much to your prejudice. Now my request is, that under these circumstances, you will give your impartial opinion of that paper.

Replying, the *Apollo*, while stoutly denying any rumours of dwindling sales, sought to suggest an affectionate literary kinship with Steele's *Tatler*.

> A. That every week we increase the number of our subscribers, all they who take in subscriptions for us will witness; nor can we be under the least apprehensions of a decrease whilst there be inquisitive people in the world,

---

[35] *Athenian News; or, Dunton's Oracle*, 21 Mar. 1710.
[36] *British Apollo*, 2 Nov. 1709.

which will most certainly continue long after our date. However, we frankly own, the universal approbation that gentleman's paper has met with may have prevented us from gaining near two thousand subscribers we might have had more, had not that been published. Yet the satisfaction we take in reading it so far vanquishes all prejudice we might be supposed to have conceived against the author, on any account whatsoever, that we shall give our opinion of it in the following manner. We believe nothing at present extent will tend so much to the improvement of morality as that paper; for by the just merit couched in the method and disposition of it, together with the alluring persuasion and delicateness of the style, the author hath gained such an ascendant over mankind that he can freely expose the vices and follies of both sexes, without the least occurring [*sic*] their displeasure.[37]

Such sentiments bear a striking similarity with J. G.'s comments in *The Present State of Wit*, published the following year. Possibly Gay, quitting the *Apollo* along with Hill, helped Smith compose this piece of flattery less in the service of the *Apollo* than as a means of furthering his own career. The *Apollo* assured its readers that 'we have no other design in all we have said, than to give a just due to merit, we being wholly strangers to his person, nor hath the least transaction of any kind ever passed between us'. This was something less than the whole truth. Though it may be true that no 'transactions' had passed between Steele and Smith, the *Apollo*'s tactic of praising the *Tatler* was clearly motivated by hopes of spurring Steele into some reciprocal gesture of support. But, despite Smith's best endeavours, Steele failed to return the compliment, never even deigning to acknowledge the *Apollo*'s existence. Ironically, Smith's paper still contrived to outlive its fashionable rival, as the *Tatler* abruptly ceased publication on New Year's Day 1711. But this appearance of relative success was illusory; Steele went on to greater things, assisting Addison with the *Spectator*, while Smith sank into debt, imprisonment, and the Mint.

By the summer of 1710 both Gay and Hill had successfully dissociated themselves from a journal whose down-market reputation had become something of an embarrassment. Pope's dismissive comments on the trade in second-hand verses indicate the kind of condescension with which the *British Apollo* was regarded in fashionable literary circles.

[37] Ibid., 3 Mar. 1710.

The same reason that furnishes Common Garden [*sic*] with those nosegays you so delight in, supplies the *Muse's Mercurys* and *British Apollos* . . . with verses. And 'tis the happiness of this age that the modern invention of printing poems for pence apiece has brought the nosegays of Parnassus to bear the same price; whereby the public-spirited Mr Henry Hills of Blackfriars has been the cause of great ease and singular comfort to all the learned.[38]

It was Henry Hills who pirated Gay's poem *Wine* in 1708, an act which helped confirm his arrival on the literary scene. But three years later Gay felt able to join Pope in disparaging the 'brown sheets and scurvy letter' of this notorious Grub Street scavenger.[39] Anxious to escape from the literary world's anonymous back-alleys, Gay was now striving to assert a more patrician literary identity. His pamphlet *The Present State of Wit* exudes a sense of relief at having emerged from the drudgery of Grub Street hack-work. Adopting the pose of a literary connoisseur, J. G. assiduously flatters those like Addison, Steele, and Swift who might further assist the upward rise of his own literary career, but affects to overlook the *British Apollo* entirely. However, as an afterthought, he adds this postscript.

Upon a review of my letter, I find I have quite forgot the *British Apollo*, which might possibly happen from its having of late retreated out of this end of the town into the city; where I am informed however, that it still recommends itself by deciding wagers at cards, and giving good advice to the shop-keepers, and their apprentices.

This condescending gesture, deliberately biting the hand that had fed him, indicates the intensity of Gay's desire for social status. *The Present State of Wit* is conspicuously date-marked '*Westminster*, May 3, 1711'. Gay thus clearly signals his identification with the fashionable West End of the capital, rather than the mercantile ethos of the city. Although providing him with his first literary employment, the *British Apollo* was still associated in his mind with a milieu from which he desperately yearned to escape. In stigmatizing its readership as city 'shop-keepers, and their apprentices' Gay was bidding a none too fond farewell to a world he wished to forget.

Hill's reign at Drury Lane was short-lived. The actors were still

---

[38] Pope to Cromwell, 7 May 1709; Pope, *Corr.* i. 56.
[39] In his dedicatory poem to Bernard Lintot's new poetical *Miscellany*.

furious at the way they had been duped and at the start of June, taking advantage of Hill's absence from London, they staged a revolt, refusing to act and threatening to remove all the theatre props and costumes. Hill returned to find himself confronted by a hostile confederacy of the actors Booth, Bickerstaff, Leigh, and Keene. Alarmed at their threats to strip the house of all its props, Hill ordered the doors of the theatre to be locked, and sent for constables to keep the peace. But, as he stood talking to his brother, he discovered that the rebel actors had entered the theatre by a side door and were charging through to confront him.

The doors were beaten open and a crowd, with Booth at their head, burst into ye office upon me, with drawn swords in their hands; with much ado I got into ye open passage, had drawn my sword and while surrounded by a crowd, some to prevent and some to increase ye tumult, Powell had shortened his sword to stab me in ye back, and has cut a gentleman's hand through, who prevented ye thrust; Leigh in ye mean time, while my brother was held, struck him a dangerous blow on ye head, with a stick from behind.[40]

With consummate theatrical timing, just in the heat of all these skirmishes, the former licence-holder, Christopher Rich, just happened to pass by. He was immediately 'huzza'd along ye passage, had his hands kissed, and was saluted by Mr Leigh. "God bless you, master, see here! We are at work for you."' Convinced that if he stayed there any longer 'murder . . . must ensue', Hill prudently withdrew, warning Collier that 'unless Booth, Powell and Leigh are taken immediately into custody, and silenced, your interest in ye playhouse will, from this time forward, be worth not one shilling'. All this took place on 5 June 1710. That night the theatre was closed, and remained closed for the rest of the season. So ended the first tumultuous episode of Hill's theatrical career.

For Gay, too, the transition from anonymous Grub Street hack to public man of letters was not accomplished without some painful traumas. Not content with merely severing his links with the *Apollo*, it seems possible he may have sought to exorcize humiliating memories by composing a curious ghost story published by the *Apollo*'s arch-enemy, Dunton, in his *Athenianisms* for 1710. The story, set in Barnstaple, among the family of Gay's school-friend Fortescue, is a supernatural tale of spectral apparitions and divine retribution. It is

---

[40] Hill to Collier, 5 June 1710; quoted in *Vice Chamberlain Coke's Papers*, 144–5.

possible, but unlikely, that Fortescue himself may have been its source. Eustace Budgell, related through marriage to both Fortescue and Addison, is another possible author; so too is Aaron Hill, but since the story appeared in a volume which contained more of Dunton's attacks on Hill's 'arrogance', this seems a remote possibility. So, although this 'Barnstaple Ghost Story' cannot be securely identified as Gay's, it seems an interesting possibility that he might have used this means of laying the ghosts of a childhood he now wished to disown.

The story, set in 1639 and allegedly deriving from 'Madam Fortescue', widow of John Fortescue of Brixham, concerns a former town clerk of Barnstaple, 'one of those whom the world called Puritans'. This man had a young apprentice called Chamberlain, who 'complains often to his master that the house was haunted, and that he was frighted with apparitions'.

Sometimes he should see a young gentlewoman about eighteen or twenty years old, all in white, with her hair dishevelled, leading a very little child up and down the room, which seemed as if it were new born; otherwhiles . . . there would come an old man in his gown and sit upon the bed by him, staring him in the face but speaked never a word. These apparitions were very troublesome and afflictive to him.

One night, while sitting up late at his work, Chamberlain is again visited by the ghost of the old man, who tells him to go into another room in the house 'and dig there up the planking, and thou shalt find four boxes, one upon the other'. The first box contains 'all sorts of wearing apparel, of silks, satins and velvet'; the second, 'abundance of good table and bed linen, very choice and fine'.

In the third there was a sum of money in gold and silver, ready coined. And two silver pots, one full of gold, which together with all the rest of those buried goods, the apparition bestows upon him. But the other pot, he commands him upon pain of death, not to look into it, but to take it and carry it into Wales to Mrs Betty, his master's daughter . . . But he bad him look to it that he did not so much as peep into that silver pot he was to carry over to her, for it was as much as his life was worth.

The next day, with his master's permission, Chamberlain does as the ghost commanded, and finds the four boxes under the floorboards, containing 'near twelve thousand pound' in money, besides the other promised goods and the mysterious silver pot.

Never did any fellow's teeth water more upon a sweet bit, or his fingers itch to meddle with prohibited wares, than Chamberlain's eyes did to be looking into the forbidden silver pot; but the fear of the spectrum's menaces awed him and kept him, much against his will, within bounds, though a thousand times a day he would be peddling about it to see what was in it.

Chamberlain takes a boat and crosses over the Severn to Wales, carrying the pot to Mrs Betty's house. He knocks at the door 'and down comes a young gentlewoman of about 27 with her breasts naked, hair dishevelled, in a very forlorn and disconsolate condition and asks him what his business is'. At first Mrs Betty refuses to accept the silver pot, but Chamberlain insists:

'Mrs Betty, if you do not it will be so much the worse for you, for I am ordered to leave it with you.' With that, fetching a deep sigh and smiting her breast, 'Ah!' saith she, 'it was not for nothing I have been so troubled all this night. I was born to be miserable.' And so, without enquiring for her parents, or inviting him in to drink, she takes the silver pot and gets up into her chamber. Chamberlain having now discharged his trust and errand, immediately returns to the seaside, where finding a boat ready for Barnstaple, he enters into it, and before it launched off from land, Mrs Betty comes down into it also, and sits just against him; but all the time they were passing over never speaks a word to him, nor he to her.

Back at her parents' house, she barely speaks to them, but 'takes a key and hammer that hung in the parlour and goes upstairs, unlocks a chamber-door, and then locks it again upon her, where she was heard beating out a board in the window, and then nailing it fast again'. That done, she insists on returning immediately to Wales. A year later, on her death-bed, Mrs Betty calls her maid to her and promises her a legacy of £700,

provided she would solemnly promise and swear to her that as soon as she was buried, she would take the first opportunity to go over to Ireland and carry that silver pot (but she must not look into it) unto her uncle the Lord Bishop of Waterford, with her dying message to him, that if he did not repent of the sin he knew himself guilty of, he should be hanged.

Within only a few hours of delivering this message, Mrs Betty dies. A Justice of the Peace, summoned to inquire into the circumstances of her death, commands that the cover should be removed from the forbidden pot, 'and, looking into it, finds the skeleton and bones of a little new-born infant'. News of this incident soon reaches Charles I, who quickly orders the arrest of the Bishop of Waterford. The story ends with the execution of this hypocritical clergyman for his secret incestuous lust.[41]

The final moral of this story, with its exposure of a lecherous priest, conformed to one of Dunton's favourite themes; but the preceding narrative has all the circumstantial detail of a well-known local tale. Clearly Gay was not the only figure in literary London brought up on Barnstaple folklore and scandal. But it was he who loved to exploit such superstitious motifs in his literary burlesques, bringing on-stage the avenging ghost of an embryo in his surreal comedy *The What D'Ye Call It*. Did Gay, anxious to sever a last link with home-bred pieties, choose this way to expose the hypocrisy of Barnstaple's godly crew? For a man set upon making his own bargain with the devil of hedonistic London society, this tale is full of dream-like resonances. Goaded by an unquiet spirit, the apprentice finds buried treasure beneath his Barnstaple floorboards, but only at the price of digging up the skeleton of long-buried sins. Analysed as a dream-fantasy, the essential underlying emotion of this fable is guilt; the guilt of knowledge, represented by the secret taboos of incest and infanticide; the guilt of complicity, represented by a domestic conspiracy of silence; and the guilt of exposure, in the uneasy compact with the devil through which secret sins are brought to light. If Gay did not write this piece, he must at least have known it, and it was a tale with a special message for a Barnstaple youth poised between the prohibitions of a puritan past and the lure of literary success. What sacrifices must he make, what ghosts must he lay, or what skeletons uncover, to gain the treasure he sought?

[41] Dunton, *Athenianism*, pt. ii, project xvii, 'The Apparition, Evidence' (1710), 351–360.

FOUR

In Attendance

And in attendance wasted years in vain.

(Rural Sports, 1713)

HILL's premature ejection from his post at Drury Lane came as something of a blow to Gay, who had probably begun work already on his first stage play, *The Wife of Bath*.[1] Hill himself was not disheartened. Although evidently unskilled in the arts of man-management, he boasted influential allies and an undoubted flair for spectacular theatrical effects. Less than six months after leaving Drury Lane Hill assumed directorship of the new Haymarket theatre, where he quickly turned his talents to the latest fashionable craze—Italian opera. His début there was predictably applauded by the *British Apollo*.

> The ruler of the stage, we find,
> A youth of vast extended mind;
> No disappointment can control,
> The emanations of his soul.[2]

The first emanation of Hill's soul was an immediate hit. He persuaded Handel, newly arrived in England, to compose his first London opera, *Rinaldo*, written in a fortnight and performed in February 1711.[3] In the

---

[1] *The Wife of Bath* was definitely completed well before the end of 1711; see Pope to Cromwell, 21 Dec. 1711; Pope, *Corr*. i. 138. There is some dispute whether the comedy referred to here is *The Wife of Bath* or *The Mohocks*, but, for the reasons set out below, *The Wife of Bath* seems the more likely candidate.

[2] *British Apollo*, 18 Dec. 1710.

[3] The libretto of *Rinaldo*, developed from Hill's own idea, was written by Giacomo Rossi, with an English translation by Hill himself.

preface Hill insisted that the principal deficiency of previous Italian operas on the English stage was a lack of histrionic spectacle: 'wanting the machines and decorations which bestow so great a beauty on their appearance, they have been heard and seen to very considerable disadvantage.' In his splendidly appointed new theatre, Hill was determined to rectify all this, promising 'to fill the eye with more delightful prospects, so at once to give two senses equal pleasure'. *Rinaldo* was a masterpiece of showmanship. In the first act a character was transported through the air in a 'chariot drawn by two huge dragons, out of whose mouths issue fire and smoke', while a black cloud descended 'fill'd with dreadful monsters spitting fire and smoke on every side'. In the second act, two mermaids sang an underwater duet, while Act III offered waterfalls, 'thunder, lightning and amazing noises'. The *Spectator*, though, was unimpressed by Hill's theatrical effects, complaining of a 'very short allowance of thunder and lightning', though conceding archly that the quantities of fire and smoke which filled the auditorium were 'exceedingly generous'.[4] In all likelihood, Gay met Handel at this time, and the extraordinary spectacle of Hill's operatic extravaganza provided his first direct experience of this beguiling and fantastical art-form.

Gay's other principal friends after quitting the *Apollo* circle included Nick Rowe, Eustace Budgell, Fortescue, and Henry Cromwell. Rowe was a constant source of fun and literary conviviality: 'Why, he would laugh all day long!', said Pope. 'He would do nothing else but laugh.' Budgell was a less jovial character who later suffered fits of insanity and eventually drowned himself, filling his pockets with stones and jumping overboard from a small boat.[5] In 1711, however, he was a very useful contact, sharing lodgings with his cousin Addison, and collaborating with him and Steele on early issues of the *Spectator*. Budgell was also related, through his father's second marriage, to Fortescue, who had left Devon on his wife's death in 1710 and opted for a legal career, with chambers in the Middle Temple. Henry Cromwell, a well-known coffee-house dandy and tavern *habitué*, was rather older than the others. A self-styled connoisseur of the whores who plied the alley-ways of Drury Lane,

---

[4] *Spectator*, 5 and 14 (6, 16 Mar. 1711).

[5] Pope to Spence; Spence, item 249; i. 109. After Budgell's suicide in May 1737, these lines were found on his desk: 'What Cato did, and Addison approved, | Cannot be wrong.'

he evidently enjoyed instructing his youthful protégés in the ways of the world and the delights of ladies of easy virtue. Favouring a full-bottomed wig built so high at the parting that, according to one female friend, it resembled the twin peaks of Parnassus, Cromwell walked with a mincing gait as if 'leading up a Spanish pavan in the minuet step'. The playwright Wycherley described Cromwell's 'creeping advances, clinging embraces', and his sallow 'satyr's face';[6] but Cromwell still retained the skill to charm his hearers with a repertoire of salacious anecdotes, such as the story of how he had once competed with Dryden for the favours of a street-walker. Aaron Hill could match such erotic adventures with his *risqué* Turkish memoirs, while Gay responded with stories from the neighbouring 'seraglio' of the New Exchange. Together this band of literary men about town haunted the bohemian *demi-monde* of taverns, bagnios, coffee-houses, and clubs around Drury Lane, affecting the rakish style and 'good qualities of the world' that Swift describes in *A Tale of a Tub*.

They writ, and rallied, and rhymed and sung, and said and said nothing; they drank and fought and whored and slept and swore and took snuff; they went to new plays on the first night, haunted the chocolate-houses . . . ate at Locket's, loitered at Will's; they talked of the drawing-room and never came there; dined with lords they never saw; whispered a duchess, and spoke never a word; exposed the scrawls of their laundress for billet-doux of quality; came ever just from court and were never seen in it; attended the levee *sub dio*; got a list of peers by heart in one company, and with great familiarity retailed them in another.[7]

The 20-year-old Pope was equally eager to participate in this pose of decadent sophistication. Writing from his parents' home near Windsor he complained to Cromwell of the lack of willing females in his neighbourhood. In London, he declared, ''tis ten to one but a young fellow may find his strayed heart again with some Wild Street or Drury Lane damsel'. But the country rake enjoyed no such recreational diversions. 'Here, where I could have met with no redress from an unmerciful virtuous dame, I must forever have lost my little traveller in a hole, where I could never rummage to find him again.'[8] As an adult Gay had a somewhat unprepossessing appear-

---

[6] See Elizabeth Thomas's autobiography, *The Life of Corinna* (1731), 53, and Wycherley's letter to Pope, 14 June 1709; Pope, *Corr.* i. 65.

[7] *A Tale of a Tub* (1704), s. ii.

[8] Pope to Cromwell, Mar. 1708; Pope, *Corr.* i. 42.

ance, fat, unhealthy, and ungainly. Pope mentions his 'laughing eyes that twinkled in his head'[9] but the surviving portraits present a pudgy, slab-like face with surprisingly little animation. Gay frequently made fun of his own corpulence and clumsiness, dubbing himself Burlington's 'fat squire', and comparing his own circumference with that of the obese physician Dr Cheyney. His clumsy step was likewise a subject of frequent ridicule, with Gay himself contributing to tales of his clownish misadventures, falling from his horse or collapsing into a palace screen. To his friends, Gay's fleshiness was proof of over-indulgence; but it seems more probable that both this and his chronic colical disorders were symptomatic of a deeper psychological unease. In later years, at Amesbury with the Queensberrys, he subjected himself to a strict remedial diet, eating salads, abstaining from wine, and taking rigorous exercise; but all to no avail. His maladroit gait, lumbering form, and intestinal ailments were enduring physical manifestations of an inner sense of awkwardness. In the elegant world of courtiers, beaux, and dilettantes Gay retained the physical appearance of a provincial clown.

It seems that Gay and Cromwell first met in London shortly after Cromwell's return from a summer trip to Lincolnshire in August 1710. Soon afterwards, Cromwell introduced Gay to Pope; in a letter the following summer Pope asked Cromwell to 'give my service to all my new friends, and to Mr Gay in particular'. From the start Pope adopted a proprietorial tone towards his new friend's literary achievements. 'Gay they would call one of my *élèves*,' he later boasted,[10] ignoring the fact that he was actually younger than his 'pupil'. For Pope, Gay was always an impetuous juvenile whose literary endeavours required careful supervision. In an early letter to Cromwell, expressing disappointment that a recent stage comedy success was not by Gay, Pope added this characteristic comment: '(had it been any way in my power) [I] should have been very glad to have contributed to its introduction into the world.'[11] Implicit in the terms of their relationship was the expectation that, in return for promoting Gay's literary career, Pope would deploy him as a willing

[9] Pope's description of Gay can be found in the collations of the *Dunciad* manuscripts made by Jonathan Richardson, Jr., before the MSS were destroyed. See Maynard Mack's '*The Last and Greatest Art': Some Unpublished Poetical Manuscripts of Alexander Pope* (Newark, Del., 1984), 104.

[10] Spence, item 150; i. 62.

[11] Pope to Cromwell, 21 Dec. 1711; Pope, *Corr.* i. 138.

lieutenant in his own literary enterprises. In particular, Pope soon adopted the habit of nominating Gay as a convenient foster-parent for literary offspring of which, in later years, he preferred not to acknowledge paternity. This same letter to Cromwell includes a poetical 'whim', inspired by reading Gay's verses on Bernard Lintot's new *Miscellany*, which concludes:

> Lintot's for gen'ral use are fit;
> For some folks read, but all folks sh—

Such ribaldry is entirely in keeping with the rakish pose that Pope affects throughout this letter. Indulging his erotic fantasies about the Blount sisters, he writes: 'How gladly would I give all I am worth, that is to say, my *Pastorals* for one of their maidenheads, and my *Essay* for the other', and fondly imagines 'the dear tremblings of the bed of bliss'. But later, in the 'official' version of his letters, Pope was anxious to banish all trace of such improper thoughts, which were, accordingly, ascribed to Gay instead.[12] Clearly, the privilege of having Gay assume responsibility for 'whims' which Pope subsequently deemed too undignified to be acknowledged as his own was part of the recompense which Pope exacted in return for promoting Gay's career.

Another role which Gay performed was to serve as Pope's faithful aide-de-camp in literary feuds. Almost as soon as they met he had an opportunity to demonstrate his usefulness in this respect. In June 1711 Pope ended another letter to Cromwell with this postscript.

Mr Lintot has favoured me with a sight of Mr Dennis's piece of fine satire before 'twas published. I desire you to read it and give me your opinion, in what manner such a critic ought to be answered?[13]

The 'fine satire' of Dennis's *Reflections on Pope's Essay on Criticism* included this vicious attack on Pope's physical deformities.

As there is a great deal of venom in this little gentleman's temper, Nature has very wisely corrected it with a great deal of dulness . . . As there is no creature in Nature so venomous, there is nothing so stupid and so impotent as a hunch-backed toad; and a man must be very quiet and very passive,

---

[12] Sherburn comments: 'Pope seems here by ambiguous placing of his footnote to try to shift the authorship of the verses . . . from himself to Gay' (Pope, *Corr.* i. 138 n.).

[13] Ibid. 125.

and stand still to let him fasten his teeth and his claws, or be surprised sleeping by him, before that animal can have any power to hurt him.[14]

Despite his affected jaunty air, Pope was deeply shocked by such violent personal abuse. Yet, just six weeks later, and shortly after his first meeting with Gay, he had changed his tone entirely about retaliation. In a letter to his Catholic friend John Caryll Pope now loftily disclaimed any intention of answering Dennis's attack.

'I shall never make the least reply to him, not only because you advise me, but because I've ever been of opinion that if a book can't answer for itself to the public, 'tis to no sort of purpose for its author to do it.'[15]

Pope now believed it would be both demeaning and counter-productive to engage personally in an acrimonious dispute with the ill-tempered critic. Yet it might still be possible to take revenge by proxy. Privately, he told Cromwell that he had recommended a 'paper' by Gay to Lewis, the publisher of his *Essay on Criticism*: 'if it be copied fairly out', he added, 'I guess he will be glad of it.' Within weeks, the *Critical Specimen*, a scurrilous lampoon on Dennis, was on sale.[16] This pamphlet, a patchwork parody of Dennis's bombastic poetry and pedantic criticism, includes a sub-Miltonic 'fragment', which ostentatiously repeats the vitriolic language of Dennis's attack on Pope.

> A baneful hunch-back'd toad, with look malign
> Glares on some traveller's unwary steps
> Whether by chance or by misfortune led
> To tread those dark unwholesome, misty fens,
> Rage strait collects his venom all at once
> And swells his bloated corps to largest size.[17]

---

[14] John Dennis, *Reflections Critical and Satirical, upon a Late Rhapsody, Called An Essay upon Criticism* (1711), 26.

[15] Pope, *Corr.* i. 132.

[16] Pope to Cromwell, 24 July 1711; ibid. i. 130. It cannot be asserted beyond question that Gay's 'paper' was indeed the *Critical Specimen*, though the likelihood is very high. Norman Ault has argued for Pope's authorship of this pamphlet, detailing several verbal parallels with Pope's letters at the time. (See *The Prose Works of Alexander Pope*, ed. N. Ault (Oxford, 1936), i, pp. xiff. and 15). Yet Pope's clear disclaimer to Caryll of any intention of retaliating against Dennis suggests that any revenge he may have taken would have been either vicarious or disguised. And Gay would have been keen to seize this opportunity to demonstrate his usefulness to his new literary mentor.

[17] 'Critical Specimen', *Pope's Prose Works*, ed. Ault, 5.

Mangled borrowings from Ariosto, Cervantes, and Milton are used to decorate this zestful caricature, in which Dennis is dubbed 'Don Rinaldo Furioso, the Critic of the Woful Countenance' a name evidently chosen to suggest affinities with Hill's recent operatic extravaganza. The hilarious depiction of 'Rinaldo Furioso' astride not Pegasus nor even Rosinante, but a poor wooden hobby-horse, hints at the *Spectator*'s gibes at the inadequacy of Hill's theatrical machinery. Dennis is reduced to a comic-opera grotesque as Gay exploits the bizarre forms of Italian opera for this satire on literary pretension.

Clearly delighted by this opportunity to consolidate his friendship with Pope, Gay returned to the attack a few months later, dedicating his tragi-comical farce *The Mohocks* 'To Mr D***'. Pope's offending lines in his *Essay on Criticism* had alluded to Dennis's failed tragedy *Appius and Virginia*:

> But Appius reddens at each word you speak,
> And stares, tremendous! with a threat'ning eye
> Like some fierce tyrant in old tapestry.   (ll. 585–7)

Gay eagerly reverts to the same theme. 'The world', he declares, 'will easily perceive that the plot of [*The Mohocks*] is formed upon that of *Appius and Virginia*, which model, indeed, I have in great measure followed throughout the whole conduct of the play.' This claim is pure spoof; happily, Gay's farce bears no resemblance to Dennis's tragedy, and the reference is merely intended as provocation. Warming to his satiric task, Gay goes on to mimic Dennis's critical jargon. The subject of *The Mohocks*, he asserts, is both 'horrid and tremendous', terms invariably associated with Dennis's pronouncements on tragedy. 'Tremendous' was Dennis's catch-phrase, widely parodied by his literary adversaries.[18] Five years later, in *Three Hours after Marriage*, Gay joined with Arbuthnot and Pope in satirizing Dennis as 'Sir Tremendous', a name which nicely mocked not only his critical theories, but also his notoriously volcanic temperament.

Clearly, by the end of 1711 Gay had made a tactical decision to ally himself with Pope. A pamphlet published the following year still named him among Hill's assistants in a new scheme for extract-

---

[18] One review of Dennis's play *Iphigenia* (1700) had concluded that 'there were many TREMENDOUS things in't; but if there be anything of tragedy in't it lies in that word, for he is so fond of it, he had rather use it in every page than slay his beloved Iphigenia'. See *A Comparison between the Two Stages* (1702), 37.

ing oil from beech-mast, but by this time Gay's interests were in a different kind of unction. In recognition of Gay's efforts on his behalf, Pope found room for two of his poems in the *Miscellany* he was editing for Lintot.[19] Gay returned the compliment with this eulogy of Pope's own 'harmonious muse':

> His steady judgment far out-shoots his years,
> And early in the youth the God appears.[20]

While there is no reason to doubt the sincerity of Gay's admiration for Pope's poetry, such hyperbole suggests not close friendship, but distant worship. There is more than a hint, in this exaggerated praise of the younger man's achievements, of the kind of self-serving sycophancy with which Gay had previously flattered Godolphin, Sunderland, and William Coward. By contrast, the chummy tone of Pope's letters to Cromwell has the authentic ring of intimacy. In December Pope asked Cromwell to pass on his thanks to Gay 'for the favour of his poem, and in particular for his kind mention of me'.[21] Clearly Cromwell was still a necessary intermediary between them, and Gay had more work to do to establish himself as Pope's favourite literary protégé.

Gay was now engaged in a determined campaign to provide himself with literary allies and/or patrons. His two poems for Lintot's *Miscellany* and his prose pamphlet *The Present State of Wit*, published earlier the same year, indicate the progress and tactics of that campaign. Subtitled 'A Letter to a Friend in the Country', and signed 'J. G.', *The Present State of Wit* provides a connoisseur's guide to current literary fashions. Ostensibly written so that the anonymous (and no doubt fictional) 'friend' 'may not be quite at a loss in conversation among the *beau monde* next winter', it provides a perfect opportunity for literary ingratiation. From the start Gay is careful to insist on his political impartiality. 'As you know', he writes, 'I never cared one farthing either for Whig or Tory.' This was a conventional, indeed a formulaic declaration, which usually implied the exact opposite of what it claimed. It was a formula particularly favoured by Swift, especially when, in the

---

[19] Advertisements for this *Miscellany* appearing in the *General Post* in early Oct. announced: 'Those who have excellent copies by them may command a place in this *Miscellany*, if sent before 1st November to B. Lintot at the Cross Keys in Fleet Street.'

[20] 'On a Miscellany of Poems', ll. 84–5.

[21] Pope, *Corr.* i. 138.

Examiner, he was writing, as J.G. notes, 'by the direction and under the eye of some Great Persons who sit at the helm of affairs'.[22] As a relative newcomer in the world of literary politics, Gay was understandably anxious not to offend potential patrons by appearing to take sides. But this was no easy task. The literary world was increasingly polarized into rival Whig and Tory camps, and even the most innocuous works were scrutinized for hints of party bias. Swift protested bitterly, and somewhat disingenuously, at the way party differences cut across literary ties. 'Mr Addison and I are different as black and white', he complained in December 1710, 'and I believe our friendship will go off by this damned business of party.'[23] *The Present State of Wit* treads warily in this territory. At one point J.G. suggests that Steele's surprise decision to 'fling up his *Tatler*' at the height of its success, can only be explained as 'a sort of submission to, and composition with the government for some past offences'. Yet he is keen to stress that the *Tatler*'s appeal extended far beyond Steele's political allies. 'Everyone read him with pleasure and good will', he writes, 'and the Tories, in respect to his other good qualities, had almost forgiven his unaccountable imprudence in declaring against them.' None of this though was enough to prevent Swift from identifying 'J.G.' as a political opponent. He read Gay's twopenny pamphlet as soon as it appeared, and summarily declared, 'the author seems to be a Whig'. He did, though, concede that he 'speaks very highly of a paper called the *Examiner*, and says the supposed author of it is Dr Swift'. In fact J.G. describes the *Examiner* as 'a paper which all men who speak without prejudice, will allow to be well writ', but it is clear that what he chiefly admires is its style rather than its content. The *Examiner*'s political subject-matter, he says, 'will admit of no great variety', yet the author 'is continually placing it in so many different lights . . . that men, who are concerned in no party, may read him with pleasure'. Swift was particularly piqued at the way *The Present State of Wit* consistently flattered the *Tatler* and *Spectator*: 'I believe Steele

---

[22] In *Examiner*, 14 (2 Nov. 1710) Swift wrote: 'It is a practice I have generally followed to converse in equal freedom with deserving men of both parties.' In fact, as J. A. Downie points out, Swift's pamphleteering on behalf of the Tory government's peace campaign represented 'the finest example of the organisation of propaganda under the Oxford ministry, (J. A. Downie, *Robert Harley and the press*, Cambridge, 1979, 148).

[23] *Journal*, i. 127.

and Addison were privy to the printing of it,' he declared. 'Thus is one treated by these impudent dogs.'[24]

Addison, now aged 40, was at the zenith of his career, an aloof literary mandarin with the virtual power to make or break any newcomer's literary reputation. Fortified with a perfect blend of literary and diplomatic skills, Addison's career had been a model of Whiggish rectitude. From Charterhouse he had gone on to distinguish himself at Magdalen College, Oxford. Early verses, dedicated to the Whig grandees Somers and Halifax, had resulted in a government pension of £200 which enabled him to make the Grand Tour. When he returned he was offered first a lucrative position in the Excise office, and subsequently promoted to an Under-Secretaryship, at £400 per year. Such were the rewards of dedicated literary loyalty. Steele was a more impulsive and feckless figure, frequently contradicting in practice the high-minded principles he preached in print. Always in debt, and endlessly quarrelsome, he had fought a duel (something which both the *Tatler* and the *Spectator* deplored) and been arrested at least once for non-payment of bills. A schoolmate of Addison's at Charterhouse and again at Oxford, he had left university (without a degree) for the army, and left the army for the stage. Where Addison was cautious, reserved and dignified, the perfect civil servant, Steele was thriftless, impetuous, and indiscreet.

Published two months before Gay's first meeting with Pope, *The Present State of Wit* was written at a time when Gay clearly calculated that his best hopes of advancement lay with these twin peaks of the Whig literary establishment. Already well acquainted with Budgell, Addison's assistant on the *Spectator*, he lavished praise on their new enterprise: 'We ... can only wonder', he declares, 'from whence so prodigious a run of wit and learning can proceed; since some of our best judges seem to think that they have hitherto, in general, outshone even the ... first *Tatlers*.' These best judges did not include Swift, who dismissed the *Spectator* as merely 'pretty', and refused to 'meddle' with it.[25] J. G. judges differently; the *Spectator*, he writes, 'was writ in so excellent a style, with so nice a judgement, and such a noble profusion of wit and humour' that it could clearly only the work of those 'two great geniuses' (i.e. Addison and Steele) 'who seem to stand in a class by themselves, so

---

[24] *Journal*, 14 May 1711; i. 269.
[25] Ibid. ii. 482.

high above all our other wits'. Indeed, he is almost lost for words to describe Steele's pre-eminence above all his literary imitators and rivals.

To give you my own thoughts of this gentleman's writings, I shall in the first place observe, that there is this noble difference between him and all the rest of our polite and gallant authors. The latter have endeavoured to please the age by falling in with them, and encouraging them in their fashionable vices, and false notions of things . . . [He] ventured to tell the town that they were a parcel of fops, fools and vain coquets; but in such a manner as even pleased them, and made them more than half inclined to believe that he spoke truth . . .

'Tis incredible to conceive the effect his writings have had on the town; how many thousand follies they have either quite banished, or given a very great check to; how much countenance they have added to virtue and religion; how many people they have rendered happy, by shewing them that it was their own fault if they were not so; and lastly, how entirely they have convinced our fops, and young fellows of the value and advantages of learning . . .

Lastly, his writings have set all our wits and men of letters upon a new way of thinking, of which they had little or no notion before; and tho' we cannot yet say that any of them have come up to the beauties of the original, I think we may venture to affirm that every one of them writes and thinks much more justly than they did some time since.

Reading this, it is not hard to see why Swift identified J. G. as a Whig, especially when he concludes the pamphlet by suggesting that 'the conjunction of those two great geniuses . . . resembled that of two famous statesmen in a late reign'. The two statesmen J. G. has in mind are Somers and Halifax, leading members of William III's Whig government. A reader of such sentiments might be forgiven for deducing that an essential ingredient of genius was loyalty to the Whig cause.

Swift would also have been dismayed, though hardly surprised, by J. G.'s summary dismissal of William Harrison's continuation of the *Tatler* as a few 'sparks of wit' beneath 'an heap of impertinencies'. Had Gay but known it, the career of Harrison, his exact contemporary, might have provided an ominous warning of the pitfalls of the literary politician's trade. A mild-mannered Fellow of New College with modest literary abilities, Harrison first met Swift in 1710, and quickly became his favourite protégé. When Steele 'flung up' the *Tatler* in January 1711, Harrison attempted to take it over. Nervously he approached Swift for an opinion of the first

issue. 'I am tired with correcting his trash,' Swift told Stella.[26]
Much as he liked the 'little brat' he could see that he lacked the
'true vein' for journalism. When this enterprise collapsed Swift was
on hand to suggest a new one. He persuaded the Secretary of State
Henry St John to offer Harrison 'the prettiest employment in
Europe', namely secretary to Lord Raby, ambassador extraordinary
at The Hague. In practice though this employment proved considerably less pretty than anticipated. Whitehall was notoriously dilatory
in the payment of salaries, and although Harrison's post was nomi-
nally worth £1,000 a year, Swift knew that he would never see 'a
groat' of it till he returned. Yet the problem was so common that it
warranted only a gentle teasing by Swift of Lord Treasurer Oxford.
'He must be three or four hundred pounds in [their?] debt,' Swift
guessed, looking forward to marching the lad round, with self-
righteous indignation, from one paymaster to the next. But when
Harrison actually returned Swift's tone changed abruptly. A depressing little letter lay on his table one night in February, informing him
that the brat had returned, but was lying ill and wanted to see him.
It was too late for a visit that night, and Swift fretted the hours
away till morning in anxious foreboding. He had obtained Oxford's
promise of an immediate payment of 100 guineas, but he knew
Oxford's promises of old. The next day he found Harrison cooped
up in squalid, airless lodgings, seriously ill with fever and inflammation. Swift immediately had him moved to the fresh country air of
Knightsbridge, and gave him £30 from Secretary St John (now
Lord Bolingbroke). All night he worried over Harrison's condition,
and, not daring to visit him himself, sent out a servant to see how he
was. 'Extremely ill' was the reply. First thing next morning Swift
went with Parnell—for he dared not go alone—to see Harrison. He
had at last a Treasury note for £100 in his pocket. 'I told Parnell I
was afraid to knock at the door; my mind misgave me. I knocked &
his man in tears told me his master was dead an hour before.'[27] Less
than two years later it was Gay's turn to be sent to Europe, on
Swift's recommendation, as secretary to another ambassador extraordinary. Swift's anxiety, at that time, to see Gay properly provided
with funds clearly reflected his bitter memories of Harrison's fate.
He was determined to ensure that another of his literary protégés
should not perish as a victim to false court promises.

[26] *Journal*, i. 162.
[27] Ibid. ii. 619–20.

Other contemporary journalists, like Mainwaring and Oldmixon, King and Ozell, are treated in *The Present State of Wit* with a perfunctory mention that indicates Gay's lack of interest in their more pedestrian enterprises. Towards Defoe's *Review* J.G. displays the kind of fashionable disdain characteristic of the *beau monde* whose tone he affects. Borrowing a phrase from Swift's *Battle of the Books* (1704) he dismisses 'this fellow' (Defoe) as 'a lively instance of those wits who, as an ingenious author says, will endure but one skimming'. *The Present State of Wit* confirms Gay's paramount desire to associate himself with the 'polite' end of the literary world, *irrespective* of party allegiances, rather than remain in the humdrum Grub Street milieu where the *Review* and the *British Apollo* plied their trade. The *Review*, with its regular discussion of trade and business matters, catered for the world of merchants and apprentices that Gay hoped he had left behind. There is an unmistakable sense of exultation in the way J.G. affects to have forgotten altogether the *British Apollo* in its down-market city retreat. Writing from the superior vantage-point of his Westminster lodgings, Gay signalled his clear intention to escape from such mercantile drudgery forever. If this meant he must write sycophantic eulogies of Steele, Addison, and Pope, then so be it. Clearly he found servility towards literary 'geniuses' less irksome than service to shopkeepers and their apprentices.

The Present State of Wit is all too clearly the work of a name-dropping literary neophyte, affecting to pass judgements while busily currying favour. Beneath its blasé tone of coffee-house sophistication, one can detect an urgent strategy of self-promotion. Six months later Gay returned to the campaign with his dedicatory verses 'On a Miscellany of Poems'. Here again, he studiously maintains a pose of political impartiality with name-dropping references that span the political spectrum, 'from a supporter of the junto Whigs (Addison) through a Harleyite (Prior) to men later to reveal Jacobite sympathies (Granville and Buckingham)'.[28] In literary terms, Gay scrupulously divides his admiration between Addison and Pope. Addison is praised for '*The Campaign*', a patriotic Whig celebration of the battle of Blenheim.

> In him, pathetic Ovid sings again,
> And Homer's *Iliad* shines in his *Campaign*. (ll. 74–5)

---

[28] Downie, 'Gay's Politics', 49.

But Pope's 'harmonious muse' reaches beyond the realms of poetic imitation to a spiritual sublimity: 'And early in the youth the God appears.' If Addison is granted the status of a modern classic, Pope is hailed as a new divinity.

The poem ends with more book-trade chatter, and knowing references to the publishers Henry Hills, Jacob Tonson, and Bernard Lintot. Gay's final line 'And Tonson yield to Lintot's lofty name' indicates his keen sense of the literary world as an arena of competing reputations, and his fascination with the rise and fall of literary stocks. But perhaps the poem's most revealing lines are these:

> Variety's the source of joy below,
> From whence still fresh revolving pleasures flow.
> In books and love, the mind one end pursues,
> And only change th'expiring flame renews.   (ll. 41–4)

Such sentiments, natural enough in the dedication to a verse miscellany, are particularly appropriate to Gay. More than any other writer, he delighted in a daring literary variety, constantly coupling tragedy with farce, and satire with sentimentality. His most successful and enduring works are surreal literary hybrids in which variety is indeed 'the source of joy'. But 'variety' was also a kind of defence; by constantly changing his tone and style, Gay carefully avoided placing all his literary eggs in one political basket. If the literary world was an exchange of constantly fluctuating stocks, Gay prudently resolved to play the market.

Gay's other contribution to Lintot's *Miscellany* was a translation of 'The Story of Arachne' from Ovid's *Metamorphoses*. This is a highly revealing choice which enabled him to hint at the psychological tensions which underlay his anxious striving for literary success. The story presents a weaving contest between the goddess Pallas and the mortal Arachne. Pallas, enraged that a mere mortal should pretend to challenge her artistic prowess, resolves to take revenge on a lowly rival 'that dares my sacred deity deride'. Like Gay, Arachne comes from a humble trading family in the provinces.

> No famous town she boasts, or noble name,
> But to her skilful hand owes all her fame;
> Idmon, her father, on his trade relied,
> And thirsty wool in purple juices dyed;
> Her mother, whom the shades of death confine,

Was, like her husband, born of vulgar line.
At small Hypaepe though she did reside,
Yet industry proclaimed what birth denied . . .   (ll. 11–18)

Pallas's fury at the presumption of this provincial upstart is undisguised: 'Wrath and disdain inflame her rolling eyes' (l. 47); but,
undeterred, Arachne willingly accepts the challenge. In her tapestry,
Pallas depicts an epic scene on Mount Olympus, with the gods and
goddesses grouped in all their awesome majesty.

Twelve deities she frames with stately mien,
And in the midst superior Jove is seen . . .
Heav'n's thund'ring monarch sits with awful grace,
And dread omnipotence imprints his face.   (ll. 102–3, 106–7)

By contrast, Arachne depicts decadent scenes of 'celestial crimes' in
which the gods, tempted by lust, assume the forms of beasts to
abuse their human prey. Jove appears as a demonic rapist, as bestial
in his appetites as in his disguises. In the form of a roaring bull he
ravishes the 'fair Europa'; disguised as a 'vigorous swan' he 'treads'
the 'dissolving Leda'; he assumes a 'serpent's form' to betray Deois,
and 'a strong satyr's muscled form' to seduce Antiope. Deconstructed
as a social allegory, this story presents a humble but honest artist
defying an Olympian artistic monopoly by daringly depicting the
violent and deceitful ways by which such monopolistic power is
maintained. 'The Story of Arachne' seems to represent a subconscious revolt against the tone of servile flattery Gay felt obliged to
adopt towards those 'two great geniuses' Addison and Steele; even
his praise of Pope's immanent divinity appears less flattering alongside these descriptions of godlike behaviour. Yet, at a deeper level,
this contest mirrors a conflict within Gay's own mind. While
evoking the jealousy of a social outsider towards those who assumed
a godlike right to literary pre-eminence, Gay appears characteristically uncertain whether to envy or deplore the attitudes they represent. For him it remained an unresolved question, whether to
champion the voice of honest industry, or to aspire to the Olympian
irresponsibility of a literary god.

Arachne pays a heavy price for her presumption. Cursed by the
angry goddess, she is transformed into a spider: 'Suspended thus to
waste thy future time.' To Swift, the spider was the perfect symbol
for the aspiring courtier, forever dangling by a slender thread of

hope, and dependent on the arbitrary whims of those in power. 'It is a miserable thing to live in suspense,' he wrote; 'it is the life of a spider.'[29] Already, it seems, Gay was anticipating the frustrating life of dependence on court favours that lay ahead of him.

In the early spring of 1712 a new terror gripped London, as a gang of fashionable young bloods, known as the 'Mohocks', took to the streets. The first report of them is contained in Swift's *Journal to Stella*. 'Did I tell you of a race of rakes called the Mohocks, that play the devil about this town every night, slit people's noses and beat them?'[30] At court, Swift heard more lurid tales of Mohock outrages. One man told how he had been set upon by the gang and 'how they ran his chair through with a sword'; another described how 'two of the Mohocks caught a maid of old Lady Winchilsea's just at the door of their house in the park . . . they cut all her face and beat her without any provocation'. According to Swift 'they are all Whigs' and he himself had been warned 'by a great lady' to take special precautions against them, 'for she had heard they had malicious intentions against the ministers and their friends'.[31]

Soon the newspapers were filled with sensational reports of Mohock atrocities: 'Grub Street papers about them fly like lightning, and a list printed of near 80 put into several prisons.'[32] On 12 March Steele devoted a whole issue of the *Spectator* to the Mohocks, describing in detail some of their sadistic tricks. Yet, as the public hysteria increased, Swift began to suspect the whole thing of being a media invention. 'I begin almost to think there is no truth or very little in the whole story.' Nevertheless, cautioned by his servant 'that one of the lodgers heard in a coffee-house publicly that one design of the Mohocks was upon me', he continued to take sensible precautions, while grumbling at these additional expenses. 'The dogs will cost me at least a crown a week in chairs.' Even this was no security, though, for Lord Oxford warned Swift that they 'insult chairs more than they do those on foot'. For more than a fortnight leading Tories were panicked by the scare, and the worst of it was that none could be sure whether they were merely the victims of a hoax. As Swift cowered in his rooms in Panton Street, bitterly

[29] 'Thoughts on Various Subjects', *Prose Works*, i. 244.
[30] *Journal*, ii. 508–9.
[31] Ibid. 509–15.
[32] Ibid. 511.

counting up how much the scare had cost him, the suspicion that he might merely be the victim of a practical joke was what annoyed him most. Finally, on 17 March, just ten days after the panic began, a proclamation was issued against the gang, offering a £100 reward for their arrest. This appears to have had the desired effect, though Swift was a little premature in his declaration that 'our Mohocks are all vanished'. Three days later he was forced to concede that 'our Mohocks go on still, and cut people's faces every night; faith, they shan't cut mine, I like it better as it is'.[33] Budgell devoted an issue of the *Spectator* to them on 8 April, but by the end of the month they were yesterday's news.

Both the suddenness of the Mohock panic, and its abrupt cessation, strongly support the view, held by both Swift and Chesterfield, that they were largely a figment of the popular imagination, created by a combination of press hysteria and public credulity. This is not to deny the ever-present reality of street robberies and violent assaults carried out nightly in the streets of London, often by organized criminal gangs whose activities provided Gay, fifteen years later, with the inspiration for his *Beggar's Opera*. But, as a phenomenon, the Mohocks seem to have belonged to that apocryphal tradition of charismatic rebels, often led by some renegade nobleman, stretching back in popular mythology to Robin Hood and including in more recent times the 'Roaring-Boys', Tity-Tues, Bugles, Hectors, Nickers, and Scourers.[34]

Apocryphal or not, the idea of this unruly fraternity of aristocratic young rakes intent on terrorizing the respectable citizens of London clearly appealed to Gay's imagination. What more appropriate parallel could there be with the crimes of the Olympians described in 'The Story of Arachne' than the exploits of this gang of privileged vandals? Gay's one-act play *The Mohocks* was published on 10 April. The title-page describes it as 'A Tragi-Comical Farce. As it was Acted near the Watch-House in Covent-Garden. By her Majesty's Servants'. Actually no performance of the play ever took

---

[33] Ibid. 524–5.

[34] Shadwell's play *The Scourers* (1691) describes the exploits of a similar confederacy of young bloods, roaming the midnight streets in pursuit of devilment. For a full account of the Mohocks, see R. J. Allen, *The Clubs of Augustan London* (Cambridge, Mass., 1933), 105–18. At several points in Gay's play *The Mohocks*, the gang is represented as a historical epiphenomenon; Justice Scruple is informed 'that there were Mohocks in Queen Elizabeth's days' (iii. 2), while Watchman Bleak remembers 'the ancient Mohocks of King Charles' his days' (ii. 119).

place, and the term 'acted' here is ironic, referring not to the play, but to the street-theatre antics of the gang itself. Although Gay's dedication maintains the pretence that this 'tragedy' had been 'rejected by the players', we should not be misled into believing that he ever intended it for production. The dedication is dated 'April 1st' and the play's non-performance is part of an elaborate April Fool's Day hoax.[35] For him the Mohocks are figures of fantasy, and what better way to dramatize them than in a performance which is itself a non-event.[36]

The Mohocks represents Gay's first attempt to create a deliberate literary freak; not only a drama never intended to be dramatized, but a 'tragi-comical farce' which mingles Miltonic parody with slapstick farce. Gay treats the Mohocks as a mock-heroic, or rather mock-demonic, fraternity, much given to theatrical hyperbole and blood-curdling schoolboy oaths. Two of the Mohock gang are called Molloch and Abaddon, names taken from *Paradise Lost* and *Paradise Regained*, while their conjuration 'That villainy, and all outrageous crimes | Shall ever be our glory and our pleasure' appears to parody Satan's oath 'Evil, be thou my good' (*Paradise Lost*, iv. 10). Yet, as in *Wine*, Gay's target is not Milton's works themselves, but the literary taste for sub-Miltonic rodomontade.[37] Dennis, who pronounced *Paradise Lost* 'the greatest poem that ever was written by man',[38] was among Milton's chief contemporary admirers and, in using the dedication of this play to recall Dennis's verbal mugging of Pope, Gay effectively turns Dennis himself into a kind of literary Mohock.

Elsewhere Gay's use of literary allusions is deliberately eclectic. Believing as he did that 'variety's the source of joy', he cheerfully juxtaposes echoes of Milton, imitations of Dryden, parodies of

---

[35] Four years earlier Swift had also chosen April Fools' Day as the date for his Bickerstaff hoax, a work which seems to have influenced Gay's ironic strategy in *The Mohocks*.

[36] It seems most unlikely that *The Mohocks* could have been Gay's 'new comedy' to which Pope refers in his letter to Cromwell of 21 Dec. 1711, since there was no mention of the Mohocks in the press before Feb. 1712. Also Pope's comments imply that Gay was seeking a production for his comedy, which would seem inappropriate for *The Mohocks*. All the evidence suggests that Pope had in mind an early draft of Gay's *Wife of Bath*.

[37] Fuller notes that 'parallels here between Gay and Milton are quite difficult to find'. He points out that the play's opening lines ('Thus far our riots with success are crowned, | Have found no stop, or what they found o'ercome') are borrowed not from Milton but from Dryden's play *Tyrannick Love*. See Fuller, i. 408.

[38] *The Grounds of Criticism in Poetry* (1704).

Dennis, and borrowings from Shakespeare. The effect of such eclecticism is a kind of hectic episodic comedy. The dialogue in *The Mohocks* is a patchwork of literary allusions and Grub Street echoes. Gay's comic constables are derived from Shakespeare, combining elements of Dogberry and Verges, Falstaff's motley crew, and the 'rude mechanicals' of *A Midsummer Night's Dream*. The watchman's account of how he 'kept nine Mohocks, with their swords drawn, at pole's length, broke three of their heads, knocked down four, and trimmed the jackets of the other six' is clearly based on Falstaff's similar feats of pugilistic and mathematical agility in recounting the Gad's Hill episode.[39] But for his more lurid details Gay plundered recent press reports. When one man describes how he saw the gang 'hook a man as cleverly as a fisherman would a great fish, and play him up and down from Charing Cross to Temple Bar', he echoes a contemporary newspaper report: 'last night a woman was very ill used and had a fish hook stuck in her cheek, with a string fastened to it, and so dragged about, till these unmerciful wretches thought fit to cut it out.'[40] Similarly Gay's suggestion of Mohock cannibalism (one member of his gang is called Cannibal) no doubt derived from Steele's suggestion in the *Spectator* that the Mohocks had borrowed their name 'from a sort of cannibals in India'.[41]

Indeed, it seems possible that *The Mohocks* was not an entirely solo work, but rather Gay's own variation on satiric themes developed by friends with whom he was seeking to establish closer ties. The many similarities between Gay's farce and Budgell's *Spectator* essay on the Mohocks (itself a response to Steele's discussions of the gang) suggest not merely that Gay had read Budgell's piece, but that he may well have been privy to its composition.[42] Steele had facetiously described the Mohocks' 'happy dexterity' in 'tipping the lion' upon innocent pedestrians, 'which is performed by squeezing

[39] *1 Henry IV*, II. iv. The same scene provides the source for Moloch's evidence: 'With these very eyes, Mr Constable, I saw him in a dark alley, where one could not see one's hand, slit a cinder wench's nose . . .'

[40] Report on the Dublin Mohocks, published in the *Supplement*, 702 (7–9 Apr. 1712); see Fuller, i. 409–10.

[41] *Spectator*, 324 (12 Mar. 1712). Most accounts derived the name Mohocks from the four Mohawk chieftains who had visited London in a colonial deputation in early 1710, and were celebrated in Pope's *Windsor Forest* (ll. 404–6); See Richmond P. Bond, *Queen Anne's American Kings* (Oxford, 1952).

[42] Budgell wrote *Spectator*, 327 (8 Apr.); Steele wrote *Spectator*, 324 and 332. Winton speculates on a possible clash with Defoe over the Mohock panic; see Winton, 22–3.

the nose flat to the face and boring out the eyes with their fingers'. But Budgell's 'Mohock Emperor' gives strict commands that 'they never tip the lion upon man, woman or child till the clock at St Dunstan's shall have struck one'. Another group of Mohocks, Steele asserts, 'are called the dancing-masters, and teach their scholars to cut capers by running swords through their legs'. Accordingly Gay has his constables take care 'that we may not be forced to cut capers against our wills – pox of such dancing-masters' (ii. 33-4). Steele's third sub-caste of the Mohock clan is made up of Tumblers, 'whose office it is to set women upon their heads, and commit certain indecencies, or rather barbarities on the limbs which they expose'. Budgell's Mohock Emperor prescribes strict limits to the exercise of this office, commanding that the Tumblers 'confine themselves to Drury Lane and the purlieus of the Temple', that is, to the familiar haunts of prostitutes. Budgell's Mohocks are public avengers, a kind of Hell's Angels, exercising their violent authority on behalf of public security. His Mohock Emperor, issuing his manifesto from 'our court at the Devil tavern' (the former haunt of Gay's tipplers in *Wine*), declares: 'We have nothing more at our imperial heart than the reformation of the cities of London and Westminister.' Gay's Mohocks are schoolboy pranksters dressed up for a satanic masquerade. He describes a city street on a windy morning after a night of Mohock face-slashing: 'all the ground covered with noses, as thick as 'tis with hail-stones after a storm.' And much of his humour is ribald slapstick. Beau Gentle's anxious plea, 'Be civil, I beg you, gentlemen, disengage your poles from my full bottom', ostensibly refers to his wig, but undoubtedly the *double entendre* is intentional.

Gay returned to the Mohock theme in a satiric broadsheet entitled 'A Wonderful Prophecy, Taken from the Mouth of the Spirit of a Person Barbarously Slain by the Mohocks'. This parodies the apocalyptic language of the Camisards, or 'French prophets', a sect of Huguenot refugees who had created a considerable stir in London when they arrived in 1708, following an unsuccessful religious revolt in the south of France. Almost certainly the Camisards' millennialist rhetoric would have recalled to Gay's mind the language of the Huguenots of Barnstaple, and there is a noticeable facility in the way the 'Prophecy' mimics their doom-laden dedication to the Book of Revelation. 'Woe! Woe! Woe!' it begins; 'Woe to London! Woe to Westminster! Woe to Southwark! and Woe to the inhabitants thereof!' Yet although this piece is skilfully contrived, it fails as a vehicle for social satire. If Gay had entertained hopes of publishing it in the *Spectator*, he had chosen badly. By 1712 the Camisards were hardly a topical theme.

Gay spent part of the summer of 1712 revisiting his family in Devon. There is an uncorroborated story that his brother Jonathan had shot himself the year before, 'after a dispute with his colonel', but no evidence of the incident survives.[43] It is certain though that Jonathan died some time between 1709 and 1711, and, as a consequence, Gay may have come into a little money, though not enough to maintain him on any kind of equal footing with his new literary friends.[44] Lintot had paid him £2. 10s. for the copyright of *The Mohocks*, and his income from other publications was similarly meagre. Accordingly, shortly after his return to London he accepted an employment which, though it relieved him of financial anxieties, only served to underline the vast chasm of social status which divided him from a literary Olympian like Addison. His new appointment was as secretary and domestic steward to the elderly Duchess of Monmouth. Pope immediately congratulated his 'good success', doing all he could to ease Gay's embarrassment at such a menial employment. 'Notwithstanding the many inconveniencies and disadvantages they commonly talk of in the *res augusti domi*,' he wrote, 'I have never found any other than the inability of giving people of merit the only certain proof of our value for them, in doing 'em some real service.' Urging Gay to adopt a philosophical attitude, he signed off with a cheery piece of Chaucerian bawdy, suggesting that, after all, an elderly duchess was a less demanding mistress than those fickle ladies the Muses: 'He who is forced to live wholly upon those ladies' favours is indeed in as precarious a condition as any he who does what Chaucer says for sustenance.' This was hardly an encouraging allusion.[45] 'What Chaucer says' in the *Cook's Tale* is: 'And swived for hir sustenance.' By implication, Gay's only choice

[43] For the story of Jonathan Gay's suicide see Phoebe Fenwick Gaye, *John Gay* (London, 1938), 47; the family genealogy in *The Visitations of the County of Devon*, ed. F. T. Colby (London, 1872), states that Jonathan Gay died unmarried in 1709.
[44] According to the entry on Gay in the *General Dictionary* (1737), 'Our author had a small fortune at his disposal, but far from sufficient to support him in that independent condition of life to which the freedom of his spirit adapted his desires' (v. 406). This account of Gay was revised by Pope before publication, and must accordingly be treated with some scepticism.
[45] Pope to Gay, 24 Dec. 1712; Pope, *Corr.* i. 169.

of livelihoods lay between being a kept man or a gigolo. Unconsciously Pope confirmed that Gay's status had hardly risen from his days as a draper's apprentice among the he-strumpets of the New Exchange.

Anne Scott, Countess of Buccleugh and Duchess of Monmouth, was 61 when Gay entered her service. A witty and vivacious woman, she had been described in her youth by the diarist John Evelyn as 'certainly one of the wisest and craftiest of her sex'.[46] Forty years on she had lost little of her sprightliness. Lady Cowper recalled that 'she had all the life and fire of youth and it was marvellous to see that the many afflictions she had suffered had not touched her wit and good nature, but at upwards of threescore she had both in their full perfection'.[47] Among the Duchess's 'many afflictions' was the forfeiture of her husband's honours and estates following his rebellion and execution in 1685. However, these were quickly restored to her by William III in 1690, and her own Scottish estates were never confiscated. In 1688 she was married again to Lord Cornwallis, who died ten years later; in 1703, at the age of 52, she took a third husband, the Earl of Selkirk, twelve years her junior. Even in her sixties she remained a wealthy and fashion-conscious woman, who loved to regale her friends at court with anecdotes of Charles II. At the Queen's Birthday party in 1711, when the nobility and gentry all appeared 'in richer habits than has been known since 1660', she created a dramatic impression by decking herself in jewels 'to the value of £50,000'.[48]

Apart from her own family estates at Dalkeith, the Duchess owned extensive properties in Lincolnshire and Hertfordshire, as well as a London residence at the upper end of Laurence Street in Chelsea. It was chiefly in this London mansion that Gay's services were required, though it seems likely that he owed his appointment to a network of Lincolnshire connections. Henry Cromwell had numerous acquaintances in the county, including Maurice Johnson, whose father was steward of the Monmouth estates. Johnson, the same age as Gay, was a lawyer and antiquarian who divided his time equally between Lincolnshire and London. In 1709 he founded the Gentleman's Society of Spalding, whose minute-book records that

[46] John Evelyn, *Diary*, ed. E. S. De Beer (6 vols., Oxford, 1955), iv. 6 (16 Mar. 1673).

[47] Mary, Countess Cowper, *Diary, 1714–1720* (London, 1864), 95, 125.

[48] Narcissus Luttrell, *A Brief Historical Relation of State Affairs from September 1678 to April 1717* (6 vols., Oxford, 1857) vi. 688.

Gay introduced him to the leading figures of literary London.

> Maurice Johnson . . . the founder of this society, who being by Mr John Gay the poet brought acquainted with Mr Pope, Addison became with Sir R Steele and others of his meeting at one Button's who had been his butler and kept a coffee-house in Covent Garden where the *Tatlers* were taken out of the Lion there receiving them and read to the company [*sic*].[49]

Gay's duties in the Monmouth household were hardly onerous, and it seems the Duchess took an interest in his literary career. Shortly after his appointment, Gay sent Johnson a copy of his newly published poem *Rural Sports*, thanking him for 'former favours' and diplomatically deferring to the literary opinions of his new patronesses. 'Her Grace and Lady Isabella', he wrote, 'seem not displeased with my offering.'[50] Some months later Johnson's brother John confirmed the Duchess's support for her new secretary's literary endeavours: 'I am told at the Duchess's Mr Gay is every day at the playhouse, morning and afternoon, seeing his play rehearsed. They don't seem displeased at it but kindly concerned for the success of it.'[51] The fact that Gay was permitted to spend so much time supervising rehearsals for his play *The Wife of Bath* suggests that his secretarial duties were easily compatible with the pursuit of a literary career.

Nevertheless, however easy the terms of his employment, Gay was still acutely sensitive about his dependent status as a paid domestic. In an essay on 'The Manner of Living with Great Men' his friend Nick Rowe reflected on the humiliating posture of the hanger-on at court in terms which might apply with equal force to the household writer-in-residence.

> What slavery it is to a ridiculous vanity to hunt after the conversation of insolent greatness! What peace, what ease, what happiness does a man forgo, who might be used as he pleases among his equals, and yet chooses to put himself upon the rack, to make a lord laugh![52]

When Samuel Johnson, a man acutely sensitive to the condescension

---

[49] Footnote in the minute-book etc. The 'Lion' refers, to the lion's head letter-box erected at Button's coffee-house for the reception of contributions to the *Guardian*, not the *Tatler*. The lion's head became the *Guardian*'s logo, a device which apparently had its desired effect in raising public awareness of the periodical.

[50] *Letters*, 2; Lady Isabella Scott was the Duchess's daughter.

[51] Irving, 70.

[52] Ibid. 17.

of aristocratic patrons, reviewed this episode of Gay's life, he did so with undisguised dismay. Portraying the Duchess as a vain woman 'remarkable for her inflexible perseverance in her demand to be treated as a princess', he abruptly telescoped the period of Gay's apprenticeship with his employment as the Duchess's secretary: 'by quitting a shop for such service', he wrote, Gay 'might gain leisure but he certainly advanced little in the boast of independence'.[53] For Johnson, Gay's apparent decision to abandon an honest trade, however humble, in favour of a role as a domestic courtier represented a reprehensible retreat from self-reliance to servility. In fact a period of four years separated Gay's abandonment of his apprenticeship from his acceptance of the post in the Duchess's household. During these four years he had indeed made strenuous endeavours to sustain an independent existence on the strength of his own literary labours. Yet the question remains a pertinent one. Throughout Gay's works the twin themes of dependence and independence constantly recur. In principle Gay's endorsement of the moral value of independence is always clearly stated, yet in practice he lived his life in the houses, and at the behest, of a succession of aristocratic patrons. Even after he had acquired sufficient wealth to set up an independent establishment of his own, he chose to remain a perpetual guest and lodger in the homes of others. It was not until the very end of his career that he acknowledged, with some nostalgia and regret, that the life of an independent tradesman, however humdrum, might be superior to that of a perpetual court jester.

It was during 1713 that Gay first became acquainted with Swift, and the two men might have found much to discuss in their shared experiences of the role of domestic secretary. Coincidentally, one of the Duchess's many far-flung estates was Moor Park in Hertfordshire, where Gay spent part of the autumn. Swift himself had spent the best part of ten years, from 1690, at another Moor Park, in Surrey, as domestic secretary to Sir William Temple. It was there, studying in the library 'at least eight hours a day', that Swift accomplished the transition from mediocre student to outstanding man of letters. Yet he always bitterly resented his dependent status in Temple's household. Years later, Temple's nephew insisted that Swift had been a mere domestic servant at Moor Park, hired 'at the rate of £20 a year and his board'. He added that 'Sir William never

[53] Johnson, 'Gay', 60.

favoured him with his conversation, because of his ill qualities, nor allowed him to sit down at table with him'.[54] Swift never forgot the humiliation of these years, and was always acutely sensitive to any hint of condescension in the demeanour of aristocratic friends. In April 1711 he warned Secretary St John 'never to appear cold to me, for I would not be treated like a schoolboy; that I had felt too much of that in my life already (meaning from Sir W[illiam] T[emple])'.[55] As soon as he was able, Swift established his own independent household, where he ruled as a domestic tyrant, even extending his imperious commands to the households of others where he consented to visit as a guest. 'I hate all people whom I cannot command,' he boasted, adding that he could only bear to live 'where all mortals are subservient to me'.[56] Swift never failed to urge Gay to follow this example of determined independence, and was constantly baffled by Gay's refusal to comply. In this, as in so many other matters, the similarities between these two men's backgrounds only underline the fundamental differences in their psychological needs.

One article in the terms of Gay's employment was particularly humiliating. It appears that, on some occasions at least, he was required to wear the household livery of blue cloth laced with silver loops. The evidence for this comes from two sources; the first, Gay himself; the other, an anonymous pamphleteer. In the mock-doggerel prologue to *The Shepherd's Week*, Gay affects the style of a country yokel, newly come to town to meet the famed royal physician Dr Arbuthnot.

> Quoth I, please God, I'll hie with glee
> To court, this Arbuthnot to see.
> I sold my sheep and lambkins too,
> For silver loops and garment blue.   (ll. 37–40)

Here the description of Gay's new livery may seem a facetious exaggeration, like the suggestion that he came to London driving a flock of sheep before him. But the description is confirmed in a pamphlet entitled *Two Letters Concerning the Author of the Examiner* which attacked the supposed authors of the Tory periodical. Among the various mountebank costumes assumed by the *Examiner*, it

---

[54] For a discussion of the exaggerated accounts of Macaulay, Thackeray, and others, see Nokes, 16.

[55] *Journal*, i. 230.

[56] Swift, *Corr.* iii. 421. 471.

suggests, are those of 'a poor whore, in petticoats and tawdry ribbons' (evidently aimed at Delariviere Manley), or 'a gown and cassock' (Swift). Sometimes, it goes on, the *Examiner* 'puts on a green ribbon and fancies himself a lord' (a gibe at the newly ennobled Bolingbroke); but at other times 'the whim will take him to write in the persona of a footman, and then he calls for his blue livery, embroidered with silver'. This is clearly aimed at Gay; but what is particularly interesting is that this pamphlet was published in November 1713, five months before *The Shepherd's Week*. The author of the *Two Letters* was thus not alluding to Gay's own mocking self-portrait, but describing the servant's uniform by which, he clearly expected, Gay would be easily identified.[57]

Soon after entering the Duchess's employment Gay published his georgic poem *Rural Sports* (January 1713), and it is tempting to assume he drew his inspiration from his recent summer visit to Devon. Yet the poem's principal sources are literary, not topographical, and this apparent celebration of bucolic themes is essentially designed to achieve metropolitan success. Dedicated to Pope, it takes as its primary model Pope's *Windsor Forest*, which, although not published until March, had been in preparation, and widely circulated among Pope's friends, for several months. On the surface, Gay's homage to his friend's work represents an act of literary deference, but certain differences between the two works indicate a significant divergence of social outlook.

The site and inspiration of Pope's georgic celebration are emphatically identified. Windsor is chosen not only for its rich associations with monarchy, which allow Pope to represent it as the heartland of national values, but also as Pope's native soil, and the inspirational source of poetic impulses which intimately identify his own mythopoeic imagination with the culture that fostered it. Although actually born in the city of London, Pope had grown up at Binfield, on the fringes of Windsor Forest, and hence takes the forest as his own poetic territory. In offering his Arcadian vision of Windsor under a Stuart monarch, he assumes the authoritative tones of one whose sense of belonging inspires an intuitive sympathy for the secret languages of nature and cultural history. Gay's perspective is very different. He writes as one not fostered in, but excluded from, an

[57] For a discussion of Gay's possible contributions to the *Examiner*, see below pp. 135–7.

Arcadian paradise. It is impossible to overlook a tinge of envy in the initial antithesis which dramatizes their contrasting situations. There is almost a hint of accusation in the emphatic opening monosyllable, 'You'.

> You, who the sweets of rural life have known,
> Despise th'ungrateful hurry of the town;
> In Windsor groves your easy hours employ,
> And, undisturbed, yourself and muse enjoy.
>
> (*Rural Sports* (1713), ll. 1–4)

While Pope enjoys the idyllic calm of an earthly paradise, pampered by admiring river-gods and indulged by a sympathetic nature, Gay's position is quite the opposite.

> But I, who ne'er was bless'd from Fortune's hand,
> Nor brighten'd plough-shares in paternal land,
> Have long been in the noisy town immured,
> Respir'd its smoke, and all its toils endured;
> Have courted bus'ness with successless pain,
> And in attendance wasted years in vain;
> Where news and politics amuse mankind,
> And schemes of state involve th'uneasy mind;
> Faction embroils the world; and ev'ry tongue
> Is fraught with malice, and with scandal hung:
> Friendship, for sylvan shades, does courts despise,
> Where all must yield to int'rest's dearer ties;
> Each rival Machiavel with envy burns,
> And honesty forsakes them all by turns;
> Whilst calumny upon each party's thrown,
> Which both abhor, and both alike disown.
> Thus have I, 'midst the brawls of factious strife,
> Long undergone the drudgery of life;
> On courtiers' promises I founded schemes,
> Which still deluded me, like golden dreams;
> Expectance wore the tedious hours away,
> And glimm'ring hope roll'd on each lazy day. (ll. 9–30)

If Pope is in heaven, Gay is in hell, condemned to a life of pointless drudgery and toil. The sense of entrapment in a Stygian underworld of noise and smoke, where strife and faction rule, and where 'each rival Machiavel with envy burns', has distinctly infernal overtones.

Most clearly of all, Gay's painful sense of being without 'paternal land' marks him out as an outsider, an interloper, a man denied the symbolic and material blessings of an identifiable home. He is mentally and emotionally displaced, occupying a sort of limbo which, as the poem demonstrates, remains a permanent enclosure, irrespective of his actual physical surroundings. All the frustrations of his years as a draper's assistant and Grub Street hack well up in his recollection of having 'courted bus'ness with successless pain'; while already his resentment at the humiliating quest for literary patrons—a theme which was to dominate so much of his later writing—is clearly stated. It is some tribute to the Duchess of Monmouth's character that she was apparently 'not displeased' by this evidence of her secretary's clear dissatisfaction with his present role. Gay enters the countryside not to recover some lost patrimonial Eden, but as a stranger, a trespasser and fugitive, fleeing from the drudgeries and humiliations of the town. Nature for him is an asylum, a place of refuge for his 'harassed mind'.

> Resolv'd at last no more fatigues to bear,
> At once I both forsook the town and care;
> At a kind friend's a calm asylum chose,
> And soothed my harassed mind with sweet repose . . .   (ll. 31–4)

The 'kind friend' was probably Fortescue, and the 'asylum' Fortescue's estate at Buckland Filleigh. Yet the word asylum suggests confinement more powerfully than liberation, and, even in this rural refuge, Gay cannot escape the besetting snares of dependency and frustrated ambition. While attempting to evoke an atmosphere of freedom and liberation, allowing his muse to 'rove through flow'ry meads and plains', he immediately contradicts himself:

> And the same road ambitiously pursue,
> Frequented by the Mantuan swain, and you.   (ll. 39–40)

That adverb, 'ambitiously', implicitly acknowledges that Gay has not left his 'glimm'ring hopes' behind him in the town, but has merely transferred them to a different setting. His muse will not in fact rove freely in the open meadows, but will be confined to the high road of literary ambition mapped out by Virgil ('the Mantuan swain') and Pope before him. The homage to Virgil and Pope is thus another form of 'attendance' on those above him, while Gay's descriptions of rural retirement assume the ironic status of another business activity.

Indeed, while on the surface Gay seems to offer a conventional contrast between the 'sweet repose' of country life, and the toil, faction, and falsehood of the town, the undercurrents of his poem suggest similarities, rather than differences, between these two worlds. Instinctively he selects images which imply affinities, rather than antitheses, between town and country mores. Treachery and betrayal, cruelty and deceit, are shown to be common to both. The first countryman he describes is a fisherman.

> The fisherman does now his toils prepare,
> And arms himself with ev'ry wat'ry snare;
> He meditates new methods to betray,
> Threat'ning destruction to the finny prey. (ll. 55–8)

'Toils' were what Gay had endured in the noisy town, but the same feelings of betrayal and entrapment remain his predominant emotions in the country. In his detailed descriptions of the angler's art, Gay presents the fisherman as a rural Machiavel, as accomplished as any courtier in techniques of deception. 'Fraud', 'deceit', 'cheat', and 'stratagem' are the key words chosen to represent the 'delusive arts' of the angler, who, as he baits his 'treach'rous hook' with the 'fallacious meat' of an impaled earthworm, becomes the rural equivalent of a London politician. And although, in proffering his sage advice on angling techniques, Gay seems to align himself with the hunter, emotionally his lines evoke the anguish of his prey.

> Soon in smart pains he feels the dire mistake,
> Lashes the waves, and beats the foamy lake,
> With sudden rage he now aloft appears,
> And in his look convulsive anguish bears;
>
> Till tired at last, despoil'd of all his strength,
> The fish athwart the streams unfolds his length.
> He now, with pleasure, views the gasping prize
> Gnash his sharp teeth and roll his bloodshot eyes;
> Then draws him t'wards the shore, with gentle care,
> And holds his nostrils in the sick'ning air:
> Upon the burthen'd stream he floating lies,
> Stretches his quiv'ring fins, and panting dies. (ll. 175–8, 189–96)

The extended simile which follows the salmon's death emphasizes the parallel between this rural sport and the chicanery of town-life.

> So the coquet, th'unhappy youth ensnares,
> With artful glances and affected airs,
> Baits him with frowns, now lures him on with smiles,
> And in disport employs her practised wiles;
> The boy at last, betray'd by borrow'd charms,
> A victim falls in her enslaving arms.   (ll. 197–202)

The country riverbank provides a new arena for those same delusive arts taught in the jilt's academy of the New Exchange. And, as Gay describes the arts of fly-fishing, he finds a new ironic application for his draper's apprentice skills.

> To frame the little animal, provide
> All the gay hues that wait on female pride,
> Let nature guide thee; sometimes golden wire
> The glitt'ring bellies of the fly require;
> The peacock's plumes thy tackle must not fail,
> Nor the dear purchase of the sable's tail.
> Each gaudy bird some slender tribute brings,
> And lends the growing insect proper wings:
> Silks of all colours must their aid impart,
> And ev'ry fur promote the fisher's art.
> So the gay lady, with expensive care,
> Borrows the pride of land, of sea, and air;
> Furs, pearls and plumes, the painted thing displays,
> Dazzles our eyes, and easy hearts betrays.   (ll. 125–38)

For Gay, the artificial fly becomes a perfect symbol for the beguiling treachery of appearances. His injunction, 'Let nature guide thee', is wonderfully ironic. Almost certainly it recalls Pope's similar prescription in the *Essay on Criticism*, 'First follow Nature . . .'; but, for all their apparent similarity, these two admonitions carry very different meanings. For Pope, nature is a model of truth:

> Unerring Nature, still divinely bright,
> One clear, unchang'd and universal light . . .   (ll: 71–2)

But for Gay nature is the great deceiver, the source and inspiration of all human affectations. The natural world is a theatre of vanities, outwardly dazzling, but built upon suffering and death. In *Windsor Forest*, Pope presents a clear distinction between natural harmony and human discord. Left to itself, he argues, nature is harmonious and benign; it is only man who perverts it into destructive acts:

> Beasts urg'd by us, their fellow-beasts pursue,
> And learn of man each other to undo.   (ll. 123–4)

Gay sees things the other way round. It is precisely through following nature that man perfects his predatory skills, since nature is the true source of deceitfulness and cruelty.

Like *Windsor Forest*, *Rural Sports* is a 'peace poem', designed in part to celebrate the Treaty of Utrecht, which put an end to twenty years of intermittent warfare in Western Europe. Although not concluded until April, negotiations for this treaty had been in progress for well over a year, while the protracted bargaining over preliminaries had been a principal preoccupation of the Tory ministry since assuming office in October 1710. In their delicate political manœuvrings to secure a speedy settlement on terms satisfactory to British, and more specifically Tory, interests, the government had been at pains to identify a set of national priorities quite distinct from the declared war aims of their allies, the Dutch, Austrians, and Catalans. In the propaganda offensive to establish these priorities and legitimize a negotiating posture which would abandon several of the allies' stated objectives, Swift's *Conduct of the Allies* (1711) and Arbuthnot's 'John Bull' pamphlets (1712) had been particularly effective. Swift represented the prolongation of the war as a self-serving conspiracy between the 'moneyed men' of the City and their confederates, the Austrian and Dutch governments, all determined to enrich themselves at the expense of British lives and Tory taxpayers. 'No nation', he thundered, 'was ever so long or so scandalously abused by the folly, the temerity, the corruption, the ambition of its domestic enemies; or treated with so much insolence, injustice and ingratitude by its foreign friends.'[58]

In the summer of 1711 rumours of a secret treaty between Britain and France leaked out when the chief negotiator, Matthew Prior, was arrested as a spy on his arrival, incognito, in England. Not surprisingly, the Whigs became increasingly suspicious of government intentions and, even after the signing of the treaty, there were bitter political recriminations and accusations that it represented a betrayal of Britain's allies. Hence, among the numerous poetical

---

[58] *Prose Works*, vi. 15.

effusions which celebrated the end of the war, it is easy to detect the poets' political allegiances. Whig poets concentrate on Marlborough's glorious victories, and on the valiant defence of Protestantism in battles overseas. Tory poets dwell on the miseries of war, contrasting the chaos of battle with the steady patriotic purpose of the government in guiding the nation back to the tranquillity of peace. Writing in the earnest tones of the Whig press chief, Addison promulgated a *Spectator* 'Edict' to discipline his loyal troops of versifiers. In it, he sternly prohibited the use of classical allusions.

I do hereby strictly require every person who shall write on this subject to remember he is a Christian, and not to sacrifice his catechism to his poetry ... I do ... positively forbid the sending of Mercury with any particular message or dispatch relating to the peace, and shall by no means suffer Minerva to take upon her the shape of any plenipotentiary concerned in this great work.[59]

In thus insisting on a Christian, rather than a classical, frame of reference, Addison reinforced Whig concerns that the war should be presented not only as a victory for Protestantism, but as the triumph of a new British imperial civilization founded on the twin pillars of free trade and constitutional monarchy. Such a civilization, confident in its own heroic values, had no need of foreign mythological imports. Instead, Addison's own poem, *The Campaign*, which described Marlborough as 'our god-like leader', became the approved model for subsequent Whig panegyrics. For Addison, the day of Blenheim was:

> The day when Heav'n designed to show
> His care and conduct of the world below.

Like William Coward before him, Addison envisaged a new tradition of English epic verse in which the Christian heroism of Marlborough's campaign would equal, not imitate, the classical heroism of Homer's works. He made this conviction explicit in a couplet which Gay had already praised in *Wine*.

> Rivers of blood I see, and hills of slain,
> An *Iliad* rising out of one campaign.

But if Marlborough was God's holy instrument, what did that make of God-fearing Tories, like Swift, who opposed him?

---

[59] *Spectator*, 523 (30 Oct. 1712).

A dutiful Whig poet like Thomas Tickell found little difficulty in obeying Addison's edict. Banishing all classical deities from his poem *On the Prospect of Peace*, he contrived to represent Britannia as the agent of divine providence.

> Her labours are to plead th'Almighty's cause,
> Her pride to teach th'untam'd barbarian laws.
> Who conquers wins by brutish strength the prize,
> But 'tis a godlike work to civilize.

Even an unswerving Tory like Joseph Trapp felt inhibited from transgressing the terms of Addison's literary prohibition, though the political message of his poem *Peace* clearly endorsed Swift's conspiracy theory of the war:

> Too long have our deluded heroes died
> For Belgic avarice and Austrian pride.

Swift dismissed Trapp's poem as 'good for nothing' even after his own attempts to improve it.[60] Gay was more generous. In a letter to Maurice Johnson which shows his first hints of Tory sympathies, he wrote: 'there are a great many good lines in the poem, and he hath here and there mixed some reflections on the late ministry.'

Reading Tickell's poem *On the Prospect of Peace*, Pope was disturbed to find several striking similarities with his own, as yet unpublished, *Windsor Forest*. Both poems sound the imperial theme and represent the 'painted kings of India' bowing down before Queen Anne.[61] Yet Pope's vision of empire has a clear Tory bias. The imperial dominion of the Stuart monarch Anne owes its authority not to recent feats of arms, but to its embodiment of timeless classical ideals. Ostentatiously ignoring the terms of Addison's edict, Pope peoples his forest with classical deities; Ceres and Pan, Flora and Pomona, Phoebus, Diana, Neptune, and Jove. Moreover, in dedicating the poem to George Granville, recently elevated to the peerage as Lord Lansdowne, one of twelve new peers suddenly created in a desperate political manœuvre to secure the passage of the peace treaty through the House of Lords, Pope signals a clear political preference. The opening section of *Windsor Forest* paints an

---

[60] *Journal*, ii. 651.
[61] Compare Tickell's lines, 'Thee, thee, an hundred languages shall claim, | And savage Indians swear by Anna's name', with *Windsor Forest*, ll. 379–84.

idyllic picture of a happy land whose subjects live in harmony with nature under the rule of a benign monarch:

> Rich Industry sits smiling on the plains
> And Peace and Plenty tell a STUART reigns.   (ll. 41–2)

This is immediately followed by a nightmare vision of the same land under Norman rule as royal killing field.

> Not thus the land appeared in ages past,
> A dreary desert and a gloomy waste,
> To savage beasts and savage laws a prey,
> And kings more furious and severe than they . . .
>
> (*Windsor Forest*, ll. 43–6)

An ingenious kind of coded Tory arithmetic is at work here, whereby William I and William II = William III; the Norman kings' reduction of Windsor forest into a private hunting ground becomes a metaphor for the Dutch King William's use of the entire kingdom as a base for protracted Continental wars. In his original draft of the poem Pope concluded this section on the savagery of the Normans with this couplet:

> Oh may no more a foreign master's rage
> With wrongs yet legal, curse a future age!

Wisely, before publication, he chose to withdraw this rash reproach against the 'foreign' heir to the throne, the Elector of Hanover. But the political iconography of the poem was clear enough for Swift, who had not yet met Pope, to tell Stella: 'Mr Pope has published a fine poem called *Windsor Forest*. Read it.'[62] Swift's literary judgements were seldom innocent of political prejudice, and he clearly saw Pope as a potential ally. Two months after publishing this poem, Pope wrote an essay attacking hunting for Steele's new journal the *Guardian*.

We should find it hard to vindicate the destroying of anything that has life, merely out of wantonness; yet in this principle our children are bred up, and one of the first pleasures we allow them, is the licence of inflicting pain upon poor animals. Almost as soon as we are sensible what life is ourselves, we make it our sport to take it from other creatures.[63]

---

[62] *Journal*, ii. 635; 9 Mar. 1713.
[63] *Guardian*, 61 (21 May 1713); Stephens, 233–7.

These are sentiments which find a ready echo in Gay's *Rural Sports*. Gay too evades the terms of Addison's edict by casting his poem in the form of a Virgilian georgic; Ceres and Flora, Jove and Phoebus, Cynthia and Aurora all jostle in his verses alongside Virgil, Machiavelli, and Pope himself. Like Pope, Gay ostensibly celebrates the peace and plenty of a tranquil land, ruled over by a beneficent Queen Anne and remote from the horrors of war.

> Oh happy plains! remote from war's alarms,
> And all the ravages of hostile arms;
> And happy shepherds who, secure from fear,
> On open downs preserve your fleecy care!
> Where no rude soldier, bent on cruel spoil,
> Spreads desolation o'er the fertile soil;
> No trampling steed lays waste the rip'ning grain,
> Nor crackling flames devour the promis'd gain; . . .
> Let Anna then adorn your rural lays,
> And ev'ry wood resound with grateful praise;
> Anna who binds the tyrant war in chains,
> And peace diffuses o'er the cheerful plains;
> In whom again the bright Astrea reigns.   (ll. 357–64, 371–5)

Yet ironically, while apparently celebrating the rural sports of peace, Gay's lines depict a perpetual state of natural warfare. Almost half the poem's episodes end with the death of some hapless victim.

> Into the thinner element he's cast
> And on the verdant margin gasps his last.   (ll. 87–8)

> When soon they rashly seize the deadly bait,
> And lux'ry draws them to their fellows' fate.   (ll. 163–4)

> Upon the burthen'd stream he floating lies,
> Stretches his quiv'ring fins, and panting dies.   (ll. 195–6)

> The scatt'ring lead pursues th'unerring sight,
> And death in thunder overtakes his flight.   (ll. 444–5)

> Now speed he doubles to regain the way,
> And crushes in his jaws the screaming prey.   (ll. 464–5)

> Till tir'd at last, he pants and heaves for breath;
> Then lays him down, and waits approaching death.   (ll. 511–12)[64]

[64] All these quotations are from the original (1713) version of the poem. In his revised version (1720), Gay intensified this ironic effect; the sixty lines leading up to 'Oh happy

While ostensibly endorsing the myth of pastoral tranquillity, Gay more powerfully represents man's role in nature as a relentless killer. Nor are these killings merely 'natural'; they are carried out with Machiavellian cunning, employing all the technology that artifice can devise to gratify a sadistic taste for murder as a kind of fatal seduction. Gay's sportsman is a 'rude soldier' out of uniform, no less bent on 'cruel spoil' than his military comrade in arms. Indeed, by emphasizing the huntsman's crafty stratagems Gay suggests that, far from being more innocent than the soldier, he may be more culpable, since he is engaged in an unequal conflict, using his skills to stalk an innocent prey, not openly confronting a human adversary. It is particularly instructive to observe how Gay, even when clearly borrowing a poetic episode from Pope, contrives to give it a very different moral value. Here they both describe the netting of a partridge:

> When milder Autumn Summer's heat succeeds,
> And in the new-shorn field the partridge feeds,
> Before his lord the ready spaniel bounds,
> Panting with hope, he tries the furrow'd grounds,
> But when the tainted gales the game betray,
> Couch'd close he lies, and meditates the prey;
> Secure they trust th'unfaithful field, beset,
> Till hov'ring o'er them sweeps the swelling net.
>
> (*Windsor Forest*, ll. 97–104)

> As in successive toil the seasons roll,
> So various pleasures recreate the soul;
> The setting dog, instructed to betray,
> Rewards the fowler with the feather'd prey.
> Soon as the lab'ring horse with swelling veins
> Hath safely hous'd the farmer's doubtful gains,
> To sweet repast th'unwary partridge flies,
> At ease amidst the scatter'd harvest lies,
> Wand'ring in plenty, danger he forgets,
> Nor dreads the slav'ry of entangling nets.
> The subtle dog now with sagacious nose

---

plains! remote from war's alarms' contain four hunting scenes, each of which concludes with a killing. See *Rural Sports* (1720), ll. 341–2; 349–50; 360–1; 386–7 (Dearing, 54–6).

Scours through the field, and snuffs each breeze that blows,
Against the wind he takes his prudent way,
Whilst the strong gale directs him to the prey;
Now the warm scent assures the covey near,
He treads with caution, and he points with fear;
Then lest some sentry fowl his fraud descry,
And bid his fellows from the danger fly,
Close to the ground in expectation lies,
Till in the snare the flutt'ring covey rise.
Thus the sly sharper sets the thoughtless squire,
Who to the town does awkwardly aspire:
Trick'd of his gold, he mortgages his land,
And falls a victim to the bailiff's hand.

(Rural Sports (1713), ll. 376–99)

It is not only that Gay's description is longer and more detailed; he turns the hunting scene into a little social vignette, a farmyard fable of vanity and deception, artifice and folly. The partridge is caught in a network of social stratagems as intricate as any ropes. Gay introduces the scene with a neat ironic touch, linking toil and pleasure, betrayal and the soul. Both 'toil' and 'betray' recall the cunning of the fisherman, yet slid between them is a line, 'So various pleasures recreate the *soul*; which seems, perversely, to dignify betrayal as a spiritual exercise. A few lines later he describes how a greyhound pursues a 'tim'rous hare';

And crushes in his jaws the screaming prey.
Thus does the country various sports afford,
And unbought dainties heap the wholesome board. (ll. 465–7)

'Wholesomeness' here is presented as the product of torture as the 'screaming prey' is transformed into a culinary 'dainty', and the word 'sports' takes on a cynical note as a euphemism for crushing the life out of a 'tim'rous' creature. The violence of the hound's bone-crushing mastication suggests a savage caricature of the 'sportsmen' themselves, at table on their 'unbought dainties'; while the financial terms 'afford' and 'unbought' expose the ruthless reality of rural economy. These table dainties have indeed been 'bought' at the cost of an innocent creature's suffering. In the country, just as in the town, exploitation rules, and there is no such thing as a free lunch.[65] Gay's authorial perspective, as observer of these country rites, is deliberately uneasy, siding more with the victim than the victor of these field sports, yet ironically lending his voice to the conventional chorus of bucolic pieties. Significantly, in his *Fables* (1727) Gay assumed the persona of the innocent hare, whose 'care was, never to offend', but who, in the final line of the volume, sees the murderous hounds approaching.

In the 'partridge' passage Gay offers a social cameo in terms of a farmyard power-struggle. His inclusion of the farmer's horse, at first sight a mere piece of background colour, is typical. 'Lab'ring . . . with swelling veins' the horse is a beast of burden, carrying the farmer's 'doubtful gains'. 'Doubtful' here refers primarily to the uncertain harvest, but at another level suggests dubious or question-able profits. Between the farmer and his horse a clear power relationship is established between labour and capital. The partridge enters this arena as a natural innocent, a fool among knaves, 'wand'ring in plenty'. But the encircling lines already depict him threatened by 'the slav'ry of entangling nets'. The subtle dog, a farmyard Machiavelli, is described in anthropomorphic terms of worldly wisdom. He has a 'sagacious nose', his movements are 'prudent' and he 'treads with caution'; animal instinct is reprocessed into the language of human social skills. Even without Gay's conclud-ing simile, which explicitly likens the relationship between dog and partridge to that between the city slicker and the country booby, the social message is clear. Gay may ostensibly be offering a charming rural scene; in reality, he is identifying the hierarchies and hypocri-sies of social exploitation. Unlike Pope, Gay does not offer rural harmony as the antithesis of military conflict, or celebrate a private pastoral Arcadia as a refuge from the treacheries of town life. For him, deceit is nature's own primary characteristic, and the predatory instinct is as deeply rooted in the country as in the town. In terms of political iconography, the poem contains both Whig and Tory indicators, but its essential political perspective is quite distinct from either party line. For Gay, both the golden age Arcadianism of the Tories and the new imperialism of the Whigs are equally deceptive myths, designed to disguise the realities of suffering and exploitation. From his lofty literary perspective Addison could

---

[65] The fact that 'unbought' is translated directly from Virgil does not lessen, but in some ways intensifies, its ironic effect here.

survey with equanimity the battlefield carnage of Blenheim, instantly transforming its 'hills of slain' into the subject of heroic myth. Gay is unable even to view a table 'dainty' like jugged hare without bringing to mind the screaming death of the animal itself.

Unlike Parnell and Trapp, who dedicated their 'peace' poems to Bolingbroke, Gay chose a fellow poet, Pope, rather than a politician, as his dedicatee. In part this represents a confirmation of his desire to escape the drudgery of attendance on great men, and a wish to elevate friendship above flattery. But it also implicitly acknowledges a kind of literary dependency. Pope already considered himself as something of an arbiter of literary fortunes. Writing to Caryll in February he announced that 'five or 6 authors have seized upon me, whose pieces, of quite indifferent natures I am obliged to consider, or falsify the trust they repose in me'.[66] Undoubtedly Gay was included among these 'five or 6' literary hopefuls and hence, even in his relationship with Pope, he remained in the role of a suppliant for favour.

Rural Sports is a highly literary poem, full of echoes and imitations of earlier bucolic works. Since for Gay this poetic representation of the countryside was essentially an exercise in cultural myth-making, his perspective often leaves it unclear whether he is describing a Devon field, or transcribing a page of Virgil:

> Here I with Virgil's muse refresh my mind,
> And in his numbers all the country find.   (ll. 290–1)

In the revised (1720) version of the poem he indicates that his imagination is chiefly inspired by 'the labours of Italian swains'; but even in the 1713 version, the detail 'Here I survey the purple vintage grow' suggests a Mantuan rather than a Devon landscape.[67] Pope's *Windsor Forest* provided a model for several passages, while Gay's detailed discussions of the various sports of cynegetics (hunting with dogs), ixeutics (fowling), and halieutics (fishing) seem to have been derived from literary sources rather than personal observation.[68]

---

[66] Pope, *Corr.* i. 174.

[67] As Gay's editors note: 'Gay gives the impression of having opened his book [Virgil's *Georgics*] at the first page' (Dearing, ii. 493).

[68] In the revised version of the poem he added a second Latin epigraph from Nemesia's *Cynegetica*; the poem also demonstrates familiarity with Ovid's *Halieutica* and the *Ixeutica* of Oppian the Cilician. Some of Gay's more detailed technical passages seem

Altogether, *Rural Sports* is a poem which could more easily have been composed in the library of Monmouth House than in Gay's temporary Devon asylum. It ends abruptly, with a farewell to the happy fields, those 'kind rewarders of industrious life', as Gay returns to his own business and confinement.

> Farewell—Now business calls me from the plains,
> Confines my fancy, and my song restrains.   (ll. 523–4)

But the truth, as Gay knows, is that he has been involved in business all the time, confining his fancy within prescribed literary limits and restraining his song to a dutiful chorus, rather than a joyful solo. Industriously misrepresenting work as play, and literary confinement as imaginative release, Gay's poem seeks the kind rewards which flow not from nature, but from the deceitful arts of the courtier-poet.

to have been borrowed from English works on fishing, such as Walton's *The Compleat Angler* (1653) and James Chetham's *The Angler's Vade Mecum* (1681). Gay's advice on choosing worms as bait for trout ('Their shining tails when a deep yellow stains | That bait will well reward the fisher's pains' (ll. 95–6) recalls Chetham's recommendation of the 'tag-tail worm' for this purpose. 'A worm of the colour of a man's hand, or a pale flesh colour, with a yellow tag on his tail, about half an inch long . . . there are anglers that affirm that there is not a better bait in the world for a trout' (Chetham, *The Angler's Vade Mecum*, 26; Dearing, 494).

FIVE

Taking Sides

I never cared one farthing either for Whig or Tory.

(J. G., *The Present State of Wit*, 1711)

SPRING 1713 was a period of intense literary and political activity. Throughout March, while Oxford prorogued parliament until the peace treaty was safely signed and sealed, new literary alliances were forming. On 12 March Steele launched his new journal, the *Guardian*, designed as a sequel to the *Spectator*, which had ceased publication the previous December. There was, however, one important difference. The *Guardian* did not, like the *Spectator*, promise 'to observe an exact neutrality between the Whigs and Tories'. On the contrary, it declared: 'the parties among us are too violent to make it possible to pass them by without observation. As to these matters, I shall be impartial, tho' I cannot be neuter.'[1] Just what Steele's 'impartiality' amounted to was made clear in May, when he delivered a fierce attack on the author of the *Examiner*, identified as either an 'estranged friend' (Swift) or an 'exasperated mistress' (Delariviere Manley).[2] In fact the current writer of the *Examiner* was William Oldisworth and Swift was greatly offended by Steele's attack. He sent a protest to Addison, demanding sulkily, 'have I deserved this usage from Mr Steele, who knows very well that my Lord Treasurer has kept him in his employment upon my intreaty and intercession?[3] There followed an angry exchange between Steele and Swift, in the course of which Steele constantly ridiculed his fellow Irishman's pretensions to be the fountain-head of patronage. 'They laugh at

[1] *Guardian*, 1 (12 Mar. 1713).
[2] Ibid. 53 (12 May 1713).
[3] Swift to Addison, 13 May 1713; Swift, *Corr.* i. 348.

you', he wrote, 'if they make you believe your interposition has kept me this long in office.' Swift, deeply goaded by this taunt, replied in bitter and self-righteous tones, before embarking to take up his new post as Dean of St Patrick's in Dublin, an appointment which he regarded as a punishment, rather than a reward, for his years of loyal service to the Tory government.

Addison did all he could to minimize, or at least disguise, such political divisions. In April his new play *Cato* was in rehearsal and he was anxious to placate potential Tory critics. On Good Friday, the day after news arrived that the peace treaty was finally signed, he and Swift joined other guests for dinner at Bolingbroke's house. Polite congratulations were offered, but then, 'in a friendly manner of party, Addison raised his objections, and Lord Bolingbroke answered them with great complaisance'.[4] Addison even presumed so far upon the general spirit of reconciliation to propose a toast to the Whig grandee Lord Somers, 'which went about', though Swift warned him 'not to name Lord Wharton' (another former leader of the Whig Junto), 'for I would not pledge it, and I told Lord Bolingbroke frankly that Addison loved Lord Wharton as little as I did'. 'So we laughed', wrote Swift, though the humour had a nervous quality to it. Three days later Addison invited Swift to a rehearsal of *Cato*, but Swift was unimpressed.

We stood on the stage and it was foolish enough to see the actors prompted every moment, and the poet directing them, and the drab that acts Cato's daughter out in the midst of a passionate part, and then calling out 'what's next?'[5]

The 'drab' in question, Mrs Oldfield, was enough to strain the credulity of even the most sympathetic spectator, playing the part of Cato's virgin daughter although already in an advanced state of pregnancy.

Pope too was involved in Addison's elaborate preparations to procure a favourable reception for his play. In February, having just read it, he sent Caryll this glowing account.

It drew tears from me in several parts of the fourth and fifth acts, where the beauty of virtue appears so charming that I believe (if it comes upon the theatre) we shall enjoy that which Plato thought the greatest pleasure an

---

[4] *Journal*, ii. 652.
[5] Ibid. 654.

exalted soul could be capable of, a view of virtue itself great in person, colour and action . . . I question if any play has ever conduced so immediately to morals as this.[6]

In retrospect, Pope told a rather different story. 'I gave him my opinion sincerely', he recalled, that the piece was 'well writ' but 'not theatrical enough'. Addison pretended to agree, but claimed 'that some particular friends of his, whom he could not disoblige, insisted on its being acted'. Such disingenuous disclaimers were part of Addison's careful strategy for disarming potential critics. He begged Pope to show the play to Bolingbroke and Oxford 'to assure them that he never in the least designed it as a party-play'. This too was pure bluff. 'Addison after made a merit of it as a party-play,' Pope bitterly recalled.

Nevertheless, Pope was persuaded to write the prologue for *Cato*, a decision which he soon had reason to regret. The timing of the play's production does little to endorse Addison's claim that it had no political motive. The bulk of the play had been written almost twenty years earlier while Addison was still an undergraduate, but suddenly, in the spring of 1713, there was considerable urgency to prepare an actable text. According to Steele, the fifth act 'was written in less than a week's time'[7] and Pope contemptuously remarked that the play's love scenes were 'flung in after, to comply with the popular taste'.

The theme of *Cato* dramatizes the conflict between liberty and tyranny, personified in the opposition between the philosopher Cato and the soldier Caesar. In its climactic scene, with Caesar's armies approaching Cato's home, the philosopher reads over Plato's treatise on the immortality of the soul before committing suicide, a martyr to the cause of freedom. For Whigs, who regarded the Utrecht treaty as a cynical betrayal of national pride and an abuse of ministerial power, the play's political significance was clear. As Tickell observed: '[Addison's] friends of the first quality and distinction prevailed with him to put the last finishing to it at a time when they thought the doctrine of liberty very seasonal.' The opening night was tense and rowdy. The best seats and boxes had all been booked at least a fortnight before. Addison himself sat with friends

---

[6] Pope, *Corr.* i. 173.
[7] Spence, i. 64–5.

in a side box 'where we had a table and two or three flasks of burgundy and champagne, with which the author (who is a very sober man) thought it necessary to support his spirits in the concern he was then under'.[8] Addison's concern was increased by the outbreak of violent political factionalism which greeted the performance. As Pope reported:

the numerous and violent claps of the Whig party on one side of the theatre were echoed back by the Tories on the other, while the author sweated behind the scenes with concern to find their applause proceeding more from the hand than the head.[9]

Forewarned by his reading of the play, Bolingbroke had contrived his own theatrical flourish to upstage Addison's Whiggish doctrines. In the interval he ostentatiously sent for Booth, the actor who played Cato, and presented him with fifty guineas, 'in acknowledgment' (as he expressed it) 'for his defending the cause of liberty so well against a perpetual dictator'. Then, as now, each party strove to claim the cause of 'liberty' as its own private property and this gesture, greeted by Tory cheers, was a calculated hit at Marlborough, who had demanded to be appointed Captain General of the army for life.

As prologue-writer, Pope was acutely embarrassed to find himself 'clapped into a staunch Whig sore against his will at almost every two lines', and relieved his feelings by composing some smutty anti-*Cato* verses.[10] Gay's anxieties at Addison's theatrical success were at least as great as Pope's, but for a different reason. He had at last completed his play *The Wife of Bath*, which was in rehearsal during April and due to follow *Cato* on the stage at Drury Lane. But Addison's triumph would be a hard act to follow. He told Maurice Johnson that his own play had already been 'put off upon account of *Cato*; so that you may easily imagine I by this time begin to be a little sensible of the approaching danger'.[11] In fact the opening of *The Wife of Bath* was twice postponed as the clamour for *Cato* continued. 'I don't know a mortal that is not gone to the play that could get places, either in boxes, pit or gallery,' remarked one

---

[8] George Berkeley to Sir John Percival, 16 Apr. 1713; Benjamin Rand (ed.), *Berkeley and Percival* (Cambridge, 1914), 113–14.

[9] Pope, *Corr.* i. 175.

[10] Ibid. i. 175. See his lines 'On a Lady who P—st at the tragedy of Cato'.

[11] *Letters*, 3.

aristocratic lady.[12] Gay clearly feared his own play would appear a sad anticlimax and commiserated with Pope on the unwelcome political applause his prologue was receiving. Happily, he observed (pleased for once to play the insider's role), 'the ministry are so far from thinking it touches them, that the Treasurer and Chancellor will honour the play with their presence'.[13] Rarely had any play attracted such an abundance of propagandist political commentary. For a young playwright hoping to achieve an impartial reception for his own first production, and still anxiously soliciting support from both Whig and Tory friends, the prospects were hardly bright.

Coincidentally, another literary event confirmed the increasing clannishness of the Whig literary establishment. Throughout April, Steele's *Guardian* published a series of essays on pastoral poetry by Addison's protégé and friend Tickell.[14] These essays lavished praise on the recent *Pastorals* of Ambrose Philips, declaring Philips the direct descendant of the true pastoral succession from Theocritus to Virgil and Spenser.[15] Strangely, though, the *Guardian* never even deigned to mention Pope's *Pastorals*, published alongside those of Philips in 1709.[16] Philips, like Tickell, belonged to the Whiggish literary coterie that congregated round Addison at Button's coffee-house, and Pope clearly resented this further demonstration of the mutual self-congratulation of Addison's 'little senate'. The implications of such political favouritism, he realized, extended far beyond the realm of pastoral poetry. In the preface to his *Pastorals* Philips noted that 'Virgil and Spenser made use of pastoral as a prelude to heroic poetry'; Pope too, coyly imitating Virgil by echoing the first line of his *Pastorals* in the last line of his georgic *Windsor Forest*, hinted at similar heroic ambitions. Clearly, by encouraging the literary careers of his acolytes Philips and Tickell, while down-playing the poetic achievements of less partisan figures like Pope and Gay, Addison was attempting to ensure that any future English

---

[12] See *Letter-Book of John Hervey, First Earl of Bristol . . . 1651–1750* ed. S. H. A. Hervey (3 vols., Wells, 1894), i. 370.

[13] *Letters*, 3.

[14] *Guardian*, 22, 23, 28, 30, and 32. The essays were published anonymously, but Tickell's authorship has been generally accepted, though, as John Nichols suggested, they were probably written 'under Addison's inspection, and perhaps with his assistance'. See *The Guardian*, printed for John Nichols (1789), quoted by Stephens, 18–19.

[15] *Guardian*, 32 (17 Apr. 1713) 137.

[16] The only glancing reference to Pope's bucolic verse is to his Chaucerian imitation 'January and May' (*Guardian*, 30 (15 Apr. 1713), 129).

epics would follow the example of his own *Campaign*, rather than the potentially Jacobite lines of Pope's celebration of Stuart virtues.

Pope was particularly disturbed to find such evidence of political bias in the *Guardian* since he had been privy to the planning of this new periodical from the start and clearly expected to be among its most regular contributors.[17] In only the second week of the new journal's publication he and Gay collaborated on a light-hearted spoof prescription for an 'Obsequium Catholicon' or 'Grand Elixir' guaranteed to fortify the heart 'against the rancour of pamphlets, the inveteracy of epigrams, and the mortification of lampoons'.[18] Yet, as Steele became more cliquish in his literary outlook, Pope and Gay found themselves increasingly excluded from the charmed circle of the *Guardian*'s contributors. Their next joint essay for the periodical was a calculated act of defiance against this new policy of Whig political correctness. *Guardian* no. 40, still on the theme of pastoral poetry, purports to be from the same hand as the previous essays on this topic, but actually parodies both Tickell's pastoral theories and Philips's pastoral practice. According to Tickell, the essential charm of pastoral poetry lay in its total lack of historical authenticity. Arcadia was neither ancient nor modern but an idealized Never Never Land where shepherds were synonymous with princes. Any author who 'would amuse himself by writing pastorals', he argued, must engage in a kind of rustic make-believe. He must 'show only half an image to the fancy . . . let the tranquillity of that life appear full and plain, but hide the meanness of it; represent the simplicity as clear as you please, but cover its misery.' Pastoral did not involve holding a mirror up to nature, but pulling a little decorative wool over the readers' eyes. Only the most conventional and stylized misfortunes could be allowed to disturb the tranquillity of this bucolic world. 'I will allow shepherds to be afflicted with such misfortunes as the loss of a favourite lamb, or a faithless mistress,' declares Tickell, promulgating literary edicts in the same mock-magisterial tones as his mentor Addison. The melancholy swain 'may, if you please, pick a thorn out of his foot, or vent his grief for

---

[17] A month before the first issue appeared he told Caryll that he had 'an affair with Mr Steele, that takes up much consultation daily' (Pope, *Corr.* i. 174).

[18] *Guardian*, 11 (24 Mar. 1713); for a discussion of Gay's contribution to this article see Stephens, 615–16. Steele subsequently attributed only six essays (out of 175) to Pope, adding that he had a hand in 'some others'. Recent editors have detected signs of his authorship in eight more essays: see Stephens, 17–33.

losing the prize in dancing'. What is most evident in these literary prescriptions is a tone of condescension. This is the voice of the sophisticated town poet, addressing his coffee-house readership and recommending the affectation of rural innocence as an amusing diversion, but implying, by his tone, that this is a paradise well lost in favour of the modern benefits of irony and city life. The only essential requirement of pastoral poetry was that it must convey 'innocence and simplicity'. These terms, together with 'tranquillity and ease', were repeated ten times in five short essays.

Seizing upon these terms in their own *Guardian* essay, Pope and Gay heap ironic praises on Philips for achieving a truly bathetic level of 'simplicity'. They cite these examples of 'that beautiful rusticity' of Philips's verse 'in which no man can compare with him'.

> 'O woful day! O day of woe, quoth he,
> And woful I, who live the day to see!'
>
> Ah me the while! ah me! the luckless day,
> Ah luckless lad! the rather might I say;
> Ah silly I! more silly than my sheep,
> Which on the flow'ry plains I once did keep.

They comment: 'How he still charms the ear with these artful repetitions of the epithets; and how significant is the last verse! I defy the most common reader to repeat them without feeling some motion of compassion.'[19] Artfully juxtaposing such puerile passages from Philips's *Pastorals* with Pope's more dignified couplets, they find no difficulty in pronouncing Philips the superior pastoralist, since Pope has miserably failed to attain this sublime height of clownish inanity. On the contrary, like Virgil, he sometimes commits the heinous fault of sinking 'into downright poetry'.

Part of the satisfaction that Pope and Gay must have experienced in contriving this ironic *tour de force* was the pleasure of tricking Steele into publishing a piece which ridiculed his two fellow Whigs Philips and Tickell and, by extension, mocked the literary pretensions of the whole Button's clique. Philips, however, recognized and

---

[19] *Guardian*, 40 (27 Apr. 1713); Stephens, 160–5. This essay, reprinted as appendix v to the *Dunciad*, is usually attributed to Pope. For a discussion of Gay's possible role in its composition see Maynard Mack, 'Two Variant Copies of Pope's *Works* . . . *Volume II*: Further Light on Some Problems of Authorship, Bibliography, and Text', *Library*, 5th series 12 (1957), 48–53.

resented the satire at once and, evidently unprovided with any of the 'Grand Elixir' to fortify his heart against such a lampoon, he reputedly hung up a rod at Button's coffee-house, threatening to use it on Pope if he should ever dare to show his face there. Even when disabused, Steele evidently failed to suspect Gay's complicity in Pope's satiric essay, since, a fortnight later, *Guardian* no. 50 (8 May) concluded with an enthusiastic puff for Gay's *Wife of Bath*. Commending the lively talents of its leading lady, Mrs Bicknell, it remarked:

if the rest of the actors enter into their several parts with the same spirit, the humorous characters of this play cannot but appear excellent on the theatre; for very good judges have informed me that the author has drawn them with great propriety and an exact observation of the manners.[20]

Such flattering support only highlights the difficult political balancing act that Gay was attempting to perform. Throughout the summer, while his friendship with Pope grew stronger, he was tempted to lend his covert assistance to several anonymous lampoons against Addison, yet wisely chose not to break cover with any public declaration of literary affiliation. As late as September, when the relationship between Addison and Pope was near to breaking-point, Gay was invited to compose a *Guardian* essay on female fashions (no. 149) as part of a sequence of essays on this topic begun by Addison the previous month. Yet, at the same time, it seems possible that he was also submitting copy to the *Guardian*'s chief political rival, the *Examiner*. This was a high-risk strategy, fraught with personal as well as political dangers. In attempting to promote his literary career, and thereby escape his servile role as the Duchess of Monmouth's secretary, Gay developed a conscious pose of political ambiguity. He was to pay a heavy price for such chameleon tactics in later years.

There is some dispute whether *The Wife of Bath* received one, two, or three performances.[21] What is not disputed is that this comedy,

---

[20] A fortnight later (22 May) *Guardian* no. 62 included this advertisement: 'This day is published *The Wife of Bath*, a comedy written by Mr Gay, author of *Rural Sports* pr. 1s 6d.'

[21] Dearing asserts that 'its one and only night' was 15 May, an author's benefit provided 'only as a favour' by the actors. Fuller says that it 'was first performed at Drury

which Gay later called his 'damned play', was something of a flop. Despite the favour of Steele's friendly puff, audiences that had flocked to *Cato* were uninspired by Gay's theatrical début. To be fair, it is difficult to make out a very strong case for the dramatic qualities of *The Wife of Bath*. On the positive side, it has charm, variety, and some lively dialogue; but against that, it is episodic, loosely constructed, and full of stock theatrical stereotypes. The main targets of Gay's ridicule are snobbery and superstition. Doggrell, a country spark turned poetaster, is equally obsessed by pedigrees and pindaric odes, and insists on ennobling his name to D'Ogrelle. Myrtilla, a lady of quality, is at the mercy of astrologers and fortune-tellers, alternating hourly in her determination to marry or become a nun according to the latest clairvoyant's prediction. The action takes place on St Agnes's Eve (20 January) at an inn 'lying on the road between London and Canterbury' where three Canterbury pilgrims, Franklin, the Wife of Bath, and Chaucer himself, become involved in the courtship comedy of a winter's night.

Chaucer was a literary interest shared equally by Gay and Pope and undoubtedly Pope's own recent modernization of *The Wife of Bath's Prologue*, published in December 1713, but drafted some years earlier, influenced Gay's choice of subject. Part of the fun of Chaucer, for both men, lay in his ready stock of ribald tales and coarse humour. Bawdy Chaucerian jokes run like a schoolboy code through much of their early correspondence, and Pope's own priapic 'Schoolboy's Tale', a youthful indulgence in mock-Chaucerian pastiche, is evidence that Chaucer's name was used to lend literary respectability to a taste for vulgarity. Even Dryden, who described Chaucer as 'a perpetual fountain of good sense', admitted that he was 'a rough diamond and must first be polished ere he shines'. In selecting tales which, in their newly polished form, were to shine in his volume of *Fables Ancient and Modern*, Dryden was careful to choose only those that 'savour nothing of immodesty'. He specifically excluded the Reeve's, Miller's, Shipman's, Merchant's, and Sumner's tales, 'and above all, the Wife of Bath in the Prologue to her Tale'. But Gay's instinct was to prefer the diamond in its uncut state, and, although clearly influenced by Pope's version of the

Lane on 12 May 1713 and received two performances in the season'. Burgess says that it was first produced on 12 May and 'ran three nights to indifferent audiences' (Dearing, i. 3; Fuller, i. 411; Letters, 3).

Prologue, his *Wife of Bath* is closer, in both vocabulary and tone, to
Chaucer's original than to Pope's refinement. Pope's Wife of Bath is
a town-rake, sophisticated in her maxims and worldly in her views.
Gay's Wife of Bath has an instinctive colloquial turn of phrase,
reducing principles to proverbs. Here, for example, she expresses
her contempt for a jealous husband. 'Would he, an old niggard, have
had ever the less light for letting a neighbour light a candle at his
lantern?' This is taken directly from Chaucer: 'He is to greet nygard
that wolde werne | A man to lighte a candle at his lanterne; | He shal
have never the lasse light, pardee' (ll. 333–5). Pope's version, by
contrast, is altogether more urbane. ''Tis but a just and rational
desire | To light a taper at a neighbour's fire' (ll. 138–9). For Pope,
the Wife's aphorism becomes an ironic instance of self-love and
social being the same; Gay's lines are more strictly localized in the
domestic comedy of a *ménage à trois*.

For its animation Gay's play relies heavily on the character of
Alison, the Wife of Bath herself. Yet, despite vigorous efforts to
invest her speech with an idiomatic raciness, her personality rarely
achieves real vitality. Her proverbial quips and frequent oaths fall
short of a convincing colloquial style and run the risk of slipping
into caricature. As a dramatist, Gay was largely uninterested in two
elements which conventionally contribute to successful drama: development of character and coherence of plot. In his later plays he
made a satiric virtue of the parodic one-dimensionality of his
characters and the burlesque non sequiturs of his plots. But in *The
Wife of Bath* he still seems torn between attempting to create a
conventional drama, and an irresistible impulse to subvert the
foundations upon which such a drama depends. It is easy to list
some of the weaknesses of dramatic construction: the hints of a
subplot concerning Astrolabe, the conjuror, come to nothing; the
laboured preparations for the servant Busy's disguise (v. i) destroy
the dramatic impact of her subsequent unmasking; and the miraculous cure of Doggrell's snobbery in the final scene, together with
Franklin's sudden captivation by 'a random glance' from Alison, are
only plausible in a drama which denies any depth of characterization.[22] In compensation for this relative unconcern with character,
the play makes ample use of pantomime and spectacle, including a

---

[22] Winton comments: 'Gay has rather more plot than he knows what to do with'
(Winton, 34).

dumb-show, conjuror's spells, and slapstick buffoonery. But *The Wife of Bath* shows Gay to be more interested in theatre than in drama. Gay no doubt hoped to find in Chaucer an appropriate source for that irreverent, demotic quality which animates his most inventive work. What he produced though was a comic tableau, rather than a play.

The failure of *The Wife of Bath* came as a severe disappointment, and Gay may have wished for a draught of his own 'Grand Elixir' that had, he claimed, cured a fellow playwright of a violent fit of the spleen 'upon a thin third night'. He received some encouragement though when Lintot paid him £25 for the copyright, a tenfold increase over that for *The Mohocks*.[23] But such modest returns still condemned him to an indefinite further period of domestic service. Meanwhile *Cato* continued its triumphal progress, following its London run with performances at Oxford, where it continued to provoke partisan reactions. It seems likely that Gay was privy—if that is the right word—to the composition of a scurrilous epigram by his two friends Pope and Rowe 'On a Lady who P—st at the Tragedy of Cato':

> While maudlin Whigs deplor'd their Cato's fate,
> Still with dry eyes the Tory Celia sat,
> But while her pride forbids her tears to flow,
> The gushing waters find a vent below . . .

In July John Dennis gave Addison's play a more thorough drenching in his *Remarks upon the Tragedy of Cato*, which denounced the play's violations of the classical rules of tragic drama. In particular, Dennis ridiculed the perfunctory love-plot, involving Cato's sons:

Is it convenient, is it consistent, or is it expected, that persons who are at first introduced as philosphers, as Romans, as lovers of their country, as dutiful and affectionate children to the best of fathers, would play the whining, amorous milk-sops upon that very day when reason is about to yield to force, liberty to tyranny, Rome to Caesar, and the sacred life of their father to that universal tyrant, death?[24]

Pope and Gay eagerly seized on this latest outburst of their old

---

[23] Nichols, *Literary Anecdotes*, 8:296

[24] John Dennis, *Remarks upon . . . Cato*, included in *The Critical Works of John Dennis*, ed. E. N. Hooker (2 vols., Baltimore, 1939), i. 54.

enemy, to 'defend' Addison with the same kind of ironic praise they had lavished on Philips in *Guardian* no. 40. Borrowing the 'quack-doctor' formula already used in *Guardian* no. 11, they collaborated to produce *The Narrative of Dr Robert Norris Concerning the Strange and Deplorable Frenzy of Mr John Dennis*, published at the end of July. In the *Narrative* Norris, a real doctor, whose advertisements appeared regularly in the *Guardian*,[25] is visited by an old woman greatly distressed by her master's mental state. He had been 'taken ill of a violent frenzy last April', she declared (the date of *Cato*'s first performance), and since then 'raves aloud, and mutters between his teeth the word "Cator" or "Cato" or some such thing. Now doctor', she continues, 'this Cator is certainly a witch and my poor master is under an evil tongue; for I have heard him say Cator has bewitched the whole nation.' Norris returns with the old woman to Dennis's seedy lodgings, where the hirsute critic is discovered in a wild and raving state. The walls of his room are hung 'with old tapestry which had several holes in it caused . . . by his having cut out the heads of diverse tyrants' (in obsessive reprisals, clearly, for Pope's offending lines in his *Essay in Criticism*). Elsewhere are 'pinned a great many sheets of a tragedy called *Cato*' annotated with the words 'Absurd, Monstrous, Execrable', and behind the door a huge heap of *Spectators*, hidden by Dennis's nurse because she believed 'they were books of the black art, for her master never read them but he was either quite moped or in raving fits'.

Though innocently posing as Addison's allies in this critical spat, Pope and Gay managed to combine mockery of *Cato* itself with ridicule of Dennis in this deft lampoon. But, unlike Steele, Addison was sharp enough to detect the undertone of contempt beneath the comradely pose. He chose a curiously circuitous means to signify his displeasure at this lampoon. On 4 August Steele wrote to Lintot:

Mr Addison desired me to tell you that he wholly disapproves the manner of treating Mr Dennis in a little pamphlet by way of Dr Norris's account. When he thinks fit to take notice of Mr Dennis's objections to his writings,

---

[25] 'Robert Norris, at the Pestle and Mortar on Snow Hill, having been many years experienced in the care of lunatics, hath convenience and suitable attendance at his own house for either sex: and persons applying themselves to him as above, may have unquestioning satisfaction and the cure shall be speedily and industriously endeavoured and (by God's blessing effected) on reasonable terms' (George Sherburn, *The Early Career of Alexander Pope* (Oxford, 1934), 106).

he will do it in a way Mr Dennis shall have no just reason to complain of. But when the papers above-mentioned were offered to be communicated to him, he said he could not, either in honour or conscience, be privy to such a treatment, and was sorry to hear of it.

Such an Olympian reproof, communicated via not one but two intermediaries, was an eloquent demonstration of Addison's aloof literary demeanour.[26] Gay's own involvement in this lampoon cannot be proved, but seems highly probable. Necessarily cautious about offending the Whig literary godfathers, the *Narrative* allowed him to take a vicarious revenge on the play which, by upstaging the production of his own *Wife of Bath*, had – or so at least he might have believed – fatally damaged his own stage début. But the chief effect of the 'Norris' episode was to mark a further downward spiral in the rapidly deteriorating relationship between the Whig and Tory literary camps. One of Steele's few personal contributions to the *Guardian* that summer was a flagrant piece of Whig propaganda insisting that the English people 'expected' the demolition of the fortifications at Dunkirk, a condition of the Utrecht treaty still unfulfilled. By this time he had abandoned even the pretence of political impartiality and, despite Addison's moderating influence, the *Guardian* was increasingly seen as a Whig party publication. This presented difficulties for contributors, like Pope and Gay, who were disinclined to find themselves so closely implicated with the opposition cause. Chided by Catholic friends for his association with such a disreputable publication, Pope argued that the problem 'is caused by the want of Mr Addison's assistance, who writes as seldom as I do, once a month or so'.[27] Presenting himself as a literary moderate, Pope insisted that he was 'no ways displeased that I have offended the *violent* of all parties already'.[28] But increasingly violence was the characteristic style of political debate. At the end of August Swift returned from Dublin and lost no time in resuming hostilities with Steele, recently elected as MP for Stockbridge. Steele too was in no mood for compromise. In October he abandoned the *Guardian* altogether and began the *Englishman*, a frankly partisan

[26] See Pope, *Corr.* i. 184. The suggestion that Steele himself may have collaborated in the satire can be discounted. Having been embarrassed by his own unwitting complicity in the *Guardian* attack on Philips, he was now clearly anxious to demonstrate his loyalty to the rules of literary decorum laid down by the Button's little senate.

[27] Pope, *Corr.* i. 180.

[28] Ibid., 179.

Whig paper. Addison attempted, unsuccessfully, to restrain him from descending further into the vulgar depths of political invective. 'I am in a thousand troubles for poor Dick', he wrote, 'and wish that his zeal for the public may not be ruinous to him.' Although a consummate politician himself, re-elected for Malmesbury in the August elections, Addison still endeavoured, in public at least, to maintain a distinction between literary taste and political prejudice. While Swift and Steele slugged it out like two journalistic prize-fighters over the still undemolished fortifications at Dunkirk, Addison made a last despairing attempt to preserve at least the semblance of literary impartiality. Throughout July and August, while Steele was electioneering at Stockbridge, Addison had assumed control of the *Guardian*, and immediately steered it away from stormy political waters into the beguiling haven of ladies' fashions. Mingling a tone of arch disapproval with coy voyeurist fantasy, he endeavoured to tempt back non-partisan readers with a series of essays on the 'unaccountable humour of stripping that has got among our British ladies'.[29] Instead of the ramparts of Dunkirk, Addison professed himself more concerned with the disappearing defences of female breasts. There is, he noted, 'a certain female ornament by some called a tucker, and by others the neck-piece' which used to cover 'a great part of the shoulders and bosom';

I must take notice, that our ladies have of late thrown aside this fig-leaf, and exposed in its primitive nakedness that gentle swelling of the breast which it was used to conceal. What their design by it is they themselves best know.[30]

'Even for a man of my character and gravity', he confesses, such exposure can have a disturbing effect. 'Every man is not sufficiently qualified with age and philosophy to be an indifferent spectator of such allurements.' When Addison describes how, 'surprised with beauties which I had never before discovered' in the exposed bosom of 'a famous she-visitant', he 'could scarce forbear making use of my hands to cover so unseemly a sight', the sense of suppressed erotic excitement comically disturbs the urbane poise of the prose. Subsequent papers contained a good deal of unacknowledged underclothes excitement, with coy observations on the 'exorbitant growth of the

---

[29] *Guardian*, 109 (16 July 1713); Stephens, 375.

[30] *Guardian*, 100 (6 July 1713); Stephens, 353.

female chest' and pseudo-learned reflections on petticoats and stays, legs and breasts. The British ladies, it seems, were not only 'letting down their stays' but also 'tucking up their petticoats which grow shorter and shorter every day'. And when Addison, discussing this exposure of the lower limbs, remarks that he 'may possibly take another occasion of handling this extremity' the *double entendre* is unmissable, and somewhat undermines the supposed moral decorum of the argument.[31]

Ladies' fashions were a topic on which Gay was well qualified to pronounce, and on 1 September the *Guardian* published his mock-treatise on the 'Art of Dress', a waggish essay loosely parodying Ovid's *Art of Love* and Horace's *Art of Poetry*. But, as with so many of Gay's early writings, the wit of this piece is spoilt by a kind of literary showing-off, as he parades knowing references to Aristotle, Ovid, Horace, Milton, and Boileau. He was more successful in treating the same theme in his poem *The Fan*, begun earlier that summer. 'I am glad your *Fan* is mounted so soon', Pope wrote to him in August, but cautioned against over-hasty publication. 'I would have you varnish and glaze it at your leisure, and polish the sticks as much as you can.'[32] Still smarting from the failure of *The Wife of Bath* Gay accepted Pope's advice, and spent much of the autumn at the Duchess's Moor Park estate, polishing his new work. In October he sent a sample to Fortescue, requesting his 'impartial opinion'. ''Tis in length about 700 lines', he told him, 'but in goodness, I'm afraid, not above 100.' Returning to Binfield in November, Pope offered further assistance, promising 'to take along with me your poem of the *Fan*, to consider it at full leisure'.[33] Finally published in December, *The Fan* offers further evidence of Gay's strategy of ingratiation by including obligatory echoes of both Pope and Addison. Pope's own verses, 'On a Fan of the Author's Design', published in the *Spectator* the previous year, provided the inspiration for the poem, while *The Rape of the Lock* supplied models for several of its set piece effects. Yet, as in *Rural Sports*, the compliment which Gay pays to Pope's imagination is mingled with an unacknowledged instinct for competition. Like *The Rape of the Lock*, *The Fan* deploys the elaborate artifice of mock-epic verse to

[31] *Guardian*, 109 (16 July 1713); Stephens, 375–7.
[32] Pope, *Corr*. i. 188.
[33] Ibid. 195.

celebrate a 'graceful toy'. But Gay exploits the elegance of the mock-heroic form for satiric effects which hint at an outsider's sense of social indignities. 'I have introduced gods and goddesses and others of little inferior dignity,' he told Fortescue, but in fact his imaginative sympathies in this poem, as in 'The Story of Arachne', are with the victims of the Olympians' whims. The poem traces the social and verbal chiasmus between one person's toy and another's toil; between a fine lady's fashionable toilette and the toilsome labours of her servants. The grotto of Venus where 'busy Cupids' labour to produce 'each trinket that adorns the modern dame', is presented as a proletarian underworld of ceaseless toil.

> A diff'rent toil another forge employs;
> Here the loud hammer fashions female toys,
> Hence is the fair with ornament supply'd,
> Hence sprung the glitt'ring implements of pride . . .
> The toilsome hours in diff'rent labour slide,
> Some work the file, and some the graver guide;
> From the loud anvil the quick blow rebounds,
> And their rais'd arms descend in tuneful sounds . . .
>
> (*The Fan*, i. 111–14, 131–4)

While there is a good deal of comic charm in this troglodyte vision of industrial labour, the social message is clear. The words 'toil' and 'toilsome', 'labour' and 'labourer', are repeated like tiny hammer blows, fashioning this female toy into a symbol of autocratic vanity. Armed with her latest deadly 'machine', the modern coquette becomes the counterpart of the artful fisherman in *Rural Sports*. His 'tortur'd worm' and 'twisted hair' become her 'tortured ringlets' and 'curling hair', but the effect of both is equally fatal.

Gay's imitation of Addison similarly contrives to spice a literary compliment with an implied ironic joke. 'In ancient times', he writes, echoing the sentiments of Addison's recent *Guardian* articles,

> when maids in thought were pure,
> When eyes were artless, and the look demure,
> When the wide ruff the well-turn'd neck enclos'd,
> And heaving breasts within the stays repos'd . . .
>
> (*The Fan*, i 197–200)

Affecting to share Addison's unease at this modern fashion for full frontal display, Gay complains: 'The bosom now its panting beauties shows.' Yet, while ostensibly lending his voice to this cover-up campaign, he cannot resist exposing the prurient undercurrent of erotic excitement in Addison's essays. Were their grandmothers really so innocent?

> Then in the muff unactive fingers lay,
> Nor taught the fan in fickle forms to play.   (i. 203–4)

The two key words here, 'muff' and 'fan', were both slang terms for the female genitals, and exploited as such by Fielding in *Tom Jones* and *Joseph Andrews*. Gay thus teasingly subverts the *Guardian's* moralistic campaign by hinting that the true source of Addison's anxiety may be an apparent shift from a covert to an overt female sexuality. A little later on Gay risks another satiric touch when describing how Cephalus, provoked by the wanton display of Aurora's charms, 'his modest hand upon her bosom warms'. This nicely mocks the inadvertent comedy of Addison's pious confession that he 'could scarce forbear making use of my hand to cover so unseemly a sight'. Such deft satiric touches are tiny, instinctive gestures of rebellion against the literary authority of those to whom Gay found he was reluctantly obliged to defer.

The form of *The Fan* recalls other well-established themes. Besought by Strephon to furnish a gift to win Corinna's heart, the goddess Venus approaches her fellow Olympians to choose the most appropriate scenes to decorate this 'fantastic engine'. The goddess Diana recommends lurid scenes of male treachery, such as Ariadne's seduction and betrayal by Theseus, or the death of Dido.

> Thus may the nymph, whene'er she spreads the fan,
> In his true colours view perfidious man.   (ii. 123–4)

The 'merry Momus' recommends scenes of covert and illicit pleasure:

> Let vig'rous Pan th'unguarded minute seize,
> And in a shaggy goat the virgin please.   (ii. 149–50)

But Minerva, whose views finally prevail, recommends cautionary vignettes in which the artifice of female vanity is seen to lead directly to the destruction of the artful temptresses themselves. Hence the poem concludes on a trite, moralistic note. Chastened by the sight of such homiletic scenes, Corinna abandons her coquettish airs and submits to matrimony. 'Strephon weds the dame, | And

Hymen's torch diffus'd the brightest flame.' The fan, customarily a symbol and accessory to female vanity and pride, is thus ironically transformed into an instrument for their correction. But such a glib and pious conclusion, though no doubt highly satisfactory to Addison, hardly suited Gay's own satiric view of human incorrigibility. Revising the poem the following year, he cheerfully scrapped this incongruous moral tag in favour of a flirtatious flourish in which vanity rules supreme.

> The gay coquette, of her last conquest vain,
> Snatches the trinket from the trembling swain,
> Then turns around with a disdainful mien,
> Smiles on the fop, and flirts the new machine.

Gay spent much of his time at the Duchess's Moor Park estate in determined efforts at polishing his literary and social skills. He began by improving his French, though with a schoolboyish facetiousness that disguised the earnestness of this enterprise. In a name-dropping letter to Fortescue he described himself as 'but a poor proficient in that polite tongue', choosing to write instead in a kind of comic *franglais*. 'I was last week a shooting with my lord Essex,' he remarked with affected nonchalance, turning these recent rural sports into a set of class-room exercises. 'When I came to the word *shooting*', he explains:

I was forced to express myself in a poetical manner by having recourse to Boileau, and call it '*Faire le guerre aux habitans de l'air*'; and when I would have told you that we owed our game to dogs called pointers, I was obliged in a tedious circumlocution to tell you, that we had dogs that lying themselves down, would direct us to the birds.[34]

This is a typical exercise in self-mockery. The official diplomatic letters which Gay penned from Hanover the following year show that his French was perfectly competent. Meanwhile the journalistic slanging-match between Swift and Steele continued unabated and it says much for the dexterity of Gay's policy of self-promotion that he contrived to maintain a position of neutrality between these two influential antagonists. It would be interesting to know for certain just when Gay and Swift first met. There is no mention of Swift in

---

[34] *Letters*, 4.

his Moor Park macaronic to Fortescue on 5 October, which contains references to Pope and Budgell. Pope, though, was clearly well acquainted with Swift before his departure for Ireland in the spring. In a letter to Gay in August, boasting of his new skills as an artist under the tutelage of the portrait-painter Charles Jervas, Pope mentions that he has already executed and thrown away 'three Dr Swifts, each of which was once my vanity'.[35] Two months later, in a letter which effectively dates the start of the 'Scriblerus' project, Pope told Gay that 'Dr Swift much approves what I proposed, even to the very title'.[36] It seems likely that Gay and Swift were first made acquainted, by Pope, sometime in mid-October, shortly after Gay's return from Hertfordshire. This was a time when Swift was deeply involved in his bitter feud with Steele, but when Gay was preparing two short poems for inclusion in Steele's forthcoming *Poetical Miscellany*. This raises interesting questions about the claim made in the *Two Letters Concerning the Author of the Examiner*, published on 1 and 7 November respectively, that Gay himself was a contributor to the Tory periodical. Ever eager to recruit new writers for the Tory cause, Swift would have had to work fast to install Gay on the *Examiner*'s staff; yet it would clearly have delighted him enormously to have snubbed Steele by doing so. Relations between the *Examiner* and the *Guardian* had never been exactly cordial, but they seldom descended to the level of scabrous abuse exchanged between the *Examiner* and Steele's new paper, the *Englishman*, that autumn. It throws a whole new light on Gay's character if we assume that, while composing meditative musings on the 'nobler aims' of a 'virtuous soul' in a poem for inclusion in Steele's *Poetical Miscellany*, he was simultaneously vilifying Steele in the *Examiner* as 'the head of the worst writers of the worst party'.[37] Such a suggestion might seem to imply an unusually devious reading of Gay's personality. But it is important to remember that this was clearly the image of Gay which the author of the *Two Letters* expected contemporaries to accept. Reading this pamphlet Gay would have been forced to recognize that he was being publicly branded as an unprincipled and ungrateful literary opportunist. His livery of blue and silver lace thus represented a twofold uniform of shame; a badge of social

---

[35] Pope, *Corr.* i. 187.
[36] Ibid. 195.
[37] See 'A Thought on Eternity', l. 27, and *Examiner*, 4/37 (9 Oct. 1713).

inferiority and a symbol of personal treachery.

Inevitably, since Gay made such strenuous attempts to conceal the facts about much of his early career, any attempt to identify his handiwork in the *Examiner* must be conjectural. Yet the possibility is worth exploring. Throughout his life Gay was tormented by a deep uncertainty of social status and ambivalence of social role. Dearing insists that an 'essential goodness' prevailed in his character, despite his numerous disappointments, 'until almost the end of his life, when finally the bitterness of his disappointments began to show a little in his writing, as it had already begun to show in the intestinal disorder that finally killed him'.[38] This suggestion, that Gay's colical ailments, which troubled him for at least the last fifteen years of his life, were a symptom of a bottled-up bitterness, might prompt us to look for other subconscious signs of repressed resentment in the body of his writing. There is a subversiveness in Gay's temperament which, though never explicitly acknowledged, inspired the ambiguous satiric tone of so many of his works. Reduced to domestic service, hanging on by his finger-nails to the fringes of literary society, he was at once desperate not to give offence, yet simultaneously itching to do exactly that. If he did indeed contribute to the *Examiner*, such an act would have been a gesture of defiance, not unlike his breaking the terms of his apprenticeship, or his mocking dismissal of the *British Apollo* in *The Present State of Wit*. It pleased him to mock *Cato* in the *Robert Norris* pamphlet, while ostensibly leaping to its defence; or to parody Addison's sexual prurience in *The Fan*, while apparently echoing his opinions. And he may well have relished the chance to lampoon the *Englishman*'s political stridency while simultaneously composing solemn verses to flatter Steele's favourite pose of poetical piety.

Gay could have made contact with the *Examiner* staff even without Swift's direct intervention, since the paper's publisher, John Morphew, had latterly shared publication of the *British Apollo*. Much of the *Examiner*'s output for 1713 consists of routine political point-scoring, but a few papers are distinguished by more idiosyncratic flourishes. The issue published on the same day as *Guardian* no. 40 contains a review of *Cato* which praises the prologue by 'the ingenious Mr Pope', but condemns the Whig faction 'who tried to

---

[38] Dearing, 3–4.

make this a party-play'.[39] The *Examiner* published on 2 March draws an analogy between the protracted war in Flanders and the interminable party-political skirmishing of the pamphlet-war at home. The author, labouring on a journalistic treadmill, longs to quit his Grub Street drudgery and 'entertain myself with all the curious landscape of antiquity'. This sounds not unlike Gay, abandoning the 'noisy town' for the Virgilian landscapes of *Rural Sports*. However, the most intriguing possibility is that Gay may have written the *Examiner* for 22 June, which treats warfare as a branch of commerce. This begins with a satiric contrast between the military fortunes of officers and other ranks. Epic poems, it complains, when describing the hardships of military life, fail to distinguish between the lot of the general 'who eats in gilt plate, sleeps in a nunnery, or brandishes his cane upon a distant rising' and that of the common foot-soldier 'lying in frost and snow, sleeping in wet trenches, being exposed to swords, mines, bombs and bullets'. The art of true generalship, the *Examiner* claims, consists less in mustering columns of men than in mastering columns of figures. War is reduced to an accounting exercise, requiring 'a competent knowledge in the course of exchange, a good venturing genius, a reasonable talent in accounts ... and of drawing out columns in order under the heading of Debtor and Creditor'. In this consistently unheroic analysis the *Examiner* undermines Addison's epic vision of martial glory and endorses Swift's view of the war as a financial conspiracy. 'War is trade,' it bluntly asserts. Many things about this *Examiner* are suggestive of Gay. Throughout his writings, the language of trade provides an ironic counterweight to the rhetoric of heroism; and the use of Peachum's account-books to satirize Walpole's network of state bribery would seem to develop naturally from this image of Marlborough as an asset-stripping profiteer. Similarly, the ironic pose of social egalitarianism is consistent with that found in several of Gay's works. It is quite in keeping with a satiric style which presents princes as clowns, and statesmen as highwaymen, to reduce military heroes to racketeers.

In November, fearing Swift's strategy of enticing the most promising young authors into the Tory camp, Addison wrote candidly to Pope:

---

[39] *Examiner*, 3/46 (27 Apr. 1713). It has to be acknowledged that the *Examiner*'s contemptuous dismissal of Garth's epilogue to *Cato* hardly squares with Gay's earlier praise of Garth as 'great ... alike in physic, as in poetry' in his dedicatory poem to Lintot's *Miscellany*.

You gave me leave once to take the liberty of a friend, in advising you not to content yourself with one half of the nation for your admirers when you might command them all. If I might take the freedom to repeat it, I would on this occasion. I think you are very happy that you are out of the fray, and I hope all your undertakings will turn to the better account for it.[40]

By implication, though, this letter acknowledges that Pope, like Gay, was already straying towards a different allegiance. The year ended with a political crisis which threw both parties into sudden panic activity. On 23 December the Queen suffered a violent ague, and over Christmas there were strong rumours of her imminent death. The Tories were in despair, while the Whigs found it hard to disguise their jubilation with a decent show of grief. The Queen's physician, Dr John Arbuthnot, became the Tory hero of the hour, nursing the monarch back to fitful health in the New Year.

It was in the spring of 1714 that meetings of a new Tory literary club began, under Swift's careful direction. Membership of the Scriblerus Club was restricted to an intimate group of like-minded literary friends, and Gay felt himself privileged to be included in a small but influential group whose other members were Pope, Swift and Arbuthnot, the Irish poet Thomas Parnell, and the Lord Treasurer, Lord Oxford. Here, for the first time, he found himself at the very heart of the literary and political establishment, and psychologically the effect of this unexpected inclusion in such an élite group was dramatic. Looking back nostalgically on the intimacy of those early Scriblerian meetings, Swift subsequently remarked to Pope:

I have often endeavoured to establish a friendship among all men of genius, and would fain have it done. They are seldom above three or four contemporaries, and if they could be united would drive the world before them. I think it was so among the poets in the time of Augustus.[41]

Pope likewise proudly recalled that their club included 'some of the greatest wits of the age'.[42] At last Gay was no longer regarded, by his friends at least, as a mere straggler in the footsteps of Virgil and Horace, but as one of their modern counterparts. He had become an Olympian.

---

[40] Pope, *Corr.* i. 196–7.
[41] Swift, *Corr.* ii. 465.
[42] Spence, i. 56.

Meetings of the Scriblerus Club were usually held in Arbuthnot's rooms at St James's, where he could be on hand to attend the Queen in case of further illness. According to Pope's recollection, Lord Oxford 'used to send trifling verses from court to the Scriblerus Club almost every day, and would come and talk idly with them almost every night'. Though Swift enjoyed this clear demonstration of the Lord Treasurer's friendship, he could not entirely approve such neglect of ministerial duties. In May he wrote that the Queen's continuing illness 'puts all in alarms, and when it is over, we act as if she were immortal. Neither is it possible to persuade people to make preparations against an evil day.'[43] It was largely for the benefit of Oxford, who liked to show off his skill in versifying in the company of professionals, that elaborate rhymed invitations to club meetings were exchanged during March and April.

> I will attend to hear your tuneful lays
> And wish your merits meet with one who pays—

wrote Oxford, with unconscious irony, in reply to one such invitation. 'I really believe . . . he will prove a very good poet,' remarked Arbuthnot of this and similar effusions. It gave Gay a particular thrill to think that his company took precedence, in the mind of such a powerful politician, over affairs of state, as Oxford signified in a later couplet:

> He that cares not to rule will not fail to obey,
> When summoned by Arbuthnot, Pope, Parnell & Gay.[44]

There were regular meetings of the club throughout the early spring, when Pope's ambitious plan for a satiric periodical was abandoned, in favour of the collection of 'hints' towards the composition of a single collaborative work. 'The design of the *Memoirs of Scriblerus*', Pope subsequently recalled, 'was to have ridiculed all the false tastes in learning, under the character of a man of capacity enough that had dipped in every art and science, but injudiciously in each.'[45] He added that 'Gay often held the pen', instinctively reducing Gay's role from that of full participant to mere secretarial assistant. But in fact the only surviving manuscript fragment of

---

[43] Swift, *Corr.* ii. 21.
[44] Pope, *Corr.* i. 217, 228.
[45] Spence, i. 56.

Scriblerian material is written in Arbuthnot's hand, not Gay's. Essentially, though, the club provided a congenial and relaxing diversion from mounting political pressures. In February Swift replied to Steele's latest pamphlet, *The Crisis*, with *The Public Spirit of the Whigs*, a blistering polemic whose violent tone provoked immediate calls for prosecution. In early March the House of Lords condemned Swift's pamphlet as a 'false, malicious libel', and the following night Swift received a cryptic note from Oxford, written in a heavily disguised hand.

I have heard that some honest men who are very innocent, are under trouble touching a printed pamphlet. A friend of mine, an obscure person, but charitable, puts the enclosed bill in your hands, to answer such exigencies as their case may immediately require.[46]

The enclosed bill, for £100, did not come a moment too soon. Within the week a reward was issued for discovery of the pamphlet's author, and Swift found himself a wanted man, with a price of £300 on his head.

Steele fared little better. In retaliation, the Tories in the Commons demanded his prosecution too, for his final truculent issue of the *Englishman*. Despite a brilliant speech in his defence, Steele was expelled from the House after barely more than a month's membership. At last the simmering antagonism between the Whig and Tory literary camps had erupted into open warfare.

Meanwhile Pope did his best to avoid the political fray by working on his revised version of *The Rape of the Lock*. ''Tis a sort of writing very like tickling,' he told one correspondent. He was, he assured John Caryll, 'the least politician in the world', despite some 'modern rumours . . . which would have represented me as more concerned in party affairs than I ever dreamed on'. One particular rumour, which named him as 'an enemy to the *grande société* at Button's', was, he insisted, 'laughed at by the chief of my Whig-friends and my Tory-friends'.[47] This was a highly disingenuous claim, since at that very time Pope was encouraging Gay in the composition of a satire that mercilessly parodied the literary pretensions of the Button's wits.

Gay's *Shepherd's Week*, published in April 1714, continued the

---

[46] Swift, *Corr.* ii. 12.
[47] Pope, *Corr.* i. 210–11.

parody of Philips begun in *Guardian* no. 40 the previous year. 'It is to this management of Philips that the world owes Mr Gay's pastorals,' Pope told Caryll, as if proudly showing off a favourite pupil's work.[48] Like *Guardian* no. 40, Gay's poem targeted those passages from Philips's *Pastorals* which had received Tickell's special praise. For poems whose supposed appeal lay in their Arcadian innocence, there was something curiously knowing about the quotations which Tickell selected as appetizers.

> Once Delia slept, on easy moss reclin'd,
> Her lovely limbs half-bare, and rude the wind:
> I smooth'd her coats, and stole a silent kiss;
> Condemn me shepherds, if I did amiss.[49]

This coy erotic hinting suggests not real innocence at all, but a form of bucolic bo-peep. Arcadia here is a kind of licensed play-area for some semi-naturist frolics, and these coy nymphs belong to the same sort of teasing fantasy which in later literature is filled with French maids and naughty schoolgirls. This is definitely a post-Eden nakedness, a world of eyeing and spying, and the poet's tone recalls the similar voyeurism of Addison's *Guardian* essays on the 'stripping ladies'. Even Philips's natural descriptions seem to hint at a complaisant human sensuality. In the phrase 'on easy moss reclin'd' the word 'easy' seems to describe Delia herself, with her 'lovely limbs' displayed, suggesting not so much easy moss as an easy Miss. Similarly the 'rude' wind seems to invite a corresponding 'rudeness' in the spectator swain (the ambiguity in that word 'rude' encapsulates the kind of knowing irony here). The phrase 'I smooth'd her coats' suggests the exact opposite and the hidden pun in 'condemn me shepherds, if I did amiss' (a Miss) turns this voyeuristic vignette into a kind of masque in *déshabillé*.

Gay happily seized upon the voyeurism of such lines, coarsening it into a kind of school-yard exhibitionism:

> On two near elms the slacken'd cord I hung,
> Now high, now low, my Blouzelinda swung.
> With the rude wind her rumpled garment rose,
> And show'd her taper leg, and scarlet hose.
>   ('Monday', ll. 103–6)

[48] Ibid. i. 229.
[49] Philips, *Pastorals*, vi. 73–6: quoted in *Guardian*, 23 (7 Apr. 1713).

Throughout *The Shepherd's Week* Gay makes his parody of Philips's work explicit. In 'Tuesday; or, The Ditty' he takes delight in making Marian 'wail' in tones borrowed directly from Philips:

> Ah woful day! ah woful noon and morn!
> When first by thee my younglings white were shorn,
> Then first, I ween, I cast a lover's eye,
> My sheep were silly, but more silly I.   (ll. 25–8)

The use of fake archaic and dialect terms, pedantically annotated; the coy erotic hints; the pseudo-folklorish superstitions; the banal repetitions and the pretentious glossary are all deliberately chosen to draw attention to the pseudo-simplicity of Philips's verses. One particular exchange in 'Monday', the first of Gay's six mock-eclogues, combines a parody of Philips's pruriency and his pedantry. Cuddy is boasting to his fellow swain, Lobbin Clout.

> As my Buxoma in a morning fair,
> With gentle fingers strok'd her milky care,
> I queintly stole a kiss; at first, 'tis true
> She frown'd, yet after granted one or two.
> Lobbin, I swear, believe who will my vows,
> Her breath by far excell'd the breathing cows.   (ll. 77–82)

Gay's footnote to the word 'queint' is a model of his satiric method. 'Queint', he observes,

has various significations in the ancient English authors. I have used it in this place in the same sense as Chaucer hath done in his *Miller's Tale*; 'As clerkes been full subtil and queint' (by which he means arch or waggish) and not in that obscene sense wherein he useth it in the line immediately following.

This is a typical Scriblerian ploy. By drawing attention to what the word *does not* mean (and by going out of his way to tell us where to find that other obscene meaning), Gay outdoes Philips's coy hints with a knowing wink of his own. The playful suggestion of cunnilingus turns these parody-yokels into disguised sexual sophisticates, and gives an added ironic twist to Cuddy's bathetic boast that his sweetheart's breath 'by far excell'd the breathing cows'.

Undoubtedly, one of the chief pleasures of *The Shepherd's Week* comes from its description of homely farmyard tasks and simple domestic life. 'Thou wilt not find my shepherdesses idly playing on oaten reeds,' Gay writes in the proem, mocking the affectations of courtly pastoral; 'but milking the kine, tying up the sheaves, or if the hogs are astray, driving them to their sties'. Indeed, at times he is so successful in creating a tone of rural idyll that some later commentators have wondered if *The Sheperd's Week* should really be considered a parody at all.

While he pursues his primary design of burlesque parody he paints rural scenes with a truth of pencil scarcely elsewhere to be met with; and even pathetic circumstances are intermixed with strokes of sportive humour.[50]

Yet even Gay's most lyrical scenes are not without a healthy blend of irony. Take this example, from 'Tuesday; or, the Ditty'.

> Whilom with thee 'twas Marian's dear delight
> To moil all day, and merry-make at night.
> If in the soil you guide the crooked share,
> Your early breakfast is my constant care.
> And when with even hand you strow the grain,
> I fright the thievish rooks from off the plain.
> In misling days when I my thresher heard,
> With nappy beer I to the barn repair'd;
> Lost in the music of the whirling flail,
> To gaze on thee I left the smoking pail;
> In harvest when the sun was mounted high,
> My leathern bottle did thy drought supply;
> When-e'er you mow'd I follow'd with the rake,
> And have full oft been sun-burnt for thy sake;
> When in the welkin gath'ring show'rs were seen,
> I lagg'd the last with Colin on the green;
> And when at eve returning with thy car,
> Awaiting heard the jingling bells from far;
> Straight on the fire the sooty pot I plac'd,
> To warm thy broth I burnt my hands for haste.
> When hungry thou stood'st staring, like an oaf,

---

[50] John Aiken, 'Letter to a Young Lady on a Course of English Poetry' (1806); quoted in R. P. Bond's *English Burlesque Poetry* (Cambridge, Mass., 1932), 114. Irving argues that Gay may have 'encouraged Pope to think' he was satirizing Philips, while actually writing a poem which endorsed a version of pastoral simplicity. Irving, 83–4.

> I slic'd the luncheon from the barley loaf,
> With crumbled bread I thicken'd well thy mess.
> Ah, love me more, or love thy pottage less! (ll. 49–72)

That last line is a good example of Gay's use of the volte-face effect, a final ironic decent into bathos to check any self-indulgent drift into romanticism. The principal quality of this description is a richly sensuous evocation of the tastes and smells, the sights and sounds, of simple rural life. The use of dialect terms here ('moil', 'misling', 'nappy') is designed not as a clever piece of literary parody, but as part of a genuinely affectionate portrait of this farm-worker's wife. Yet, at the end, having beguiled us with this charming rural scene, Gay undermines it, with a neat ironic touch, as though laughing at himself, and us too, for indulging such a piece of bucolic fantasy.

The bathetic effect of this 'love in a pottage' motif is repeated several times throughout the eclogues. Typically, it is used to draw a comic analogy between the direct physical appetites of the farm animals, unmodified by the forms and conventions of art, and the more stylized aspirations of the swains, which affect an elevated pseudo-literary 'simplicity'. Several eclogues conclude with just such an ironic volte-face. In 'Monday' Cloddipole suddenly appears, and puts an end to the rival boasting of Cuddy and Lobbin Clout:

> Your herds for want of water stand adry.
> They're weary of your songs—and so am I. (ll. 123–4)

In 'Tuesday', Marian's lovesick ditty is interrupted by a cruder form of sexual union:

> Thus Marian wail'd, her eye with tears brimfull,
> When Goody Dobbins brought her cow to bull.
> With apron blue to dry her tears she sought,
> Then saw the cow well served, and took a groat. (ll. 103–6)

In 'Friday; or, The Dirge', 158 lines of plangent elegy are suddenly overturned by three chirpy couplets cheerfully reasserting life.

> Thus wail'd the louts in melancholy strain,
> Till bonny Susan sped across the plain;
> They seiz'd the lass in apron clean array'd,
> And to the ale-house forced the willing maid;

> In ale and kisses they forgot their cares,
> And Susan, Blouzelinda's loss repairs. (ll. 159–64)

Certain stock motifs reappear in these concluding couplets. One is the antithesis of moisture and dryness. 'Excessive sorrow is exceeding dry' is Gaffer Treadwell's convivial motto in 'Friday', as he recommends a cheering autumnal beverage of 'cider mulled with ginger warm'. The prolongation of any lofty stylization of feelings (usually dismissed as 'wailing') leads to a certain monotonous aridity at odds with natural appetites. In 'Monday' it is the herds that are dry; in 'Friday' it is the louts; but in both, the promptings of nature undermine the hyperboles of art. The predictability of these volte-face effects may perhaps appear glib or even cynical. The ease with which 'bonny Susan' can fill the place of Blouzelinda may seem to go beyond a mere parody of elegiac conventions and suggest a certain brutishness in rural mirth and manners. But it is worth comparing these lines from Swift's *Verses on the Death of Dr Swift*:

> Here shift the scene to represent
> How those I love my death lament.
> Poor Pope will grieve a month; and Gay
> A week, and Arbuthnot a day. , (ll. 205–8)

Here, Arbuthnot's brevity of mourning does not signify indifference, but a cheerful love of life. In the same way, Blouzelinda is best honoured not by an ostentatious grief but by the cheerful continuation of all those natural joys which she embodied in life. Enjoyment is the essential quality of all these concluding couplets, a physical enjoyment that implies continuity. The effectiveness of these volte-faces comes from the fact that, while rhythmically and artistically they enclose the eclogues which they conclude, they simultaneously open them out in terms of feeling. They provide a final chink of light, or life, to disturb the comic stereotypes and pastoral parodies.

For the urban artist, country subjects compose themselves all too easily in a series of familiar motifs; 'rural sports', 'country life', 'Arcadia', 'the hay-wain'; there is a whole set of bucolic stereotypes, from wily straw-chewing gaffers to pert milkmaids, to decorate the courtier's day-dreams. *The Shepherd's Week* parades them all. There are allusions to contending pastoral theories; there are imitations of Theocritus and Virgil, and echoes of Chaucer, Spenser, and Milton; there is a thesaurus of proverbial folklore and a chorus of popular ballads. Artfully combining all these elements, Gay confirms the arbitrary power of the artist to see-saw happily from style to style, and from stereotype to stereotype, creating a satiric territory of his own out of the juxtaposition of contrasting genres. Sometimes parodic, sometimes lyrical, his poetry transgresses the stylistic boundaries of established literary forms, making good his earlier contention that 'variety's the source of joy'. At times his wailing swains affect a mock-Virgilian sublimity, or 'seiz'd with a religious qualm' sing 'the hundredth psalm'; at others they descend to lusty ballads, schoolboy pranks, or the bathetic doggerel of Philips. Adorning the poem with mock-learned footnotes and a glossary of dialect terms, Gay deliberately displays all the colours of the pastoral rainbow, dressing himself sometimes in the clown's smock, and sometimes in the courtier's ribbons and bows. But underneath it all are the rhythms of birth, copulation, and death; the rising and setting of the sun; the cycle of the seasons and the alternation of happiness and despair.

Elsewhere, more personal preoccupations mingle with Gay's satire of the Button's wits. In the prologue he represents his own move from Devon to London as a progress from countryman to courtier.

> I sold my sheep and lambkins too
> For silver loops and garment blue.
> My boxen haut-boy, sweet of sound,
> For lace that edg'd mine hat around.   (ll. 39–42)

Typically, Gay's emphasis is on the financial terms of this transaction, *selling* his sheep to purchase the trappings and trimmings of a court lackey's costume. But within such a patchwork of parodies, social satire comes disguised as literary burlesque. The episode in 'Wednesday' where Sparabella presents herself as the victim of attempted rape is a good example.

> Ah! didst though know what proffers I withstood,
> When late I met the squire in yonder wood!
> To me he sped, regardless of his game,
> While all my cheek was glowing red with shame;
> My lip he kiss'd, and prais'd my healthful look,
> Then from his purse of silk a guinea took,
> Into my hand he forc'd the tempting gold,
> While I with modest struggling broke his hold.

> He swore that Dick in liv'ry strip'd with lace,
> Should wed me soon to keep me from disgrace;
> But I nor footman priz'd nor golden fee,
> For what is lace or gold compar'd to thee? (ll. 75–86)

As a satiric vignette of social exploitation this portrait of the hunting
squire has all the classic ingredients. The description of Sparabella's
cheek 'glowing red with shame' not only emphasizes her distress,
but also continues the suggestion of a blood sport. 'Healthful' nicely
catches a tone of threatening euphemism in this compliment from a
depraved superior to his youthful prey. The violence of the words
'forc'd' and 'struggling' is undisguised. To complete the humiliation,
the squire promises to fix up a marriage for Sparabella with his
footman, whose bondage is signalled by his livery: 'in liv'ry strip'd
with lace.' The echo of Gay's description of his own livery of lace
and loops and garment blue is not coincidental. This costume is the
uniform of humiliation. 'Strip'd' also conveys the suggestion of
stripes or lashes, continuing the hints of violence and blood throughout the passage. In context, however, all this satiric force is controlled
and contained by a burlesque style which presents all such set-piece
literary effects as potentially self-parodic. So Sparabella's description
of her plight takes on the cliché style of a familiar motif: the country
maiden seduced by the wicked squire. There is satire here, certainly;
but it is a self-conscious satire qualified by its own status as a
literary stereotype.

Biographically, the most interesting of the eclogues is the last one,
'Saturday; or, The Flights', in which the ballad-singer Bowzybeus
entertains the swains at harvest in the fields. His first appearance,
appropriately, is as a phallic joke, like the serpent in the garden.

> To the near hedge young Susan steps aside,
> She feign'd her coat or garter was untied,
> Whate'er she did, she stoop'd adown unseen,
> And merry reapers, what they list, will ween.
> Soon she rose up, and cried with voice so shrill
> That echo answer'd from the distant hill;
> The youths and damsels ran to Susan's aid,
> Who thought some adder had the lass dismay'd.
> There, fast asleep, they Bowzybeus spied . . . (ll. 13–21) [51]

---

[51] In this last eclogue the main target of Gay's literary parody shifts from Philips to

Bowzybeus becomes the incarnation of rustic revelry, a drunken
pied piper, or vagabond Autolycus, peddling his fairground trinkets
and catch-penny tunes. Like the Beggar in the *Beggar's Opera*,
Bowzybeus is Gay's anarchic *alter ego*, a mischievous latter-day Pan
mingling seductiveness and satire in his beguiling repertoire of
country airs. Like the Beggar, Bowzybeus diverts his hearers with a
lively medley of ballads, catches, folk-songs, psalms, and anthems,
mingling jingoism with pathos, ribaldry with piety.

> For Buxom Joan he sung the doubtful strife,
> How the sly sailor made the maid a wife.
> To louder strains he rais'd his voice, to tell
> What woeful wars in Chevy Chase befell . . .
> Then he was seiz'd with a religious qualm,
> And on a sudden, sung the hundredth psalm.
> He sung of Taffy Welch, and Sawney Scot,
> Lillibulero and the Irish Trot . . .   (ll. 99–102, 113–16)

The Shepherd's Week echoes throughout with popular ballad airs,
testifying to Gay's enduring fascination with this rich subculture of
song. Offered in parody of the rarified bucolic style of pseudo-
Virgilian pastoral, these songs represent the authentic poetry of
peasant life. 'Hang Sorrow', 'Gillian of Croydon', 'Over the Hills
and Far Away', 'Buxom Joan', 'Chevy Chase', 'Lillibulero', and
'Sawney Scot' are used here, as in the *Beggar's Opera*, to embed
Gay's satire of the incongruously stylized forms of 'high' art in the
beguiling idioms of a 'low', popular alternative.

Addison had lent a certain dignity to the appreciation of some of
the more celebrated old English ballads with his extended discussion
of 'Chevy Chase' and 'Two Children in the Wood' in the *Spectator*.[52]
'The old song of *Chevy Chase*' he declared, 'is the favourite ballad of
the common people of England', and reminded his readers that 'Ben
Jonson used to say he had rather have been the author of it than of all his
works'. He singled out some stanzas for special praise. 'What can be
greater than either the thought or the expression in that stanza:

William Coward's favourite, Sir Richard Blackmore. See J. R. Moore, 'Gay's Burlesque
of Sir Richard Blackmore's Poetry', *Journal of English and Germanic Philology*, 50 (1951),
83–9. Dearing, though, is unconvinced that the eclogue parodies Blackmore. The parallels,
he claims, 'are too vague and commonplace to establish a purposeful connection' (Dearing,
ii, 536).

[52] *Spectator*, 70, 74, 85, 179.

> To drive the deer with hound and horn
> Earl Percy took his way;
> The child may rue that was unborn
> The hunting of that day.'[53]

These were sentiments which Gay evidently shared, finding in 'Chevy Chase' not the bathetic affectation of simplicity offered by Philips's *Pastorals*, but, in Addison's words, that 'majestic simplicity . . . that is the delight of the common people'. Bowzybeus's medley includes the very stanza from 'Chevy Chase' that the *Spectator* had praised. Nevertheless, Addison still felt uneasy about admitting to so 'Gothic' a taste, and insisted on justifying his praise for 'Chevy Chase' by extensive comparisons with the acknowledged classics. 'I feared my own judgement would have looked too singular on such a subject', he confessed, 'had not I supported it by the practice and authority of Virgil.' Consequently, it was not Addison but Tom D'Urfey who did most to popularize a taste for native ballads, which, though they could claim little affinity with Virgil, found a ready audience from the royal palace to the street singer and tavern balladeer. And it is D'Urfey, the despised collector of vulgar ballads and folk-songs, rather than Theocritus or Virgil, Spenser or Philips, whose influence most conspicuously pervades *The Shepherd's Week*.

No other writer had so great an influence on Gay as D'Urfey. The two men shared a love of popular ballads, a delight in bizarre theatrical effects, and a mischievous satiric flair for political and cultural burlesque. Yet it was an influence which Gay would only acknowledge by off-hand and often condescending allusions. D'Urfey, a particular favourite with Charles II, liked to boast that he stayed on good terms with five monarchs. 'I myself', Addison recalled in the *Guardian*, 'remember King Charles the Second leaning on Tom D'Urfey's shoulder more than once, and humming over a song with him.'[54] But in literary circles D'Urfey was regarded as a 'low' poet, despised for dealing in such plebeian wares. It was a symptom of the debasement of the court, not of D'Urfey's respectability, that royalty should share his vulgar tastes. Pope's attitude was typical. 'I would as soon write like D'Urfey', he told Cromwell in August 1709, 'as live like Tidcombe; whose beastly, laughable life

---

[53] Ibid. 70 (21 May 1711) and 74 (25 May 1711).
[54] *Guardian*, 67 (28 May 1713).

is (if you will excuse such a similitude) not unlike a fart, at once nasty and diverting.'[55]

Now aged about 60, D'Urfey had fallen on hard times after a lifetime of congenial but ill-paid literary labours.

After having written more odes than Horace, and about four times as many comedies as Terence, he was reduced to great difficulties by the importunities of a set of men who, of late years, had furnished him with the accommodations of life, and would not, as we say, be paid with a song.[56]

Though a Tory, whose popular ballad 'The King's Health' 'gave the Whigs such a blow' during the time of the Exclusion crisis that 'they were not able to recover that whole reign', D'Urfey found unlikely champions in Addison and Steele, who promoted a special benefit performance of his play *A Fond Husband* at Drury Lane on 15 June 1713. What delighted Addison, and Gay too, was the extraordinary inventiveness, good humour, and impartiality of a man who could create the most ingenious literary and musical metamorphoses. For his ballad 'The King's Health' D'Urfey had adapted a tune by Farinelli, prompting Addison to claim that he had 'made use of Italian tunes and sonatas for promoting the Protestant interest, and turned a considerable part of the Pope's music against himself'. Such an example of transforming an Italian musical work into a popular, and political, English ballad was not lost on Gay. Among his many other talents, D'Urfey was also an accomplished fisherman. 'My old friend angles for a trout the best of any man in England,' Addison observed: 'May flies come in late this season, or I myself should, before now, have had a trout of his hooking.' Whether D'Urfey benefited from the angling advice contained in *Rural Sports*, though, we cannot tell.

Unlike Pope, Gay was never entirely happy ambitiously pursuing the Virgilian high road. He was, said Johnson, a poet 'of a lower order', never more successful than when evoking the same native ballad traditions that D'Urfey kept alive. While affecting to share Pope's snobbish disdain for the old balladeer, privately he found a constant source of inspiration in D'Urfey's literary output. The very first issue of the *Tatler* in April 1709 praised D'Urfey's irrepressible

---

[55] Pope, *Corr.* i. 71. See also Pope's letter to Cromwell, 10 Apr. 1710; Pope, *Corr.* i. 81.

[56] *Guardian*, 67 (28 May 1713).

inventiveness: 'who, besides his great abilities in the dramatic, has a peculiar talent in the lyric way of writing, and that with a manner wholly new and unknown to the ancient Greeks and Romans, wherein he is but faintly imitated in the translations of the modern Italian operas.' It was this instinct for literary novelty and surprise, and a relish for a native tradition of surreal comedy which outdid even the histrionic appeal of Italian opera, which appealed to Gay. He would undoubtedly have known D'Urfey's popular ballad collections, *Wit and Mirth; or, Pills to Purge Melancholy*,[57] and we know that D'Urfey's bizarre satiric comedy *Wonders in the Sun* had a profound effect upon him. This play, which draws eclectically from Aristophanes' *The Birds*, Cyrano de Bergerac's *Voyage dans la lune*, Aphra Behn's *The Emperor of the Moon* (1687), and Elkanah Settle's *The World in the Moon* (1697), is a glorious theatrical fantasy. Much of the action takes place in 'the Land of Artificials', where apples are made of stone, and mouth-watering peaches prove to be tennis-balls; 'fine tempting cherries too, bobbing at my nose, when I thought to regale upon them, were nothing but brittle berries of red glass'.[58] The language of the kingdom is surreal gobbledegook: 'A kondibuly melikka, flownce gowtry yawna verokta Belch hander van dan Soiterkino.' The resulting work, as its most recent editor remarks, 'is basically unclassifiable, a unique mixture of fantasy, low comedy, song and satire which that mistress of surrealist drama, the Duchess of Newcastle, might well have envied'.[59] Much of the play's surreal comic appeal lies in its lively operatic parodies. With his love of native ballads, D'Urfey had been among the first to latch on to the satiric potential of the new vogue for Italian opera. In the prologue to his earlier play *The Old Mode and the New* (1703), he wrote:

> If comic scenes could please like cap'ring tricks,
> Or could be sounded with Italian squeaks,
> We might suppose this play would last six weeks.

In *The Wonders in the Sun* D'Urfey mingles barnyard ballads with

---

[57] The volumes of *Wit and Mirth; or, Pills to Purge Melancholy* first appeared between 1698 and 1706; they were gathered together by D'Urfey in a six-volume edition in 1719–20. See the facsimile edition, with an introduction by Cyrus L. Day (New York, 1959).

[58] *Wonders in the Sun; or, The Kingdom of the Birds* (1706), Augustan Reprint Society edition 104, ed. W. W. Appleton (Los Angeles, 1964), 10.

[59] Ibid., p. ii.

pastiche passages from Stanzani's *Arsinoe* and *The Loves of Ergasto*, both performed in London the previous year. The play's editor comments:

It would be pleasant to find a link, musical or textual, between *Wonders in the Sun* and that triumphant example of English comic opera, *The Beggar's Opera*, but to do so would be to strain the argument. Gay's Newgate pastoral, with its razor-sharp satire and consistent point-of-view is incomparably finer. It is also a *pasticcio* in the use that it makes of ballad airs, but of striking originality in its bitter-sweet blend of mordant lyrics and tuneful melody.[60]

However, links between *Wonders in the Sun* and *The Beggar's Opera* are not so hard to find. In the preface to *The What D' Ye Call It* Gay cites the precedent of D'Urfey's play to justify his own bizarre theatrical hybrid. In *The Wife of Bath*, the affectations of the poet Doggrell, who insists on styling himself D'Ogrelle, are partly intended to ridicule D'Urfey's similar pretensions. According to one well-known anecdote, D'Urfey had once reprimanded King Charles himself for mispronouncing his name: 'My name is not Durfey, but De-Urfey. Oh! very good, said the king; pray friend De-Urfey, will you help me to a slice of De-umplin, just by you there.'[61] In *The Wife of Bath, The What D' Ye Call It*, and *Three Hours after Marriage*, Gay followed Pope in mocking D'Urfey's stutter, something which the actor Penkethman, who performed in all three plays, had made into a little party-piece. But such slight satiric touches disguise a deeper sense of imaginative kinship which Gay, ever anxious about his own social status, was reluctant to acknowledge. 'The town may da-da-damn me for a poet', said D'Urfey, 'but they si-si-sing my songs for all that.'[62]

An awareness of D'Urfey's writings and reputation permeates many of Gay's most successful works, and none more so than *The Shepherd's Week*. The mock-invocation to D'Urfey in 'Wednesday', hailing him as a patron muse, is clearly intended to be comic:

> A while, O D'Urfey, lend an ear or twain,
> Nor, though in homely guise, my verse disdain . . .

[60] *Wonders in the Sun*, p. iv.

[61] See *Pasquin*, 112 (28 Feb. 1724).

[62] *The Fourth and Last Volume of the Works of Mr Thomas Brown* (1715), 117. D'Urfey stuttered except when singing or swearing.

But it was the rich tradition of popular ballads, which D'Urfey preserved, that inspired Gay's imaginative rejection of the pseudo-bucolic inanities of courtier-pastoralists like Philips and Tickell. D'Urfey's ballads restored the authentic voice of the common people, in the strong colloquial rhythms and native wit of traditional songs. Gay may have found it diplomatic to present himself as a pretender to the Virgilian tradition, but his instinctive allegiance was to the voice of common experience which D'Urfey was not ashamed to present. In *Spectator* no. 70 Addison wrote: 'an ordinary song or ballad that is the delight of the common people, cannot fail to please all such readers as are not unqualified for the entertainment by their affectation or ignorance.'[63] Such sentiments were to remain among the guiding principles of Gay's literary career.

In literary terms *The Shepherd's Week*, published on 15 April 1714, was Gay's most accomplished and original work to date. Politically, however, it proved a less adroit performance. In his jaunty pseudo-rustic prologue to the poem, Gay facetiously presents himself as a country Cloddipole, newly come to town to thank the 'skilful leach' Arbuthnot for saving the Queen's life: 'For well I ween, | He sav'd the realm who sav'd the Queen.' He also praises those two 'worthy wights' Oxford and Bolingbroke, for their able conduct of state affairs. The poem in fact is dedicated to Bolingbroke, whose interest in the work is represented thus:

> There saw I St John, sweet of mien,
> Full steadfast both to church and Queen.
> With whose fair name I'll deck my strain,
> St John, right courteous to the swain;
> For thus he told me on a day,
> Trim are thy sonnets, gentle Gay,
> And certes, mirth it were to see
> Thy joyous madrigals twice three,
> With preface meet, and notes profound,
> Imprinted fair, and well y-bound.
> All suddenly then home I sped,
> And did ev'n as my lord had said.   (ll. 75–86)

[63] 21 May 1711.

If, as seems likely, Bolingbroke did indeed encourage Gay's publication of *The Shepherd's week*, it was almost certainly in an attempt to counteract Oxford's greater influence and intimacy with the close-knit group of Tory wits. During the early months of 1714 the relationship between the two leaders of the Tory ministry, never exactly cordial, had degenerated into open hostility. Bolingbroke, the 'man of mercury' was young, charismatic, and impetuous, whereas Oxford, 'the dragon', was increasingly devious, secretive, and slow. Furious that his peerage, a viscountcy, finally granted to him in the summer of 1712, was a lesser honour than Oxford's earldom, Bolingbroke told Swift that henceforward he would 'never depend upon the earl's friendship as long as he lived, nor have any further commerce with him than what was necessary for carrying on the public service'.[64] Swift constantly laboured to engineer a reconciliation between the two men, contriving, one day in late 1713, to send them down to Windsor in the same coach.[65] But all such efforts at *détente* were unavailing. If Gay's prologue was intended as a similar diplomatic manœuvre it misfired badly. In such an atmosphere of mutual jealousy and suspicion, the hint of favouritism towards Bolingbroke could only antagonize Oxford, while dismaying Gay's Whig friends with the suggestion that he had gone over to the 'high-flying' Tory extremists. When, the following year, Bolingbroke fled to France to head the Pretender's Jacobite government-in-exile, Gay's fulsome expression of political approval became a serious embarrassment.

Reviews of *The Shepherd's Week* were not especially favourable. One anonymous versifier pictured Apollo sitting in judgement on the claims of all the rival pastoralists.

> In haste the summon'd wits from Button's came,
> Each ready to support his fav'rite's claim:
> Steele with a train of ten supporters near,
> Forc'd to the head, and would in front appear,
> And D'Urfey with a song brought up the rear.
>   The court now sat; Apollo, looking round,
> Many strange unpoetic faces found,
> And asking Prior whence that medley crew,
> Whom nor the muses, nor his godship knew,

---

[64] See Nokes, 167.
[65] Swift, *Corr.* v. 45–6.

> The bard replied, with an Horatian grin,
> They're wits, and have Steele's ticket to come in.
> Steele's ticket! cried the God. And is that all?
> And so bid critic Dennis clear the hall.

Philips appears, backed by Budgell and Tickell, offering a petition signed by twenty friends. Pope, called from a corner where he has slunk 'to jest and rally with a merry Dean', comes forward to repeat his 'Winter Song'. Finally Gay appears, to receive the God's harsh judgement.

> He courted ev'ry muse Parnassus knew,
> And from him, ev'ry muse he courted, flew;
> And now repeated loud Bowselus hight,
> And Blouzelinda in her apron white.
> But soon the God, to stop the killing lay,
> Cried out,—Whate'er Lord Bolingbroke may say,
> Full silly are thy sonnets, gentle Gay.[66]

The first break in the regular pattern of Scriblerian meetings came a week after the publication of *The Shepherd's Week* when Pope and Parnell left to work on Homer at Pope's family home near Windsor. From there they wrote deploring 'this miserable age . . . sunk between animosities of party and those of religion'.[67] Gay, though, was in high spirits. The rump of the club continued to meet in Arbuthnot's apartments, and he wrote to assure Parnell that 'Martin still is under the Doctor's hands, and flourishes'.[68] Gay himself was toying with a Scriblerian *jeu d'esprit* under the pseudonym of 'Esdras Barnivelt', one of several aliases the club assumed for its joint compositions. 'Mr Barnivelt', he told Parnell, 'was here this evening, and entered into a learned conference with me concerning Homer. He tells me he very much suspects the accounts we have of that poet and doubts whether there ever were such a person in being.'[69] This theory, which would find wide acceptance now, was hardly congenial to Gay's two friends, who, by their own admission, had 'grown so grave' in their studious preoccupation with Homer

---

[66] 'The Judgement of Apollo upon the Present Set of Poets', *Poems on Several Occasions* (1714), 35.
[67] Pope, *Corr.* i. 220.
[68] *Letters*, 7.
[69] Ibid.

that 'we have not condescended to laugh at any of the idle things about us this week'. Pope was intensely anxious that no injudicious witticism should prejudice the reception of his forthcoming translation of the *Iliad*, and, though affecting to mock his own solemnity on the subject, was irredeemably solemn. 'I have contracted a severity of aspect from deep meditation on high subjects', he told Gay, 'equal to the formidable front of black-brow'd Jupiter . . . In a word, Young himself has not acquired more tragic majesty in his aspect by reading his own verses than I by Homer's.' This being the case, he went on: 'I cannot consent to your publication of that ludicrous trifling burlesque you write about. Dr Parnell also joins in my opinion, that it will by no means be well to print it.' Typically enough, Gay assented to this ban. Pope himself subsequently assumed the pseudonym of 'Esdras Barnivelt' for his *Key to the Lock* (1715), but there is no record of Gay's own burlesque, written under the same name.

Otherwise, Gay was chiefly engaged in playing the part of the man about town. In February he saw Nick Rowe's new play *Jane Shore*, which was to provide the source for much knockabout theatrical parody in his own play *The What D'Ye Call It*. He was also, as usual, putting in appearances at court, accompanied by either Swift or Arbuthnot, and doing his best to ingratiate himself with those whose influence he sought. 'Oh dear Dr Parnell', he wrote in early May,

What's all your trees, your meadows, your streams and plains, to a walk in St James's Park? I hope you won't be so profane as to make any comparison of the sight of a cow and a calf to a beau and a belle? Do you imagine a place beneath a shady back of equal value to a place at court?

He included some brief verses on the diversions of the town, including 'Ye operas with voices sweet' and 'Ye balls, assemblies, tea and ombre | And other pleasures without nombre'.[70] Parnell replied with a sly allusion to the rather less rosy picture of town life contained in the opening lines of *Rural Sports*: 'Since by your letter we find you can be content to breathe in smoke, to walk in crowds, and divert yourself with noise . . . we should give you up as one abandoned to a wrong choice of pleasures.' He invited Gay to join them at Binfield, but if not, 'pray leave to tempt us with your

[70] *Letters*, 7.

description of the court; for indeed humanity is frail . . .'.[71] Pope, though, was less deceived by Gay's affectation of gaiety, sensing, beneath the pose of nonchalance, certain enduring anxieties. 'Above all other news', he urged him to 'send us the best, that of your good health, if you enjoy it; which Mr Harcourt made us very much fear'.[72] Already, it is clear the ill health which was to dog Gay throughout the rest of his career was a genuine source of concern, though Gay himself did his best to conceal it. Almost certainly, one partial cause for that ill health was his persisting and so far unsuccessful quest for a place at court. In his facetious chatter with Parnell ('Do you imagine a place beneath a shady back of equal value to a place at court?') he does his best to make light of what was, in reality, a source of deep anxiety. His decision to remain in town, rather than follow them to Binfield, was not, as he liked to pretend, in order to flirt with the ladies in St James's Park, but rather to haunt the levees of the great, in hopes of some more dignified employment. Pope and Swift well understood his uneasiness in this respect. At the end of May, Pope was still urging Parnell to bring 'the true genuine shepherd, John Gay of Devon' down to Binfield with him, though already he suspected that Gay's ambitions lay in another direction. Swift, who also remained in London throughout May, still anxiously endeavouring to patch up the divisions in the Tory ministry, used part of his time soliciting on Gay's behalf. At last, at the beginning of June, 'weary to death of courts and ministers, and business and politics', Swift stole away from London to stay at a friend's rectory at Letcombe Bassett in the Berkshire countryside. But not before he had recommended Gay for a mission which, with luck, might be the making of his future career.

[71] Pope, *Corr.* i. 222.
[72] Ibid. 223.

PART II

The Modes of the Court
(1714–1727)

SIX

Envoy Extraordinary

. . . you must not expect from me any arcanas of state.

(Gay to Swift or Arbuthnot, Aug. 1714)

FOR several months relations between Queen Anne's court and that of her nominated Protestant successor, George Ludwig, Elector of Hanover, had been somewhat strained. In April Baron Schutz, the Hanoverian representative in England, demanded that a writ be issued summoning the Electoral Prince (afterwards George II) to take his seat in parliament as Duke of Cambridge. The Queen was furious at this presumption and Bolingbroke seized the opportunity to gain her favour by insisting that the writ be refused. Oxford, recognizing the legality of the claim, was caught in a dilemma. Reluctantly agreeing to the issue of the writ, he simultaneously dispatched his cousin, Thomas Harley, on an informal mission of conciliation to the Elector. In a long, coded letter he told his cousin, 'I never saw her majesty so much moved in my life. She looked upon it as that she is treated with scorn and contempt.'[1] His ploy was only partially successful. The Elector, anxious not to exacerbate the situation, repudiated Schutz's actions and recalled him from duty. But the Queen was unforgiving and transferred her support from Oxford to his younger rival. In a desperate attempt to recoup his position, Oxford decided to send an 'Envoy Extraordinary' to Hanover to defuse the situation. Anyone undertaking such a task would find it not only difficult but almost certainly thankless. Too great a *rapprochement* with the Elector would risk alienating the Queen,

[1] HMC Portland MSS (1899), v. 418.

while any apparent coldness towards George would put an end to all hopes of preferment under the future monarch.

Oxford's first choice for the post was Lord Paget, former ambassador in Constantinople. Without positively refusing the job, Paget did all he could to avoid it. In a flurry of letters from his house in Jermyn Street during April and May, he offered one excuse after another, until finally, on 22 May, after his commission and official yacht had already been prepared, he requested 'that your lordship may recommend somebody else for ye service'.[2] That 'somebody else' was Edward Hyde, Earl of Clarendon, formerly Governor of New York, where he had caused some consternation by appearing at state functions dressed in women's clothes, in order, so he said, to represent the Queen more exactly.

Within days of Clarendon's commission, Gay was appointed as his official secretary. Writing to Swift on 8 June, he gratefully acknowledged Swift's help in obtaining the post. It was, he said, 'by making use of those friends which I entirely [owe] to you' that Clarendon had 'accepted me for his secretary'.[3] The publisher John Barber assured Swift that Gay was 'very well pleased with his promotion'[4] and, indeed, there is an unmistakable note of liberation in Gay's announcement to Swift that 'I am quite off [from] the Duchess of Monmouth'.[5] Pope also, still evidently regarding Gay as his own special protégé, thanked Swift, on Gay's behalf: 'I can't name Mr. Gay, without all the acknowledgements which I shall ever owe you, on his account.'[6] Nevertheless, those besetting anxieties of Gay's career, a self-consciousness about social status and an embarrassing lack of money, continued to cast a shadow over the excitement of this new appointment. Acknowledging 'the many favours I have received from you', he went on to beg Swift for one favour more.

If 'twas possible, that any recommendation could be procured to make me more distinguished than ordinary during my stay at that court I should

---

[2] BL MSS, Portland Loan 29/203, fo. 253.

[3] Although Gay's patroness the Duchess of Monmouth was distantly related to Hyde by marriage, it seems unlikely that she was instrumental in securing him this post. It was at first intended that Parnell too might accompany the expedition as chaplain, but in the hurry of preparation there was not time for his appointment to be confirmed.

[4] Swift, *Corr.* ii. 29.

[5] *Letters* 8.

[6] Pope, *Corr.* i. 231.

think myself very happy if you could contrive any method to procure it; for I am told their civilities very rarely descend so low as the secretary.[7]

As usual, Gay feared he might be relegated to the status of liveried attendant, rather than literary companion. Only the previous Saturday he had enjoyed the privilege of the Lord Treasurer's company at a lively Scriblerian gathering, but he clearly anticipated that no such informal camaraderie would be possible in the more hierarchical Hanoverian court. His chronic lack of funds posed an even more pressing problem. Forewarned by the sad fate of Swift's former protégé Harrison, Gay forced himself to resume the role of uniformed court-swain in tackling Oxford on the subject.

The Epigrammatical Petition of John Gay

I'm no more to converse with the swains
But go where fine people resort
One can live without money on plains,
But never without it at court.
If when with the swains I did gambol
I arrayed me in silver and blue
When abroad & in courts I shall ramble
Pray, my Lord, how much money will do?[8]

Even in such an ostensibly light-hearted petition those two key terms, *money* and *court*, which sound throughout so much of Gay's writing, are strongly emphasized. Gay was particularly anxious since Clarendon's expedition was something of a rushed affair and he was due to depart in less than a week. Two days later he wrote again to Oxford, gently reminding him of his 'Shepherd's Petition' and adding that 'my Lord Clarendon tells me, he sends his things down the water tomorrow and embarks on Saturday. The time to provide myself is very short.'[9] On Saturday, just two days before the appointed date of departure, Arbuthnot was still reporting that 'My Lord Treasurer has promised to equip him . . . & he is now dancing attendance, for money to buy him shoes, stockings and linen.'[10] Swift was only too painfully familiar with such promises, and wrote back, enquiring cynically, 'was the money paid, or put off till the day after

[7] *Letters*, 9.
[8] Ibid. 8.
[9] Ibid. 9.
[10] Swift, *Corr.* ii. 34.

he went?'[11] However, Gay was more fortunate than the ill-fated Harrison. On 26 June Arbuthnot assured Swift that 'Gay had a hundred pound in due time, [and] went away a happy man'.[12]

Plainly elated by the adventure of this new appointment, Gay sent high-spirited reports back to his friend Charles Ford at White-hall. In the first, sent from the official yacht *Henrietta* while still moored in Margate roads, he declares, 'you can scarce imagine the happiness I have had since I came aboard';[13] this despite the fact that the letter was scribbled down between violent bouts of seasick-ness. A week later he wrote again, this time from The Hague, where, still suffering the after-effects of 'a day or two's sea-sickness', he was nevertheless full of the excitement of being in the midst of 'treaties & negotiations, plenipotentiaries, ambassadors & envoys'.[14] These letters are typical of Gay in enthusiastic mood, mingling snippets of name-dropping gossip with an ostentatious flourish of literary allusions. Above all they show him already cultivating a fantasy role as a great connoisseur of the ladies. At Margate he recalls his 'wistful looks' watching Clarendon's daughter, 'my lady Theodosia', leaving their vessel without casting 'one pitying look behind'. At The Hague he declares his time is 'wholly taken up with observing the ladies' who 'are pretty enough while they are in Holland; but should they once appear in Kensington Gardens, they must resign all their pretensions to beauty'.[15] In all such comments Gay's role is essentially passive, a pastoral swain commenting on 'nymphs' who are less real-life individuals than contemporary copies of classical types. If Ford should meet his 'Venus' in a wood, Gay writes, he trusts he will behave as 'a man of honour and modesty— think not of hairs less in sight or any hairs but these'; this coy allusion to Pope's *Rape of the Lock* suggests less sexual *savoir-faire* than literary self-consciousness.[16]

Clarendon's party finally set sail from Sheerness on 30 June, reaching The Hague on Sunday, 4 July, where they stayed for several days, before going on to Amsterdam and reaching Hanover

[11] Swift, *Corr.* ii. 36.

[12] The official *Newsletter* for 8 June 1714 reported: 'A warrant is passed the Privy Seal appointing the Earl of Clarendon's allowance for going to the Court of Hanover £50 for his equipage and £5 a day.'

[13] *Letters*, 10.

[14] Ibid. 11.

[15] Ibid.

[16] Ibid.

on 21 July. To sustain him in his new diplomatic role Gay carried with him not only his £100 allowance, but also a letter of advice in statecraft from Swift. Complimenting Gay on the sly wit of his *Epigrammatical Petition* (it proved, he said, that Gay was beginning 'to be an able courtier'), Swift prescribed a crash course in political skills.

Pray learn to be a manager, and pick up languages as fast as you can, and get Aristotle upon Politics, and read other books upon government; Grotius *De Jure belli et pacis*, and accounts of negotiations & treaties &c and be a perfect master of the latin, and be able to learn everything of the court where you go.[17]

In addition, Swift had contacted Thomas Harley, lately returned from Hanover, to furnish Gay with a general letter of introduction to the court. But chiefly, Swift advised Gay to use this opportunity to demonstrate his political value to the administration. 'Keep correspondence with Mr Lewis, who if you write letters worth showing, will make them serviceable to you with [the] Lord Treasurer.'[18] Almost certainly Gay intended to follow this advice. Writing to Ford he denied 'having, as yet entered the lists of politicians', but his letter concludes with a postscript: 'Mr Lewis shall hear from me soon.'[19] Arbuthnot and Bolingbroke both report seeing further letters from Gay, and in diplomatic circles he was clearly regarded with some suspicion. The Hanoverian ambassador Count Bothmar reported back from The Hague on 16 June that he was annoyed (*fâché*) at the sending of 'Le Comte de Clarendon et son secrétaire jacobite'.[20] But Gay's hopes of proving useful as a political spy were quickly frustrated. At the end of July, barely a week after Clarendon's arrival at Hanover, Oxford was finally ousted from power by his younger rival. Bolingbroke's triumph was short-lived. Just four days later, on 1 August, Queen Anne died, setting the political world in turmoil. 'What a world is this', Bolingbroke complained bitterly to Swift, 'and how does fortune banter us?'[21] Suddenly Whigs were appointed to all the key positions on the new Council of Regents, with Addison in the pivotal role of Secretary to the Council.

[17] Swift, *Corr.* ii. 33.
[18] Ibid.
[19] *Letters*, 13.
[20] BL Stowe MSS 227, fo. 119.
[21] Swift, *Corr.* ii. 101.

Politically, Clarendon's mission was doomed from the start. Although news of the Queen's death did not reach Hanover for another week, there was little opportunity for either him or his secretary to be, as Secretary Bromley had hoped, the 'happy instrument' for 'settling the friendship [between the Queen and the Elector] upon a firm & lasting foundation'.[22] Meanwhile, in Whitehall, the ever-prudent Erasmus Lewis was already busily destroying any politically sensitive material, possibly including letters received from Gay.

Typically, Gay's surviving letters from Hanover disguise any covert efforts at political espionage he may have made with a facetious display of ridicule at all such political manœuvres. In a letter to Arbuthnot and Swift he pokes fun at Swift's earnest attempts to coach him in the skills of a secret agent. 'You remember', he begins, 'that I was to write you abundance of letters from Hanover; but as one of the most distinguishing qualities of a politician is secrecy, you must not expect from me any arcanas of state.' He has, as Swift instructed, 'made it my business to read memoires, treaties, &c', but with the intention not of following their principles, but of parodying their style. 'I think the King of France hath established an academy to instruct the young Machiavellians of his country in the deep and profound science of politics,' he comments, implicitly comparing his would-be mentor Swift with the old spy-master Richelieu. There follows a brief Scriblerus-style spoof, a 'Compendium, or the Ambassador's Manual, or Vade Mecum' for the benefit of 'young politicians'. Written in the form of a political catechism, this 'learned treatise' implicitly mocks Swift's diligent efforts to school him in just the same manner.

POLITICIAN. What are the necessary tools for a prince to work with?

STUDENT. Ministers of State.

POLITICIAN. What are the two great qualities of a Minister of State?

STUDENT. Secrecy and dispatch.

POLITICIAN. Into how many parts are the Ministers of State divided?

STUDENT. Into two. First, Ministers of State at home: secondly, Ministers of State abroad, who are called foreign ministers.

[22] BL Stowe MSS 227, for 154–5.

POLITICIAN. Very right. Now, as I design you for the latter of these employments, I shall waive saying anything of the first of these. What are the different degrees of foreign ministers?

STUDENT. The different degrees of foreign ministers are as follows: first, plenipotentiaries; second, ambassadors extraordinary; third, ambassadors in ordinary; fourth, envoys extraordinary; fifth, envoys in ordinary; sixth, residents; seventh, consuls, and eighth, secretaries.[23]

And so on. Having sneaked himself in at the very tail end of this classified list of diplomatic emissaries, Gay offers a few more flourishes of terms of statecraft, before concluding with his only snippet of genuine political intelligence: 'My Lord Clarendon is very much approved of at court, and I believe is not dissatisfied with his reception.' The fact that this piece of information was already obsolete is a nice, unconsciously ironic conclusion to a letter which implicitly satirizes the solemn rituals of such 'arcanas of state'.

The chief exercise of Gay's diplomatic skills was in the area of personal ingratiation, rather than state policy. Determined to make himself 'more distinguished than ordinary' he set himself to cultivate the arts of the accomplished courtier. In a letter to Ford he describes happy conversations with the Princess Caroline and her lady-in-waiting the Countess of Picbourg. 'I go every night to court at Herrenhausen,' he boasts, already presenting himself as something of a favourite. Even if Clarendon's mission was doomed, this need not imply that Gay's own fortunes must be blighted. 'The court have a notion that I am to reside here upon his lordship's return, and I have received many compliments upon that occasion.'[24] Evidently Gay was doing all he could to secure the literary favours of the ladies of the future royal house. 'The princess and the countess of Picbourg have both subscribed to Pope's *Homer*,' he reported, 'and her Highness did me the honour to say she did not doubt it would be well done, since I recommended it.' However, with his usual lack of forethought, Gay had neglected to take with him any poetry of his own, so that, when the Princess graciously asked to see some, he had none to show her. In urgent letters to

---

[23] *Letters*, 14.
[24] Ibid. 12.

Arbuthnot and Ford he asked them to send some over. 'If the books are not sent with expedition I shall lose my credit.'[25] This little incident caused much amusement to his more politically experienced friends. 'Is he not a true poet,' Arbuthnot wrote to Swift, 'who had not one of his own books to give to the Princess that asked for one?'[26] Despite Gay's protestations to the contrary, Swift and Arbuthnot were still convinced that Gay had much to learn in the arts of self-promotion.

Gay's official duties as Clarendon's secretary took up little of his time, though, in his letters home, he made sure to mention them. He told Ford that 'I had a design of writing to the Dean, but my Lord Clarendon hath just this minute sent me a long letter to copy, so that I shall be able to write nothing to him this post.' This long letter, never previously published, is printed in full for the first time in the Appendix.

Undoubtedly the most important contact Gay made during his time in Hanover was with Henrietta Howard. She had married, while still very young, Charles Howard, third son of the earl of Suffolk, a man whom Hervey describes as 'wrong-headed, ill-tempered, obstinate, drunken, extravagant, brutal'.[27] Despite their aristocratic connections, the couple were very poor, and Henrietta underwent extraordinary privations in efforts to conceal the state of their impoverishment from their courtly friends. In depositions which supported her plea for a formal separation from her husband in 1727 (by which time she had long been the mistress of the new King George II), she produced witnesses to the secret miseries and cruelty she had endured in the months before Gay first met her. Mrs Anne Hall, her landlady in East Street in 1713, testified to having let out lodgings to the Howards for eight shillings a week. 'One particular night', she recalled, she had 'assisted ye sd Mrs Howard in carrying a grate with a red hot fire in it out of one room into another twice ye same night, wch was in ye presence of ye sd Mr Howard who saw & suffered his wife to do it.'[28] She added that 'ye sd Mrs Howard's garb & dress was as beggarly & mean as any of this [deponent's] servants will wear'. Mrs Ann Sell also remembered the Howards lodging in

---

[25] Ibid. 13.
[26] Swift, *Corr.* ii. 122–3.
[27] Lord Hervey, *Memoirs*, ed. R. Sedgwick (3 vols., London, 1931), i. 40.
[28] BL Add. MSS 22627, fo. 43.

East Street, where 'they went by the name of Smith . . . for fear
of being arrested'. One day she had gone with Mrs Howard 'to
Shugg Lane in order to dispose of their goods & furniture, beds
& bedding not excepted, where they were actually sold'.[29] But
selling her bed and bedding was not the worst of Henrietta
Howard's indignities. In her own 'Book' of complaints addressed
to her husband she recalled: 'Amongst other expedients to raise
money I went to sell my hair and after having been with Mr Sell
at several periwig makers and only 18 guineas offer'd, all ye
thought fit to say was you wonder'd I had not sold it for ye
thought it was more than it was worth.'[30] By the sale of all their
furniture the Howards had managed to raise enough money to
make their way to Hanover, where they endeavoured, successfully,
to ingratiate themselves with the incoming royal family. But
change of scene had brought little relief from her domestic miseries. She recalled, 'I performed the journey in the meanest and
most fatiguing manner and when I came to H[anover] and hoped
to enjoy some respite of my troubles, I found ye uneasiness of yr
temper render'd me void of almost a moment's rest wch was so
visible as to be remark'd by all our acquaintances.' She detailed
constant acts and threats of physical violence:

You have called me names and have threatened to kick me and to brake my
neck. I have often laid abed with you when I have been under apprehension
of yr doing me a mischief and sometimes I have got out of bed for fear you
shou'd.[31]

It should of course be remembered that the woman who assembled
such a dossier of complaints was seeking to establish grounds for a
formal separation from her brutish husband in order to consolidate
her waning influence over the new King of England. Swift, whom
Mrs Howard flattered with empty courtiers' promises, took a more
jaundiced view of her character. She was, he wrote, 'a most unconscionable dealer', a charming but deceitful politician.

She abounds in good words and expressions of good wishes, and will
concert a hundred schemes for the service of those whom she would be
thought to favour: Schemes that sometimes arise from them, and sometimes

---

[29] Ibid., fos. 43/45.
[30] Ibid., fo. 41.
[31] Ibid., fo. 42.

from herself; although, at the same time, she very well knows them to be without the least probability of succeeding.[32]

It is clear, though, that, when Gay first met Henrietta Howard at Herrenhausen, he was struck by finding something of a kindred spirit. Here was another victim of poverty and neglect, inured to suffering the insults of domestic humiliation, and pinning all her hopes on brighter prospects under a new regime. 'We have not much variety of diversions,' Gay reported; 'what we did yesterday & today we shall do tomorrow, which is, go to Court and walk in the gardens.'[33] On their long evening strolls together through the gardens at Herrenhausen, this ambitious but impoverished pair found pleasure in concocting schemes for their mutual advancement. Mrs Howard was a beguiling ally, and her influence on Gay's long and tantalizing quest for court preferment was profound. Even when he came to recognize the truth of Swift's attacks on her vain and ineffectual stratagems, Gay could not disown a friendship with a woman with whom he could share more openly than with anyone else the intimate frustrations and humiliations of court life.

News of the Queen's death finally reached Hanover on 17 August (New Style), just one day after Gay had dispatched his facetious letter to Arbuthnot and Swift. All at once the slow nuances of diplomatic manoeuvres gave way to sudden activity. Secretary Bromley informed the Envoy Extraordinary that the Privy Council now desired the Elector's presence in England with all speed, and 'for the safety and convenience of his passage a squadron of Men of War is appointed to attend his pleasure on the coast of Holland'.[34] In a set of measures 'for maintaining the public tranquillity' the Council demanded the seizure of 'the horses and arms of Roman Catholics' and required all local authorities 'to keep a watchful eye on suspected persons'. Regiments throughout the British Isles and Flanders were put on alert 'to prevent any disturbance' and an embargo placed on all ships not to sail without a special government warrant.[35]

In England, Gay's friends received the long anticipated blow with

---

[32] 'Character of Mrs Howard', *Prose Works*, v. 214–15. Swift wrote this 'Character' in 1727, at the same time that Mrs Howard, now Countess of Suffolk, was compiling her 'Book' of grievances.

[33] *Letters*, 15.

[34] BL Stowe MSS 242, fo. 156.

[35] Ibid.

varying degrees of stoicism and panic. Swift made plans for a hasty departure to Ireland. According to him the Whigs had not even bothered to conceal their glee at the Queen's demise with a decent pretence of mourning: 'She was not prayed for even at her own chapel at St James's, and what is most infamous stocks rose three per cent in the city.' In this new political world, he complained, 'I have no interest even with the footmen of anybody now in power.'[36] Arbuthnot, peremptorily deprived of his post as royal physician, exchanged his lodgings in St James's for a house in Dover Street, but retained his customary equanimity. His case, he said, was 'not half so deplorable' as that of many of the Queen's former servants, who were like 'poor orphans, exposed in the very streets'.[37] Ford was one such orphan; ejected from his post as Gazetteer, he soon left England for the Continent. Pope protested at the injustice of penalizing loyal English Catholics for the actions of Catholic potentates abroad.[38] His 'greatest fear', he said, 'under the circumstances of a poor papist is the loss of my poor horse', but consoled himself with Job-like resignation: 'if they take it away . . . I thank God I can walk.' Together with Parnell he retreated from London to Binfield, where they concerned themselves with the fate of Homeric, not Hanoverian, dynasties. Arbuthnot tried to lift their spirits by dreaming up more Scriblerian schemes. 'Pray remember Martin, who is an innocent fellow', he told Swift, 'and will not disturb your solitude.'[39] But Swift was in no mood for diversions, and sent this damning report on their joint satiric schemes:

To say the truth, Pope who first thought of the hint has no genius at all to it, in my mind. Gay is too young; Parnell has some ideas of it, but is idle; I could put together and lard and strike out well enough, but all that relates to the sciences must be from you.[40]

In fact, as noted earlier, Pope was actually the youngest of the group.

Throughout the following year, and beyond, all these men were 'suspected persons', whose intimacy with the former Tory leaders carried with it the suspicion of Jacobitism. Official surveillance of their

[36] Swift, *Corr.* ii. 94, 119.
[37] Ibid. 136.
[38] Pope, *Corr.* i. 241.
[39] Swift, *Corr.* ii. 42.
[40] Ibid. 46.

activities intensified after March the following year, when Bolingbroke took his reckless gamble of fleeing to France and joining forces with the Pretender. In July 1715 Lord Oxford was committed to the Tower, where he remained imprisoned for two years. Letters to and from Swift were regularly intercepted by post office spies acting under the supervision of Addison and Budgell, as the new Whig government sought evidence to implicate him in Jacobite plots. In public Pope always affected a lofty indifference to such matters. 'I thank God that as for myself, I am below all the accidents of state changes by my circumstances, and above them by my philosophy.'[41] Yet, though rigorously excluding political comments from his correspondence, he was on close terms with several leading Jacobites. In January he spent some days in the country with Bolingbroke, who was already contemplating his flight to France. In August a planned trip to Sir William Wyndham's country seat had to be abandoned when Wyndham was arrested and sent to the Tower.

Still in Hanover, where he was busily cultivating the favour of the new royal family, Gay had a rather different perspective on events. In the circumstances it may have been fortunate that he did not have any copies of *The Shepherd's Week* to show the Princess, since the flattering prologue to Bolingbroke could only have confirmed Bothmar's suspicions of him as Clarendon's 'secrétaire jacobite'. By mid-September his English friends were eagerly anticipating his return from his aborted mission. 'Is Gay come over?' Pope asked Parnell, immediately resuming his habit of making plans on Gay's behalf. First, Pope thought, a little recreation might be in order: 'Could we get Gay with us to Bath?' he wondered. In the event, Gay was too late to accompany his Scriblerian friends on a visit to Bath which, for Pope at least, was less than an unalloyed delight. 'I am damnably in the spleen,' he told Ford, after three weeks of 'pump-assemblies, the walks, the chocolate houses, raffling shops, plays, medleys &c'. What he longed for was a 'quiet indolent station by your fireside, with a nightcap on, which is a thousand times more to be preferred than this way of catching cold for my health'.[42]

The new King embarked for England in mid-September attended by a 'squadron of English and Dutch Men of War' and landed at

[41] Pope, *Corr* i. 247.
[42] Ibid. 259.

Greenwich on 18 September, accompanied by his son, the Electoral Prince.[43] Judging by the evidence of Gay's later poem *Mr Pope's Welcome from Greece* (1720), which follows the route of this royal progress, it seems probable that Gay travelled in their entourage and was able to witness at first hand the carefully stage-managed triumph of the new King's arrival.

The King and Prince went into a barge in Long-Reach, and arriv'd at Greenwich about six o'clock in the evening, being saluted by all the guns on board all the ships in the river, and welcom'd by the loud acclamations of the multitudes of people that crowded everywhere the banks.

As the royal party neared the capital, the Whig demonstration of welcome achieved new heights of political street theatre.

Above two hundred coaches of the nobility and gentry, all with six horses, preceded his Majesty's. When the King came to St Margaret's Hill in Southwark, he was met by the Lord Mayor, Aldermen, Recorder, Sheriffs, and Officers of the City of London; in whose name Sir Peter King, Recorder, made a congratulatory speech ... The royal pomp continu'd till his Majesty's arrival at his palace at St James's, and the shining show was still brighten'd by as fair a day as ever was known in that season of the year. The streets from the Stone's End to St James's, as many miles as they were in length, were thronged with joyful spectators; the balconies all along adorn'd with tapestries, and fill'd with the brightest beauties in England who, particularly from Ludgate to Temple Bar, made an appearance equally surprising and charming ... It was observable that the Duke of Marlborough's coach ... was attended by great numbers of the populace, and shouts of acclamation from Greenwich to St James's; and that the Earl of Oxford was hiss'd in several places ...[44]

Not to be outdone, a few days later Pope wrote from Bath greeting the newly returned Gay with this effusive letter of welcome.

Dear Mr Gay,—Welcome to your native soil! Welcome to your friends! thrice welcome to me! Whether returned in glory, blest with court-interest, the love and familiarity of the great, and fill'd with agreeable hopes; or melancholy with dejection, contemplative of the changes of fortune, and doubtful for the future: whether return'd a triumphant Whig or a desponding Tory, equally All Hail! equally beloved and welcome to me! If happy, I

[43] See John Oldmixon, *The History of England during the Reigns of ... George I* (London, 1735), 572–3.
[44] Ibid.

am to share in your elevation; if unhappy, you have still a warm corner in my heart, and a retreat at Binfield in the worst of times at your service. If you are a Tory, or thought so by any man, I know it can proceed from nothing but your gratitude to a few people who endeavour'd to serve you, and whose politics were never your concern. If you are a Whig, as I rather hope, and as I think your principles and mine (as brother poets) had ever a bias to the side of liberty, I know you will be an honest man and an inoffensive one. Upon the whole, I know you are incapable of being so much of either party as to be good for nothing. Therefore once more, whatever you are, or in whatever state you are, all hail![45]

This is an interesting letter in many ways. While there is no reason to question the sincerity of Pope's welcome, his bantering questions about Gay's current political allegiances hint at some of Pope's own anxieties as he set about the tricky business of soliciting subscriptions for Homer. While ostensibly deferring to Gay's freedom of political opinion, he implicitly offers counsel, and even coaching in the formulas of a politically correct neutrality. Pope himself affected a similar pose of diplomatic neutrality in a letter to Charles Jervas, where he attributed his friendship with Swift to simple gratitude, with no partisan significance.

For all that pass'd betwixt Dr Swift and me, you know the whole (without reserve) of our correspondence: the engagements I had to him were such as the actual services he had done me, in relation to the subscription for Homer, obliged me to. I must have leave to be grateful to him, and to any one who serves me, let him be never so obnoxious to any party.[46]

In later years, Pope's fabricated version of his correspondence demonstrated his revisionist skills in the art of rewriting history. But this letter to Jervas already suggests a tendency to deny former friends in accordance with the prevailing political climate. No doubt, as a prominent Catholic and known associate of Bolingbroke, Pope feared his letters would be intercepted by government spies. This would account for his ringing declaration of Whiggish principles ('ever a bias to the side of liberty') to Gay. Sentiments like these, echoed in many of Pope's letters at the time, were evidently intended to instruct Gay in the correct political responses. Pope's roguish depiction of Gay as a dashing ladies' man suggests a similar

[45] Pope, *Corr*. i. 254.
[46] Ibid. i. 245.

exercise in image-making. 'Come and make merry with me in much feasting', he writes.

> We will feed among the lilies. By the lilies I mean the ladies, with whom I hope you have fed to satiety: Hast thou passed through many countries, and not tasted the delights thereof? Hast thou not left thy issue in divers lands, that German Gays and Dutch Gays may arise, to write pastorals and sing their songs in strange countries?[47]

There is something both sad and preposterous about Pope's relentless attempts to present himself and Gay as such a pair of rakes. The nearest Pope himself came to an amorous adventure during his stay at Bath was penning suggestive letters to Teresa Blount in which he imagined her 'modestly half-naked', like the ladies whose attitudes and postures 'something betwixt swimming and walking' in the Roman baths he evidently watched with some erotic pleasure.[48]

Characteristically, Pope ends his letter with a straightforward 'word of advice in the poetical way. Write something on the king, or prince, or princess', he urged him. 'On whatsoever foot you may be with the court, this can do no harm.' A few days later, having received no reply from Gay, Pope wrote to Ford, enquiring, 'Is Gay our countryman, or a High Dutch Squire? I have heard not a syllable of his adventures.' If Gay was afraid of corresponding with Tories 'tell him I am a Whig' and, 'if he wants consolatory discourses, pray give him what encouragement you can'.[49] In fact Gay was doing what he could to follow Pope's advice by composing some panegyric verses for the new Princess Caroline. Without the support of his former position in the Duchess of Monmouth's household, his financial situation was again precarious. As Arbuthnot reported to Swift: 'poor Gay is much w[h]ere he was only out of the Duchesses family & service.'[50] He did, however, have 'some confidence in the Princess and Countess of Picbourg', which Arbuthnot hoped 'may be significant to him'. The doctor seconded Pope's advice in urging Gay 'to make a poem upon the princess before she came over, describing her to the English ladies, for it seems the princess does not dislike that; (she is really a person that I believe will give great

---

[47] Ibid. 255.
[48] Ibid. 257.
[49] Ibid. 259.
[50] Swift, *Corr*. ii. 137.

content to everybody)'.[51] To Gay's friends his best course of action
was obvious enough. He had both the occasion and the opportunity
for some flattering panegyrical verses which might earn him the
place at court he so much desired. But to Gay, it was the obviousness
of this stratagem which inhibited him. It was not that he did not
like the Princess, on the contrary, it was because he *did* like her that
he found it difficult to flatter her in this insincere and mercenary
way. He was, said Arbuthnot, 'in such a groveling condition, as to
the affairs of the world, that his muse would not stoop to visit
him'.[52] At last, though, his muse did stoop to the task, but too late
to provide the welcoming fanfare that Arbuthnot had recommended.
The Princess landed in England on 11 October, and made her
triumphal entry into London two days later, accompanied by the
Prince: 'The Tower Guns fired as they came over the Bridge, and
those in the Park when they alighted at St James's. And at Night
there were Illuminations and Bonfires, with all other publick Demonstrations of Joy.'[53] Alas, these demonstrations of joy did not include
Gay's poem, *A Letter to a Lady, Occasion'd by the Arrival of her
Royal Highness the Princess of Wales*, which was not published till
the following month. Nor is it the kind of poem that Gay's friends
had hoped for. In place of the usual court flattery, Gay attempted to
strike a note of amiable intimacy with the Princess by mocking such
ritual effusions. Instead of writing a panegyric he deconstructs one,
parodying the usual formulas of the genre. The poem opens in
conversational manner suggesting that the Princess herself is among
those urging him to put pen to paper for his own good.

> Madam, to all your censures I submit,
> And frankly own I should long since have writ:
> You told me, silence would be thought a crime,
> And kindly strove to tease me into rhyme.   (ll. 1–4)

Summoned thus for what is virtually a royal command performance,
Gay calls 'th'unwilling muses to my aid' and buckles down to the
task of fabricating a standard eulogy. First he offers a sample
selection of allegorical special effects:

> Here I to Neptune form'd a pompous Pray'r,

[51] Swift, *Corr.* ii. 137.
[52] Ibid.
[53] *The Present State of Europe*, 25 (1714), 411–20.

> To rein the Winds, and guard the Royal Fair;
> Bid the blue Tritons sound their twisted Shells,
> And call the Nereids from their pearly Cells. (ll. 21–4)

Next, he ransacks classical literature for some off-the-peg metaphors, until an unnamed friend protests at such second-hand stuff.

> For shame, says he, what, imitate an Ode!
> I'd rather ballads write, and Grubstreet lays,
> Than pillage Caesar for my patron's praise. (ll. 34–6)

Finally, Gay tries his hand at following Arbuthnot's advice, by introducing the Princess to the English ladies.

> Ladies, to you I next inscrib'd my Lay,
> And writ a Letter in familiar way:
> For still impatient till the Princess came,
> You from description wish'd to know the Dame.

The thirty lines of poetic tribute which follow are the most sustained piece of panegyric in the whole poem, and show some real skill in this kind of idealized portraiture. In a letter to Ford from Hanover Gay had commented that the Princess would 'take a pleasure in speaking English', and in this poem he compliments her on her accent: 'Such Harmony upon her tongue is found, | As softens English to Italian sound' (ll. 57–8); her beauty, wit, and piety are all praised, but most of all she is celebrated for her dynastic role.

> Oft have I seen her little Infant Train,
> The lovely Promise of a future Reign;
> Observ'd with pleasure ev'ry dawning Grace,
> And all the Mother op'ning in their Face. (ll. 69–72)

More of this might well have improved Gay's prospects of a court place. What this section of the poem does *not* do, however, is what it claims; it does not describe the Princess to the English ladies. When Pope enclosed a copy of Gay's poem to Martha Blount he felt it necessary to add one neglected detail: 'She is very fat.'[54] However, before Gay's poem was completed, the Princess herself had arrived, rendering his poetic introduction superfluous:

---

[54] Pope, *Corr.* i. 269.

Behold the bright Original appear,
All Praise is faint when CAROLINA'S near.
Thus to the Nation's Joy, but Poet's Cost,
The Princess came, and my new Plan was lost.   (ll. 85–8)

Baulked again, Gay haunts the court, anxiously seeking some sign of favour.

Pensive, each Night from Room to Room I walk'd,
To one I bow'd, and with another talk'd;
Enquir'd what News, or such a Lady's Name,
And did the next day, and the next, the same.
Places, I found, were daily giv'n away,
And yet no friendly Gazette mention'd Gay.   (ll. 91–6)

Increasingly desperate, he asks one court friend after another how best to succeed, yet shows more skill in satirizing their responses than in following them.

I ask'd a friend what method to pursue,
He cry'd, I want a place as well as you.
Another ask'd me, why I had not writ:
A poet owes his fortune to his wit.
Strait I reply'd, with what a courtly grace
Flows easy verse from him that has a place! . . .
You must, cries one, the ministry rehearse,
And with each patriot's name prolong your verse.
But sure this truth to poets should be known,
That praising all alike, is praising none.
Another told me, if I wish'd success,
To some distinguish'd lord I must address . . .
Still ev'ry one I met in this agreed,
That writing was my method to succeed;
But now preferments so possess'd my brain,
That scarce I could produce a single strain:
Indeed I sometimes hammer'd out a line,
Without connection as without design.
                    (ll. 97–102; 111–16; 125–30)

In such a context of desperate, mercenary verse-grinding, the scraps and snippets of eulogy which Gay does manage to squeeze out inevitably sound like parody. Recommended to praise the 'high virtues' of some 'distinguish'd lord', Gay picks on the Duke of Argyle, but his formulaic phrases come perilously close to satire. Similarly, his brief epigrams in praise of the King's heroism and the Princess's piety, intended to strike a note of informality, actually suggest that this is as much of such stuff as he can bring himself to utter.

The poem thus undermines itself with almost every line. Unable to take such rote-like rhapsodies seriously, Gay gambles that the Princess may have wit enough to prefer his kind of jesting honesty to any amount of pompous public-relations verse. In fact, although the poem is dedicated to the Princess, it is Gay himself, not Caroline, who is the subject here. Instead of a panegyric, he produces a little comic sketch, with himself centre-stage, as jester, innocent, clown, trying one gambit after another, but all to no avail. Implicit in this clown-like pose is some, perhaps subconscious, mockery of his over-solicitous friends. Gay's repeated failures to follow the career advice of his well-intentioned friends were not due, as they fondly believed, to indolence, naïvety, or inadequacy, but rather to a deeper sense of his own integrity. What is most eloquently presented in this poem is the humiliation of dependence, the venal insincerity of those who crowd in to fawn and flatter the leaders of the new regime. Gay presents himself torn, as so often, between the imperatives of financial need, and the instinct for honesty. Implicitly the poem argues that, if the Hanoverian court is to be worthy of the sudden praises heaped upon it, it must have the sense to discriminate between mere flattery and genuine tribute. One particular couplet stands out:

> But now preferments so possess'd my brain,
> That scarce I could produce a single strain:

The tantalizing and desperate search for preferment has a paralysing effect upon him, making it almost impossible for him to write at all. In the event, Lintot paid him £5. 7s. 6d. for the copyright to the poem, which was sufficiently well liked to go through four editions in the year. But this modest success was far from the rich harvest of favour that Gay had hoped for.[55]

By the end of the year Gay's hopes of a court place were practically dead. On 30 December he wrote to Charles Ford in Paris

[55] Irving, 107.

enclosing some sample lines from an early draft of *Trivia*. Work
on the poem was already well advanced, by which progress, he
cynically observed, 'you may imagine . . . that I have not been
interrupted by any place at court'. The note of weariness and
depression in Gay's voice is unmistakable as the letter tails off
into silence. He recounts how, at a Christmas ball at Somerset
House, he had seen his former patroness, the Duchess of Monmouth, and watched the Prince and Princess of Wales dancing
'our English country dances'. He concludes: 'I have been studying
these two or three minutes for something [else] to write to you,
but I find myself at a loss, and can't say anything . . .' Once
again the paralysing obsession with lost preferments so possessed
his brain that he found himself unable to write at all. To have
seen not only his former patroness, but also the royal couple on
whom he had depended for future advancement, would have been
bad enough; but to watch them dancing 'our English country
dances', the very airs that Gay sought to make his courtly stock-
in-trade, must have made the sting of exclusion especially sharp.

The modest fee which Gay obtained from Lintot for his poem on
the Princess was little enough to sustain him, and in the New Year,
recovering somewhat from his lassitude and disappointment, he set
himself to work with unaccustomed discipline. In January he wrote
to the ailing Parnell with news of his recent literary activities. 'I
have writ one book of the walking the streets [i.e. *Trivia*], & among
us we have just finish'd a farce in rhyme, of one act, which is now
ready for the stage.' This one-act farce, *The What D'Ye Call It*, was
one of Gay's happiest performances. The idea for the play, as he
reminded Parnell, had been with him since he wrote *The Shepherd's
Week*, to which it bears many striking parallels. ''Tis upon the
design I formerly have mention'd to you of a country gentleman's
having a play acted by his tenants.' He enclosed some sample lines,
written with a lively air that belies his former depression. 'After this
is play'd', he confidently predicted, 'I fully design to pursue the
Street Walking with vigour, & let nothing interfere but a place,
which at present, I have little prospects of, so that I must rub on as
well as I can in hope that Gazettes will some time or other be my
friend.'[56] Clearly he had not abandoned all hopes of a place at court,
and, obsessively scanning the pages of the *Gazette*, he could not

[56] *Letters*, 18.

help noticing how others were being favoured. Nick Rowe, now Clerk to the Prince's Council, was offering his latest play *Lady Jane Grey*, to the playhouse managers while Ambrose Philips, recently appointed paymaster to one of the lotteries, was about to publish a new *Miscellany*.[57] Their success merely confirmed what Gay had asserted in his *Letter to a Lady*: 'With what a courtly grace | Flows easy verse from him that has a place!' It should come as little surprise that two of the playwrights whose works are most frequently parodied in *The What D'Ye Call It* are Rowe and Philips. For Gay, in his present plight, a lottery seemed almost his best hope of financial survival. 'All the politicians are employ'd in elections,' he remarked, 'and they search the newspapers for whigs & tories just as I do the lottery-paper for my chance of one ticket.'[58]

With his customary lack of self-assertion, Gay described *The What D'Ye Call It* as another collaboration, written 'among us'. His detractors were always quick to seize on such admissions and Cibber's celebrated retort, 'What, does Mr Pope make knives too?', perpetuated the image of Gay as Pope's stooge. But this allegation, made several years later owes more to the gossip and animosities surrounding the later comedy *Three Hours after Marriage* than to any inside knowledge.[59] In fact it is clear not merely from the frequent echoes of *The Shepherd's Week*, but from the protean form of this incongruous dramatic hybrid, that the work is essentially Gay's. In a letter to Caryll describing the play's triumphant reception, Pope specifically names Gay as the one 'who has wrought all the above said wonders'.[60] However, Pope and Arbuthnot undoubtedly encouraged him to write it, while Pope made use of his connections not only to secure an early performance, but also to ensure a good house. Writing to Caryll a week after the play's opening night, Pope thanked him for epistles sent 'in Mr Gay's behalf ... attended with a competence of tickets, to my Lord

---

[57] Philips advertised for contributions for this projected new *Miscellany* in the *London Gazette*, 8 Jan. 1715, inviting 'such gentlemen as were willing to appear' in it to direct their poems to Tonson. Gay evidently recognized that contributions from him would not be welcome.

[58] *Letters*, 18.

[59] Cibber's assertions that the play was 'in Pope's own handwriting' and that 'when it was read to the players, Mr Pope read it, though Gay was by' sound like malicious fabrications, intended to damage equally both Pope and Gay.

[60] Pope, *Corr.* i. 282–3.

Waldegrave and Mr Plowden . . . You have obliged my friend and me beyond all power, and even decency of expression.'[61]

The What D'Ye Call It opened at Drury Lane on 23 February when it was performed as the afterpiece to Rowe's *Jane Shore*. It was an immediate success and received twenty-one further performances during the year. Just as important, from Gay's point of view, it turned out to be a money-spinner. 'He will have made about an £100 of this farce,' Pope told Caryll, when the play was still only half-way through its initial run.[62] It is worth noting that he says 'he' not 'we', a clear indication that Pope regarded the play as Gay's property.

Subtitled 'A Tragi-Comi-Pastoral Farce', *The What D'Ye Call It* revels in its own freakishness. It is a magnificent hybrid, a literary riddle, and a theatrical tease. There is a new note of confidence in Gay's display of literary virtuosity here, self-consciously 'interweaving the several kinds of drama with each other, so they cannot be distinguished or separated'. From the provocative assertion in the preface that 'the sentiments of princes and clowns have not in reality that difference which they seem to have', to the terse tongue-in-cheek epilogue ('Our stage play has a moral—and no doubt | You all have sense enough to find it out'), Gay's burlesque of literary hierarchies carries with it a gibe at the social pretensions which such ritual hyperbole sustains. In fact *The What D'Ye Call It* was such a literary enigma that audiences were in some difficulties to find out the moral: 'some looked upon it as a mere jest upon the tragic poets, others as a satire upon the late war.'[63] Pope's old companion Henry Cromwell, now rather deaf, was particularly puzzled: 'hearing none of the words and seeing the action to be tragical, was much astonished to see the audience laugh.' Even the cast were in some difficulties interpreting Gay's intentions, with the result, as he complained, that 'the parts in general were not so well played, as I could have wished'. Johnson, in the role of Filbert, was particularly ill at ease, though 'Penkethman [Peascod] did wonders; Mrs Bicknell [Kitty Carrot] performed miraculously, and there was much honour gained by Miss Younger tho' she was but a parish child'.[64] Critics who had come with a premeditated intention to damn the play 'confessed they were forced to laugh so much that they forgot the

---

[61] Pope, *Corr*. i. 282.
[62] Ibid. 283.
[63] Ibid. 282–3.
[64] *Letters*, 20.

design they came with'. Others (Pope calls them 'the common people of the pit and gallery') 'received it at first with great gravity and sedateness, some few with tears; but after the third day they also took the hint, and have ever since been very loud in their claps'. The first two nights of *The What D'Ye Call It* were 'court nights' attended by the Prince and Princess of Wales, together with others of 'the first quality' who entered 'in a very particular manner . . . into the jest'. Much encouraged by their reaction, and by the receipts of his benefit night, Gay boasted that the play had 'met with more success than could be expected from a thing so out of the way of the common taste of the town . . . the galleries who did not know what to make of it, now enter thoroughly into the humour, and it seems to please in general better than at first'.[65]

Only Dennis, and a few 'grave sober men', refused to enter into the jest, and seemed 'determined to undeceive the town at their own proper cost, by writing some critical dissertations against it'. Nothing could have pleased Gay better than to provoke Dennis into print, and he did all he could to egg him on: 'to encourage them in which laudable design, it is resolved a preface shall be prefixt to the farce in the vindication of the nature and dignity of this new way of writing.' This preface is a deliberate piece of literary incitement. Defending his heterogeneous work, Gay innocently observes that 'we have often had tragi-comedies upon the English theatre with success'. This was a dig at Addison, who had famously condemned tragi-comedy as 'one of the most monstrous inventions that ever entered into a poet's thought'.[66] 'Even among the best critics', Gay went on, it was still disputed 'whether a tragedy may not have a happy catastrophe'. The 'best critics' he had in mind were Addison and Dennis, who had clashed on this very point. Addison had famously poured scorn on Dennis's 'ridiculous doctrine' of 'poetical justice' which insisted that tragedy had a moral duty to present the final triumph of good over evil. *King Lear* 'as Shakespeare wrote it', Addison declared, 'is an admirable tragedy . . . but as it is reformed [by Tate] according to the chimerical notion of poetical justice, in my humble opinion it has lost half its beauty'.[67] Sadly, even all this goading could not tempt Dennis to respond, though Thomas

---

[65] Ibid.
[66] *Spectator*, 40. (16 Apr. 1711).
[67] Ibid. In the *Narrative of Dr Robert Norris* it was this issue of the *Spectator* which provoked Dennis's 'deplorable frenzy'.

Burnet's *Grumbler* obliged with some carping comments. Gay sounds positively boastful when he speaks of provoking 'the fury of Mr. Burnet, or the German Doctor'.[68] Both he and Pope affected to regard such attacks as a form of stimulus: 'For poets assailed by critics are much like men bitten by tarantulas: they dance on the faster the deeper they are stung, till the very violence and sweating makes 'em recover.'[69] Indeed, not content with the meagre ration of critical outrage that he had already provoked, it seems probable that Gay combined with Pope to simulate some synthetic outrage of his own, publishing a hoax attack on his own play in *A Complete Key to the Last New Farce, The What D'Ye Call It.* Under the guise of deploring the play's 'unjust' and 'invidious' parodies, this ingenious spoof, or 'double jest', amplifies Gay's literary satire by gleefully identifying all the targets of his ridicule.[70]

Structurally *The What D'Ye Call It* makes use of the 'play-within-a-play' format successfully employed in Buckingham's *Rehearsal* (1681) and enthusiastically developed in Fielding's later theatrical burlesques. Unusually, though, Gay chooses not to set his framing play in a London playhouse, but in a country justice's hall. In the 'inner' play, performed for the benefit of two local country justices, the servants of Sir Roger enact a comic impromptu in which the barbarity of war, the injustice of the law, and the sexual dishonesty of the great are all exposed to mock-bucolic satire.

---

[68] *The What D'ye Call It* was attacked by Thomas Burnet in the *Grumbler* (17 Mar. 1715) and by Philip Horneck in *The High-German Doctor* (1719): see Irving, 112–13. Burnet had also criticized Pope in his *Homerides; or, A Letter to Mr Pope Occasion'd by his Intended Translation of Homer.* In Addison's support, Steele, as patentee of Drury Lane, let it be known that 'the farce should not have been acted if he had not been in town' (Pope, *Corr.* i. 287).

[69] Pope, *Corr.* i. 286–7.

[70] Not everyone agrees that the *Complete Key to . . . the What D'Ye Call It* was written by Pope and Gay themselves. Pope asserts that it was written by 'one Griffin a player, assisted by Lewis Theobald' (Pope, *Corr.* i. 288 n.). Among modern scholars who have accepted this attribution are W. H. Irving (p. 113); R. F. Jones (*Lewis Theobald* (New York, 1919), 16–17); George Sherburn (*The Early Career of Alexander Pope* (Oxford, 1934) 137–9); J. V. Guerinot (*Pamphlet Attacks on Alexander Pope, 1711–1744* (London, 1969), 29); and V. A. Dearing, i.). However, when examined carefully, their arguments for supporting Pope's claim are far from convincing. Irving, who describes the pamphlet as 'a vicious attack on Pope and Gay', insists that 'Theobald's hand is clear enough . . . as Mr R. F. Jones has shown'. But what Jones actually writes is that 'the evidence' for this attribution 'is indeed slight'. Sherburn, while accepting Pope's word about the authorship, is still puzzled why Theobald, who 'was still on friendly terms with both Gay and Pope . . . should have joined a combination against [them]'. In fact, readers

The protean quality of Gay's wit is evident in all features of the play. It is not merely that he switches, from scene to scene, between comedy and tragedy, pastoral and farce; the promiscuous and parodic mingling of genres occurs simultaneously within a single scene or speech. The aunt's tirade before the local justices (I. i. 33 ff.) is identified by the *Key* as a parody of *The Distressed Mother:* 'his repetition of relations alludes to the 3d act of the *Distressed Mother*, where Andromache repeats all the miseries of Priam's family: "But how can I forget it? How can I | Forget, &c"'.[71] But it also includes an eloquent indictment of the Press Act, the game laws, the poor laws, and rural exploitation, all the more damning for their bathetic homely details.

> O tyrant Justices! have you forgot
> How my poor brother was in Flanders shot?
> You press'd my brother—he shall walk in white,
> He shall—and shake your curtains ev'ry night.
> What though a paltry hare he rashly kill'd,
> That cross'd the furrows while he plough'd the field?
> You sent him o'er the hills and far away;
> Left his old mother to the parish pay,
> With whom he shar'd his ten pence ev'ry day.
> Wat kill'd a bird, was from his farm turn'd out;
> You took the law of Thomas for a trout:
> You ruin'd my poor uncle at the 'sizes,
> And made him pay nine pounds for *Nisiprises*.

of the pamphlet at the time regarded it not as a 'vicious attack' on Pope and Gay but as an ingenious hoax. As Burnet wrote in the *Grumbler* (3 May 1715): 'Another obliges the world with a *Key* to his own *Lock* [i.e. *The Rape of the Lock*] . . . the same arch wag, a little before this, gave us a *Complete Key* to his farce.' The idea that the *Key* was actually an ironic work concocted by the Scriblerians themselves is supported by Kerby-Miller, who argues that it is 'largely, if not wholly, the work of Pope and Gay' (*The Memoirs of Martinus Scriblerus*, ed. Charles Kerby-Miller (New York, 1966), 44). Fuller (i. 419) partially inclines to this view, but with some reservations: 'For myself, I find that if one makes some sort of distinction between the severe preface and the *Key* itself, Kerby-Miller's theory seems credible.' I too believe that Burnet and Kerby-Miller have got it right, and that the *Key* is another Scriblerian exercise in mock self-censure, similar to the ironic disparagement of Pope's *Pastorals* in their *Guardian* no. 40. The apparent severity of the preface is a typical piece of disorientation, or a 'double bluff', something which the authors of the *Key* themselves cheekily acknowledge: 'A *Key to the What D' Ye Call It* is a double jest; and one would have imagined that so lucky a thought could not have escaped the inventive heads of its composers.' This is a fairly heavy hint, from such masters of ironic deception, that what follows is not a criticism, but a celebration of the play's parodic style.

[71] *Complete Key*, 4; see *The Distressed Mother*, III. vi.

> Now will you press my harmless nephew too?
> Ah, what has conscience with the rich to do!   (I. i. 33–48)

The faint echo of the familiar ballad 'O'er the hills and far away' reinforces this bitter-sweet tone.[72] This ballad, already used in *The Shepherd's Week*, was clearly one of Gay's favourites and is included in *The Beggar's Opera*. But the song's wistful nostalgia and pledge of loyalty had been given an ironic twist by Farquhar in *The Recruiting Officer*, where Kite leads his country recruits, Pearmain and Appletree, in this sardonic version.

> We all shall lead more happy lives,
> By getting rid of brats and wives,
> That scold and brawl both night and day,
> Over the hills and far away. Over &c.   (II. ii. 6–10)

Gay would seem to bring both versions of this song, the sentimental and the sardonic, to mind, in this speech of mingled social satire and literary burlesque. *The What D'Ye Call It* is full of wonderful moments of theatrical parody. There is the glorious comic scene when the two lovers, Filbert and Kitty, are parted and dragged off either side of the stage.

KITTY. Yet one look more—
FILBERT.   One more ere yet we go.
KITTY. To part is death.—
FILBERT.   'Tis death to part.
KITTY.   Ah!
FILBERT.   Oh!

The *Key* comments on the 'whimsicalness of these concluding groans':

'Tis further observable that these great masters in sighs and groans have so far preserved the delicacy of them, and distinguished the feminine softness that they have made Kitty tenderly breathe an 'Ah!'—and sturdy Filbert more hoarsely a deep bass 'Oh!'[73]

---

[72] This ballad, properly entitled 'Jockey's Lamentation', appears in D'Urfey's *Wit and Mirth* (1719?), v. 316. The aunt's speech was the sample from the play that Gay included in his Jan. letter to Parnell. Fuller observes that the play contains 'as much criticism of social injustice as one's belief in the characters can bear' (Fuller, i. 19).

[73] *Complete Key*, 10. The source for Gay's parody here was Steele's *Tatler*, where 'Dick Easy' remarked of his friend Ned Softly's line 'For Ah! it wounds me like his dart'

In later editions of the play Gay even changed the 'Oh!' in Kitty's earlier line, 'Oh! good your worships, ease a wretched maid' (I. i. 7) to the more feminine 'Ah!', to underline the *Key's* satiric point. There is a ludicrous ghost scene (I. iv), parodying *Richard III* and imitating D'Urfey's *Wonders in the Sun*, which ends with the 'tyrant justices' scampering from the stage pursued by the 'hoopings and hobblings' of a ghostly chorus comprised of their judicial victims.[74] The second act contains the beautiful ballad ''Twas when the seas were roaring', with music possibly supplied by Handel, which Cowper found so moving that he refused to believe Gay could have written it unaided.[75] But even here, Gay safeguards the ballad's fragile sentimental charm by being the first to poke fun at its conventions: the scene begins and ends with parodies of the standard 'mad scene' in which a distracted tragic heroine gives vent to suicidal fantasies, while a chorus 'of Sighs and Groans' croon their 'oh's' and 'ah's' like a backing-group.

Parodies of Philips abound. 'O rueful day! . . . O woeful day!' laments Kitty, echoing lines from Philips's *Pastorals* already ridiculed by Pope and Gay.[76] A few lines earlier, Kitty is on her knees before the justices, begging for Filbert's freedom: 'Behold how low you have reduced a maid.' This, the *Key* declares, 'is an invidious parody of Mr Philips' Andromache in *The Distressed Mother* where she, kneeling to Pyrrhus, says thus: "Behold how low you have reduced a queen".'[77] However, the fact that Rowe's *Jane Shore* is another favourite target raises an interesting question about Gay's satiric intentions.[78] Although Gay was clearly envious of Rowe's

---

that 'he would rather have written that "Ah!" than to have been the author of the *Aeneid*' (*Tatler*, 163 (25 Apr. 1710)).

[74] *The What D'Ye Call It*, I. iv; see *Richard III* (v. iii) and Orpheus' song in the prologue to D'Urfey's *Wonders in the Sun*. Defending his use of 'the speaking ghost of an embryo', Gay, in the preface, recalls that 'Mr D'Urfey . . . has given all the fowls of the air the faculty of speech equal with the parrot' (in *Wonders in the Sun*).

[75] Letter to William Unwin, 1783; *William Cowper: Selected Letters*, ed. James King and Charles Ryskamp (Oxford, 1989), 73. For a detailed discussion of the sources of this ballad, its popularity, and the question of Handel's possible composition of the setting, see Fuller, i. 432–4.

[76] Here the *Key*, which suggests a source in *Romeo and Juliet*, is deliberately misleading. Contemporaries familiar with *Guardian* no. 40 and *The Shepherd's Week* could not have failed to spot the parody of Philips.

[77] *Complete Key*, 5; *The Distressed Mother*, III. vi.

[78] The rushed preparations for the deserter Peascod's summary execution ('Draw out the men: | Quick to the stake; he must be dead by ten.') are, as the *Key* informs us, 'an

success (he was elevated to the post of Poet Laureate later that same year) the two men were still on friendly terms, and relished each other's wit. There was, wrote Pope, a 'vivacity and gaiety of disposition' about Rowe's character 'which renders it impossible to part from him without that uneasiness and chagrin which generally succeeds all great pleasures'.[79] Pope himself had composed an epilogue for *Jane Shore* and, at about the time *The What D'Ye Call It* was performed, Rowe invited him to write a prologue for his new play *Lady Jane Grey*.[80] There is no evidence that Rowe resented Gay's parodies of his work; on the contrary, it seems he entered whole-heartedly into the spirit of the jest. No doubt he took the view that parody of this kind was indeed the sincerest form of flattery, and that a farce which so wittily burlesqued his own work alongside Chaucer, Shakespeare, Bunyan, Addison, and Philips could only add to his literary celebrity. Probably he also shared Pope's desire to assist the fortunes of a fellow writer whose prospects, under the new regime, seemed so markedly different from his own.[81]

There is sometimes a certain naïvety in critical discussions of satire and its effects. Most politicians are well aware that it is far preferable to be satirized than to be ignored, and many have mastered the art of turning the lampoons of their opponents to self-promotional effect. Both Gay and Rowe knew the importance of publicity and Gay's parody of Rowe's play may well have worked to their mutual advantage, by keeping *Jane Shore* in the Drury Lane repertoire. Indeed, the fact that *The What D'Ye Call It* often appeared as an afterpiece to the very plays it parodied, especially *Jane Shore* and *The Distressed Mother*, suggests some inventive programming on the part of the Drury Lane

ironical imitation of the hasty orders for Hastings's death in *Jane Shore*: "GLOUCESTER: Seize him, and bear him instantly away. | He shall not live an hour."' *Complete Key* 19; *Jane Shore*, IV. i. 245–6.

[79] Pope to Edward Blount, 10 Feb. 1716?; Pope, *Corr.* i. 329–30. This is a fabricated letter, hence the date is uncertain though the sentiments are not in doubt. On Pope's friendship with Rowe see Ault, 128–55.

[80] Pope's epilogue for *Jane Shore* was not used because the actress, Anne Oldfield, refused to deliver it. But even this did not sour relations between himself and Rowe. In his poem *A Farewell to London: In the Year 1715*, Pope writes in genial vein: 'To drink and droll be Rowe allow'd | Till the third watchman toll.' For a full discusion of relations between Pope, Gay, and Rowe, see Ault, 129–55.

[81] It even seems possible that Rowe may have lent a hand in the composition of the *Key* to *The What D'Ye Call It*.

management.[82] The resulting controversy boosted audiences, provoked discussion, and produced handsome financial receipts.

Addison was less amused by Gay's parody of *Cato*. Faced with
the firing-squad, the deserter Peascod is offered the consolation of a
'good book'.

PEASCOD. Lend me thy handkercher—*The Pilgrim's Pro-*
[*Reads and weeps*

(I cannot see for tears) *Pro-Progress-* Oh!
The Pilgrim's Progress- eighth edi-ti-on
Lon-don-prin-ted-for -Ni-cho-las Bod-ding-ton
With new ad-di-tions never made before.
Oh! 'tis so moving. I can read no more.

[*Drops the book*

'These lines', declares the *Key*,

are the most unjust abuse of the famous *Cato*, a play whose scenery is so
universally known that 'tis almost impertinent to remember the reader that
in the fifth act thereof, preparatory to his designed murder of himself, the
hero is introduced reading the treatise of Plato on the immortality of the
soul, and from which he draws the finest soliloquy that ever appeared on
the stage: 'It must be so,—Plato thou reason'st well'.

Not content with pointing out this parallel, the *Key* goes on to spice
the jest by adding what Gay *intended* to write, before 'modesty'
restrained him.

The authors had designed to change this verse conformable to their
thought of the *Pilgrim's Progress*, to 'Bunyan, thou reason'st well'; but on a
second deliberation they found the parody so flagrant that they expected it
would entail the curse of an audience, and for that reason grew more
modest.[83]

Addison though had ample means for taking his revenge. Many
years later Pope told this story to Spence:

---

[82] It was performed three times as the afterpiece to *Jane Shore* and twice to *The
Distressed Mother*.

[83] *Complete Key* 16, *Cato*, v. i. '*Cato* had at the time run to eight editions, all of which
had appeared in 1713 (the eighth edition of Boddington's Bunyan was published in 1682).
The joke was borrowed by Thomas Tickell in 'A Poem in Praise of the Hornbook' (1726),
71 ff.' (Fuller, i. 429.) See Gay's letter to Caryll, (Letters, 23).

A fortnight before Addison's death Lord Warwick came to Gay and pressed him in a very particular manner to 'go and see Mr Addison', which he had not done for a great while. Gay went, and found Addison in a very weak way. Addison received him in the kindest manner and told him that 'he had desired this visit to beg his pardon, that he had injured him greatly, but that if he lived he should find that he would make it up to him.'

Pope interpreted Addison's apology thus:

Gay, on his going to Hanover, had great reason to hope for some good preferment, but all those views came to nothing. It is not impossible but that Mr. Addison might [have] prevent[ed] them from his thinking Gay too well with some of the great men of the former ministry. He did not at all explain himself in what he had injured him, and Gay could not guess at anything else in which he could have injured him so considerably.[84]

As Secretary to the Council of Regents, Addison was certainly in a powerful enough position to have prevented Gay's advancement. Some authorities even suggest that 'it was in Addison's power to have been Secretary of State at the Accession', an eminence which he did not in fact reach until three years later.[85] Certainly the terms of Gay's praise of Bolingbroke in his prologue to *The Shepherd's Week* may have made Addison, like Bothmar, doubt whether Gay wholly subscribed to the Whiggish principles that Pope was so eager to attribute to him. Read in such a context, the back-handed compliments of his *Letter to a Lady* might have sounded less like an attempt at honesty than an ungracious lampoon. If Addison had not already determined on frustrating Gay's hopes of a court place, this parody of *Cato* could only strengthen his sense of animosity. As Pope later observed: 'Addison [was] very vain.'[86]

The What D'Ye Call It is Gay's first theatrical triumph. Inventive and spontaneous, it is above all gloriously funny, audaciously flouting all the rules, but always retaining a perfect instinct for comic timing and burlesque detail. Repudiating the drudgery of panegyric verse, Gay produced this little comic *tour de force* as testimony to the

---

[84] Spence, i. 79–80; The earliest manuscript is even more explicit: 'The present Family had made great promises to Gay at Hanover, wch had no effect wn they came over.'

[85] *An Historical Essay on Mr Addison* (Tyers, 1783), 53.

[86] Spence, item 157; i. 66.

independence of his own imagination. *The What D'Ye Call It* has the virtuosity of the best and most original satiric revue, and belongs in the same category of theatrical burlesque as Fielding's *The Tragedy of Tragedies*, Sheridan's *The Critic*, and Stoppard's *Real Inspector Hound*.

The success of the play did much to recover Gay's spirits, though he had still not abandoned his hopes of a court place. In late March Pope told Caryll that 'Mr Gay expects a present from the Princess',[87] but at least he was no longer moping despondently over the columns of the *Gazette*. Now he had the confidence, and the cash, to idle his time in literary haunts and high society. One day, seated 'amidst clouds of tobacco' in Williams's coffee-house, keeping his eye on passers-by for material for *Trivia*, he found time to pen a gossipy letter to Caryll while Pope paid a diplomatic visit to Charles Jervas's studio, where Addison was having his portrait painted. Gay's letter is filled with all the latest coffee-house chatter, including Whiston's millennialist lectures, Lord Peterborough's banishment from the court, and Rowe's new play. He also mentions the *Key . . . to The What D'Ye Call It*, a 'sixpenny criticism' whose author 'with much judgment & learning calls me a blockhead, & Mr Pope a knave'.[88] Apparently, says Gay with poker-faced solemnity, Peascod's reading of *The Pilgrim's Progress* in *The What D'Ye Call It* is supposed to parody Cato's reading of Plato in Addison's play. He no doubt took a particular pleasure in this oblique form of self-congratulation, confident that Pope was at that very moment assuring Addison that no such parody had been intended.

The weather had been very rainy of late, creating a general dampness in Lintot's publishing house, where the printed sheets of Pope's Homer were so slow drying that publication was again postponed. Lintot, said Gay, was 'now endeavouring to corrupt the curate of his parish to pray for fair weather, that his work may go on the faster'.[89] Meanwhile, both he and Pope were doing the social rounds. Pope promised to introduce Gay to 'a lord and two ladies' while Gay agreed to introduce Pope to the Duchess of Monmouth,

---

[87] Pope, *Corr*, i, 287.

[88] *Letters*, 23.

[89] It is not clear where Gay was living, but he uses both Jervas and Lewis as a post office; see his postscript to Pope's letter to Caryll *c.* 19 Mar. 1715 (Pope, *Corr*. i. 287): 'I have given the book [*The What D'Ye Call It*] to Lewis to be sent to you the first opportunity.'

with whom, apparently, he was now back on friendly terms. Both
men were eagerly anticipating a visit to Ladyholt, Caryll's country
estate in Sussex, as soon as Homer was published. Gay looked
forward to rambles in the parkland of 'one of the pleasantest seats in
England', where he might, as the mood took him, 'celebrate a
milkmaid, describe the amours of your parson's daughter, or write
an elegy upon the death of a hare'.[90]

But Gay's hopes of such bucolic recreations were sadly premature.
Suddenly on 2 March Bolingbroke fled to France. Immediately all
his former friends found themselves under suspicion. Every day the
Whigs strengthened their stranglehold on the administration, filling
places with their most loyal supporters and keeping a watchful eye
on those they distrusted. Lewis had already dispatched a brief and
urgent cautionary note to Swift 'that if you have not already hid
your papers in some private place in the hands of a trusty friend, I
fear they will fall into the hands of your enemies',[91] and no doubt
offered Pope and Gay the same prudent counsel. Prior's papers had
already been seized, and he himself had been impeached as Tories
everywhere were hounded from office. In May Pope left the 'dear,
damn'd, distracting town' and retreated with some reluctance to
bury himself in his Homeric labours at Binfield. He marked his
departure with his poem *A Farewell to London*, in which he is
careful to make a parade of his Whig friends, including the genial
Rowe, the 'good Christian' Dr Garth, and the deceased Lord
Halifax. For the present, politics had poisoned the conviviality of
the town with rumours and suspicions. 'My friends, by turns, my
friends confound, | Betray and are betray'd.' In Ireland, Swift wrote
to his friend Knightley Chetwode, who had just been ejected from
his position as a commissioner of the peace: 'it seems there is a trade
going of carrying stories to the government and many honest folks
turn the penny by it.'[92]

Pope hoped that Gay might be persuaded to join him at Binfield,
forsaking the gourmet pleasures of Lord Burlington's 'lobster-nights'
for 'salads, tarts and peas' *chez* Pope.

> Adieu to all but Gay alone,
> Whose soul, sincere and free,

---

[90] *Letters*, 24.
[91] Swift, *Corr*, ii. 156.
[92] Ibid. 174–5.

Loves all mankind, but flatters none,
And so may starve with me.

But for the moment Gay preferred to stay in London with Arbuthnot and Jervas, working hard on *Trivia* and scrutinizing the columns of the *Gazette*. Pope made the best of Gay's decision: 'It is not the worse for me that Gay did not accompany me hither', he told Caryll, 'for whatever the world may think of my love to the muses, I never keep 'em company when I can have that of a friend.' After only a few days, though, he was feeling isolated and weary. 'My Muse is now an old stale wife', he complained, 'and I make bitter dry drudgery of it.'[93]

The combination of unrelenting poetical drudgery, political anxieties, and his nervousness awaiting the publication of the *Iliad* made him quite ill. At last, on 6 June the first four volumes of his translation were published and distributed to subscribers. They were headed by a preface which included this statement.

Mr Addison was the first whose advice determin'd me to undertake this task, who was pleas'd to write to me upon that occasion in such terms as I cannot repeat without vanity.[94]

But, in the intervening years, Addison's attitude to Pope had changed, soured by what he regarded as Pope's desertion to Swift and the Tories. As Thomas Burnet later recalled: 'I have [often] seen Addison caressing Pope, whom at the same time he hates worse than Beelzebub.'[95] Even so, Pope had no inkling of the revenge that Addison intended. Suddenly, just two days after the publication of Pope's *Iliad*, a rival translation appeared. Pope was thunderstruck. Secretly concocted by Tickell and Addison, *The First Book of Homer's Iliad* was a deliberate spoiling tactic, designed to upstage

---

[93] Pope, *Corr*. i. 292.

[94] A letter sent from Addison to Pope in Oct. 1713 would seem to confirm this claim. In it, Addison promises his full assistance in 'forwarding' Pope's translation: 'you cannot lay a greater obligation upon me than by employing me in such an office. As I have an ambition of having it known that you are my friend, I shall be very proud of showing it by this, or any other instance. I question not but your translation will enrich our tongue and do honour to our country . . . The work would cost you a great deal of time, and unless you undertake it will I am afraid never be executed by any other, at least I know none of this age that is equal to it besides yourself' (Pope, *Corr*. i. 196). On the problems of sorting out the facts of this episode from Pope's fabrications, see Ault, 103–27.

[95] *Letters of Thomas Burnet to George Duckett, 1712–1722*, ed. D. Nichol Smith (Roxburghe Club, 1914), 99.

Pope's work. Lintot immediately sent him a copy of Tickell's volume, assuring him that it was 'already condemned here and the malice & juggle at Buttons is the conversation of those who have spare moments from politics'.[96] But the 'malice & juggle' of Addison's little senate at Buttons were now inseparable from the political hostilities which divided not only the literary world, but the nation. The Whigs were back in power, and intent on taking revenge on all their adversaries. Lintot concluded his letter with the ominous note, 'Lord Bolingbroke is impeach'd this night. The noise the report makes does me some present damage.'[97] In fact, on 10 June the House of Commons voted the impeachment of both Oxford and Bolingbroke, and a month later Oxford was imprisoned in the Tower. 'They say the Whigs do not intend to cut off Lord Oxford's head,' wrote Swift, 'but that they will certainly attaint poor Lord Bolingbroke.'[98] In the preface to Homer Pope had paid a particular compliment to Bolingbroke, which was seized on by his Whig enemies as further proof of disaffection. 'The Whigs say, Bolingbroke is the hero of your preface,' Jervas reported, advising him, with his customary diplomatic pragmatism, to 'make room for Walpole in your next, to keep the balance of power even'. In Dublin, Swift too was surprised by Pope's daring: 'you were pretty bold in mentioning Lord Bolingbroke in that preface.'[99] The gossip was that, although the rival Homer bore Tickell's name, it was in fact in part, if not wholly, the work of Addison, and Pope was furious at such a calculated attempt at literary sabotage. Charles Jervas was dismissive of the 'Tickell' version: 'I fancy I could make a more poetical translation in [a] fortnight.'[100] He also passed on the latest Whig chatter which insisted that 'Tickell's *Iliad* sample was intended 'as a specimen of his ability for the *Odyssey*'. In response to this absurd claim, Fortescue had dreamt up the perfect satiric rejoinder, namely that Gay should 'publish a version of the first book of the *Odyssey* & tell the world 'tis only to bespeak their approbation & favour for a translation of Statius or any other poet'.[101] This time, however,

---

[96] Pope, *Corr.* i. 294. The copy of 'Tickell's' Homer which Lintot sent him is still preserved among Pope's books at Hartlebury Castle. It is heavily annotated and scored through with angry comments.

[97] Ibid. 294–5.

[98] Swift, *Corr.* ii. 173.

[99] Pope, *Corr.* i. 301–2.

[100] Ibid. 296.

[101] Ibid.

Gay did not immediately leap to Pope's aid. The accusation that Tickell had merely served as Addison's mouthpiece was uncomfortably close to the frequent allegation that Gay himself served the same function for Pope, thus allowing the two literary principals to remain aloof from the fray conducted by proxy among their protégés. He did, however, as promised, leave off walking the streets of London to spend the last week of June with Pope at Binfield. *En route*, instead of visiting the convivial wine merchant William Rollinson as expected, Gay went out of his way to call on Lady Bolingbroke at Bucklebury, a few miles west of Binfield. This was a gesture of defiance which did not go unnoticed in London. It was as if Gay, still earnestly hoping for court favour, wished to place it on record that he was not one of those prepared to trade friends for places. Even Pope was a little disturbed by such cavalier behaviour. In an effort of diplomatic fence-mending he told Jervas: 'You may tell Mr Rollinson that Gay was not sure he should go to Lady Bolingbroke's when he came hither; or help him to some excuse, for his neglect was scandalous, and has given him much vexation of spirit.'[102] Just as in his 'welcome home' letter, Pope continued to school Gay in the diplomatic language of excuses and compromise. Yet in the very same letter Pope makes a heroic virtue of his own championing the cause of a supposed underdog: 'If the Whigs say now B[olingbroke] is the hero of my preface, the Tories said (you may remember) three years ago, that Cato was the hero of my poetry. It looks generous enough to be always on the side of the distressed.' Pope liked to reserve the dignity of such flourishes to himself, while privately doing all he could to retain the favour of both parties. He was irritated that Gay should thus bid to rival him in a public gesture of dangerous heroics.

In France, Bolingbroke, angered by the news of his impeachment, reacted by taking the ultimate gamble, accepting the post of Secretary of State to the Old Pretender. This placed his former intimates under even greater suspicion. At Binfield Pope and Gay discussed the deepening political crisis and their reaction to 'Tickell's' Homer. Pope continued to pester his London friends with queries ('Pray tell me if you hear anything said about Mr Tickell's or my translation'[103] but, as he rather feared, the town was preoccupied

---

[102] Ibid. 303.
[103] Ibid. 304.

with other, weightier skirmishings. Lintot reported, 'those whom I expected to be very noisy on account of your translation are buried in politics'.[104]

----

[104] Pope, *Corr.* i. 298.

SEVEN

Trivial Pursuits

Our stage-play has a moral—and no doubt
You all have sense enough to find it out.

(Epilogue to *The What D'Ye Call It*)

BACK in London at the start of July, Gay was not left in any doubt about the official Whig line on the rival *Iliads*, which he communicated to Pope directly.

—I have just set down Sir Samuel Garth at the opera. He bid me tell you, that everybody is pleased with your translation, but a few at Button's; and that Sir Richard Steele told him, that Mr Addison said Tickell's translation was the best that ever was in any language. He treated me with extreme civility, and out of kindness gave me a squeeze by the sore finger. I am inform'd that at Button's your character is made very free with as to morals, &c. and Mr A[ddison] says, that your translation and Tickell's are both very well done, but that the latter has more of Homer. I am, &c.

The curious formality of this letter, of which no manuscript survives, makes it somewhat suspect.[1] Apart from the detail of Garth squeezing Gay's sore finger, there is none of the usual gossip that characterizes letters between Pope and Gay. Both the roll-call of titles (Steele had only recently received his knighthood) and the formality of the phrasing give it the air of an official bulletin. For Addison to pose in this way as an impartial arbiter was transparently disingenuous. According to Pope, even Steele conceded that 'not Mr. Tickell but Mr. Addison himself was the person that translated this book'.[2] But

---

[1] The letter, dated 8 July 1715, was first printed as an 'excerpt' in the 1735 edition of *Letters of Mr. Pope, and Several Eminent Persons*.
[2] In the preface to his edition of Addison's comedy *The Drummer*.

politics now outweighed all other literary considerations. As Pope told one correspondent: 'the busy part of the nation are not more divided about Whig and Tory, than these idle fellows of the feather about Mr. Tickell's and my translation.' It pleased him though to reverse the usual party labels.

If our principles be well consider'd, I must appear a brave Whig, and Mr Tickell a rank Tory; I translated Homer for the public in general, he to gratify the inordinate desires of one man only.[3]

As a relief from all this political feuding, Pope and Gay planned a summer expedition to Devon, in company with Fortescue and Jervas. But even this was put in jeopardy as the newspapers filled with threats and rumours of an imminent Jacobite invasion. Hyde Park became an armed camp, covered with the tents of Coldstream and Grenadier Guards. Bad weather further hindered their plans and, eventually, Gay and Fortescue went on ahead, hoping to meet up with their London friends in the West Country. At last, in mid-August Charles Jervas sent Pope a detailed itinerary, complete with meticulously itemized contingency arrangements for clean shirts, spare horses, night clothes, etc., all the way from Hyde Park Corner to Bath.[4] Travelling with Pope was rarely a spontaneous event. Yet this still proved an impossibly ambitious programme. Suddenly Sir William Wyndham was arrested as a Jacobite plotter, throwing the plans of these 'rambling associates' into disarray. Pope and Arbuthnot lingered in Oxford, Jervas went on to Bath, while Gay and Fortescue remained in Devon.

Deprived of Pope's company, Gay made good use of his time, completing a first draft of his poem *Trivia*. It appealed to his *goût de travers* that he should thus have written his bucolic eclogues *The Shepherd's Week* in town, and his town georgic in the country. Among other rural pleasures, he ate 'two dishes of toadstools of my own gathering, instead of mushrooms'.[5] Any ill effects were presumably remedied at Bath, where he finally caught up with Pope, before returning to London in October. In Devon too Gay enjoyed a peaceful respite from the political tensions that gripped the capital. This was despite the fact that in October, and again in December,

---

[3] Pope, *Corr* i. 306.
[4] Ibid. 312.
[5] *Letters*, 25.

the Duke of Ormonde made two unsuccessful attempts to land an invasion fleet in the county. Even after the outbreak of the Jacobite rebellion in Scotland, another Devonshire friend was able to report that 'the genius that reigns in our country [i.e county] . . . is happily turn'd to preserve peace and quiet among us'.[6]

From the start the Jacobite rising of 1715 was marked by mishaps, misjudgements, and mistrust. In November two Jacobite armies were defeated at Preston and Sheriffmuir, and by the end of December, when James himself finally landed at Peterhead, he found only 4,000 demoralized troops and his cause already in ruins. In March he dismissed Bolingbroke from his service, and by April the whole invasion scare was over. In their correspondence at the time Pope and Gay maintain a silence concerning the activities of their former friend. Pope joined with Sir William Trumbull in 'wishing quiet to our native country' while maintaining a studious neutrality:

I can pray for opposite parties, and for opposite religions, with great sincerity. I think to be a lover of one's country is a glorious elogy, but I do not think it so great an one as to be a lover of mankind.[7]

Such high-sounding sentiments fall somewhat short of a ringing pledge of loyalty to the current regime. As Pope wrote to Swift the following year, 'this is not a time for any man to talk to the purpose. Truth is a kind of contraband commodity which I would not venture to export.'[8]

On a lighter note, the best gossip of the winter concerned the death-bed marriage of the 76-year-old dramatist William Wycherley, who chose this expedient to prevent his nephew from inheriting his estate. He was outmatched, though, in deviousness by his young bride, Elizabeth Jackson, who, three months after Wycherley's demise, pocketed her widow's settlement and promptly married the man she really loved. Meanwhile Pope, whose profits from his *Iliad* translation amounted, despite Addison's spoiling tactic, to a vast fortune of some £5,000, now reckoned himself something of an expert in the lucrative process of subscription publishing.[9] He

---

[6] Pope, *Corr.* i. 320.

[7] Ibid. i. 324.

[8] Ibid. 342.

[9] He made a similar amount from his translation of the *Odyssey*. In 1975 David Foxon estimated these profits to be worth about £200,000 in current money; by 1985, Brean Hammond estimated that inflation would have raised this figure to 'nearer £500,000'; B. Hammond, *Pope*, (Brighton, 1986), 121.

quickly busied himself in procuring a 'pretty tolerable number' of people prepared to subscribe for Gay's forthcoming volume of *Trivia* at the rate of a guinea a book. 'I believe it may be worth £150 to him in the whole,' he told Caryll.[10] In addition, Lintot paid Gay £43 for the copyright to the poem, which was published on 26 January. A month later Arbuthnot remarked that Gay 'has got so much money by his art of walking the streets, that he is ready to set up his equipage', a joke which clearly appealed to Gay's own sense of the ridiculous, since he repeated it to Parnell: 'what I got by walking the streets, I am now spending in riding in coaches.'[11] In a light-hearted tavern letter, Arbuthnot also reported that the newly wealthy Gay was 'just going to the bank to negotiate some exchequer bills', though Gay's own drunken contribution to this facetious joint missive hardly suggests a man in a state for dealing with bankers. Indeed, he assured Parnell that 'as I draw on the bank but seldom & with much caution, I believe [I] will scarce break it'. He did, however, find new lodgings in town with the appropriately named Mrs. Bouzer, and felt for the first time like a man who had finally made his mark in the literary world. Despite his disappointment at being denied a court place, his receipts over the last year from his *Letter to a Lady*, *The What D'Ye Call It*, and now *Trivia* totalled nearly £300. In the advertisement to the poem Gay addressed himself to critics who had formerly 'allowed me an honour hitherto only shown to better writers: that of denying me to be the author of my own works'. The repeated insinuations that Pope was the real author of *The What D'Ye Call It* had clearly annoyed him and fuelled the single-mindedness with which he had completed the present poem. Yet while giving notice of his refusal to play Tickell to Pope's Addison, he simultaneously acknowledges a debt for 'several hints' in the poem, to Swift. 'I hope my performance will please the Dean,' he told Parnell, evidently finding the advice of a literary mentor over the water in Ireland more comfortable than the constant solicitude of one in whose shadow he usually wrote. Gay's poem did indeed please Swift, who, though much preoccupied with ecclesiastical politics, found time later that year to send Gay, via Pope, a useful literary 'hint'.

[10] Pope, *Corr.* i. 327.
[11] *Letters*, 29.

There is a young ingenious Quaker in this town who writes verses to his mistress, not very correct, but in a strain purely what a poetical Quaker should do, commending her look and habit, &c. It gave me a hint that a set of Quaker-pastorals might succeed, if our friend Gay could fancy it, and I think it a fruitful subject; pray hear what he says. I believe further, the personal [pastoral] ridicule is not exhausted; and that a porter, foot-man, or chair-man's pastoral might do well. Or what think you of a Newgate pastoral, among the whores and thieves there?[12]

Praise or encouragement from Swift always gave Gay a particular pleasure. His letters to Parnell never fail to conclude with the request to 'pray give my humble service to [the Dean]', though he clearly felt diffident about addressing himself to Swift directly. On this occasion he lost no time in following up Swift's advice about a Quaker pastoral, although it was a dozen years before he developed Swift's idea for a satiric 'Newgate pastoral'.

In April, anticipating a new bout of anti-Catholic legislation, Pope's family moved from their beloved Binfield to a rented house at Mawson's Buildings in Chiswick.[13] He and Gay took their sad farewells of the old house at the end of March, with Gay regretting that 'the trees of Windsor Forest shall no more listen to the tuneful reed of the [Popian] swain'.[14] The chief attraction of this new location was that it lay 'under the wing of my lord Burlington' just a short walk from Chiswick House. Pope and Gay had been introduced to Richard Boyle, Earl of Burlington, by Jervas, who accompanied the young lord on the Grand Tour in 1714–15. When he returned to London in May 1715 Burlington, still aged only 21, was bursting with ideas for an English artistic renaissance. His retinue included 'the sculptor G. B. Guelfi, the violinist Pietro Castrucci, the cellist Filippo Amadei, a goodly number of Italian craftsmen, and 878 trunks and crates containing works of art, besides two Paris-made

---

[12] Swift, *Corr.* ii. 215.

[13] On 23 June one of Pope's Catholic friends informed him that 'Yesterday the bill to oblige papists to register their names and estates passed the Lords'. This legislation, entitled 'An Act for appointing Commissioners to inquire into the estates of certain traitors, and of Popish recusants, and of estates given to superstitious uses, in order to raise money out of them severally for the use of the public', received the royal assent on 26 June. 'In anticipation of this device to increase taxes on Catholics and possibly because of questionable title to the house and land at Binfield (for Catholics were not allowed to buy land and the Popes had a sort of concealed ownership of the place at Binfield) the Popes had sold out and moved to Chiswick, there renting a new house' (Sherburn in Pope, *Corr.* i. 344).

[14] *Letters*, 29.

harpsichords, an instrument on which Burlington himself was apparently a tyro performer'.[15] Soon Pope and Gay were enjoying the hedonistic atmosphere of Burlington's lavish hospitality both at Chiswick and more especially at Burlington House in Piccadilly. In his freewheeling *Farewell to London, 1715*, written just weeks after Burlington's return, Pope salivated over the pleasures of the young Earl's table:

> Laborious lobster-nights, farewell!
> For sober, studious days;
> And Burlington's delicious meal,
> For salads, tarts and peas!

Back in town the following spring, the two men were quickly reinstated among Burlington's favourites. 'We ... walk, ride, ramble, dine, drink, & lie together. His gardens are delightful, his music ravishing.'[16] In *Trivia* Gay paid his own compliment to the congenial artistic atmosphere of the Earl's splendid Piccadilly palace.

> Beauty within, without proportion reigns.
> Beneath his eye, declining art revives,
> The wall with animated picture lives;
> There Handel strikes the strings, the melting strain
> Transports the soul, and thrills through ev'ry
>   vein;
> There oft' I enter (but with cleaner shoes)
> For Burlington's belov'd by ev'ry muse.   (ll. 494–500)

In Richard Boyle Gay found not just a patron, but a friend and kindred spirit whose enthusiasm for the arts extended from a love of classical simplicity, to a fascination with more exotic and cosmopolitan art-forms. In 1719 Burlington was the leader of the sixty-plus subscribers to the new Royal Academy of Music, contributing £1,000 for the establishment of an institution dedicated to the encouragement of Italian opera. With Handel as its 'Master of Music' commissioned to recruit a team of star operatic performers, 'Count' Heidegger as general manager, and Paolo Rolli as librettist and artistic consultant, the Academy, which enjoyed an annual royal

[15] Mack, 286.
[16] Pope to Martha Blount, Pope, *Corr*. i. 338.

grant of £1,000, sought to naturalize a musical taste still widely regarded as profoundly, and dangerously, un-English. Before long the two men were on terms of intimacy, and Gay enjoyed the kind of artistic encouragement from Burlington which emboldened him to persevere with the style of travesty theatrical productions that he loved best. It was not, of course, a friendship of equals, and in letters and poems to Burlington Gay is careful to strike the right blend of informality and deference. In fact his relationship with Burlington has striking parallels with that of William Kent, whom Burlington had met in Rome the previous year. When, five years later, Kent returned to England, he quickly became like Gay and Handel, one of the earl's regular house-guests, spending long periods as a lodger at one of Burlington's mansions, in Piccadilly, Chiswick, or Londesborough in Yorkshire. The prevailing homo-erotic atmosphere of Burlington's artistic coterie has already been mentioned. Charges of effeminacy and unmanliness were constantly levelled against Italian operas with their castrati singers and travesty roles; and the fascination with which both Burlington and Gay regarded 'gender-bending' literary parodies suggests a certain impatience with conventional sexual stereotypes. Part of the outrageousness of Gay's theatrical parodies in *The What D'Ye Call It* and *Three Hours after Marriage* comes from a kind of camp delight in literary promiscuity; his is a hermaphrodite art, delighting in its own freakish refusal to conform to standard notions of normality. This does not mean that we should take literally Pope's reference to their 'lying together' when describing their 'three or four days in high luxury' at Burlington House in March 1716. Despite the sexual awkwardness so often evident in Pope's letters to female friends, there is nothing to suggest that Pope's constant wish for the consolations of male friendship had anything sexual about it.[17] The man who was 'sorry

---

[17] See G. S. Rousseau, 'The Pursuit of Homosexuality in the Eighteenth Century', in R. P. Maccubbin (ed.), *'Tis Nature's Fault: Unauthorized Sexuality during the Enlightenment* (Cambridge, 1987), 132–68: 'No one sensible could possibly consider the writings of Irvin Ehrenpreis or Maynard Mack cowardly or prudish, but even they—the best biographers of Pope and Swift—have remained rather reticent about the frequent homoerotic correspondence and friendship of these men; so too for others of the Scriblerian circle, especially John Gay, who never married and whose psychological attachment to the older, if occasionally paternal, Pope merits more attention than it has received. These men were probably *not* homosexual (certainly there is no evidence of genital activity), but they were homosocial and homoerotic by any definition, and their biographers might wish to adopt a less reticent attitude towards their sexuality' (p. 134).

to say' that 'Addison and Steele [were] a couple of h——s [i.e.
hermaphrodites]', and who vilified Lord Hervey 'Sporus' with the
same charge, was unlikely to have done anything but repress any
similar instincts in himself. But with Gay the case is different. From
him we find no intimately emotional letters to female friends like
Pope's to the Blount sisters and Lady Mary Wortley Montagu. On
the contrary, his gallantries to 'the ladies' all have the exaggerated
facetiousness of a well-studied act, and his genuine friendships with
several ladies of the court, Henrietta Howard, Mary Bellenden, and
Mary Lepell, were maintained precisely because of the absence of
any dangerously sexual charge. In Gay's friendships with women we
find him adopting a quasi-female personality, just as many of his
poems and plays adopt a female perspective. The terms of his
relationship with Burlington strike quite a different note. Writing to
a friend in August 1721 he remarks, 'I live almost altogether with
Lord Burlington and pass my time very agreeably.'[18] The letter
which he sent to Burlington from Bath the following year has an
emotional intensity in its expressions of 'love' which suggests far
more than the customary flattery of a client towards his patron.[19]

At about this time a new edition of Mattaire's *Horace* was published
by Tonson and Watts. Continuing to coach his 'élève' in literary
matters, it was no doubt Pope who encouraged Gay to study and
annotate this new work.[20] Gay's copious annotations have the air of
schoolboy exercises dutifully undertaken to propitiate an exacting
master. *Reticulum* in the first satire of the first book is pedantically
glossed as 'a bag made with network in which they used to carry
their provision'. Likewise, in the sixth satire, he notes (l. 27): 'The
senator's shoes were drawn up to the middle of the leg fastened
there with little buckles. They were inconvenient, which makes
Horace use *impedit*.' Only a few annotations escape this atmosphere
of the schoolroom. Sometimes, when glossing transvestite or homosexual terms, Gay's comments have a certain bawdy relish, though
even these suggest something of the naughty schoolboy. He un-

[18] *Letters*, 39.
[19] Chatsworth MSS 173. 0.
[20] Gay's annotated copy of Horace, *Quinti Horatii Flacci opera, Londinii ex officina
Jacobi Tonson & Johanns Watts, MDCCXV*, is now in the Forster Collection of the
Victoria and Albert Museum (12.Q 17). It is signed 'J. Gay' on the title-page, and the fly-
leaf has a note: 'This copy of Mattaire's Horace L.P. has the autograph & MSS notes of
Gay.'

squeamishly renders *hunc perminxerunt calones* (*Satires*, 1. 2. 44) as 'the slaves have buggered this fellow'; he annotates *discipularum* (*Satires*, 1. 10. 89–90) thus:

Demetrius and Tigellius were effeminate fellows who read nothing but love verses, as those of Calvus and Catullus mentioned in this same satire. 'Tis for this reason he says *discipularum*, among the women.[21]

And he seems particularly fascinated by the diaphanous costume of the courtesans, glossing '*Cois*' (*Satires*, 1. 2. 101) thus: 'Coan garments were only worn by courtesans. They were so thin that they truly shew'd the naked body. It was made of a thin transparent kind of gauze made in the island of Cos.' About half the volume is annotated in this detailed fashion, which suggests that Gay may have been planning a translation of his own, though in the event he made little obvious use of all these textual labours. Perhaps appropriately, it was only in his *Epistle to Burlington* (1715), loosely modelled on Horace's Satire 1. 5, that he was stimulated to draw a parallel between his own experiences and those of the Augustan poet.[22]

In his own *Epistle to Burlington*, published in 1731, the year before Gay's death, Pope celebrates Burlington as the symbol of all that is judicious and correct in artistic taste, combining natural good taste with an enlightened classical perspective.

> You show us, Rome was glorious, not profuse,
> And pompous buildings once were things of use . . .
> 'Tis use alone that sanctifies expense,
> And splendour borrows all her rays from sense.   (ll. 23–4, 179–80)

Such expressions of cultural correctness are part of the same process by which *The Beggar's Opera* was subsequently recruited into the xenophobic campaign against Italian opera as a patriotic blast against a dangerous foreign corruption. But in the years immediately following Burlington's return to England in 1715, his artistic influence was regarded rather differently. In 1724 Hogarth's print *Masquerades*

---

[21] 1. 2. 44: The Loeb version is more discreet: 'another [has] been abused by stable-boys.' *Horace: Satires, Epistles and Ars Poetical*, with an English translation by H. Rushton Fairclough (Loeb Classical Library, London, 1926, repr. 1978), 21. 1. 10. 89–90: 'Demetri, teque, Tigelli, | discipularum inter iubeo plorare cathedras' ('But you, Demetrius, and you, Tigellius, I bid you go whine amidst the easy chairs of your pupils in petticoats!' Loeb translation, 123).

[22] The poem is annotated: 'Horace describes his journey from Rome to Brundisium.'

and Operas, originally titled *The Bad Taste of the Town*, shows Burlington presiding over an institutionalized cultural decline. To the left of the picture a fool and satyr lead a throng into the Haymarket Opera-House, home not just of operas but of masquerades, conjuring-shows, and lotteries; to the right we see Lincoln's Inn Fields theatre, where John Rich thrived on topical pantomimes. In the centre a woman-pedlar pushes a barrowload of discarded books, the works of Shakespeare, Dryden, Congreve, crying 'Waste paper for shops!'; while at the back, surveying the whole scene with a kind of élite amusement, stands Burlington, lord of misrule, before the gate of his sumptuous new mansion in Piccadilly.

Like all the best of Gay's writings, *Trivia* defiantly resists generic classification. This is not because its literary models and antecedents are in any way obscure. On the contrary, Gay not only parades literary sources from Virgil and Juvenal to Ned Ward and Swift, but makes clear his basic structure is borrowed, once again, from Virgil's *Georgics*. In formal terms, then, the poem is a town georgic; what is elusive is its tone. Some commentators have read its descriptions of the London streets as an exercise in topographical realism; while others regard it as 'a purely literary artifact', claiming, 'our experience of it is filtered almost entirely through allusions, recollections, imitations—of Virgil, Juvenal, Dryden'.[23] Some find a tone of celebration in its description of the busy, dirty town, while others read it as a moral satire. Thus one writes that 'all the genuine activities of the town ... take on the quality of a ballet or a pageant',[24] while another insists that these same London streets appear as 'the very type and habitation of moral disorder, depravity, and disease'.[25] Pat Rogers endeavours to resolve these contradictions by finding in the poem's elusive tone a subtle combination of literary, social, and moral themes: '*Trivia* is no more a straightforward mock-heroic than it is straight reportage ... the poetry employs social observation to make permanent moral comment; it employs moral emblems, such as the Fleet, to state a sociological truth.'[26] Most recently, contradiction itself has been taken as the poem's most essential quality, enabling it to occupy a variety of different

---

[23] Max Byrd, *London Transformed* (New Haven, Conn., 1978), 62.
[24] John Chalker, *The English Georgic* (London, 1969), 177–8.
[25] Martin C. Battestin, *The Providence of Wit* (Oxford, 1974), 127–40.
[26] Pat Rogers, *Grub Street* (London, 1972), 162.

and at times mutually exclusive positions simultaneously'.[27] Many of these contradictions derive from the ambiguous relevance and status of the georgic form itself. In his influential essay on the *Georgics* (1697) Addison praised the poet (Virgil) who could invest 'the meanest of his precepts with a kind of grandeur' and suffuse a poetic treatise on husbandry with a genuine patriotic and inspirational dignity. Yet in borrowing a form rooted in the celebration of rural labour to describe the mercantile activities of the town, certain ironies were inevitable. 'Virgil's poem of rural labour could not be translated without a certain awkwardness into the terms of an economic system increasingly dependent on capitalism and the city.'[28] Gay's earlier georgic, *Rural Sports*, in which he cast himself in the role of a literary connoisseur of bucolic motifs, had already confronted this contradiction between the dignity of agricultural labour and the cultivation of genteelly murderous country 'sports'. In *Trivia* likewise it is the ambivalent status and perspective of the poet which gives the poem its contradictory tensions. Addison found no difficulty in exploiting classical idioms to dignify the claims of commerce. In *Spectator* no. 69 he boasted: 'There is no place in the town which I so much love to frequent as the Royal Exchange', celebrating this 'grand scene of business' as the 'Emporium for the whole Earth'.[29] But Gay, who excludes the Royal Exchange from the topography of *Trivia*, felt no such enthusiasm for identifying stock-jobbers as the modern equivalent of Virgil's sturdy peasantry. Nor, though he offers sympathetic portraits of boot-blacks, sempstresses, apprentices, and fruit-sellers, can he adopt the viewpoint of the urban poor. Instead he creates a specific role and status for himself as a 'walker', investing the whole business of walking with the mock-earnest seriousness of a practised skill or craft. 'Walking' becomes what agriculture was for Virgil, a purposeful activity, equally beneficial to individual and society, which serves as a metaphor for social cohesion. In offering his advice on the best and safest means of walking the streets of London, Gay often strikes a note of public service:

---

[27] Stephen Copley and Ian Haywood, 'Luxury, Refuse and Poetry: John Gay's *Trivia*', in Lewis and Wood, 67.

[28] Tom Woodman, '"Vulgar Circumstance" and "Due Civilities": Gay's Art of Polite Living in Town', in Lewis and Wood, 83.

[29] *Spectator*, 69, (19 May 1711).

> Now venture, Muse, from home to range the town,
> And for the public safety risk thy own.　(ii. 5–6)

Throughout the poem he draws a sharp contrast between the public virtues of the walker and the private vices of the aristocrat lolling in his coach or chair. Walking is synonymous with health and honesty:

> Rosie-complexion'd health thy steps attends,
> And exercise thy lasting youth defends.　(i. 73–4)

Coach-riding is a recipe for disease and decay.

> In gilded chariots while they loll at ease,
> And lazily insure a life's disease . . .　(i. 69–74)

The walker is openly charitable while the coach-rider is insensitively mean:

> Proud coaches pass, regardless of the moan,
> Of infant orphans, and the widow's groan;
> While charity still moves the walker's mind,
> His lib'ral purse relieves the lame and blind.　(ii. 451–4)

The very appearance of a coach becomes a symbol of decadence and vice.

> See, yon bright chariot on its braces swing,
> With Flanders mares, and on an arched spring,
> That wretch, to gain an equipage and place,
> Betray'd his sister to a lewd embrace.
> This coach, that with the blazon'd 'scutcheon glows,
> Vain of his unknown race, the coxcomb shows.　(ii. 573–8)

Rather than ride in such dishonourable pomp, Gay declares:

> O rather give me sweet content on foot,
> Wrapt in my virtue, and a good surtout!　(ii. 589–90)

Coach-riding is not only harmful to the individual (leading apparently to rheumatic pains, jaundice, asthma, gout, and the stone, ii. 505–10), but pernicious to the public. The poem dwells at length on the traffic hazards of Hanoverian London, with recklessly driven coaches crashing into carts, coach-wheels crushing pedestrians' feet, drivers' whips cutting their eyes, coach-horses mercilessly beaten, and a pile-up in a narrow street leading to a full-scale battle.

Now oaths grow loud, with coaches coaches jar,
And the smart blow provokes the sturdy war;
From the high box they whirl the thong around,
And with the twining lash their shins resound:
Their rage ferments, more dang'rous wounds they try,
And the blood gushes down their painful eye.   (iii. 35–40)

Envying even the 'floating town' of Venice (usually itself a symbol of decadence), whose watery thoroughfares preclude such traffic hazards, Gay longs nostalgically for the days when

Coaches and chariots yet unfashion'd lay,
Nor late invented chairs perplex'd the way:
Then the proud lady trip'd along the town,
And tuck'd up petticoats secur'd her gown;
Her rosie cheek with distant visits glow'd,
And exercise unartful charms bestow'd.   (i. 103–8)

Now, all is changed:

Now gaudy pride corrupts the lavish age,
And the streets flame with glaring equipage . . .
In saucy state the griping broker sits,
And laughs at honesty, and trudging wits.   (i. 113–18)

This contrast between walking and riding is maintained with such consistency throughout the poem, and invested with such a weight of moral and social significance, that it is impossible to deny that, at some level, it represents an important conviction. At the same time there is considerable irony in the way Gay thus confers upon his role as 'walker' a kind of heroic dignity. Certainly his Scriblerian colleagues found something richly comic in this assumption, by their corpulent, indolent friend, of such an energetic persona. Arbuthnot's quip that Gay had 'got so much money by his art of walking the streets, that he is ready to set up his equipage'[30] became a standing joke. Many years later Swift was still pointing out the contradictions between Gay's rhetorical and private personas in this respect:

You pretend to preach up riding and walking . . . yet from my knowledge of you after twenty years, you always joined a violent desire of perpetually

---

[30] *Letters*, 27.

shifting places and company, with a rooted laziness, and an utter impatience of fatigue. A coach and six horses is the utmost exercise you can bear, and this only when you can fill it with such company as is best suited to your taste, and how glad would you be if it could waft you in the air to avoid jolting.[31]

Similar contradictions are easy to find. In book i of *Trivia* Gay remarks, moralistically:

> While softer chairs the tawdry load convey
> To court, to White's, assemblies, or the play.   (i. 71–2)

White's was a celebrated chocolate-house and gambling club in St. James's, described by Swift as 'the common rendezvous of infamous sharpers and noble cullies'.[32] Yet by 1721, if not before, Gay was using the club as his London address for correspondence, while his attendances at court, assemblies, and the playhouses were even more regular. In other words, in creating this rhetorical persona of the walker, Gay satirizes the very social milieu to which he aspired. The walker, like the pastoral swain, is a fantasy projection whose contradictory attitudes embody Gay's own ambivalence, torn between the provincial work-ethic of his Barnstaple background, and the self-indulgent hedonism of his new life in London. One recent critic puts it well:

For 'Walking' in this poem is actually the sign of a deliberate non-involvement in the economic system. It is a leisure pursuit as much as a form of labour. The walker has time to remark on all he sees, to stop and browse at bookstalls and to taste oysters. Walking thus has a fairly precise class orientation as a golden mean between *nouveau riche* selfishness and idleness and the vulgar labours of the lower classes. But it can hardly be taken seriously as a georgic activity. Gay cannot find a convincing form of work as the georgic art of living in his period, and it is for this reason that he needs the saving grace of mock georgic.[33]

Much of this 'mock-georgic' effect is located in a self-conscious irony surrounding the moral attitudes of the walker himself, and his claim to be performing a dangerous public duty. Both at the beginning and the end of the poem, Gay offers his work as an enduring monument to his own dedication to public service.

---

[31] Swift, *Corr.* iv, 15–16.
[32] *Intelligencer*, 9 (1728).
[33] Woodman, '"Vulgar Circumstance"' 88.

My youthful bosom burns with thirst of fame,
From the great theme to build a glorious name,
To tread in paths to ancient bards unknown,
And bind my temples with a civic crown;
But more, my country's love demands the lays,
My country's be the profit, mine the praise.   (i. 17–22)

This is richly ironic. The 'civic crown' refers to the 'corona civica', a Roman honour bestowed on those who saved the lives of fellow citizens in battle, as Gay here pretends to save his fellow walkers from the perils of the streets. Gay also purports to offer himself as a candidate for the title of 'city-poet' of London, an office currently held by the truly pedestrian Elkanah Settle and regarded by the Scriblerians as the ultimate badge of literary ineptitude. Even his professed stance of selfless patriotism ('My country's be the profit') parodies the rhetoric of Whig poets whose banging of the patriotic drum was designed more to serve their own interests than the country's.

This ironic camouflage of self-interest as social concern is evident in Gay's mock-heroic presentation of the walker as a latter-day hero, fearlessly risking the dangers of the city streets to serve the public good. Crossing the road becomes a perilous epic adventure.

Now man with utmost fortitude thy soul,
To cross the way where carts and coaches roll; . . .
                    On either hand
Pent round with perils, in the midst you stand,
And call for aid in vain; the coachman swears,
And carmen drive, unmindful of thy prayers.
Where wilt thou turn? ah! whither wilt thou fly?
On ev'ry side the pressing spokes are nigh.
So sailors, while Charybdis' gulf they shun,
Amaz'd, on Scylla's craggy dangers run.   (iii. 169–84)

Elsewhere the intrepid walker is compared to Theseus lost in the minotaur's labyrinth (ii. 83–6); to Orpheus, charming the powers of hell (i. 204); to Aeneas searching for his bride (iii. 92) or bearing his father on his back (iii. 368); and to Oedipus at the fatal crossroads (iii. 215). There is a knowing and ironic exaggeration about all these epic similes, as Gay playfully presents himself as a latter-day

Odysseus and invests the pursuit of sauntering through the London streets with the purposeful aura of a heroic quest.

As in Pope's *Dunciad*, the sense in which the London streets of *Trivia* are both topographically real, and literary metaphors, gives the poem an animation and vitality of reference which defiantly resist any simple reading. This interpenetration of the mundane and the heroic, so characteristic of eighteenth-century art, is a technique which twentieth-century artists have been slowly reacquiring. It is there in Hogarth's paintings. When these are at their most realistic, they are also often at their most allusive; the cunningly observed domestic detail or street incident, taking ironic force from its recollection of an Old Master model. At its best this permeation of the real with the imaginary can acquire a strange visionary and surreal quality which lends satire a disturbing imaginative force. Right at the centre of *Trivia* Gay offers such a vision in his lengthy mock-heroic digression on the birth and life of a boot-black boy. Decoded, this can be read as an extended social reflection on the inequalities of wealth and power in busy streets where aristocrats and urchins are in daily close proximity. But the literary framing of this episode, which has its model in Virgil's account of the art of engendering bees from putrid cattle blood, lends the social satire an additional ironic force.[34] The episode begins and ends with the street-boy's cry 'Clean your honour's shoes', echoing along the streets where he plies his trade. His is the ever-present 'voice of industry', though it is the muse, 'fatigu'd amid the throng', who feels the need for rest.

The boy's story begins, in epic fashion, with the infatuation of a deity for a mortal: 'great Jove (grown fond of change) | Of old was wont this nether world to range | To seek amours . . .' (ii. 107–9). In this realistic urban setting Jove's metamorphosis assumes a social colouring and he appears as an aristocratic rake, cruising the alleyways of London for 'rough trade'. Soon there is quite a fashion among the Olympians for one-night stands with proletarians: 'ev'n the proudest goddess now and then | Would lodge a night among the sons of men.' Amid all this promiscuity none is more promiscuous than Cloacina '(Goddess of the tide | Whose sable streams beneath the city glide)'. In a footnote Gay informs us that 'Cloacina was a goddess whose image Tatius (a king of the Sabines) found in

[34] See Dearing, ii, 557.

the common sewer, and not knowing what goddess it was, he called it Cloacina from the place in which it was found, and paid to it divine honours'. More prosaically, Cloacina here is the Fleet Ditch, the city's main open sewer, and her 'promiscuity' is an appropriate metaphor for the common receptacle for all the city's refuse. The sewer thus becomes the city's central symbol, a dark, subterranean goddess, receiving her tributes from rich and poor alike. Roving through the town (the poem accurately traces the sewer's path) the goddess falls in love with a 'mortal scavenger' or sewage-worker.

> The muddy spots that dried upon his face,
> Like female patches, heighten'd ev'ry grace:
> She gaz'd; she sigh'd. For love can beauties spy
> In what seem faults to ev'ry common eye.   (ii. 119–22)

Assuming the 'black form of a cinder-wench' the goddess consummates her proletarian amour in a dark alley and, nine months later, 'beneath a bulk she dropt the boy'.[35] Anxious for the child's future, the goddess prevails upon her fellow Olympians to provide him with the tools of his trade.

> With the strong bristles of the mighty boar
> Diana forms his brush; the God of day
> A tripod gives, amid the crowded way
> To raise the dirty foot, and ease his toil;
> Kind Neptune fills his vase with fetid oil
> Press'd from th'enormous whale; the God of fire,
> From whose dominions smoky clouds aspire,
> Among these gen'rous presents joins his part,
> And aids with soot the new japanning art:
> Pleas'd she receives the gifts; she downward glides,
> Lights in Fleet-ditch, and shoots beneath the tides.   (ii. 156–68)

The effect of this richly sensuous vocabulary is to create what Joyce would call an 'epiphany', a literary evocation of divinity within the most humble of human activities. Gay accurately describes the mundane tools of the boot-boy's trade, yet invests them with all the ritual and mystique of a religious ceremony. Just as Belinda's toilette-table in the *Rape of the Lock* becomes a mock-sacred display case for the products of the East India Company's commercial

---

[35] A bulk is the stall in front of a shop.

exploitation ('Unnumber'd Treasures ope at once, and here | The various Off'rings of the World appear', i. 29–30), so the boot-boy's stand becomes an altar to the spirit of Industry. A Mandevillian sense of irony is at work here, as Gay celebrates the apotheosis of trade not, like Addison, in the genteel transactions of the Royal Exchange, but in a subterranean world of scavenging and begging. In *The Fable of the Bees* Mandeville, tracing the public benefits of national wealth back to the private vices of greed, corruption, and luxury, presents the dirtiness of the capital city as an emblem of its opulence.

There are, I believe, few people in London, of those that are at any time forc'd to go a-foot, but what could wish the streets of it much cleaner than generally they are; while they regard nothing but their own clothes and private conveniency: but when once they come to consider, that what offends them is the result of the plenty, great traffic and opulency of that mighty city, if they have any concern in its welfare, they will hardly ever wish to see the streets of it less dirty. For if we mind the materials of all sorts that must supply such an infinite number of trades and handicrafts, as are always going forward; the vast quantity of victuals, drink and fuel that are daily consumed in it, the waste and superfluities that must be produced from them; the multitudes of horses and other cattle that are always daubing the streets, the carts, coaches and more heavy carriages that are perpetually wearing and breaking the pavement of them, and above all the numberless swarms of people that are continually harassing and trampling through every part of them: If, I say, we mind all these, we shall find that every moment must produce new filth; and considering how far distant the great streets are from the river side, what cost and care soever be bestowed to remove the nastiness almost as fast as 'tis made, it is impossible London should be more cleanly before it is less flourishing. Now would I ask if a good citizen, in consideration of what has been said, might not assert, that dirty streets are a necessary evil inseparable from the felicity of London, without being the least hindrance to the cleaning of shoes, or sweeping of streets, and consequently without any prejudice either to the blackguard or the scavengers.[36]

Gay's *Trivia* offers an ironic analysis of Mandeville's perception of an inseparable link between the 'necessary evil' of dirt and the 'felicity' of wealth in a flourishing commercial capital. Much of the poem's advice is devoted to instructing his fellow walkers how best

---

[36] *The Fable of the Bees*, ed. F. B. Kaye (2 vols., Oxford, 1924), i. 10–12; quoted in Copley and Haywood, 'Luxury, Refuse and Poetry', 68–9.

to avoid the filth and refuse that threatens to assail them on all sides. The barber's apron 'soils the sable dress' (ii. 28); chimney-sweeps and small-coals-men smear clothes with smuts and soot-stains (ii. 32–6); fish-stalls leave evil-smelling stains (iii. 106); 'the dustman's cart offends thy clothes and eyes' (ii. 37); the chandler's basket 'with tallow spots thy coat' (ii. 40); the hooves of dray-horses spatter clothes with mire and 'muddy blots' (ii. 293); mud and rain pose constant threats to hosiery and wigs alike (i. 200–2). But perhaps the greatest danger to maintaining a cleanly appearance comes from the open sewers or 'kennels' running down the city streets. After a heavy downpour, he warns,

> You'll hear the sounds
> Of whistling winds, e'er kennels break their bounds;
> Ungrateful odours common sewers diffuse,
> And dropping vaults distil unwholesome dews   (i. 169–72)

The most notorious of these open sewers, the Fleet Ditch, was described by Defoe in 1722 as a 'nauseous and abominable sink of public nastiness'.[37] But Gay invests this stinking locale, the trysting-place of his dark goddess Cloacina, with a pseudo-mythological dignity, transforming it from a private nuisance into the topos of Mandeville's consumer society.

> The goddess rose amid the inmost round,
> With wither'd turnip tops her temples crown'd;
> Low reach'd her dripping tresses, lank and black
> As the smooth jet, or glossy raven's back;
> Around her waist a circling eel was twin'd,
> Which bound her robe that hung in rags behind.   (ii. 195–200)

This incongruous deity, herself a kind of literary detritus, made up, like so much of Augustan 'culture', from wastes and scraps of art and nature, becomes the poem's animating force. 'Go thrive', she commands (ii. 203), bestowing on the boot-boy the tools of his future trade. Thus happily equipped, the boy, whose street-cry 'Clean your honour's shoes' resounds from Charing Cross to Whitehall, becomes the symbol of a society in which the simulacra of classical art provided an acceptable face for an entrepreneurial spirit

---

[37] 'Due Preparation for the Plague', in *The Works of Daniel Defoe*, ed. G. H. M[aynadier] (16 vols., Boston, 1903–4), v. 29.

based on luxury, exploitation, and waste. Refuse, in a classical disguise, is the presiding deity of this capital of industry.[38]

Gay's ambivalence towards the city's refuse is typical of his stance throughout this poem. On the one hand he offers fastidious advice for maintaining a cleanly appearance, while on the other he depicts filth and waste as the mythological source for a flourishing industry. The 'walker' is neither a plebeian tradesman nor an aristocrat lolling in his coach. He is an informed spectator of human affairs and for the most part appears as a consumer, offering useful advice on the delights and hazards of the town. But as the author of the poem, he is also a producer, offering his work for sale for the benefit and entertainment of a discerning public. The poem concludes on a characteristic note.

> And now compleat my gen'rous labours lie,
> Finish'd, and ripe for immortality.
> Death shall entomb in dust this mould'ring frame
> But never reach th'eternal part, my fame.   (iii. 407–10)

While his body may become just another waste-product (dust), his 'fame', that is, his poem, will achieve immortality. Such is the classical commonplace; *ars longa, vita brevis.* Yet even as he writes this, Gay implicitly subverts it. 'Labours' suggests an industrial rather than an inspirational process, and the organic metaphor 'ripe' (for immortality) carries the obvious implication that what is 'ripe' at one time will subsequently rot. The final lines make this clearer.

> When critics crazy bandboxes repair,
> And tragedies, turn'd rockets, bounce in air;
> High-rais'd on Fleetstreet posts, consign'd to fame,
> This work shall shine, and walkers bless my name.   (iii. 413–16)

Literary labours, like any other, have to be brought to market, hawked and advertised at booksellers' shops, to become part of the consumer life of the capital. And, since literary works are made of paper, the most distinguished of them, epics and tragedies, may find an ignominious end as a commercial waste-product, lining a band-box, binding a rocket, or by some even more lowly use be returned to the goddess Cloacina of Fleet Ditch. Gay's final irony is that, in

---

[38] The whole Cloacina episode is to some extent a burlesque parody of the Aristaeus episode in the fourth book of the *Georgics.*

writing a mock-classical poem, he is actually only bringing another perishable commodity to market; like the boot-black boy he is a scavenger of the literary sewers and alley-ways of Olympus to create a decorative ornament for his own consumer society. As Gay evokes the boot-boy's plaintive cry, there is more than a hint of self-portraiture.

> But I, alas! hard Fortune's utmost scorn,
> Who ne'er knew parent, was an orphan born!
> Some boys are rich by birth beyond all wants,
> Belov'd by uncles, and kind good old aunts;
> When time comes round, a Christmas-box they bear,
> And one day makes them rich for all the year.   (ii. 181–6)

Though not born an orphan, Gay had become one by the age of 10, and clearly felt himself deprived of Fortune's blessings, and the generous favours of indulgent aunts and uncles. Though he had never cleaned the shoes of the wealthy, he had cut and measured their clothes. And even now, as he attended their levees, laughed at their jokes, and flattered them with verses, he felt a certain kinship with the suppliant street-urchins, spattered by the gilded chariots of those who 'loll at ease'.

Throughout the spring and early summer of 1716 the friendship between Pope, Gay, and Burlington flourished as work on the new Burlington House went on apace. 'His gardens flourish, his structures rise, his pictures arrive,' reported Pope, surrounded by the constant activity of 'Italian chymists, fiddlers, brick-layers and opera-makers'.[39] It was with some regret that Gay made his usual summer journey to Devonshire that year, forsaking the excitement of Piccadilly and the hedonistic pleasures of Chiswick, 'Where Pope unloads the bough within his reach, | Of purple grape, blue plum, or blushing peach'. 'Within his reach' is a nice touch, taking Pope's diminutive stature as a measure of nature's spirit of accommodating indulgence to all wishes in Burlington's bower of bliss. The Earl's orchard extended a similar hedonistic indulgence to that connoisseur of indolence James Thomson, whom Mrs. Piozzi recalled 'lounging round Lord Burlington's garden, with his hands in his waistcoat pockets, biting off the sunny sides of the peaches'.[40]

---

[39] Pope, *Corr.* i. 347.
[40] James Sambrook, *James Thomson: A Life* (Oxford, 1991), 208.

Having established his reputation in *Trivia* as a poetic walker, Gay never failed to draw ironic attention to his new status as a horse-rider. In preparation for the Devon trip his friend Fortescue sent him word of 'a very easy [goi]ng little horse, which you may have [for] 5 guineas',[41] adding that '[if] you don't succeed with my Lord Burlington, [you] may at least with him'. Evidently, Gay did succeed with Lord Burlington, who seems to have procured for him a horse from the Blount sisters at Mapledurham suitable for such an inexperienced rider. In his *Epistle to Burlington*, subtitled *A Journey to Exeter*, Gay expressed his thanks, observing, 'You knew fat bards might tire, | And, mounted, sent me forth your trusty squire'. But even this specially chosen steed proved unequal to the task, as Pope told Teresa Blount in August: 'Mr. Gay has had a fall from his horse, & broken his fine snuffbox.'[42] This little comic incident was later included in Gay's brief satiric pamphlet *God's Revenge against Punning*, published in November, which concludes with this joking self-portrait: 'A Devonshire Man of Wit, for only saying in a jesting manner, "I get up-pun a horse", instantly fell down, and broke his snuff-box and neck, and lost the horse.'[43]

This self-deprecating comedy suggests the sense of social awkward-ness which Gay experienced in his promotion from pedestrian to equestrian status. By posing as Burlington's 'fat bard' or 'squire' he preserves a sense of social deference, and by falling from his horse draws attention to his lack of gentlemanly skills. But Gay's instinct for self-abasement went even further. In an extraordinary letter to the Blount sisters, he describes his journey to the West Country from the viewpoint not of the gentleman rider but of the weary horse, 'who had the misfortune to be sent into Devonshire with a poet on my back'. Taken together, these two descriptions of Gay's trip to Devon offer a fascinating dual perspective on his ambivalent sense of identity and status.

The *Epistle* takes the form of a verse Baedeker, entertainingly describing Gay's westward itinerary in the topographical manner of *Trivia*.[44] Leaving London one Sunday morning with two unnamed

---

[41] Pope, *Corr* i. 341.

[42] Ibid. 350.

[43] For a discussion of the 'James Baker' pamphlets see Ch. 8 n. 54.

[44] Although not published till 1720, the *Epistle* was already circulating in manuscript soon after Gay's return to London in the autumn. It provided the ostensible model for an anonymous imitation *A Walk from St. James's to Covent-Garden, the Back-Way* (1717), which was in reality a rejoinder to *Trivia*.

companions, Gay's route took him through Hyde Park, Kensington, and Turnham Green, (just north of Burlington's Chiswick estate). He jogged on through the dirty streets of Brentford, 'a tedious town', ferried the Thames at Staines (the bridge had been destroyed in winter floods), avoided the highwaymen of Bagshot Heath (one of Macheath's favourite spots) and spent the night at Hartley Wintney. Rising late, the travellers rode twelve miles in the noonday heat to Popham-Lane, a symbolic meeting-place of town and country values, where country mothers reconstituted themselves as London 'maids' by farming out their illegitimate offspring.

> Here unown'd infants find their daily food
> For should the maiden mother nurse her son,
> Twould spoil her match when her good name is gone.
> Our jolly hostess nineteen children bore,
> Nor fail'd her breast to suckle nineteen more.
> Be just, ye prudes, wipe off the long arrear;
> Be virgin still in town, but mothers here.   (ll. 40–6)

Next on to Stockbridge, formerly Steele's parliamentary seat, but now no longer the site of regular vote-buying binges following the passage, a few months earlier, of the Septennial Act.

> Sad melancholy ev'ry visage wears;
> What, no election come in seven long years! . . .
> Our streets no more with tides of ale shall float,
> Nor cobblers feast three years upon one vote.   (ll. 51–2, 55–6)[45]

At Salisbury Gay recalls former days as a draper's apprentice, praising not only the town's 'proud cathedral' but also its rag-trade fame:

> What sempstress has not prov'd thy scissors good?
> From hence first came th'intriguing riding-hood.   (ll. 73–4)

Similarly, at Honiton, he mentions the town's reputation for fine lace; but it is at Aximinster that fondest memories of his former intimacy with women's clothes are revived. A friendly chambermaid

---

[45] The Septennial Bill, extending the life of a parliament from three years to seven, was introduced on 10 Apr. 1716, and the Act was signed on 7 May. In the days of triennial parliaments the seventy Stockbridge electors usually sold their votes for £60 each—see Irving, 123 n.

lends Gay her own smock to sleep in, inspiring some transvestite fantasies.

> The maid, subdu'd by fees, her trunk unlocks,
> And gives the cleanly aid of dowlas smocks.
> Mean time our shirts her busy fingers rub,
> While the soap lathers o'er the foaming tub.
> If women's gear such pleasing dreams incite,
> Lend us your smocks, ye damsels, ev'ry night!   (ll. 103–8)

The word 'subdu'd' invests this simple laundry arrangement with the air of a rakish conquest, and a similar coy eroticism runs throughout the poem. Salisbury's three boarding-schools 'well stock'd with misses' ensure that these 'knights errant' do not 'starve for want of kisses'. But the chief erotic thrills come from a kind of passive tactile fetishism; the stimulating sensation of sleeping in a country-girl's smock; the excitment of watching her fingers rub the soap into a lather; the delicious intimacy of being shaved by a female barber:

> Smooth o'er our chin her easy fingers move,
> Soft as when Venus strok'd the beard of Jove.   (ll .113–14)

With his regal plural ('our chin') and Jove-like pose, Gay, attended at his toilette by this gold-bedecked female servant, leaves behind the world of courtiers' antechambers and ascends, in his fantasy, to the status of a god.

The poem is full of charming informal details; Gay's own unskilful attempts to draw his companions sprawled out asleep and snoring in elbow-chairs; their Bridport landlord's theft of a coat of arms from a passing hearse to adorn his hall; the rain cascading from their hat-brims. Also, like any good travel-guide, Gay offers details of the hospitality *en route*. At Hartley Wintney their jovial host keeps a good cellar; Stockbridge offers a pleasant lunch of locally caught trout and rich metheglin wine; while their thieving Bridport landlord dresses a lobster almost as well as Burlington's own chef. The poem concludes with a tilt at a familiar literary target, Sir Richard Blackmore. Spying some doggerel verses on an inn sign, Gay hints that the Whig Laureate may have missed his true vocation.

> How rhyme would flourish, did each son of fame
> Know his own genius, and direct his flame!   (ll. 127–8)

The *Epistle to Burlington* is an accomplished literary exercise.[46] However, like *Trivia*, which it closely resembles, the poem hovers uncertainly between sophisticated wit and deferential naïvety. Leaving his new adopted 'home' at Burlington House for his 'happy native land', Gay is once again uncertain about his loyalties. He is careful in this poem never to undercut his own self-portrait with farcical mishaps. He does not fall from his horse, but rather is a 'knight errant', a pseudo-Jove, even venturing into the lists against Sir Richard Steele and Sir Richard Blackmore.[47] But the pose adopted in his simultaneous 'horse' letter to the Blounts is altogether more self-deprecating, making fun of these quasi-seigneurial pretensions.[48] Here it is Gay, not the landlord, who is fat, and the horse jogs on 'a good hard trot the better to reduce him into shape at his return to London'. While Gay, in the *Epistle*, enjoys the pleasures of the table, the horse travels on 'very melancholy, for what horse could do otherways, when he saw such delicate cocks of hay lie spoiling on ev'ry side of him?' And while Gay enjoys the kisses of Salisbury schoolgirls, the horse endures a far more tantalizing fate:

the last day I travell'd in company with a very beautiful dappled mare, which made me more than ever regret the melancholy circumstances of a gentleman that I often heard you talk of, (I think they call him Nicolini) and myself.

Nicolini, the Italian opera star, and another of Burlington's favourites, was a castrato, implying that the horse is a gelding. But why should Gay choose to assume the perspective of a castrated beast of burden? The horse's impotent voyeurism provides an intriguing counterpoint to Gay's hints of rakishness in the *Epistle*. Here, the horse describes one of his master's amorous encounters.

One day he lighted from me to kiss a damsel by the wayside, her lips were like a scarlet poppy, her complexion was fair as the daisy, her eyes black as the sloe, and her cheeks shining like the brass bosses of a new bridle, her

---

[46] Blackmore had recently attacked Swift in a volume of essays, which may have provoked Gay's retaliation here.

[47] Sutherland describes the poem as 'a minor triumph of the politely familiar mode'; see James Sutherland, 'John Gay', in *Pope and his Contemporaries* (Oxford, 1949), 212.

[48] This 'horse' letter, which is found among the Blount papers at Mapledurham House, was first transcribed and printed (with some errors) by Maynard Mack in *Scriblerian*, 11/1 (Autumn 1978), 1–3. The idea may have been partly suggested by the speech of Achilles's horse at the end of *Iliad*, 19. The following summer (Sept. 1717) Pope told Edward Blount he was 'very well prepared to translate with belief and reverence the speech of Achilles's horse' (Pope, *Corr* i. 425).

breath was as sweet as a cow's, for you must know that I once kiss'd one by
mistake in the dark. In the struggle her straw hat fell off, which, being at
that time very hungry, and having nothing else to do, I happen'd unluckily
to eat up. I saw my master give her half a guinea which I suppose was to
make her amends.

There are echoes here of *The Shepherd's Week*, where Cuddy
assures Lobbin Clout that the sweetness of Buxoma's breath 'far
excell'd the breathing cows' ('Monday', l. 82). And, in his 'struggle'
with the country damsel, offering her money 'to make her amends',
Gay seems to imitate the behaviour of the lecherous squire in
'Wednesday'. But these are hardly flattering comparisons, and in
making them Gay seems to mock his own pseudo-patrician pretensions. In 'Wednesday' he adopts the voice of the victim, Sparabella;
in this letter, the voice of an impotent voyeur, the horse. What he
never assumes is the voice of the rake himself. The little comic
detail of eating the girl's hat is a revealing touch. In his own
innocent way the horse adds to and accomplishes the girl's 'ruin'
since the loss of her hat is the only visible evidence of her seduction.
Yet, deprived of hay, and sexually impotent, his appetite is natural
enough, as is his naïve assumption that the half-guinea is to pay for
the hat. It is tempting to speculate that Gay himself, a social
inferior, who frequently mocked his own obesity and whose poems
are filled with sensuous details of homely and exotic foods, had
grown similarly accustomed to sublimating sexual tastes which were,
for whatever reason, unsatisfied. Or he may have felt that, like
Nicolini, he had been emasculated by the need to produce the
required sweetness of voice of a courtier-poet.

The *Epistle* concludes with praise for his 'happy native land' but
the sentiments here are entirely formulaic, and are anyway preceded
by Gay's gibe at Blackmore, designed to cause excitement in literary
London. Pope told Jervas, 'Gay . . . has broke forth in a courageous
couplet or two upon Sir Richard Bl——. He has printed it with his
name to it, and bravely assigns no other reason, than that the said
Sir Richard had abused Dr. Swift.'[49] There is something characteristically patronizing about Pope's repeated emphasis on Gay's 'brav-
ery' and 'courage'. It was exactly this role, as a literary aide-de-
camp, that the loyal work-horse Gay was accustomed to perform.
Even the 'horse' letter itself was a form of vicarious gallantry,

[49] Pope, *Corr.* i. 371.

flattering the Blount sisters on Pope's behalf. The horse declares that his highest ambition was 'the honour of drawing your ladyships' [coach]'. For Gay the uncertainty still persisted, whether to aspire to the cavalier role of a literary knight, or accept the humble status of an amiable hack.

Early in 1715 Pope and Gay became acquainted with Lady Mary Wortley Montagu, the most celebrated and outspoken of the female wits. Now 26, Lady Mary's early life had been the stuff of romance. The daughter of an influential Whig politician, she had, while still only a child, been elected the reigning beauty of the year by members of the Kit-Cat Club. On that occasion 'she went from the lap of one poet, or patriot, or statesman, to the arms of another, was feasted with sweetmeats, overwhelmed with caresses, and, what perhaps already pleased her better than either, heard her wit and beauty loudly extolled on every side'.[50] At 23 she had eloped with Edward Wortley Montagu, another Whig politician, after a clandestine courtship of intrigues, stratagems, and parental threats that rivalled anything in fiction. Years later, living in lonely retirement in Italy, she remarked of Richardson's *Clarissa* that the first two volumes 'touched me, as being very resembling to my maiden days'.[51] But, as her modern biographer notes, 'the aftermath of her elopement did not match Clarissa's. Wortley was not Lovelace; he lacked his charms as well as his vices.'[52] By 1715 the couple had installed themselves in Duke Street on the east side of St. James's Park, where they lived in a state of genteel estrangement. Wortley busied himself with the pursuit of high political office, while Lady Mary entertained a salon of wits, painters, and poets.

Gay had recently begun composing a series of 'town eclogues', the first of which was inspired by Swift's suggestion for a Quaker pastoral.[53] *The Espousal: A Sober Eclogue, between two of the People called Quakers* pokes fun at the outward rituals of this pious sect. Tabitha, a Quaker maid, upbraids her sweetheart Caleb, a recent convert to the sect, for former vanities when, 'beguil'd by Popish shows'

---

[50] Letter to Edward Wortley Montagu, 9 Apr. 1711; Wortley MSS, i. 186; Halsband (1961), 4.

[51] Letter to Lady Bute, 22 Sept. 1755, Wortley MSS, ii. 285.

[52] Halsband (1961), 28.

[53] *The Espousal* also has some affinities with D'Urfey's 'Quaker's Song' (*Wit and Mirth* (6 vols., 1719–20), v. 105–6) and with Denham's 'News from Colchester', to which Gay had alluded in 'Saturday' of *The Shepherd's Week*.

he had doted 'on ribbons, flounces, furbelows'. He, eagerly confessing 'the frailties of my youthful days', insists that now it is nature only, not vanity, that guides his passion.

> Beloved, see how all things follow love,
> Lamb fondleth lamb, and dove disports with dove.   (ll. 7–8)

But for Tabitha, nature itself is potentially whorish, offering gaudy emblems of Man's fallen state; macaws (mockaws) appear 'all deck'd in scarlet pride'; even the rainbow's 'tawdry dyes' are a symbol of falshood. The poem's ironic charm comes from the localization of nature's temptations as a secret Eden planted in the sect's own backyard; Caleb describes peaches from Newington 'painted' by the sun and lips red as Kentish cherries. For both of them, sinfulness is largely a matter of satin and soft furnishings. Tabitha scorns to 'be drest | In flaring di'monds and a scarlet vest' (ll. 75–6), while Caleb shuns lords 'Whose couches creak with whoredom's sinful shame, | Whose velvet chairs are with adult'ry lame' (ll. 93–4).

On one Duke Street visit Gay brought with him a new satiric 'town eclogue' *The Toilette*. Intrigued, Lady Mary suggested a few extra lines, and began drafting some 'town eclogues' of her own. Throughout the autumn she, Pope, and Gay collaborated on a trio of similar poems, in which identifiable London figures were ridiculed under a pseudo-Virgilian fancy-dress. For several months these poems were handed round in manuscript for the amusement of like-minded friends. But before long copies were circulating more widely and had acquired a certain notoriety since Montagu's satires, unlike Gay's, specialized in scandal. Montagu subsequently made clear her contempt for much of the Hanoverian court. The King's character, she wrote, could be 'comprised in a very few words':

In private life he would have been called an honest blockhead; and Fortune, that made him a king, added nothing to his happiness, only prejudiced his honesty, and shortened his days ... He could speak no English, and was past the age of learning it. Our customs and laws were all mysteries to him, which he neither tried to understand, nor was capable of understanding if he had endeavoured it.

She was even more disparaging about the ladies of the court. The King's mistress, Mlle Schulenberg, she declared, was 'duller than himself, and consequently did not find out that he was so'; but Montagu's sharpest comments were reserved for the Princess Caroline. The Princess's chief quality, she wrote, was 'a low cunning, which gave her an inclination to cheat all the people she conversed with'. But even in this she lacked finesse, 'not having understanding enough to observe that falsehood in conversation, like red on the face, should be used very seldom and very sparingly, or they destroy that interest and beauty which they are designed to heighten'.[54] Montagu's mock-eclogue *The Drawing-Room* included a portrait of the Princess 'learn'd in all the courtly arts | To cheat our hopes, and yet to gain our hearts'. In December Lady Mary suffered a serious attack of smallpox which left her face badly pitted. 'Pitted but not pitied' was the smart remark among those who had already felt the sharpness of her tongue. A few weeks later Lady Loudoun reported:

Lady Mary is now very well. I do not think she ever was in danger, but the town said she would die two days together, upon which a friend of hers (I do not know who it was) showed a poem she had entrusted them with upon the Court. I have not yet seen it, but I'm told it is very pretty and not a little wicked. I'm promised it in a day or two. The Princess has seen it. Poor Lady Mary will not know how to come to Court again. This would put a body with a good assurance out of countenance. How will her modesty go through with it?[55]

James Brydges, who found the poem 'very entertaining', sent copies of it to friends, adding that it would surely wreck her husband's hopes of political advancement. Inevitably, copies of all three ec-logues soon fell into the hands of the pirate publisher Edmund Curll. In March 1716 he brought them out in a volume of *Court Poems* with a coy preface teasing readers as to their authorship. At St. James's Coffee-House, he asserted, 'they were attributed . . . to be the productions of a lady of quality' (i.e. Montagu); at Button's 'the poetical jury there brought in a different verdict; and the foreman strenuously insisted upon it that Mr. Gay was the man'; but 'a gentleman of distinguished merit who lives not far from Chelsea' (i.e. Addison) pronounced them to be the work of 'the judicious translator of Homer [i.e. Pope]'. Pope immediately retali-ated. Meeting Curll at Lintot's shop he offered him what purported to be a conciliatory glass of sack, into which he had slipped a violent emetic. As he remarked coolly to Caryll, 'I contrived to save a fellow a beating by giving him a vomit.'[56] Pope took evident pleasure in

[54] 'Account of the Court of George I', in *Essays and Poems and 'Simplicity, a Comedy'*, ed. R. Halsband and I. Grundy (Oxford, 1993), 83–94.

[55] Lady Loudoun, 3 Jan. 1716; see George Sherburn, *The Early Career of Alexander Pope* (Oxford, 1934), 208 n.; and Halsband (1961), 52.

[56] Pope, *Corr.* i. 339.

writing up the incident in a Grub Street pamphlet *A Full and True Account of a Horrid and Barbarous Revenge by Poison, on the Body of Mr. Edm. Curll*, dwelling at some length on the anatomical consequences of the vomit. But Curll was a dangerous adversary and Pope's satisfaction was short-lived. Throughout the following spring and early summer, while Jacobite rebels were tried and executed, Curll kept up a constant sniping attack on Pope, insinuating that he harboured Jacobite sympathies and stigmatizing his Homer as a covert piece of Catholic propaganda. In May Curll published a pirate version of Pope's facetious scatological lampoon of Mr John Moore, 'Author of the celebrated Worm Powder', describing it as an obscene heresy.[57] In June he published Pope's mildly bawdy parody of Sternhold's version of the First Psalm, which he denounced as a 'lewd, prophane, uncleanly' blasphemy. But Curll's most stinging retaliation came in two savage pamphlet attacks. *The Catholic Poet* vilified 'This Papish Dog . . . [who] has translated HOMER for the Use of the PRETENDER', while *A True Character of Mr. Pope*, by Dennis, delivered a brutal assault on Pope's works, character, and physical disability:

the deformity of this libeller, is visible, present, lasting, unalterable, and peculiar to himself. 'Tis the mark of God and Nature upon him, to give us warning that we should hold no society with him, as a creature not of our original, nor of our species.[58]

All this, and much more, Pope had brought on himself by his schoolboyish prank against Curll. Yet in fact Pope himself had had little part in composing the offending eclogues. Two of the poems, *The Bassett-Table* and *The Drawing-Room*, were written almost entirely by Lady Mary, while, as Pope told Spence, '"Lydia" [*The Toilette*] is almost wholly Gay's; and is published as such in his works.'[59] Pope's act of revenge, which became an exercise in self-martyrdom, was thus undertaken in a misguided spirit of chivalry. Already indulging amorous fantasies about Lady Mary, it gratified

[57] Gay may have had a hand in composing this verse lampoon. See his letter to Parnell (*Letters*, 28–31), first described and dated by C. J. Rawson in *Review of English Studies*, NS 10 (1959), 380–3.

[58] 'A True Character of Mr Pope', included in *Pamphlet Attacks on Alexander Pope, 1711–1744*, ed. J. V. Guerinot (London, 1969), 40–5.

[59] Spence, i. 104.

his fantasy self-image to act as her champion in this affair, administering a physical rebuff to her tormentor and suffering wounds on her behalf which only added to the gallantry of his gesture. But the chief loser in this affair was Gay, for whom the publication of such scandalous private verses was a disaster. Years later, in *The Curliad*, Curll reported that Pope's alleged reason for retaliation had been a concern that 'Mr. Gay's interest at Court, would be greatly hurt by publishing these pieces'. Yet it is difficult to see how such a visceral act of reprisal could be expected to retrieve Gay's fortunes. Gay found himself an innocent third party in a dispute, fought allegedly on his behalf, but in which he became the principal victim. His own eclogue, *The Toilette*, was an entirely inoffensive piece, a deft and subtle poem of gentle ironies, containing nothing scandalous or subversive. In it Lydia, a former society beauty, now past her prime, moons in her dressing-table mirror and laments her lost youth. Instead of beaux and admirers she is surrounded by decorative household pets.

> Around her wait Shocks, monkeys and mockaws,
> To fill the place of fops, and perjur'd beaux;
> In these she views the mimickry of man,
> And smiles when grinning Pug gallants her fan.   (ll. 9–12)

Miniaturizing the ritual displays of social life into this kind of domestic menagerie is one of Gay's favourite techniques. His imagination has a natural tendency to focus on some modish detail, an oriental fan or pet parakeet, and transform it from a mere accessory into a metaphor for the world it adorns. Many details derive from Pope's *Rape of the Lock*; Lydia is a superannuated Belinda, and her pug, Shock, has the same name as Belinda's favourite lap-dog. Lydia's voice though has an authority which Belinda's lacks. Here she comments, with authentic asperity, on her husband's latest mistress:

> 'Tis true, this Chloe boasts the peach's bloom.
> But does her nearer whisper breathe perfume?
> I own her taper shape is form'd to please.
> Yet if you saw her unconfin'd by stays!   (ll. 33–6)

Her tone moves easily from derision to despair as she contemplates the emptiness of her days.

What shall I do? how spend the hateful day?
At chapel shall I wear the morn away?
Who there frequents at these unmodish hours,
But ancient matrons with their frizzled tow'rs,
And gray religious maids? my presence there
Amid that sober train would own despair;
Nor am I yet so old; nor is my glance
As yet fixt wholly to devotion's trance.   (ll. 43–50)

Gay sympathetically conveys the restlessness of a personality, unhappy, unregarded, and displaced in a society where religion is the
last refuge of the *démodé*. When Lydia resolves to cheer herself up
with a shopping expedition she returns to the dressmakers' shops
'through all the Change' where Gay first learnt to observe the
loneliness of such lives. The sudden fluctuations of Lydia's moods
from self-pity to satire and from misery to revenge are not offered,
as in Pope's *Epistle to a Lady*, as stereotypical exempla of the
essential fickleness of women. Instead they suggest the fragility and
instability of a personality under stress. The poem ends with a
characteristic volte-face. Suddenly Lydia's maid appears with a
handsome new head-dress.

How charmingly you look! so bright! so fair!
'Tis to your eyes the head-dress owes its air.
Strait Lydia smil'd; the comb adjusts her locks,
And at the play-house Harry keeps her box.   (ll. 103–6)

The poem concludes all smiles as Lydia resumes her place in the
gallery of social stereotypes. Yet the disturbance at the heart of the
poem remains. This is not happiness, but merely a return to the
merry-go-round of human monkeys and mockaws. No one would
claim that *The Toilette* is a profound poem. Its tone is light and
ironic, and its satire never violates the polite style of *vers de société*.
Yet, compared with *Araminta*, written three years earlier, it shows
considerable poetic development. The style and setting of both
poems are practically identical. Araminta denounces her rival Delia
whose 'rich stays her taper shape confine' (l. 18), just as Lydia rails
at Chloe. Both women complain of the faithlessness of their former
lover. Yet while Araminta always remains a literary stereotype,
Lydia becomes a character. Two other 'town eclogues' written at
this time confirm Gay's fascination with the emptiness of female

lives reduced to a set of ritualized motifs. Written in dialogue form, *The Tea-Table* and *The Funeral* are like miniaturized comedies of manners. In *The Tea-Table*, Doris and Melanthe exchange scandalous gossip, while in the distance St. James's bell tolls for noon day prayers. In *The Funeral* the widowed Sabina lies pensive 'on the couch of state', mourning her dead husband. *The Tea-Table* specializes in elegant innuendo, as Doris and Melanthe dissect the morals of their friends. Laura's reputation for Christian self-sacrifice is confirmed by her having taken her footman as a secret lover.

> Her soul to gen'rous acts was still inclin'd;
> What shows more virtue than an humble mind?   (ll. 64–5)

Sylvia's charitable acts are on an even more generous scale.

> Her favours Sylvia shares among mankind,
> Such gen'rous love should never be confin'd.   (ll. 91–2)

The two ladies continue with such casual backbiting until Laura and Sylvia arrive, when, naturally, all four profess themselves the best of friends.

Reading through the light social satires which Gay wrote at this time, it is impossible not to acknowledge a certain sameness in language, attitude, and form. Similar motifs and phrases are repeated in poem after poem. Monkeys, lap-dogs, and parrots ('mockaws' or 'perroquets') constantly reappear as analogies for fops and beaux. *The Espousal* has 'mockaws, all deck'd in scarlet pride'; *The Toilette* has 'monkeys and mockaws'; The *Epistle to William Pulteney* describes Parisian high society in these anthropological terms:

> In Paris, there's a race of animals,
> (I've seen them at their Operas and Balls)
> They stand erect, they dance when-e'er they walk,
> Monkeys in action, perroquets in talk;
> They're crown'd with feathers, like the cockatoo . . .   (ll. 31–5)

The lap-dog Shock, borrowed from *The Rape of the Lock* to decorate *The Toilette*, reappears in *The Funeral*, where it appears alongside China jars and matador cards also taken from Pope's poem, and again in *An Elegy on a Lap-Dog*. Even fashion details are repeated. In *The Tea-Table* Doris comments on Phillis's 'gold-clock'd stockings', which in the *Epistle to William Pulteney* (ll. 172, 190) are twice mentioned as the height of Paris fashion. There is a formulaic quality in Gay's satire of this social world, reflecting his own ambivalence towards it. While hinting at the moral emptiness of the world of fashion he describes, he does so with a designer air, presenting his own poems as toys and trinkets, modish accessories to the world they mock.

EIGHT

The Confederates

He makes a foe who makes a jest.

(*Fables* (1727), XLVI)

WHEN Gay returned from the West Country that autumn he was relieved to find his friends at court had not deserted him. Whatever Princess Caroline may have thought of the *Court Eclogues*, her maids of honour were evidently highly amused by them and soon regarded Gay as something of a favourite. In December Pope reported that Gay 'dines daily with the maids of honour', an intimacy that was to prove extremely timely.[1] Other evenings were spent in less convivial company. Pope describes a dinner with a gluttonous 'old beauty', probably Gay's former employer the Duchess of Monmouth.

She appeared at the table like a death's head enamelled. The Egyptians, you know, had such things at their entertainments; but do you think they painted and patched them? However the last of these objections was soon removed; for the lady had so violent an appetite for a salmon, that she quickly eat all the patches off her face. She divided the fish into three parts; not equal, God knows; for she helped Gay to the head, me to the middle, and making the rest much the largest part took it herself and cried very naively, 'I'll be content with my own tail'.[2]

In November a new plague hit London. Worse than the pestilence of 1665 or the Great Fire of 1666, this latest epidemic was even more contagious than the recent plague of playhouse obscenity which had, allegedly, provoked 'infants [to] disfigure the walls of holy temples with exhorbitant representations of the members of

---

[1] Pope, *Corr.* i. 379.
[2] Ibid., 380.

generation.' What was this dreadful visitation? 'The woeful practice of PUNNING'. So wrote 'James Baker', the pseudonymous author of *God's Revenge against Punning*, and almost certainly the latest alias of the Scriblerian triumvirate, Pope, Arbuthnot, and Gay.[3] 'James Baker' was sufficiently familiar with the details of Gay's recent trip to Devon to include his equestrian misadventures as a telling instance of providence's revenge against punsters. He also attacked Eustace Budgell, who, working under Addison's instructions in Ireland, continued to intercept Swift's mail. 'Eustace, Esq.,' he pronounced, 'for the murder of much of the King's English in Ireland, is quite depriv'd of his reason.'[4]

The epidemic of which 'James Baker' complained had been predicted five years earlier by Addison. 'I do very much apprehend', he intoned sadly, 'that our posterity will in a few years degenerate into a race of punsters.'[5] At court the plague raged fiercely, especially among the Princess of Wales's entourage. At Leicester House, Chesterfield reported:

Puns are extremely in vogue, and the licence very great. The variation of three or four letters in a word breaks no squares, in so much that an indifferent punster may make a very good figure in the best companies.[6]

The Scriblerians, who devoted a whole chapter of *The Memoirs of Martinus Scriblerus* to Crambe's virtuoso display of the art, all caught the punning bug,[7] but Dennis was predictably immune: 'He

---

[3] Ibid. 379. Authorship of *God's Revenge against Punning* is attributed to Gay by Irving (pp. 144–5) and to Pope by Ault. 'James Baker' was the name both of a well-known gambler, and of the publisher of the *White-Hall* and *St James's Journals*. (See G. A. Aitken, 'Pamphlets by John Gay', *Athenaeum*, 49/321 (7 Sept. 1889); George Sherburn, *The Early Career of Alexander Pope* (Oxford, 1934) 183.) For discussion of Gay's possible authorship of 'James Baker' works see n. 54 below.

[4] The title of this lampoon parodied John Reynold's evangelical best seller *The Triumph of God's Revenge against the Crying and Execrable Sin of Murther*, though its subject-matter is entirely secular and social. Reynold's classic work, which had reached its sixth edition in 1679, was still extending its influence on Fielding as late as 1752. See Fielding's work *Examples of the Interposition of Providence in the Detection and Punishment of Murder* (1752), in *An Enquiry into the Causes of the Late Increase of Robbers, and Related Writings*, ed. Malvin R. Zirker, Wesleyan Edition of the Works of Henry Fielding (Oxford, 1988), 175–217. A sequel work, God's *Revenge against the Crying and Execrable Sin of Adultery*, filled with yet more lurid examples, had been published in 1708.

[5] *The Spectator*, ed. D. F. Bond (5 vols., Oxford, 1965), i. 259–63; 61 (10 May 1711).

[6] W. H. Wilkins, *Caroline the Illustrious, Queen-Consort of George II* (London, 1901), i. 289.

[7] Together Swift and Sheridan produced *Ars punica, sive flos linguarum: The Art of Punning, or the Flower of Languages . . . in Thirty-Four Rules*, by Tom Pun-sibi (1719).

that would pun', he solemnly pronounced, 'would pick a pocket.'[8] Shortly after *God's Revenge* came the reply, *An Heroi-Comical Epistle from a Certain Doctor to a Certain Gentlewoman, in Defence of the Most Ancient Art of Punning.* This six-page verse epistle, almost certainly the work of Arbuthnot, extended the original joke into a satire on the government's mania for detecting cryptic Jacobite codes in the most innocuous forms of wit.[9]

> Dear Nanny, all the world are running
> Stark-mad against our vein of punning;
> But I regard not their James Baker,
> So much as barking dog or Quaker; . . .
> But, dearest Nann, I smell the bottom
> Of all our anti-punsters (rot'em;)
> It is a Papist-Jesuit plot,
> By Tory Jacobites begot . . .

Whatever encouragement the maids of honour gave him to believe that a court place might still be possible, Gay was careful to provide himself with an alternative means of support. Following the pattern of recent years he devoted most of the autumn to writing, to ensure that he had a new work ready for the New Year. In December, Pope told Martha Blount:

Gay is well at court and more in the way of being served than ever. However, not to trust too much to hopes, he will have a play acted in four or five weeks, which we have driven a bargain for.[10]

Pope's wording here is significant. He makes it clear that this play, *Three Hours after Marriage*, was essentially Gay's, but that he had lent a helping hand in its promotion. Pope's phenomenal success in marketing his *Iliad* translation had rightly earned him something of a reputation for financial acumen among his friends, and Gay no doubt appreciated his assistance in negotiating with the theatre management at Drury Lane.

Three Hours after Marriage is one of those works whose backstage dramas are almost as celebrated as the play itself. Ten days before it opened, on 16 January 1717, a rumour was already circulating that

---

[8] Note to *Dunciad* (1729), i. 61.
[9] For the authorship of this *Epistle* see *The Prose Works of Alexander Pope*, ed. Norman Ault (Oxford 1936), i, pp. cx–cxiv, and Irving, 145–6.
[10] Pope, *Corr.* i. 379.

'Pope is coming out with a play in which every one of our modern poets are ridiculed'.[11] Expectations like these provoked an instinct for retaliation and inspired a confederacy of the dunces to damn the play at birth. Between January and March at least eight pamphlets appeared attacking its alleged obscenity and vindictiveness. Although highly prejudiced, these offer a fascinating glimpse of Gay's public image and reputation at the time.[12] Most pamphlets adopted the familiar tactic of treating Gay's name on the title-page as a mere subterfuge by Pope. In his verse satire *The Confederates*, J. D. Breval (alias 'Joseph Gay') presented Pope gloating alone in a room at the Rose tavern in Covent Garden.

> POPE. This very night, with modern strokes of wit,
> I charm the boxes, and divert the pit;
> Safe from the cudgel, stand secure of praise;
> Mine is the credit, be the danger Gay's.[13]

Similary 'E. Parker, Philomath', in the prologue to his *Complete Key to . . . Three Hours after Marriage*, asserted:

> The play is damn'd, and Gay would fain evade
> it,
> He cries 'Damn Pope and Arbuthnot who made
> it.'[14]

Such assertions seemed justified by Gay's own admission in the advertisement to the play: 'I must farther own the assistance I have received in this piece from two of my friends', he wrote, 'who, tho' they will not allow me the honour of having their names joined with mine, cannot deprive me of the pleasure of making this acknowledgment.' This guileless statement was seized on by Pope's enemies, who presented Gay as Pope's oafish underling. In the first scene of

[11] Burnett to Duckett, 6 Jan. 1717; *Letters of Thomas Burnet to George Duckett, 1712–1722* ed. D. Nichol Smith (Roxburghe Club, 1914), 119–20.

[12] These pamphlets include *The Drury Lane Monster; A Satyr on the Present Times; A Complete Key to . . . Three Hours after Marriage; The Weekly Journal; A Letter to Mr Gay; Palaemon to Celia, at Bath; The Confederates*; and an essay in Sir Richard Blackmore's *Essays on Several Subjects* (1717). For further details of these pamphlets see George Sherburn's article 'The Fortunes and Misfortunes of *Three Hours after Marriage*', *Modern Philology*, 24 (1926), 91–109.

[13] *The Confederates*, 2.

[14] E. Parker, 'Philomath', *A Complete Key to the New Farce, Call'd Three Hours after Marriage* (1717), title-page.

The Confederates Breval has Pope disparage Arbuthnot's contributions to the play.

> Know, Caledonian, thine's a simple part,
> Scarce anything but some quack-terms of art,
> Hard words and quibbles; but 'tis I that sting,
> And on the stage th'Aegyptian lovers bring;
> Miss Phoebe, Plotwell, Townley, all are mine,
> And Sir Tremendous:—Fossile's only thine.

Written in a knockabout cartoon-style, *The Confederates* delights in imagining violent backstage rows between Pope and his hapless henchman. Arbuthnot, absurdly represented as a burly Highland chieftain with his kilt, claymore, and targe, threatens to beat Pope's brains out, cursing him in a thick Glasgow accent as a 'vain pigmy'. Terrified, the diminutive Pope retracts his abusive comments.

> POPE. I was to blame; forgive me, gentle Scot,
> Why should Pope differ with his Arbuthnot?
> Thoughtful and anxious for our first essay,
> I lost my reason and took thee for Gay . . .[15]

Throughout Breval's farce, Gay himself is depicted as a lumbering stage buffoon. His entrance to the Green Room is heralded by the actress Mrs Oldfield with these words: 'But hark! Who's entering here? I'll run away; | For by the clumsy tread it should be Gay.' All the pamphlets agree in denouncing *Three Hours after Marriage* as an artistic and commercial failure, a play so malicious and obscene that the actors themselves mutinied against performing it. Yet, as Sherburn has demonstrated, such confident pronouncements on its 'failure' suggest a premeditated campaign, rather than impartial judgement. In fact *Three Hours* played to packed houses for seven nights together, which was the largest number of consecutive performances at Drury Lane that season. And, as Fuller comments, 'there is every reason to believe that the play would have had earlier and more frequent revivals if it had not been for the quarrel with Cibber, or possible pressure put upon Steele or the actor managers'.[16] Even the attacks on *Three Hours* hint at its crowd-pleasing appeal. *The*

---

[15] *The Confederates*, 6.
[16] Sherburn, 'Fortunes and Misfortunes', 97–109; Fuller, i. 25. Winton suggests that

Drury Lane Monster, a broadside composed apparently the day before the play was published, describes it as 'for five days together the talk of the town'; and 'Timothy Drub', the pseudonymous author of *A Letter to Mr John Gay*, berates the Drury Lane audiences for 'suffering their judgement to be over-ruled' by a vulgar taste for such a 'low, insipid performance'.[17] In April a 'new dramatic entertainment' at Lincoln's Inn Fields 'of dancing, in grotesque characters' entitled *The Jealous Doctor; or, The Intriguing Dame* stole all its main characters (Fossile, Townley, Plotwell, Underplot, and Ptisan) from Gay's play, attesting to their continuing box-office appeal.[18]

Three Hours after Marriage is a theatrical oddity; an episodic and allusive satire whose loose dramatic structure is underlined by Gay's apparent indecision whether it should be performed in three acts or five.[19] The plot, such as it is, involves the marriage of an antiquarian physician, Dr Fossile (based on Arbuthnot's old adversary Dr John Woodward), to a coquettish and promiscuous bride, Mrs Townley. Throughout the action of the play, Townley is pursued by two rakish admirers, the actors Plotwell and Underplot, disguised in increasingly ludicrous costumes as quack doctors, virtuosi, a crocodile, and an Egyptian mummy. Other characters include Fossile's niece, the mad poetess Phoebe Clinket, and the irascible critic 'Sir Tremendous', a caricature of Dennis. Gay makes little attempt to conceal the play's eccentric structure. The appearance of Sir Tremendous in Act I is an isolated satiric cameo with little dramatic relevance to the plot; similarly, the implausible conclusion, which

Steele, a friend of Woodward and governor of Drury Lane, may have been partly responsible for the play's early closure. See Winton, 54.

[17] *The Drury Lane Monster* was advertised in the *Post Boy* as published 22 Jan. 1717.

[18] This entertainment had at least six performances, advertised in the *Daily Courant* for 29 Apr.; 1, 3, 4, 7, 21 May.

[19] In the advertisement to the play Gay writes: 'It may be necessary to acquaint the reader that this play is printed exactly as it is acted; for, tho' the players in compliance with the taste of the town, broke it into five parts in the representation; yet as the action pauses, and the stage is left vacant but three times, so it properly consists but of three acts, like the Spanish comedies.' Fuller prints the three-act version of the play and defends his decision (i. 436–7); John Harrington Smith, reprinting a five-act version of the play first published in *A Supplement to the Works of Alexander Pope, Esq.* (Dublin, 1758) for the Augustan Reprint Society (Los Angeles, 1961), argued that this derived from 'an authentic acting MS of the play' (p. 9). In my own edition of the play (World's Classics) I have followed Fuller in printing a three-act version, but with new scene divisions to help to make better dramatic sense of Gay's episodic structure.

leaves Fossile literally holding the baby, is contrived as a deliberate affront to any notion of dramatic *vraisemblance*. Yet such apparent structural incoherence is not the result of laziness, inadequacy, or the problems of collaborative composition; rather it represents a conscious, and characteristic, satiric ploy. *Three Hours after Marriage* continues the assault on dramatic conventions begun in *The Mohocks* and *The What D'Ye Call It*. In *A Letter to John Gay* 'Timothy Drub' insisted that Gay's 'design was to write the worst play that could be wrote', which is a negative way of acknowledging that Gay deliberately subverts all established notions of what a play should be. *Three Hours after Marriage* is composed according to Phoebe Clinket's *goût de travers*, a form of inspiration explained in the Scriblerians' own spoof poetic manifesto *The Art of Sinking in Poetry* (1728) as 'a most happy, uncommon, unaccountable way of thinking'. Based on a series of farce motifs and satiric conceits, it operates like a theatrical raree-show in which a series of comic freaks appear to perform their novelty routines. Hence any attempt to regularize the plot risks compromising its essential idiosyncrasy.[20] Gay, if not the inventor of theatrical surrealism (he borrowed many of his bizarre effects from Aristophanes and D'Urfey), was at least among its earliest practitioners, and *Three Hours after Marriage* is a play which benefits from productions which exploit, rather than exclude, its exuberant randomness. A glance at the dramatis personae reveals a list of characters, either 'real' or diguised, more appropriate to a Bedlam freak-show than to a drawing-room or bedroom comedy: a crackpot scientist, a mad poetess, a smouldering critic, an eccentric Polish professor, a quack doctor, an Egyptian mummy, a crocodile, an absent-minded judge, and a jolly Jack Tar. Most of these figures pop up and disappear with only the most marginal relevance to the plot. In radio terms the most obvious modern parallel might be with *The Goon Show*; theatrically its descendants include *One Way Pendulum* and *Ubu Roi*.

As a result of all the critical attention that the play received, we have an almost unparalleled, if highly unreliable, record of its performances. On the opening night the Drury Lane theatre was packed. One disappointed commentator 'could not find the least

[20] A recent BBC radio production, by Glyn Dearman in 1987, sought to clear away much of the clutter of satiric detail and turn the play into a conventional beaux' stratagem.

room; every door that was opened to me diffused more heat than a baker's oven'.[21] In *The Confederates* (scene i) Breval has Gay report to his collaborators on the first night audience:

> Betimes, the better to conceal my face,
> In th'eighteen-penny row I chose a place;
> Whence, unobserv'd, I might attend the play,
> And the loud critics of the pit survey.
> So vast a throng took up the spacious round,
> Scarce for a mouse, or you [to Pope], had room been found;
> Heroes and Templars here were mix'd with wits,
> There bawds and strumpets, with a group of cits;
> Rang'd in each box were seen th'angelic fair,
> Whose footmen had since two been posted there.
> Round me I gaz'd with wonder and delight,
> And wish'd that this had been the poet's night.
>
> ARBUTHNOT. It promis'd well
> GAY.   It did; but mark the end:
> What boots a crowd, unless that crowd's your friend?
> The prologue finish'd, in the Doctor came,
> And with him, hand in hand, th'intriguing dame.
> Silent awhile th'attentive many sat,
> The men were hush'd, the women ceas'd their chat.
> But soon a murmur in the pit began,
> And thence all round the theatre it ran;
> The noise increasing as along it mov'd,
> Grew loud at last, and to a hiss improv'd.
> Nor wit, nor humour could their rage appease,
> Clinket and Plotwell strove in vain to please;
> Each smutty phrase, and every cutting line,
> Was thrown away and lost, like pearls on swine.[22]

But according to the author of the 1758 *Key* to the play, first reactions to the play were far from universally hostile. The next morning, he reports:

I strolled to several coffee-houses, where I knew the wits and critics met like surgeons, to dissect the body of any new piece; but I found more opinions among them than there are sectaries in the world. So I resolved to

[21] Letter included with *Three Hours after Marriage* (Dublin, 1761), 210.
[22] *The Confederates*, 9.

venture a sweating the next evening and be my own judge.

He offers this account of the second night.

The play was acted like a ship tossed in a tempest; yet notwithstanding, through those clouds of confusion and uproar, I, as one of the neutral powers, could discover a great many passages that gave me much satisfaction; and while the inimitable Oldfield was speaking the epilogue . . . the storm subsided—And to speak poetically, my friend—'The billows seem'd to slumber on the shore'. But when the play was given out for the third night, (tho' the benefit of the author was not mentioned) the roar burst out again, like sudden thunder from two meeting clouds; but I with pleasure observ'd, the roar of applause overcame and triumphed.[23]

Returning again the third night, the same reviewer 'saw the comedy performed to a numerous and polite audience with general applause'. As Fuller observes, 'the house may have been packed for the author's benefit' that night, or perhaps 'the critics felt they had already done their worst, and had retired to pen their keys and diatribes'.[24] On the fourth night, slapstick mishaps on-stage added to the general uproar. Penkethman, playing the part of Underplot, and disguised in a crocodile costume, 'boasting much in the beauty of his long tail', swung round so clumsily that he knocked Sarsnet (Mrs Hunt) flat on the stage, where 'she discovered more linen than other habiliments, and more skin and flesh than linen'. Shortly afterwards Penkethman, who was well known for his comic ad libs, further disrupted the performance by falling backwards into the Egyptian mummy's case where he became so firmly wedged that it took the stage carpenters half an hour to free him. The audience were apparently so delighted by all this knockabout that they called for a repetition the following night.[25] Penkethman's antics would seem to confirm that the main reason for the play's alleged 'failure' was less the concerted opposition of a critical faction than sabotage by the players themselves. Breval's *Confederates* alleges that the actresses Oldfield and Bicknell were so affronted by the hostile reception they received on the opening night that they refused to go on again without more money. Faced with this mutiny, Gay is at his wits' end, when suddenly help arrives in the form of a 'purse of

---

[23] Letter included with *Three Hours after Marriage* (1761), 210.
[24] Fuller, i. 27–8.
[25] 'Letter' (Dublin, 1761), 221–2. On Penkethman's fondness for ad libbing see Winton, 31.

gold' from his three female admirers, the maids of honour, Mary
Bellenden, Molly Lepell, and Miss Griffin. Parker in his *Complete Key*
even specifies the amount (400 guineas) that their purse of gold
contained.[26] In gratitude for such magnificent generosity Breval has
Pope promising to record the three ladies' names in a ballad. And, sure
enough, a fortnight after the play's first night Pope published his *Court
Ballad*, a gallant *jeu d'esprit* which pays handsome compliment to the
sprightly wit and independent opinions of the three court ladies.

> In truth by what I can discern,
>   Of courtiers from you three,
> Some wit you have and more may learn,
>   From court than Gay or me;
> Perhaps in time you'll leave high diet,
> And sup with us on mirth or quiet,
>   With a fa.

The story of this dramatic rescue by the maids of honour is one of the
traditional anecdotes of Gay's career, though its authenticity has
frequently been questioned.[27] If Gay did indeed receive a gift of 400
guineas (worth more than £10,000 in 1994 values), it would have
represented a huge increase to his income, since Lintot only paid him
£43 2s. 6d for the copyright to the play. But though Gay's friendship
with the maids of honour grew and blossomed at this time, his
continuing pleas of poverty hardly suggest the outlook of a man who
has enjoyed a windfall profit. Sadly this story of the purse of gold,
however attractive, must be treated with a certain scepticism.

Oldfield and Bicknell were not the only mutinous members of the
Drury Lane cast. Gay's most audacious satiric stroke in *Three*

---

[26] *Complete Key*, 50.

[27] Many scholars have questioned the story of the ladies' purse of gold, and the notion
that Pope's *Court Ballad* was intended as a tribute to their generosity. Sherburn, who
describes *The Confederates* as 'a well-fused mixture of prejudice and fact', writes:
'Breval's story is substantially found in Parker's *Key* where we are told that Gay
"modestly gives out that . . . the very Ladies of Honour raised him four hundred
guineas" because of the play's merits. Breval is sufficiently explicit with regard to their
names, which possibly he took from Pope's *Court Ballad* (published two weeks after
Three Hours was first acted), and which were Griffin, Bellenden and Lepell. The *Court
Ballad*, then, becomes a lively expression of avowed intimacy and of covert gratitude for
patronage to Gay when in difficulties' (pp. 101–3). Sherburn goes on to point out that Pope
recalled the incident in his *Sixth Epistle of the First Book of Horace Imitated by Mr Pope*
(1738), where he writes: 'His wealth brave Timon gloriously confounds; | Ask'd for a groat,
he gives a hundred pounds; | Or if three ladies like a luckless play, | Takes the whole

1. *John Gay* by Michael Dahl, *c.*1729.

2. *Alexander Pope* by Charles Jervas, *c.*1717.

Earl of Burlington

3. *Richard Boyle, 3rd Earl of Burlington* by Jonathan Richardson, *c.*1718.

4. *Lady Mary Wortley Montagu*, attributed to Jonathan Richardson, *c*.1725.

5a. *The Beggar's Opera*, by William Hogarth *c*.1729.

5b. *The Beggar's Opera III, xi*, by William Hogarth.

6a John Gay, *Fables* (1727); Fable X, *The Elephant and the Bookseller*;
plate designed by William Kent.

6b John Gay, *Fables* (1727); Fable XIV, *The Monkey who had seen the World*;
plate designed by William Kent.

7a John Gay, *Fables* (1727); Fable XXIV, *The Butterfly and the Snail*;
plate designed by William Kent.

7b John Gay, *Fables* (1727); Fable L, *The Hare and many Friends*;
plate designed by John Wootton.

H. Gravelot, inv. et delin.   G. Scotin Sculp.

Published Sep. 29. 1738. by J. & P. Knapton & J. Cox.

8. John Gay, *Fables* (1738); Fable X, *The Degenerate Bees*;
plate designed by Hubert François Gravelot.

Hours after Marriage was to ridicule the actor-manager Colley Cibber in the part of Plotwell, and then get Cibber to play the part himself. At first it seems that Cibber failed to realize he was the target of his own lines; but when he did, he was naturally indignant. He did not have long to wait before taking his revenge. On 7 February, a fortnight after *Three Hours after Marriage* had been withdrawn, he staged a revival of Buckingham's burlesque play *The Rehearsal*, 'which had lain some years dormant'. Cibber played the part of Bays, a role which customarily involved some ad-libbing on topical theatrical themes. This is his record of what followed.

I, Mr Bays, when the two kings of Brentford came from the clouds into the throne again, instead of what my part directed me to say, made use of these words, viz. 'Now, Sir, this revolution I had some thoughts of introducing by a quite different contrivance; but my design taking air, some of your sharp wits, I found, made use of it before me; otherwise I intended to have stolen one of them in, in the shape of a mummy, and t'other, in that of a crocodile'. Upon which . . . the audience by the roar of their applause

house upon the poet's day' ll. 85–8. 'This', Sherburn writes, 'can hardly be an allusion to anything except the "three ladies known full well" who liked the luckless play of *Three Hours after Marriage*' (p. 103). Fuller concedes that 'the gift is by no means impossible', but argues that 'the tradition . . . connecting the *Ballad* with the play was finally killed by Ault' (pp. 26–7). However, Ault's arguments (pp. 177–82) are far less conclusive than Fuller suggests. Ault merely states, accurately enough, that 'there is nothing in the poem to give the slightest colour to that suggestion'. Yet the absence of any specific reference to the play or the 'purse of gold' in the *Court Ballad* does not, *ipso facto*, disprove the theory that the poem was intended as a gesture of gratitude. Discretion may have led Pope to omit any explicit mention of the money, and the *Ballad* is full of more generalized expressions of obligation. Internal evidence proves that the *Court Ballad* was written between 12 Dec. 1716 and 19 Jan. 1717 (the final stanza contains the line 'God send the King safe landing' and the King actually landed back in England on 19 Jan.). Breval's account implies that the ladies' gift was made on 17 or 18 Jan., which would have provided the perfect occasion for Pope to pen this handsome tribute the following day. However, since both accounts of the ladies' gift, by Parker and Breval, were published *after* the appearance of the *Court Ballad* (published on 31 Jan.), it is not impossible that the *Ballad* was the inspiration for the story, rather than vice versa. (Parker's *Key* was advertised for sale on 2 Feb., but *The Confederates* was not published till 30 Mar.) Three weeks after its first publication, Pope's *Court Ballad* was incorporated into a small book, accompanied by six short epigrams, entitled *Epigrams, Occasion'd by an Invitation to Court*. The fifth of these reads: 'On Sunday at six, in the street that's call'd Gerrard | You may meet the two champions who are no Lord Sh[erra]rd.' It is clear that Breval seized on this epigram to lend authenticity to the invitation which he imagines the ladies sending along with their purse of gold. Breval's lines are these: 'Then pray accept this little purse of gold, | And let us be among your friends enroll'd. | You, and your Brethren, we'll be glad to see, | In street call'd Gerrard when we drink our tea.'

showed their proportionable contempt of the play they belonged to . . . Surely to have used the bare word *mummy* and *crocodile* was neither unjust nor unmannerly; where then was the crime of simply saying there had been two such things in a former play? But this, it seems, was so heinously taken by Mr Pope that, in the swelling of his heart, after the play was over, he came behind the scenes, with his lips pale and his voice trembling, to call me to account for the insult: And accordingly fell upon me with all the foul language that a wit out of his senses could be capable of . . . When he was almost choked with the foam of his passion, I was enough recovered from my amazement to make him (as near as I can remember) this reply, viz. 'Mr Pope—you are so particular a man, that I must be ashamed to return your language as I ought to do. But since you have attacked me in so monstrous a manner, this you may depend upon; that as long as the play continues to be acted, I will never fail to repeat the same words over and over again.'[28]

Cibber did not write this account until 1742, and it diverges in some details from contemporary reports of the same incident. Another witness offered this colourful version:

I don't know whether you heard, before you went out of town, that *The Rehearsal* was revived . . . Cibber interlarded it with several things in ridicule of the last play, upon which Pope went up to him and told him he was a rascal, and if he were able he would cane him; that his friend Gay was a proper fellow, and if he went on in his sauciness he might expect such a reception from him. The next night Gay came accordingly, and, treating him as Pope had done the night before, Cibber very fairly gave him a fillip on the nose, which made them both roar. The guards came and parted them and carried Gay away, and so ended this poetical scuffle.[29]

This story was quickly picked up and embellished by critics of *Three Hours* itself, though most commentators at least gave Gay the honour of emerging victorious from the backstage scuffle. 'Drub' described Gay as a 'boxing bard', summoned by Pope to give Cibber a thrashing, and Breval concluded *The Confederates* with 'A Congratulatory Poem, inscribed to Mr Gay on his valour and success behind Drury Lane scenes'. Whatever the precise details of this backstage brawl, it had grim consequences for Gay's career. In

---

[28] *A Letter from Mr Cibber to Mr Pope, Inquiring into the Motives that might Induce him in his Satirical Works to be so Frequently Fond of Mr Cibber's Name* (1742).

[29] Montagu Bacon to James Montagu; in *Mr Pope: By George Paston* (i.e. E. M. Symonds) (2 vols., London, 1909), i. 197.

thus recklessly antagonizing London's leading actor-manager, he could hardly have chosen a more certain way of sabotaging his own future prospects as a dramatist.

The sustained critical mauling which *Three Hours after Marriage* received, both at the time and since, has inevitably tarnished its reputation. The hysterical chorus of complaints against its alleged obscenity helped to ensure that revivals were few and far between.[30] Few now though would take exception to its harmless *double enten-dres* and bawdy innuendoes. At one point Clinket asks her uncle Fossile, 'How do the Platonics and Cartesians differ?' 'The Platonics', he replies, 'are for ideas; the Cartesians for matter and motion.' 'This', splutters Drub, 'is bringing the very *act* before our eyes, and speaking home to the very point of lewdness.' 'E. Parker, Philomath' objected to the same speech: 'This vile obscenity is called humour . . .' And Drub even claimed that the players themselves 'left out a considerable load of obscenity and profaneness, which tho' you were not ashamed to print, they had so much modesty as not to speak'.[31] Gay's immediate instinct was for revenge. Angered at the absurdly exaggerated outcries against his play's so-called 'obscenities', he set himself to write a satiric reply in the form of a 'Letter from a Lady in the City to a Lady in the Country'.

In it he quoted the passages which had been most exclaimed against, and opposed other passages to them from Addison's and Steele's plays. These were aggravated in the same manner that they had served his; and appeared worse. Had it been published, it would have made Mr Addison appear ridiculous, which he could bear as little as any man.[32]

Pope, though, who had already suffered enough from Gay's literary recklessness, was deeply unhappy at this further planned act of provocation, and 'prevailed on Gay not to print it'. Recounting this episode to Spence in 1738, six years after Gay's death, Pope told him: '[I] have the manuscript now by me,' proud of this further proof of his success in perpetuating his pupil's reputation for inoffensiveness.

[30] In fact the play was not revived until 1737, and was acted again in 1746 and at Bath in 1765. No edition of the play was published between 1807 and 1961: see Fuller i: 24, 72. Among those loudest in their protests at its alleged obscenity were Addison, Blackmore, Leonard Welsted, and Giles Jacob.

[31] *A Letter to John Gay*, 8; *Complete Key*, 50. Harrington Smith (*Three Hours after Marriage* (1961), 6) identifies a two-page quotation in 'Drub' from Jeremy Collier, and even suggests that 'Drub' might be Collier, the tireless reformer of the stage, himself.

[32] Spence, item 238; i. 104.

Protests against the play's supposedly malicious and vindictive satire were equally exaggerated. In choosing to ridicule Dennis (Sir Tremendous) and Woodward (Fossile), Gay selected well-known satiric targets less out of personal hostility than as a gesture of Scriblerian solidarity. Notoriously vain, ill-tempered, and belligerent, Woodward and Dennis had long been, and would long remain, among the favourite butts of contemporary satiric lampoons. Woodward, who reappears as Cornelius Scriblerus in the *Memoirs of Scriblerus*, was the perfect model of the mad scientist, with his dogmatic theories on a range of subjects, from fossils, vomits, and the 'biliose salts' to Greek and Roman antiquities.[33] But the Scriblerians were not alone in mocking a man whose intellectual arrogance, extravagant theories, and frequent feuds with fellow scientists made him a standing joke.

[Woodward] was extraordinarily rude, ill-tempered, arrogant, suspicious, jealous and combative. As a result, every stage of his career was marked by violent and disgraceful quarrels which . . . won him . . . Hooke's mantle as the most detested scientist of his generation.[34]

Arbuthnot's own feud with Woodward had begun some twenty years earlier in a geological dispute concerning Noah's flood. In his *Essay towards a Natural History of the Earth* (1695) Woodward argued that, at the time of the flood, the entire substance of the Earth had been dissolved, and subsequently resettled according to the specific gravity of its component elements. For Woodward (alias Fossile) the study of fossils was thus not merely an eccentric hobby, but a means of proving the authority of Genesis.[35] In his lighthearted *Examination of Dr Woodward's account of the Deluge* (1697) Arbuthnot poked fun at the many implausibilities of Woodward's hypothesis. Why, he asked, were 'shells, teeth and bones', the fossil remains upon which Woodward placed so much reliance, not dissolved when rocks were? More playfully, he enquired about the timing of the flood:

[33] *The Memoirs of Scriblerus* were not published till 1741, but were compiled over many years before that.

[34] *The Memoirs of Martinus Scriblerus*, ed. Charles Kerby-Miller (New York, 1966), 204. Among Woodward's most protracted feuds were those with Hans Sloane, Richard Mead, and John Freind.

[35] Parker, in his *Complete Key*, asserts that Gay hit upon the name after hearing that Woodward had 'enquired of two labourers whom he saw at work at Kensington gravel-pits, whether in their digging, they had discovered any fossils'.

Now the Deluge happening, according to the Doctor, in the month of May, few plants must have remained but such as were seeded at the beginning of that month, or the latter end of April . . . I believe the barley, after the waters were off, would have made better malt than seed corn; and Noah might have made merry with strong beer, rather than stayed so many years 'till vines grew up . . .[36]

In *Three Hours after Marriage*, Phoebe Clinket's play 'The Universal Deluge; or, the Tragedy of Deucalion and Pyrrha' continues this parody of Woodward's theory. Her stage directions include descriptions of fields 'over-flowed' with water and 'cattle and men swimming'. 'The tops of steeples rise above the flood', she declares, 'with men and women perching on their weather-cocks—' But Sir Tremendous interrupts her with a query surely inspired by Arbuthnot: 'Begging your pardon, . . . if stones were dissolved, as a late philosopher hath proved, how could steeples stand?'

In fact, Gay was notably restrained in his gibes at Woodward. Within months Woodward published *The State of Physic and Diseases*, which contained, *inter alia*, dire warnings against the noxious political influence of such pernicious beverages as tea and coffee. Woodward's new theory of 'vomition' led to violent public quarrels with his fellow physicians Richard Mead and John Freind and eventually to a street affray and duel. This latest controversy sparked off a spate of unsavoury lampoons devoted not to Woodward's theories, but to his alleged sexual proclivities. In one pamphlet, *The Life and Adventures of Don Bilioso de L'Estomac*, the hero, 'Don Bilioso' (alias Woodward), is described as 'a great lover of boys'; one chapter of his forthcoming treatise (a parody of Woodward's *The State of Physic and Diseases*) is outlined thus.

Chapter XV: How *Don Bilioso* gave a dose of opium to a troublesome bedfellow, and after he was asleep with what caution and humanity he attacked him behind and made an evacuation in his body.[37]

Another pamphlet, *An Account of the Sickness and Death of Dr W—*

---

[36] John Arbuthnot, 'Examination . . .', in *The Miscellaneous Works of the Late Dr Arbuthnot* (2 vols., Glasgow 1750–1), ii. 207.

[37] This parodies pp. 129–30 of *The State of Physic*, where Woodward prescribes the use of opium 'to overpower and subdue . . . the emotions of the bile and other vicious principles'. 'Every wise physician', Woodward goes on, 'that has due humanity, will not unnecessarily go to storm a distemper, and make an evacuation in a body that hath been so long harassed.'

dw—d, contains this obvious innuendo:

I should say something for the satisfaction of the ladies who will be inquisitive of what sex he died; the account of his dissection will inform them in this particular, and altho' from the softness of his voice something may have been suggested to his disadvantage in their esteem . . .[38]

Significantly, despite its alleged obscenity and vindictiveness, *Three Hours after Marriage* contains no insinuations of this kind. Although Gay's play seems to relish just about every other conceivable form of the *goût de travers*, it offers no hint at all of Woodward's sexual deviancy. Nor do the accounts of the play's performance suggest that Johnson acted the part in an effeminate manner. There are details of Penkethman's suggestive stage business as he boasts of the magnificent erection of his crocodile's tail, but no indication that Fossile's role involved camp or epicene gestures. Had the play really been as obscene as its enemies pretended, it would hardly have missed such an opportunity as this. But in fact, although subject to constant ridicule, Fossile retains a kind of comic dignity throughout and his eccentricities are treated with a certain compassion. In the play's denouement Fossile emerges as the victim, not the villain, of the piece, and his final soliloquy, cradling Clinket's illegitimate baby in his arms, is full of a rueful humanity.

FOSSILE. What must be, must be. [*Takes up the child*] Fossile, thou didst want posterity; here, behold, thou hast it. A wife thou didst not want; thou hast none. But thou art caressing a child that is not thy own. What then? A thousand and a thousand husbands are doing the same thing this very instant, and the knowledge of truth is desirable and makes thy case the better. What signifies whether a man beget his child or not? How ridiculous is the act itself, said the great emperor Antoninus! I now look upon myself as a Roman citizen. It is better that the father should adopt the child, than that the wife should adopt the father.

[38] Both *The Life and Opinions of Don Bilioso de L'Estomac* and *An account of the Sickness and Death of Dr W——dw——d* are included in Arbuthnot, *Works*, although the accuracy of these attributions has been seriously challenged by Aitken: See *The Life and Works of Dr John Arbuthnot*, ed. G. A. Aitken (Oxford, 1892). The name 'Don Bilioso' is chosen as a mock-Cervantic way of mocking Woodward's belief in the importance of the 'bilious salts' for maintaining a healthy body.

Undoubtedly Gay would have been aware of the rumours surrounding Woodward, but deliberately eschewed the kind of homophobic smear that others used against him. It may be too much to assume that Gay's avoidance of such an obvious source of satiric attack implies anything about his own sexual preferences. But it seems at least possible that, in portraying the homosexual Woodward as a proud foster parent, Gay may have touched upon a private fantasy of his own.

Phoebe Clinket, the mad poetess, has likewise frequently been cited as a malicious slur on one or more female writers of the day. Parker confidently identifies her as a caricature of the Countess of Winchilsea, while others have suggested Susannah Centlivre or the Duchess of Newcastle as more likely targets.[39] In fact it seems clear that Clinket is designed as a composite portrait, drawn from several different models, and not excluding ironic hints of Scriblerian self-portraiture. For actually it was Pope himself who, as an adolescent, began an epic on the subject of Deucalion's flood, which bears a striking similarity to Clinket's tragedy. 'The scene of it', he recalled, 'lies at Rhodes and some of the neighbouring islands, and the poem opened under water . . .'[40] Equally, Clinket's appeal for sympathetic literary encouragement seems to echo Gay's own heartfelt pleas:

CLINKET. What struggles has an unknown author to vanquish prejudice! Suppose this play acts but six nights, his next may play twenty. Encourage a young author, I know it will be your interest.

The player's rebuke to this request has the authentic sound of a rejection that Gay had heard many times in his career.

2ND PLAYER. I would sooner give five hundred pounds than bring some plays on the stage. An audience little considers whether 'tis the author or the actor that is hissed; our character suffers.

Three Hours after Marriage was Gay's most ambitious and experimental work to date, and the critical uproar which it provoked had profound consequences on him and on his relationship with his Scriblerian colleagues. For Pope, the supposed 'honour' of having his name joined with Gay's in the advertisement to the play had

---

[39] *Complete Key*, 5.
[40] Spence, i. 16.

proved particularly embarrassing. The whole episode, including the brawl with Cibber, had been a public relations disaster. He complained to Parnell that 'Gay's play' (as he pointedly described it) 'has cost much time and long suffering, to stem a tide of malice and party that certain authors have raised against it'.[41] For his part, Gay was abject in his apologies for the pain his ill-judged compliment had caused his friends. In a penitent letter he offered himself as a willing sacrifice to the wrath of their enemies.

Dear Pope,
　　Too late I see, and confess myself mistaken in relation to the comedy, yet I do not think, had I followed your advice and only introduced the mummy, that the absence of the crocodile had saved it. I can't help laughing myself, (though the vulgar do not consider that it was designed to look very ridiculous) to think how the poor monster and mummy were dashed at their reception, and when the cry was loudest, thought that if the thing had been wrote by another, I should have deemed the town in some measure mistaken: and as to your apprehension that this may do us future injury, do not think it; the Doctor has a more valuable name than can be hurt by anything of this nature, and yours is doubly safe. I will (if any shame there be) take it all to myself, as indeed I ought, the motion being first mine, and never heartily approved of by you . . . I beg of you not to suffer this, or anything else, to hurt your health. As I have publicly said that I was assisted by two friends, I shall continue in the same story, professing obstinate silence about Dr Arbuthnot and yourself.[42]

Had Breval glimpsed this letter it would have confirmed all his suspicions. Once again Gay was forced to assume the role of the innocent Ajax shielding a malevolent Teucer. His letter is an interesting blend of contrition and bravado. Though he confesses himself 'mistaken' in insisting on his surreal menagerie of the crocodile and mummy, there is nothing in his tone that suggests real regret. In *The What D' Ye Call It* he had successfully defied audience expectations; in *Three Hours* the same attempt had been defeated by a hostile alliance of players and critics. But there is nothing here to suggest that he will abandon such high-risk strategies in favour of Pope's more circumspect style. Indeed, his immediate impulse for retaliation against the Button's clique demonstrates an instinct for self-justification rather than self-criticism; but, as so often happened,

---

[41] Pope, *Corr.* i. 395.
[42] *Letters*, 31–2.

Pope intervened to persuade him into a more submissive style. Clearly Gay was worried that Pope's apprehension of 'future injury' might cause a rift between them, and his airy attempts to dismiss such fears carry little force. Though he signs himself off with a flourish, 'I am (not at all cast down), your sincere friend, John Gay', he too had reason for low spirits. Reading through the voluminous criticisms of the play, he would have found himself depicted in a depressingly familiar and ignominious role. One of the play's off-stage characters, the hypochondriac Countess Hippokekoana, is identified thus by Parker:

The Countess of Hippokekoana is the Duchess of Monmouth. To whom Gay was a serving-man, and never hoped for any higher preferment than holding a plate at a side-board, till Pope took him into his protection . . . Gay justly deserves a cudgel for abusing a lady . . . who took him in when he was destitute of meat, drink and clothes.

Breval took up the same line, imagining Gay's melancholy soliloquy as the catcalls ring out:

> Oh that contented with my servile state,
> At some buffet I still had held a plate.[43]

Once again Gay saw himself represented as a jumped-up servant, a clumsy, semi-literate clown who had advanced himself by syco-phancy to become Pope's lackey, stooge, and bully. Though he may have affected to laugh off such caricatures, their effect on a man with such a deep sense of social inferiority, must have been profoundly hurtful.

Already Pope's apprehensions of 'future injury' were proving true. He heard ominous rumours that 'my person is in some danger', and entrusted over £1,000 in Gay's hands to be left for Martha Blount as a security 'against accidents'. Meanwhile his 'old enemy' (probably Dennis) was uttering all kinds of dire threats, though Gay affected to laugh these off. 'You will live to prove him a false prophet, as you have already a liar,' he told Pope, adding: 'whether I shall do so or no, you can best tell, for with the continuance of your dear friend-ship, and assistance, never yet withheld from me, I dare promise as much.' In the event, Pope chose a more oblique form of literary

---

[43] *Complete Key*, 11; *The Confederates*, 22.

retaliation, seizing upon Parnell's recently completed *Remarks of Zoilus* as 'the best revenge upon such fellows'. He even arranged that the profits from this pamphlet should go to Gay as some compensation for his loss of earnings from the play.[44] But the £16. 2s. 6d. copy money which Gay received from Lintot on 4 May was little enough compensation for the public ridicule he had suffered. And the very pettiness of this charitable hand-out could only have underlined his continuing sense of literary dependence.

Gay's obvious state of poverty at this time lends little credence to the story of the gift of 400 guineas from the maids of honour; but he and Pope continued to visit them often at Gerrard Street, Leicester House, and Hampton Court. In Pope's *Court Ballad* the two men resume their customary fantasy pose as a pair of rakish ladies' men.

> To one fair lady out of court
>   And two fair ladies in
> Who think the Turk and Pope a sport
>   And Wit and Love no sin,
> Come these soft lines with nothing stiff in
> To Bellenden, Lepell and Griffin
>   With a fa . . .
>
> In truth by what I can discern,
>   Of courtiers from you three,
> Some wit you have and more may learn,
>   From court than Gay or me;
> Perhaps in time you'll leave high diet,
> And sup with us on mirth or quiet,
>   With a fa.
>
> In Leicester Fields, in house full nigh,
>   With door all painted green,
> Where ribbons wave upon the tye,
>   (A milliner's I ween)
> There may you meet us, three to three,
> For Gay can well make two of me.
>   With a fa.

While Gay flirted innocuously with the maids of honour, Pope sent coyly suggestive letters to Lady Mary *en route* to Constantinople and

---

[44] *Letters*, 32; Pope, *Corr.* i. 396.

to Martha Blount at Mapledurham. The tone of this correspondence has the bashful erotic innuendo of despairing sexual fantasy. Pope pictured Lady Mary in 'the land of jealousy, where the unhappy women converse with none but eunuchs, and where the very cucumbers are brought to them cut';[45] he teased Teresa Blount, who sent him money to invest on her behalf, as an 'abandoned creature . . . who has so lately prostituted herself to a man in a sheet of paper'.[46] In fact the intimacy which Pope and Gay enjoyed with these women was due to the fact that they posed no sort of sexual threat. As the *Court Ballad* coyly intimates, there was 'nothing stiff' in their exchanges. The typical self-deprecating allusion to their appearances ('For Gay can well make two of me') emphasizes that neither man presented the physical appearance of a genuine sexual predator. Part of the danger of such play-acting was that the deep sense of sexual inadequacy which disguised itself as superficial gallantry could easily degenerate into cynicism. Equally, this habit of romantic fantasy threatened to sublimate all forms of personal aspiration into a kind of make-believe. Gay's hopes of a court place are often treated, by both himself and Pope, as the same kind of elusive dream. Whereas, in *Three Hours after Marriage* Gay had demonstrated a bold and reckless theatrical daring, in his personal life, under Pope's supervision, he appears timid and unsure. The *Court Ballad* dangles the temptations of a place in the Prince of Wales's court at Leicester House, only to settle for the country consolations of celibacy and a simple diet.

The spring of 1717 was a time of intense political manoeuvring and intrigue. In April a sharp rift within the ruling Whig clique led to Townshend's dismissal from the Lord-Lieutenancy of Ireland, followed in quick succession by the resignations from the government of Walpole, Methuen, and Pulteney. A few weeks later Pope wrote to Lady Mary:

The political state is under great divisions, the parties of Walpole and Stanhope as violent as Whig and Tory. The K[ing] and P[rince] continue two names: there is nothing like a coalition, but at the masquerade; however the Princess is a dissenter from it, and has a very small party in so unmodish a separation.[47]

---

[45] Pope, *Corr.* I. 368.
[46] Ibid. 375.
[47] Ibid. 407.

With consummate political opportunism, Walpole and Pulteney immediately set about the task of cultivating new allies among their former Tory enemies, while in France Bolingbroke seized on the situation to renew his efforts at political rehabilitation with extravagant protestations of loyalty. From Paris, the English ambassador Lord Stair sent secret messages to Marlborough in London, indicating that Bolingbroke was prepared to purchase a pardon by betraying former Jacobite associates.

He orders me to tell you that he will have no reserves of any kind with you, that he will tell you all he knows . . . He will likewise tell the King everything he knows, and do everything to deserve his Majesty's pardon.[48]

Even in Dublin, rumours that Bolingbroke was now 'following the trade of an informer' were freely circulating. Swift's archbishop concluded a long letter with this insidious afterthought: 'We have a strong report that my Lord Bolingbroke will return here & be pardoned, certainly it must not be for nothing. I hope he can tell no ill story of you.'[49] Gay, who has too often been dismissed as a political *naif*, was among the first to recognize and exploit the opportunities of this changed political landscape. In the aftermath of *Three Hours after Marriage*, he lost no time in cultivating the friendship of new potential benefactors, as a defence against the malice of his enemies and the possible disaffection of former friends. Soon both Methuen and Pulteney were included among his influential contacts at the Prince of Wales's alternative court at Leicester House. In letters, he presents himself as something of an *habitué* at Hampton Court, the Duke of Dorset's, and Mr Pulteney's.

Gay's new friendship with Pulteney is an important indicator of his willingness to trim his political opinions in pursuit of personal gain. Just one year older than Gay, William Pulteney had hitherto appeared as a model of Whig orthodoxy. Elected to parliament in 1705, he had vehemently opposed Harley's peace policy, and had made something of a reputation for himself, on Queen Anne's death, as a scourge of the Jacobite rebels. He supported the proposal of a reward of £100,000 for capturing the Pretender; he moved the impeachment of the Jacobite Lord Widdrington, and opposed the idea of extending a royal pardon to former Scottish rebels. As a

---

[48] Blenheim Palace, Marlborough MSS BII-27, 7 June 1716.
[49] Swift, *Corr.* ii. 227–8, 237–8.

reward for such conspicuous displays of loyalty to the new regime he was appointed Secretary at War and was also a key member of the committee of secrecy investigating the conduct of Harley's peace negotiations. It was to this powerful committee that all intercepted papers, including those of Oxford, Bolingbroke, and Swift, were sent with a view to prosecutions. Pulteney was not only powerful, he was also rich, having augmented the considerable wealth and property which he inherited on his father's early death by an advantageous marriage in 1714 to Anna Maria Gumley (a 'vixen', according to his enemies). In the early days of the new Whig government it was Pulteney, together with Walpole and Stanhope, who were regarded as the grand triumvirate in charge of state affairs. When in 1717 he resigned from office, replaced as Secretary at War by James Craggs, he and Walpole represented a dangerous destabilizing influence on the Whig back benches, and a potential nucleus of disaffection for politicians of all parties.

The basis of the friendship between Gay and Pulteney was essentially literary. Pulteney had a genuine love both of the classics and of literary ephemera. In his old age it was said to be a sure sign of his declining powers when he desisted from Greek and punning.[50] He happily took part in punning games with the maids of honour, and relished the wit of hoaxes like *God's Revenge*. However, Pulteney may also have regarded Gay as a useful go-between with Bolingbroke, and in their convivial literary evenings at Leicester House the two men began to toy with the outlines of a new grand political alliance. Faced with continuing poverty and uncertain literary prospects, it is little wonder that Gay should have sought a change of fortune through acquaintance with one of the most powerful politicians in the realm. To Pope, suspicious of this change of companions, Gay wrote: 'tho' I am to mix with quality, I shall see nothing half so engaging as you, my dear friend.' But this was one of his increasingly formulaic professions of friendship; in fact Gay was already seeking engagements elsewhere.

Other literary friends faced even bleaker prospects. Erasmus Lewis described to Swift the plight of Matthew Prior, who, like the Earl of Oxford, had been imprisoned on a charge of treason but was now released.

Our friend Prior having not had the vicissitudes of human things before his

---

[50] Lord Stanhope, *History of England*, &c (5th edn., London 1858), ii. 75.

eyes is likely to end his days in as forlorn a state as any other poet has done before him, if his friends do not take more care of him than he has done of himself. Therefore, to prevent the evil which we see is coming on very fast, we have a project of printing his *Solomon* & other poetical works by subscription, one guinea to be paid in hand, & the other at the delivery of the books. He, Arbuthnot, Pope & Gay are now with me & remember you; it is our joint request that you will endeavour to procure some subscriptions.[51]

In a similar spirit of benevolence Pope sought to foster a literary friendship between Gay and Sir Samuel Garth, who was currently preparing a handsome new English edition of Ovid's *Metamorphoses* with a distinguished cast of translators, old and new, including Dryden, Addison, Pope, Congreve, and Rowe. Pope had already translated 'The Fable of Dryope' from book 9 and he now encouraged Gay to translate the rest of the book. But Gay seems to have regarded this commission as journeyman work. Although grateful to be included among such celebrated company, he suspected that his own assignment, filling in the surrounds of Pope's set piece, would only reinforce the public perception of him as Pope's under-strapper. His translation is fluent and competent enough but shows less ingenuity and flair than his earlier translation of 'The Story of Arachne'. At one point an allusive *hommage* to Pope's *Rape of the Lock* teeters on the brink of parody. When Gay writes,

> Foot strove with foot, I prone extend my breast,
> Hands war with hands, and forehead forehead prest.

he seems to recall Pope's couplet:

> Where wigs with wigs, with sword-knots sword-knots strive,
> Beaux banish beaux, and coaches coaches drive.   (i. 101–2)

But by echoing Pope's mock-heroic style Gay risks reducing his own labours (and, incidentally, those of Hercules) to a kind of comic pastiche. Officiously supportive as ever, Pope made it his business to make a public display of Garth's gratitude for Gay's contribution. Among the poems included in his *Poems on Several Occasions*, published the same month, was an 'Anacreontick to Mr Gay. By Dr Garth' which concludes:

[51] Swift, *Corr.* ii. 245.

> The graces held the lyre,
> Th' harmonious frame, the muses strung,
> The loves and smiles compos'd the choir,
> And Gay transcrib'd what Phoebus sung.

By publishing this testimonial among his own collected verse Pope was clearly undertaking to maintain his role as Gay's literary mentor. But while such efforts of mutual support might mitigate the worst effects of political disfavour, the changed political climate seemed to promise better prospects for Gay's long-term security. Erasmus Lewis's letter to Swift envisaged a benevolent self-help network operating among the old Tory faithful. But the old alliances were changing and Gay was not prepared to live forever on nostalgia and hand-outs from his friends.

Following his resignation from office, Pulteney promptly decided to take his wife on a relaxing Continental jaunt. He extended the same invitation to Gay, who was delighted to accept. Pope viewed this unexpected foreign excursion with mixed feelings. Writing to Caryll he apologized on Gay's behalf for his being unable to pay a promised visit to Ladyholt that summer: 'Gay is to be excused on account of [a] strange desire to see foreign lands.'[52] Pope no doubt harboured memories that Gay's previous Continental expedition, to Hanover, had failed to repay the eager hopes of advancement he had invested in it. More personally Pope, whose fragile constitution would not permit him to risk the dangers of sea travel, felt increasingly isolated with so many of his friends in foreign lands. Letters arrived from Lady Mary in 'Belgrade Village'; from Swift and Parnell in Dublin; while Bolingbroke maintained a diplomatic silence in France. Meanwhile Pope was a housebound invalid at Chiswick, living on a valetudinarian diet of ass's milk, salads, and herbs, and 'under the directions and operations of an eye-doctor, who drops nine drops a day into each eye'. 'Gay is going for France next week,' he wrote gloomily to Parnell, adding: 'I remain within four miles of London, a man of business and poetry, from both of which I pray to be delivered.'[53]

Gay and the Pulteneys were due to set out for the Continent in early June. Pope told Parnell on 7 June that they were already 'upon

---

[52] Pope, *Corr.* i, 413.
[53] Ibid. 414–16.

the wing for Aix-la-Chapelle'. But fresh political skirmishes imposed
an unexpected delay. Lord Cadogan, formerly Marlborough's
quarter-master and only recently ennobled, was now a leading figure
in the new Whig administration. Walpole and Pulteney, placing
themselves at the head of an opposition coalition, had high hopes of
inflicting a defeat on the new administration with an attack on
Cadogan's alleged corruption as commander of the forces which put
down the Jacobite rebellion. Pulteney himself opened the parliamentary attack while Gay, eager to consolidate his friendship with the
former Secretary at War, assisted with a savage verse lampoon of
Cadogan, written under the pseudonym 'James Baker'.[54] This
pseudo-Horatian satire, nasty, brutish, and short, ridicules Cadogan's newly acquired title and concentrates on the new lord's
lowly origins.

---

[54] Dearing denies Gay's authorship of this poem, *Horace, Epod. IV: Imitated by Sir
James Baker, Kt. To Lord Cad—n*, and does not include it in his edition of the *Poetry and
Prose*. His reasons are very briefly set out in his introduction, where he treats all the
'James Baker' poems together. 'I accept Pope's statements and Norman Ault's ascriptions
to Pope of the following: *God's Revenge Against Punning*, the commendatory poem signed
"James Baker" in the second and following editions of *A Key to the Lock* . . . If Gay is
not the author of *God's Revenge*, whose reputed author is "James Baker", or of the
"Baker" commendatory poem, there seems to be no reason to connect him with the other
"James Baker" pieces, *An Admonition Merry and Wise to the Famous Mr Tr[ap]p*, *A Letter
to a Buttonian K[nigh]t*, *Horace Epod. IV. Imitated*, and *A Letter from Sir J—B—to Mr.
P—*, *upon Publishing of a Paper, Entituled, God's Revenge* . . ., a vicious attack on Pope'
(p. 17). However, lumping all these 'James Baker' pieces together in this way involves a
logical difficulty which Dearing appears not to appreciate. If, as he claims, Pope was the
author of *God's Revenge*, this might seem to imply that Pope was likewise responsible for
the other 'James Baker' pieces too, including *A Letter from Sir J—B—to Mr P—*,
which Dearing describes as 'a vicious attack on Pope'. In fact, of course, there is no
reason to assume that all these pieces were written by the same person at all. The
pseudonym 'James Baker', like so many other Grub Street personas, identifies not an
individual but a satiric style. In seeking to establish the authorship of such ephemera,
each one must be considered separately. The evidence for Gay's participation in the
composition of *God's Revenge* is set out above (p. 232 and Ch. 8 n. 3). The case for Gay's
authorship of *To Lord Cad—n* is even stronger. Much of the evidence is summarized by
Faber (pp. xxxi and 638), who includes the poem in his list of 'Poems of Doubtful
Authenticity', where he concludes: 'On the whole I believe the following piece to be
Gay's' (p. 638). The strongest evidence for this ascription is circumstantial. Gay, keen to
cement his new alliance with Pulteney, had compelling reasons to demonstrate his
usefulness to his new friend and may, as Faber suggests, have written the poem 'at
Pulteney's instance'. Internal evidence too supports this notion. The poem opens in the
ironic fable mode Gay was to make peculiarly his own: 'As tender lambs with wolves
agree . . .'; the parish-badge (l. 18) and hunted hare (l. 27) recall motifs from *The What
D'Ye Call It* (II. iv. 12) and *Rural Sports* (ll. 294–8). Perhaps most persuasive of all is the
prevalence of clothing imagery as Gay contrasts the 'coarse paternal frize' of Cadogan's
humble origins with the gaudy robes, scarlet sash, and plume of his new eminence.

Thou dar'st not surely plead thy blood,
It runs thro' such *plebeian* mud,
No title can refine it:
It had, my friend, been much more wise,
To wear thy coarse paternal frize,
Than thus in robes to shine it.

'Baker' goes on to compare Cadogan with Marlborough as two masters not of military strategy but of mercenary self-interest:

Slaves think thee an important lord,
In senate and at council-board,
In camps a son of thunder;
But sure, as I'm a valiant knight,
If Marlb'rough taught thee not to fight,
He taught thee how to plunder.

This is a harsh, unsubtle caricature, but its very crudity may suggest something of the intensity of Gay's desire to impress his new political patron. Part of the suppressed anger of his intended attack on Addison is released in this covert assault on another Whig placeman. While Pope attempted to smother Gay's expressions of dangerous resentment, Pulteney encouraged him to channel them into political invective. In the event, the new unstable coalition of opposition forces was defeated in parliament by just ten votes; 204 to 194. But all was not lost. Three weeks later the House of Lords met to debate the impeachment of Lord Oxford, but Marlborough, Cadogan, and Sunderland, sensing the change of mood, prudently absented themselves. As a result, impeachment proceedings were dropped 'by the unanimous consent of all the lords present'.[55] By the time that Gay and the Pulteneys finally set sail in late July, Oxford was released from his imprisonment in the Tower and happily installed once more in his house at St James's. Meanwhile, in France, Bolingbroke wrote again to Lord Stair:

If his Majesty is so good as to pardon me, let it be done with all the air possible of an unconditional mercy and with [all] grace possible, not for my, [but] for ye public good.[56]

---

[55] Swift, *Corr.* ii. 273.
[56] 20 June 1717; Baratier, 40.

Gay was not alone in seeking personal rehabilitation from the changed state of public affairs. *En route* for the channel ports the three travelling companions spent a weekend at Canterbury, where they penned some frivolous after-dinner verses to their absent friends, the maids of honour.

> My dear Belladine,
> O'er a glass of wine
> We send you this line
> On purpose to tell
> You & Miss Lepell
> We are all very well.
> If news we should send you from Canterbury,
> That news to be sure you would think is a lie;
> And therefore we'll say what before you did know,
> That we are your servants wherever we go.
> Ann Pulteney
> Wm. Pulteney
> J. Gay

Pope, though, who continued to enjoy the company of the maids of honour, found little relish in their way of life:

We all agreed that the life of a Maid of Honour was of all things the most miserable; & wished that every woman who envied it had a specimen of it. To eat Westphalia ham in a morning, ride over hedges and ditches on borrowed hacks, come home in the heat of the day with a fever, & what is worse a hundred times, a red mark in the forehead with a beaver hat; all this may qualify them to make excellent wives for fox-hunters, & bear abundance of ruddy-complexioned children. As soon as they can wipe off the sweat of the day, they must simper an hour, & catch cold, in the Princesses apartment; from thence *To dinner, with what appetite they may*— And after that, till midnight, walk, work, or think, which they please?[57]

---

[57] Pope to the Blount sisters, *Corr.* i. 427.

NINE

The Beast of Blois

... despise great beasts, such as Gay; who now goes by the
dreadful name of *The Beast of Blois* ...

(Pope, letter, Oct. 1717)

GAY kept up a lively correspondence with friends in England
during his travels on the Continent though sadly none of his letters
has survived. Always somewhat vague about the details of his own
correspondence, he thanked Pope for a letter which was never
written, prompting his more meticulous friend to keep an inventory
on his behalf. In addition to letters sent to Fortescue and himself,
Pope confirmed that the Duchess of Hamilton, Lord Stanhope, Mrs
Bellenden, Lord Warwick (twice), and Mrs Lepell (thrice) had all
received letters from him. 'And I can't tell who else', he added,
unsuccessfully affecting to mimic Gay's own carelessness in this
respect.[1]

Aix-la-Chapelle, where the travellers spent the latter part of the
summer, was the Bath of the Low Countries, an increasingly fashionable spa town drawing visitors from all parts of Europe. Following a
fire in 1656 which had destroyed much of the old part of the town
including twenty churches and some 5,000 houses, the centre of the
town had been rebuilt in a new, more grandiose style. According to
the *Description de la ville d'Aix-la-Chapelle*, published in 1700, the
town 's'embellit journellement de plus en plus, ainsi qu'elle s'aug-
mente en puissance & en richesses, par l'affluence du monde qui
vient tous les ans y prendre les bains'.[2] The fashionable season at
Aix extended throughout May and June, and then again from mid-

---

[1] Pope, *Corr.* i. 450.
[2] *Description de la ville d'Aix-la-Chapelle* (1700), 24.

August till the end of the September, which was when Gay and the Pulteneys made their visit. The two fountains from which one took the waters (officially described as 'sulphureuses, nitreuses & chaudes') were both encircled by elegant galleries and promenades; the first, in the 'Bain de l'Empereur', dignified by a statue of the Emperor Charlemagne, the other by the figure of the Virgin Mary. Away from the baths the guide suggested visitors might care to examine the town's collection of holy relics; these included a chemise belonging to the Virgin Mary together with a lock of her hair; a cloth in which the severed head of John the Baptist had been wrapped; pieces of the Holy Cross, and Charlemagne's mummified left arm.

Gay would have found more congenial advice on the town's diversions in a scurrilous 'alternative guide' entitled *Les Bains d'Aix ou les amours secrètes des dames qui vont prendre les eaux à Aix-la-Chapelle*. This roguish rake's handbook presents the town as the perfect hunting-ground for gigolos and fortune-seekers.[3] Written in a racy Sternian peek-a-boo style of interruptions and innuendoes, it makes clear the main attraction of a town visited by so many sexually frustrated upper-class young ladies: 'Les Eaux, Madame, donnent des libertez qu'on n'oserait prendre ailleurs.' Taking a survey of the pale beauties who haunt the pump-room galleries, each one with a waxen complexion, lowered eyes, 'la bouche mourante & phisionomie amoureuse', the author, 'Le Chevalier De M——', has no difficulty in diagnosing their unhappy condition. While their old, impotent, jealous husbands are taking the waters in hopes of restoring their lost virility, the Chevalier offers the ladies his own alternative prescription. Water will never satisfy their needs, he writes: 'il faut quelque chose de plus solide, de plus succulent & de plus substantieux.' He recommends 'a young, healthy, vigorous male, to be taken twice daily, morning and evening for the first fortnight, and thereafter at will'.[4] Concerning the spa-water itself the Chevalier is uncompromising in his contempt: 'Malepeste! qu'elle est dégoutante!' If, as seems likely, Gay knew this work, he would have been particularly amused by the Chevalier's Rabelaisian description of Aix's pissing nuns (beguines), which has the same scurrilous

---

[3] The book enjoyed something of a vogue, going through at least three editions in the first decade of the century.

[4] p. 18: 'un mari de 25 à 30 ans, sain, jeune & vigoureux que vous vous appliquerez les 15 premiers jours le soir & le matin & le reste du tems comme vous pourrez . . .'

tone as Gay's own mock-Chaucerian *Answer to the Sompnour's Prologue* published earlier that year.[5]

Whatever Gay's own opinion of the remedial properties of the waters, they were not, he complained in another lost letter, particularly conducive towards the writing of verse. Pope was less inclined to blame the waters, attributing Gay's summer idleness to other distractions. Writing, he suggested, was equally difficult with or without the assistance of the waters. He fancied it was 'not writing but thinking' that presented a problem in the spa town's hedonistic atmosphere. Aix-la-Chapelle though did have another reputation. As a favourite resort for foreign travellers it was a known rendezvous for spies and Jacobite sympathizers. We know for certain that Bolingbroke was in Aix in May the following year, staying at the Lion d'Or, where Swift had plans to visit him. It seems likely that Gay and Pulteney either met or hoped to meet him there during their summer visit.[6]

Gay did manage to complete one poem during the summer. His *Epistle to William Lowndes* is one of his wittiest and most accomplished verse satires, and he sent a copy over for the amusement of Lord Burlington. Part of the poem's success comes from the simplicity of its ironic strategy, based upon a modest pun on the word 'author'. The full title of the poem is: *To my Ingenious and Worthy Friend W[illiam] L[owndes] Esq; Author of that Celebrated Treatise in Folio, Called the* LAND-TAX BILL. As Secretary to the Treasury Lowndes was the man responsible for 'writing' the annual Land Tax Bill; this makes him, in Gay's ironic estimation, the most successful author of this or any other era. For while most authors would be pleased to earn a few guineas for their efforts (even Pope, the most bankable poet of his generation, only gained £5,000 for his *Iliad* translation), Lowndes's compositions raked in an annual return of between £1 million and £2 million.[7] By presenting Lowndes as the most successful 'author' of his generation Gay goes to the heart of his society's uneasy attempt to celebrate capitalist values in a

---

[5] 'Voyez, elles s'en vont toutes pisser par compagnie. Il faut avouer que les béguinnes sont de franches pisseuses: elles rendent toujours au double toutes les eaux qu'elles prennent, leur fontaine ne tarit jamais, c'est une source seconde, un flux & reflux continuel, un coulant d'eau vive, enfin un puits, ou plutôt un abîme . . .'.

[6] Swift, *Corr.* ii. 318; Baratier, 100.

[7] Gay himself had recently assisted in the successful marketing and promotion of Prior's poems through a subscription edition which netted the poet some 4,000 guineas.

borrowed classical iconography. In *Spectator* no. 3 Addison had
offered his vision of Public Credit as the inspiring deity of his
imagination; for him commerce was what daffodils were to Words-
worth. He drew his inspiration from the stock market: 'an assembly
of countrymen and foreigners consulting together upon the private
business of mankind.'[8] In such a society, is not the true epic author
the man whose prose inscribes the essential financial dynamic of the
State, represented in its taxes? Certainly the stately roll-call of
names in Lowndes's lines has a an authentically Homeric ring.

> If the blind poet gain'd a long renown
> By singing ev'ry Grecian chief and town;
> Sure L [owndes] his prose much greater fame requires,
> Which sweetly counts five thousand knights and squires,
> Their seats, their cities, parishes and shires.   (ll. 13–17)

However, Gay decides that Lowndes's chief literary talent is not
epic but satire; for whose writings have a more direct and chastening
effect than the tax man's? In *A Tale of a Tub* Swift complained
there was not 'in all nature another so callous and insensible a
member as the world's posteriors, whether you apply to it the toe or
the birch'.[9] But as a satirist Lowndes hits the world where it really
hurts, not on the posteriors but in the pocket-book. Pope was
explicit about the satirist's duty to name names: 'To attack vices in
the abstract, without touching persons, may be safe fighting indeed,
but it is fighting with shadows.'[10] But even in *The Dunciad* Pope
did not name a fraction of the individuals identified in Lowndes's
comprehensive charge.

> No. Satire is thy talent; and each lash
> Makes the rich miser tremble o'er his cash;
> What on the drunkard can be more severe,
> Than direful taxes on his ale and beer?   (ll. 30–3)

Praising Gay's poem, Pope remarked that Lowndes had 'lately
become an inoffensive person to me' since, with the sale of Binfield,
he no longer paid any land-tax. Yet his words can bear another
interpretation, an ironic refusal to be offended by Gay's teasing

---

[8] *Spectator*, 3 (3 Mar. 1711).
[9] *A Tale of a Tub* (1704), 'The Preface'.
[10] Pope, *Corr.* iii. 419

suggestion that Lowndes, not he, was both the true Homer and the leading satirist of the age.

The poem ends with the expression of political sentiments which confirm Gay's strong desire to impress his new political patron. Commissioners named in the land-tax acts also doubled as commissioners for recruiting; hence Lowndes had the power not only to raise money but also to raise armies. But Gay sides with those arguing against the maintenance of a peacetime standing army.

> Thy labours, L [owndes], can greater wonders do,
> Thou raisest armies, and canst pay them too.
> Truce with thy dreaded pen; thy annals cease;
> Why need we armies when the land's in peace?
> Soldiers are perfect devils in their way,
> When once they're rais'd, they're cursed hard to lay.   (ll. 52–7)

This was precisely the issue on which the opposition chose to harry the government in the new session of parliament. As Prior noted, now that the Jacobite rebellion was long since over 'Whigs and Tories begin to think there are not a sufficient number disbanded'.[11] In December Walpole led the opposition attack, demanding that land forces should be reduced to 12,000 men. The campaign culminated on 4 January 1718 in a spirited resistance to a clause in the annual Mutiny Bill which made desertion (Peascod's crime in *The What D'Ye Call It*) punishable by death. Among those who spoke against the government was Gay's distant relative Sir Thomas Hanmer, but, as before, the ministry scraped a narrow victory by 247 votes to 229.

After Aix, the travellers spent some time in France, first at Blois, where Gay eagerly snapped up more scandalous anecdotes of lecherous priests for use in his later ribald tale *Work for a Cooper*, and then at Paris. In October Pope wrote in facetious vein to the Duchess of Hamilton advising her to 'despise great beasts, such as Gay; who now goes by the dreadful name of *The Beast of Blois*, where Mr Pulteney & he are settled, & where he shews tricks gratis to all the beasts of his own country, (for strangers do not yet understand the voice of the beast.)'[12] In Paris the travellers were visited by Burlington, who complimented Mrs Pulteney on having

---

[11] HMC Bath, iii. 450.
[12] Pope, *Corr.* i. 438.

'as much outshin'd all the French ladies, as she did the English before'.[13] His remark set the tone for Gay's verse epistle *To the Right Honourable William Pulteney Esq*, which takes as its theme the superiority of all things English to all things French. Pulteney evidently had suggested Gay might try his hand at a Parisian *Trivia*:

> Shall he (who late Britannia's city trod,
> And led the draggled Muse, with pattens shod,
> Through dirty lanes, and alleys doubtful ways)
> Refuse to write, when Paris asks his lays! (ll. 11–14)

Gay's response is unenthusiastic: 'Well then, I'll try.' The result is uninspired and unattractive, a complacent exercise in Francophobia, adopting the prejudiced voice of the Englishman abroad and offering only a set of Gallic stereotypes (French foppishness, hypocrisy, vanity, and lasciviousness). The poem's trite conclusion, 'All French-men are of *petit-maître* kind', is a perfect embodiment of the very snobbery it pretends to condemn. Affecting the pose of an intrepid explorer in strange lands Gay falls back on over-familiar motifs, presenting high society in terms of exotic beasts:

> Monkeys in action, perroquets in talk;
> They're crown'd with feathers, like the cockatoo,
> And like camelions, daily change their hue. (ll. 34–6)

His depiction of *alfresco* adulteries in the Bois de Boulogne, where 'ev'n court ladies sin in open air', recalls Rochester's *Ramble in St James's Park*. One high-born lady engages with 'three abbots in one night' while another 'with the cardinal her nights employs, | Where holy sinews consecrate her joys' (ll. 176–8). But Gay's sharpest satire is directed at the Paris opera:

> But hark! the full orchestra strike the strings;
> The hero struts, and the whole audience sings.
> My jarring ear harsh grating murmurs wound,
> Hoarse and confus'd, like Babel's mingled sound.
> Hard chance had plac'd me near a noisy throat,
> That in rough quavers bellow'd ev'ry note.
> Pray sir, says I, suspend awhile your song,
> .Th'opera's drown'd; your lungs are wondrous strong;

---

[13] Pope, *Corr*. i. 451.

I wish to hear your Roland's ranting strain,
While he with rooted forests strows the plain.
Sudden he shrugs surprise, and answers quick,
Monsieur apparement n'aime pas la musique. (ll. 191–202)

This reference to the mad scene in Lully's opera *Roland* (IV. vii), in
which the hero 'brise les inscriptions, & arrache des branches
d'arbres, & des morceaux de rochers', confirms Gay's fascination
with operatic motifs as a source of literary parody.[14] Significantly, it
is specifically *French* opera that he attacks, no doubt influenced by
Burlington's predilection for the Italian style; but it is also noticeable
that the only performer he chooses to praise is Anastasia Robinson,
the leading *English* opera-singer, rather than one of the Italian super
stars.

O sooth me with some soft Italian air,
Let harmony compose my tortur'd ear!
When Anastasia's voice commands the strain,
The melting warble thrills through ev'ry vein. (ll. 205–8)

At some point during the winter, if not before, the travellers
would have contrived to see Bolingbroke, who was now attempting
to bribe Lord Stair with gifts of wine.[15] But, ever vigilant to pre-
empt any new alliance between crypto-Jacobites and disaffected
Whigs, Stair kept a watchful eye on Pulteney's movements, sending
back regular reports to the new Secretary of State in London, James
Craggs. On 25 April he reported: 'Whatever project ye Jacobites
have you may be assured it is not yet ripe for they don't propose to
leave France till ye end of May or ye beginning of June.' He went
on:

Mr Pulteney goes into England in a fortnight. I have taken a good deal of
pains with him and he seems to be very well disposed at present; he speaks
very respectfully and kindly of ye king, and he thinks ye ministers have

---

[14] *Roland* (1743), 57. This opera was performed in Mar. 1718, which strongly suggests
that Gay was still in Paris at that time. On 23 May Lord Oxford's nephew Winnington
wrote to the Earl from Vienna: 'I have endeavoured in my travels to find something
curious, and of your lordship's *goût*. There is a description of Languedoc, written by Mr
Bavil, with another little book of the canal, which Mr Gay will remit into your hands.'
HMC Portland MSS (1899), v. 560. Despite Irving's caution that 'the Gay mentioned . . .
may not be the poet at all' (Irving, 168) this would seem to confirm that Gay remained in
Paris throughout the spring.
[15] 12 Jan. 1718; Baratier, 52.

been acting a good and honourable part for ye nation.

Clearly Stair was less than convinced by such protestations of political loyalty. Three weeks later he wrote again:

Pulteney sets out for England on Monday next; ye man leaves very sensible of ye folly of those who left ye king's service . . . but after all I dare not answer for ye part he'll play in England. He seems to have a *mauvaise honte* to leave his friends.[16]

In the conclusion to his *Epistle to Pulteney* Gay turns from the empty pretensions of French civilization to a patriotic celebration of those twinned concepts, Britain and liberty, whose mythic synonymity was to become a central theme of James Thomson's verse.

> Happy, thrice happy shall the monarch reign,
> Where guardian laws despotic power restrain!
> There shall the plough-share break the stubborn
>   land,
> And bending harvests tire the peasant's hand;
> There liberty her settled mansion boasts,
> There commerce plenty brings from foreign coasts.
> O Britain, guard thy laws, thy rights defend,
> So shall these blessings to thy sons descend!　(ll. 247–54)

Though echoing Pope's lines in *Windsor Forest* ('Rich Industry sits smiling on the plains, | And Peace and Plenty tell a STUART reigns'), Gay deliberately transforms Pope's Tory eulogy of the Stuart Queen Anne into an orthodox Whig panegyric to the Hanoverian Prince of Wales. In these lines Gay makes a bid not merely to endorse the political sentiments of his new friend and patron Pulteney, but also to recommend himself once more to the service of his future king. Pope viewed the desperation of such efforts at political ingratiation with the resigned amusement which came from his relatively more affluent circumstances. He concluded his November letter with this barbed remark: 'I wish you joy of the birth of the young prince, because he is the only prince we have from whom you have had no expectations and no disappointments.'[17] It was just as well that Gay did not have hopes of the young Prince George William. Born on 3 November, he died just three months later.

*

---

[16] Stair to Craggs, Paris, 25 Apr., 14 May 1718; BL Stowe MSS 246, fos. 87, 97.
[17] Pope, *Corr.* i. 451.

Gay was a perpetual nomad. Not merely did he never own a home of his own, but for most of his life he appears not to have had any settled lodgings either. He spent his life as a permanent house-guest, lodging sometimes with Burlington, sometimes with Pulteney, sometimes with Charles Jervas in Cleveland Court or with Pope at Chiswick. His summers were peripatetic, rambling from one great lord's house to another, visiting Devon, or touring the spa towns of England and the Continent. A sense of displacement, and the house-guest's enforced habit of ingratiation, are among the most conspicuous features of all his writing and help to distinguish his satiric perspective from that of either Pope or Swift. For Pope the sense of *place*, the identification with a specific topos, both allegorical and physical, provided a key element in the psychological defences from which he launched his satiric attacks. After the sale of Binfield, whose landscape area provided the psychic home for Pope's mythopoeic vision in *Windsor Forest*, Pope was, for all the convenience of Chiswick, imaginatively less independent until, with his move to Twickenham, he recreated a domestic world in which art and nature were consciously configured as symbolic representations of classical authority. For Swift too, though he never actually *owned* a property himself, the Deanery of St Patrick's represented a mental fortress. 'I hate all people whom I cannot command,' he wrote, insisting he could only live 'where all mortals are subservient to me'.

Gay was never where he could command, but was always at the command of others. The reasons for this choice of life were not merely circumstantial. Gay was never wealthy, but could certainly have maintained a modest set of lodgings in town had he so chosen. The motives for his instinctive habit of casting himself in the role of household dependant lie deep in his personality. Although they never married, both Pope and Swift project satiric personalities which are secured within a known domestic setting.[18] Their households express their values, and from their correspondence we gain a sense not merely of their friends among the great, but of their domestic routines, their servants and daily rituals. With Gay all this is a blank. As far as we know he had no servant, at least none has been identified; and this is hardly surprising since, without a fixed

---

[18] Swift, *Corr.* iii. 421, 471. I accept the tradition that Swift agreed to a secret marriage ceremony with Stella (Hester Johnson), but that they never cohabited. For a discussion of this point see my biography *Jonathan Swift: A Hypocrite Reversed* (Oxford, 1985), 217–18.

address, Gay would have nowhere for a servant to live. Homelessness implies all sorts of other questions. Where did Gay keep his books, his letters, his clothes? No doubt friends and patrons provided storage for some of these, but to a large extent he must have lived out of a trunk, carrying with him the essentials he would need to equip himself for his permanent adopted role as guest. His apparent carelessness about letters becomes less remarkable when understood in the context of such constant upheavals. Above all there is a sense of loneliness about Gay's life. He had, undoubtedly, a knack of gaining and keeping friends, yet the genial persona which sustained his way of life, and which has led to his depiction in our own century as 'an Augustan Peter Pan', always seems to teeter on the brink of a desperate facetiousness. His letters profess friendship but imply little *intimacy*; there is an element of performance within even their most candid jesting, and a veiled undercurrent of despair.

One reason why Gay travelled, from the age of 40 onwards, was for his health, in attempts to cure the chronic colical disorder which grew increasingly disabling in his later years. Many of his letters are sent from Aix and Spa, Tunbridge and Bath, the fashionable spa towns where each year he spent a longer period taking the waters. The atmosphere of these towns had a kind of superficial gaiety which Gay grew to despise. Although outwardly projecting the image of a witty, gregarious gallant, Gay was in fact overweight, unwell, deeply private, and consumed with an overpowering sense of social inferiority. It was the irony of Gay's life that he constantly subjected himself to living in exactly the kind of milieu of court-gossip and social pretension that his satires most often derided.

Pope was certainly pleased at Gay's return from France. The previous autumn he had suffered the death of his father as well as a certain strain in relations with the Blount sisters. 'My natural temper is pretty much broke', he told Lady Mary, '& I live half a hermit within five miles of London.'[19] At the playhouse the hit of the season was Cibber's *The Non-Juror*, a play whose populist propaganda ('we stare and roar and clap hands for K. George and the government') did nothing to raise Pope's spirits. In June he persuaded Gay to join him in an extended visit to Stanton Harcourt, Lord Harcourt's country place near Oxford which his lordship had placed at their disposal (Harcourt himself lived nearby at

---

[19] Pope, *Corr.* i. 469.

Cokethorpe). Still hard at work on the final volumes of his *Iliad* translation, Pope found the sombre tranquillity of this half-disused house a perfect retreat from the distractions of London. He described its Gothic atmosphere in detail.

> The great hall within is high and spacious, flanked on one side with a very long table, a true image of ancient hospitality: the walls are all over ornamented with monstrous horns of animals, about twenty broken pikes, ten or a dozen blunderbusses, and a rusty matchlock musket or two, which we were informed had served in the civil wars. Here is one vast arched window beautifully darkened with divers scutcheons of painted glass: one shining pane in particular bears date 1286, which alone preserves the memory of a knight whose iron armour is long since perished with rust, and whose alabaster nose is mouldered from his monument. The face of dame Eleanor in another piece owes more to that single pane than to all the glasses she ever consulted in her life. After this, who can say that glass is frail, when it is not half so frail as human beauty, or glory! and yet I can't but sigh to think that the most authentic record of so ancient a family should lie at the mercy of every infant who flings a stone.[20]

With its 'broken-belly'd virginal' its 'mildewed pictures of mouldy ancestors', its crop of mushrooms growing in chinks of the floor-boards, and owls flitting in by night, the house was a perfect story-book retreat. And, for entertainment, the 'starched grey-headed steward' took pleasure in regaling his guests with appropriately Gothic legends.

> He then led us up the tower by dark winding stone-steps, which landed us into several little rooms one above another. One of these was nailed up, and our guide whispered to us as a secret the occasion of it: It seems the course of this noble blood was a little interrupted about two centuries ago, by a freak of the Lady Frances, who was here taken in the fact with a neighbour-ing prior, ever since which the room has been nailed up, and branded with the name of the Adultery-chamber. The ghost of lady Frances is supposed to walk there, and some prying maids of the family report that they have seen a lady in a farthingale through the key-hole; but this matter is hushed up, and the servants are forbid to talk of it.

The two friends passed much of the summer in this curious house, with occasional jaunts to Cokethorpe, Oxford, and Lord Bathurst's country seat at Cirencester. Erasmus Lewis and Matthew Prior were also among Bathurst's summer guests, and together they represented,

---

[20] Ibid. 509.

in Pope's opinion, 'the best company I ever knew'. Gay apparently was so charmed by the landscape of Bathurst's estate that, with his now practised skill in flattering aristocratic hosts, he set about celebrating it in a (fortunately) lost pastoral. Pope told Bathurst:

> Mr Gay is as zealously carried to the bower by the force of imagination as ever Don Quixote was to an enchanted castle. The wood is to him the Cave of Montesinos: He has already planted it with myrtles, & peopled it with nymphs. The old woman of the pheasantry appears already an Urganda; & there wants nothing but a crystal rivulet to purl through the shades, which might be large enough to allay Mr Lewis's great thirst after water.[21]

Literary role-play was evidently the mood of the group with the pedantic Lewis playing prosaic Sancho Panza to Gay's Quixotic fantasies. To Lewis, Bathurst's well-maintained estate presented not the woods of romance but the cultivated landscape of sensible estate management.

> A wood? quoth Lewis: and with that,
> He laughed, and shook his sides so fat:
> His tongue (with eye that marked his cunning)
> Thus fell a reas'ning, not a running.
> Woods are (not to be too prolix)
> Collective bodies of straight sticks.
> It is, my lord, a mere conundrum
> To call things woods, for what grows und'r'em;
> For shrubs, when nothing else at top is,
> Can only constitute a coppice.
> But if you will not take my word,
> See anno quart. of Edward, third.
> And that they're coppice call'd, when dock'd,
> Witness ann. prim. of Henry Oct.

In July Pope and Gay interrupted their country vacation with a short visit to London. Parnell had recently returned from Dublin, and with Lord Oxford now released from the Tower the four men made a nostalgic attempt to revive the spirit of former Scriblerian meetings. As in the old days, their reunion dinner was heralded by doggerel verse invitations sent from the Ship tavern at Charing Cross.

---

[21] Pope, *Corr.* i. 477. Urganda appears in *Amadis de Gaula*.

To the Right Honourable the Earl of Oxford.

One[a] that should be a saint,	[a] Parnell
and one[b] that's a sinner	[b] Gay
And one[c] that pays reckning	[c] Pope
but ne'er eats a dinner,	
In short Pope and Gay (as	
you'll see in the margin)	
Who saw you in Tower, and since	
your enlarging,	
And Parnell who saw you not since	
you did treat him,	
Will venture it now—you have	
no stick to beat him—	
Since these for your jury, good	
and true men, vous avez;	
Pray grant us admittance,	
and shut out Miles Davies.[22]	

Later the same month Pope and Gay returned to Stanton Harcourt, where they were joined by Pope's mother, still grieving for the death of her husband. With customary hushed tones Pope pictured himself to Lady Mary watching over the 'last precarious days' of his mother's life 'as a melancholy recluse watches the last risings & fallings of a dying taper'.[23] It was to be a long vigil; Mrs Pope lived on for a further fifteen years. The two men were immediately plied with invitations. Dr William Stratford, Canon of Christ Church, wrote to Edward Harley on 31 July: 'Your friend Steady, being so eminently ingenious, has got the company of two wits for his entertainment, Pope and Gay. Lord Harcourt lends them Stanton Harcourt to live in this summer.'[24] Even in their rural retreat Pope and Gay soon made themselves a focus of literary attention, returning just in time to transform reports of a local accident into a bucolic *Liebestod*. On the last day of July two young lovers, caught out in the fields in a sudden summer storm, were killed by a bolt of lightning while sheltering by a haystack. The two descriptions of the incident which Pope and Gay simultaneously sent to friends are so

---

[22] Ibid. 478. Miles Davies: not the jazz musician, but the antiquarian (or his ghost; *DNB* claims that Davies died in 1715).

[23] Ibid. 469.

[24] HMC Portland MSS (1899), vii. 239.

carefully crafted, and so similar in both phrasing and tone, that they are clearly joint compositions. Of the two, that attributed to Gay and sent to 'Mr F——' (probably Fortescue) is marginally the less florid.

Stanton Harcourt, Aug. 9, 1718.

. . . John Hewet was a well-set man of about five and twenty; Sarah Drew might be rather called comely than beautiful, and was about the same age. They had passed thro' the various labours of the year together with the greatest satisfaction; if she milked, 'twas his morning and evening care to bring the cows to her hand; it was but last fair that he brought her a present of green silk for her straw hat, and the posy on her silver ring was of his choosing. Their love was the talk of the whole neighbourhood; for scandal never affirmed that they had any other views than the lawful possession of each other in marriage. It was that very morning that he had obtained the consent of her parents, and it was but the next week that they were to wait to be happy. Perhaps in the intervals of their work they were now talking of the wedding clothes, and John was suiting several sorts of poppies and field flowers to her complexion, to choose her a knot for the wedding-day. While they were thus busied, (it was on the last of July between two and three in the afternoon) the clouds grew black, and such a storm of lightning and thunder ensued that all the labourers made the best of their way to what shelter the trees and hedges afforded. Sarah was frightened and fell down in a swoon on a heap of barley. John, who never separated from her, sat down by her side, having raked together two or three heaps the better to secure her from the storm. Immediately there was heard so loud a crack as if heaven had split asunder; every one was now solicitous for the safety of his neighbour, and called to one another throughout the field. No answer being returned to those who called to our two lovers, they stepped to the place where they lay. They perceived the barley all in a smoke, and then spied the faithful pair; John with one arm about Sarah's neck, and the other held over her, as to screen her from the lightning. They were struck dead and stiffened in this tender posture. Sarah's left eye-brow was singed, and there appeared a black spot on her breast; her lover was all over black, but not the least signs of life were found in either. Attended by their melancholy companions, they were conveyed to the town, and the next day interred in Stanton Harcourt church-yard. My Lord Harcourt, at Mr Pope's and my request, has caused a stone to be placed over them, upon condition that we furnish'd the epitaph, which is as follows;

> When Eastern lovers feed the funeral fire;
> On the same pile the faithful fair expire;

Here pitying heaven that virtue mutual found,
And blasted both, that it might neither wound.
Hearts so sincere th'Almighty saw well pleas'd,
Sent his own lightning, and the victims seiz'd.[25]

There is a studied formality to this description, consciously transforming the incident into a literary set piece, and the echoes of Gay's own *Shepherd's Week* merely underline the absence of his usual parodic humour. Pope's letter makes clear that it was he alone who composed the lovers' epitaph, and it is very much Pope's sensibility, deliberately 'stiffening' the 'faithful pair' into a 'tender posture', that strikes us in 'Gay's' letter. The only authentic sound of Gay's own voice comes in a final sentence where he notes that Lord Harcourt 'is apprehensive the country people will not understand' Pope's epitaph; in which case 'Mr Pope says he'll make one with something of scripture in it, and with as little of poetry as Hopkins and Sternhold'. This concluding comic touch offers the only relief from an otherwise lapidary tone.

For much of the summer Pope worked at revising both the epitaph and his sentimental representation of the scene. On 1 September he wrote to Lady Mary, now in Paris, expressing a hope that she might honour the lovers 'with a tear from the finest eyes in the world' by adding some lines of her own to the 'little monument' he designed for them. 'I know you have tenderness,' he wrote.[26] Her reply was not what he expected. Unlike Gay, Lady Mary was not coerced by Pope's sentimentality into contributing to this exercise in mawkish idealization. In a brisk, no-nonsense satire she punctured his sentimental fantasy. While ironically applauding his 'good nature' for supposing the lovers would have 'lived in everlasting joy and harmony, if the lightning had not interrupted their scheme of happiness', she begs to differ.

I see no reason to imagine that John Hughes and Sarah Drew were either wiser or more virtuous than their neighbours. That a well-set man of twenty-five should have a fancy to marry a brown woman of eighteen is nothing marvellous; and I cannot help thinking that, had they married, their lives would have passed in the common track with their fellow-parishioners. His endeavouring to shield her from a storm was a natural action, and what he would have certainly done for his horse, if he had been

[25] Pope, *Corr.* i. 482–3.
[26] Ibid. 496.

in the same situation. Neither am I of opinion that their sudden death was a reward of their mutual virtue. You know the Jews were reproved for thinking a village destroyed by fire more wicked than those that had escaped the thunder. Time and chance happen to all men. Since you desire me to try my skill in an epitaph, I think the following lines perhaps more just, tho' not as poetical as yours.

> Here lies John Hughes and Sarah Drew;
> Perhaps you'll say, What's that to you?
> Believe me, friend, much may be said
> On that poor couple that are dead.
> On Sunday next they should have married;
> But see how oddly things are carried!
> On Thursday last it rain'd and lighten'd,
> These tender lovers, sadly frighten'd,
> Shelter'd beneath the cocking hay
> In hopes to pass the time away.
> But the BOLD THUNDER found them out
> (Commision'd for that end no doubt)
> And seizing on their trembling breath,
> Consign'd them to the shades of death.
> Who knows if 'twas not kindly done?
> For had they seen the next year's sun,
> A beaten wife and cuckold swain
> Had jointly curs'd the marriage chain;
> Now they are happy in their doom,
> For POPE HAS WROTE UPON THEIR TOMB.[27]

In this devastating satiric salvo Montagu blows away all the pious nonsense of Pope's bucolic idyll. Pope liked his nature artistically methodized; his rustic lovers not alive, promiscuous and knowing, but aesthetically deceased, sentimentalized and frozen into a classical attitude of Arcadian innocence. But Montagu's tart rejoinder goes further than rejecting the cult for pastoral pathos. The urbane irony of that condescending parenthesis on the 'bold thunder' '(Commission'd for that end no doubt)' mocks the pious providentialism which lies at the heart of Pope's later attempts to prove 'All Nature is but Art, unknown to thee; | All Chance, Direction, which thou canst not see.'[28] And her argument that the man's attempt to shield

---

[27] Ibid. 523.
[28] *Essay on Man*, i. 289–92.

the woman 'was a natural action, and what he would have certainly done for his horse' recalls a bathetic formula used several times by Gay in both *The Shepherd's Week* and *The What D'Ye Call It*.[29] Almost certainly, left to his own responses, Gay, always suspicious of literary attempts to refashion the realities of rural life into a series of decorous motifs, would have found more in common with Montagu's attitude than with Pope's. But while she was writing from the salons of Paris, Gay was immured at Stanton Harcourt. In the solemn 'romantic' atmosphere of that old house, and in the company of the recently bereaved Mrs Pope, he could not bring himself to mock his friend's evident need for a transcendent symbol.

In this case, however, Pope had the last word. His Arcadian version of the incident became a favourite, and much-anthologized, literary motif. It was included by James Thomson in *The Seasons* and by Goldsmith in *The Vicar of Wakefield* and 'for a long time no collection of model letters was complete without it'.[30]

In addition to his pastoral celebration of Oakley Woods, Gay collaborated with Handel on the masque or 'pastoral entertainment' *Acis and Galatea*. The two men may have met as early as 1711, at the time of Aaron Hill's lavish production of *Rinaldo*. They had certainly become well acquainted at Burlington House, where Handel had been living, on and off, since 1710, dividing his time between London and Hanover, where he held the post of court conductor. Superficially, the similarity of age and background between Gay and Handel might have appeared to put them on an equal footing. Just six months older than Gay, Handel also came from a provincial petty bourgeois family with a mother, like Gay's, descended from a long line of Protestant clergymen. But, as court composer to the King, Handel enjoyed not only the favour of the court but also a secure artistic status within Burlington's cultural ménage. A private set of rooms was set aside for him within Burlington House, where he was very much his own master, coming and going between London and Hanover as he wished, even when Burlington himself was away on extended trips.

The story of Acis and Galatea had fascinated Handel for several

---

[29] Compare Kitty Carrot's lines: 'Pigs in hard rains I've watched, and shall I do | That for the pigs, I would not bear for you?' (*The What D'ye Call It*, I. i. 80–1).

[30] Irving, 171.

years. As early as 1708 in Naples he had composed the short musical
sketch *Aci, Galatea, e Polifemo* to celebrate a princely wedding.
Now, ten years later, he returned to the same theme and, assisted by
Gay, transformed his youthful essay into a mature masterpiece. The
story derives from book 13 of Ovid's *Metamorphoses*, Dryden's
translation of which had been reissued in Garth's edition the previous year. In preparing his libretto Gay clearly worked with Dryden's
text before him, creating a lyrical and dramatic version which
retains many echoes of Dryden's vocabulary. Other phrases are
borrowed from the fourth volume of Pope's *Iliad*, which had appeared just as the two men were setting out for Stanton Harcourt.[31]
Yet, although unashamedly derivative in its language, Gay's text is
not without distinctive qualities. His particular talent was to orches-
trate and dramatize the story in a way which would provide the
greatest tonal variations and depth of character for the composer to
exploit. Slight as it may appear on the page, Gay's *Acis* and *Galatea*
is a tribute to the librettist's art. Resisting the self-contained closure
of a literary text, it offers the vocal and dramatic basis for a set of
musical opportunities. The happy effect of such self-effacing skills is
evident in modern descriptions of the work as 'an incomparable
masterpiece saturated with exquisite musical poetry . . . every musical phrase a jewel and every turn a miracle'.[32]

---

[31] *Acis and Galatea*, ii. 6, 'the mountains nod, the forests shake!' clearly echoes 'the
lofty mountains nod, | The forests shake!' (Pope, *Iliad*, 13. 29–30). However the
suggestion by Ault and Butt (*Alexander Pope: Minor Poems* (London, 1954), 217) that this
and similar echoes indicate Pope's hand in *Acis and Galatea* is merely a further instance
of the scholarly habit of attributing, wherever possible, Gay's works to one of his more
celebrated colleagues.

[32] Lang, 206, 259. Paul Lang best describes the differences between *Acis and Galatea*
and Handel's earlier treatment of the same theme. 'The greatest difference from the early
Italian setting of this pastoral theme, and one that in fact was an altogether new departure
for Handel, was the use of the chorus. With "Wretched lovers" he far exceeds the
boundaries of the serenata and is within the region of the choral music drama. The
incentive came, of course, from English poetry . . . Even this master of choral writing
seldom achieved such a dramatically "through-composing" scene as this. The beginning,
a slow dirge in which the contrapuntal parts are loath to release the suspensions,
introduces something new in Handel's artistic world: this, in tone and attitude, is the
chorus of Attic tragedy. Once the contemplative and commentary part ends, the pace
quickens and so does the excitement, until the intricate counterpoint is replaced by
shouts. Handel charged the bucolic atmosphere with tragedy, but realising that despite all
its expressive beauty this chorus could destroy the spirit of the pastoral, with a master
stroke he removed the anguish by the simple means of not taking the raging Polyphemus
too seriously. In less subtle hands Polyphemus would have become a plain villain. Handel
made the ungainly giant fierce but in a blustery way, and this monster is also amorous; his

At some point in 1718 Handel left Burlington House to take up residence at Cannons, the Edgware mansion home of James Brydges, Earl of Caernarvon (later Duke of Chandos). Brydges, who had made his fortune as paymaster-general to the army, was another opera lover who set out to rival Burlington as a patron of musical tastes. He already employed Pepusch as his 'director of music' and, by recruiting Handel as his 'resident composer', signalled an intention to turn Cannons into a centre for the new musical taste. Almost certainly *Acis and Galatea* received its first performance at Cannons soon after Handel came into residence there, but exact information is lacking, and we have no way of knowing whether Gay was present to see the work performed.[33] Later that August Pope and Gay returned to Oakley Wood, where Pope fondly hoped the Blount sisters would join them. He suggested that Mrs Pope, Gay, and himself could meet them '& show you Blenheim by the way . . . our roads are very good all September, come, stay and welcome'. But the sisters were not persuaded, and, disappointed of their company, Pope resigned himself to such woodland amusements as gathering nuts 'which I believe Gay & I shall oft'ner crack than jokes'. In September Gay returned to London, leaving a still melancholy Pope to spend his days in 'dry walks' through Oakley Bower, his evenings playing cards, and his nights in erotic fantasies of the Blount sisters '& those white bums which I die to see'.[34]

Emerging from his rural isolation, Gay now happily resumed the social round, enjoying songs with the maids of honour, politics with Pulteney, and drinking-sessions with Lord Warwick, whose mother, much to Warwick's chagrin, had recently married Addison. He also spent much time with Warwick's Piccadilly neighbour Burlington,

confession of love, "O ruddier than the cherry" restores the fairy tale atmosphere. The opening chorus, "Oh the pleasures of the plains", is the quintessence of the pastoral, the drone bass and the lightly floating recorders creating a bit of Arcadia straight from Sicily. But "Hush, ye pretty warbling choir" is English pastoral *in excelsis*. Acis's love songs are also affectingly lyrical. In the closing scene the spectators, again the Greek chorus, are seized with grief, blurting their lines between long pauses as if they cannot collect themselves. The trio "The flocks shall leave the mountains" admirably sums up the dramatic situation. It is a genuine ensemble, remarkably varied in the combination of expression, sound, rhythm, and dynamics, in which each figure retains its individuality, though as a character portrayal Polyphemus towers over the others.' Ibid. 273–4. As usual, there is no acknowledgment of Gay's role in facilitating the achievement of such a musical triumph.

[33] The work received no public performance until 1732, the year of Gay's death.
[34] Pope, *Corr.* i. 515.

now deeply engaged in his campaign to revolutionize the architectural, musical, and artistic taste of the town. In 1717 the first
volume of Colen Campbell's *Vitruvius Britannicus* had appeared,
denouncing the old baroque style with its 'capricious ornaments' as
obsolete. Burlington promptly commissioned Campbell to take over
the renovation work on Burlington House, replacing the Tory James
Gibbs, whose designs Gay had praised in *Trivia*.[35] When Kent
returned from Italy Burlington set him to work on interior decorations, supervising and supplanting work already begun by the Italians
Marco and Sebastiano Ricci. Throughout the year both Pope and
Gay were very much caught up with all the excitement of these
developments. For several months Pope even toyed with the idea of
building his own matching *palazzato* just behind Burlington House,
'on the same plan & front with Lord Warwick's, so as not to clash
with any regular designs'. However, the cost of Colen Campbell's
proposals ('200 pound above what I am pretty well assured I can
build the same thing for') gave him cause to hesitate.[36]

In October Eustace Budgell once more came to Gay's attention.
Recently dismissed from his post as chief secretary to the Lords
Justices of Ireland, Budgell attempted to reclaim his reputation in a
lengthy pamphlet of self-justification entitled *A Letter to the Lord
***** . . . Throughout the pamphlet Budgell refers repeatedly to 'the
honour I have of being so nearly related to Mr Addison', but by
now Addison felt it something less than an honour to be so nearly
related to this sad, self-righteous figure. Over a dozen pages of
Budgell's pamphlet are filled with flattery of King George: 'this
great and good prince . . . wise in his counsels, brave in the field,
resolute in his undertakings, and graceful in his person'. This is
rather too much to take in a pamphlet which concludes by assuring
readers 'that I will not flatter any Great Man. I was never a mighty
admirer of the panegyric . . .' Such a work clearly invited parody
and was soon answered by *A Letter to a Buttonian Knight . . . from*

---

[35] In vol. iii of *Vitruvius Britannicus* (1725) Campbell writes of Burlington House: 'the
stables were built by another architect before I had the honour of being call'd to his
lordship's service, which obliged me to make the offices opposite conformable to them.
The front of the house, the conjunction from thence to the offices, the great gate and
street wall, were all designed and executed by me'—see Lees-Milne, 117. The influence
of the new architectural fashion was confirmed in 1718, when Sir Christopher Wren was
replaced as surveyor-general to HM Board of Works by the amateur Palladian William
Benson.

[36] Pope, *Corr.* i. 516.

Sir James Baker, Admirer-General of the Fair Sex. Almost certainly this 'James Baker' pamphlet can be ascribed to Gay since, apart from Budgell, it also mocks two other estranged friends, Aaron Hill and Richard Steele, both of whom had diversified from literary enterprises into utopian joint-stock ventures worthy of the academicians of Lagado. 'Baker's' treatment of Steele's fish-pool scheme and Hill's beech-mast project has much in common with Gulliver's later description of the projector who 'had been eight years upon a project for extracting sun-beams out of cucumbers'.[37] That Gay should take this opportunity to ridicule his former friends and colleagues should not be taken as evidence of bad faith. Such reversals were part of the essential dynamic of both the literary and political worlds. One of Budgell's more congenial duties in Ireland had been intercepting Swift's correspondence. Hill had recently attacked Pope, echoing Dennis's denunciations of him as 'a kind of foe to everybody but yourself'. Walpole, former scourge of Tories, was now courting Tory allies to challenge the Whig ministry, while in France Bolingbroke, the former Jacobite, was eagerly betraying erstwhile Jacobite friends. Within months even those closest of literary allies, Addison and Steele, would be savaging each other in print over the Peerage Bill. Gay, who had every reason to suspect the Button's clique of sabotaging his own hopes of court preferment, viewed all such opportunist alliances with an ironic detachment. Men like these were practised self-apologists, and he took an obvious relish in the spectacle of their current disarray.

Politically the autumn was a time of considerable instability, as the infighting continued within Whig ranks. James Craggs, another drinking-companion of Warwick's, took over the Southern Department from Addison while Stanhope gave up the Treasury to Sunderland in exchange for the Northern Secretary's post. Meanwhile the opposition, led by Walpole and Pulteney, began to notch up some successes. When Stanhope introduced a Peerage Bill aimed at limiting the creation of new titles, Walpole seized the opportunity for a powerful political attack. Addison, supporting the ministry, was more than matched by Steele writing for the opposition and in April 1719 the Bill was dropped. Walpole, Pulteney, Townshend, and the Prince of Wales had won their first significant victory.

Arbuthnot had spent much of the summer in France and returned

---

[37] *Gulliver's Travels* (1726), bk. iii, ch. v.

full of anecdotes and gossip. In particular he related the story of Nelly Bennet, a young Irish cousin whom he had introduced at the French court, where 'she was admired beyond all the ladies in France for her beauty' and, among other amorous favours, invited to kiss the young King's cat.[38] Gay, amused by a story which confirmed his view of French courtiers as two-legged domestic pets, promptly turned it into a lively bawdy ballad.

> For when as Nelly came to France,
> (Invited by her cousins)
> Across the Tuileries each glance
> Kill'd Frenchmen by whole dozens.
> The king as he at dinner sat,
> Did beckon to his hussar,
> And bid him bring his tabby cat,
> For charming Nell to buss her.
>
> The ladies were with rage provok'd,
> To see her so respected;
> The men look'd arch, as Nelly strok'd,
> And Puss her tail erected.
> But not a man did look employ,
> Except on pretty Nelly;
> Then said the Duke de Villeroy,
> *Ah! qu'elle est bien jolie!*[39]

Arbuthnot had also taken his two daughters with him to France, and the ballad's most *risqué* moment comes when Gay imagines a French courtier attributing the doctor's jealous regard for these young ladies to incestuous motives.

> *Ma foy!* (quoth then a courtier sly,)
> He on his child does leer too;
> I wish he has no mind to try
> What some papa's will here do.

---

[38] Swift, *Corr.* ii. 300.

[39] The poem was first published in the so-called 'last' volume of the Pope–Swift *Miscellanies* (1728) and so its authorship is not beyond dispute. Lester Beattie, denouncing it as 'an extraordinarily coarse and insinuating poem' (*John Arbuthnot: Mathematician and Satirist* (Cambridge, Mass., 1935), 287), is anxious to deny Arbuthnot's hand in it. Irving, less hysterical, detects in the ballad Gay's characteristic fondness for 'obscene fun' (p. 174). Citing the evidence of Gay's own recent experience of the French court, and the fact that he 'was busy at this time writing some of his very best songs', Irving concludes: 'I have no doubt that Gay wrote the verses.'

The ballad concludes on a triumphant note of sexual patriotism; the French may like their goddesses as ornamental symbols, naked beauties carved in stone and shamelessly exposed to public view in ornamental gardens. Gay's English taste is more discreet, preferring fleshly goddesses whose finer points are only revealed by more intimate topographical explorations.

> Were Nelly's figure mounted there,
> 'Twould put down all th'Italian:
> Lord! how those foreigners would stare!
> But I shou'd turn Pygmalion:
> For spite of lips, and eyes and mien,
> Me, nothing can delight so,
> As does the part that lies between
> Her left toe, and her right toe.

Meanwhile, at the Haymarket theatre, the ugly Swiss-born impresario 'Count' Heidegger presented a troupe of French and Italian comedians performing acrobatic harlequinades. Heidegger's Haymarket masquerades had a reputation for disorderliness and debauchery which Gay chose to satirize in a bawdy ballad which introduced Heidegger's double, the devil, as a lively hermaphroditic participant.[40]

---

[40] This poem is not included in Dearing's collected edition of Gay's *Poetry and Prose*. The manuscript (Duke of Portland MS Pw V351) was first discovered and published by P. J. Croft in *Autograph Poetry in the English Language* (2 vols., London, 1973), i. 64–7. The poem is fifteen stanzas long and can be dated from internal evidence, such as the references to Thomas Killigrew's play *Chit-Chat*, performed at Drury Lane in Feb. 1719. The authenticity of the ballad is accepted by Pat Rogers (*Literature and Popular Culture in Eighteenth Century England* (Brighton, 1985), 55, 68), who points out that the devil was 'a favourite [masquerade] costume, which is prominent in Hogarth's print [*Masquerades and Operas* or *The Bad Taste of the Town*] at the head of the queue entering the theatre'; *Literature and Popular Culture*, 55. See also my own article, 'Pope and Heidegger: A Forgotten Fragment', *Review of English Studies*, 23 (1972), 308–13. In 1729 Lord Egmont complained of the depravity of Heidegger's productions: 'These masquerades are the corruption of our youth and a scandal to the nation, and it were well to be wished the king would not encourage them. The bishops have addressed in a body against them . . . but all to no purpose.' *Diary of Viscount Percival, afterwards First Earl of Egmont*, Historical Manuscripts Commission (3 vols., London, 1920–3), 23 Jan. 1729. Twenty years later Heidegger's masquerades still had the same reputation for promiscuous depravity. The ballad *Marriage A-la-Mode* (1746) included these lines: 'Blest H[eide]g[ge]r, that could invent, | A Scheme both sexes to content! | What longing wife, what melting maid, | Who sighs not for a masquerade?'

8

He tempted in all shapes, maids, widows and wives,
Who ne'er did such frolics before in their lives
   And as they tell me,
   Some husbands [may] still see
The print of his black hand above their wives' knee
Oh Heidegger &c.

11

Who took him for woman, might find by the smell
That their fingers had been in the devil of hell.
   If man's shape he chose,
   And touch'd a *belle chose*
He burnt lady's smocks, and singed their domino's
Oh Heidegger &c

Although ostensibly deploring such licentious antics, Gay's lines clearly relish the devil's polymorphous perversity. There is a mischievous relish in these lines, which culminate with the roof of the theatre exploding in orgasmic excitement. The writing of ballads like these, relaxed, bawdy, and teasing, represented a welcome relief from the solemn Arcadian formality of the Stanton Harcourt pair.

By the end of the year Gay's circle of literary friends was reduced by the deaths, in quick succession, of Parnell, Garth, and Rowe. In June the following year Addison also died, but not without some final scenes of death-bed sententiousness. First, he summoned his dissolute stepson, Lord Warwick, to his sick-room to 'see in what peace a Christian can die'.[41] Then, as part of his final Christian peacemaking, he sought a reconciliation with Gay. Sending for him in a solemn manner he made a penitent confession: 'that he had injured him greatly, but that if he lived he should find that he would make it up to him.'[42] This was how an Olympian took his leave; but it would have come as little consolation to Gay to receive such a belated and sanctimonious apology. Addison had had four years in which he might have repaired the wrong he had done him. Now, when it was too late, this conscience-salving gesture only added insult to the injury it confessed.

---

[41] Edward Young, *Conjectures on Original Composition* (1759), 101–2.
[42] Spence, item 187; i. 79.

With Pulteney once more preoccupied with political affairs, Gay now spent most of his time in company with Pope, Arbuthnot, and the Blounts. But even the Blount sisters were toying with the idea of an overseas adventure. Letters from their friend Mary Dering in Charleston, Carolina, tempted them with the prospect of American admirers:

If you want lovers, quit those dull assemblies & masquerades for our new world. The men shall own your merit & your beauty & make you mistress of a hundred slaves & Indian kings shall daily be employed to feast your taste. We have ortolans in vast abundance.[43]

When Burlington too decided in the summer of 1719 to leave England for a trip to Italy Gay decided there was little reason for him to stay in London.

We have virtually no information about Gay's activities in 1719. All we know for certain is that he was in Dijon in September, from where he wrote to Mrs Howard. Burlington met Kent by prearrangement at Genoa and it seems likely that Gay may have accompanied him on the first part of his journey, though his letter to Mrs Howard makes no mention of such an arrangement. Without Burlington's assistance, though, it is difficult to see how Gay would have financed a lengthy Continental trip which included a month recovering from a fever at Spa and visits to Lyons, Montpellier, and Paris. It is possible that Pulteney may have dispatched him as an emissary to Bolingbroke, who continued to bombard Lord Stair with professions of loyalty. In February Bolingbroke had had a meeting with 'Mr Arbuthnot' and in April the following year was back at Aix-la-Chapelle. But, though the likelihood is strong, there is no definite evidence of a meeting between himself and Gay.[44]

[43] Letter from Mary Dering to Martha Blount, Charleston, Carolina, 18 Feb. 1718; Mapledurham MSS. Dering, though, was unsentimental in her account of the Indian character. 'With all this seeming innocence, [they] are as envious & revengeful as the world that boasts their hypocrisies, & are from children taught to disguise their thoughts. An instance of it has lately happened. The Cherokees, a vast Indian nation, have a conjuror called Cherokee-Aga & a war-captain called Caesar, (all the nations have two such useful men amongst them). Caesar was always friend to the English, Cherokee-Aga not; but however, coming into alliance with them some years ago, the English treated him, as Caesar thought, with too much respect, for which he vowed revenge, which he has now performed, having shot him as they were going together into the mountains.' Such behaviour is sharply at odds with the nobility of Thomas Southerne's Oroonoko, another Indian prince nicknamed 'Caesar': *Oroonoko* (1696), I. ii. It would be interesting to know if Gay was familiar with this account before composing his idealized version of the Indian character in *Polly*, a work clearly influenced by Southerne's *Oroonoko*.

Burlington and Kent set about their cultural expedition with a crusading zeal. 'I hope', Kent wrote to a former patron, 'by his lordship's encouragement and other gentlemen who may have a better gusto, than that damned gusto that's been for this sixty years past [*sic*].'[45] By contrast Gay's travels have a desultory, forlorn air; he himself describes them as 'tedious'—rambling from spa to spa in pursuit of health and congenial companions. We have no word of other letters, and since Gay complains that his preoccupation with such mundane matters as fever, 'a very bad physician', and bed-bugs 'which are exceeding familiar to strangers' make him a dull correspondent, it seems unlikely that he sent many. Even Pope, who had moved to Twickenham in March, was for once too much taken up with his own domestic affairs to spend time keeping track of his friend's movements.

What Gay does write in his letter from Dijon may offer some clue to the surrounding silence. His continuing failure to secure a place at court led to low spirits which quickly turned to ill health. The itinerary of his journey has a decidedly remedial air, less a Grand Tour than a convalescent cure, and he was in danger of becoming something of a connoisseur of spring-water remedies. Back home the following year he recommended the efficacy of Spa water to Pope, who, in turn, passed on the prescription to Congreve. Yet whatever benefits Gay may have gained from the waters at Spa, the wines of Burgundy, or the Montpellier sun were undermined by feelings of loneliness. One anecdote in his letter to Mrs Howard is particularly revealing:

Last night at an ordinary I was surprised by a question from an English gentleman whom I had never seen before; hearing my name, he asked me, if I had any relation or acquaintance with myself and when I told him I knew no such person, he assured me that he was an intimate acquaintance of Mr Gay at London.[46]

Gay here disowns all knowledge of himself. The literary 'Mr Gay' of London is a person quite distinct from this lonely *habitué* of French boarding-houses and spas. The rest of the letter is taken up with snippets of overheard conversation.

---

[44] Baratier, 86–7, 100. 'Mr Arbuthnot' was almost certainly Dr Arbuthnot's brother, a wine-seller and banker in Rouen.

[45] Lees-Milne, 122. [46] *Letters*, 36.

There was a Scotch gentleman who all supper time was teaching some French gentlemen the force and propriety of the English language, and what is seen very commonly, a young English gentleman with a Jacobite governor. A French Marquis drove an Abbé from the table by railing against the vast riches of the church, and another Marquis who squinted endeavoured to define transubstantiation . . .

It is noticeable that Gay presents himself as saying nothing; he is a spectator, not a participant, eavesdropping from a separate table and drinking his wine (the only positive comment in the letter is his praise of the local vines). It is a letter from a man who feels himself an outsider, on the fringe of things, unable even to acknowledge his own name and reputation which seem, at this distance, to belong not to him but to some fictional *alter ego*. He concludes by asking to be remembered to Mrs Lepell and Mrs Bellenden. No male friend is mentioned in the letter at all. Possibly this silence was designed to outwit post office spies, but it also corresponded with Gay's over-whelming sense of isolation.

It seems reasonable to assume that Gay spent part of his time in France working on the play which he had ready for the stage shortly after his return to England in November. That play was *Dione*, his five-act pastoral tragedy, and the first independent full-length play he had attempted since his ill-fated *Wife of Bath* in 1713. According to the Lord Chamberlain's records for 16 February 1720, Gay had already obtained an order for the Drury Lane managers, Wilkes, Cibber, and Booth, to stage the play. The Lord Chamberlain's instruction is quite categoric: 'I do hereby order and direct that Mr Gay's pastoral tragedy be immediately acted after Mr Hugh's.'[47] Yet despite this order, the play was refused a performance. Hughes's *The Siege of Damascus* appeared as expected on 17 February, but was not followed by *Dione*. This failure to get the play performed must have been a severe disappointment. *Dione* is a long and carefully wrought verse drama which must have cost him much intellectual labour to complete. Perhaps that was part of the problem. Gay's happiest productions, like *The Shepherd's Week* or *The What D'Ye Call It*, have an anarchic spontaneity. But *Dione* is a highly contrived piece, laboriously correct and classically designed, which is now best remembered, if it is remembered at all, for Johnson's celebrated criticism:

[47] PRO document LC 5/157, p. 287; quoted by Nicoll (p. 275).

A pastoral of an hundred lines may be endured, but who will hear of sheep and goats, and myrtle bowers and purling rivulets, through five acts? Such scenes please barbarians in the dawn of literature, and children in the dawn of life; but will be for the most part thrown away, as men grow wise, and nations grow learned.[48]

Johnson's comments are unduly severe but do point to the central problem of the play, namely, its monotonous artificiality of tone. The real puzzle is how the man who had so brilliantly parodied the mummified motifs of both tragedy and pastoral in *The What D'Ye Call It* could have so lost his touch to produce this frozen museum-piece. *Dione* is full of the kind of lines which the *The What D'Ye Call It* parodied. At the start of Act II, scene iv, Parthenia begins her soliloquy with the line, 'This melancholy scene demands a groan'. From Gay's usual audiences a groan is exactly what it would have received; and he should have known it. Gay not only suspends his own sense of the ridiculous; he also purges it from his literary sources. The influence of Motteux's translation of *Don Quixote* is detectable in several places, but Gay systematically sublimates Cervantes's ironic version of pastoral motifs into pure Arcadian myth.

Nevertheless, it is difficult to say why this play should have been thought unworthy of performance when Addison's *Cato* (described by Johnson as 'a splendid exhibition of artificial and fictitious manners') had been such a hit.[49] The taste for Arcadian escapism was at least as well established as that for stoic classical heroism, as Lady Mary Wortley Montagu's recent descriptions of the pastimes of Greek shepherds indicate.

The young lads generally divert themselves with making garlands for their favourite lambs, which I have often seen painted and adorned with flowers, lying at their feet while they sung or played. It is not that they ever read romances. But these are the ancient amusements here, and as natural to them as cudgel-playing and football to our British swains; the softness and warmth of the climate forbidding all rough exercises, which were never so much as heard of amongst them, and naturally inspiring a laziness and aversion to labour, which the great plenty indulges.[50]

Possibly Cibber had not forgiven Gay for *Three Hours after Marriage* and took this means of revenge; or possibly the Drury Lane managers

---

[48] Johnson 'Gay', 69.
[49] The Plays of William *Shakespeare*, ed. S. Johnson (1765), 'preface'.
[50] Pope, *Corr.* i. 396–402.

simply despaired of making such an elaborately literary play work on-stage. For whatever reason, *Dione* was not performed and all Gay's literary labours went unrewarded.[51]

Such a serious misjudgement of London theatrical taste would seem the consequence of Gay's lonely evenings in European spas. *Dione* represents a deliberate attempt to take himself seriously, yet what it betrays is a lack of understanding of his own identity and voice as a writer. It is the work of a man who cannot acknowledge himself as Mr Gay of London. It was about this time that Gay penned his own self-mocking epitaph:

> Life's a jest; and all things show it.
> I thought so once; but now I know it.[52]

He was just about to find out how true that could be.

---

[51] As a literary text it was apparently sufficiently well liked to be issued separately in 1733 and again in 1763 and translated into German: see Irving, 177.

[52] First published in his *Poems on Several Occasions* (July 1720).

TEN

Bubbled

POLLY. I'm bubbled.
LUCY . I'm bubbled.
POLLY. O how I am troubled!
LUCY. Bamboozled, and bit!
(*The Beggar's Opera*, air 36)

No rhetorical motif is more common in Swift's political journalism than the antithesis between the narrow sectional interest of the 'monied men' in the City (Whigs) and the broad national interest of the landed gentry (Tories). He constantly castigates the selfish myopia of those who 'conceived the world to be no wider than Exchange-Alley', or 'mistake the echo of a London coffee-house for the voice of the kingdom'.[1] 'By this means', he complains, 'the wealth of the nation, that used to be reckoned by the value of land, is now computed by the rise and fall of stock.'[2] Yet, however useful for polemical purposes, this antithesis was a considerable over-simplification. Many Tory squires owned stocks and just as many Whig financiers used their trading profits to buy up landed estates. As early as 1711 Robert Harley had sought to ensure a Tory voice in the City by establishing the South Sea Company as a rival to the Whig-dominated Bank of England and East India Company. Over the years the Company's status steadily increased until in the early months of 1720 a Bill was passed 'privatizing' the National Debt by converting government annuities into the equivalent value of South Sea stock. James Craggs, one of the Bill's promoters and a new neighbour of Pope's at Twickenham, encouraged Pope to get in early on what he predicted would be a rapidly rising market. On his advice Pope bought £500 of South Sea stock in March, when its value stood at 200; by June he was gratified to see that value climb to over 1,000.

---

[1] *Prose Works*, iii. 134; vi. 53.
[2] Ibid. iii. 6.

All this came as little consolation to Gay, who was still encumbered with debts. Denied the potential profits from a staging of *Dione* he was thrown back once more upon the support of friends and, under Pope's management, 'cabals were formed our Johnny's debts to clear'. The subscription edition of Prior's *Poems*, from which the author had gained some £4,000, provided the perfect business model, and within weeks a similar network of patrons and well-wishers was being formalized into an effective subscription list for Gay's *Poems on Several Occasions*. It was no doubt highly gratifying to Gay, and not merely in financial terms, to see how generously his friends rallied round to support the scheme. In mid-June he dined with the Duke of Buckingham 'at a sort of *convivium poeticum*',[3] where the other guests included Pope and Prior. They were all in a relaxed and contented mood; Prior, still basking in the success of his edition; Pope buoyant at having finally completed his *Iliad* translation; Gay greatly relieved and gratified at the swelling list of subscribers for his just completed volume of poems.

The subscription list for Gay's *Poems on Several Occasions* provides us with the best evidence of the range of his acquaintances. And it is an impressive roll-call. Running to some 364 names, the subscribers read like a *Who's Who* of court and social life, politics, and the arts. Headed by the Prince and Princess of Wales, it clearly identifies Gay's principal patrons. Burlington and Chandos both subscribed for fifty copies, followed by Pulteney, who took twenty-five. In addition, Bathurst, Henry Pelham, the Earl of Warwick, and James Craggs (proudly identified as 'His Majesty's principal Secretary of State') all subscribed for ten copies each. Multiple subscriptions like these were in fact a form of private subsidy, since aristocratic subscribers rarely demanded their full quota of books in return. Thus Gay eagerly wrote to thank his friend the Earl of Warwick:

Sir, I have sent you only two copies of my poems though by your subscription you are entitled to ten, whatever books you want more Tonson or Lintot upon your sending will deliver. I cannot neglect this occasion of returning you my thanks for the benefits you have done me & I beg you to believe that I have a just sense of them. If you even could think of doing more for me, you could not engage me further to you, for 'tis impossible to owe you more love & gratitude than I do already.[4]

---

[3] Prior to Harley, HMC MSS of the Marquis of Bath (1904), iii. 482.
[4] This letter, first published in 1931, has always hitherto been wrongly identified as

The list also includes the names of several leading politicians from both government and opposition ranks. Stanhope subscribed for five books, with other members of his family taking another five; Townshend, Lord President of the Council, took three; Robert Walpole took two, the Duke of Newcastle took two, and Spencer Compton, Speaker of the Commons, took three. Family and friends are also well represented: Gay's cousin Joseph Gaye subscribed for three books and his sister Mrs Baller for one more; Fortescue and his family took four copies; Arbuthnot and family took three; the Blount sisters took one each. Perhaps the most interesting group of subscribers are Gay's fellow artists, whose presence on the list helps to define the extent of the Burlington–Chandos circle of cultural patronage. Congreve, Handel, Heidegger, Lord Hervey (five books), Jervas, Kent, Kneller, Lady Mary Wortley Montagu, Pope, Prior, Jonathan Richardson, Anastasia Robinson, Horace Walpole, and Edward Young all subscribed. Equally significant is the absence of certain names, most notably of the 'Button's' Whigs Steele, Budgell, Philips, and Tickell. More ominous for Gay was the absence of playhouse supporters. Although the volume included his unperformed *Dione*, none of the Drury Lane managers Cibber, Wilks, or Booth chose to subscribe. Neither did Aaron Hill, who, although anxiously attempting to repair relations with Pope, did not take this opportunity to assist that process by subscribing for his old school fellow's poems.

Just as Gay was basking in the revenues and recognition that such a list provided, he received yet more financial support, when James Craggs made him a handsome present of South Sea stock.[5] In addition, thanks to the business-like canvassing of supporters on his behalf, Gay received the bulk of his subscription money by June, just in time to invest it in the share issue of South Sea stock which closed on 22 June. Clearly Gay had been caught by the infectious

---

addressed to Addison, and hence also wrongly dated in 1713; see *Letters*, 5–6. It was Vinton A. Dearing (ii. 601) who first recognized its correct recipient as Addison's stepson, Edward Henry Rich, seventh Earl of Warwick. Interestingly, more women subscribed for Gay's *Poems* than for any of the other major subscription editions of the period (which included Prior's *Poems*, Pope's *Iliad*, *Odyssey*, and *Shakespeare*, and Addison's *Works*). Also the average age of Gay's subscribers was younger than that for any other comparable edition. See Pat Rogers, 'Pope and his Subscribers', in *Essays on Pope* (Cambridge, 1994), 209–27.

[5] Spence, item 241; i. 105.

spirit of speculative mania which had seen South Sea shares take a fivefold leap in value, and could not wait to join in the general prosperity. For a few weeks he forsook the salons and spas for the stock-jobbers' shops, allowing himself to indulge dreams of making his fortune. On the 24th Pope wrote to Fortescue: 'Pray, if it is possible to remember a mere word of course in such a place as Exchange Alley, remember me there to Gay, for anywhere else (I deem) you will not see him as yet.'[6] By the following week Pope and Gay were indulging visions of themselves as contented Devonshire landowners, and Pope wrote again to Fortescue for details of suitable properties.

From an information given me by Mr Gay, correspondent with what I formerly heard from you, that estates were yet to be had in Devonshire at 20 & 25 years purchase, I beg it of you as a particular kindness to interest yourself so much in my affairs as to get (if possible) about the yearly value of two hundred £ entirely, or in the parcels, (as it falls out & as to your judgement shall seem meet.) If Mr Gay & I by this means become effectually your countrymen, we hope (in conjunction with you) to come in time to represent Devonshire itself.[7]

It is a revealing insight into Gay's psychology that his first instinct, when offered the prospect of a fortune, was to purchase property in his native Devon. For the displaced youngest son of a younger son, the man who in *Rural Sports* wrote feelingly, 'But I who ne'er was bless'd from Fortune's hand, | Nor brighten'd plough-shares in paternal land', the desire to recover a lost patrimony was clearly a strong driving ideal. As a rural squire in his native county, not the hired shepherd who sells his sheep to buy a court livery, he would at last have the independence he so much desired. When Pope speaks of coming 'in time to represent Devonshire itself' he articulates Gay's dream of an end to his wanderings.

That July of 1720 was a heady time for Gay. The subscription edition of his poems provided him not only with much-needed funds; it also offered him the security and satisfaction of seeing the large number of friends in high places who were happy to have themselves identified and numbered among his subscribers. The disappointment of *Dione* and the frustrations of his lonely months

[6] Pope, *Corr.* ii. 48.
[7] Ibid. 49.

rambling from spa to spa were forgotten in the warmth of a high summer of dreams of plenty. All things seemed to conspire to bring about this change of fortune. The very proximity of James Craggs, main proponent of the South Sea scheme, as Pope's friend and neighbour at Twickenham seemed to presage a new era of civilization when art and commerce might go hand in hand. Pope's friend Robert Digby caught the new mood in a letter sent at the end of the month.

I congratulate you, dear sir, on the return of the golden age, for sure this must be such, in which money is showered down in such abundance upon us. I hope this overflowing will produce great and good fruits, and bring back the figurative moral golden age to us. I have some omens to induce me to believe it may; for when the Muses delight to be near a court, when I find you frequently with a great minister, I can't but expect from such an intimacy an encouragement and revival of the polite arts.[8]

For others though the speculative frenzy of what now was called the South Sea Bubble represented not a new golden age but a kind of mass hysteria. A sudden rash of 'Bubble' companies were spawned by promoters keen to cash in on the investing public's eagerness to join the get-rich-quick phenomenon.

Schemes reported (real or fantastic) include one to extract butter from beech trees; one for insurance on horses; one for drying malt by the air; a flying engine; a 'night machine', that is, a burglar alarm; a machine for powdering periwigs; a scheme to make salt water fresh; a wheel for perpetual motion; a hospital for illegitimate children; ... a fish-pool (a different scheme from Steele's); and an engine to remove South Sea House to Moorfields, that is, Bedlam ... Perhaps the most vivid to the imagination of all these wild ideas (it has rightly been termed a 'Swiftian apparatus') was James Puckle's machine-gun, omnipresent in Bubble satires. According to the patent specification, it possessed a convenient attachment for firing either round or square cannon balls, 'according to whether the enemy were Christians or Turks'.[9]

Suddenly none of the normal, prudent rules seemed to apply when there were paper fortunes to be made overnight. Lady Bristol reported that 'Mrs Howard has got £20,000, & [Sophie] Howe

<hr>

[8] Ibid. 51.
[9] Pat Rogers, *Eighteenth Century Encounters* (Brighton, 1985), 18.

£10,000.' The printer John Barber was said to have made £20,000 and the Duke of Chandos made £30,000.[10] Suddenly, too, Exchange Alley was the most fashionable place in town.

> Our greatest ladies hither come,
>   and ply in chariots daily,
> Oft pawn their jewels for a sum
>   to venture't in the alley.[11]

'The demon of stock-jobbing is the genius of this place,' wrote Edward Harley. 'This fills all hearts, tongues and thoughts, and nothing is so like Bedlam as the present humour which has seized all parties.' 'One can hear nothing else talked of,' his sister Abigail agreed. 'Exchange Alley is the place of greatest resort now; there they call this end of the town Wapping.'[12] The most sensational rise in South Sea stock—from 610 to 870—happened in the first two days of June, prompting the government to introduce the 'Bubble Act', passed into law on 9 June, to restrain some of the more obviously fraudulent enterprises. Walpole was among the prudent minority expressing doubts about the security of the mushrooming South Sea speculation, but as yet his warnings went unheeded.

Although hardly sharing Digby's golden-age dreams, Pope experienced considerable feelings of satisfaction at having finally completed his six-year labour of translating the *Iliad*. To mark his friend's monumental achievement Gay composed a celebratory poem which compared Pope's literary 'exile' in Homeric lands with the real-life exile of such absent friends as Swift and Bolingbroke. *Mr Pope's Welcome from Greece* imagines Pope's triumphant home-coming as a hero's return to his native land, fêted by admiring crowds of well-wishers, as his stately bark makes its ceremonial progress up-river, from the shores of Kent to the capital.

> Cheer up, my friend, thy dangers now are o'er
> Methinks—Nay, sure the rising coasts appear:

---

[10] *Letter Books of John Hervey, First Earl of Bristol, 1651–1750* (3 vols., Wells, 1894), ii. 131–2; Edward Harley to Abigail Harley, 25 Feb. 1720, HMC Portland MSS (1899), v. 593.

[11] 'A South-Sea Ballad; or, Merry Remarks upon the Exchange-Alley Bubbles', song II. in *The Shepherd's Garland: Compos'd of Four New Songs* (1720).

[12] HMC Portland MSS (1899), v. 593, 599.

Hark how the guns salute from either shore
As thy trim vessel cuts the Thames so fair.
Shouts answering shouts from Kent and Essex roar,
And bells break loud thro' every gust of air.
Bonfires do blaze, and bones and cleavers ring,
As at the coming of some mighty king.

Borrowing its format from Ariosto, *Mr Pope's Welcome from Greece* is an accomplished and intriguing poem, yet for some reason Gay chose not to include it in his *Poems on Several Occasions*.[13] There are at least two possible reasons for this. The poem is of immense biographical interest since its 168 lines are chiefly taken up with brief thumbnail sketches of friends who are imagined lining the route of Pope's triumphal progress. This gives the poem a special feeling of intimacy, as if identifying the membership of a heroic band. And Irving may be right to suggest that such exclusivity may have made the poem seem more appropriate for circulation in manuscript: 'Presumably [Gay] felt that it would be of interest only to his friends, and modestly underestimated [its] poetic qualities.'[14] However, closer inspection of this Popeian 'fan-club' reveals a striking similarity with the list of subscribers for Gay's own *Poems*. Forty-five of the eighty people named also appear on Gay's list, including six of the seven individuals who had subscribed for ten or more copies.[15] A few others, glimpsed among the crowds of cheering spectators (e.g. Dennis, Gildon, Steele, and Tickell), are there not as friends but enemies. Some names are dropped in jest; thus Oxford is characteristically registered as an absence ('Oxford by Cunningham hath sent an excuse'), giving his nonappearance in Gay's subscription list at least the merit of consistency. The absences of Bolingbroke ('to foreign climates he's confined') and Swift ('When will thou bring back wit and humour here?') make a more serious point, suggesting a political definition to the literary band depicted. In all, excluding such enemies and absentees, something like 70 per cent of those named in the poem were subscribers to Gay's *Poems*, which suggests that Gay may partly have intended it as a vicarious 'thank you' letter to his own

---

[13] The poem, which imitates canto XLVI of *Ariosto's Orlando Furioso*, was first published in Stevens's *Additions to the Works of Alexander Pope, Esq* (1776).

[14] Irving, 181.

[15] The only missing name is that of Henry Pelham.

supporters. And if, as seems likely, he compiled the poem's extensive list of acknowledgements from the 'target list' of names for his own edition, this may in part explain his reluctance to publish it. For there remain about a dozen friends named in the poem whose absence from the list of Gay's subscribers is something of a puzzle. These include Henry Boyle, Thomas and John Dancastle, 'Duke' Disney, Thomas Southerne and John Tidcombe. Gay may have anticipated a certain embarrassment on the part of those identified as members of an exclusive literary fellowship who had neglected to stump up the subscription fee.

But there is another more serious reason why Gay may have felt it more prudent to reserve this poem for private circulation. In imagining Pope's triumphal procession, Gay seems ironically to be recalling what he had witnessed of the carefully stage-managed political welcome for the new King George when he first arrived in England six years earlier.[16] In 1714 the new King had spent his first night in England at Greenwich, where he was 'saluted by all the guns on board all the ships in the river, and welcomed by loud acclamations of the multitudes of people that crowded everywhere the banks.'[17] He was also greeted by the Lords of the Regency and, the following morning, held his first state levee in the Greenwich palace apartments. In 1720 likewise, Gay imagines Pope's first home-coming reception taking place at Greenwich:

> where dwells the friend of human kind,
> More visited than or her park or Hall,
> Withers the good; and (with him ever joined)
> Facetious Disney, greet thee first of all.
> I see his chimney smoke, and hear him say;
> Duke! that's ye room for Pope and that for Gay.

In London, the King's route was decorated as a street festival:

The streets from the Stone's End to St James's, as many miles as they were in length, were thronged with joyful spectators; the balconies all being adorned with tapestries and filled with the brightest beauties in England, who, particularly from Ludgate to Temple-Bar, made an appearance equally suprizing and charming.[18]

---

[16] I am indebted for this suggestion to Pat Rogers's excellent short article 'Satire in Disguise' in *Eighteenth Century Encounters*, 93–9.

[17] John Oldmixon, *The History of England during the Reigns of . . . George I* (1735), 572–3.   [18] Ibid.

Pope's imagined welcome is no less heroic or majestic.

> O what a concourse swarms on yonder quay!
> The sky re-echoes with new shouts of joy:
> By all this show, I ween, 'tis Lord Mayor's day,
> I hear the voice of trumpet, and haut-boy.
> No, now I see them near; oh, these are they
> Who come in crowds to welcome thee from Troy.
> Hail to the bard whom long as lost we mourned
> From siege, from battle and from storm returned.
>
>   7
> Of goodly dames, and courteous knights I view
> The silken petticoat and broidered vest;
> Yea, peers and mighty dukes with ribbands blue
> (True blue, fair emblem of unstained breast.) . . .   (ll. 41–52)

Such a parallel is not merely decorative or playful, for the six years of Pope's Trojan 'exile' corresponded exactly with the six years of George's 'exile' from his native Hanover. The political subtext of Gay's poem is clearly adumbrated in the opening stanza.

> Long hast thou, friend, been absent from thy soil,
> Like patient Ithacus at siege of Troy:
> I have been witness of thy six years' toil,
> Thy daily labours, and thy night's annoy,
> Lost to thy native land with great turmoil . . .   (ll. 1–5)

'George had found his "six years' toil" in Britain distinctly uphill work. He was always hankering after a return to Hanover, and looked on the restrictions placed upon him as intolerable.'[19] Starting in 1716 the King disturbed his supporters by making several lengthy visits to Hanover. 'Once he threatened not to return from Hanover at all . . . But of all his unpopular jaunts, the most ill-timed was that begun on 15 June 1720, when the South Sea Bubble was at its height.'[20] For Pope, the triumphal progress which Gay envisages from Greenwich through cheering crowds lining the banks of the Thames all the way to London is a home-coming, an entry into his birthright. For George, the same progress had been the opposite;

---

[19] Rogers, *Eighteenth Century Encounters*, 98.
[20] Ibid.

not a release from exile, but a life sentence. If, as seems likely, this poem was written shortly after the King's latest escape back to his native land, its political message, however playfully advanced, was potentially subversive. A foreign king gone, and in his place a warrior hero returned at the head of his Homeric armies, to receive the adulation of the people. Of course it was all a piece of literary fantasy, but even fantasies can be dangerous in a time of political uncertainty. A central accusation in Dennis's vituperative *Remarks upon Mr Pope's Translation of Homer* (1717) was that Pope's *Iliad* was a piece of Jacobite propaganda: 'I regard him as an enemy, not so much to me, as to my King, to my country, to my religion, and to that liberty which has been the sole felicity of my life.' Gay's poem ironically transforms Dennis's paranoia into comic verse: a native Catholic hero enthroned at the head of Homeric forces, while Dennis's king abandons London, England, and the South Sea Company in favour of his Hanoverian mistresses. Such writing is great fun, but hardly tactful for someone still hoping to obtain a place at court. There should be little surprise that Gay chose not to include the poem in his *Poems on Several Occasions*.

Although essentially a retrospective collection, Gay's *Poems on Several Occasions*, issued as a handsome quarto volume in a joint publication by Tonson and Lintot, contains several interesting new works. Among the most successful is his *Epistle to the Right Honourable Paul Methuen, Esq*, a poem that returns to Gay's most enduring preoccupation—patronage, and what lies behind patronage, the enabling power of money. Gay is the poet of money; it is the theme his works return to again and again. He does not, like Pope in his *Epistle to Bathurst*, metamorphose currency into a parody of nature; or, like Swift in the first of his *Drapier's Letters*, devalue the coinage into a symbol of servitude. His emphasis is both simpler and more consistently ironic. For Gay the social world is a market-place, and all its honours and achievements are commodities to be traded. Seizing on Addison's vision of Public Credit as the presiding deity of a new consumer culture, he constantly weighs moral value against market price, like a lady of quality cheapening silks in a shop at the New Exchange.

Paul Methuen was a man with all the courtly advantages Gay envied. He was not only very wealthy, an MP and former diplomat, but also a noted literary connoisseur and something of a dandy.

According to Lady Mary, Methuen had been 'picked out' by Lord Halifax as a lover for the King's mistress Mme Kilmansegg, in a manœuvre designed to further both men's political careers. He was, she wrote:

handsome and well-made; he had wit enough to be able to affect any part he pleased, and a romantic turn in his conversation that could entertain a lady with as many adventures as Othello,— and it is no ill way of gaining Desdemonas. Women are very apt to take their lovers' characters from their own mouths; and if you will believe Mr Methuen's account of himself, neither Aramantes nor Oroondates ever had more valour, honour, constancy and discretion.[21]

Methuen was a subscriber to Gay's *Poems* and also appears among Pope's friends in *Mr Pope's Welcome from Greece*, where he is celebrated for feminine rather than philandering qualities: 'Methuen of sincerest mind | . . . grave, yet soft as woman kind' (ll. 55–6).[22] At the time this poem was published (June 1720) Methuen, who had resigned from government along with Walpole and Pulteney in 1717, was hastily reappointed as Comptroller of the Household as the growing crisis of the South Sea Bubble swept Walpole's friends back to office. For Gay, caught up in the uncertainties of the financial situation, it was an opportune moment to make this courtly gesture of friendship.

Yet the poem is far from a simple panegyric. In it Gay pulls off the trick which he had failed to achieve in his *Letter to a Lady* six years earlier: that is, he manages to flatter a potential patron while simultaneously parodying the forms of literary flattery. He begins by listing the ways that poets are exploited by their patrons.

> Yet there are ways for authors to be great;
> Write ranc'rous libels to reform the state:
> Or if you choose more sure and ready ways,
> Spatter a minister with fulsome praise;
> Launch out with freedom, flatter him enough;
> Fear not, all men are dedication-proof.
> Be bolder yet, you must go further still,

---

[21] Lady Mary Wortley Montagu, 'Account of the Court of George I', in *Essays and Poems and 'Simplicity, a Comedy'*, ed. R. Halsband and I. Grundy (Oxford, 1993), 92.

[22] Pope made use of Methuen's diplomatic offices to facilitate his correspondence with Lady Mary in Turkey.

Dip deep in gall thy mercenary quill.
He who his pen in party quarrels draws,
Lists, an hired bravo, to support the cause;
He must indulge his patron's hate and spleen,
And stab the fame of those he ne'er has seen.
Why then should authors mourn their desperate case?
Be brave, do this, and then demand a place.
Why art thou poor? exert thy gifts to rise,
And banish tim'rous virtue from thy eyes.   (ll. 19–34)

All this was familiar territory to Gay and he makes no claim to innocence in respect of such acts of literary prostitution. On the contrary, he writes as one who knows only too well this world of hireling hack-work. In his time, Gay had spattered half a dozen ministers with fulsome praise and, on Pulteney's behalf, had stabbed the fame of Cadogan, a man whom he had almost certainly never met. Even the subscription edition, in which this poem appeared, was part of the same self-serving racket.

Yet let not me of grievances complain,
Who (though the meanest of the Muse's train)
Can boast subscriptions to my humble lays,
And mingle profit with my little praise.   (ll. 43–6)

What Gay has managed here is the perfect con-man's patter: of course he is no better than all the others, but at least he is honest about it. From now on, honesty was Gay's stock-in-trade. If all literature was merely a form of commerce, then Gay chose honesty as his own best-selling line. His most deceptively 'honest' device in this poem is to ignore one name altogether. Although dedicated to Methuen this verse epistle fails to mention its dedicatee at all. Such a silence can be interpreted two ways. On the one hand, it respects Methuen's good taste by refusing to spatter him with ritual praise; on the other, it ironically turns the poem into the very thing it satirizes, a mercenary exercise available for hire to any dedication-proof grandee.

The poem's central proposition is that Britain is a land of potential greatness and artistic talent, currently languishing for want of enlight-ened sponsorship. Why is it that Handel must scour Italy for operatic performers? The answer is not lack of native talent, but lack of money.

'Tis not th'Italian clime improves the sound.
But there the patrons of her sons are found   (ll. 13–14).

Again, 'Why didst thou, Kent, forgo thy native land, | To emulate in picture Raphael's hand?' The answer, according to Gay, is the more generous sponsorship of the arts to be found in Rome. It hardly matters that Gay's facts here are at best tendentious.[23] What this question-and-answer format provides is an easy platform for his praise of such new enlightened patrons as Burlington and Chandos as patriotic heroes. In striving to domesticate a taste for Continental art such patrons simultaneously revive the true national spirit of cultural supremacy. Thus Gay, who preferred the singing of Anastasia Robinson to that of her Italian rivals, contrives to naturalize such foreign influences into a patriotic celebration of native talent. He depicts a heroic fellowship of connoisseurs, artists, and patrons, all dedicated to a single noble ideal. What binds these cultural crusaders together is the common aim of 'doing good'. They appear as a courageous band of pioneers, undeterred by the sneers of their enemies.

> Censure will blame, her breath was ever spent
> To blast the laurels of the eminent.
> While Burlington's proportioned columns rise,
> Does he not stand the gaze of envious eyes?
> Doors, windows are condemned by passing fools,
> Who know not that they damn Palladio's rules.
> If Chandos with a lib'ral hand bestow,
> Censure imputes it all to pomp and show;
> When if the motive right were understood,
> His daily pleasure is in doing good.   (ll. 65–74)

The poem ends with a brief fable, whose moral, that virtue is enslaved while empty pretension goes unharmed, is presented as a strutting crow flatters a lark.

> What force of lungs! how clear! how sweet you sing!
> And no bird soars upon a stronger wing.

---

[23] Dearing takes issue with Gay's assertions, arguing that most Italian patronage 'was personal, and subject to the current whim and income of the patron: "the salary that Monteverdi received in Mantua was exceedingly low" (Manfred F. Bukofzer, *Music in the Baroque Era*, 1947, p. 401)': Dearing, ii. 587.

The lark, who scorn'd soft flattery, thus replies,
True, I sing sweet, and on strong pinions rise;
Yet let me pass my life from envy free,
For what advantage are these gifts to me?
My song confines me to the wiry cage,
My flight provokes the falcon's fatal rage.
But as you pass, I hear the fowlers say,
To shoot at crows is powder flung away.   (ll. 89–98)

The irony here though has a more bitter tinge. Try as he might to enrol himself among the heroic company of stoic idealists, Gay was never able to 'pass [his] life from envy free'.

If, as Gay claimed, 'variety's the source of joy', then his *Poems on Several Occasions* were calculated to bring considerable joy to his subscribers. Apart from *Wine* and his recent translations of Ovid, this volume includes all his major poems to date, and gives a good sense of the eclecticism of his literary repertoire.[24] Among the more interesting new works are five 'Tales' and four songs which emphasize his talent in the less formal literary genres. Johnson famously described him as a poet 'of a lower order',[25] meaning by that phrase not a poet of inferior quality, but one who specialized in the minor or 'lower' literary forms, intended to raise a glass or a smile. Combining bawdy humour with anti-clerical satire, these new 'Tales' abandon the Chaucerian pastiche of his earlier *Answer to the Sompner's Prologue in Chaucer*, in favour of a more generalized pseudo-fabliau style. Several of the settings contain reminders of his recent travels. The haunted inn in *A True Story of an Apparition* seems to recall something of the spooky dilapidation of Stanton Harcourt:

Here towers and antique battlements arise,
And there in heaps the moulder'd ruin lies;
Some lord this mansion held in place of yore,
To chase the wolf, and pierce the foaming boar:
How chang'd, alas, from what it once had been!   (ll. 53–7)

Similarly he chooses Blois, where he stayed in 1718, as the setting for *Work for a Cooper*, a tale of monkish lust. A favourite erotic

---

[24] The volume includes his five town eclogues, only one of which, *The Toilette*, had been published before.
[25] Johnson, 'Gay', 67.

motif is the fantasy of a young servant-girl, equally compliant in buttery and bed.

> Get you a lass that's young and tight,
> Whose arms are, like her apron, white; . . .
> She might each morn your tea attend,
> And on your wrist your ruffle mend;
> Then if you break a roguish jest,
> Or squeeze her hand, or pat her breast,
> She cries, oh dear sir, don't be naught!
> And blushes speak her last night's fault.   (*Cooper*, ll. 21–30)

The coy eroticism of Gay's comic verse always has a kind of peep-show quality; a schoolboy voyeurist fantasy of something naughty and forbidden. In *Work for a Cooper* the lascivious priest fearing his favourite wine-cask has sprung a leak is aided in his search by his willing maid, who climbs up on the barrel.

> She straddles wide, and downward bends;
> So low she stoops to seek the flaw,
> Her coats rise high, her master saw—
> I see—he cries—(then clasped her fast)
> The leak through which my wine has passed.   (ll. 147–51)

A similar ribald fascination with bodily apertures is evident in the *Answer to the Sompner's Prologue*, where a friar, having fastened and bolted every entry to his house against night-faring sprites, is still surprised by a sodomite Satan.

> He turneth the freere upon his face downright,
> Displaying his nether cheeks ful broad and white.
> Then quoth Dan Sathanas as he thwacked him sore,
> Thou didst forget to guard thy postern door.
> There is an hole which hath not crossed been:
> Farewel, from whence I came I creepen in.   (ll. 61–6)

The brief verse epistle *To A Young Lady, with some Lampreys* is a good example of the way Gay toys with sexuality. Aphrodisiacs, those culinary cupids which reduce human desire from a noble emotion to an irresistible craving, are the subject of the poem, though less as the seducer's accessory than the prude's excuse. The young lady's aunt presents herself as a helpless victim of seafood stimulation:

Should I tonight eat sago cream,
'Twould make me blush to tell my dream;
If I eat lobster, 'tis so warming,
That ev'ry man I see looks charming; . . .
Who has her virtue in her power?
Each day has its unguarded hour;
Always in danger of undoing,
A prawn, a shrimp may prove our ruin!   (ll. 29–32, 37–40)

Presented as a kind of rake's recipe-book (the aunt compares the inflaming effects of lobsters and lampreys to that of Rochester's verses), the poem is both an exercise in erotic arousal and a satire on social hypocrisy. The virtue which can be undone by a prawn or shrimp is not very secure. The poem ends, like the ballad on Nelly Bennet, with a rejection of all such artificial (and hypocritical) forms of sexual stimulation:

For when I see you, (without joking)
Your eyes, lips, breast, are so provoking,
They set my heart more cock-a-hoop,
Than could whole seas of craw–fish soup.

For Gay, sexuality is always a handy vehicle for social satire. In *The Mad-dog* he contrasts the prude's pious vocabulary with her insatiable carnal appetite; but the poem ends by taking her insatiable libidinous itch as a metaphor for the compulsive vices of statesmen and courtiers. Even his ghost story *A True Story of an Apparition* concludes on a similar note:

What is the statesman's vast ambitious scheme,
But a short vision, and a golden dream?
Power, wealth, and title elevate his hope;
He wakes. But for a garter finds a rope.   (ll. 139–42)

The songs included in this volume helped to confirm Gay's success as a lyricist, already indicated by the popularity of the ballad ''Twas when the seas were roaring'.[26] 'Damon and Cupid' was apparently composed shortly after Gay had left Pope lamenting the absence of

[26] This ballad was republished several times, with music attributed to Handel. For the details of its popularity, and the evidence of Handel's composition of the music, see Fuller, i. 432–4. In 1784 it was translated into Latin as 'Nympha Lugens'. *Daphnis and Chloe* had already appeared as a printed broadside earlier in 1720, but 'The Lady's

the Blount sisters in Oakley Bower. It presents Damon similarly bewailing the lack of female company as he wanders through the groves.

> Will ne'er a nymph be kind,
> And give me love for love?

Cupid tells him to leave the country and 'hast away to town', since:

> At Court I never fail
> To scatter round my arrows,
> Men fall as thick as hail;
> And maidens love like sparrows.

Cupid's favourite haunt is with the maids of honour, and he advises Damon to 'readily resort | To B[ellende]n's or L[epe]ll's'. But by the time this volume was published, both these former maids of honour had made advantageous marriages. Molly Lepell, 'youth's youngest daughter, sweet Lepell', was secretly married to Lord Hervey, 'fair of face', in May (though their union was not acknowledged publicly till October); Mary Bellenden, having escaped the attentions of the Prince of Wales, married John Campbell, later fourth Duke of Argyll. Both husbands subscribed to the volume (Hervey for five copies) but may have been dismayed by a compliment which identified their new brides as women who 'love like sparrows'.

Without doubt the most popular of these new songs was the charming sea-shanty 'Sweet William's Farewell to Black-Ey'd Susan'. Circulating for some time before its publication in *Poems on Several Occasions*, this ballad was already sufficiently well known to be parodied by an answering ballad, 'Blue-ey'd Lucy to the Tune of Black-Ey'd Susan'. Within the year it was set to music by four different musicians and reprinted in the form of a broadside ballad.[27] The appeal of the song lies in its lyrical simplicity, its lack of literary pretension, and its bitter-sweet blend of innocence and loss. Poised

---

Lamentation' ('Love in cities never dwells, | He delights in rural cells') and 'Damon and Cupid', with its somewhat ambivalent compliment to Bellenden and Lepell, first appeared in *Poems on Several Occasions*.

[27] The musicians were Carey, Leveridge, Haydon, and Sandoni. 'Blue-ey'd Lucy' can be found in *Tunbridgalia; or, Tunbridge Miscellanies for the Year 1719*'. As Irving notes: 'The parodies are innumerable in succeeding years'; for the details of these, and of the ballad's subsequent reappearance in musical miscellanies, see Irving, 179–80, and Dearing, ii. 596.

on the rocking billows, which simultaneously symbolize the shifting tides of change and the returning motion of constancy, the lovers' parting embrace becomes the focus of the world's oscillation between fidelity and faithlessness. As William swears his love to Susan, he describes her in terms of a seductive female rival, the world.

> If to far India's coast we sail,
> Thy eyes are seen in di'monds bright;
> Thy breath is Africk's spicy gale,
> Thy skin is ivory, so white.
> Thus ev'ry beauteous object that I view.
> Wakes in my soul some charms of lovely Sue.

Even the ship that carries him away is another rival, with her sails swelling like ample breasts.

> The boatswain gave the dreadful word,
> The sails their swelling bosom spread,
> No longer must she stay aboard:
> They kiss'd, she sigh'd, he hung his head.
> Her less'ning boat, unwilling rows to land:
> Adieu, she cries! and waves her lily hand.

The finality of that 'adieu' and the fragility of the lily hand (not permanent like ivory, but a symbol of perishability) adds to the poignancy of the scene. This is a beautifully modulated ballad. Avoiding the pastoral condescension and literary knowingness that comes with the use of Arcadian names (Damon, Daphnis, Chloe, Phillida), Gay creates two vulnerable individuals, swearing their fidelity in the midst of a world where nothing is permanent. As in the parting of Polly and Macheath in *The Beggar's Opera*, Gay creates a moment of private tenderness, made poignant by a context of public irony.[28]

All through the heat of summer the South Sea stock continued to float on a buoyant current of optimism. The streets of the capital were thronged with new-made millionaires building castles in the air. With parliament in recess, the King returned to Hanover, and Sir Robert Walpole retired to Norfolk, a kind of fevered holiday

---

[28] It has been suggested that the song's final stanza may have been inspired by the memory of Lady Theodosia's sad farewell to the ship which carried Gay to Hanover.

atmosphere turned the streets into a permanent carnival. Such an 'inundation of wealth', Robert Digby predicted, must give rise to monsters 'as various as those of Nile . . . What will become of the play-house?' he asked: 'Who will go thither when there is such entertainment in the streets?'[29] But this heady atmosphere of casual affluence provided a fertile breeding-ground for monsters of a more familiar kind. On the night of 18 July, as they were travelling back to town, the lords Burlington and Bruce were attacked and robbed in Richmond Lane. With lords and ladies of quality pawning their jewels for ready cash to speculate on the stock market, there were rich pickings for footpads, and, according to the report in *Applebee's Weekly Journal*, Burlington's assailants carried off a sizeable haul.

We are informed that on Monday night last the Earl of Burlington, his brother-in-law, the lord Bruce, and another person of quality, were set upon by two highwaymen in Richmond Lane, who took from them about six hundred guineas, a large blue sapphire ring of great value and 3 gold watches. Two gentlemen mounted on horseback and two servants stood by and were idle spectators.[30]

Burlington promptly did what any sensible person would do in the circumstances; he applied to Jonathan Wild. As the principal god-father of the London underworld, Wild was at this time at the height of his powers, running a criminal protection racket for the capital which was a perfect model of business efficiency. First he instructed his gang members where and what to steal and received the stolen goods from them at a profit; simultaneously he advertised a 'finder's service', offering to retrieve stolen goods and return them to their rightful owners for a handsome fee. Any independently minded felons who refused to co-operate with his organization were easily caught and framed by Wild, who sent more than sixty of them to the gallows.[31] Naturally, it was this 'public service' aspect of his role which he chose to emphasize, assuming for himself the grandiose title of 'Thief-Taker General of Great Britain and Ireland'. And, in the absence of any effective police service, Wild's cynical system of

---

[29] Pope, *Corr.* ii. 51.

[30] *Applebee's Weekly Journal*, Saturday, 23 July 1720.

[31] For the list of sixty-four men and one woman whom Wild claimed to have brought to justice, see my edition of Fielding's *Jonathan Wild* (Harmondsworth, 1982), 259–63. This also contains a note of seventeen publications concerned with Wild which appeared in the period of his trial and execution.

'private vices/public benefits' was not merely condoned, but actively encouraged. Earlier the same year the Privy Council had urgently consulted Wild about methods for checking the recent increase in highway robberies. Unsurprisingly he advised an immediate increase in the rewards paid for apprehending highwaymen. Accordingly in May a Royal Proclamation had raised the recommended level of the reward from £40 to £100, thereby providing Wild himself with a handsome increase in profits.[32]

Much of Wild's success was due to a remarkable flair for publicity. Reports like the following presented him as a fearless law-enforcement agent, travelling the country in pursuit of wrongdoers:

Jonathan Wild, the British Thief-Taker, going down last week into Oxfordshire with a warrant from the Lord Chief Justice to apprehend two notorious highwaymen who infested that country, met them within a few miles of Oxford on the road. But they hearing of his design met him, and one of them fired a pistol at him: but Jonathan having the old proverb for armour, received no hurt, and then he discharged a pistol at them, which wounded one of them so terribly that his life is in great danger: the other was pursued and taken and committed to Oxford gaol, and Jonathan has given security to appear the next assizes to justify his conduct.[33]

Since Gay was currently spending much of his time as Burlington's guest at Chiswick, the Earl's involvement with the 'Thief-Taker' afforded a perfect opportunity to observe Wild's methods at first hand. Within a few months Wild had identified and tracked down the highwayman, James Wright, and handed him over for prosecution. Thereupon Burlington authorized his agent George Graham to offer Wild ten guineas 'for his expense and trouble in the apprehending and prosecuting of ye said Wright'.[34] But, as Graham noted, the Thief-Taker was affronted at the offer of such a paultry sum: 'Wild wd not take 10 guineas but demanded £25.' Accordingly, on another page in the accounts we find this receipt in Wild's own hand:

Recd this 8th of Janry 1721 of ye Rt Honoble ye Earl of Burl by the same hands Twenty-five pounds in full of my bill for the taking and securing James Wright the highwayman yt rob'd his Ldp. I say recd by order by me | Joth Wilde. £25.

Wright's case came on at Kingston assizes the following August,

[32] But in *The Beggar's Opera* the figure mentioned is still £40.
[33] *Weekly Journal*, 13 June 1719.
[34] Chatsworth: account-book of Graham and Collier (Burlington's stewards), 19, 33.

where he was among seven men and three women sentenced to
death. But a week later, and possibly at Wild's connivance, all ten
prisoners were reprieved. For Wright the reprieve was all too brief.
He and Nathaniel Hawes were again condemned to death at the
Old Bailey in December. Hawes refused to plead, whereupon he was
'carried back to the Press Yard . . . stript naked, and ty'd down to
the ground; but when 250 pound weight was laid upon his breast, in
about seven or eight minutes he consented to plead . . .' Wright's
exit, on the gallows at Tyburn, was itself a little piece of theatre:
'who, to the great surprize of the spectators, went with a shroud on
him, and with no shoes or stockings on.'[35]

It seems that Gay spent part of August at Cannons, where one of
Handel's Chandos Anthems received its first performance in the
Duke's newly embellished chapel on the 29th.[36] He may also have
followed Burlington to Yorkshire, where, recovered from his recent
attack, the Earl, with Kent and Bruce, was hurriedly making arrangements for the first season of their new Royal Academy's operatic
programme. Their principal anxiety was the inconvenient pregnancy
of their leading lady, Signora Margherita. But a fortnight later they
had more urgent concerns. In the first few days of September the
value of South Sea stock began to slip. The slip quickly became a
slide, and the slide became a tumble. By the end of the month the
value of the stock, which had touched 1,000 when Gay bought in at
the end of June, had slumped to just 200. Pope, who as late as 22
August had passed on a tip from Craggs to Lady Mary that she
'might depend upon it as a certain gain, to buy the South Sea stock
at the present price, which will certainly rise in some weeks, or less',
saw the whole episode as a salutary moral lesson: 'Methinks God has
punished the avaricious as he often punishes sinners, in their own
way, in the very sin itself: the thirst of gain was their crime, that
thirst continued became their punishment and ruin.'[37] He did,
however, recognize that in this case divine retribution had been
exacted with a somewhat indiscriminate force.

Indeed the universal poverty, which is the consequence of universal avarice,
and which will fall hardest upon the guiltless and industrious part of

---

[35] *Applebee's Journal*, 16/23 Dec. 1721.
[36] Irving (p. 184) suggests that the performance was of Handel's oratorio *Esther*, but
Deutsch (p. 113) questions this idea.
[37] Pope, *Corr.* ii. 52–3.

mankind, is truly lamentable. The universal deluge of the S. Sea, contrary to the old deluge, has drowned all except a few unrighteous men.

Congratulating himself on his relative good fortune in having retained at least half of his speculative gains, he was content to share Arbuthnot's whimsical fantasy, that

the government and South Sea Company have only locked up the money of the people upon conviction of their lunacy, (as is usual in the case of lunatics) and intend to restore 'em as much as may be fit for such people, as fast as they shall see 'em return to their senses.[38]

Others took a far less philosophical view of a catastrophe in which many leading families had lost their entire fortunes. The librettist Antonio Rolli was in no doubt that it was the directors of the South Sea company who needed to be locked up.

What ruination has the South Sea crash caused! The whole nobility is at its last gasp; only gloomy faces to be seen. Great bankers are going bankrupt, great shareholders just disappear and there is not an acquaintance or friend who has escaped total ruin. These rogues of company directors have betrayed everybody and I assure you the tragic worst is feared.[39]

Suddenly all the gossip was not of sudden riches but of instant ruin. 'They say the noble Chandos is reduced to be three days in borrowing eight hundred pounds,' reported Lord Harley.[40] Simultaneously with the bursting of the South Sea Bubble came the threat of plague, which was already raging in Marseilles and much of Provence. Throughout the following winter the newspapers were filled with stories of these two analogous distempers, often describing the South Sea crash in terms of an infection. On 1 October *Mist's Journal* reported: 'Exchange Alley sounds no longer of thousands got in an instant, but on the contrary, all corners of the town are filled with the groans of the afflicted.' In December *Applebee's Journal* developed the plague metaphor further:

In a sick body, when the mass of blood is corrupted, when the constitution of the body is subverted, and the motion of the spirit stopped and stagnated, the patient finds no benefit by medicine; he must be left to the

---

[38] Ibid. 54.
[39] Rolli to Riva, 23 Sept. 1720; trans. Deutsch, 113.
[40] HMC Portland MSS (1899), v. 613.

secret operations of Nature, either for life or death. The body of the South
Sea people seem to be in just such a crisis at this time; the distemper is
strong upon them;—they sink under it, and 'tis vain to offer reasons or
arguments to them; the patient must be left to Nature, and to the ordinary
operations of his own demented understanding.[41]

The columns of these and other papers carried reports of a spate of
deaths and suicides in the wake of this economic disaster. In
February Stanhope died of 'apoplexy' following a vigorous interroga-
tion in the House of Lords; a few days later James Craggs died,
allegedly of smallpox, though there were rumours that both deaths
were really due to a drunken binge: 'The great debauch which killed
Stanhope and Craggs was at the Duke of Newcastle's. They drank
excessively of new tokay, champagne, visney and barba water,
thirteen hours as it is said.'[42] A month later, Craggs's father
committed suicide by taking laudanum.

This feverish atmosphere of panic and recrimination quickly
turned to political crisis as it became apparent that ministers and
their minions had been involved in manipulating the market for
personal gain. Rumours that the absent monarch had made a killing
before selling out his stock at the top of the market even rekindled
thoughts of a new Jacobite rebellion. The Whig MP Arthur Onslow,
a future Speaker of the Commons, later claimed that if James Stuart
had at that time landed in the City 'he might have rode to St
James's with very few hands held up against him'.[43] When the
Commons reassembled in December it was the chance for Robert
Walpole, as the man with clean hands, to take charge of affairs. On
the 21st he presented his rescue package with a scheme allowing
almost half the South Sea Company's capital to be exchanged for
Bank of England and East India stock, with a capital subsidy of £9
million from public funds to compensate for losses. Directors of the
Company were forbidden to leave the country and in January two of
them were imprisoned for corruption.

The extent of Gay's own financial losses is difficult to assess.
Since he had bought at the top of the market, in late June, using
£1,000 of subscription money for *Poems on Several Occasions*, it

---

[41] For a detailed comparison of the reporting of the plague and the South Sea Bubble
see Pat Rogers, 'This Calamitous Year', in *Eighteenth Century Encounters*, 151–67.

[42] Lord Harley to Lord Oxford, 18 Feb. 1721: HMC Portland MSS (1899), v. 616.

[43] HMC Onslow Papers, 14:9, p. 504. Quoted in Bruce Lenman, *The Jacobite Risings
in Britain, 1689–1746* (London, 1980), 258.

would seem probable that he suffered a considerable loss. Certainly in October he was unable to pay his publishers Lintot and Tonson the proportion of the subscription money due to them and replied with some asperity to Tonson's dunning letter:

> I cannot think your letter consists of the utmost civility, in five lines to press me twice to make up my account just at a time when it is impracticable to sell out of the stocks in which my fortune is engaged.

Acknowledging that, in strict terms, his contract had required him 'to make the whole payment in the beginning of September, had it been in my power', he concludes with evident irritation:

> I can assure you I am as impatient & uneasy to pay the money I owe, as some men are to receive it, and tis no small mortification to refuse you so reasonable a request, which is, that I may no longer be obliged to you.[44]

The sourness of Gay's tone here is a clear indication of his severe disappointment that his dreams of country estates should have so abruptly terminated in debts and dunning letters. As Pope later reported, Gay 'was once worth £20,000, but lost it again'.[45] Johnson was in no doubt that Gay was ruined, both financially and physically, by the South Sea Bubble.

> Gay in that disastrous year had a present from young Craggs of some South Sea stock, and once supposed himself to be master of twenty thousand pounds. His friends persuaded him to sell his share; but he dreamed of dignity and splendour, and could not bear to obstruct his own fortune. He was then importuned to sell as much as would purchase an hundred pounds a year for life, *which*, says Fenton, *will make you sure of a clean shirt and a shoulder of mutton every day*. This counsel was rejected; the profit and principal were lost, and Gay sunk under the calamity so low that his life became in danger.[46]

It should be noted though that Johnson's confident summary here embodies two familiar motifs: first, the presentation of Gay as an impractical *naïf*; secondly, his own favourite theme, the vanity of human wishes. In fact, despite Pope's assertion, there are reasons to suspect that Gay, like Pope himself, may have managed to salvage something from the South Sea débâcle. In the rush to present Gay as a helpless victim of financial forces he failed to understand, more

---

[44] *Letters*, 37–8.
[45] Spence, item 241; i. 105.
[46] Johnson, 'Gay', 63.

has depended on myth, and not enough on a thorough analysis of the somewhat complex contractual terms of the stocks he held. Apart from whatever shares he may have received as a present from Craggs, the stock which he bought was part of the company's 'third' subscription share issue, which went on sale on 15 June and closed a week later. Subscription shares like these were bought on margin:

buyers paid only 10 per cent down, contracting to pay the balance in instalments. They bought the stock at 1000, that is, at ten times its redemption value and interest base, but there was an interval of just over a year before the first of the nine half-yearly instalments was due, during which time two interest payments would accrue.[47]

Gay's £1,000 investment was thus a speculative purchase, binding him to pay a further £9,000, which, he naturally assumed, would be more than covered by interest payments and the increase in the capital value of the stock. However, under Walpole's government-imposed settlement of the South Sea Company's affairs, the price of the stock was marked down from 1,000 to 300 and instalments were eliminated; thus, although the market value of Gay's investment was reduced, he was also freed from any further liability: '£1,000 invested in the third subscription simply bought £333 6s 8d of stock in a now viable company.'[48] During the intervening period Gay continued to draw his half-yearly dividend from stocks which, though severely depleted in value, were never worthless. In a note sent on 24 February 1721 he instructed Charles Lockyer, accountant for the South Sea Company, to 'pay to Tho. Glegg my dividend due at Christmas & midsummer last on South Sea stock, being £110'. Two months later, on 1 May, he wrote again to Lockyer with a new instruction: 'Sir, | Please to place to the account of Alexander Pope Esqr. all such stock as is due to me for one thousand pounds of the third subscription paid in upon my name for the sale of South Sea stock.'[49] It is impossible to guess how much Pope may have paid Gay for this transfer of stock since, just a few months earlier, Pope himself had been reluctantly forced to call in a debt from Caryll, being then 'in more necessity for present money than I ever yet was'.[50] Yet it is difficult to believe Pope would have paid less than

---

[47] Dearing, ii. 608.
[48] Ibid.
[49] *Letters*, 38.
[50] Pope, *Corr.* ii. 60.

the current market value—something over £300. For his original investment of £1,000, then, it seems reasonable to assume that Gay realized something over £400; a loss, certainly, but by no means a financial catastrophe. As late as June 1722 he still retained some of his original stock in the restructured company, and wrote to the new cashier, Conrad de Gols, requiring him to 'pay to Mr Henry Watson the dividend on all my stocks in your books due at Christmas last'.[51]

In his poem 'The Birth of the Squire' Gay pictured the life of the country squire, born to a patrimony of family retainers and extensive estates. As if in revenge for his own lack of paternal land, Gay predicts for the young squire a career, not of glorious achievements, but of blundering shame. First, the fathering of a bastard child; next, a collar-bone cracked in a hunting accident; finally, the ultimate abasement:

> He shall survive; and in late years be sent
> To snore away debates in parliament.

If Gay now found himself denied the wished-for honour to 'represent Devonshire itself', he might at least take consolation from escaping this ale-befuddled fate.[52]

> Methinks I see him in his hall appear,
> Where the long table floats in clammy beer,
> 'Midst mugs and glasses shatter'd o'er the floor,
> Dead-drunk his servile crew supinely snore;
> Triumphant, o'er the prostrate brutes he stands,
> The mighty bumper trembles in his hands;
> Boldly he drinks, and like his glorious sires,
> In copious gulps of potent ale expires.

Both Pope and Gay lost money in the South Sea fiasco. It was Gay's opinion that Pope's decision, in early 1723, to translate the *Odyssey* was motivated 'rather out of a prospect of gain than inclination, for I am persuaded he bore his part in the loss of the South Sea'.[53] Yet for neither of them did these losses amount to a disaster, and it is clear that both men, taking advantage of Walpole's rescue scheme to stabilize the markets, managed, through the effective rescheduling of debts and transfer of liabilities, to minimize the impact of these

---

[51] *Letters*, 40.
[52] Included in *Poems on Several Occasions* (1720).
[53] Gay to Swift, 3 Feb. 1723; *Letters*, 43.

losses. In fact, making a virtue of necessity, they even managed to take some moral credit from their monetary debts. It was Bishop Atterbury who first suggested this way of thinking:

Let me add one reflection to make you easy in your ill luck. Had you got all that you have lost beyond what you ventur'd (perhaps £7,000 or £8,000), consider that your superfluous gains would have sprung from the ruin of several families that now want necessaries. A thought under which a good and good-natured man, that grew rich by such means could not, I persuade myself, be perfectly easy.[54]

Soon Pope was repeating these same sentiments as his own, earnestly assuring Caryll: "'Tis a serious satisfaction to me to reflect, I am not the richer for the calamities of others, which (as the world has gone) must have been the case nine times in ten.'[55] It became a sign of virtue not to have benefited from this corrupt speculative mania of the moneyed men, and Pope and Gay were content to draw moral capital from their wasting financial assets.

In fact Gay's main reaction to the 'Bubble' episode, as reflected in his *Panegyrical Epistle to Mr Thomas Snow*, was not bitter but ironic. Published on 8 February 1721, before the terms of Walpole's rescue package were finalized, and when Gay still held over £1,000 worth of potentially worthless stock, this poem demonstrates not the rancour of a ruined man but the wry humour of a stoic comedian. The Bubble had turned finance into fantasy, transforming the sober business of investment into a surreal flight of the imagination. Change Alley, rather than Parnassus, was the new haunt of the monetary muses.

> No wonder, if we found some poets there,
> Who live on fancy and can feed on air;
> No wonder they were caught by South Sea schemes,
> Who ne'er enjoyed a guinea but in dreams;
> No wonder they their third subscription sold,
> For millions of imaginary gold.   (ll. 19–24)

As in his *Epistle to Lowndes*, which presented the Treasury Secretary as the supreme poet of the age, Gay here casts the sombre banker

---

[54] Atterbury to Pope, 28 Sept. 1720: *Corr*. ii. 56.
[55] Pope, *Corr*, ii. 60.

Snow, with his black pen, sable locks, and hands 'black with gold', as the arch-magus and impresario of a new visionary golden age. Like Digby, imagining empty playhouses as the spirit of fantasy took to the streets, Gay presents the Bubble mania as a kind of Eldorado romance. The topography of the poem emphasizes a sense of Ovidian metamorphosis, transforming the mundane institutions of London – Change Alley, Temple Bar, and Bedlam – into beguiling South Sea islands. Stocks and shares become 'rocks and shelves' where 'thousands drowned | When credit sunk . . .'. Snow himself presides over it all, tantalizingly, like an Inca chief: '(an Indian king in size and hue) | Thy unexhausted shop was our Peru.' The poem's central 'moral tale' presents the trance-like transaction between a banker and a poet as a Hogarthian Bedlam fable. The banker, raising imaginary castles out of piles of straw, offers to sell them to the poet.

> The banker cried, 'Behold my castle walls,
> My statues, gardens, fountains, and canals;
> With land of twenty thousand acres round!
> All these I sell thee for ten thousand pound.'
> The bard with wonder the cheap purchase saw,
> So signed the contract (as ordains the law.)
> The banker's brain was cooled, the mist grew clear;
> The visionary scene was lost in air.
> He now the vanished prospect understood,
> And feared the fancied bargain was not good.
> Yet loth the sum entire should be destroyed;
> 'Give me a penny, and thy contract's void.'
> The startled bard with eye indignant frowned.
> 'Shall I, ye gods, (he cries), my debts compound!'
> So saying, from his rug the skewer he takes,
> And on the stick ten equal notches makes.
> With just resentment flings it on the ground;
> 'There, take my tally of ten thousand pound!   (ll. 54–71)

The joke here is clearly on himself, for having imagined himself, however briefly, 'once worth £20,000' and the potential possessor of a Devonshire estate. Only in the monopoly-money of Bedlam could Gay ever have owned such a property. Yet the poem is without anger; what it expresses, above all, is a grudging admiration for the mesmerizing powers of enchanters like Snow. As he sat, amusing himself by turning his worthless stock-certificates into paper kites, Gay was diverted by the thought that the true visionaries of his age were not poets and tragedians, but politicians and bankers whose make-believe enchanted and deluded millions.

By now fashionable society was at last tiring of the enticements of Change Alley and returning to more customary entertainments.

> At length, the phrenzy of the realm is o'er,
> And the wide-spreading mischief reigns no more:
> Lured by false prospects, and misguided long,
> At last to balls and theatres you throng.[56]

The most chic of these new entertainments were the operas of Burlington's Royal Academy, founded by subscription the previous year. Interestingly, the Academy's subscription list bears striking similarities with that for Gay's *Poems on Several Occasions*. Burlington and Chandos were the chief patrons of both and exactly half of the sixty-two original subscribers to the Academy also appear on Gay's list. Among the Academy's directors the proportion was even higher. Minutes of a meeting of the court of the Royal Academy held on 27 November 1719 reveal that eight of the twelve directors present (Dr Arbuthnot, Mr Blathwayte, Mr Bruce, Mr Fairfax, Mr George Harrison, Mr Heidegger, Mr Smith, and Mr Whitworth) were subscribers to Gay's poems.[57] Established by Royal command and supported by an annual royal subsidy of £1,000, the aim of the new Academy was quite explicit: 'the encouragement of operas for and during the space of twenty-one years.' As music master, Handel received royal instructions to recruit star performers of Italian opera to sing at the Haymarket theatre in London. In particular it was ordered 'that Mr Handel engage Senesino as soon as possible to serve the said company for as many years as may be'.[58]

On the supposed evidence of *The Beggar's Opera*, Gay has traditionally been presented as an enemy to Italian opera. Yet his patrons were the principal supporters of Italian opera in England, and several of his closest friends were among its most active promot-

---

[56] Leonard Welsted, *Prologue to the Town, as it was Spoken at the Theatre in Little Lincoln's Inn Fields* (1721). 'These lines were written for a special performance of *Measure for Measure*, which did not take place' (Irving, 188).

[57] Burlington and Chandos each subscribed £1,000 to the new Academy. For the list of directors see Deutsch.

[58] Deutsch, 90.

ers. Apart from Burlington himself, Arbuthnot was a director of the Academy and Pope was invited 'to propose a seal with a suitable motto' for the new institution.[59] Gay himself had collaborated with Handel and was a friend of Anastasia Robinson, one of the Academy's principal singers.[60] In subsequent years, as feuds and rivalries broke out between supporters of Handel and Bononcini, or between the rival sopranos Cuzzoni and Faustina, Gay would often ridicule the extravagancies and affectations of opposing operatic claques; but he did so with the instincts of an insider. His parodies of Italian opera were written, not in a spirit of nationalistic moral outrage, but with the wit and detail of an amused devotee.

Subscriptions to the Academy took the form of shares which could be traded on the market like the stocks of any other company. Inevitably, comparisons were drawn with the South Sea Company and, during the early months of 1720, satirists made frequent play with the relative share-values of those two latest forms of modish speculation. In his weekly journal the *Theatre*, Steele, a long-standing opponent of Italian opera, noted sardonically: 'Yesterday South Sea was 174. Opera Company 83 and a half. No transfer.' A week later he developed the idea. 'At the rehearsal on Friday last, Signior NIHILINI BENEDITTI rose half a note above his pitch formerly known. Opera stock from 83 and a half when he began; at 90 when he ended.'[61]

Disillusioned and in debt, it has been suggested that Gay began the New Year with an ill-considered act of literary revenge. In January, Cibber's latest play was performed at Drury Lane. Entitled *The Refusal*, it was freely plagiarized from Thomas Wright's *The Female Virtuosoes* (1692), though crudely updated with a few topical 'South Sea' references. Meanwhile, at Lincoln's Inn Fields, there appeared a rival version of Wright's play, entitled *No Fools like*

---

[59] Minutes, 2 Dec. 1719. Deutsch, 97. Apparently Pope failed to comply with this request.

[60] In 1722 this friendship was further strengthened by her clandestine marriage to the Earl of Peterborough, himself a subscriber to Gay's poems and an intimate acquaintance of the whole Scriblerian group. Anastasia's sister Margaret (Peg) later married Arbuthnot's brother George, 'an event duly chronicled in Gay's own correspondence. The Robinsons were Catholics, and hence it was Pope who kept most closely in touch with them. But Gay was well acquainted with both the Earl and his wife; we need not take seriously the story that he composed love letters to Mrs Howard in the Earl's name' (Rogers, 'Gay and the World of Opera', in Lewis and Wood, 156).

[61] *Theatre*, 1 and 8 Mar. 1720; the fictitious name of the singer is a conflation of Nicolini and Benedetto.

Wits. No copy of this play, first performed on 10 January, survives, though both Irving and Fuller assert that it was written by Gay.[62] Winton, however, dismisses such claims as 'a tissue of improbabilities'. The traditional account, repeated by Fuller, insists that *No Fools like Wits* was 'acted against Mr Cibber's *Refusal*'; but the dates tell a rather different story. Cibber's play was in fact performed a month *after* the production of *No Fools like Wits* in January 1721. 'Are we to suppose', Winton enquires, 'that Cibber generously supplied Gay with the promptbook in advance, so that he could write his attack?'[63] Neither play was a great success and the only one to benefit from this latest theatrical spat was Edmund Curll, who took the opportunity to rush out a reprint of Wright's original play with a cast-list 'Cibberiz'd' (i.e. cut) from thirteen to ten, and a preface, addressed to Cibber himself. In this, while cheekily reminding the actor-manager that Wright's play was itself plagiarized from Molière, Curll solemnly rebuked both playwrights for taking liberties with their sources. *The Refusal*, he concluded, was like 'a sampler, whereon Monsieur Molière's stitching may be easily perceived from Mr Cibber's canvas'; but *No Fools like Wits* was even worse, a play 'such . . . as can only be called *Monstrum & Horrendum*'.[64] These terms, 'monstrum & horrendum', may well have been intended to recall *Three Hours after Marriage*, and it seems possible that Curll (and maybe Cibber too) believed that Gay had written *No Fools like Wits*. As Fuller notes:

It is significant that in 1721 there were no performances of *The What D'Ye Call It*, although it had previously been in the repertoire at Drury Lane

---

[62] Irving, 188–90; Fuller, i. 31.

[63] See Winton, 69, 188. Mottley's *Complete List of all the English Dramatic Poets* (1747) describes *No Fools like Wits* thus: 'A Comedy, acted at the theatre in Lincoln's Inn Fields in the year 1720. It is an alteration of a comedy called *The Female Virtuosoes*; and acted against Mr Cibber's *Refusal*, which was partly taken from the same play.' Fuller states as a fact that Gay 'rewrote Wright's *Female Virtuosoes* (1692) as *No Fools like Wits* . . . intending to expose Cibber's plagiarism from the same play in his *The Refusal*' (Fuller, i. 31).

[64] *Biographia dramatica* agreed with Curll's verdict. *No Fools like Wits*, it asserted, was a mere 'republication' of Wright's original, set up and acted for three nights in opposition to Cibber's *Refusal*, 'which was partly borrowed from the same play, or at least from the same original, viz. the *Femmes Scavantes* of Molière. No one, we believe, will think this comedy equal in merit to *The Refusal*' (London, 1812), iii. 86. First issued on 14 Jan. 1721, Curll's reprint ran into a second edition the following month. Interestingly the British Library copy of this second edition originally belonged to Gay himself.

every year since its first performance: it is as though Cibber could not bear to put it on, popular as it was.[65]

Since no copy of *No Fools like Wits* survives, it is impossible to be conclusive about this point. But it is difficult to believe that Gay, anxious to recoup his South Sea losses, should have thus gone out of his way to damage further his relationship with the principal manager of one of the town's two leading theatres. Already he feared that, if he wished to see his works performed on stage, he must cultivate the favour of Burlington's operatic clique. In April he composed a brief motto for Rolli's opera *Muzio Scaevolo* which must have seemed peculiarly appropriate.

> Who here blames words, or verses, songs or singers,
> Like Mutius Scaevola will burn his fingers.[66]

For much of the spring and early summer Gay was Burlington's guest at Chiswick. 'I live almost altogether with Lord Burlington', he told his friend Francis Colman, 'and pass my time very agreeably'. Yet, however agreeable the company and surroundings, Gay resented being reduced once more to the role of a dependant, and his breezy tone breaks down as he confesses to Colman: 'You must think that I cannot be now and then without some thoughts that give me uneasiness, who have not the least prospect of ever being independent'.[67] The Pulteneys paid him a visit at Chiswick, but they, like Burlington, had more pressing concerns than Gay's employment prospects. Colman, Pulteney's relative by marriage,[68] had just been appointed British Resident in Florence. Writing to congratulate him, Pulteney urged him to stay a night or two at Chevening *en route* to Dover, adding: 'If you could persuade John Gay to come on horseback with you I shall be glad of it, because the affair is over which was to have brought me to town, so that he cannot return with me.'[69] The air of afterthought here is typical of the way that Gay appears in the correspondence of his influential friends.

---

[65] Fuller, i. 31.

[66] This opera, performed at the King's theatre in the Haymarket on 15 Apr., was intended as a showcase for all the Academy's leading talents, with music by Amadei for the first act, by Bononcini for the second, and by Handel for the third.

[67] *Letters*, 39.

[68] Colman's wife, née Mary Gumley, was Ann Pulteney's sister.

[69] *Posthumous Letters from Various Celebrated Men to Francis Colman and George Colman the Elder* (London, 1820), 1.

Pulteney would be glad of his company, but only so long as no effort was required to procure it. In the event, Gay was not included in the Chevening party and wrote to Colman in August regretting 'I had not the opportunity of seeing you before you left England'. No doubt he envied Colman's appointment. 'My friends do a great deal for me', he admitted, 'but I think I could do more for them.'[70] Dependency bred despondency which in turn led to a serious deterioration in his health. At the end of July, frustrated and complaining again of the 'colical humour in my stomach', Gay left Chiswick to take the waters at Bath. He anticipated only a short stay: 'I expect a summons very suddenly to go with Lord Burlington into Yorkshire,' he declared. But that 'summons' (the word is revealing) did not come. The Pulteneys had had some thoughts of joining him at Bath 'but I fancy their journey is put off'.[71] As August gave way to September he became increasingly gloomy. Henrietta Howard received a letter from her friend Mrs Bradshaw describing his despondent state.

I would fain persuade Mr Gay to draw his pen; but he is a lost thing, and the colic had reduced him to pass a hum-drum hour with me very often. I desired him to club a little wit towards diverting you, but he said it was not in him; so I chose rather to expose myself, than not put you in mind of a poor sick body that has taken physic today and not seen the face of a mortal.[72]

A fellow lodger wrote to a friend that 'Gay the poet lodges in our house, so he has supt with us', but in the main Gay avoided much company.[73] Part of his melancholy was the result of a deep depression following the death of his close friend, the young Earl of Warwick. 'I lov'd him', he told Colman, 'and cannot help feeling concern whenever I think of him. Dear Colman be as cheerful as you can, never sink under a disappointment.'[74] Gay's grief at the Earl's death was well known in Bath, though some took a more cynical view of the nature of his 'disappointment'. The Countess of Bristol—Molly Lepell's new mother-in-law—wrote to her husband:

[70] *Letters*, 39.
[71] Ibid.
[72] Mrs Bradshaw to Mrs Howard, Bath, 30 Aug. 1721; BL Add. MSS 22627, fo. 123.
[73] *Political and Social Letters of a Lady of the Eighteenth Century, 1721–1771*, ed. Emily F. D. Osborn (London, 1890), 22. Letter to Robert Byng, Bath, 30 Aug. 1721.
[74] *Letters*, 39–40.

Poor Gay is exceeding melancholy for the death of his friend, Lord Warwick, who died (as they say) without a will; so all goes to Lady Betty, his aunt, who married a country attorney, & poor Rich, of our family, is an earl without a groat.[75]

The fact that it is now impossible to determine whether financial disappointment or emotional loss played the greater part in Gay's 'melancholy reflections' is a good example of the difficulties we encounter in trying to establish a fixed interpretation of Gay's character. For those wishing to see him as an 'Augustan Peter Pan', such open expressions of grief are eloquent confirmation of his tender and sentimental nature. But for those who view his career as a constant struggle for financial security, Warwick's death without a will represents another failed investment, another bubble burst. Warwick's life had been notoriously licentious, and it was generally reported that he, like Craggs, had 'killed himself with his debauchery'.[76] It was Warwick who had inveigled Pope into a whore-house in 1715; and it was Warwick who had provided Gay with a companion willing to share and able to sponsor the pleasures of drunken binges and obscene songs as a release from the life of spa-water remedies and pastoral purity. A bequest from Warwick, Addison's stepson, would have gone some way to compensate Gay for the injury that Addison himself had done to his career.

This materialist interpretation of Gay's 'disappointment' at Warwick's death would seem to be confirmed by the speed with which he set about replacing one dead patron by a new live patroness. After a month of drinking the waters and moping in his room, he began frequenting the pump room and public assemblies when the Duchess of Queensberry arrived in Bath. On 19 September Mrs Bradshaw complained to Mrs Howard about Gay's changed attitude. 'He is always with ye Duchess of Queensberry, for we are too many for him.'[77] Once again Gay allowed himself to indulge the hope of better prospects.

[75] *Letter-Book of John Hervey, First Earl of Bristol . . . 1651–1750*, ed. S. H. A. Hervey (3 vols. Wells, 1894), ii. 161.

[76] G. E. Cokayne (ed.) *The Complete Peerage of England, Scotland, Ireland* (rev. and enlarged edn., 12 vols., London, 1910–59), XII. ii. 418.

[77] Mrs Bradshaw to Mrs Howard, Bath, 19 Sept. 1721, BL Add. MSS 22627.

ELEVEN

A Will of my Own

... what will become of me I know not, for I have not and fear never shall have a will of my own.

(Gay, letter, 1724)

W HEN Gay arrived back in London in the autumn he was promptly plunged back into a new form of literary drudgery. The *Weekly Journal or Saturday Post* for 18 November 1721 carried the following advertisement: 'The celebrated Mr. Pope is preparing a correct edition of Shakespeare's Works, that of the late Mr. Rowe being very faulty.' Pope himself had little enthusiasm for this new task. In a letter to Caryll he described himself descending 'by due gradations of dulness, from a poet a translator, and from a translator a mere editor'.[1] In fact he arranged for the work to be done on a kind of factory system, while he devoted most of his creative energy to planning the grounds and interior of his Twickenham house. In September, he told Tonson, he had 'got a man or two here at Oxford to ease me of part of the drudgery of Shakespeare';[2] but as the months went by, more of Pope's literary acquaintances found themselves called in to assist on the production line. In May he wrote assuring Tonson the work was well in hand, despite his absences at Twickenham during the planting season. 'I'm resolved to pass the next whole week in London, purposely to get together parties of my acquaintance every night, to collate the several editions of Shakespeare's single plays, 5 of which I have engaged to this design.'[3] Inevitably Gay, who suspected that both Shakespeare and

---

[1] Pope, *Corr.* ii. 140.
[2] Ibid. 81.
[3] Ibid. 118.

the *Odyssey* translation were pot-boilers undertaken to offset Pope's South Sea losses, felt compelled to lend a hand. Yet he felt a distinct uneasiness at being reduced to a mere paid assistant in Pope's expanding literary industry. The *Odyssey* was even more a production-line process than Shakespeare, with Pope's unacknowledged assistants William Broome and Elijah Fenton providing him with raw translations which he polished into heroic verse. Broome was glad that it was Fenton who had translated the first book: 'You stand in the front of the battle,' he told him, 'and the array of critics will naturally fall first upon you. I have translated the second, and shall therefore, like Teucer, be sheltered behind the shield of an Ajax.'[4] Had Gay seen this letter it might have given him further cause for disquiet, since the same analogy had been used so often to describe his own relationship with Pope. The payment he received from Tonson for this journey-work, £35. 17s. 6d., was undoubtedly useful, and only slightly less than Rowe had received for his whole edition. But Rowe had also received the credit of an edition standing in his own name, whereas Gay, like Broome and Fenton, was merely an anonymous hired help. He was only too well aware how easily his name could be forgotten, overshadowed by those of his more famous friends. In October Pope had written to ask if Lord Oxford would be prepared to accept the dedication of a posthumous edition of Parnell's poems. Oxford's reply was both gracious and nostalgic. Recalling their Scriblerian gatherings, he wrote: 'I look back, indeed, to those evenings I have usefully & pleasantly spent with Mr Pope, Mr Parnell, Dean Swift, the Doctor, &c. I should be glad the world knew you admitted me to your friendship.'[5] The name he overlooks is Gay's, reduced to a mere '&c'.

When at last the house, gardens, and grotto at Twickenham were completed to Pope's satisfaction Gay sent him a letter of congratulation. Pope replied with a gushing verse epistle, full of sentimental rhapsodies to Lady Mary Wortley Montagu. The lady was not amused and determined to put a stop to such embarrassing outpourings. 'I stifled them here,' she told a friend in Paris, enclosing a copy of the offending verses, 'and I beg they may die the same death at Paris, and never go further than your closet.'[6]

---

[4] Ibid. 121.
[5] Ibid. 91.
[6] *The Letters of Lady Mary Wortley Montagu*, ed. Robert Halsband (3 vols., Oxford, 1965), ii. 15.

The spring elections produced a handsome majority for Walpole's ministry, returning some 379 Whigs as against 178 Tories, and Walpole used every effort to consolidate his hold on power. Already he had earned the title 'Screen-Master General' for his devoted efforts to shield the Hanoverian ruling clique from implication in the South Sea scandal. Now he determined to entrench his position further by *un*-screening potential enemies to the crown. His success at the elections was largely due to an effective deployment of smear tactics to discredit the Tories as crypto-Jacobites. And in May the outpourings of his propaganda-machine were confirmed when his spies brought evidence of a fresh Jacobite plot headed by Pope's friend Francis Atterbury, the Bishop of Rochester. The plan was to combine a Jacobite invasion from France with a simultaneous rising in London as soon as George I left the capital for his usual summer vacation in Hanover. Through his network of spies Walpole had sufficient warning to head off any real military threat, but by skilfully orchestrating the atmosphere of rumour and panic he exploited the conspiracy to strengthen his own authority. In parliament he proposed a set of emergency measures, suspending the Habeas Corpus Act, imposing on Roman Catholics a punitive £100,000 fine, and, in 'a classic example of the use of armed forces not to defend but manipulate a society',[7] establishing an encampment of thousands of troops in Hyde Park. By August Walpole had gathered enough evidence to move against the leading conspirators. On 9 August Atterbury, as Dean of Westminster, presided over the grand state funeral of the Duke of Marlborough, a public event which the Whigs turned into a political exhibition of homage to a great leader shamefully treated by the Tories ten years before. Two weeks later Atterbury was arrested and sent to the Tower; his Deanery and country house at Bromley were ransacked for evidence to be used at the political show trial which Walpole planned for the following year.

These events placed both Pope and Gay in a difficult position. Throughout the previous autumn and spring the Bishop had been in regular correspondence with Pope, and, although their letters deal mainly with literary topics, 'it is possible to surmise', as Sherburn writes, 'that Lord Bathurst and even Pope were not altogether unaware of the "transactions" concerning the Pretender in which

---

[7] Bruce Lenman, *The Jacobite Risings in Britain, 1689–1746* (London, 1980), 201.

Atterbury was embarked'.[8] At the time of Marlborough's funeral Pope stayed overnight with Atterbury at the Deanery, 'to moralize one evening with you on the vanity of human glory'. Yet both Pope and Gay also had friends among Atterbury's prosecutors. It was Pulteney who, on behalf of the ministry, presented a report from the Secret Committee compiling evidence of the plot. Now back in power, he, like Walpole, had little further interest in courting disaffected Tories and had reverted to his former political stance of fierce anti-Jacobitism. Yet, at the same time, he maintained his intimacy with Gay, Burlington, and their circle. During the election hustings he boasted to Burlington of his skills as a campaigner in a typical ribald pun: 'By two balls, and a great deal of gallantry I have gained the hearts of all the ladies', he wrote, '& they assure me that no other member shall stand for them whilst they have any influence in the corporation.'[9] After all the 'fatigue, noise & hurry' of campaigning, Pulteney was pleased to retire for a week to the tranquillity of Burlington's Yorkshire estate at Londesborough.

Gay's response was characteristically diplomatic, not to say opportunistic, in promptly moving to distance himself from any suspicion of Jacobite sympathies. Seizing upon the occasion of Marlborough's death, he quickly addressed a poem of condolence to the Duke's surviving daughter. *An Epistle to her Grace Henrietta, Duchess of Marlborough* is a piece of fulsome panegyric which lavishes on the dead Duke superlatives borrowed from Addison's *Campaign*. The Duchess does not grieve alone, he assures her: 'When Marlbro' died, a nation gave a groan.'

> Could I recite the dang'rous toils he chose,
> To bless his country with a fixed repose,
> Could I recount the labours he o'ercame
> To raise his country to the pitch of fame,
> His councils, sieges, his victorious fights,
> To save his country's laws and native rights,
> No father (ev'ry gen'rous heart must own)
> Has stronger fondness to his darling shown.
> Britannia's sighs a double loss deplore,
> Her father and her hero is no more. (ll. 9–18).

[8] Pope, *Corr.* ii. 87.
[9] Chatsworth MSS 169.0.

Like Addison before him, Gay now portrayed the Duke's heroic achievements as the stuff of epic literature.

> Yet, shall he not in worthy lays be read?
> Raise Homer, call up Virgil from the dead.
> But he requires not the strong glare of verse,
> Let punctual history his deeds rehearse,
> Let truth in native purity appear,
> You'll find Achilles and Aeneas there.   (ll. 41–6).

This poem may be taken as clear evidence of the single-mindedness with which Gay was now pursuing his prime purpose of securing some kind of court employment. Only four years earlier at Pulteney's behest he had been happy to denounce both Marlborough and his deputy Cadogan in tones of righteous indignation. But now that Pulteney was back within the Whig fold, Gay was quick to demonstrate his versatility in adapting to the new party line. Even so, he cannot quite resist one tiny touch of conscience-salving irony amid the panegyric chorus, by hinting at sexual infidelities he is too tactful to spell out.

> Is it not barb'rous to the sighing maid
> To mention broken vows and nymphs betray'd?   (ll. 51–2)

That apart, the *Epistle to her Grace Henrietta, Duchess of Marlborough* is an entirely formulaic work, virtually devoid of authorial personality but still, in its vacuous panegyric phrases, an eloquent testimony to Gay's hunger for advancement. Now aged 37, in poor health and still suffering the financial consequences of his involvement in the South Sea fiasco, he was anxious to find some kind of financial security. If that meant he must descend to writing this kind of flummery, then so be it. If Pulteney was content to further his own political fortunes by time-serving shifts of allegiance, why should not Gay do the same?

Once again Gay spent the summer at Bath, arriving in mid-August and remaining there for some eleven weeks in the desperate hope of obtaining some relief from his increasingly debilitating illness. He was pleased to find the company there far more congenial than the previous year. In addition to Arbuthnot, Congreve, and Dean George Berkeley, the Pulteneys were his regular companions until the end of September. The Duchess of Queensberry, with whom he had now established a firm friendship, was another welcome presence, as was the young Duchess of Marlborough, who no doubt found ways of expressing her gratitude for his recent poetic flattery. Pope, ever solicitous for his friend's health, suspected the presence of so many congenial dining-companions might not be entirely beneficial, and soberly cautioned against following too closely the example of the gourmandizing doctors Arbuthnot and Cheyne:

Now I speak of those regions about the abdomen, pray dear Gay, consult with him [Arbuthnot] and Dr Cheyne, to what exact pitch yours may be suffered to swell, not to outgrow theirs, who are yet your betters.[10]

Pope here echoes Gay's own self-mocking joke in *Mr Pope's Welcome from Greece*, where he pictures himself among corpulent companions: '(Gay, Maine, & Cheney, boon companions dear, | Gay fat, Maine fatter, Cheney huge of size)' (ll. 133–4). Still preoccupied with the fate of Atterbury, Pope even attempted to turn the Bishop's plight into a culinary joke:

Pray tell Dr Arbuthnot that even pigeon-pies and hogs-puddings are thought dangerous by our governors; for those that have been sent to the bishop of Rochester are opened and profanely pried into at the tower: 'Tis the first time dead pigeons have been suspected of carrying intelligence.[11]

Beneath Pope's bantering tone lies a deep sense of unease and there is more than a hint of moral reproach in the contrast he draws between the card-playing gluttons of Bath and the Bishop in his prison cell. Declaring himself 'a most unfortunate wretch' he tells Gay: 'I no sooner love, and upon knowledge, fix my esteem to any man; but he either dies like Mr Craggs or is sent to imprisonment like the bishop.' Almost certainly Pope knew that Pulteney was among those drawing up evidence against Atterbury and throughout this letter to Gay there is a kind of latent accusation of betrayal. He concludes with a ringing assertion of the Bishop's innocence.

God send him as well as I wish him, manifest him to be as innocent as I believe him, and make all his enemies know him as well as I do, that they may love him and think of him as well!

These words amount less to a testimony of fact than a profession of

---

[10] Pope, *Corr*. ii. 133.
[11] Ibid. 133–4.

personal loyalty. And, by implication, Pope's final barbed sentence calls Gay's own loyalty into question. 'If you apprehend this period to be of any danger in being addressed to you, tell Mr Congreve or the Doctor it is writ to them.' The suggestion is that Gay, as an avowed place-seeker, might be unable to afford the upright moral principles which Pope prides himself, Arbuthnot, and Congreve on sharing. This might seem a reasonable response to the opportunist sentiments of Gay's *Epistle to the Duchess of Marlborough*, but nevertheless implies a considerable slur on Gay's integrity. And Gay might have been forgiven for feeling that, in aligning himself with such dubious martyrs to principle as the architect of the South Sea Bubble, and a Jacobite conspirator, Pope was hardly demonstrating the most impeccable political judgement. Some time later, in response to a letter from Gay, Pope wrote again, still worrying over the same issues, and seeking to assure Gay of his unswerving friendship: 'I not only frequently think of you, but constantly do my best to make others do it, by mentioning you to all your acquaintance.'[12] In return all he asks is that Gay should 'do the same for me to those you are now with'; meaning not only Arbuthnot and Congreve, but, more pertinently, Pulteney. Once again the letter amounts to a request for a pledge of loyalty, though its awkward phrasing betrays a suspicion that Gay may find it politically tactful to disavow their friendship.

Do me what you think justice in regard to those who are my friends; and if there are any whom I have unwillingly deserved so little of as to be my enemies, I don't desire you to forfeit their opinion or your own judgement in any case.

There is more than a hint of emotional blackmail in this letter, which begins with the bleak statement: 'The truth is, I have never been in [a] worse state in my life.' Lonely, unwell, and politically isolated, Pope clearly viewed with suspicion the idea of former friends feasting in Bath with his potential persecutors.

Another visitor to Bath that summer, 'Duke' Disney, raised hopes that Swift might come over from Dublin to join them, but this proved a false rumour. Instead, Gay spent his time with Arbuthnot and Congreve, playing ombre and sketching out satirical diversions. Arbuthnot, who had devoted much of the spring to preparations

---

[12] Pope *Corr.* ii. 137–8.

against the plague, now turned his hand to more light-hearted prognostications. His spoof astrological prophecy *Annus Mirabilis* solemnly predicted a general metamorphosis of the sexes resulting from the conjunction of Jupiter, Mars, and Saturn on 29 December 1722. Pope affected to be displeased when, as usually happened, this piece was attributed to him. He wrote to Gay protesting: 'Dr Arbuthnot is a strange creature; he goes out of town, and leaves his bastards at other folks' doors.'[13] But Gay rather liked the doctor's squib, and in the weeks that followed the two of them had fun composing a scurrilous sequel addressed to their old enemy Woodward. *An Epistle to the most Learned Doctor W[oo]d[war]d; from a Prude* recycles many jokes left over from *Three Hours after Marriage*. The prude of the title, appalled at her sudden anatomical transformation (which occurs, appropriately enough, at the opera), appeals to Woodward to forget his fossils and attend to her plight.

> Let not old Egypt's monarchs plague your head,
> For what's a mummy to a modern maid?   (ll. 13–14)

In a reversal of penis-envy, the prude, coyly exploring her/his impertinent new appendage, begs Woodward to remove the offending member.

> Whilst both hands I employ to screen my face,
> Put on your spectacles,—and view my case.
> Your judgment so profound can best decide
> If I in love must bridegroom prove or bride.
> I dare not view this guest, so new, so strange,
> I scarce have courage yet to feel the change;
> Somewhat there is—(a badge of my disgrace)—
> Impertinently perks up in my face.
> By female dress its boldness I oppose,
> In petticoats the monster bolder grows,
> And bears aloft my hoop—'spite of my nose.
> These horrid pangs no longer I'll endure,
> Oh! cut it off—or bring some other cure.   (ll. 99–111)

In Freudian terms it is tempting to see this poem as an expression of Gay's anxieties about his own sexuality. A connoisseur of 'female dress', his satire often seems at its boldest when perking up from

---

[13] Ibid. i. 133.

petticoats.[14] Although he did not join in the homophobic smears against Woodward, his imagination is clearly stimulated here by this image of hermaphrodite travesty.

In October the Pulteneys, Arbuthnot, and Berkeley all left Bath, but Gay stayed on for another month. His health had still not improved. 'I have now drank the waters six weeks', he complained to Burlington, 'but have still my daily complaint.'[15] Congreve likewise seemed little improved by the Bath water regimen and had recently suffered 'a severe fit of the gout'. However the main benefit of Gay's long summer visit was the chance it gave him to consolidate his relationship with the Duchess of Queensberry. By October, when he wrote to Burlington, he was already clearly regarding himself as her literary attendant. After taking just a few days' welcome respite from the sulphurous taste of the waters, he intended to 'begin them again, & continue to drink them till the Duchess leaves this place, which I guess will not be till about three weeks hence'.[16] Gay's new policy was to maximize his prospects of advancement by maintaining his credit with as many potential patrons as possible, and hence he was careful not to give the impression that he no longer needed Burlington's aid. On the contrary, his letter concludes with a fulsome expression of gratitude and affection.

I hope you will not forget me, for I know my heart so well that it will be always sensible of your favours, though I must own I love you more for

---

[14] Authorship of this poem has been disputed, but I have no doubt that Irving (pp. 195–6) and Kerby-Miller (*The Memoirs of Martinus Scriblerus*, ed. Charles Kerby-Miller (New York, 1966), 48) are correct in ascribing it either to Gay alone or, more likely, to a collaboration of Gay and Arbuthnot. Faber, including it among his collection of 'Poems of Doubtful Authenticity', suggests that it is 'probably by Arbuthnot' (pp. xxxi–xxxii; 639), but nevertheless points out a 'remarkable parallelism between the opening passage of the *Epistle from a Prude* and lines 19–27 of the *Epistle to a Lady on her passion for old China*' (p. xxxii). Faber's suggestion that 'the expression in the *Old China* piece is infinitely more pointed and capable . . . the work of a professional writer', whereas the *Epistle from a Prude* seems more like 'the work of an amateur – such as Arbuthnot was, for all his wit and invention', fails to acknowledge the variations of tone and subtlety throughout Gay's work. Irving may be exaggerating his case when he argues that 'in technical facility the verse itself is quite beyond [Arbuthnot]' (p. 197), but certainly there is a confidence to the verse which suggests a more practised hand. Both style and treatment are consistent with Gay's 'naughty schoolboy' vein of bawdy verse elsewhere. Dearing's decision to exclude the poem from his edition on the technical grounds that 'it has an Alexandrine as the second line of a couplet (line 44), a device that Gay and Arbuthnot seem entirely to have avoided in their later verse' (p. 17), seems unduly peremptory.

[15] Chatsworth MSS 173.0.   [16] Ibid.

what I see in yourself that for what you have done for me, which is much more than I can ever deserve.[17]

It is difficult not to find something embarrassing in the expression of such doggy-like devotion. The fact that Gay needed to be thus explicit in asserting his love for Burlington tends to undermine the sentiments themselves. The letter begins by declaring: 'whatever I might say or do can never sufficiently acknowledge my obligations; I believe I need not say this for I hope your Lordship knows me; if you do, you must know that I love you'. Yet if Gay had truly believed that he 'need not say this' he would not have done so. The letter aspires to an intimacy which its suppliant style actually contradicts. Had he been on a footing of genuine intimacy with the Earl, Gay might surely have risked a more bantering, less slavish, tone. This is the letter of an underling, a would-be favourite, and the 'love' which it professes is a commodity to be bargained for protection and support.

The letter had its desired effect and, arriving back in London in November, Gay was able to resume his former lodgings as Burlington's guest in Piccadilly. Pope meanwhile, anticipating an unseasonable winter climate 'much heated by politics and plots', had taken refuge in the solitude of his Twickenham grotto.[18] A conversation with Berkeley, just returned from Ireland, put Gay once more in mind of Swift, whose promised company at Bath that summer he had greatly missed. Even after an interval of eight years' silence between them, Gay still regarded Swift as a friend and mentor to whom he could speak with frankness. Three days before Christmas he wrote him a brief letter, describing candidly the frustrations of a life forever spent in hopes of great men's favours. He had, he admitted, 'received many civilities from many great men, but very few real benefits. They wonder at each other for not providing for me, and I wonder at 'em all.'[19]

For Swift, returning home after a short Christmas ramble, Gay's letter brought on a wave of nostalgia. Since leaving England, his years in Dublin had been a period of almost unrelieved vexations;

---

[17] Ibid.
[18] Pope, *Corr.* ii. 145.
[19] *Letters*, 41.

harassed by political surveillance, beset by ecclesiastical wrangles, and tormented by emotional crises in his tangled relationships with Stella and Vanessa. 'The best and greatest part of my life', he declared, 'I spent in England; there I made my friendships, and there I left my desires.' In reawakening memories of those happier times, Gay's letter only served to exacerbate his sense of loss. 'I am condemned forever to another country,' he complained ruefully. 'What can be the design of your letter but malice, to wake me out of a scurvy sleep?' Identifying all too easily with the frustrations of Gay's dependence on great men's promises, Swift offered these reflections:

I have been considering why poets have such ill success in making their courts since they are allowed to be the greatest and best of all flatterers; the defect is they flatter only in print and writing, but not by word of mouth. They will give things under their hand which they make a conscience of speaking, besides they are too libertine to haunt antechambers, too poor to bribe porters and footmen, and too proud to cringe to second-hand favourites in a great family.[20]

After careful consideration, Swift decided that Gay's 'surest course' might be to persuade Burlington 'to recommend you to the next Chief Governor who comes over here [i.e. to Dublin] for a good civil employment, or to be one of his secretaries'. Having spent most of his letter bemoaning the miseries of Dublin life, there was something richly ironic in presenting this as Gay's best prospect. But, in hopes of gaining a congenial companion, Swift did his best to make it sound tolerable.

The wine is good and reasonable, you may dine twice a week at the Deanery house. There is a set of company in this town sufficient for one man, folks will admire you because they have read you, and read of you, and a good employment will make you live tolerably in London, or sumptuously here, or if you divide between two places it will be for your health.

Even Budgell, he reminded Gay, 'got a very good office here' and only lost it 'by great want of common politics'. In Swift's view, Gay's 'original sin' had also been political, namely his dedication of *The Shepherd's Week* to Bolingbroke at a time when he should have

---

[20] Swift, *Corr.* ii. 442–3.

been pursuing his fortune with the Hanoverians: 'by the force of too much honesty, or too little sublunary wisdom, you fell between two stools.' Torn between offering cynical advice on strategies for self-advancement, and expressing admiration for the integrity that re-fused such subterfuges, Swift concluded by urging Gay to be 'less modest and more active'. Failing that, he might be reduced to the last and most desperate expedient of all, 'turn parson, and get a bishopric here'. In Swift's eyes there could be no greater humiliation than that.

Interestingly Gay had shown Pope his letter to Swift before sending it, but Pope declined to add any message of his own, merely allowing Gay to pass on the assurance that he would 'never forget his obligations' to the Dean. Swift found this silence puzzling; surely 'he might have added three lines of his own'?[21] In fact it was not until the following August, and after the Atterbury trial, that Pope wrote again to Swift. Only too well aware of the penalties for political 'original sin', it seems probable that Pope was being deliber-ately circumspect about writing to those who, like himself, were under suspicion of disaffection.

Happily complying with Swift's request for more news of his old friends, Gay wrote back in February assuring him that Congreve, Arbuthnot, and Lewis were all unanimous in believing a visit to England would 'be very good for your health'. The mood of this letter is quite different from his previous one six weeks earlier, and the reason is not hard to find. At last all Gay's patient flattery of the great had paid off. 'I shall this year be a commissioner of the State Lottery', he announced, 'which will be worth to me a hundred & fifty pounds'; and, he went on, 'I am not without hopes that I have friends that will think of some better & more certain provision for me'.[22] Almost certainly it was Burlington whose influence had secured him this useful sinecure since Pulteney, on whom his larger hopes depended, was finding difficulty in providing for himself. Ever jealous of potential rivals, and suspicious of Pulteney's political volatility, Walpole drew back from offering Pulteney any ministerial position, and in the end only granted him the minor office of Cofferer to the royal household. Unusually, Gay's hopes of a 'better & more certain provision' also proved well founded. Within months

---

[21] Ibid. 442.
[22] *Letters*, 43.

the Earl of Lincoln, a subscriber to Gay's *Poems*, succeeded in obtaining rent-free lodgings for him at Whitehall. Now, for the first time in his life, Gay had a regular income and settled lodgings of his own. A tangible sense of relief breathes through his high-spirited letter to Swift and signifies a sudden renewal of good humour. Although an income of £150 a year was hardly a fortune, it was a respectable sum and freed him from the ignominious obligations of casual private patronage and literary journey-work. In the lottery of public fortunes Gay had at last drawn a winning ticket.

The duties of Gay's new office were hardly onerous. Commissionerships of this kind, which imposed few obligations, were a recognized form of state patronage for writers in the era before Arts Council grants. Philips had been paymaster for lotteries in 1715, and, at different times in their careers Congreve had been commissioner for hackney carriages and Steele for stamp duty. Lotteries to raise funds for such worthwhile public purposes as the building of Westminster Bridge or the British Museum were held at regular intervals from 1694 to 1826, but the state lottery, as a revenue-raising institution, dated from 1710. Together Swift and Addison had gone to witness the first draw at the Guildhall, where 'the jackanapes of blue-coat boys gave themselves such airs in pulling out the tickets, and shewed white hands to the company to let us see there was no cheat'.[23] During the period of Gay's commissionership the lottery attracted little public criticism; and it may be significant that it was not until the year of his removal, 1731, that Fielding began his satiric campaign against it as a disreputable and dishonest institution.[24]

Something of the new sense of release Gay felt with the security of his government salary is evident in the way he now felt tempted to make fun of Burlington's pet project, the opera. The arrival of the Italian star soprano Cuzzoni that winter set off a new opera craze. Newspapers carried rapturous reports of her début role as Teofane in Handel's opera *Ottone* on 12 January. For the second performance, three nights later, half-guinea tickets were changing hands for five or six times their face-value 'so that it is like another Mississippi or South Sea Bubble'.[25] Before long the *London Journal* was reporting

[23] *Journal*, i. 19.
[24] See *The Lottery* (1732) and Martin Battestin, *Henry Fielding: A Life* (1989), 124.
[25] M. De Fabrice, quoted in Deutsch, 147.

that opera tickets were being traded 'at the other end of the town, as much as lottery tickets are in Exchange Alley'.[26] At the same time the opera became the focus of fresh political hostilities. When Burlington had persuaded Bononcini to join Handel as a composer for the Royal Academy in 1720, the directors had viewed it as something of a coup. By now though the two composers had become firm rivals, and the rift between them had taken on a clear political dimension. Conciliatory devices like the opera *Muzio Scaevolo* for which Handel, Bononcini and Amadei had each composed a single act merely added to the atmosphere of competition. In January De Fabrice reported; 'there exist two factions, the one supporting Handel, the other Bononcini; the one for Senesino and the other for Cuzzoni. They are as much at loggerheads as the Whigs and Tories.'[27] Gay's remarks to Swift on the operatic craze, usually wrenched out of context and used to preface his operatic parodies in *The Beggar's Opera*, are frequently cited as evidence of his hostility to Italian opera. Read in context, however, they suggest a more complex reaction.

As for the reigning amusement of the town, tis entirely music; real fiddles, bass viols and hautboys, not poetical harps, lyres and reeds. There's nobody allowed to say 'I sing' but an eunuch or an Italian woman. Everybody is grown now as great a judge of music as they were in your time of poetry; and folks that could not distinguish one tune from another now daily dispute about the different styles of Handel, Bononcini and Attilio. People have now forgot Homer and Virgil & Caesar, or at least they have forgot their ranks; for in London and Westminster in all polite conversations, Senesino is daily voted to be the greatest man that ever lived.[28]

As Pat Rogers writes:

It would be idle to deny that this echoes the most common anti-operatic attitudes of the time; John Dennis could not have expressed much more clearly the fear that serious 'high' literature would be supplanted by popular 'low' entertainment in the shape of the opera. And it may well be that Gay was beginning to have doubts concerning the form: the kind of admiration for London opera (and especially the singing of Anastasia Robinson), which he had expressed in his *Epistle to Pulteney* (1717), has

[26] *London Journal*, 2 Mar. 1723; Deutsch, 150.
[27] De Fabrice to Count Flemming (translated), London, 15 Jan. 1723; Deutsch, 147–8.
[28] *Letters*, 43.

been replaced by a conventionalized jokiness at the expense of the dominance of Italianate music.[29]

Nevertheless, as Rogers also notes, what Gay is really ridiculing here is not opera itself, but the *cult* of opera and sudden babble of media excitement. In personal terms too, what these cheeky and irreverent comments represent is a new feeling of freedom. If one contrasts the sense of fun here with the desperate, pleading intensity of Gay's letter to Burlington just five months earlier, one can see how much more confidence he has in his newly independent status. The opera was Burlington's darling project, and in voicing these mocking comments Gay signals a desire to put behind him the hushed dutiful tones expected from a client. Opera did have its comic side and at last Gay was free to say so.

It is also worth noting that Gay does not offer to take sides in the rivalries between Handel and Bononcini, or between Senesino and Cuzzoni; rather he positions himself above the factions and observes their heated squabbles with a kind of amused detachment. This was both an instinctive and a tactical reaction. The world of opera bred fiercely partisan loyalties, and many of Gay's closest friends were involved on one side or the other. He might naturally have been expected to be a supporter of Handel, with whom he had collaborated and who had subscribed to his *Poems on Several Occasions*. But several of his friends were passionate Bononcini fans; the Duke and Duchess of Queensberry each subscribed for twenty-five copies of Bononcini's *Cantate* in 1721, and Pulteney subscribed for ten copies.[30] The big operatic news-story of the following winter season (1723–4) was Senesino's alleged insult to Anastasia Robinson during a performance of Bononcini's *Farnace*. Lady Mary Wortley Montagu reported that 'The 2nd heroine [Anastasia] has engaged half the town in arms from the nicety of her virtue, which was not able to bear the too near approach of Senesino in the opera.'[31] Challenged by the lady's champion (and secret husband) the Earl of Peterborough, Senesino had been obliged to confess on his knees that Anastasia was a 'paragon of virtue and beauty'. In this confused

---

[29] Pat Rogers, 'Gay and the World of Opera', in Lewis and Wood, 159.

[30] At the time this subscription was mounted, Bononcini was living at Twickenham, and Rogers suggests that Pope may have assisted with it. Arbuthnot subscribed for one copy of the *Cantate* (ibid. 158 and Pope, *Corr.* ii. 99).

[31] Letters of Lady Mary Wortley Montagu, ed. Halsband, ii. 37.

hothouse world of sudden feuds and theatrical passions, Gay's ironic aloofness was a sane perspective. Even now, though commentators are all agreed that opera-house rivalries assumed a political dimension, there is some confusion about the exact nature of respective allegiances. Deutsch asserts that 'The Whigs were, in fact, Bononcini's patrons, while the Tories favoured Handel'; but this is flatly contradicted by Lang, who argues that Handel's supporters, headed by the King, were found mainly among the Whigs, and it was the Tories who espoused Bononcini's cause.[32] Rogers points out that Bononcini's *Cantate* contained a fulsome dedication to George I, but that 'it was the opposition nobility, pinning their reversionary hopes on the Prince of Wales, who showed their "strong partisanship" in rallying to Bononcini's cause.'[33] Having just extricated himself from the demands of one set of party-political squabbles, Gay had no desire to plunge into the feuding claques of rival divas. The fact that such tribal loyalties could become the stuff of high political drama struck him in much the same way as it did Swift when satirizing the fierce contentions between the high heels and low heels of Lilliput. Or, as Pope and Swift wrote in their *Miscellanies*:

> Strange! all this difference should be,
> Twixt Tweedle-Dum, and Tweedle-Dee![34]

The Atterbury trial was political theatre of a far more solemn nature. Despite strenuous endeavours, Walpole's agents had been unable to gather sufficient evidence against the Bishop to be certain of gaining a conviction in a court of law; instead he was subjected to a parliamentary prosecution under a Bill of Pains and Penalties. The trial, in other words, was political, not judicial, and since the Whigs held clear majorities in both Houses, the result, as Atterbury complained to Pope in April, was 'already determined'. It began on 6 May; four days later Pope was summoned as a witness and resolutely denied ever having seen or heard anything to suggest the Bishop's involvement in a Jacobite plot. The next day it was the turn of Atterbury, who dwelt on the lack of direct evidence against him:

---

[32] Deutsch, 148; Lang, 177.
[33] Rogers, 'Gay and the World of Opera', 158.
[34] Pope and Swift, *Miscellanies: The 'Last' Volume* (1727).

After a twelve month's search for the contrivers and conductors of this scheme, no consultations appear to have been held, no money to have been raised, and (which is stranger) no arms, officers or soldiers, to have been provided . . . A poor bishop has done all, and must suffer for it.[35]

That night Pope wrote to congratulate him on this 'noble defence', declaring the honour that he felt 'in this great and shining incident . . . to enter, as it were, my protest to your innocence, and my declaration of your friendship'.[36] Four days later the Bill was passed against him and he was banished in perpetuity. On Atterbury's last night in England, Pope again contrived to see him and was given the Bishop's bible as a souvenir of their friendship. The next day Atterbury was taken aboard a ship which carried him to Calais, where this little political drama had its final ironic scene. Waiting at Calais, but counterfeiting illness to avoid a meeting, was the former exile Bolingbroke, who had at last obtained permission to return to England. Atterbury's comment was succinct: 'Then I am exchanged!'[37]

While all this was going on Gay kept out of the way, busying himself with his new affairs of office. But he was quick to pass on his compliments to Bolingbroke, via Pope, as soon as he returned. Bolingbroke himself was careful to maintain his hard-won reputation as a reformed character, no longer the womanizing politician, but a sober faithful philosopher.[38] Not to be outdone, Gay made great play with Swift's hint that he should set up for a parson. In visits to Richmond Lodge he boasted to Henrietta Howard how much he loved to 'frequent the church'.[39]

Clearly Gay still had hopes of a more substantial court employment and was already privately complaining that the salary from his commissionership was insufficient to his needs. That summer he forsook Bath in favour of Tunbridge Wells, but the choice was not his own. The Burlingtons had decided to spend the summer there and Gay, resuming his familiar role as a dependant, travelled as their companion. Mrs Howard was not entirely convinced by his familiar pleas of poverty; though, as a consummate court tactician

[35] Francis Atterbury, *Miscellaneous Works*, ed. John Nichols (5 vols., 1788–9), v. 387.

[36] Pope, *Corr.* ii. 168–9.

[37] Quoted by Mack, 402.

[38] See e.g. Bolingbroke's letter to Swift, Aug. 1723, Swift, *Corr.* ii. 460–3.

[39] *Letters of Henrietta, Countess of Suffolk*, ed. J. W. Croker (2 vols., London, 1824), i. 106.

herself, she understood and approved his decision to spend the summer at Burlington's expense, rather than his own. 'I applaud your prudence (for I hope it is entirely owing to it), that you have no money at Tunbridge,' she wrote, adding: 'It is easier to avoid the means of temptation, than to resist them where the power is in your own hands.'[40] She herself was long skilled in the arts of supplying her wants from the pockets of others. Gay was one of the few to whom she confided that she had successfully inveigled a secret gift of some £12,000 out of the Prince of Wales to assist with her pet project of building a villa at Marble Hill. 'Never mention the plan which you found in my room,' she begged him; 'there is necessity yet to keep that whole affair secret, though (I think I may tell you) it is almost entirely finished to my satisfaction.'[41]

Nevertheless, there is a new jauntiness in Gay's tone at Tunbridge. Instead of keeping to his room like an impoverished and melancholy invalid, he resumed his former pose as a self-styled rake. Pope wished him 'success as a fisher of women at the Wells, a rejoicer of the comfortless and widow, an impregnator of the barren, and a playfellow of the maiden'.[42] Mrs Howard was equally encouraging. 'Take my word for it', she wrote, 'many a fine lady has gone there to drink the waters without being sick, and many a man has complained of the loss of his heart who had it in his own possession.'[43] As if not to disappoint her, Gay was soon claiming to have lost his heart to a plump teenage heiress, with £30,000 to her credit. The chief distinction of this charming 'wheatear' was her insatiable love of ale.[44] 'Her shape', he confessed, 'is not very unlike a barrel . . . and the form of the universe itself is scarce more beautiful, for her figure is almost entirely circular.' Money, though, was a powerful aphrodisiac. 'You see what thirty thousand pounds can do, for without that I could never have discovered all these agreeable particularities.' Mrs Howard was not much impressed by the charms of this ale-guzzling heiress. 'I have taken some days to consider of your wheat-ear,' she replied; 'but I find I can no more approve of your having a passion for that, than I did of your turning parson;

[40] Ibid., 5 July 1723.
[41] Ibid. 106–7.
[42] Pope, *Corr.* ii. 182.
[43] *Letters of the Countess of Suffolk*, i. 107–8.
[44] Wheatear: a small fat bird of the thrush family, much esteemed as a table delicacy in the 18th century. The name is a corruption of 'white arse'.

but if ever you will take one, I insist upon your taking t'other. They ought not to be parted, they were made from the beginning for each other.'[45] As usual, though, Gay's infatuation was pure fantasy, concocted more for the epistolary amusement of his friends than for any personal gratification, whether sexual or financial. The truth was, as he sheepishly confessed, 'I have not as yet drank with her.' His friends though played their part in maintaining the pretence and Mrs Howard recommended 'the full enjoyment of . . . this wonderful phenomenon'. Gay thanked her for her opinion.

As to your advice that you give me in relation to preaching and marrying, and ale; I like it extremely, for this lady must be born to be a parson's wife, and I never will think of marrying her till I have preach'd my first sermon.[46]

It is revealing that even in his erotic fantasies Gay does not allow himself to pursue a sexually desirable woman. In casting himself in the role of would-be suitor to this female freak, this 'barrel' or 'lump of fat', he confirms that his rakish pose is essentially a piece of clownish self-parody. The real intimacy which Gay experienced with women, as these letters to Mrs Howard demonstrate, was not as a predatory male, but as an honorary female, sharing their sense of dependence on the favours of more powerful men. The final sentence of his letter is highly revealing: 'I fancy I shall not stay here much longer, though what will become of me I know not, for I have not and fear never shall have a will of my own.'[47] Gay's position as a subsidized companion of aristocratic patrons is an emasculated one; he is a kept man, just as Mrs Howard, as the Prince of Wales's mistress, is a kept woman. Yet, though he complains constantly at the powerlessness of this role, it was still his choice to maintain it, even though his commissioner's salary now offered an alternative of relative independence. He was indeed a man without a will of his own, and financial self-sufficiency did not alter this basic psychological trait.

Henrietta Howard was one of the few friends who understood Gay's self-imposed dependency culture. Drawn together at the court of Hanover by their shared hopes of court favour, they maintained

---

[45] BL Add. MSS 22626, fo. 31; Howard to Gay, 22 July 1723 (not in Croker's edn.).
[46] *Letters*, 46.
[47] Ibid. 47.

an intimate relationship based on a mutual fascination with the mechanisms of court advancement and the rise and fall of favourites. But it was a relationship based on a form of role-play, in which Gay acted the part of the honest *ingénu*, while Howard affected the style of the guileful court lady and consummate politician. Even Gay's supposed passion for his ale-drinking heiress was part of the same charade. What he loved, Gay claimed, was her shameless sincerity: 'I cannot help being fond of a lady who has so little disguise of her practice, either in her words or appearance.' Howard's reponse was a predictably worldly rebuke: 'I don't like to have you so passionately fond of everything that has no disguise,' she protested:

I (that am grown old in courts) can assure you; sincerity is so very unthriving that I can never give consent that you should practise it, (excepting to three or four people that I think may deserve it from you; I am in that number).[48]

Swift loved to bait Howard on her expression of such sentiments. Some years later he sent her this ironic endorsement: 'For as to friendship, truth, sincerity, and other trifles of that kind, I never concerned myself about them, because I knew them to be only parts of the lower morals which are altogether useless at courts.'[49] Gay's choice of the role of 'honesty' was synonymous with an instinctive acceptance of impotence, of remaining forever a man without 'a will of my own'. For Howard, by contrast, knowledge was a powerful capital asset. Swift offered this acerbic comment on her style of dealing at court:

The credit she hath is managed with the utmost thrift; and whenever she employs it, which is very rarely, it is only upon such occasions where she is sure to get much more than she spends.[50]

Howard viewed Gay as an inefficient promoter of his own talents; having taken the trouble to establish influential connections, he should be more assiduous in exploiting them for profit: 'if my power were equal to theirs', she assured him, 'the matter should soon be determined.'[51]

Even when Gay set out to prove his own skills in the tricks of the

[48] BL Add. MSS 22626, fo. 31.
[49] Swift, *Corr.* iii. 424–5.
[50] *Prose Works*, v. 214.
[51] *Letters of the Countess of Suffolk*, i. 106.

courtier's trade, he showed more consciousness of ignoble means than profitable ends. Where Howard, in Swift's terms, was careful 'to get more than she spends', Gay always found moral liabilities outweighing political gains. From Tunbridge that summer he sent her his own version of the courtier's creed:

if you have any friendship with any particular one you must be entirely governed by his friendships and resentments not your own; you are not only to flatter him but those that he flatters, and if he chances to take a fancy to [a] man whom you know that he knows to have the talents of a statesman, you are immediately to think both of them men of the most exact honour. In short, you must think nothing dishonest or dishonourable that is required of you, because if you know the world you must know that no statesman has or ever will require anything of you that is dishonest or dishonourable.[52]

Although generalized in expression, these observations owed their particular force to the acrobatic feats of political agility required in faithfully following the volte-faces of Pulteney's political career. Having assisted Walpole in the prosecution of Atterbury, Pulteney, smarting at his failure to receive the reward of high political office, was already realigning himself for the move which, in eighteen months' time, would lead him to join Bolingbroke in opposition to Walpole.

For as men of dignity believe one thing one day, and another the next, so you must daily change your faith and opinion. Therefore the method to please these wonderful and mighty men, is never to declare in the morning what you believe 'till your friend has declared what he believes, for one mistake this way is utter destruction.[53]

Political cynicism like this made Howard almost despair of Gay's prospects at court, yet she continued to insist that even these eloquent scruples, rightly managed, might serve his purpose.

I am resolved you shall open a new scene of behaviour next winter; and begin to pay in coin your debts of fair promises. I have some thoughts of giving you a few loose hints for a satire; and if you manage it right (and not indulge that foolish good nature of yours) I don't question but I shall see you in good employment before Christmas.[54]

[52] *Letters*, 45–6.
[53] Ibid. 46.
[54] BL Add. MSS 22626, fo. 31.

As it happened Gay already had more than a few loose hints for satires of his own. Three weeks before Christmas the death of the Regent of France provoked a characteristic lampoon on the sycophantic pantomime of court life. *The Quidnuncki's* draws a familiar anthropomorphic comparison between statesmen and baboons:

> On either bank, from bough to bough,
> They meet and chat (as we may now).
> Whispers go round, they grin, they shrug,
> They bow, they snarl, they scratch, they hug;
> And, just as chance, or whim provoke them,
> They either bite their friends, or stroke them. (ll. 19–24)[55]

In Ireland Swift dreamt of a cultural coup, in which the satirist's pen would finally prove mightier than the politician's purse. Drawing his inspiration from 'the poets in the time of Augustus' he pictured their old Scriblerian fellowship as a heroic guerrilla band. He told Pope:

I have often endeavoured to establish a friendship among all men of genius, and would fain have it done. They are seldom above three or four contemporaries and if they could be united would drive the world before them.[56]

Already the outlines of such a literary revolt were taking shape, though still heavily disguised. Swift himself was writing on 'the most trifling subjects', such as 'a country of horses' and 'a flying island'.[57] Meanwhile Gay, mulling over his recent first-hand observations of Jonathan Wild's methods, was giving fresh thought to Swift's suggestion for a Newgate pastoral. In a letter to Mrs Howard, he made it clear he was well on the way to establishing the plan for his *Beggar's Opera*.

I cannot indeed wonder that the talents requisite for a great statesman are so scarce in the world, since so many of those who possess them are every month cut off the prime of their age at the Old Bailey. How envious are statesmen! and how jealous are they of rivals! A highwayman never picks

---

[55] First printed in the *Weekly Journal or Saturday Post* for 14 Mar. 1724. I agree with Irving (pp. 206–7) and Dearing (ii. 612), who both accept Gay's authorship of *The Quidnuncki's*, while summarizing the evidence for its attribution variously to Pope, Swift, and Arbuthnot.

[56] Swifts, *Corr.* ii. 465.

[57] Ibid. 442, iii. 5.

up an honest man for a companion, but if such a one accidentally falls in his way; if he cannot turn his heart he like a wise statesman discards him.[58]

Evidently sentiments like these were rather more forthright in their satire than Howard considered diplomatic. And, as if confirming his lack of 'a will of my own', Gay was once again easily persuaded to abandon his own ideas in favour of a more elevated political drama. The play which he wrote that autumn, and on which, once again, he pinned his hopes of court favour, contained only the mildest and most generalized strokes of satire, aiming not at subversion but political correctness.

The Captives represents one of Gay's most earnest and deliberate bids to attract court favour. Everything about this heroic tragedy suggests that both its composition and presentation were stage-managed by Mrs Howard in accordance with her promise to 'see you in good employment before Christmas'. The plot, which demonstrates the magnanimity of a monarch towards a group of rebel conspirators, treads a prudent political line. While including enough generalized allusions to recent Jacobite scares to constitute a compliment to George, it carefully avoids the kind of detailed characterization which would identify individual rebels. If some were tempted to see the exiled conspirator Hydarnes, who attempts to buy his freedom by betraying former allies, as a portrait of Bolingbroke, then this was a 'false scent' which Gay was happy to lay.[59] As a result, the pro-government paper *Pasquin* was pleased to praise the play as combining 'the justness and exactness of an ancient, and the spirit and variety of a modern'. Yet, at the same time, Gay allowed himself some mild strokes of satire (such as Mrs Howard might approve) aimed at Walpole's machinations against Atterbury. *Pasquin* itself referred to the government decipherers who had investigated Atterbury's papers as the 'dreadful Magi'.[60] In *The Captives*, Gay brings these 'Magi' on-stage, uttering their dire predictions 'Of deep-laid treasons, ripe for execution'.[61] Even the loyal Orbasius is driven to protest at their devious stratagems:

[58] *Letters*, 45.
[59] Fuller, i. 41.
[60] *Pasquin*, 63, (6 Sept. 1723).
[61] *The Captives*, I. ii. 21.

Our priests are trained up spies by education,
They pry into the secrets of the state,
And then, by way of prophecy reveal 'em;
'Tis by such artifice they govern kings . . .   (I. v. 8–11)

In the same way Swift, in *Gulliver's Travels*, drew attention to 'the kingdom of Tribnia' (i.e. Britain), where

the bulk of the people consisted wholly of discoverers, witnesses, informers, accusers, prosecutors, evidences, swearers; together with their several subservient and subaltern instruments; all under the colours, the conduct, and pay of ministers and their deputies.[62]

Yet, while permitting himself this gibe at Walpole's spies, Gay maintains a political line designed to attract support from both government and opposition. 'The keynote of *The Captives* is the concept of liberty,' a term whose political ambivalence made it peculiarly slippery as a partisan term.[63] Famously, Addison's lines on liberty in *Cato* had drawn Whig cheers and Tory counter-cheers at Drury Lane, as both parties sought to identify themselves with this noble ideal. In *The Captives* Gay attempts a similar balancing act, presenting liberty as a political goal which transcends all other loyalties. Araxes, the loyal Medean (i.e. Hanoverian) general, acknowledges the moral case of his political enemies in their pursuit of this ideal.

Captivity's a yoke that galls the shoulders
Of new-made slaves, and makes them bold and resty.
He that is born in chains may tamely bear them;
But he that once has breathed the air of freedom
Knows life is nothing when deprived of that.
Our lord the King has made a people slaves,
And ev'ry slave is virtuously rebellious.
I fear the Persian Prince.   (I. iii. 13–19)

This concept of 'virtuous rebellion' is potentially subversive, though Gay is careful to ensure that nothing in Araxes' arguments conflicts with orthodox Whig doctrine. When Orbasius assures him that

---

[62] *Gulliver's Travels* (1726), bk. iii, ch. vi.
[63] J. A. Downie, in Lewis and Wood, 51. I am indebted to Professor Downie's arguments here.

Sophernes, the Persian Prince, is virtuous, Araxes replies:

> Who suspects his virtue?
> 'Tis not dishonest to demand our right;
> And freedom is the property of man.   (I. iii. 26–8)

Lines like these might have been taken from the Whig political bible, Locke's *Two Treatises of Civil Government* (1690); but, considered in the context of recent Whig legislation to restrict the rights of Catholics, they might assume a more controversial significance. In the coming years the 'Patriot' opposition, led by Bolingbroke and Pulteney, would increasingly attempt to portray Walpole's one-party state as an incipient tyranny. Writing to Pulteney, Swift feared he 'might outlive liberty in England'; while he confessed to Gay that he took 'great comfort to see how corruption and ill conduct are instrumental in uniting virtuous persons and lovers of their country of all denominations'.[64] This, as Downie writes, 'sounds remarkably like the virtuous rebellion outlined by Araxes'.[65] Gay's political stance in *The Captives* is a subtle one; articulating political ideals to which no right-thinking Whig could object, he offers loyalty to the Hanoverian regime, but in artfully coded terms. So long as Britain and liberty remain, as in his *Epistle to Pulteney*, synonymous terms, he is happy to celebrate their twin virtues. But, as he presents it, the real threat to that happy equilibrium came not from virtuous slaves in exile, but from the conspiratorial magi within the inner sanctums of government.

Since Mrs Howard had interested herself so conspicuously in the successful promotion of Gay's play, there seems little reason to doubt she helped arrange the audience at which he read it to Princess Caroline, to whom it was subsequently dedicated. However, the anecdote describing Gay's clown-like performance at this reading must be treated with caution; not published till many years after Gay's death, it sounds like a well-polished comic set piece designed to confirm the legend of his gaucheness.

Mr Gay had interest enough with the late Queen Caroline, then Princess of Wales, to excite Her Royal Highness's curiosity to hear the author read his play to her at Leicester House. The day was fixed and Mr Gay was commanded to attend. He waited some time in a presence chamber with his

---

[64] Swift, *Corr.* iv. 336, iii. 506.
[65] Downie, in Lewis and Wood, 52.

play in his hand; but being a very modest man, and unequal to the trial he was going to, when the door of the drawing-room, where the Princess sat with her ladies, was opened for his entrance, he was so much confused and concerned about making his proper obeisance, that he did not see a low footstool that happened to be near him, and stumbling over it, he fell against a large screen, which he overset, and threw the ladies into no small disorder. Her Royal Highness's great goodness soon reconciled this whimsical accident, but the unlucky author was not so soon clear of his confusion.[66]

Since Gay had been an *habitué* of the court for ten years since his days at Hanover, and was a familiar guest at both Leicester House and Richmond Lodge, it seems unlikely that he would have been quite so awestruck by such an occasion. The main significance of this anecdote, repeated by Johnson in his 'Life of Gay', was the part it played in consolidating the image of Gay as socially inept and politically naïve. In fact Gay's management of the launch of *The Captives*, which opened at Drury Lane on 15 January 1724, demonstrated a considerable flair for public relations. On the opening night he borrowed a tip from his electioneering friends with a liberal distribution of tots of brandy. The critic for the *Briton* was not amused by this ploy:

Sir: I was a spectator, the first night, at the representation of the last new play, called *the Captives*; when I was witness to a ceremony, which I can never judge to be either beneficial to the author, or contribute much to the entertainment of the town. There were large quantities of brandy distributed amongst the footmen in the boxes, and that in so plentiful a manner, that several of them were carried out of the house dead drunk. This, it seems, is called 'christening a play'; but I think it is such a christening as ought not to be suffered in a civilized country, unless it were at the performance of a lackey-poet. I assure you, I have no prejudice to the author, but heartily wish him, and every other gentleman who takes pains to divert the town, all the success they can propose to themselves. But I am afraid, if this Hottentot custom prevails, it will be far from proving a support to polite writing; for the same expedient may, with greater probability of success, be made use of to the detriment, than the advantage of an author.[67]

[66] This anecdote was first published by Benjamin Victor in *The History of the Theatres of London and Dublin* (1761), ii. 155–7, although it seems in part to derive from the detailed comic account of a similar incident in the *Adventurer*, 52 (5 May 1753), which does not name the hapless author. Gay's reputedly 'clumsy tread' had been satirized by Breval in *The Confederates* (1717; ii. 64) and Horneck in *The High-German Doctor* (1719; ii. 186), which may have encouraged Victor to identify him as the subject of the story.

[67] *Briton*, 22 Jan. 1724.

A week later Gay took care to ensure himself a second benefit performance by buying up tickets for the previous night. Elijah Fenton was somewhat sniffy about this device. In the postscript to a letter from Pope to Broome, he noted: 'Gay's play had no success. I am told he gave thirty guineas to have it acted the fifth night.'[68] But Fenton's comment may be taken as the jealous put-down of a literary rival. His own play *Mariamne* came on the following month and he was evidently keen to insist on equal status with Pope's favourite protégé. Pope himself took pains to maintain at least the appearance of parity of esteem towards his two playwright friends. Attempting to explain his refusal to supply a prologue for Fenton's play, he told Broome:

He knows ... my reasons and inability ... As to my writing one, were it to be engaged for as the greatest of secrets, I have learnt by experience nothing of that kind is ever kept a secret; ... I would most gladly make the prologue, tomorrow, could it be done without any man's knowing it.[69]

However, it seems that Pope did lend a hand with the epilogue to Gay's play, but then did all he could to deny it. In an urgent letter to Tonson sent just two days before the publication of *The Captives*, he wrote:

Mr Gay & myself think it absolutely necessary that you should cancel that leaf in which the epilogue is printed, or if it falls out wrong, cancel both leaves rather than fail. It must necessarily be inserted, after the title, *Epilogue* (*Sent by an unknown Hand.*). Whatever charge this cancelling will cost, shall be paid.[70]

In fact Gay's ploy made perfect financial sense, since the profits of the sixth performance amply compensated for his outlay on the fifth.[71] A few weeks later Edward Young told Lady Mary Wortley Montagu that *The Captives* had earned Gay 'above £1,000'. This was truly a handsome profit for a play which only ran for seven nights. Even Thomas Southerne, the box-office specialist, whose

---

[68] Pope, *Corr.* ii. 216.

[69] Ibid. 134.

[70] Ibid. 215. Ault (pp. 207–14) argues that this proves Pope's authorship of the epilogue; Sherburn (Pope, *Corr.* ii. 215) and Fuller (i. 459) are less convinced, but offer no alternative explanation for Pope's insistence that the epilogue should appear as 'sent by an unknown hand'.

[71] Playwrights took the profits from every third night of a play's performance. The receipts from other performances were distributed among the players and the theatre management.

Oronooko provided part of the inspiration for *The Captives*, only boasted of having 'cleared seven hundred pounds' by one particularly successful play.[72] Such impressive proceeds were clearly the result of Gay's enterprising self-promotion; Princess Caroline attended the first night, and a donation from her, in return for the dedication, no doubt contributed to his £1,000 profit. Indeed, properly managed, this was a period when writing for the stage could be highly lucrative, and Fenton's *Mariamne*, acted seventeen times that season, 'brought its author above £1,500'.[73] In comparison with attempting to anticipate and flatter the fickle prejudices of a political patron, the rewards for theatre-writing came to seem increasingly attractive. A run of seven nights, though quite respectable, was hardly an unqualified triumph, and *Pasquin*, while praising the play, admits that it 'seems to have miscarried, and to have been sacrificed purely to the prevalent folly of the times'. Even Elizabeth Harrison, in her enthusiastic *Letter to Mr John Gay, on his Tragedy Called The Captives*, concedes that the play was 'much criticised'.[74] Yet, if a relative failure of this kind could still earn him £1,000, Gay may have been stimulated to speculate on the likely rewards of a genuine theatrical triumph.[75]

The play itself shows ample evidence of Gay's recent enforced immersion in Shakespeare. The opening scene, a taut, conspiratorial night-time encounter, bristling with broken lines and whispered queries, contains echoes of *Macbeth* and *Julius Caesar*. Other parallels, with Dryden's *Aureng-Zebe*, confirm the conventional nature of Gay's theme and style, though even Fenton conceded the story of *The Captives* was Gay's 'own invention'.[76] The clearest parallel though is with Southerne's *Oronooko*, revived at Drury Lane the previous September.[77] Like Southerne, Gay presents a bond of

---

[72] The secret of Southerne's financial success was well-known: 'Mr Southerne was not beneath the drudgery of solicitation, and often sold his tickets at a very high price, by making applications to persons of distinction'. Theophilus Cibber, quoted in *The Lives of the Poets of Great Britain and Ireland* (5 vols., London, 1753), v. 328–9.

[73] *Letters of Lady Mary Wortley Montagu*, ii. 11.

[74] 21 Jan. 1724.

[75] *The Captives* was at least sufficiently well known to be included as an object of parody in Fielding's *Tom Thumb*.

[76] Pope, *Corr.* ii. 215. The successful revival of *Aureng-Zebe* at Drury Lane in Dec. 1721, with Mrs Porter as Nourmahal and Mrs Oldfield as Indamora, may have influenced Gay in creating the similar roles of Astarbe, the passionate Persian queen, and Cylene, the loyal Medean wife, for these two actresses to play.

[77] *Oronooko* was performed again just ten days after the ending of *The Captives*' run.

sympathetic understanding between a noble captive and his captors, a thematic similarity underlined by the fact that Booth played the leading role in both plays. The resemblance was picked up by the reviewer in *Pasquin*, who declared however that Gay 'has much surpassed his original'.[78] Where *The Captives* particularly surpasses the rote-like 'love versus duty' formulas of so much contemporary tragedy is in the delineation of a quality of mercy as the ultimate prerogative of power. The fits and starts of disloyal passions which threaten civil and marital harmony are constantly defused by the expression of transcendent ideals (liberty, sympathy, mercy) which bind together victor and vanquished, traitor and traduced. Just as Araxes understands the noble sentiments which inspired his enemies to be 'virtuously rebellious', so Orbasius pleads for mercy towards those wrongly accused:

> Of all the pleasures that a monarch tastes,
> Sure mercy is most sweet! 'Tis heav'nly pleasure
> To take the galling chains from off the hands
> Of injur'd innocence! That privilege
> O'er-balances the cares that load a crown.   (III. i. 21–5)

The implication was clear: 'If Bolingbroke could be pardoned and allowed to return from exile, so could Atterbury.'[79]

It may be worth pausing to reflect at this point on the validity of Gay's constant protests of poverty. With the £1,000 from *The Captives*, added to his annual salary of £150 as commissioner for lotteries, Gay now enjoyed a relatively comfortable financial state. He had rent-free lodgings in Whitehall, and continued to spend his summers as the subsidized guest of aristocratic patrons. That July, Pope noted, 'Gay is, and will be, at Chiswick' (i.e. staying with Lord Burlington). In September Gay was once again at Bath, where he had attached himself to the entourage of Lord Scarborough. Nevertheless, a year later, Gay was again bitterly lamenting his failure to secure a more lucrative employment, and complaining, in familiar terms, of his continuing 'disappointments'. In life as in death Gay's friends all fostered the fiction of his penury as a proof of his much quoted 'honesty'. For Swift it was axiomatic that Gay was 'too proud to cringe to second-hand favourites'; Mrs Howard chided his

---

[78] *Pasquin*, 105 (4 Feb. 1724).
[79] Fuller, i. 42.

'foolish good nature', while the Duke of Buckingham thought him 'too modest' to publicize his worth.

> H—hs, F—ton and G—y, came last in the train,
> Too modest to ask the crown they would gain:
> Phoebus thought them too bashful, and said they
>   would need
> More boldness if ever they hoped to succeed.[80]

All these people agreed that it was Gay's very virtues which precluded him from obtaining the kind of court office that he sought. Yet poverty is always a relative condition; and it could be argued that Gay not only possessed the diplomatic talents necessary for social advancement, but that he exercised them with considerable success, skilfully 'networking' his friends and connections to gain both money and status. Never without a titled patron, he was able to assemble a subscription list for his *Poems on Several Occasions* which included the cream of artistic and political society. Unlike Hogarth or Fielding, Defoe or Marshall Smith, Gay never knew the inside of a debtors' prison. Hob-nobbing constantly with dukes and earls no doubt reinforced his sense of relative social disadvantage, and provoked his constant complaints of 'disappointment'. It is true that he lacked the funds (and, more importantly, the will) to purchase his own Thames-side villa alongside those of Pope or Mrs Howard. But Gay was never a beggar, though it suited his satiric purposes to adopt the style of one.

---

[80] 'The Election of a Poet Laureate in 1719', *The Works of John Sheffield, Duke of Buckingham* (1723), i. 199.

TWELVE

The Hare and Many Friends

A hare, who, in a civil way,
Complied with ev'rything, like Gay
(*Fables*, 1727)

THE year 1724 saw the climax of Jonathan Wild's career as Thief-Taker General. In February the cockney housebreaker Jack Sheppard was arrested and imprisoned in St Giles's Roundhouse. He promptly escaped and Wild was hired to track him down. In May Wild was successful; Sheppard was again arrested and imprisoned, this time in the New Prison. Within a week he had escaped again. Wild recaptured him in July. This time Sheppard was tried, convicted, and placed in the security of Newgate's condemned hold. But on 30 August, the night the death warrant arrived for him, he managed to escape once more. By this time the rivalry between the charismatic escapologist and his wily pursuer had taken hold of the popular imagination. Sheppard was a minor celebrity and his quips—such as 'a file is worth all the bibles in the world'—were circulated as catch-phrases. He was free for ten days only, until some of Wild's men discovered him on Finchley Common. This time Sheppard was placed in the 'Castle', the strongest room in Newgate, and chained to the floor with manacles and fetters. Five nights later, when he escaped again, there were general celebrations throughout the underworld taverns of London. Ballads were written; Defoe interviewed the incredulous turnkeys, who demonstrated that Sheppard had not only broken loose from chains and padlocks but had got through six iron-barred doors, several of them padlocked on the outside. Wild though was just as determined to capture Sheppard as Sheppard was to escape. The pursuit began again and eventually, at the end of October, Wild located his man in a Drury Lane gin-shop. Sheppard was placed in the middle stone room of Newgate and loaded with 300 lb. of iron. There he was visited by hundreds of society tourists, evangelical clergymen, and even the fashionable portrait painter Sir James Thornhill, who did him in oils, all of them paying 1*s.* 6*d.* for the privilege of meeting the famous escapologist. At last, on 16 November, Sheppard was hanged and Wild received his reward.[1]

This episode had an ominous impact on Wild's public reputation; Sheppard's status as a popular hero cast Wild not in the role of public defender but as a story-book villain. Wild's increasing ruthlessness in meting out 'justice' to criminal rivals, together with his barely concealed contempt for the legal authority under which he was ostensibly operating, began to undermine his position. At the same time as he was pursuing Sheppard, Wild also contrived the breakup of the notorious Carrick gang, arresting twenty-one of its members between 23 July and 4 August. At first this was a coup which gained him considerable public credit and over £800 in reward money. But, much to Wild's annoyance, one member of the gang, Joseph 'Blueskins' Blake, was released. Wild immediately determined to hunt him down. Arrested again in October, Blake was quickly tried, convicted, and sentenced on evidence framed by Wild. But, when Wild added insult to injury by gloating over his victim in the condemned cell, Blake rebelled and, as the *British Journal* reported, 'seized Wild by the neck, and with a little clasp-knife cut his throat in a very dangerous manner'.[2] The incident became instant folklore, the subject of prints, moralizing broadsheets, pantomimes, and ballads, one of them by Gay.

Ever since his encounter with Wild in 1720, Gay had been following the 'Thief-Taker General's' career with interest. What fascinated him was the barefaced hypocrisy of Wild's dual role which allowed an acknowledged criminal to pose as a public defender. This made him, in Gay's eyes, the perfect model of a politician.

This parallel, first mentioned in his letter to Mrs Howard the previous September, did not originate with Gay. Newspaper reports

[1] For a modern account of Wild's career, see Gerald Howson, *Thief-Taker General* (London, 1970).
[2] *British Journal*, 17 Oct. 1724.

throughout the year frequently juxtaposed Walpole's Jacobite-hunting manœuvres with the thief-catching devices of Wild, and the comparison of criminals and courtiers soon became a standard motif of opposition satire.[3] In his ballad *Newgate's Garland* Gay seized on the instance of Blake's near-fatal assault on Wild as a metaphor for the deviousness of rival politicians, ruthlessly sacrificing former allies for a share of public spoils.

> When to the Old Bailey this Blueskin was led,
> He held up his hand, his indictment was read,
> Loud rattled his chains, near him Jonathan stood,
> For full forty pounds was the price of his blood.
> > Then hopeless of life,
> > He drew his penknife,
> > And made a sad widow of Jonathan's wife.
> But forty pounds paid her, her grief shall appease,
> And every man round me, may rob, if he please.
>
> Some say there are courtiers of highest renown,
> Who steal the king's gold, and leave him but a crown
> Some say there are peers, and some parliament men,
> Who meet once a year to rob courtiers again.
> > Let them all take their swing,
> > To pillage the king,
> > And get a blue ribbon instead of a string.
> Now Blueskin's sharp penknife hath set you at ease,
> And every man round me may rob, if he please.[4]

In the final stanza of *Newgate's Garland*, Gay directed a comradely nod towards the political campaign Swift was currently waging in Ireland, citing Wood's halfpence as the latest most blatant example of official robbery under the privilege of a royal patent. The allusion was both topical and pertinent: Wood was Wild's courtly counterpart, a corrupt profiteer trading under the cover of public service.

Newgate's Garland was included in *Harlequin Sheppard*, the latest

---

[3] See W. R. Irwin, *The Making of Jonathan Wild* (New York, 1941).

[4] I agree with Irving (pp. 204–6) and Dearing (ii. 613–14) in accepting Gay's authorship of this ballad. Arguments attributing it, either wholly or in part, to Swift place undue emphasis on references to Wood's halfpence in the final stanza, yet as Irving rightly remarks: 'the scandal about Wood's half-pence . . . was known in London as well as Dublin, perhaps better. The king's mistress was involved, and the government distinctly embarrassed. Wood was the thief of the hour in high places, as Jonathan Wild was at the Old Bailey. Gay could have found no better name to point his moral.'

in John Thurmond's series of Drury Lane pantomimes. Just a few months earlier the epilogue to *The Captives* had poked fun at Thurmond's crowd-pleasing *Harlequin Doctor Faustus*, an afterpiece whose popularity provoked Rich to reply in December with the even more successful *The Necromancer; or, Harlequin Doctor Faustus* at Lincoln's Inn Fields. The epilogue to *The Captives* is somewhat sniffy about the pseudo-moral pretensions of these competing subliterary spectacles.

> What tragedy can take, like Doctor Faustus?
> Two stages in this moral show excel,
> To frighten vicious youth with scenes of hell;
> Yet both these Faustuses can warn but few,
> For what's a conjuror's fate to me—or you?

However, the topical success of *Harlequin Sheppard*, produced less than two weeks after Jack Sheppard's hanging, may have prompted Gay to take a less aloof view of such mountebank productions. Never entirely happy working within the formal dramatic constraints of either tragedy or comedy, Gay was seeking an appropriate travesty form for his next stage satire and Thurmond's pantomime may have provided just the inspiration he required.

For all his apparent successes, Wild's position was becoming increasingly precarious. In 1718 the laws relating to the receiving of stolen goods had been tightened, with his own activities in mind. His obsessive pursuit of Jack Sheppard had damaged his popular reputation, and he was also beginning to lose some of his support in high places. Advertisements such as the following, in the *Daily Post* for 2 November 1724, continued to appear, but Wild was now treading on dangerous ground.

Lost, the 1st of October, a black shagreen pocket-book, edged with silver, with some notes of hand. The said book was lost in the Strand, near the Fountain tavern, about 7 or 8 o'clock at night. If any person will bring the aforesaid book to Mr Jonathan Wild, in the Old Bailey, he shall have a guinea reward.

Such a notice was really an elaborate code. What it signified was that Wild already possessed the pocket-book and was prepared to return it for an appropriate fee. Mention of 'notes of hand' implies that he already knew the owner's name and, since the Fountain tavern was a notorious brothel, probably hints at a threat of blackmail. The advertisement is an example of Wild's method at its most sophisticated, and at the point when the precarious balance he maintained between law-breaking and law-enforcement was about to topple over into disaster. In August Wild made a serious tactical error in stealing a vast haul of jewels from aristocrats attending the instalment ceremony for Knights of the Garter at Windsor. According to legend it was on this occasion that he and Gay met. A note in the *Flying Post* asserted that the two men talked familiarly together, and that Wild, boasting of his success, happily instructed Gay in 'all the knavish practices and intrigues of the thieving trade'.[5] Defoe certainly was acquainted with Wild's techniques. In his *True and Genuine Account of . . . the Late Jonathan Wild* (1725) he gave a lively account of Wild's business patter.

He openly kept his compting-house, or office, like a man of business, and had his books to enter everything in with the utmost exactness and regularity. When you first came to him to give him an account of anything lost, it was hinted to you that you must first deposit a crown; this was his retaining fee. Then you were asked some needful questions, that is to say needful not for his information, but for your amusement; as where you lived, where the goods were lost, whether out of your house, or out of your pocket, or whether on the highway, and the like. And your answers to them all were minuted down, as if in order to make a proper search and enquiry, whereas perhaps the very thing you came to enquire after was in the very room where you were, or not far off. After all this grimace was at an end, you were desired to call again, or send in a day or two, and then you should know whether he was able to do you any service or no, and so you were dismissed. At your second coming you had some encouragement given you, that you would be served, but perhaps the terms were a little raised upon you, and you were told the rogue that had it was impudent, that he insisted it was worth so much, and he could sell it when he would for double the money you offered; and that if you would not give him such a sum, he would not treat with you. 'However' says Jonathan, 'if I can but come to the speech of him, I'll make him more reasonable.' The next time he tells you, that all he can bring the rogue to is that—guineas being paid to the porter who shall bring the goods, and a promise upon honour that nothing

<hr />

[5] 11 Jan. 1729. Further evidence of such a meeting is missing and on the whole the story must be treated as apocryphal, although it is worth noting that *The Beggar's Opera* (III. v) specifically mentions 'instalments' as prime opportunities for plunder. But, as Sutherland notes, the publication of such a story, during the turbulent political aftermath of the banning of *Polly*, may be 'merely another of the numerous attempts to discredit Gay's character by exposing him as an intimate of thieves and rogues': J. R. Sutherland, "The Beggar's Opera", *TLS*, 25 Apr. 1935, p. 272.

shall be said to him, but just take and give; the gold watch, or the snuff-box, or whatever it is, shall be brought to you by such a time exactly; and thus upon mutual assurances the bargain is made for restoring the goods. But then it remains to be asked what Mr Wild expects for his pains in managing this nice part, who answers with an air of greatness, he leaves it to you; that he gets nothing by what is to be given the porter, that he is satisfied in being able to serve gentlemen in such a manner, so that it is in your breast to do what you think is handsome by Mr Wild, who has taken a great deal of pain in it to do you service.[6]

Not all Wild's methods were so elegant. In February 1725 Wild used force to rescue a gang member, Roger Johnson, from custody. It was a rash move, for which he himself was arrested a few days later. Even in Newgate he continued to advertise for business, apparently unconcerned at threats of prosecution. But the mood had shifted against him. Just a few days before his arrest Bernard Mandeville had begun publishing a series of thoughtful letters in the *British Journal* on methods of crime prevention.[7] Now, emboldened by Wild's imprisonment, his former associates began to bring forward the necessary evidence to convict him. Wild's trial was quickly concluded and on 24 May he was taken for execution at Tyburn. The crowd which lined the route of his final progress from Newgate to Tyburn was of quite unprecedented proportions. 'Never was there seen so prodigious a concourse of people before, not even upon the most popular occasions of that nature.' What was remarkable, according to the eye-witness Defoe, was the crowd's universal detestation of the man who was to be executed.

In all that innumerable crowd, there was not one pitying eye to be seen, nor one compassionate word to be heard; but, on the contrary, wherever he came, there was nothing but hollowing and huzzas, as if it had been upon a triumph.[8]

So ended the career of the most notorious criminal of his generation, the gang leader, receiver, and racketeer who had elevated criminality, if not quite to the status of an art, at least to that of a branch of politics. But the death of Wild the man was only the beginning of Wild the legend. For several weeks the press was full of elegies,

---

[6] Henry Fielding, *Jonathan Wild*, ed. David Nokes (Harmondsworth, 1982), including Defoe's *True and Genuine Account . . . of the Late Jonathan Wild*, 243–4.

[7] Subsequently reprinted as a pamphlet, *An Enquiry into the Causes of the Frequent Executions at Tyburn*, Augustan Reprint Society 105 (Los Angeles, 1964).

[8] Fielding, *Jonathan Wild* (1982), introduction, p. 7.

epitaphs, 'last farewells', narratives, satires, histories, and lives of Wild. And already Gay was planning his own satiric tribute to the legendary career of this Alexander of crime.[9]

However, it would be wrong to exaggerate the level of Gay's political involvement. In Dublin, Swift, addressing the fourth in his series of *Drapier's Letters* 'To the Whole People of Ireland', was consciously inciting a nation-wide campaign of civil disobedience. Gay's political satire was more ambivalent in its purpose, designed as much to amuse those whom it lampooned as to agitate for their removal. The force of his attack on the venality of courtiers is inevitably compromised by the sense that what really fuelled his indignation was less a righteous anger at a corrupt system than a strong ambition to benefit more fully from its spoils.

After spending the early summer with Burlington at Chiswick, Gay went to Bath in September, where he successfully attached himself to the Earl of Scarborough's party. His chief companions there were Arbuthnot and his brother, and Dean George Berkeley, just returned from Ireland and keen to recruit converts for his utopian Bermuda project. Gay's gossipy name-dropping letter back to Mrs Howard indicates his continuing campaign to cultivate aristocratic connections. The breathless social-diarist tone in which he records Lord Somerville's marriage, Lord Essex's private ball, and Lord Fitzwilliam's winning ticket in the lottery suggests not the disaffection of a radical spirit, but the aspirations of a social climber. Snippets of upper-class chatter are retailed with an eavesdropper's fascination: 'Lady Fitwilliam wonders she has not heard from you, and has so little resolution that she cannot resist buttered rolls at breakfast, though she knows they prejudice her health.'[10]

That winter saw the end of work on Pope's *Shakespeare* and the *Odyssey*, or 'Homerland', as Gay called it.[11] In January Pope was busy supervising newspaper advertisements for both, insisting they should stand 'at the head of the more vulgar advertisements, at least ranked before eloped wives, if not before lost spaniels & strayed geldings'.[12] Gay's own poetic output was more modest: *To a Lady*

---

[9] Eighteen years later Wild's reputation was still sufficiently fresh for Fielding to use him as the eponymous hero of a mock-heroic novel satirizing the political machinations of 'great men'. See *Jonathan Wild* (1743).

[10] *Letters*, 47.

[11] Swift, *Corr.* iii. 39.

[12] Pope, *Corr.* ii. 285.

on her Passion for Old China is a conventional exercise in light social verse. Taking its cue, like so many of Gay's occasional poems, from Pope's *Rape of the Lock*, it reiterates the well-worn analogy between the fragility of chinaware and female honour:

> Vessels so pure, and so refin'd
> Appear the type of woman-kind:
> Are they not valued for their beauty,
> Too fair, too fine for household duty? . . .
> She who before was highest prized
> Is for a crack or flaw despised.   (ll. 31–4, 39–40)

The extension of this concept of brittleness to include the promises of courtiers is equally commonplace:

> Are not Ambition's hopes as weak?
> They swell like bubbles, shine and break.
> A courtier's promise is so slight,
> 'Tis made at noon, and broke at night.   (ll. 57–60)

It seems possible that the lady of the title was Mrs Howard, whose Marble Hill villa was now nearing completion (in September Pope reported, 'Marble Hill waits only for its roof,—the rest finished').[13] But a poem so conventional in form and content hardly requires a specific subject.

Freed from the 'dull duties' of Shakespeare and Homer, Pope was in a more light-hearted mood and joined with Arbuthnot in cooking up a little hoax for Gay's amusement. He told Fortescue: 'Gay is made to believe that I had a clap, of which I fancy you'll hear his sentiments in that ludicrous way which God has given him to excel all others in.'[14] In June Pope and Gay joined a house-party of Lord Bathurst's friends at Riskins Park, where they cheered up a wintry summer with chimney-corner gossip and fighting off an invasion of ducks. To the amusement of the other guests, Gay proved himself somewhat less proficient as a fisherman than his confident pronouncements in *Rural Sports* would have suggested. Robert Digby promptly urged Pope to bring Gay with him to his country house on the river Wye near Hereford, 'where his art may take (if fortune cross him

---

[13] Ibid. 257.
[14] Ibid. 290

not) some huge salmon of dimensions worthy to be recorded by his
own pencil on the kitchen wall, & where it may remain a trophy of
his skill in fishery'.[15]

In fact, as all his friends were well aware, Gay was angling for a
different kind of trophy, and unwilling to spend too long away from
the courtiers he affected to despise. Mrs Howard had made it widely
known that she believed this summer would at last bring Gay the
long sought-after court employment. In August Martha Blount
wrote to her saying she was 'very glad Mr Gay has yet a chance of
getting from those lords and ladies that so very ill deserve his
company. I can only wish him well which I sincerely do, but it is, I
am sure, more in your power to persuade him than in any others.'[16]

Digby clearly understood Gay's need to remain near the Prince
and Princess of Wales: 'I would not wish Gay so far from Richmond
to the ruin of any interest he may have begun to make there by a
close attendance.'[17] Yet once again the summer passed and still 'no
friendly Gazette mentioned Gay'. At the start of September Arbuthnot was dangerously ill with an imposthume of the bowels, and Gay
was in regular attendance, sending detailed bulletins to Pope on the
doctor's condition. A week later the crisis had passed, and Gay left
for a visit to the Duke and Duchess of Queensberry at Amesbury,
though not without a final call on Mrs Howard to assess likely
prospects. He had hardly arrived at Amesbury when the expected
summons came. The death of a court placeman created a fortuitous
vacancy and Gay quickly scurried back to Twickenham to be on
hand to press his claims. Despite the encouragement of Mrs Howard,
he was not unduly optimistic. 'I cannot say I have any great
prospect of success,' he wrote to Fortescue; 'but the affair remains
yet undetermined, and I cannot tell who will be his successor.'[18] As
usual, he attempted, somewhat lamely, to assume a philosophical
tone: 'One would think that my friends use me to disappointments,
to try how many I could bear; if they do so they are mistaken, for as
I don't expect much, I can never be much disappointed.' Pope,
contributing the second half of this joint-letter, adopted a more

---

[15] Ibid. 305
[16] Suffolk Papers, BL Add. MSS 22626, fo. 9. Dated 'August 23'. The year can be
deduced from the fact that Pope has just returned from Lord Cobham's, and is planning
to assist Mrs Howard with landscaping the grounds of Marble Hill.
[17] Pope, *Corr.* ii. 305.
[18] *Letters*, 48–9.

impassive, not to say complacent, air: '"Blessed is the man who expects nothing, for he shall never be disappointed,"' was his high-minded quip. This, he claimed, 'was the ninth beatitude which a man of wit (who, like a man of wit, was a long time in gaol), added to the eighth'. He had, he boasted to Fortescue, 'long ago' preached this *contemptus mundi* homily to Gay, but to little avail:

I have *preached* it, but the world and his other friends *held it forth*, and exemplified it. They say Mr Walpole has friendships, and keeps his word; I wish he were our friend's friend, or had ever promised him anything.

Although no doubt designed as consolation, there is an air of self-satisfaction about Pope's reaction here. As Swift, quoting La Roche-foucauld, was later to observe: 'In the adversity of our best friends, we find something that doth not displease us.' Pope, who shared something of Swift's distrust of Mrs Howard's self-proclaimed political skills, was not entirely displeased to find in Gay's adversity a confirmation of the undependability of such court friends. Pope made a virtue of not seeking out ministers. On the contrary, as he described it, it was they who sought him out. 'I have never . . . returned Sir R[obert] W[alpole]'s visit. The truth is, I have nothing to ask of him; and I believe he knows that nobody follows him *for nothing*.' In fact, just four months earlier, Pope had sought Walpole's assistance in securing a place for his early friend and benefactor Father Southcote. By contrast, Mrs Howard's only successful recent solicitation had been entirely selfish, applying for an enlargement of her Marble Hill estate by taking over some neighbour's land: 'Mr Walpole swore by G—d, Mrs Howard should have the grounds she wanted.' The contrast is clear. Pope presents himself as a man independent of the court, concerned only for the happiness of others, while Mrs Howard, who boasted of her court connection, confined her influence to her own self-interest.[19]

Swift was dismayed but unsurprised to hear the court continued to keep Gay 'at hard meat', and wrote renewing his suggestion that

[19] Actually Pope was secretly maintaining a private contact with Walpole, with whom he dined again in Feb. Later the same year he accepted a £200 grant from the Treasury, 'that is, from Walpole's government though technically from the King, which he kept discreetly quiet about' (Winton, 90). The details of this grant can be found in PRO T.29/25, p. 26: '£200 to Mr Pope as his Ma[jesty]'s encouragement to his translation of Homer's *Odyssey* and to the subscriptions making for the same.' See also PRO T.60/12, p. 391; and T.52/52/33, p. 324.

he should seek a job in Ireland. Pope replied that Gay was used 'as friends of Tories are by Whigs, (and generally by Tories too)'.[20] In his view, and from what he may have gleaned from Walpole, Gay's original sin was not his former flattery of Bolingbroke, but his present affinity with Swift: 'Because he had humour, he was supposed to have dealt with Dr Swift, in like manner as when anyone had learning formerly, he was thought to have dealt with the devil.'

Swift's response was cynical: 'He would better find his account in dealing with the devil than with me, who have not one friend at court.'[21] Pope went on to say that Gay 'puts his whole trust at court in that lady [i.e. Mrs Howard] whom I described to you, and whom you take to be an allegorical creature of fancy'. Swift affected to be mystified by this allusion, a pose of *faux-naïveté* which has succeeded in misleading some later commentators. 'Mr Ford hath explained to me your allegorical lady,' he wrote back; 'she is our friend Gay's steward.'[22] In retrospect Swift derided Pope and Gay as 'a couple of simpletons' for putting so much trust in Mrs Howard's promises, describing Gay as 'one of her led captains'.[23] In fairness, though, Mrs Howard's professions of friendship were more than mere court affectation. When Mrs Pope was ill with jaundice that autumn, she wrote several times to Gay, who was helping Pope to take care of her. 'I should have been more uneasy for Mr Pope', she wrote, 'if you had not been with him, for he wanted a friend and I am sure you are so much his, as to have a particular satisfaction in

---

[20] Pope, *Corr.* ii. 332.

[21] Ibid. 343.

[22] Ibid. 332, 343. The allegory is easily explained by tracing back the two men's recent correspondence. On 14 Sept. Pope had written describing a lady 'who is as deaf, though not so old as yourself . . . considerable at court, yet no party-woman' (ii. 322). Swift would easily recognize this lady as Mrs Howard, but affected to make a mystery of her identity. 'The lady whom you describe to live at court, to be deaf and no party woman, I take to be mythology, but know not how to moralize it. She cannot be Mercy, for mercy is neither deaf nor lives at court. Justice is blind and perhaps deaf but neither is she a court lady. Fortune is both blind and deaf and a court lady, but then she is a most damnable party woman and will never make me easy as you promise. It must be riches, which answers all your description; I am glad she visits you but my voice is so weak that I doubt she will never hear me' (Swift, *Corr.* ii. 326). To this Pope replied, 'I wish she really were Riches, for [Gay's] sake' (Pope, *Corr.* ii. 332). Pope continued the game of mystification in his letter of 14 Dec. 1725 (Pope, *Corr.* ii. 350). Both men knew very well whom they had in mind (though their allegorical disguise deceived Elrington Ball into thinking 'Gay's steward' must be the Duchess of Queensberry). In referring to Mrs Howard in this delphic manner, they parodied her own delight in the allusive confidences of court intrigue.

[23] Swift, *Corr.* iv. 98–100.

giving him this proof of it.'[24] However, as a court 'steward', Mrs Howard was now well past her prime. Forty-four years old and deaf, her hold on the Prince's affections had waned, and her powers of persuasion were no match for Walpole's efficient network of state patronage. By October Gay knew that his hopes had once again proved groundless, and at the end of the month he wrote with an air of grimly determined cheerfulness on the vanities of human wishes to his old friend Brigadier James Dormer, now Envoy Extraordinary at Lisbon. 'I have been this summer at Amesbury with the Duke of Queensberry; I came away from there post upon one of my usual prospects, & met with my usual success—a disappointment.' Yet the familiar gossip-column tone of his letter indicates that Gay was still anxiously keeping track of all his potential patrons:

Mrs Pulteney is brought to bed of a son; they are both very well, & Mr Pulteney is the happiest man alive; Lord and Lady Burlington are returned to Chiswick from Yorkshire. Kent is employed in making vast alterations in Newcastle House in Lincoln's Inn Fields. I dined with him today at Williams his coffee-house . . . Mr Pelham came to town yesterday for the birthday today from the Duke of Grafton's, as did several others of the court, who will leave us again in a day or two . . . By what I hear, I think the King is not expected till after Christmas.[25]

By this time Gay was so used to penning pieces of court flattery, what Swift called 'little flams',[26] that he had come to distrust his own tone in the expression of any kind of sincere affection. When he writes to Dormer 'I hope I have no occasion to make any professions of friendship to you, because I have really more of it than I can profess' one can hear the self-doubt of a man for whom 'friendship' itself had become a court euphemism. Gay's life had become a profession of friendship, and he was losing the sense of what genuine friendship might mean.

Now 40 years old, Gay was a man on a treadmill of his own making; unable to abandon the masochistic quest for court patronage, yet increasingly fatalistic about his constant rebuffs. For more than eight years, since the staging of *Three Hours after Marriage*, his literary ambitions had effectively taken second place to his social

---

[24] Suffolk Papers, BL Add. MSS 22626, fo. 61; see also fo. 62; both these letters are undated, and since Mrs Pope suffered recurring illnesses throughout the 1720s, the proposed date, Nov. 1725, can only be conjectural.

[25] *Letters* 51–2.

[26] Pope, *Corr*. ii. 326.

aspirations; what he wrote was determined less by any settled sense of literary purpose, than by the desire to charm patrons or, in fits of disillusionment, to vent his frustration in satires which still retained an inhibited obliqueness. The result is an eclectic collection of mediocre occasional pieces in which social tact muzzles artistic imagination, and in which he himself appears most often as the butt of his jokes. The social awkwardness of many of these pieces gives them the air of elocution exercises, performances offered to prove his social *savoir-faire*, but which, paradoxically, achieve exactly the opposite effect, by demonstrating his painful sense of inferiority.

In the summer of 1725 Gay resolved to make one last literary bid for royal favour. A year earlier Pope had written to Fortescue, 'the little prince William wants Miss Fortescue, or to say truth, anybody else that will play with him'.[27] The future Butcher of Culloden was at this time a 4-year-old toddler whom Gay would often have met on visits to Mrs Howard at Richmond. As a self-styled *ingénu* within the charmed circle of the court, it seemed appropriate that Gay should volunteer for the role of the young prince's entertainer. In October he told Dormer:

What I am about is a Book of Fables, which I hope to have leave to inscribe to Prince William. I design to write fifty, all entirely new, in the same sort of verse as Prior's Tales. I have already done about forty, but as yet there are very few of my friends know of my intention.[28]

Gay's defensiveness in admitting to his latest literary project was no doubt due to fears of the ridicule he might suffer for attempting what might seem both a puerile and sycophantic activity. Pretty soon all his friends knew about it, and Pope's reaction was fairly typical. He told Swift:

Gay is writing Tales for Prince William. I suppose Philips will take this very ill for two reasons; one, that he thinks all childish things belong to him; and the other, because he'll take it ill to be taught that one may write things to a child without being childish.[29]

Although expressed in neutral tones, the mention here of Philips carries a hint of warning. Evidently Pope suspected (rightly as it

---

[27] Ibid. 257.
[28] *Letters*, 52.
[29] Pope, *Corr.* ii. 350.

proved) that Gay's adoption of such a kindergarten role might earn him not kudos, but condescension. Irving, who likes to see Gay as 'the little chap's playmate', argues that the inscription 'invented for his amusement' which Gay finally placed in his dedication to *The Fables* (1727) 'is a statement of plain fact, not merely an effort to flatter the attention of an indulgent mother'.[30] But there is no evidence to support this assertion. Irving also asserts that 'Gay's love of children is one of the many amiable aspects of his character' but again fails to provide proof for such a claim. Statements like these, perpetuating Gay's 'Peter Pan' image, rely not on document-ary, or even anecdotal, evidence, but on a subsequent tradition of patronizing commentary. The fact that Gay's *Fables* became some-thing of a nursery classic is no proof that he loved children; *Gulliver's Travels* was another children's favourite, but that did not prevent Thackeray (unfairly) asserting that Swift 'enters the nursery with the tread and gaiety of an ogre'.[31]

One day in early March, full of anticipation, Swift sailed back to England, carrying with him the manuscript of *Gulliver's Travels*. Travelling via Oxford he reached London about the middle of the month, and took up familiar lodgings in Bury Street, a short stroll from Gay's apartments 'over the gate' in Whitehall and Arbuthnot's house in Cork Street, just behind Burlington House. These three were soon joined by Pope, who was delighted to find Swift in perfect health and good spirits, 'the joy of all here who knew him as he was'.[32] The next fortnight was taken up with a happy series of reunions as Arbuthnot took the Dean on 'a course of visits through the town', in company with Chesterfield and Pulteney.[33] Swift spent time at Bolingbroke's newly acquired residence, Dawley, and visited Pope at Twickenham. He observed the 'wild boy', a natural Yahoo found walking on all fours in a German forest, who had been placed under Arbuthnot's care. Most of his time was taken up with old friends and reminiscences, but the *Drapier's Letters* had made Swift a major political figure, and he soon found himself wooed by self-styled admirers of every political persuasion.

---

[30] Irving, 213.
[31] *The English Humourists of the Eighteenth Century* (1853; Everyman edn., London, 1920), 29.
[32] Pope, *Corr.* ii. 372.
[33] HMC Portland MSS (1899), vii. 431.

For several months Bolingbroke had been strenuously denying rumours that he was 'caballing' against the government with Pulteney.[34] As usual, the truth was rather different. Denied the position of Secretary of State by Walpole, Pulteney had shifted sides once more, and was now leader of the Whig parliamentary opposition. Together with Jacobites like William Shippen, and Tory grandees like Bathurst, he and Bolingbroke were attempting to forge a new opposition alliance and were keen to enlist Swift's aid in their political offensive. Princess Caroline and Mrs Howard both plied Swift with invitations to visit them. As usual Swift played hard-to-get, and later boasted that the Princess had sent for him eleven times before he consented to obey her summons. His reluctance was not entirely feigned, for though his friends did all they could to make him feel at home, he was instinctively suspicious of so many new court friends and politicians' protestations of friendship. 'Your people are very civil to me,' he wrote back to the Whig Tickell in Dublin, 'and I meet a thousand times better usage from them than . . . in Ireland.'[35] Early in April Swift dined with Walpole, and used the occasion 'to represent the affairs of Ireland to him in a true light'. Their meeting was immediately the subject of rumours by cynics who believed Swift had come over to make his peace with the ministry at the price of an English bishopric. Walpole though made no new concessions. He may have intercepted a letter from Swift to Arbuthnot which hinted at an intention of deceiving him with flattery, and the two men approached each other with wary distrust. Afterwards Swift told Peterborough, 'I failed very much in my design.'[36] In retrospect, and partly as a means of purging his own reputation of any taint of political tergiversation, Swift presented this celebrated interview with Walpole in a very different light. Just a week after Gay's death he wrote insisting the main aim of his conversation had been not the plight of Ireland but the plight of Gay.

Some time before there came out a libel against Mr Walpole, who was informed it was written by Mr Gay, and, although Mr Walpole owned he was convinced that it was not written by Gay, yet he never would pardon him, but did him a hundred ill offices to the princess. Walpole was at that time very civil to me, and so were all the people in power. He invited me and some of my friends to dine with him at Chelsea. After dinner I took an

---

[34] Pope, *Corr.* ii. 291.
[35] Swift, *Corr.* iii. 128.
[36] Ibid. 132.

occasion to say what I had observed of princes and great ministers, that, if they heard an ill thing of a private person who expected some favour, although they were afterwards convinced that the person was innocent, yet they would never be reconciled. Mr Walpole knew well enough that I meant Mr Gay. I afterwards said the same thing to the princess, with the same intention, and she confessed it a great injustice. But Mr Walpole gave it another turn: For he said to some of his friends . . . that I had dined with him, and had been making apologies for myself . . . Mrs Howard was then in great favour, and openly protected Mr Gay; at least, she saw him often and professed herself his friend: But Mr Walpole could hardly be persuaded to let him hold a poor little office for a second year, of commissioner to a lottery.

Though there may be some partial truth in this account, the acknowledged purpose of the letter in which it appears was 'to justify myself'.[37] The eradication of any hint of time-serving, by representing his conversation with Walpole as a piece of pure altruism on Gay's behalf, is a key element in that process of self-justification. Already, just a month after his death, Gay had assumed the convenient symbolic status, in his friends' self-righteous correspondence, of neglected innocence. He was, Swift concluded, 'as honest and sincere a man as ever I knew; whereof neither princes nor ministers are either able to judge or inclined to encourage'.[38] Politically, it was far easier, for both Pope and Swift, to champion the posthumous claims of such a mythic paragon than to justify in detail every tack of their own political careers.

From May till July Swift, Pope, and Gay kept up a hectic round of social engagements, 'rambling' from London to Twickenham, and from Twickenham to Lord Bathurst's Riskins Park estate. On one such ramble the three of them put up for the night at the Rose in Wokingham, where they clubbed together on some comic verse in praise of the landlord's daughter. The resulting poem, 'Molly Mog', was published in *Mist's Weekly Journal* on 27 August 1726, just a few days after Swift's return to Ireland. In form, this poem is a 'crambo' or rhyming game, responding to the challenge of the previous week's *Mist's* editor (appropriately 'Incog.') who had promised a reward 'to whoever can furnish another rhyme' to follow his own specimen stanzas, ending with *Og* and *shog*.[39] Three weeks

---

[37] Swift to Lady Betty Germain, Jan. 1733, Swift, *Corr.* iv. 99.

[38] Swift, *Corr.* iv. 100.

[39] Though clearly a joint effort, Gay was generally acknowledged as the principal author of 'Molly Mog'; see Faber, 189; Dearing, ii. 616–18.

later the game was still running, with contributors sending in stanzas culminating in *dialogue, catalogue, hog,* and *nog*. The poem itself is an ephemeral *jeu d'esprit*, though the light-hearted lilt of its verses caught the public imagination, spawning several imitations and additions.

iv

The schoolboy's desire is a play-day;
The schoolmaster's joy is to flog;
The milk-maid's delight is on May day,
But mine is on sweet Molly Mog . . .

vii

The heart when half wounded is changing
It here and there leaps like a frog;
But my heart can never be ranging,
'Tis so fixed upon sweet Molly Mog.   (ll. 13–16, 25–8)

Pulteney and Chesterfield were among those who prolonged the game, turning it into a little court satire, as Arbuthnot reported to Swift:

I gave your service to Lady Hervey. She is in a little sort of a miff about a ballad that was writ on her, to the tune of Molly Mog, and sent to her in the name of a begging poet. She was bit, and wrote a letter to the begging poet, and desired him to change two double entendres, which the authors, Mr Pulteney and Lord Chesterfield, changed to single entendres. I was against that, though I had a hand in the first. She is not displeased, I believe, with the ballad, but only with being bit.[40]

However, as with all Gay's best songs, the popularity of the ballad extended far beyond the court circuit. The barmaid who inspired it became a minor celebrity, earning an obituary notice in the *Dublin Gazette* when she died in 1766.[41]

Pleasant as it was to renew so many old friendships, Swift was soon fatigued from leading 'so restless and visiting and travelling and vexatious a life'. In particular, he was finding Pope's officiousness as a host somewhat wearing. To the Earl of Oxford he

---

[40] Swift, *Corr.* iii. 179. Lady Hervey was Gay's friend, the former maid of honour Mary Lepell who had married John Hervey, afterwards Lord Hervey of Ickworth, in 1720.

[41] *Dublin Gazette,* 18–22 Mar. 1766.

complained: 'He prescribes all our visits without our knowledge, and Mr Gay and I find ourselves often engaged for three or four days to come, and we neither of us dare dispute his pleasure'.[42] Much of Swift's uneasiness stemmed from his deep anxieties about Stella, who was dangerously ill in Dublin. He begged his vicar John Worrall to send regular weekly bulletins on her condition. 'I am determined not to go to Ireland to find her just dead or dying. Nothing but extremity could make me so familiar with those terrible words applied to such a dear friend.'[43] His Scriblerian friends did their best to divert him from such gloomy thoughts. Lord Oxford joined them in nostalgic reminiscences of happier times; there were dinners with Bathurst, Congreve, and Bolingbroke; visits to the opera, where the latest Italian diva, Faustina Bordoni, had just made her début. Bolingbroke wrote saluting Pope, Swift, and Gay as the 'three Yahoos of Twickenham', wishing them 'mirth be with you' and dubbing Swift himself 'professor of divine science, la bagatelle'. All this was too much for Swift to bear. To his friend Tom Sheridan in Dublin, he wrote:

This is the first time I ever was weary of England, and longed to be in Ireland, but it is because go I must; for I do not love Ireland better, nor England, as England, worse; in short you all live in a wretched dirty dog-hole and prison, but it is a place good enough to die in.[44]

Swift was relieved to retire from the enforced gaiety of London to the tranquillity of Twickenham, but unfortunately Pope was unwell, and his frail condition caused Swift further anxiety. Soon he could no longer bear to witness the daily struggles of his well-intentioned host, and in August he returned to London, where he stayed at Gay's Whitehall lodgings while he made final preparations for the publication of *Gulliver's Travels*.[45]

The short period at the start of August that Swift stayed at Gay's Whitehall lodgings had a profound effect on Gay. It is clear that Swift had felt increasingly uncomfortable at Twickenham. 'Two sick friends never did well together,'[46] he remarked by way of excuse the

---

[42] Swift, *Corr.* iii. 136–7.
[43] Ibid. 141.
[44] Ibid. 140.
[45] Ibid. 149.
[46] Ibid. 242.

following year, when he had again felt the necessity of quitting Pope's house suddenly. Something about Pope's over-solicitous manner made it impossible for Swift to broach the subject that was most on his mind, namely Stella's illness. With Gay he felt more relaxed and could be more confidential. In letters back to Ireland he spoke of the advisability of Stella visiting Montpellier, Bath, or Tunbridge for her health. These were all places Gay knew intimately, and he was well able to offer an opinion of their relative merits. Politically too, Swift seems to have valued Gay's advice. Of all Swift's friends, Gay had the longest and closest acquaintance with Pulteney, who had been courting Swift's support all summer and to whom he now finally wrote before returning home to Dublin. Swift certainly drew upon Gay's intimate knowledge of Pulteney's switchbacking political career in deciding his own level of commitment to the new opposition campaign. Moreover, Gay was a witness, if not a party, to the final secretive manœuvres surrounding the printing of *Gulliver's Travels*. On 8 August one 'Richard Sympson', supposed cousin to Lemuel Gulliver, sent one book of the *Travels* to the publisher Benjamin Motte, demanding 'a bank bill of two hundred pounds' in return should be delivered 'to the hand from whence you receive this, who will come in the same manner exactly at 9 o clock on Thursday'.[47] When Motte protested he was unable to find so much money at short notice 'Sympson' agreed to payment in six months' time. A few nights later, Motte received the rest of the manuscript 'he knew not from whence, or from whom, dropped at his house in the dark, from a hackney coach'. Whether Gay himself was Swift's agent in these clandestine operations is unknown; but certainly he would have shared in the secret excitement of dealing with such potentially dangerous satiric material.

For Gay, Swift's visit marked a turning-point in his career. Psychologically it represented a significant role-reversal; for once he was the host, and his celebrated friend the guest. How unusual this was is clear from the fact he had to borrow sheets for Swift to sleep in from Charles Jervas.[48] Yet although Swift could have enjoyed better-appointed London accommodation with Jervas, Arbuthnot, or Burlington, it was with Gay that he felt he could be most himself in a period of intense emotional pressure. In return, it would appear

[47] Swift, *corr*. iii. 153.
[48] *Letters*, 56.

that Gay talked candidly to Swift about his own literary and social ambitions. Despite, or possibly because of, his professed solicitude for Gay's welfare, Pope was never able to escape a certain supervisory air when considering his friend's projects. It is clear, for example, that he viewed Gay's work on the *Fables* with some scepticism, and even advised him not to write them.[49] Swift was altogether more encouraging and less prescriptive in his advice, treating Gay not as one of his élèves, but as a literary equal. And almost certainly, as the two men prepared for the publication of *Gulliver's Travels*, Gay would have discussed with Swift his further thoughts about a satiric 'Newgate pastoral'.

From the time of Swift's visit to England, there is a new determination in Gay's literary career, a virtual abandonment of light courtly verse in favour of the major works upon which his subsequent reputation largely depends. From this point too, Swift replaced Pope as his principal ally and mentor in both literary and political matters. This fact is easily substantiated by an analysis of the sudden and remarkable change in the pattern of Gay's correspondence. Gay was the first person Swift wrote to when he reached Dublin, and from that point the two men remained in regular contact. Of Gay's eighty-two personal letters which survive (excluding the official letters which he penned as Clarendon's diplomatic secretary), less than half (thirty-nine) were written during the twenty-one years of his adult life from 1705 till Swift's visit in 1726; the rest (forty-three) were written during the last six years of his life, and of these almost three-quarters (thirty) were written to Swift. It is dangerous to draw too firm conclusions from these statistics since Gay's carelessness with letters was legendary,[50] and a large number of the letters which he both sent and received have been lost. But the general trend is clear, and shows an abrupt change in his epistolary priorities. Burgess detects a continuing immaturity in Gay's frequent letters to Swift, which, he argues, 'so often adopt the tone of an undergraduate writing home'.[51] However, this is to confuse their affectionate intimacy with the dutiful *bonhomie* that so frequently mars Gay's earlier correspondence. Clearly Gay wrote in obedience to Swift's request for regular news from London: 'If I write to you once a quarter, will you promise to send me a long

[49] Ibid. 66.
[50] See Pope to Fortescue, 2 Apr. [1726], *Corr.* ii. 373.
[51] *Letters*, 59 n.

answer in a week, and then I will leave you at rest till the next quarter day.'[52] Gay eagerly complied, sending enthusiastic bulletins on the newsworthy activities of all Swift's friends. But he did so in a spirit of literary comradeship, not of conscious inferiority. The bond between them was sufficiently clear to Swift's Irish friends that Tom Sheridan could imagine no higher place in Swift's affections than as a substitute Gay:

> Let me be your Gay, and let Stella be Pope,
> We'll wean you from sighing for England, I hope.[53]

The chief impact of Swift's visit was to encourage Gay to take himself, and his literary ambitions, *seriously*. Pope's literary advice, however well meant, always had the effect of undermining Gay's self-confidence, reducing him to the status of a literary aide-de-camp. Swift urged him to follow his own instincts, and trust his own literary judgements. The difference can best be seen in Gay's assertion of a new literary autonomy, the inspiration for which he attributes to Swift. Writing to Swift in July 1731 he declared: 'You and I are alike in one particular, (I wish to be so in many), I mean that we hate to write upon other folks hints. I love to have my own scheme and to treat it in my own way . . .'[54] This is a far cry indeed from the abject confession of dependency in his letter to Mrs Howard just seven years earlier: 'I have not and fear never shall have a will of my own.'[55] Whether Gay was entirely justified in laying claim to such literary originality is a moot point. *The Beggar's Opera* itself was undoubtedly inspired by Swift's own 'hint', all those years before, of a 'Newgate pastoral'; Swift obliquely reminded him of the fact when he wrote back to say that 'sometimes a friend may give you a lucky one [i.e. hint] just suited to your own imagination'.[56] But the important point is that Gay now *felt* himself to be independent; he no longer wrote with a conscious sense of obligation to literary friends or political patrons. As an author he had come into his own. Paradoxically the greatest debt that Gay owed to Swift was his liberation from the sense of indebtedness.

*

[52] Swift, *Corr*. ii. 444.
[53] 'An Invitation to Dinner, from Dr Sheridan to Dr Swift', Swift, *Poems*, iii. 1049.
[54] *Letters*, 113.
[55] Ibid. 47.
[56] Swift, *Corr*. iii. 495.

Outwardly, there was little obvious change in the pattern of Gay's life. Having returned the borrowed sheets to Jervas, 'mended, finely washed, & neatly folded up',[57] he spent the early part of September 'upon the ramble' with the Duke and Duchess of Queensberry, in Oxfordshire, at Petersham, and 'wheresoever they would carry me'. When they returned to Amesbury for the autumn, Gay took himself to Twickenham, where Pope was recovering from a nasty coach accident which had almost severed two of his fingers and left him unable to write for several weeks. Inevitably Gay found himself once more in the role of Pope's amanuensis on early drafts of the *Dunciad*, which, as he told Swift, 'you know is no idle charge, & I have read about half Virgil, & half Spenser's *Faery Queene*'.[58] Pope clearly viewed this as a far better use of Gay's time than his customary pastime of eavesdropping on court gossip. Still Gay worked hard at keeping up all his influential connections, writing to the Burlingtons in Paris to wish them a safe return to England, visiting Pulteney at Isleworth, and dining with the Bolingbrokes at Lord Berkeley's house at Cranford. Pope's political manœuvres were of a more discreet kind. Shortly after Swift got back to Dublin he received a somewhat surprising report from Pope on a private conference with Walpole.

He said he observed a willingness in you to live among us; which I did not deny; but at the same time told him, you had no such design in your coming this time, which was merely to see a few of those you loved; but that indeed all those wished it, and . . . wished you loved Ireland less, had you any reason to love England more.[59]

This was a pretty broad hint to the Great Man, who, naturally enough, promised nothing. From the other side of the political divide, Pulteney was even more anxious to secure Swift's goodwill, replying to his letter in fulsome terms. 'I would rather not have you provided for yet, than provided for by those that I don't like,' he declared in typical politician's style, clearly worried that Walpole might attempt to buy off Swift's opposition.[60] 'When we meet again', he went on, 'I flatter myself we shall not part so soon, & I am in hopes you will allow me a larger share of your company.'

---

[57] *Letters*, 56.
[58] Ibid. 59.
[59] Pope, *Corr*. ii. 395.
[60] Swift, *Corr*. iii. 162.

Pulteney was convinced that any letter from himself to Swift was liable to government interception, so he would only hint at 'something which I would willingly have communicated'. Almost certainly what he had in mind was the new opposition paper the *Craftsman*, masterminded by himself and Bolingbroke, whose first issue appeared in December. Meanwhile Pope cherished the fantasy that the old Scriblerian fellowship might live together as philosophers, contemptuous of the world, if not in England, then 'in Wales, Dublin or Bermudas'.[61] Gay, too had lost much of the air of desperation that had tormented him in the months before Swift's visit. In particular he had taken Swift's advice regarding Mrs Howard, and now treated the promises of his court 'steward' with a healthy scepticism. 'I have not seen Mrs Howard a great while,' he told Swift in mid-September, adding archly, 'which you know must be a great mortification and self-denial'.[62]

Much of his time Gay spent with Kent, and the two of them had great amusement making fun of a Bartholomew Fair performance of Elkanah Settle's *The Siege of Troy*. 'I think the poet corrected Virgil with great judgement in the poetical justice which he observed,' Gay reported; 'for Paris was killed upon the spot by Menelaus, and Helen burnt in the flames of the town before the audience.'[63] The sight of the Trojan Horse, 'large [as] life and extremely well painted', prompted the pair of them to take a river-trip the following day 'to compare it with the celebrated paintings at Greenwich'. There, as Gay told Lady Burlington, though Kent 'did not care to reflect upon a brother of the pencil', his repertoire of 'hums & hahs and little hints . . . seemed to give the preference to Bartholomew Fair'. This was hardly surprising, since there was a long-standing rivalry between Kent and Sir James Thornhill (or Cornhill, as Kent called him), who had decorated the Great Hall of the Royal Naval Hospital with an elaborate allegory of the Protestant Succession. Thornhill was notorious for haggling over prices and in 1722 had demanded £800 to decorate the Cube Room in Kensington Palace. Kent promptly underbid him by £500 and, championed by Burlington, succeeded in gaining the commission instead.[64] In response,

[61] Pope, *Corr*. ii. 395.

[62] *Letters*, 56.

[63] Ibid. 53.

[64] George Vertue, Vertue Note Books, vols. xviii, xx, xxii, xxiv, xxvi, xxix (Walpole Society Publications, 1930–47).

Hogarth, Thornhill's assistant and son-in-law, identified Burlington and Kent as principal exponents of 'The Bad Taste of the Town' in his satiric print *Masquerades and Operas*. Kent and Gay took evident delight in ridiculing the showman's patter of the guide who led them on a tour of Thornhill's paintings. His description of King William's entourage, including 'the four cardinals of virtue', struck Gay as a particularly whimsical solecism. It was not merely the notion of there being four virtuous cardinals (as opposed to four cardinal virtues) which amused him; but also the unwitting heresy 'that there should be four cardinals attending a Protestant prince'. When the guide went on to show them 'the Princess of Savoy and the Queen of Persia' Gay again took pleasure in correcting him, 'by telling him, that they might indeed be more like those two ladies, but that certainly Sir James meant them for the Princess Sophia and the Queen of Prussia.'[65] On the face of it such smart-alec remarks seem little more than intellectual snobbery, yet they bear an interesting similarity to ideas that Pope was currently developing in the *Dunciad*. Settle's *Seige of Troy* was a regular play-booth favourite at Smithfield's annual Bartholomew Fair, and Settle himself figures as a pseudo-Anchises to Theobald's Aeneas in Pope's poem. Since Sir James Thornhill was Serjeant-Painter to the King, Gay's facetious comments seem to hint at the progress of Dulness which Pope proclaimed as his theme in the *Dunciad's* opening couplet:

> Books and the man I sing, the first who brings
> The Smithfield muses to the ear of Kings.[66]

Gay himself was currently annotating the *Aeneid* for Pope's use in the poem, and was consequently quick to point out where Settle's fairground hit had 'corrected' Virgil. All such comments serve to confirm how far the identification of cultural degeneracy was a matter of partisan affiliations. For Hogarth, it was the Burlington House set, with their newfangled architectural theories, and their patronage of the 'outlandish' Italian opera, who represented the depravity of modern taste. While for Pope and Gay it was plebeian 'city-poets' like Settle, 'word-catcher' critics like Dennis, Theobald, and Bentley, Grub Street pirates like Curll, and vain actor-managers

[65] *Letters*, 54.
[66] i. 1–2: See Pat Rogers, 'Booths and Theatres: Pope, Settle and the Fall of Troy', in *Literature and Popular Culture in Eighteenth Century England* (Brighton, 1985), 87–101.

like Cibber whose activities heralded a new dark age of Dulness. Such judgements owed more to personal prejudice than to clear aesthetic standards. There was just as much vain artistic pretension about the opera stars whom Burlington patronized as about either Settle or Thornhill. And it could be argued there was a degree of hypocrisy about the high-minded defence of cultural values by the Scriblerians who themselves revelled in travesty forms. In the *Dunciad* Pope ridicules the dunces' literary miscegenation: 'How tragedy and comedy embrace; | How farce and epic get a jumbled race . . .' (i, 67–8), yet his own mock-heroic style revels in such parodic effects. Gay liked to mock Settle, D'Urfey, and the pantomimes of Rich, yet his own most successful dramatic ventures are glorious theatrical hybrids which deliberately drew upon the 'jumbled race' of such popular idioms.

Towards the end of September Pope, Gay, Bolingbroke, Mrs Howard, Pulteney, and Arbuthnot rounded off a convivial meal by composing a joint or 'cheddar' letter to Swift enclosing a rhymed recipe for a dish of stewed veal, devised by Pulteney's cook, versified by Pope, and penned by Gay. Like much of the correspondence of the time, its laborious facetiousness reads like a deliberate hoax, designed to tease Walpole's post office spies with hints of a Jacobite code. Replying in kind, Swift advised Pope and Gay to enquire 'whether the mice who ate up your buttons were Whigs or Tories, or . . . they may perhaps be some of knight Robert's mice to pay you a visit'.[67] In October Gay was at the Guildhall for the draw of the state lottery, and saw the Duchess of Queensberry's ticket win a £1,000 prize, from which he, no doubt, later benefited in compensation for the cold he caught supervising the proceedings. Pulteney was still eagerly awaiting Swift's reply concerning the *Craftsman* project, though Gay himself disavowed all political ambitions. 'I still despise court perferments,' he declared disingenuously, 'so that I lose no time upon attendance on great men.' This claim was flatly contradicted by Pope, who told Swift: 'The Dr [Arbuthnot] goes to cards, Gay to court; one loses money, one loses his time.'[68] The fact that Gay had carefully noted that 'the Prince and his family come to settle in town tomorrow' effectively undermines his pretence of disinterest. In reality Gay was still torn between offering flattering

[67] Pope, *Corr.* ii. 407.
[68] *Letters*, 59; Pope, *Corr.* ii. 395.

tit-bits to Sir Robert's mice, and identifying himself openly with Bolingbroke and Pulteney's opposition. 'Next week I shall have a new coat & new buttons for the [King's] birthday,' he wrote, adding ironically, 'though I don't know but a turncoat might have been more to my advantage'.

In the first week of November *Gulliver's Travels* was published, and was an instant success. The whole first edition was sold off in a week. Arbuthnot, finding the book 'in everybody's hands', predicted it would have 'as great a run as John Bunyan'. For the next few days and weeks the letters of Swift's friends were filled with Gulliverian allusions. Mrs Howard reported that an English female Yahoo 'has brought forth four perfect black rabbits' and hoped in time another such prodigy might 'produce a race of Houyhnhnms'.[69] Lord Peterborough eagerly anticipated a 'neighing duetto' in the following season's operatic repertoire.[70] Gay rushed to be among the first to congratulate Swift on his triumph. 'From the highest to the lowest it is universally read, from the cabinet-council to the nursery.' Yet, amid all his excitement at *Gulliver's* success, he attempted to maintain the charade of the author's anonymity. After two pages of praise he adds solemnly:

Perhaps I may all this time be talking to you of a book you have never seen, and which hath not yet reached Ireland. If it hath not, I believe what we have said will be sufficient to recommend it to your reading, and that you order me to send it to you.[71]

Reporting on the London scene for Dormer in Lisbon at the end of the month Gay showed once again just how difficult he found it to shake off the courtier's habit of equivocation. *Gulliver*, he declared, was 'the whole conversation of the town', though people varied widely in their judgements of it; 'some think it hath a great deal of wit, but others say it hath none at all.' He does not venture an opinion of his own. The Burlingtons were back from Paris, and among other new arrivals in town Gay mentions Voltaire, banished from France after his quarrel with the Chevalier de Rohan, and a troupe of Italian comedians at the opera-house who 'are very little

[69] Swift, *Corr*. iii. 186; A reference to Mary Tofts, the fraudulent 'Rabbit-Woman' of Godalming.
[70] Swift, *Corr*. iii. 191.
[71] *Letters*, 60–1.

approved of, for the Harlequin is very indifferent'. Again, this is not a personal opinion, but the affected voice of the town. Yet, despite all his cultivation of diplomatic tact, Gay was still disregarded: 'I have as little prospect of being provided for as ever, so that I have not had the least good fortune to make me some amends for the loss of your company.'[72] Though he claimed to despise the court, Gay's tone remained that of the courtier *manqué*.

By the time *Gulliver's Travels* was published Gay's *Fables* were nearing completion. He had been working on them since early the previous year, and already by October 1725 had completed some forty of the fifty fables in the volume. But the final work of revision and preparation for publication took rather longer than anticipated. First there was the business of obtaining permission to dedicate the volume to the young Prince William; then there was the problem of allocating each fable to its appropriate place in the completed sequence. Swift grew impatient with such interminable delays. 'How comes friend Gay to be so tedious?' he wrote to Pope; 'another man can publish fifty thousand lies sooner than he can publish fifty fables.'[73] Part of Gay's hesitation was because the *Fables* were very much his own idea; Pope's attitude was lukewarm, and other friends were less than enthusiastic. Gay though was becoming more territorial about his own literary ambitions, determined to shake off his reputation as Pope's under-strapper. As he writes in fable x:

> No author ever spared a brother,
> Wits are game-cocks to one another.

By October the volume was completed and waited only for the engraving of Kent's and Wootton's illustrations to be published 'soon after Christmas'. By the end of November printing had begun but was further delayed by the engravers, 'who are neither very good or expeditious'.[74] Three months later Gay was still waiting. 'My *Fables* are printed,' he told Swift, 'but I cannot get my plates finished, which hinders the publication.' All these postponements brought on a predictable fit of depression. 'I expect nothing, & am

[72] *Letters*, 62.
[73] Pope, *Corr.* ii. 417.
[74] *Letters*, 63.

like to get nothing.' At last, by March, the work was completed and the volume finally appeared.[75]

No other work of Gay's has remotely approached the long-running popularity of the *Fables*, which went through more than 350 editions, most of them before 1890. For most modern readers Gay is mainly, if not exclusively, known as the author of *The Beggar's Opera*, but it was the *Fables* which sustained his reputation from the time of his death till the end of the nineteenth century. In the beast-fable Gay found a genre peculiarly suited to his poetic talents. With his fondness for rural motifs, animal metaphors, and proverbial lore, he had little difficulty in transforming the farmyard world of fable into his own satiric Lilliput. Translations of Aesop, like that by L'Estrange in 1691, were both plentiful and popular; fables by Mandeville and Locke, La Motte and La Fontaine, Swift and Prior had all confirmed the genre's continuing appeal. Gay, who had already used the fable form in his *Epistle to Paul Methuen*, *The Quidnuncki's*, and several of his *Tales* knew fables from India, in the collection of Bidpai, classical fables, native English fables, and fables from Italy and France. But whereas the traditional fable tended to retell a familiar tale, Gay's *Fables* were 'all entirely new'. His verse form too was his own. Though he claimed to be writing 'in the same sort of verse as Prior's tales', his frequent use of enjambment and distinctive aphoristic style are his own original contributions to a traditional poetic form.[76]

Among nineteenth-century readers, such originality often went unnoticed. The enduring popularity of Gay's *Fables* owed less to their fresh ironic wit than to their conventional proverbial wisdom. Young parsons made gifts of them to their sweethearts, pleased by their capacity to encapsulate heart-warming truths; 'to mark our faults and not offend us'.[77] The *Fables'* blend of anthropomorphic fantasy and homiletic sententiousness quickly earned them the status of a nursery classic. When in 1828 a certain Ingram Cobbin sought to explain in his *Elements of Arithmetic for Children* how to write a bill, the items he chose to enumerate included a ream of paper, a stick of wax, an almanac, a bible, a prayer-book, and Gay's *Fables*. As Irving writes: 'The Victorians might disapprove

---

[75] It was not listed in the *Monthly Catalogue* till June.
[76] *Letters*, 52. For a description of the verse form of the *Fables* see Dearing, p. 621.
[77] Myles Cooper, *Poems on Several Occasions* (Oxford, 1761), 149.

of *Nelly* or *Work for a Cooper*, but they read *The Fables* with pleasure.'[78]

Yet Gay's apparent disregard for the didactic conventions of the fable form disturbed some critics. Johnson, overcoming his distaste for the irrationality of a genre in which brute beasts and even inanimate objects were 'for the purposes of moral instruction, feigned to act and speak with human interests and passions', still complained that Gay failed to stick to the rules. 'For a fable he gives now and then a tale or an abstracted allegory; and from some, by whatever name they may be called, it will be difficult to extract any moral principle.'[79] Warton was even more scathing:

His fables, the most popular of all his works, have the fault of many fable-writers, the ascribing to the different animals and objects introduced, speeches and actions inconsistent with their several natures. An elephant can have nothing to do in a bookseller's shop. They are greatly inferior to the fables of *La Fontaine*, which is perhaps the most unrivalled work in the whole language.[80]

But the erudite elephant in the bookshop (fable x), like the crocodile and the Egyptian mummy in *Three Hours after Marriage*, adds that surreal touch of freakish humour that Gay loved. Unlike Warton, for whom each animal had its own appointed 'nature' and prescribed domain, Gay saw monkeys at court and parakeets in parliament. Other fables contain similar bizarre and comic details; there is the semi-domesticated stag of fable xiii, dining al fresco on the clothes-line ('Munches the linen on the lines, | And on a hood or apron dines'), or the well-bred wasp of fable viii, taking tea in fashionable society. In fable xvi a pin quarrels with a needle, and in fable xxxv a dung-hill vies with a barley-mow.

At the start of the *Fables* Gay sounds a conventional homiletic note. The sententious shepherd of the introductory fable promises to instruct us in 'nature's laws', drawing traditional moral lessons from the examples of the industrious bee, the careful ant, and faithful dog, apparently untroubled by Gay's earlier parodies of such bucolic lore.[81] In the dedicatory fable to Prince William (no.

---

[78] Irving, 222–4.
[79] Johnson, 'Gay', 68.
[80] Joseph Warton, *An Essay on the Genius and Writings of Pope* (5th edn., London, 1806), ii. 245.
[81] Cf. in *The Shepherd's Week*.

1), a tyrant lion, chided by a man for his aggressive ways, tamely accepts a sober lecture in social behaviour. 'Be lov'd', the man tells him; 'Let justice bound your might.' To which the lion, like an attentive prince, replies, 'You reason well,' and agrees to change his ways. But before long such simplistic moralizing gives way to satire. In a couple of lively comic fables (XXVII and XXIX) Gay ridicules the pious notion of sudden conversion or death-bed repentance. In XXIX an expiring fox, haunted by guilty visions of his victims in the spectral forms of 'murder'd geese' and 'bleeding turkeys', gathers his sons to his bedside to deliver some sanctimonious advice. 'Ah sons, from evil ways depart', he tells them; 'Restrain inordinate desire . . . Let honesty your passions rein.' To which his sons retort that since foxes will always be accused of robbing hen-roosts, they might as well have the booty as well as the blame. Confounded, the fox allows his moral scruples to yield once more to instinct.

> Nay then, replies the feeble fox,
> (But, hark! I hear a hen that clocks)
> Go, but be mod'rate in your food;
> A chicken too might do me good.   (ll. 47–50)

Similarly in fable XXVII a dying man, anxious to atone for the cruelty of a life of avarice, seeks to buy his way into heaven with some charitable posthumous bequests. An angel warns him that only money given in his lifetime will purge his guilt.

> Now, while you draw the vital air,
> Prove your intention is sincere:
> This instant give a hundred pound;
> Your neighbours want, and you abound.   (ll. 35–8)

But like the expiring miser Euclio in Pope's *Epistle to Cobham* (which this fable closely resembles), the man remains a slave to his ruling passion.

> While there is life, there's hope, he cried;
> Then why such haste? so groan'd and died.   (ll. 49–50)[82]

Politically, the dedication of these *Fables* to the young Hanoverian Prince gives their social observations a peculiar piquancy. There is

---

[82] Compare *Epistle to Cobham*, ll. 256–61. Possibly Gay had Addison's death-bed repentance in mind.

bitter proleptic irony in the fact that Gay should have chosen to dedicate a lecture on regal clemency to the future Butcher of Culloden. The lion's 'regal den' is daubed with the blood of his victims; his proud description of the trophies of war that litter his domain bears an eerie likeness to later descriptions of the Highland battlefield massacre of April 1746:

> These carcasses on either hand,
> Those bones that whiten all the land
> My former deeds and triumphs tell,
> Beneath these jaws that numbers fell. (ll. 57–60)

'Cowards are cruel,' Gay tells the prince; 'but the brave | Love mercy.' In fable IX, whose theme is the education of a 'fav'rite boy', he returns to the subject of cruelty. A mastiff exults in his heroic blood-lust:

> Like heroes of eternal name,
> Whom poets sing, I fight for fame:
> The butcher's spirit-stirring mind
> To daily war my youth inclin'd,
> He train'd me to heroic deed,
> Taught me to conquer or to bleed. (ll. 23–8)

The bull despairs of such deep-rooted belligerence.

> Curst dog, the bull replied, no more
> I wonder at thy thirst of gore,
> For thou (beneath a butcher train'd,
> Whose hands with cruelty are stain'd,
> His daily murders in thy view,)
> Must, like thy tutor, blood pursue. (ll. 29–34)

Trying to dissuade a modern prince from 'heroic' acts of butchery, Gay implies, is like asking foxes to forsake chickens.

The dedicatory fable demonstrates another favourite device, flattering the young Prince by warning him against flattery. 'Princes', Gay observes,

> like beauties, from their youth
> Are strangers to the voice of truth:
> Learn to contemn all praise betimes;
> For flattery's the nurse of crimes. (ll. 5–8)

When he adds, 'Must I too flatter like the rest, | And run my morals to a jest?', the irony is clear. This is the praise that mocks praise, the sententiousness which deconstructs itself as satire. Even the language of morality, as Gay presents it, had been hijacked as part of the flatterer's patter; for as Plutus claims in fable VI: 'Ev'n virtue's self by knaves is made | A cloak to carry on their trade.' Throughout the *Fables*, flattery and court lies remain central preoccupations. In fable II a sycophantic spaniel debates with a time-serving chameleon which is the more accomplished courtier. In fable XXXIII, a courtier claims greater dexterity in capricious political mutations than the god Proteus himself. In fable XVIII a penniless artist finds instant fame and fortune when he abandons honest lifelike portraiture and depicts each wealthy sitter as a modern Venus or Apollo. In fable XIV 'The Monkey who had seen the world' returns to his simian brothers to instruct them in the ways of courts and men.

> Seek ye to thrive? In flatt'ry deal,
> Your scorn, your hate, with that conceal;
> Seem only to regard your friends,
> But use them for your private ends,
> Stint not to truth the flow of wit,
> Be prompt to lie, whene'er 'tis fit;
> Bend all your force to spatter merit;
> Scandal is conversation's spirit.   (ll. 43–50)

The capriciousness of courtiers is depicted not merely as a modish insouciance, but as a form of sadism. In ironic contrast with the first fable, where man preaches mercy and justice to the tyrant lion, fable XV presents man as the most barbarous beast of all creation. A hen pheasant speaks:

> Sooner the hawk or vulture trust
> Than man; of animals the worst;
> In him ingratitude you find,
> A vice peculiar to the kind.
> The sheep, whose annual fleece is dyed,
> To guard his health, and serve his pride,
> Forc'd from his fold and native plain,
> Is in the cruel shambles slain.
> The swarms, who, with industrious skill,
> His hives with wax and honey fill,

> In vain whole summer days employ'd,
> Their stores are sold, the race destroy'd   (ll. 25–36)

This exploitation of the bees' labours contrasts ironically with the shepherd's homiletic claim in the introductory fable: 'The daily labour of the bee | Awake my soul to industry.' In fable XVII a wolf defends his predatory behaviour as mildness itself, when contrasted with the callousness of man.

> A wolf eats sheep but now and then,
> Ten thousand are devour'd by men.
> An open foe may prove a curse,
> But a pretended friend is worse.   (ll. 31–4)

Fable VII, 'The Lion, the Fox and the Geese', develops the theme that 'a dog's obeyed in office'. Lear-like, a weary lion 'tir'd with affairs of state' resolves to forsake the cares of government, 'In peace to pass his latter life'. The lion nominates a fox as his viceroy, to whom all the other animals immediately offer their compliant praises.

> The crowd admire his wit, his sense,
> Each word hath weight and consequence.   (ll. 12–13)

Foremost among the flatterers is another fox, adept in all the customary eulogistic phrases.

> How vast his talents, born to rule,
> And train'd in virtue's honest school!
> What clemency his temper sways!
> How uncorrupt are all his ways! . . .
> What blessings must attend the nation
> Under this good administration!   (ll. 19–22, 27–8)

Comparing these servile blandishments with Gay's own flattery of the young Prince William in fable I, we recognize a familiar self-parodic strategy. His own lines read:

> But shall I hide your real praise,
> Or tell you what a nation says?
> They in your infant bosom trace
> The virtues of your royal race,
> In the fair dawning of your mind
> Discern you gen'rous, mild and kind,

> They see you grieve to hear distress,
> And pant already to redress.
> Go on, the height of good attain,
> Nor let a nation hope in vain.
> For hence we justly may presage
> The virtues of a riper age.   (ll. 19–30)

As Gay wryly admits: 'He who hath power is sure of praise.' And though foxes may expect to flourish under a fox's rule, a goose offers a very different perspective.

> Whene'er I hear a knave commend
> He bids me shun his worthy friend.
> What praise! what mighty commendation!
> But 'twas a fox who spoke th'oration.
> Foxes this government may prize
> As gentle, plentiful and wise;
> If they enjoy these sweets, 'tis plain,
> We geese must feel a tyrant reign.
> What havoc now shall thin our race!
> When ev'ry petty clerk in place,
> To prove his taste, and seem polite,
> Will feed on geese both noon and night.   (ll. 31–42)

If instead of 'geese' we substitute Irish peasants, who, as Swift reported, starved to death in their thousands over the following decade, the full force of Gay's attack on the self-seeking ministerial clique becomes clear.

Yet, though the *Fables* are often serious, they are never solemn. With a deft, self-mocking skill, Gay exploits the nursery charm of his animal philosophers, creating a farmyard Lilliput where social satire blends with the magical delights of childhood fantasy. There are beguiling echoes too of *Trivia* in the vivid glimpses of urban diversions. Fable XL provides an animated picture of the circus acts of Southwark fair, while fable XLII celebrates the legerdemain of a fairground conjuror.

> He shakes his bag, he shows all fair,
> His fingers spread, and nothing there,
> Then bids it rain with showers of gold,
> And now his iv'ry eggs are told,

> But when from thence the hen he draws,
> Amaz'd spectators hum applause.   (ll. 21–6)

The aphoristic fable form also provides the perfect vehicle for a series of succinct satiric one-liners. 'He who hath power is sure of praise' (fable VII), 'For envy is a kind of praise' (fable XLIV), and 'He makes a foe who makes a jest' (fable XLVI).

Unsurprisingly, the *Fables* contain several verbal echoes and anticipations of Pope and Swift. When in fable XLI a farmer derides an owl as 'thou dull important lump of pride' he seems to recall Gulliver's final judgement of Yahoo-kind: 'a lump of deformity . . . smitten with pride.' Other fables anticipate themes and expressions in Pope's *Essay on Man*. In fable XLIX Gay ridicules the human vanity that treats the whole of Creation as a private pleasure-ground.

> When I behold this glorious show,
> And the wide watry world below,
> The scaly people of the main,
> The beasts that range the wood or plain,
> The wing'd inhabitants of air,
> The day, the night, the various year,
> And know all these by heav'n design'd
> As gifts to pleasure human kind,
> I cannot raise my worth too high;
> Of what vast consequence am I!   (ll. 29–38)

Pope echoes these sentiments:

> Ask for what end the heav'nly bodies shine.
> Earth for whose use? Pride answers, 'Tis for mine:
> For me kind Nature wakes her genial pow'r,
> Suckles each herb, and spreads out ev'ry flow'r; . . .
> Seas roll to waft me, suns to light me rise;
> My foot-stool earth, my canopy the skies.
> (*An Essay on Man*, i. 131–4, 139–40)

Clearly, in the literary borrowings between master and pupil, the debts were not all one way.[83]

---

[83] For other parallels, compare fable IV (ll. 31–40) with the *Essay on Man*, i. 173–206; fables VI and XXVII show similarities with parts of Pope's *Epistle to Bathurst* and *Epistle to Cobham*.

Often the *Fables'* farmyard allegories hint at personal preoccupations. In two fables (XXIV and XXXV) Gay tackles the theme of the social upstart. In fable XXIV a supercilious butterfly, 'proudly perking on a rose', disavows all former acquaintance with his 'forgotten friend, a snail', and exhorts the gardener to crush it. Furious, the snail reminds the butterfly of his own ignominious origins:

> Since I thy humbler life survey'd,
> In base, in sordid guise array'd;
> A hideous insect, vile, unclean . . .
> I own my humble life, good friend;
> Snail was I born, and snail shall end.
> But what's a butterfly? At best,
> He's but a caterpillar, dressed . . .   (ll. 33–5, 39–42)

Similarly, in fable XXXV, an arrogant barley-mow protests at being placed so close to a dung-hill, and commands the farmer to remove the vile thing from its sight. 'Insult not thus the meek and low'; replies the dung-hill, noting that upstarts 'to support their station, | Cancel at once all obligation'. The point is reiterated in Gay's commentary:

> Proud rogues, who shar'd the South-Sea prey,
> And sprung like mushrooms in a day!
> They think it mean to condescend
> To know a brother or a friend;
> They blush to hear their mother's name,
> And by their pride expose their shame.   (ll. 3–8)

For most of his adult life Gay had done exactly that, striving to conceal lowly origins while fashioning a new identity for himself among the aristocratic and cultural élite. His letters make no mention of his family, of Barnstaple, or of his apprenticeship in Willet's shop; on the contrary, they are filled with name-dropping references to the Duke of this or the Earl of that, to the court, clubs, and coffee-houses. It is impossible to ignore a sense of guilt in these two fables with their awkward acknowledgement of the upstart's social subterfuges. Yet even this takes the form, not of moral self-reproach, but of social self-consciousness.

> All upstarts, insolent in place,
> Remind us of their vulgar race.   (XXIV, ll. 1–2)

In betraying his meek and lowly origins Gay was also betraying himself. The more he strove, vainly, to affect the style of a social butterfly, the more he revealed the instincts of a discontented snail.

Similar doubts about his social status can be discerned in fable XLIII, 'The Council of Horses'. In this 'Animal Farm' fable, a headstrong colt rebels against the servitude that horses endure under the tyranny of Man.

> Good Gods! how abject is our race,
> Condemn'd to slav'ry and disgrace!
> Shall we our servitude retain,
> Because our sires have born the chain?
> Consider, friends, your strength and might;
> 'Tis conquest to assert your right . . .
> How feeble are the two-legg'd kind!
> What force is in our nerves combin'd!
> Shall then our nobler jaws submit
> To foam and champ the galling bit?   (ll. 11–16, 23–6)

The influence of Swift's Houyhnhnms is evident in this revolt against Yahoo rule. But the colt's rallying cry is countered by the 'grave and solemn' advice of an equine Nestor who expresses gratitude for human care. Counting the blessings of his bondage, he cites food, water, and a dry stable as the benefits of a life of docility. 'Appease your discontented mind,' he counsels the young colt; 'And act the part by Heav'n assign'd.' His view prevails and the fable concludes on a note of submission:

> The tumult ceas'd. The colt submitted,
> And, like his ancestors, was bitted.   (ll. 63–4)

But how ironically should we take the sentiments of this four-legged Uncle Tom? For Gay these were very pertinent questions. Should he choose independence or dependence? Should he accept self-censorship as the price of a life of domestic ease in the homes of his aristocratic friends? Or should he give satiric voice to his sense of moral and social indignation, and thereby risk the extinction of any lingering hopes of a court place? The emphatic feminine rhyme that marks the headstrong colt's submission, 'submitted/bitted', suggests enforced conformity rather than willing consent. Ten years earlier, in his curious 'horse' letter, Gay had presented himself as not only bridled and bitted, but gelded too. For him the cost of social comfort was an enduring sense of personal emasculation.

Gay reserves his most open expression of disillusionment for the final fable in the volume, 'The Hare and Many Friends', where his attack on the hypocrisy of court friends is given an undisguised personal intensity.

> A hare, who, in a civil way,
> Comply'd with ev'rything, like Gay,
> Was known by all the bestial train,
> Who haunt the wood, or graze the plain:
> Her care was, never to offend,
> And ev'ry creature was her friend.   (ll. 7–12)

Here Gay's sense of personal emasculation is made explicit. He not only chooses to characterize himself as a helpless, inoffensive creature, but, more specifically, as a *female* creature. His instinctive sense of social vulnerability finds its most natural expression in the adoption of a female persona. This is highly characteristic. Throughout Gay's writings there is a conspicuous lack of masculine assertiveness, and the pattern of deferential behaviour which he customarily exhibits (passive rather than active; submissive rather than assertive) conforms most obviously to the contemporary social definition of a feminine role. Criticizing Gay's lack of self-determination, Swift frequently depicted him in female terms: 'He hath as little foresight . . . as a girl of fifteen,' he told Pope; he was like 'a she-cousin of a good family . . . passing months among all her relations . . . till she grew an old maid, and everybody weary of her'.[84] Such descriptions offer eloquent confirmation of Gay's instinctive tendency to assume an androgynous, feminized role. In this fable the hare, tamely enjoying the 'dew-besprinkled lawn', is terrified to hear the distant sound of baying hounds. Imitating her counterpart in *Rural Sports*, she makes desperate efforts to escape:

> She starts, she stops, she pants for breath,
> She hears the near advance of death,
> She doubles, to mis-lead the hound,
> And measures back her mazy round;

---

[84] Swift, *Corr.* iii. 417.

> Till fainting in the public way,
> Half dead with fear she gasping lay.   (ll. 17–22)[85]

One by one her friends, all male, pass by, observing her desperate plight. But, heedless of her pleas, they all excuse themselves from offering assistance. The horse airily assures her:

> Be comforted, relief is near;
> For all your friends are in the rear.   (ll. 31–2)

The 'stately bull' has an amorous assignation with his 'fav'rite cow':

> And when a lady's in the case,
> You know, all other things give place.   (ll. 41–2)

The goat pleads indisposition; the sheep is afraid of the hounds himself; while the youthful calf protests that it would seem presumptuous for him to help her when 'older and abler' friends had passed her by.

> Should I presume to bear you hence,
> Those friends of mine might take offence.
> Excuse me then. You know my heart.
> But dearest friends, alas, must part!
> How shall we all lament! Adieu.
> For see the hounds are just in view.   (ll. 59–64)

As Gay observed to Swift five years before, all his court friends 'wonder at each other for not providing for me, and I wonder at 'em all'.[86]

Anxious at the long delays to the *Fables*' publication, and apprehensive of their public reception, Gay's health deteriorated. For most of the winter he was 'very much out of order' with constant headaches, coughs, and stomach pain. As remedies, he tried bleeding, long two-hour walks in St James's Park, and, most penitential of all, the occasional abstention from the gourmandizing pleasures of Burlington House. To Congreve, such abstemiousness was a virtual denial of Gay's identity. Gay, he declared, was 'a great eater. As the French philosopher used to prove his existence by *cogito ergo sum*,

---

[85] Cf. *Rural Sports* (1720): 'New stratagems and doubling wiles she tries, | Now circling turns, and now at large she flies; | Till spent at last, she pants, and heaves for breath | Then lays her down, and waits devouring death' (ll. 384–7).

[86] *Letters*, 41.

the greatest proof of Gay's existence is *edit, ergo est*.'[87] Nor was this Gay's only attempt to transform the received view of his identity. He told Swift that he was daily growing in 'contempt of the world':

I now begin to be richer and richer, for I find I could every morning I wake be content with less than I aimed at the day before. I fancy in time I shall bring myself into that state which no man ever knew before me, in thinking I have enough.[88]

This *contemptus mundi* theme was a favourite motif of the correspondence of Bolingbroke, who never failed to preface his schemes for regaining political power with high-minded disavowals of all such worldly ambitions. Gay's pretence that his residual ambitions were prompted solely by the expectations of others is similarly disingenuous:

I really am afraid to be content with so little, lest my good friends should censure me for indolence, and the want of laudable ambition; so that it will be absolutely necessary for me to improve my fortune to content them. How solicitous is mankind to please others!

Gay's stomach cramps and constant headaches were proof, if proof were needed, that it was not the potential censure of 'good friends' which drove his ambitions, but a relentless gnawing urge for recognition, too personal and too fundamental to be openly acknowledged.

Initial reactions to the *Fables* were somewhat mixed; they were widely read and much quoted, but regarded in some literary circles with critical condescension. The poet Young wrote to Tickell: 'Gay has just given us some fables, 50 in number & about five are tolerable.'[89] At court, though, his prospects seemed a good deal brighter. Appropriately it was Gay's female friends who responded to the challenge of his verses. According to Swift, a few weeks after the accession of George II (in June 1727), Queen Caroline told Mrs Howard 'that she would take up the hare' and bade her 'to put her in mind, in settling the family to find some employment for Mr Gay'. In a letter to Gay that autumn, Mrs Howard assured him that 'by my consent you shall never be a *hare* again'.[90]

---

[87] *Spence*, item 242; i. 106.
[88] *Letters*, 65.
[89] R. E. Tickell, *Thomas Tickell and the Eighteenth Century Poets (1685–1740)* (London, 1931), 131.
[90] Swift, *Corr.* iv. 99. *Letters of Henrietta, Countess of Suffolk*, ed. J. W. Croker (2 vols., London, 1824), i. 284.

During the winter Pope had been busy editing the *Miscellanies in Prose and Verse* by Swift and himself. In March the first two volumes were printed and Pope wrote to Swift declaring himself 'prodigiously pleased' by this joint work 'in which methinks we look like friends, side by side, serious and merry by turns, conversing interchangeably, and walking down hand in hand to posterity'.[91] Work on the third or so-called 'Last' volume of the *Miscellanies*, which included a few minor pieces by Gay, was delayed for some more months, to meet the requirements of Pope's exacting editorial policy, which insisted there must be 'a character in every piece, like the mark of the elect'.[92] Whether the ballad of Nelly Bennet carries such a 'mark of the elect' is a moot point, but Pope relented at least to the extent of allowing it, and three more of Gay's minor poems, to join him in his élite literary fraternity with Swift. Steele, editing his own latest volume of *Poetical Miscellanies*, adopted a less exclusive policy, and Gay's charming ballad 'The Coquet Mother and Coquet Daughter' found a place there alongside other writings of the non-elect.

Both Pope and Gay were eagerly anticipating Swift's early return to England to bask in his new celebrity status following *Gulliver's* success. Gay hoped he would come '*cum hirundine prima*, which we modern naturalists pronounce ought to be reckoned . . . the end of February'.[93] Swift himself sounded a less enthusiastic note. 'Going to England is a very good thing', he told Pope, 'if it were not attended with an ugly circumstance of returning to Ireland.'[94] He added, 'it is a shame you do not persuade your ministers to keep me on that side, if it were but by a court expedient of keeping me in prison for a plotter'. He asked Mrs Howard to tell Walpole 'that if he does not use me better next summer than he did last, I will study revenge, and it shall be *vengeance ecclésiastique*', a threat which casts further doubt on his subsequent claim that his negotiations with Walpole were solely on Gay's behalf.[95] England still excited Swift and, despite all the disappointments of his visit the previous year, he relished the opportunity to prove himself as good as the best of them, politicians, satirists, or peers. Meanwhile he and Pope continued to congratulate

---

[91] Pope, *Corr.* ii. 426.
[92] Ibid.
[93] *Letters*, 61–2.
[94] Swift, *Corr.* iii. 189.
[95] Ibid. 196.

each other on seeking no special favours from the great. 'We care not three pence whether a prince or minister will see us or no,' declared Swift with ringing disingenuousness.[96] In England, his friends busied themselves with arrangements to welcome him in style, composing a sequence of 'Gulliverian' verses for inclusion in the second edition of *Gulliver's Travels*, published that May. Although Pope wrote most of these, there is some evidence that Gay may have had a hand in them. *The Lamentation of Glumdalclitch* contains appropriately magnified echoes of *Rural Sports*, as Glumdalclitch describes how she 'twined the silver eel around thy hook'; *The Grateful Address of the Unhappy Houyhnhnms* recalls the theme of Gay's fable XLIII; and it is even possible that Gay published his own independent Brobdingnagian skit, *The Man-Mountain's Answer to the Lilliputian Verses*, playing with the difference in size between himself and Pope.[97] Bolingbroke sent Swift an enthusiastic letter enclosing the first issues of the *Craftsman*. 'Your deafness must not be a hackney excuse to you', he insisted. 'What matter if you are deaf? . . . You are not dumb, and we shall hear you, and that is enough.'[98] Bolingbroke's hail-fellow tone was hardly to Swift's taste, especially when he added that his wife was sending over some Gulliverian fans 'which you will dispose of to the present Stella, whoever she be'. Happily promiscuous and having recently rid himself of his wife in order to marry his mistress, Bolingbroke was ill equipped to understand the more complex emotional strains of Swift's relationship with Stella, who was still dangerously ill. Meanwhile in London the political climate grew constantly warmer. 'If you were with us, you'd be deep in politics,' said Pope, sounding a warning note. 'People are very warm, and very angry, very little to the purpose.'[99] For his own part Pope remained quietly at Twickenham, 'without so much as reading newspapers', while Gay practised his new-found contempt for the world. It is noticeable how insistent all the Scriblerians were about their lack of interest in politics, just as the political situation seemed set to suck them in.

---

[96] Nokes, 310.

[97] The most comprehensive discussion of the authorship of these 'Gulliver' poems is contained in Ault, 231–42. Ault attributes overall responsibility for all the poems to Pope, but acknowledges the possibility that Gay may have contributed to their composition. See also Faber, pp. xxxiv and 214.

[98] Swift, *Corr.* iii. 200.

[99] Pope, *Corr.* ii. 426–7.

On 7 April Swift requested a six months' leave of absence from Dublin, planning, if possible, to travel on to Aix-la-Chapelle, perhaps with Gay, after his stay in England. A proxy was arranged for the next episcopal visitation; a rogue of a Deanery proctor, who had cost Swift some £600, was dismissed; the 'ladies' (Stella and Rebecca Dingley) were safely installed in the Deanery for the summer, and on the 9th Swift set sail for England.

As soon as he arrived in London Swift found himself plunged into politics. The *Craftsman* group, headed by Bolingbroke and Pulteney, had taken 'a firm resolution to assault the present administration, and break it, if possible'. Bolingbroke had been admitted to an audience with the King, and Swift found himself treated with 'high displeasure' by Walpole, who suspected him of greater involvement in opposition journalism than was actually the case. Much of his time in London he stayed with Gay, his 'Whitehall landlord'. As usual, Swift's letters were intercepted, but now there were rumours of more serious threats against him; friends warned him 'not to go to France (as I intended for two months) for fear of their vengeance in a manner which they cannot execute here'.[100] The implication of this advice is ominous indeed, though no doubt friends like Bolingbroke were keen to magnify the dangers of foreign travel as a way of keeping Swift in England as a political ally. But when at last he did contribute a *Letter* for inclusion in the *Craftsman*, Bolingbroke was unhappy with its tone, and urged more polemic revisions. 'I would have you insinuate there, that the only reason Walpole can have . . . is the authority of one of his spies . . .'[101] At this late stage in his political career Swift would not submit to such editorial control, and preferred to abandon politics in favour of more restful pursuits with Gay. 'They are gone a fishing,' Pope told the Earl of Oxford as Swift and Gay, like Glumdalclitch and Grildrig, baited their hooks for more innocuous prey.[102] Together they exchanged anecdotes from their family histories, and compared the quality of cider apples from Herefordshire, where Swift's grandfather had been plundered by 'Cromwell's hellish crew', with those of Devonshire, where Gay's grandfather had been similarly persecuted for his faith. They discussed the *Beggar's Opera* and Swift urged Gay to visit Newgate prison to soak up the atmosphere of the place. But, perhaps

[100] Swift, *Corr.* iii. 207.
[101] Ibid. 211.
[102] Pope, *Corr.* ii. 431.

remembering his late aunt Martha's imprisonment there, Gay was reluctant to try the experiment, even as a visitor. On another occasion, walking in St James's Park, Swift introduced Gay to Miss Drelincourt, daughter of the recently deceased Dean of Armagh. Miss Drelincourt now lived in Greek Street, in the Soho district of Westminster, with her mother, who was anxious to secure Swift's help in finding a publisher for a friend's translations. Swift though was not impressed by the friend's manner of 'threatening and ill language', and declined to help in publishing a book in which 'Mr Pope was openly reflected on by name'.[103] However, both he and Gay were much taken by Miss Drelincourt herself, who made 'a good figure on the Mall'. If Gay ever thought of taking a wife, Miss Drelincourt might be the perfect candidate. Swift even suggested, in some mock-pastoral verses, that 'Plump Johnny Gay will now elope'.[104] But Gay was currently more preoccupied with courts than courtship. He thanked Swift for the introduction, and promised to give the matter further consideration.

Realizing that Swift would not be of any great assistance to him, Bolingbroke ceased to feed him dismal stories of the dangers of travelling in France and instead offered him letters of introduction to friends in Paris. Voltaire, whom he and Gay visited in London, furnished further introductions. *Gulliver's Travels* had just been translated into French and Swift had high hopes of repeating his London triumph in Paris. However, just as he was about to leave, news came which altered all their plans. King George, on a journey to Hanover, had died at Osnabrück on 12 June. Bolingbroke wrote immediately to insist that 'there would not be common sense in your going into France at this juncture'.[105] His letter trembled with barely concealed excitement. Swift must on no account contemplate 'such an unmeaning journey . . . when the opportunity of quitting Ireland for England is, I believe, fairly before you'. Although Bolingbroke made a token nod towards stoicism, he could not conceal his hunger for power.

to hanker after a court is fit for men with blue ribbands, pompous titles, gorgeous estates. It is below either you or me, one of whom never made his

---

[103] Swift, *Corr.* iii. 227–8.
[104] *A Pastoral Dialogue between Richmond Lodge and Marble Hill*, in Swift, *Poems*, ii. 409.
[105] Swift, *Corr.* iii. 215.

fortune, and the other's turned rotten at the very moment it grew ripe. But without hankering, without assuming a suppliant dependent air, you may spend in England all the time you can be absent for Ireland, & *faire la guerre a l'orgueil.* There has not been so much inactivity as you imagine.[106]

Simultaneously Gay was receiving the same optimistic message from Mrs Howard, with whom he and Swift would 'sponge a breakfast once a week' at Marble Hill.[107] Only Pope affected to remain aloof from all the political turmoil: 'Whatever our friend Gay may wish as to getting into court,' he told Mrs Howard, 'I disclaim it, and desire to see nothing of the court but yourself.'[108] Although already detecting a familiar strain of make-believe in all the sudden Tory euphoria, Swift allowed himself to be dissuaded, by the 'great vehemence' of the entreaties of Bolingbroke and Mrs Howard, from leaving England and went instead to stay with Pope at Twickenham. Within days a more realistic tone had crept into Bolingbroke's correspondence. 'I wish John Gay success in his pursuit', he wrote, 'but I think he has some qualities which will keep him down in the world.' Troubled by an untimely 'defluxion of rheum' in both eyes, Bolingbroke was roused to Hamlet-like musings.

Good God, what is man? Polished, civilized, learned man? A liberal education fits him for slavery, and the pains he has taken give him the noble pretensions of dangling away life in an ante-chamber . . . or of making his reason & his knowledge serve all the purposes of other men's follies and vices.[109]

Swift was even more frustrated with all the rumours and court intrigues. 'There are, madam', he wrote to Mrs Howard,

thousands in the world, who if they saw your dog Fop use me kindly, would, the next day in a letter tell me of the delight they heard I had in doing good; and being assured that a word of mine to you would do anything, desire my interest to speak to you, to speak to the Speaker, to speak to Sr R. Walp[ole], to speak to the King &c. Thus wanting people are like drowning people, who lay hold of every reed or bulrush in their way.[110]

---

[106] Swift, *Corr.* iii. 215–16.
[107] Swift, *Poems*, ii. 409.
[108] Pope, *Corr.* ii. 436.
[109] Swift, *Corr.* iii. 216.
[110] Ibid. 223.

Gay was just one such person in imminent danger of drowning. 'Toss John Gay over the water to Richmond, if he is with you [i.e. at Twickenham]', Bolingbroke suggested. The *Craftsman* now called on the new monarch to replace Walpole, and the Tories put forward the Speaker of the Commons, Spencer Compton, as their candidate to head a new administration. But this genial nonentity proved unable to form a ministry, or even to draft a King's speech, without Walpole's assistance. Throughout the summer Walpole worked hard at re-establishing his political position, promising the King an increased Civil List, securing the new Queen Caroline as his ally, and gradually clawing his way back to power. Tory contempt for the incompetent Compton can be glimpsed in another of Swift's letters to Mrs Howard which pokes fun at his own deafness and ill handwriting, as a means of making some satiric points. 'I make nothing of . . . knights of a share for knights of a shire, monster for minister; in writing speaker I put an "n" for a "p" and a hundred such blunders.'[111] This political humiliation coincided with the worst bout of deafness Swift had ever experienced, brought on by some devastating news from Ireland that Stella was again danger-ously ill. He became unhappy and restless at Twickenham, where it again pained him to see Pope's awkward attempts to entertain him. In desperation he resolved to move back, either to Gay's lodgings at Whitehall, or to Greenwich, where he could he nursed by his relations the Lancelots. Swift spent his last week in London, moving hither and thither, from Hammersmith to Whitehall, and from Greenwich to Bond Street, in a panic that drove him to avoid the consolation of well-meaning friends. Finally, on 18 September, deaf, giddy, exhausted, and wretched, he left London for the last time in his life.

Both Pope and Gay were disappointed that Swift should steal away 'so unexpectedly, and in so clandestine a manner'.[112] Pope, in particular, was 'sorry to find you could think yourself easier in any house than in mine'. Swift wrote back to apologize, explaining, 'I find it more convenient to be sick here, without the vexation of making my friends uneasy.' His thoughts though were still with them, and especially with Gay. 'I hope my Whitehall landlord is nearer to a place than when I left him,' he wrote; 'as the Preacher

---

[111] Ibid. 233.
[112] Pope, *Corr.* ii. 454.

said, "the day of judgement was nearer, than ever it had been before." [113]

In fact for Gay the day of judgement came even sooner than Swift guessed. Within the week the list of new appointments in the royal household was published, and at last Gay's name was included. The lawyer Fazakerly was named as Gentleman Usher to the Princess Mary, and Gay as Gentleman Usher to the 2-year-old Princess Louisa.

[113] Swift, *Corr.* iii. 242–3.

PART III

A Free Man
(1728–1732)

THIRTEEN

The Company of Beggars

I own myself of the Company of Beggars . . .
(Introduction, *The Beggar's Opera*)

FOR Gay, the offer of such an ignominious post came as a bitter disappointment. The salary of £150 per annum was no improvement on his stipend as commissioner of lotteries, but the real humiliation was the invitation to become a 2-year-old's attendant. Receiving the news at the Queensberrys' house, he summoned up the best counterfeit of a courtly manner he could command, and wrote back directly to Queen Caroline, informing her he was now too 'far advanced in life' to accept such a post. All the pent-up frustrations of his wasted years of court ingratiation burst from him in a despairing letter to Pope.

Dear Mr Pope,
  My melancholy increases, and every hour threatens me with some return of my distemper; nay, I think I may rather say I have it on me. Not the divine looks, the kind favours and expressions of the divine duchess, who hereafter shall be in place of a Queen to me, (nay, she shall be my Queen) nor the inexpressible goodness of the Duke, can in the least cheer me. The drawing-room no more receives light from those two stars. There is now what Milton says is in hell, 'darkness visible'. O that I had never known what a court was! Dear Pope, what a barren soil (to me so) have I been striving to produce something out of! Why did I not take your advice before my writing fables for the duke, not to write them? Or rather, to write them for some young nobleman? It is my very hard fate, I must get nothing, write for them or against them. I find myself in such a strange confusion and depression of spirits, that I have not strength even to make my will; though I perceive, by many warnings, I have no continuing city here. I begin to look upon myself as one already dead; and desire, my dear

Mr Pope, (whom I love as my own soul) if you survive me, (as you certainly will) that you will, if a stone should mark the place of my grave, see these words put upon it:

> Life is a jest, and all things show it;
> I thought so once, but now I know it . . .[1]

The abject tones of this letter recall Gay's similarly self-recriminatory outburst to Pope ten years earlier, following the 'failure' of *Three Hours after Marriage*. What both letters demonstrate is a sudden collapse of confidence and the annihilation of a painfully constructed persona of cheerful optimism. Gay's hold on his own sense of self-determination was always precarious at best. In his letter to Pope in 1717, he ceded all sense of self-defence by volunteering for the role of scapegoat. Ten years later, even that performance is beyond him. Now he sees himself as a dead man; his identity reduced to a self-mocking epitaph. It is particularly revealing that, in these moments of despair, it is Pope that Gay turns to. Much of Gay's literary career was an attempt to escape from the shadow of being one of Pope's *élèves*. But, in these moments of psychic breakdown, it was Pope's support and consolation, almost Pope's forgiveness, that he sought, and the letters are filled, like those of an erring pupil, with desperate apologies for having ignored Pope's wise advice. Pope replied immediately, though his consolatory letter, couched in lofty tones of moral superiority, contains as much public moralizing as personal sympathy, and does not scruple to remind Gay of the stoic homily Pope had preached to him several years before.

I have many years ago magnified in my own mind, and repeated to you, a ninth beatitude, added to the eight in the scripture; *Blessed is he who expects nothing, for he shall never be disappointed.* I could find in my heart to congratulate you on this happy dismission from all court-dependence. I dare say I shall find you the better and honester man for it, many years hence; very probably the healthfuller, and the cheerfuller into the bargain. You are happily rid of many cursed ceremonies, as well as of many ill and

---

[1] *Letters*, 65–7. The date of this letter is contested. Sherburn (Pope, *Corr.* iii. 19) follows Ayre's lead (William Ayre, *Memoirs of the Life and Writings of Alexander Pope, Esq.* (1745), ii. 118) in dating it in Mar. 1729, after the banning of *Polly* and the Duchess of Queensberry's banishment from court. Burgess, however (*Letters*, 65–6), presents cogent arguments in favour of this earlier date. There is no conclusive way to determine the question, but Burgess's arguments are highly persuasive, and the letter makes better sense in the context of Gay's despair following his refusal of the post of Gentleman Usher. It also provides the trigger for Pope's reply of 16 Oct. 1727.

vicious habits, of which few or no men escape the infection who are hackneyed and tramelled in the ways of a court. Princes indeed, and peers (the lackeys of princes) and ladies (the fools of peers) will smile on you the less; but men of worth, and real friends, will look on you the better. There is a thing, the only thing which Kings and Queens cannot give you (for they have it not to give), Liberty, which is worth all they have; and which, as yet, I hope Englishmen need not ask for from their hands. You will enjoy that, and your own integrity, and the satisfactory consciousness of having *not* merited such graces from them, as they bestow only on the mean, servile, flattering, interested, and undeserving . . .[2]

And so on. Pope's letter continues in this sententious vein for another couple of paragraphs, concluding, somewhat oddly, 'Dear Gay, adieu', as if bidding farewell to someone who has served his purpose as a moral object lesson. Indeed, through his sudden, if temporary, loss of a sense of identity, Gay conveniently turned himself into what his friends most required of him, a moral symbol. It was at this time that he wrote his mournful *Elegiac Epistle*, addressed either to Pope or Fortescue, in which he seemed to wish for death as a final welcome relief from a life of constant disappointments.

i

Friend of my youth, shedd'st thou the pitying tear
    O'er the sad relics of my happier days,
Of nature tender, as of soul sincere,
    Pour'st thou for me the melancholy lays?

ii

O! truly said! – the distant landscape bright,
    Whose vivid colours glitter'd on the eye
Is faded now, and sunk in shades of night,
    As, on some chilly eve, the closing flow'rets die.

iii

Yet had I hop'd, when first, in happier times,
    I trod the magic paths where Fancy led,
The Muse to foster in more friendly climes,
    Where never Mis'ry rear'd its hated head.

iv

How vain the thought! Hope after hope expires!
    Friend after friend, joy after joy is lost;

[2] Pope, *Corr.* ii. 453.

My dearest wishes feed the fun'ral fires,
    And life is purchas'd at too dear a cost.

Not published until 1773, this poem, with its melancholy variations
on the 'vanity of human wishes' theme, might have struck Johnson
as a more seemly valedictory than Gay's chosen epitaph, to which
he took such exception. Yet for Gay the poetic expression of
such sepulchral despondency was uncharacteristic and demonstrates, more than anything, a temporary surrender to the sensibility
of Pope, whose letters are increasingly filled with such morbid
sentiments.[3]

   Actually, Pope made no secret of his view that this latest snub
was in fact a liberation. 'Gay is a free man,' he told Swift, adding, 'I
writ him a long congratulatory letter upon it. Do you the same: It
will mend him, and make him a better man.' Swift promptly
obliged, not only congratulating Gay on refusing so lowly a post,
but intimating that Walpole himself was responsible for this latest
snub: 'I am confident you have a firm enemy in the ministry,' he
wrote, going on to offer his own reflections on court life:

I have known courts these 36 years, and know they differ, but in some
things they are extremely constant: First, in the trite old maxim of a
minister never forgiving those he hath injured; secondly, in the insincerities
of those who would be thought the best friends; thirdly in the love of
fawning, cringing and tale-bearing. Fourthly, in sacrificing those whom we
really wish well to a point of interest or intrigue. Fifthly, in keeping
everything worth taking for those who can do service or disservice. I could
go on to four-and-twentythly . . .[4]

Four years later, when Swift came to write his poem *To Mr Gay*
(1731), the episode had already acquired a legendary status:

    Say, had the court no better place to choose
    For thee, than make a dry nurse of thy muse?

---

   [3] The poem was first published in the *Miscellaneous Works* of 1773, and attributed to
Gay partly on the authority of Aaron Hill (see Dearing, ii. 640 and Ault, 238). It is
possible, but unlikely, that the 'Friend of my youth' mentioned in the first line was Hill
himself, but Fortescue or Pope (who did not in fact meet Gay until he was 26) are more
likely candidates. The date of the poem, as of the preceding letter, is inevitably
conjectural. It could possibly have been composed during Gay's severe illness in spring
1729, following the banning of *Polly*, but since its mood seems to echo that of Gay's
funereal letter to Pope, it has been placed here, along with that letter.
   [4] Pope, *Corr.* ii. 455; Swift, *Corr.* iii. 250.

How cheaply had thy liberty been sold,
To squire a royal girl of two years old!
In leading-strings her infant steps to guide;
Or, with her go-cart, amble side by side.   (ll. 7–12)

Soon the chorus of self-righteous outrage on Gay's behalf was almost deafening. Just as Gay reduced himself to a sardonic epitaph, so his friends seized on his 'disappointment' as a cautionary satiric motif.[5]

Gay did not feel like a free man. As he told Swift, 'So now all my expectations are vanished; and I have no prospect but in depending wholly upon myself and my own conduct.' Under Pope's direction, he did his best to see the whole thing as a blessing in disguise: 'As I am used to disappointments I can bear them, but as I can have no more hopes, I can no more be disappointed, so that I am in a blessed condition.'[6] This was putting a brave face on it; instinctively his condition felt anything but blessed.

Yet, despite the chorus of outrage among Gay's friends, it is not entirely clear why he should have regarded the offer of the usher's place as such an abject humiliation. From Queen Caroline's point of view it must have appeared an apt, even an imaginative appointment. It was Gay himself, after all, who had chosen to make his latest appeal for court favour in the form of *Fables* dedicated to the infant Prince William. Did this not suggest the conduct of a man who might relish the tutelage of another of the royal children? And, while Gay's feminized portrait of himself as the compliant hare might have raised questions about his suitability as an attendant to an increasingly rowdy boy, it qualified him perfectly to squire the infant princess. Courtier-like, he had sought to charm the Princess by flattering her children; monarch-like, she rewarded him with the offered post of poet-nanny in chief.

It is tempting to regard Gay's refusal of the post of Gentleman Usher to Princess Louisa as marking the end of an ignominious chapter in his career. At last the long, frustrating years of court

[5] Swift, *Poems*, ii. 531; see also the lines on Gay's rejection of 'a servile usher's place' in *A Libel on D—D—* (1730), ll. 53–60; *Poems*, ii. 481–2; also Swift's letter to Carteret, 18 Jan. 1728: 'Your friend Walpole hath lately done one of the cruellest actions I ever knew, even in a minister of state, these thirty years past; which, if the Queen hath not intelligence of, may my right hand forget its cunning' (Swift, *Corr.* iii. 260).

[6] *Letters*, 68–9.

sycophancy were over. The morbidity of the *Elegiac Epistle* might thus be taken to represent a kind of symbolic death, the necessary extinction and purification required before Gay's imaginative rebirth the following year. And, as if to prove it, the success of *The Beggar's Opera*, just three months later, represented the triumphant creativity of a free man replacing the servile cringing of a courtier. The reality is rather less straightforward. Despite all his protestations to the contrary, Gay had still not finally relinquished all thoughts of obtaining a respectable court place. His formulaic declaration of hopelessness ('now all my expectations are vanished') was a familiar cry, uttered in similar terms on several previous occasions.[7] Even Swift, despite his ritual denunciations of court perfidy, urged Gay not to abandon hope entirely. 'Upon reasoning with myself', he wrote, 'I should hope they are gone too far to discard you quite, and that they will give you something, which although much less than they ought will be as far as it is worth, better circumstantiated.'[8] Mrs Howard was even more emphatic, regarding the contretemps over the usher's place not as a final humiliation but merely as a minor set-back. Her immediate advice to Gay was to be more hard-headed. Aware that his *Beggar's Opera* was finished, but apparently having little inkling of its content, she confidently assured him that another theatrical triumph would provide the final seal of court approval. 'Now for yourself, John', she wrote:

I desire you will mind the main chance, and be in town time enough to let the opera have play enough for its life, and for your pockets. Your head is your best friend; it would clothe, lodge and wash you; but you neglect it, and follow that false friend, your heart, which is such a foolish tender thing, that it makes others despise your head that have not half so good a one upon their own shoulders. In short John, you may be a snail, or a silkworm, but by my consent, you shall never be a *hare* again.[9]

This was advice which Gay took to both head and heart. In his catalogue of court vices Swift had included the ministerial habit of 'keeping everything worth taking for those who can do service or disservice'. Up till now Gay's tactic had been to offer service:

---

[7] See letters to Swift, 22 Dec.1722, and to Fortescue, 23 Sept. 1725; *Letters*, 41, 49.
[8] Swift, *Corr.* iii. 250.
[9] *Letters of Henrietta, Countess of Suffolk*, ed. J. W. Croker (2 vols., London, 1824), i. 284.

> A hare, who, in a civil way,
> Complied with ev'rything, like Gay . . .

However, he had learnt that such docility produced only condescension. Now, in a change of strategy, he determined to adopt a policy of *disservice*, hoping to attract ministerial recognition not as the reward for servility, but as the price of independence. Forcing himself into a more up-beat frame of mind, he made plans for his long-delayed trip to Newgate, 'to finish my scenes the more correctly'. For, as he explained, 'I have no attendance to hinder me.'[10]

Ever jealous of her claims to court influence, Mrs Howard was particularly concerned lest Gay's sense of disappointment should drive him into the rival camp of his new 'queen', the Duchess of Queensberry. Adopting a somewhat bitchy tone she cautioned him to beware the counterfeit pretensions of this rival patroness. 'Don't let her cheat you in the pencils,' she warned; 'she designs to give you nothing but her old ones: I suppose she always uses those worst who love her best.' Her obsessive cavils at the Duchess's behaviour betray a consciousness of waning powers, and a desperate desire to retain the loyalty of her most faithful follower. Her letter concludes:

We go to town next week. Try your interest and bring the duchess up by the birthday. I did not think to have named her any more in this letter; I find I am a little foolish about her: don't you be a great deal so; for if *she* will not come, do you come without her.[11]

Swift shared the hope that *The Beggar's Opera* would retrieve Gay's fortunes, but had a shrewder eye to its likely political repercussions. Far from furthering Gay's court ambitions, he hoped it would prove an apt revenge against those politicians who had thwarted and humiliated him. 'I am very glad your opera is finished', he wrote; 'and hope your friends will join the readier to make it succeed, because you are used by others so ill.'[12] His chief advice was that Gay should be less concerned with chasing new resources than with securing those he already had. 'I beg you will be thrifty and learn to value a shilling,' he urged him. 'Get a stronger fence about your £1,000, and throw the inner fence into the heap.' Convinced, like

---

[10] *Letters*, 69.
[11] *Letters of the Countess of Suffolk*, 282.
[12] Swift, *Corr.* iii. 250.

Howard, that Gay was too tender-hearted for his own good, he exhorted him to follow the example of more business-minded friends. 'Be advised by your Twickenham landlord and me about an annuity.' But Gay had already invested too much in his assumed persona of hapless financial incompetence to be seen to benefit from such sensible advice. A month later Arbuthnot reported:

There is certainly a fatality upon poor Gay . . . He had made a pretty good bargain, that is a Smithfield one, for a little place in the custom house which was to bring him in about a hundred a year. It was done as a favour to an old man, & not at all to Gay. When everything was concluded, the man repented, & said he would not part with his place.[13]

In episodes like this Gay can be seen playing up to his own self-mocking persona, presenting himself as the helpless fool of circumstances for the amusement of his friends. 'I have begged Gay not to buy an annuity upon my life.' Arbuthnot joked; 'I'm sure I should not live a week.' It was Gay's constant 'inoffensive' ploy to maintain his celebrated 'honesty' by assuming the role of innocent in a world of conniving rogues. 'You are [the] most refractory, honest, good-natured man I ever have known,' wrote Swift, with rueful amusement at his friend's allegedly disaster-prone career. In reality, Gay's accumulated capital of £1,000 suggests he was rather less of a fool in financial matters than he liked to appear.

William Hogarth had scored his first popular success as a graphic satirist in February 1724 with his print *The Bad Taste of the Town*, better known as *Masquerades and Operas*, which depicted Burlington and his opera-loving friends as the impresarios of cultural degeneracy.[14] Clearly, the moralistic outcry which greeted Italian opera at its first appearance in London almost fifteen years earlier had by no means abated by the mid-1720s. If anything, it had increased, and taken on a political dimension. By his lavish annual subsidy of a foreign art-form still widely represented as a debasement of English cultural values, the Hanoverian monarch provided opponents with a perfect satiric metaphor. An early issue of the *Craftsman* declared:

---

[13] *Shift, Corr.* iii. 253.

[14] For a detailed discussion of this print see Ronald Paulson, *Hogarth* (3 vols., Cambridge, 1992), i. 111–20 and Pat Rogers, *Literature and Popular Culture in Eighteenth Century England* (Brighton, 1985) 40–3.

Operas and masquerades, and all the politer elegancies of a wanton age, are much less to be regarded for their expense (great as it is) than for the tendency which they have to deprave our manners. Music has something so peculiar in it, that it exerts a willing tyranny over the soul into whatever shape the melody directs.[15]

But on this, as on so many other matters, the opposition was divided. Amongst those included in, or sympathetic to, the *Crafts-man*'s cause were numbered some of the opera's leading supporters such as Arbuthnot and Pulteney. The most audacious lampoons directed against particular performers often came from partisan insiders in the bitter feuds that racked the operatic world. By the start of 1727 the directors of the Royal Academy, fondly hoping that the acrimonious rivalry between Handel and Bononcini had finally been put to rest, invited Bononcini to compose a new opera, 'the animosities against that great master being worn off'.[16] But just as one feud abated, another and even more newsworthy one began. The huge salaries paid to singers were a constant subject of news-paper gossip, and the emergence of an operatic 'star' system provided journalists with plentiful opportunities for invidious comparisons. In March 1723 the *London Journal* reported that, for Cuzzoni's benefit performance in *Ottone*, 'some of the nobility gave her 50 guineas a ticket'. However, it went on:

As we delight so much in Italian songs, we are likely to have enough of them, for as soon as Cuzzoni's time is out, we are to have another over; for we are well assured Faustina, the fine songstress at Venice, is invited, whose voice, they say, exceeds that we have already here; and as the encouragement is so great, no doubt but she will visit us, and, like others, when she makes her exit, may carry off money enough to build some stately edifice in her own country, and there perpetuate our folly.[17]

In fact opera lovers had to wait another three years for Faustina Bordoni's first appearance in London when, with her annual salary reputed to match Cuzzoni's £2,500, the stage was set for a superstar clash of prima donna temperaments. Throughout the spring and summer of 1727 the papers carried reports of the two women's on- and off-stage spats, their feigned indispositions, and the disruptive

[15] *Craftsman*, 13 Mar. 1727.
[16] *Flying Post*, 31 Jan. 1727.
[17] *London Journal*, 30 Mar. 1723.

manœuvres of their rival claques. At one performance in April Cuzzoni was catcalled 'to such a degree in one song, that she was not heard one note, which provoked the people that like her so much, that they . . . would not suffer the Faustina to speak afterwards'. Lord Hervey commented sardonically on these singers' arrogant pretensions and mercenary motives:

I suppose you have heard already that both Cuzzoni and Faustina were so hissed and cat-called last Tuesday that the Opera was not finished that night: nor have the directors dared to venture the representation of another since. They both threaten to go, but after a little bullying will infallibly stay. 1500 guineas are mediators whose interposition they'll never be able to resist.[18]

It was, Hervey concluded, a perfect symbol of the current depravity of English taste that they should give 'these women . . . £3000 a year to come there to have the pleasure of hissing them off [the stage] when they are there, and prefer their conversation in a barge to their voices in a theatre'. Cuzzoni in particular was frequently portrayed as a conniving foreign gold-digger. After one performance of *Ottone*, attended by the King, the *London Journal* reported, with an unmistakable sexual innuendo, 'She is already jumped into a handsome chariot, and an equipage accordingly. The gentry seem to have so high a taste for her fine parts, that she is likely to be a great gainer by them.'[19] The show-cloth hanging from the opera-house in Hogarth's print depicts her being offered an £8,000 bag of gold.

The most notorious on-stage confrontation between Faustina and Cuzzoni occurred just a few days before the death of George I in June 1727. According to the *British Journal*:

The contention at first was only carried on by hissing on one side, and clapping on the other; but proceeded at length to cat-calls, and other great indecencies: And notwithstanding the Princess Caroline was present, no regards were of force to restrain the rudenesses of the opponents.[20]

For weeks afterwards this incident, the model for the on-stage spat of Lucy and Polly in Gay's *Beggar's Opera*, was the subject of pamphlet recriminations. *The Devil to Pay at St James's; or, A Full*

---

[18] *Lord Hervey and his Friends 1726–38*, ed. the Earl of Ilchester (London, 1950), 18–19. See also the letter of Mary, Countess of Pembroke, to Mrs Charlotte Clayton, quoted in Deutsch, 207.

[19] *London Journal*, 19 Jan. 1723.

[20] *British Journal*, 10 June 1727.

and True Account of a Most Horrible and Bloody Battle between Madame Faustina and Madame Cuzzoni declared:

It is not now, (as formerly), i.e. are you High Church or Low, Whig or Tory; are you for Court or Country, King George or the Pretender: but are you for Faustina or Cuzzoni, Handel or Bononcini. There's the question. This engages all the polite world in warm disputes; and but for the soft strains of the opera, which have in some measure qualified and allayed the native ferocity of the English, blood and slaughter would consequently ensue.[21]

'Apart from the death of George I a week later, it was the biggest news story of 1727.'[22] 'All publicity is good publicity' and, in terms of opera-house profits, the value of so many gossip-column inches far outweighed the negative impact of their lofty censorious tone. There has been a certain naïvety in the assessment of the supposed 'hostility' to Italian opera in England. The opera, then as now, thrived on scandal and controversy, and the publicity generated by lampoons, pamphlets, and newspaper attacks, much of it inspired by *aficionados* themselves, only reinforced the opera's raffish reputation for gloriously histrionic excess and financial extravagance. *The Rape of Proserpine*, Lewis Theobald's pantomime performed at Rich's Lincoln's Inn Fields theatre in February, contains a song, 'The Raree-Show', which includes these lines:

> Here be de Hay-Market, vere de Italian opera,
>   Do sweetly sound,
> Dat cost a de brave gentry no more as
>   Two hundred thousand pound.

The Scriblerians, who had supplied their own spoof *Key* 'attacking' *The What D'Ye Call It*, were well aware of the media value of this kind of fake indignation. And when Gay seized on the notion of parodying Italian opera to provide the formal structure for his latest theatrical satire, he did so not in the xenophobic spirit of cultural élitism of a John Dennis, but with a sense of exultation in the glorious absurdity of this most histrionic of forms. Simultaneously Pope, in the *Dunciad*, was identifying the opera-house as a dunces' showcase, including the rival arias of Cuzzoni and Faustina

---

[21] June 1727; quoted in Deutsch, 211.
[22] Rogers, *Literature and Popular Culture*, 113.

in the general competitive cacophony of the votaries of Dulness.

> 'Hold' (cried the Queen), a cat-call each shall win;
> Equal your merits! equal is your din!   (ll. 233–4)

For Gay, the comic spectacle of the opera with its vain, pretentious superstars affecting the grand airs of gods and heroes, while inciting their supporters to outbursts of partisan spite, provided the perfect topical metaphor for court life.

For much of November and December Gay remained with the Duke and Duchess of Queensberry, working on *The Beggar's Opera*. His hosts, it should be remembered, were themselves both keen opera lovers, and partisans of Bononcini, but clearly felt no embarrassment at encouraging him in a mock-opera which parodied some of Bononcini's airs. Mrs Howard meanwhile felt increasingly excluded from his confidence, and sent a number of tart reflections on his 'kind landlady's' hospitality: 'Pray take care not to command too much where you are, lest it should give you an ill habit.' She continued to assure him of her earnest endeavours on his behalf, though admitting, 'I have never had an opportunity to know how far my plot would succeed'. In the mean time he should exploit his freeloader's opportunities (she spoke as an expert): 'I advise you to make free with towels and napkins, that you may have the less occasion for 'em in town.'[23] Much of Mrs Howard's acerbic tone may be attributable to a crisis in her own domestic affairs. Her marriage was on the point of final breakdown and she spent most of the year accumulating evidence for a formal separation from her ill-tempered, drunken husband. In May she drew up her 'Book' of grievances against him, citing, among other accusations, his 'continual obloquy and slander thrown upon me, in ye most inveterate and public manner', and his brutality: 'You have called me names and have threatened to kick me and to break my neck.'[24] Throughout November she was busy obtaining sworn depositions from her former East Street landlady concerning her husband's cruelty in the poverty-stricken days of 1713. Mrs Hall vividly recalled that Mrs Howard's clothes were then 'as beggarly and mean' as any of her own servants would wear. No wonder Mrs Howard advised Gay should 'not go quite so thinly clad, for fear your want of fires in

---

[23] Suffolk Papers, BL Add. MSS 22626, fo. 64.
[24] Ibid., BL Add. MSS 22627, fos. 37, 41–2.

town should hereafter be said to proceed from your kind landlady's care of your health'.[25] Meanwhile Lord Bathurst expressed disquiet at Gay's new intimacy with the notorious Jacobite Will Shippen, who had recently proposed cuts in the royal Civil List, a move which Gay, in his current mood, might have heartily supported.[26]

By the end of the year Gay was back with Pope at Twickenham, where the two men saw in Christmas with high spirits, hangovers, and sal volatile.[27] This Christmas break, though, was only a brief distraction from Gay's eager preparations for *The Beggar's Opera*, and soon Pope was also protesting at being neglected in the hurry of his friend's theatrical preoccupations. In January he told Swift he had seen nothing of Bathurst, Bolingbroke, Arbuthnot, Lewis, or Gay for some weeks, and was clearly irked by Gay's sudden abandonment of his role as faithful literary aide-de-camp. 'I've ten times spoken to Gay to give him the note to send to [Motte], and he was within this week so careless as not to have done it,' he grumbled. His comments on the opera itself were appropriately equivocal.

John Gay's Opera is just on the point of delivery. It may be call'd (considering its subject) a jail-delivery. Mr Congreve . . . is anxious as to its success, and so am I; whether it succeeds or not, it will make a great noise, but whether of claps or hisses I know not. At worst it is in its own nature a thing which he can *lose* no reputation by, as he lays none upon it.[28]

In his recollections to Spence, Pope was more explicit about his reservations concerning the opera's chances of success.

When it was done, neither of us [i.e. Pope and Arbuthnot] thought it would succeed. We showed it to Congreve, who, after reading it over, said, 'It would either take greatly, or be damned confoundedly'.[29]

By Boswell's time legend had transferred these delphic sentiments to the Duke of Queensberry. According to James Thomson, 'his Grace's observation was, "This is a very odd thing, Gay; I am satisfied that it is either a very good thing, or a very bad thing."'[30]

---

[25] Ibid., fo. 43; BL Add. MSS 22626, fo. 64.
[26] Pope, *Corr.* ii. 465.
[27] Ibid. 466.
[28] Ibid. 468–9.
[29] Spence, i. 107.
[30] *Boswell's Life of Johnson*, ed. G. Birkbeck Hill and L. F. Powell (6 vols., Oxford, 1934), 18 Apr. 1775, ii, 368.

In the event, as we know, *The Beggar's Opera* was a phenomenal success, enjoying a run of sixty-two performances in its opening season, and inspiring a host of imitations, parodies, and Beggarmania bric-à-brac ranging from playing cards to fans, fire-screens, and toys all adorned with scenes from the opera. As the most conspicuously successful of Gay's works, *The Beggar's Opera* has inevitably been the focus of many of the best-known legends that attach themselves to his career. Among the most lasting, and injurious, of these is the impression created by his friends and enemies alike, that Gay was not the opera's sole author. Broome regarded it as merely the latest example of Pope using his complaisant friend as a decoy. 'I have seen Mr Gay's mock-opera,' he told Fenton in May.

Johnny is a good-natured, inoffensive man. I doubt not, therefore, but those lines against courts and ministers are drawn, at least aggravated, by Mr Pope, who delights to paint every man in the worst colours. He wounds from behind Gay, and like Teucer in Homer, puts Gay in front of the battle, and shoots his arrows lurking under the shield of Ajax.[31]

The actor Charles Macklin, whose *Memoirs*, compiled by William Cooke in 1804, contain lively but unreliable anecdotes of the opera's genesis and early performances, ascribed many of its most celebrated songs to Pope, Swift, and several others. Authorship of the first song in particular, 'Through all the employments of life', has been attributed variously to both Swift and Pope. The *Universal Spectator and Weekly Journal* (24 January 1730) confidently asserted: 'People think Mr Gay was not the sole author of *The Beggar's Opera*; and they go so far as to say the first song in that performance was Dr Swift's.' Scott in his *Life of Swift* repeated this claim:

About this time [1727] Swift is supposed to have supplied Gay with the two celebrated songs, after ingrafted in *The Beggar's Opera*, beginning 'Through all the employments of life' and 'Since laws were made for every degree' [air 67].

He added that 'Mr Deane Swift and Mrs Whiteway [Swift's housekeeper] uniformly declared they were written by the Dean.'[32] However, William Ayre in his *Memoirs of Pope* insisted that it was Pope

[31] Pope, *Corr.* ii. 489.
[32] *Memoirs of Jonathan Swift* (Edinburgh, 1814), i. 351.

who was responsible for supplying at least the final couplet of this first song, while Pope himself, in his remarks to Spence, claimed that he and Arbuthnot had helped to polish up the final version of the opera: 'As he [Gay] carried it on he showed what he wrote to both of us, and we now and then gave a correction or a word or two of advice, but 'twas wholly of his own writing.'[33] Gay, though, denied seeking Arbuthnot's advice in the opera's composition. Writing to him on 28 February, Swift enquired: 'How is the Doctor? Does he not chide that you never called upon him for hints?'[34] Macklin's *Memoirs* go much further in denying Gay's responsibility for many of the opera's most successful elements. In addition to ascribing air 44, 'The modes of the court', to Lord Chesterfield, air 6, 'Virgins are like the fair flower', to Sir Charles Hanbury Williams, air 30, 'When you censure the age', to Swift, and air 24, 'The gamesters and lawyers are jugglers alike', to Fortescue, Macklin also denies that there was any intrinsic satiric design in Gay's choice and usage of music in the opera.

To this opera there was no music originally intended to accompany the songs, till Rich the manager suggested it on the second last rehearsal. The junto of wits, who regularly attended, one and all objected to it; and it was given up till the Duchess of Queensberry, (Gay's staunch patroness) accidentally hearing of it, attended herself the next rehearsal, when it was tried and universally approved of.[35]

What is so characteristic and revealing about this anecdote is the way that Gay himself is ignored. Rich, the Duchess of Queensberry, and the 'junto of wits' are the ones who decide the matter, not, apparently, the author. In fact, as many recent studies have shown, the subtlety of Gay's operatic parodies in *The Beggar's Opera* is as much musical as literary, and there is no more reason to deny Gay's conscious imitations of Purcell, Handel, and Bononcini than to suppose him ignorant of the echoes of *Julius Caesar* and *Twelfth Night*. The very originality of the opera's hybrid form, about which Pope was so sceptical, is eloquent testimony that it was, in both conception and detail, Gay's own work. He alone among the Scriblerians had the proven facility for writing popular song lyrics and,

---

[33] *Memoirs of Pope*, ii. 115; Spence, i. 107.
[34] Swift, *Corr.* iii. 267.
[35] Macklin, *Memoirs*, 60.

according to legend at least, was proficient on the flute.[36] Equally, his experience of the machinations and frustrations of court life was sufficient to provide him with ample material for his satire on courtiers' promises, without enlisting the aid of either Pope or Swift. And, while Swift's hint many years earlier for a 'Newgate pastoral' may well have provided an initial inspiration, it was the popularity of more recent 'Newgate' works, such as Thurmond's *Harlequin Sheppard* (1724) and Christopher Bullock's *A Match in Newgate* (1727), which confirmed his choice of subject.[37] It is clear Gay was not short of advice from those around him, all seeking to influence the form and style of *The Beggar's Opera*: Mrs Howard, for one, insisted, 'You shall begin and end your play with a riddle.'[38] But it is equally clear that for once Gay was determined to have a will of his own, and to create a work which, for good or ill, was the unique product of his own imagination.

Even when Gay's authorship of *The Beggar's Opera* has been grudgingly acknowledged, there has been a further disparaging tendency to regard the opera's initial success as something of a fluke, produced by a set of fortuitous circumstances rather than intrinsic merit. Thus Macklin's *Memoirs* present the felicitous casting of Tom Walker in the role of Macheath as another last-minute accident.

Quin was first designed for this part, who barely sung well enough to give a convivial song in company . . . the high reputation of Gay, however, and the critical junto who supported him, made him drudge through two rehearsals. On the close of the last, Walker was observed humming some of the songs behind the scenes, in a tone and liveliness of manner which attracted all their notice . . .[39]

However, according to traditional showbiz legend, it was not Walker, but Lavinia Fenton in the role of Polly Peachum, who rescued *The*

---

[36] Winton, who attempted to verify the legend that Gay played the flute, found it 'an especially frustrating inquiry'. He writes: 'Both Fiske and Irving assume it as fact, without providing documentation.' Winton, 191. (Roger Fiske, *English Theatre Music in the Eighteenth Century* (2nd edn., Oxford, 1986).)

[37] The dedication to the second edition of Bullock's play *A Woman's Revenge; or, A Match in Newgate* (1728) accused Gay of plagiarism: '*The Beggar's Opera* Mr Gay stole from Mr Bullock . . .'; but, as Schultz (p. 168) observes, this charge 'seems merely the expression of envy at the success of *The Beggar's Opera*'.

[38] BL Add. MSS 22626, fo. 64.

[39] Macklin, *Memoirs*, 277–8.

Beggar's Opera from potential disaster on its opening night and went on to steal the show. There is general agreement that the opera's reception on that first night (29 January 1728) was initially in doubt. According to one report, trouble started before the performance had even begun.

The first night of *The Beggar's Opera* was played at the Lincoln's Inn Fields theatre, the audience not being then much acquainted with the nature of operas, expected the usual music before the drawing up of the curtain—finding themselves (as they imagined) likely to be bilked out of their first and second music, they expressed great disapprobation, insomuch that Jack Hall [Lockit] was sent on to apologise for the omission, by explaining it was a rule to have no music prior to the overture. Jack made his obeisance with a tolerable grace, but being confounded at the general silence which so suddenly ensued on his appearance, blundered out—'Ladies and gentlemen, we—we beg you'll not call for first and second music, because—because you all know, that there is never any music at all in an opera.' This bull put the house in good humour, and the piece proceeded.[40]

Pope reported:

We were all at the first night of it, in great uncertainty of the event, till we were very much encouraged by overhearing the Duke of Argyle, who sat in the next box to us, say, 'It will do—it must do! I see it in the eyes of them.' This was a good while before the first act was over.

Macklin's *Memoirs* claim it was not until the second act that success was assured, 'when, after the chorus song of "Let us take the road", the applause was as universal as unbounded'.[41] But the best-known account insists it was Lavinia Fenton's rendition of Polly's comic-pathetic song 'O ponder well!' in Act I which won the audience over. By the time Boswell heard the story from Richard Cambridge, her performance had already acquired the legendary status of a magical moment in theatre history. [He] was told by Quin 'that

[40] William Oxberry, *Dramatic Biography* (London, 1825), iv. 177; quoted by Schultz, 4. John Hall, a former dancing-master, went on to be proprietor of the Old Smock Alley theatre in Dublin.

[41] Spence, i. 107; Macklin, *Memoirs*, 57. 'Let us take the road' (air xx) was adapted from the march in Handel's first English opera *Rinaldo* (1711) with a libretto by Aaron Hill. However, as Schultz (p. 319) remarks, the tune had already gained wider popularity through its metamorphosis into a drinking-song, 'Let the waiter bring clean glasses'.

during the first night of its appearance it was long in a very dubious state; that there was a disposition to damn it, and that it was saved by the song, "O ponder well! be not severe!", the audience being much affected by the innocent looks of Polly, when she came to those two lines, which exhibit at once a painful and ridiculous image: "For on the rope that hangs my dear, | Depends poor Polly's life" '.[42]

All these anecdotes have the ring of a familiar Hollywood scenario. First we have the eccentric and dejected author, turned away by the theatrical establishment,[43] and whose friends privately despair at the rash unconventionality of his work. Then, with rehearsals going badly, and disaster looming, there is the chance discovery of the perfect leading man, overheard backstage humming the opera's tunes. This is followed by the last-minute entrance of a benign patroness (the Duchess of Queensberry in the role of fairy god-mother) who, in a moment of sublime inspiration, hits on the final element (music) to pull the whole work together. Lastly we have the fairy-tale climax in which a young *ingénue*, nervously confronting a packed and hostile audience, wins them over with a song, and goes on not merely to become an overnight star, but to conquer the heart of a duke. All this makes a wonderful fiction, but the facts may be somewhat more prosaic. The *Daily Journal* was unambiguous not merely in praising the opera's success from the start, but in attributing that success to Gay's own imagination.

On Monday was represented for the first time at the Theatre Royal in Lincoln's Inn Fields, Mr Gay's new English opera, written in a manner wholly new, and very entertaining, there being introduced instead of Italian airs, above 60 of the most celebrated English and Scotch tunes. There was present then, as well as last night, a prodigious concourse of nobility and gentry, and no theatrical performance for these many years has met with so much applause.[44]

The subsequent success of *The Beggar's Opera* down the centuries confirms that it was not merely the performances of Fenton, Walker, *et al.*, however talented, which made for the opera's triumph, but rather the roles which Gay created for them. Similarly, since operatic parody forms such an intrinsic and essential part of *The Beggar's*

---

[42] Boswell, *Life of Johnson*, 18 Apr. 1775.

[43] Cibber refused to perform *The Beggar's Opera* at Drury Lane, partly for personal reasons and partly on account of its satire against the court.

[44] *Daily Journal*, 1 Feb. 1728.

Opera's composition (just as parody of heroic tragedy did in *The What D' Ye Call It*), the idea that music was a fortuitous late addition to the work makes nonsense of its satiric structure. *The Beggar's Opera* was a highly original work, but all the component elements of its cross-cultural satire can be traced back to origins in Gay's earlier works; to the mock-pastoralism of *The Shepherd's Week*, to the surreal theatrical parodies in *The What D' Ye Call It* and *Three Hours after Marriage*, and to the love of folk-songs and popular ballads evident throughout Gay's career.

However, as the surprise theatrical triumph of the season it was inevitable *The Beggar's Opera* should spawn not merely a spate of imitations and rival attempts at ballad-operas but also a flurry of newspaper gossip which fed on such apocryphal tales. Amid all the instant publicity which surrounded the opera perhaps the most innocuous was the fascination with the meteoric rise to stardom of Lavinia Fenton. She was celebrated in ballads, depicted in prints, toasted in drinking-songs, and courted by the Duke of Bolton. According to Macklin's *Memoirs*, 'Not a print-shop or fan-shop but exhibited her handsome figure in her Polly's costume, which possessed all the characteristic simplicity of the modern Quakers, without one meretricious ornament.' The poet Young, reporting on her instant fame in a letter to Tickell, was rather less flattering:

Polly a wench that acts in *The Beggar's Opera* is the publica cura of our noble youth. She plays her Newgate part well & shews the great advantage of being born and bred in the Mint; which was really the case. She, 'tis said, has raised her price from one guinea to 100, tho' she cannot be a greater whore than she was before, nor, I suppose a younger.[45]

In fact Lavinia Fenton was born Lavinia Beswick in 1708, the daughter of a naval lieutenant and a mother who kept a coffee-house near Charing Cross. She had made her début at the Haymarket theatre two years earlier in Otway's *The Orphan*, followed by the part of Cherry in *The Beaux' Stratagem*. Rich was so impressed by her 'figure, simplicity and archness' in this role that he poached her from the Haymarket company with 'the tempting offer of fifteen shillings per week'.[46] For the part of Polly her salary was doubled to

---

[45] Macklin, *Memoirs*, 44; Young to Tickell, Mar. 1728; included in R. E. Tickell's *Thomas Tickell and the Eighteenth Century Poets (1685–1740)* (London, 1931), 144.
[46] Macklin, *Memoirs*, 44.

thirty shillings, a considerable income for a young actress, but far from the figure which Young alleges, or which the divas at the opera-house commanded. In fact, despite her enormous success, Fenton only played one season in *The Beggar's Opera*, thereafter retiring with her admirer the Duke of Bolton. In July Gay reported: 'The Duke of Bolton I hear hath run away with Polly Peachum, having settled £400 a year upon her during pleasure, and upon disagreement £200 a year.'[47] Hogarth, who created no less than six versions of his painting of one of the opera's prison scenes (III. xi), drew ironic attention to this romantic 'play-without-the-play', by tracing the eye-line of the suppliant Polly, on her knees before her father Peachum, to rest on the admiring gaze of Bolton in his box at the side of the stage.[48] 'There is a mezzo-tinto print published today of Polly, the heroine of *The Beggar's Opera*,' Gay told Swift in March, adding that she 'was before unknown, and is now in so high a vogue, that I am in doubt whether her fame does not surpass that of the opera itself'.[49] Gay was naturally delighted with the opera's enormous and unprecedented success and wrote excitedly to Swift with regular bulletins of its progress. Ever anxious to promote his friend's financial well-being, Swift had counselled him to choose some appropriate dedicatee for the opera, and thereby get 'the usual dedication-fee of 20 guineas'. In reply, writing on 15 February, the opera's 'fifteenth time of acting', Gay reported that he had no need of such devices:

the playhouse hath been crowded every night . . . I have made no interest either for approbation or money, nor hath anybody been pressed to take tickets for my benefit, notwithstanding which, I think I shall make an addition to my fortune of between six and seven hundred pounds.[50]

Nevertheless Gay was careful to ensure that his aristocratic patrons were given privileged attention. Three days earlier he had been forced to tell the Earl of Oxford that all the boxes for the 15th 'are taken up already, but if your lordship would be so good as to send a

<hr/>

[47] *Letters*, 76. On the death of his wife in 1751 the Duke and Fenton were married.
[48] See Ronald Paulson, *Hogarth*, i: *The 'Modern Moral Subject'* (Cambridge, 1991), 172–85.
[49] *Letters*, 72–3; the mezzotint was by John Faber the Younger after a painting by John Ellys, a student of Thornhill's and later co-director with Hogarth of the Academy in St Martin's Lane.
[50] Ibid. 70.

servant to the box-keeper, I hope I shall have the honour of Lady Oxford's presence in the very box she chooses'. Two tickets were reserved in Gay's name on 19 February and picked up by Lady Oxford's servant on 26 February. A month later he wrote again.

The Beggar's Opera hath now been acted thirty-six times, and was as full the last night as the first, and as yet there is not the least probability of a thin audience ... On the benefit day of one of the actresses last week, one of the players falling sick, they were obliged to give out another play or dismiss the audience. A play was given out, but the people called out for *The Beggar's Opera*, and they were forced to play it, or the audience would not have stayed. I have got by all this success between seven and eight hundred pounds, and Rich, (deducting the whole charges of the house) hath cleared already near four thousand pounds.[51]

This last remark effectively reverses the terms of the familiar *bon mot* that *The Beggar's Opera* 'made Gay rich and Rich gay'. Swift was furious that the unscrupulous impresario should gross so much more than the author.

I think that rich rogue Rich should in conscience make you a present of 2 or 3 hundred guineas. I am impatient that such a dog by sitting still should get five times more than the author.

Even in this, Gay's greatest triumph, Swift still saw his ingenuous friend as the victim of a swindle.

You told me a month ago of £700, and have you not quite made up the eight yet? I know not your methods. How many third days are you allowed, and how much is each day worth, and what did you get for the copy?[52]

In fact Rich was doing all in his power to maximize profits for himself and his author by cramming spectators into every space he could find.

On the 23rd of March for example, the *Opera* grossed £194, with 238 spectators in the boxs, 98 (!) on the stage, 302 in the pit, 65 in the slips (extensions of the boxes), 440 compressed into the first gallery, 196 in the second gallery, and 2 paying customers in a category not yet explained by scholarship, but the comfort of which imagination can conjure up: 'pidgeon holes.' A total of 1,341 in the audience.[53]

[51] Ibid. 69–70; 72.

[52] Swift, *Corr.*, iii. 276.

[53] Winton, 102. These totals are taken from *The London Stage, 1660–1800*, ii: *1700–1729*, ed. Emmett L. Avery (2 vols., Carbondale, Ill., 1960).

The same day Pope wrote to Swift, assuring him that Gay was prospering nicely.

Mr Gay's opera has acted near forty days running, and will certainly continue the whole season. So he has more than a fence about his thousand pounds: he'll soon be thinking of a fence about his two thousand.[54]

To Swift, increasingly obsessed with the necessity of financial self-sufficiency, this was welcome news indeed. He followed a maxim which, he claimed, should be written in letters of diamond, 'that a wise man ought to have money in his head, but not in his heart', and promptly wrote back to Gay:

Will you desire my lord Bolingbroke, Mr Pulteney and Mr Pope to command you to buy an annuity with two thousand pounds that you may laugh at courts and bid ministers kiss etc.—and ten to one they will be ready to grease you when you are fat.[55]

As usual, though, Gay's friends were convinced he would fritter away his new fortune as quickly as he had lost his illusory South Sea gains. In May Martha Blount commented, 'Mr Gay's fame continues, but his riches are in a fair way of diminishing: he is gone to the Bath.' In mock-exasperation Swift wrote to Pope:

I suppose Mr Gay will return from the Bath with twenty pounds more flesh, and two hundred less in money. . . . He hath as little foresight of age, sickness, poverty, or loss of admirers as a girl of fifteen.[56]

Such a comment eloquently illustrates the tenacity with which Gay's friends held to and promoted the image of him as a perpetual adolescent. Though he had just achieved a financial and political coup with the most effective and popular satiric work since Swift's own *Gulliver's Travels*, his friends persisted in regarding him as both too 'inoffensive' to be a real satirist, and too naïve to be trusted with money. Though Swift was unquestionably delighted at *The Beggar's Opera*'s political impact, both his comments and Pope's betray a certain *frisson* of condescension at seeing themselves displaced by their protégé's success. '*The Beggar's Opera* hath knocked down *Gulliver*, I hope to see Pope's Dulness [i.e. *The Dunciad*]

---

[54] Pope, *Corr.* ii. 480.
[55] Swift, *Corr.* iii. 328, 276.
[56] Ibid. 284, 294.

knock down *The Beggar's Opera*, but not till it hath fully done its job,' Swift wrote to Gay, emphasizing the sense of an orchestrated Scriblerian onslaught. But to Pope he wrote that 'wealth is liberty, and liberty is a blessing fittest for a philosopher—and Gay is a slave just by two thousand pounds too little'.[57]

In fact Gay gained £693. 13s. 6d. from the production of *The Beggar's Opera*, with a further ninety guineas from Tonson and Watts for the copyright to the opera and *The Fables*.[58] There is no evidence that he frittered this money away either at Bath or elsewhere; on the contrary, he appears to have invested it wisely and lived with a thrift which even Swift might have admired. Three years later, after the *succès de scandale* of *Polly*, he was able to boast to Swift that his fortune 'amounts to at present (all debts paid) above three thousand four hundred pounds', and his estate when he died was worth over £6,000. Not bad for a feckless Peter Pan with, as we are so often assured, no head for finance.

Amid all the gossip and hullabaloo surrounding *The Beggar's Opera*, three main topics, apart from the fame of Lavinia Fenton, quickly came to dominate public discussion. These were its alleged ridicule of Italian opera, its reputed attack on Walpole's government, and its apparent glamorization of criminals and whores. Each of these charges has been the subject of considerable controversy, both at the time and since, and they are worth examining in detail.

Soon after *The Beggar's Opera*'s opening, Mrs Pendarves wrote from Somerset House to her sister Ann Granville.

Yesterday I was at the rehearsal of the new opera composed by Handel: I like it extremely, but the taste of the town is so depraved, that nothing will be approved of but burlesque. *The Beggar's Opera* entirely triumphs over the Italian one.

She went on to add, 'I have not yet seen it, but everybody that has

---

[57] Ibid. 278, 294.

[58] These figures are taken from 'the original Account-book of the manager, C. M. Rich'; see *Notes and Queries*, 1st series 1/178–9 (19 Jan. 1850); see also 8th series 7/501 (29 June 1895). Winton disputes the apparent certainty of these figures: 'every student knows', he writes, that the patent companies deducted the house charge—by this time about £50—from every benefit performance. He concludes that Gay may well have received some £200 less than the figure usually quoted: 'the famous £693 13s 6d is moonshine and nothing else.' Winton, 174.

seen it, says it is very comical and full of humour.'[59] A few weeks later Mrs Pendarves was even more gloomy about the pernicious influence of Gay's work, regarding it as proof of the philistine English public's lack of appreciation for serious music.

The opera will not survive after this winter ... the English have no real taste for music; for if they had, they would not neglect an entertainment so perfect in its kind for a parcel of ballad singers. I am so peevish about it that I have no patience.[60]

On 17 February Handel's *Siroe* opened at the Haymarket theatre, in a performance attended by the King, Queen, and Princess Royal, but its appeal was clearly far less than Gay's rival production at Lincoln's Inn Fields. On 23 March the *London Journal* echoed Mrs Pendarves's lament:

As there is nothing which surprises all true lovers of music more than the neglect into which the Italian operas are at present fallen; so I cannot but think it a very extraordinary instance of the fickle and inconstant temper of the English nation.

Most of the press though took a different perspective, adopting a stridently xenophobic tone in praising Gay's apparent triumph over the foreign competition. Fourteen years earlier Steele had called for the banishment of Italian opera from the London stage:

Begone, our nation's pleasure and reproach!
Britain no more with idle trills debauch;
Back to thy own unmanly Venice sail,
Where luxury and loose desires prevail.[61]

Now at last, it seemed, Steele's wishes had been fulfilled. *Thievery-a-la-Mode*, a pamphlet published in June 1728, was typical of many similar works in its confident pronouncements on Gay's satiric intentions. *The Beggar's Opera*, it declared,

was intended by the author a satire on the inconsistencies and unnatural

---

[59] *The Autobiography and Correspondence of Mary Granville, Mrs Delany*, ed. Lady Llanover (6 vols., 1861–2), i. 158. The date of this letter, given by the editor as 19 Jan., is impossible, since *The Beggar's Opera* did not open until 29 Jan., and Handel's new opera *Siroe* could not have been in rehearsal much before that date. Deutsch (p. 220) suggests 29 Jan. as a more likely date, while Schultz (p. 149) opts for 19 Feb.

[60] *Autobiography of Mrs Delany*, 29 Feb. 1728.

[61] *Miscellany* (1713).

conduct of the Italian opera, which tho' they charm the eye with gay dresses and fine scenes, and delight the ear with sound, have nothing in them either to reform the manners, or improve the mind, the original institutions of the stage.[62]

Numerous ballads proudly proclaimed the superior English charms of Polly Peachum over those of her Italian rivals:

> Of all the Belles that tread the stage,
>   There's none like pretty Polly,
> And all the music of the age,
>   Except her voice, is folly.
>
> Compared with her, how flat appears
>   Cuzzoni or Faustina?
> And when she sings, I shut my ears
>   To warbling Senesino.[63]

The *Daily Journal* carried an advertisement for 'A Song on Polly Peachum. To the tune of *Sally in our alley*' which included similar sentiments.

> There's Madam Fustina, Catso,
>   And eke Madam Cuzzoni;
> Likewise Mynheer Senesino,
>   Are *tutti abandoni*:
> Ha, ha, ha, ha, do, re, mi, fa,
>   Are all but farce and folly;
> We're ravished all with toll, toll, toll,
>   And pretty, pretty, Polly . . .[64]

The proliferation of such sentiments quickly established a tradition of patriotic commentary which, by the end of the century, had achieved the status of an accepted fact of cultural history. In his *Hogarth Illustrated* (1791) John Ireland declared:

Gay must be allowed the praise of having attempted to stem Italia's liquid stream which at that time meandered through every alley, street and square

---

[62] *Thievery-a-la-Mode; or, The Fatal Encouragement* (1728).
[63] From 'Polly Peachum, a new ballad. To the tune of *Of all the girls that are so smart*' in the *Craftsman* on 13 Apr.
[64] *Daily Journal*, 1 May. 1728.

in the metropolis,—the honour of having almost silenced the effeminate
song of that absurd, exotic Italian opera.[65]

For Ireland, Gay like Hogarth was a cultural nationalist, proudly
proclaiming the superiority of robust British folk-songs over their
effete Italian rivals. As recently as 1964 Oliver Warner was still
championing *The Beggar's Opera* in similarly nationalistic terms:

The public had grown sick of the fashionable Italian opera, sung by often
unattractive people in the language the groundlings could not understand.
Refreshingly, Gay's English was as clear as a stream, and although he
employed a German, Dr, Pepusch, to write bases [*sic*], the tunes were
familiar and beloved.[66]

More recent commentators, clearly embarrassed by this xenophobic
reading of Gay's intentions, have sought to rescue him from such
flag-waving fans by emphasizing instead Gay's own fascination with
opera, his collaborations with Handel, his intimate acqaintances
among Burlington's opera set, and the affectionate tone of his
operatic parodies. 'Intrinsically, there is nothing in *The Beggar's
Opera* which even approaches significant criticism of serious opera,'
writes Bertrand Bronson; '[it] may more properly be regarded as a
testimonial to the strength of the opera's appeal to John Gay's
imagination than as a deliberate attempt to ridicule it out of existence'.[67] Pat Rogers agrees, dismissing Warner's comments above as
'inept' and 'offensive', and preferring to regard *The Beggar's Opera*
as 'an insider-trading job' designed not to ridicule, still less to
scupper opera itself, but rather to mock the fads and crazes of opera
fans.[68] Peter Lewis offers this pertinent analogy:

Just as Jane Austen objected much less to the Gothic novel *per se* than to the
excessive seriousness with which it was taken by impressionable members of
the reading public, Gay condemns not Italian opera but the completely
uncritical theatregoers who had turned it into a fashionable cult.[69]

Yet, whatever Gay's intentions, the success of his mock-opera
undeniably posed a serious, indeed a lethal, threat to its Italian rival,

---

[65] *Hogarth Illustrated* (3 vols., London, 1791–8), ii. 575.

[66] Oliver Warner, *John Gay*, 'Writers and their Work' series (London, 1964), 27.

[67] Bertrand H. Bronson, '*The Beggar's Opera*', in J. Loftis (ed.), *Restoration Drama:
Modern Essays in Criticism* (New York, 1966), 314.

[68] Lewis and Wood, 148.

[69] Peter Lewis, *John Gay: The Beggar's Opera* (London, 1976), 23.

coinciding as it did with a general decline in support for the opera. The whirligig of fashion had moved on, and what had once been the last word in musical taste had now lost much of its modish appeal. By 1728 the Royal Academy was facing a severe financial crisis. The popularity of *The Beggar's Opera* undoubtedly hit attendances at the opera-house, bringing to a head problems which had been accumulating for some time. On 1 June the Academy's last operatic season came to an end; four days later the General Court of the Academy met in a final formal session,

to consider of proper measures for recovering the debts due to the Academy and discharging what is due to performers, tradesmen, and others; and also to determine how the scenes, clothes etc. are to be disposed of if the operas cannot be continued.[70]

From this point the Academy became merely the landlords, not the managers, of the Haymarket theatre, handing over responsibility for productions to Handel and Heidegger. At the same time Handel himself, sensing the shift in public taste, began to turn from Italian opera to the composition of English oratorios. Operas continued to be produced, but their high point was over. In April 1730 Mrs Pendarves wrote to her sister: 'Operas are dying, to my great mortification.'[71]

In a sense then it is true that *The Beggar's Opera* did kill off the vogue for Italian opera, though we cannot say with any confidence that this was Gay's intention in writing it. There is, however, ample proof that he derived a certain mischievous satisfaction from the effect he had created and did nothing to repudiate his popular reputation as the demolisher of Italian opera. In his letters to Swift he unashamedly crows over the way *The Beggar's Opera* has displaced its 'outlandish' rival as the talk of the town.

The outlandish (as they now call it) opera hath been so thin of late that some have called that the Beggars Opera and if the run continues I fear I shall have remonstrances drawn up against me by the Royal Academy of Music.[72]

This same letter concludes with the news that Arbuthnot's brother George was to marry Peggy Robinson, sister of the opera star,

[70] Notice in the *Daily Courant*, 31 May 1728; the same notice appeared in the *London Journal*, 1 June 1728; see Deutsch, 226.
[71] 4 Apr. 1730; *Autobiography of Mrs Delany*, i. 253.
[72] *Letters*, 71.

reminding us of Gay's close contacts within the world of opera. Yet his intimacy with members of the opera set does not in itself prove that he felt no resentment towards some of its performers and promoters. Familiarity can breed contempt and there is circumstantial evidence to suggest that Gay may have become increasingly disenchanted with the operatic obsessions of one promoter in particular, his former patron the Earl of Burlington. As chief shareholder and leading public figure-head of the Academy, Burlington had much to lose from the demise of an institution in which he had invested so much prestige. Gay's spoof mention of public 'remonstrances' to be drawn up against him may be a way of hinting at private remonstrances he was receiving from the Earl. A month later he resumed the same bantering tone, ironically reporting: 'there is a discourse about the town that the directors of the Royal Academy of Music design to solicit against [*The Beggar's Opera*] being played on the outlandish opera days, as it is now called.'[73] Since these directors included Burlington and Pulteney, men who had promised much but performed little in furthering Gay's career, one may reasonably deduce a certain malicious satisfaction at being the subject of solicitations from those upon whose favours he had for so long been dependent. It seems clear that the impact of *The Beggar's Opera* precipitated a serious rift between Gay and Burlington. From this point on there are no more letters between them.[74] Equally revealing is the fact that Gay never again mentions either the Earl or Countess of Burlington in his correspondence. When listing his friends and well-wishers he mentions Bathurst, Queensberry, Bolingbroke, and Pulteney but not Burlington. As a house-guest of aristocratic friends we find him staying with the Earl of Essex at Cassiobury Park or at Amesbury with the Queenberrys, but not at Chiswick or Burlington House. 'Direct to me at the Duke of Queensberry's in Burlington Gardens near Piccadilly,' he tells Swift, underlining the estrangement from his former patron and neighbour. In January 1732 he wrote to Swift while Pope went out 'to try to find Lord Burlington, within whose walls I have not been admitted this year and a half, but for what reason I know not'.[75] This is less than candid. Burlington was well known for his fickleness in freezing out former protégés:

---

[73] *Letters*, 72.

[74] This in itself is hardly a decisive point since only two letters survive from their years of intimacy.

[75] *Letters*, 119.

Guelfi was supplanted by Rysbrack and Gibbs dumped in favour of
Campbell. Gay should have anticipated the sudden coldness which
resulted from his impertinent ridicule of the Earl's darling project.

Pope, who remained on intimate terms with Burlington, sought to
maintain a diplomatic neutrality between these two disaffected parties. Writing to Burlington in early 1729, after the banning of *Polly*,
he sought advice from Fazakerly, the Earl's lawyer, to minimize the
dangers of *The Dunciad* suffering a similar fate.

Indeed I could be glad of the decisive opinion of Mr Fazakerly, it will
otherwise be impracticable to publish the thing before Mr G.'s and I am
grown more prudent than ever, the less I think others so.[76]

The implied criticism of Gay's *imprudence* is clear, as is Pope's very
deliberate attempt to distance himself in Burlington's eyes from his
friend's scandalous work. Equally significant is the apparent absence
of Burlington's name from the roll-call of subscribers to the published version of *Polly*. Unfortunately it is impossible to be absolutely
categorical about this point. *Polly* was not in a technical sense a
subscription edition, like *Poems on Several Occasions*, with its list of
subscribers printed prominently at the front. It was a private
publication, printed 'for the author' at Gay's own expense, but
underwritten by well-wishers who subscribed at least a guinea a
copy for this six-shilling work. Gay told Swift that the Duchess of
Marlborough, in a flamboyant gesture of defiance, 'hath given me a
hundred pound for one copy, and others have contributed very
handsomely but as my account is not yet settled I cannot tell you
particulars'.[77] Irving, however, writing as if the subscription list
were a verifiable document, pretends to supply these particulars.
'All the old names appear,' he declares: 'Mr and Mrs Pulteney,
Pope, Mrs Blount, Mr and Mrs Rollinson, Lord and Lady Bolingbroke, Lewis, Lord Bathurst, Sir William Wyndham, Lord Gower
... and Lord Oxford.'[78] In fact these are the names which appear
in Gay's letter to Swift as a roll-call of those who have 'showed me
the strongest proofs of friendship'.[79] It may be fair to infer that
what Gay means by 'the strongest proofs of friendship' is that these
were the principal subscribers to *Polly*. But even this does not

excuse Irving's casual remark that 'all the old names appear'. In fact, compared with the list of subscribers to *Poems on Several Occasions*, there are some conspicuous omissions. Gay's most notable benefactors in 1720 were the Earl of Burlington and the Duke of Chandos, but neither of these opera lovers is named as a supporter of *Polly*. Handel and Kent also subscribed to *Poems on Several Occasions*, but their names too are missing from the list of Gay's well-wishers in 1729.

Swift, who was always Gay's strongest supporter during the political controversies that surrounded *The Beggar's Opera* and *Polly*, felt no inhibitions about sounding a chauvinist note: *The Beggar's Opera*, he declared, had exposed

with great justice, that unnatural taste for Italian music among us which is wholly unsuitable to our Northern climate, and the genius of the people, whereby we are over-run with Italian effeminacy and Italian nonsense. An old gentleman said to me, that many years ago, when the practice of an unnatural vice grew frequent in London, and many were prosecuted for it, he was sure it would be a fore-runner of Italian operas and singers; and then we should want nothing but stabbing or poisoning to make us perfect Italians.[80]

In Swift's view there were 'few good judges in music; and that among those who crowd the operas, nine in ten go thither merely out of curiosity, fashion or affectation'.[81] In this outspoken public defence of *The Beggar's Opera* Swift may, in pursuit of his own polemical purposes, have gone further than Gay would have wished; but there is no evidence that Gay ever repudiated or reproved his friend's sentiments. Those who wish to acquit Gay of crowd-pleasing xenophobia need not only to overlook the crude anti-French sentiments of his *Epistle to William Pulteney* ('All Frenchmen are of *petit-maître* kind'), but his expressions of gratitude to Swift for championing his interests ('knowing you interest yourself in everything that concerns me so much').[82] Swift had already fallen out with Burlington over the costs of repairing a monument to one of the Earl's ancestors in St Patrick's Cathedral. He now seized on this second reason for linking Burlington with Mrs Howard, as false

---

[80] *Intelligencer*, 3 (25 May 1728); *Prose Works*, xii. 37.
[81] *Prose Works*, xii. 33.
[82] Gay to Swift, 6 July 1728, *Letters*, 76.

friends who had betrayed Gay with specious promises. 'I cannot be angry enough with my lord Burlington,' he told Gay, and, knowing Pope designed to address one of his four Moral Essays to Burlington, threatened to publish some angry 'moral letters' of his own to both Burlington and Howard.[83] Pope, diplomatic as ever, patiently dissuaded him from this design: 'As to your writing to Lord Burl. I would by no means have you, 'twill tend to no good, and only show anger, not amend.'[84] But it seems that in this simmering antagonism he was siding increasingly with Burlington, rather than with Swift and Gay. 'Mr Pope talks of you as a perfect stranger,' Swift wrote to Gay in early 1730.[85]

The likelihood is that Gay, having danced attendance at Burlington's cultural court for a dozen years, had grown increasingly weary of the sense that his own talents were undervalued in comparison with the huge salaries and fashionable status enjoyed by such pampered favourites as Cuzzoni, Faustina, and Senesino. Indeed, it is Gay's intimate familiarity with the milieux he satirizes which gives *The Beggar's Opera* its peculiarly seductive power. For fifteen years he had lived on courtiers' promises, and hence no word is used with greater frequency, or contempt, than *courtier*. For ten years he had lived in close proximity with the stars and promoters of the craze for Italian opera; hence the seductive detail of his operatic parodies. In *The Shepherd's Week* Gay had breathed ironic life into a native tradition of popular songs, rural dialects, and proverbs, as a way of ridiculing the affectations and artifice of court pastoral. In *The Beggar's Opera* his strategy is much the same, mingling operahouse arias and street ballads in a parody of cultural pretension.

Yet there is no sign of any hostility towards individual composers. His operatic parodies (with music arranged by Johann Christoph Pepusch) take the form of affectionate pastiche. Two well-known tunes were borrowed from Handel; the march from *Rinaldo* (air 20) and the song ''Twas when the seas were roaring' (air 28), which had already been used in *The What D' Ye Call It*.[86] But there is no

---

[83] Swift, *Corr.* iii. 361, 374–5.

[84] Pope, *Corr.* iii. 102.

[85] 19 Mar. 1730; Swift, *Corr.* iii. 380.

[86] Handel's composition of this air is not beyond question; see Fuller, i. 432–4. Further possible Handelian echoes occur with the parting of Macheath and Polly at the end of Act I, which parallels the similar conclusion of the first act of Handel's *Floridante*; in air xxxiv (Polly's 'Thus when the swallow, seeking prey'), which has affinities with the

evidence that these borrowings caused any serious rift with Handel, who returned to reworking *Acis and Galatea* in 1732. Gay's ridicule, as Bronson notes, 'does not go beyond poking affectionate fun at conventions'.[87] Nearly a third of the airs in *The Beggar's Opera* are taken from known composers, including Purcell, Handel, Bononcini, Sandoni, Akeroyde, and Leveridge, but the prevalence of such operatic motifs 'may more properly be regarded as a testimonial to the strength of the opera's appeal to John Gay's imagination than as a deliberate attempt to ridicule it out of existence'.[88] Gay does not seek to make polemical capital out of the rivalry between Handel and Bononcini; nor, apart from the Beggar's knowing aside in his introduction, does he exploit the more violent antagonism between Faustina and Cuzzoni. Indeed, one of the most overt parodies alludes not to an opera at all, but to one of the heroic tragedies which Gay had already ridiculed in *The What D'Ye Call It*. Macheath's exit to the scaffold to the sound of a tolling bell (III. xv) clearly echoes Pierre's similar departure in the final act of Otway's *Venice Preserved*, a parallel which would have been underlined by the fact that Walker, in the part of Macheath, had played Pierre a few weeks previously. In his introduction the Beggar offers a mock apology that 'I have not made my opera throughout unnatural, like those in vogue', an admission which offers the best key to Gay's satiric strategy. The hybridization of folk-songs with *opera seria*, domesticating high art in the cells of Newgate, creates the perfect musical setting for the opera's social satire, as described in the Beggar's final speech.

Through the whole piece you may observe such a similitude of manners in high and low life, that it is difficult to determine whether (in the fashionable vices) the fine gentlemen imitate the gentlemen of the road, or the gentlemen of the road the fine gentlemen.[89]

The title *The Beggar's Opera* is itself an oxymoron; beggars do not normally write or attend operas. In the mock-democratism of this satiric formula, Gay ironically seeks to locate the origins of

aria 'Lamentando mi corro a volo' in Handel's *Scipione*; and Macheath's patchwork medley of songs (III. xiii), which may be intended to parody the use of recitative in Italian opera.

[87] Bronson, '*The Beggar's Opera*', 314.
[88] Ibid.
[89] *The Beggar's Opera*, III. vxi.

opera's seductive appeal in the tragi-comic instincts and passions of ordinary men and women. His main musical sources are not operas, but the ballads of D'Urfey's *Wit and Mirth; or, Pills to Purge Melancholy* (1719–20), and he shows equal skill in reworking D'Urfeyesque lyrics as in rewording Handelian tunes. Mrs Peachum's song 'A maid is like the golden ore, | Which hath guineas intrinsical in't' (air v) would have had additional bite for those familiar with the original version, 'The Mousetrap', which describes a wife as a 'very bad bargain' and marriage as a painful snare.

> We're just like a mouse in a trap,
> Or vermin caught in a gin;
> We sweat and fret, and we try to escape,
> And curse the sad hour we came in.[90]

Similarly Macheath's use of the song 'Over the hills and far away' (air XVI) to promise fidelity to Polly (I. xiii) takes on an ironic dimension when compared with its original, 'Jockey's Lamentation', a complaint against female infidelity.[91] Gay was skilful and precise in the way he juxtaposed operatic and ballad motifs. His design was never merely polemical, but aimed at a far more beguiling exposure of the shared vanities, affectations, and vulnerabilities linking operatic divas and street singers, highwaymen and statesmen. By setting Handel's anthems alongside D'Urfey's ballads he did not seek to invalidate the former or elevate the latter, but rather to cast an ironic reflection on the way human life, at all levels, presents a set of parallel and symbiotic motifs.

Contemporary pundits and subsequent commentators have shown equal confidence in identifying Prime Minister Walpole as another principal target of Gay's satire in *The Beggar's Opera*. When Peachum, listing the members of his gang, mentions 'Robin of Bagshot, alias Gorgon, alias Bluff Bob, alias Carbuncle, alias Bob Booty' (I. iii) we are assured that 'this was immediately understood to refer to Walpole, whose opponents constantly claimed that he was enriching himself at his country's expense, and the name "Bob Booty" was to stick to him for the rest of his career'.[92] Cooke reports that 'the

[90] *The Merry Musician* (1716), i. 216; *Wit and Mirth* (1719).

[91] *Wit and Mirth*, v. 316–19; see also Gay's use of this song in *The What D' Ye Call It*, and Farquhar's version of it in *The Recruiting Officer*, above p. 186.

[92] *The Beggar's Opera*, ed. Bryan Loughrey and T. O. Treadwell (Harmondsworth, 1986), introduction, 26–7.

quarrelling scene between Peachum and Lockit, (II. x) was so well understood to allude to a recent quarrel between the two ministers, Lord Townshend and Sir Robert, that the house was in convulsions of applause'.[93] Even Macheath's prison lament when confronted by his rival 'wives', 'How happy could I be with either, | Were t'other dear charmer away' (air 35, II. xiii) was reputedly taken as an allusion to Walpole's *ménage à trois* with his wife and Maria Skerrett, his mistress.[94]

Swift, who persisted in believing that Walpole had personally intervened to sabotage Gay's hopes of court preferment, was keen to regard *The Beggar's Opera* as Gay's revenge. 'Does W[alpole] think you intended an affront to him in your opera?', he asked; 'Pray God he may, for he has held the longest hand at hazard that ever fell to any sharper's share.'[95] At the earliest opportunity Swift eagerly bought a sixpenny Dublin reprint of the opera but found it was 'so small printed that it will spoil my eyes'. In March it opened in Dublin, where it enjoyed another successful run, playing to full houses. Among its political admirers were Lord Carteret, Walpole's former rival for power and now Lord Lieutenant of Ireland. 'He hath seen it often', Swift confided to Pope, 'and approves it much.'[96] In London the production quickly became the toast of opposition politicians. The *Craftsman* kept up a constant commentary on its success from February to July.[97] In the issue for 17 February (no. 85) 'Phil. Harmonicus' undertook to prove 'beyond all dispute' that Gay's opera was 'the most venomous allegorical libel against the g[overnmen]t that hath appeared for many years past'. But even he could not decide whether Peachum, Lockit, or Macheath represented the main attack on Walpole. 'Some persons', he noted, 'esteem Lockit the keeper or *prime minister* of Newgate', particularly as he was 'set forth on the stage, in the person of Mr Hall, as a very corpulent, bulky man'. Moreover, Peachum and Lockit, like ministers of state, 'have a numerous gang ... under their direction ... whom they either *screen* or *tuck up* as their own interest and the

    [93] Macklin, *Memoirs*, 54.

    [94] See Lord Hervey, *Memoirs of the Reign of George the Second*, ed. J. W. Croker (1884), I. iii. 115 n.

    [95] Swift, *Corr.* iii. 267.

    [96] Ibid. iii. 269, 285.

    [97] There are references to *The Beggar's Opera* in seventeen of the twenty-four issues of the *Craftsman* published between 3 February (no. 83) and 13 July (no. 106).

present occasion requires'. On the whole, though, 'Phil. Harmonicus' rejected this interpretation, arguing that it was the 'Great Man' Macheath who chiefly represented 'somebody in authority', heading a gang of robbers pledged 'to stand by him against all the enquiries and coercive force of the law'. 'An opinion obtains', Swift remarked ironically in the *Intelligencer*, 'that in the *Beggar's Opera*, there appears to be some reflection upon courtiers and statesmen, whereof I am by no means a judge.'[98] As an astute politician Walpole did his best to draw the sting of such attacks by professing to enjoy the opera's satire. In March Swift wrote:

We hear a million of stories about the opera, of the encore at the song, 'That was levelled at me' [air 30], when 2 great ministers were in a box together, and all the world staring at them.[99]

Cooke perpetuated these stories, claiming that one of the two great ministers was Walpole, who, in a brilliant tactical gesture, encored the song himself, a ploy which 'brought the audience into so much good humour with him, that they gave him a general huzza from all parts of the house'.[100] Sadly, there is no reliable evidence to confirm this anecdote, though it has the ring of authenticity as an example of 'Bluff Bob's' own skills in political theatre. In the *Intelligencer* Swift remarked that 'even ministers of state' appeared at the theatre, 'to convince the world how unjust a parallel malice, envy and disaffection to the government have made'.[101]

Despite such face-saving manœuvres, it is clear that Walpole did regard *The Beggar's Opera* as a dangerous political attack, and did his utmost to prevent a repeat performance by banning its sequel *Polly*. Yet most modern commentators profess themselves at a loss to identify in Gay's opera the personalized attack on Walpole which was apparently so clear to his contemporaries. Neither the highwayman Macheath nor the gang leader Peachum is consistently presented as a symbol of prime ministerial corruption; and the most unambiguous Walpolean allusion to 'Robin of Bagshot, alias Gorgon, alias Bluff Bob, alias Carbuncle, alias Bob Booty' refers to a character who only has one line. As Peter Lewis rightly observes: 'No single character in *The Beggar's Opera* corresponds to Sir Robert

[98] *Intelligencer*, 3 (25 May 1728); *Prose Works*, xii. 34.
[99] Swift, *Corr.* iii. 276.
[100] Macklin, *Memoirs*, 54.
[101] *Intelligencer*, 3 (25 May 1728); *Prose Works*, xii. 35.

Walpole.'[102] The ministerial quarrel between Walpole and Towns-hend, allegedly parodied in the quarrel between Peachum and Lockit, actually took place in 1729, *after* the appearance of *The Beggar's Opera*;[103] even Swift, despite his avowed determination to regard Gay's opera as a snub to Walpole, detected no parallels, either literary or political, in that particular scene.[104]

In fact, Gay was careful not to narrow his attack to a simple *ad hominem* lampoon. His satire is directed not at individuals, but at a wider political culture, though he was powerless to prevent audiences and reviewers from interpreting it in strictly partisan terms. The notoriety which such interpretations conferred was not unwelcome, and Gay did little to repudiate the reputation he thus acquired as a hero of the opposition. But, disentangling the opera itself from the choruses of partisan praise which greeted and promoted its initial success, it is possible to discover a more ambiguous, original, and inventive work, which has retained its popularity in the theatrical repertoire precisely because it is not limited by topical allusions and contemporary feuds.

Still one of the best-known and most influential essays on *The Beggar's Opera* is that by Empson in *Some Versions of Pastoral*. For him, the work celebrates an ironic collaboration between aristocrat and swain at the expense of the bourgeois. Peachum and Lockit, he argues, are the villains of the piece, not the cavalier Macheath. 'Gay meant Peachum to be the villain . . . Gay dislikes him as a successful member of the shopkeeping middle class, whereas Macheath is either from a high class or a low one.'[105] What is surprising though is how much the language and idioms of this despised shopkeeping class, from which Gay himself was descended, permeate the opera and colour the motives of all its characters. Indeed, to judge by the vocabulary of the work it might more appropriately be called *The Business Man's Opera*. The word 'business' occurs fifteen times in

[102] *The Beggar's Opera*, ed. Peter Elfred Lewis (Edinburgh, 1973), 15.

[103] See Schultz (p. 371), who refers to William Coxe's *Memoirs of Walpole* (1768, i. 332 ff.). This point is also discussed by Charles E. Pearce, *'Polly Peachum': Being the Story of Lavinia Fenton [Duchess of Bolton] and 'The Beggar's Opera'* (London, 1913), 90 and by Jean B. Kern in 'A Note on *The Beggar's Opera*', *Philological Quarterly*, 17 (1938), 411–13.

[104] Swift, *Corr.* iii. 276. See the correspondence on this subject between J. A. Downie, David Hunt, and Yvonne Noble in *TLS* 21 Oct. and 11 Nov. 1983, pp. 1151, 1247.

[105] William Empson, 'Mock-Pastoral as the Cult of Independence', in *Some Versions of Pastoral* (London, 1935), 203.

the opera; 'money' occurs nineteen times, along with its variants and synonyms, fees, guineas, price, garnish, and so on. 'Account' is used nine times, and other financial words, 'interest', 'profit', 'debt', and 'credit', run all through it. But it is not simply the frequency of such terms which is remarkable; as Pat Rogers observes, 'the method of the entire *Opera* is to make language spill the beans—betray the hidden attitude and the real drives'.[106] Rogers notes a typical process whereby 'persons often become the objects of commercial verbs', citing, as an example, the agreement of Peachum and Lockit 'to go halves in Macheath'. This tendency to treat people and relationships in commodity terms permeates the whole work. 'Money, wife,' declares Peachum, 'is the true Fuller's earth for reputations, there is not a spot or stain but what it can take out' (I. ix); 'A man who loves money might as well be contented with one guinea as I with one woman,' asserts Macheath. Yet such satiric *bons mots* are only the tip of an iceberg of commercializing nouns and verbs which freeze-dries all relationships into market opportunities. Characters are invariably valued in trading terms, that is, according to how much may be 'got' by them. In the opening scenes Peachum promises to save Betty Sly from transportation only because 'I can get more by her staying in England'; he confesses that he hates 'a lazy rogue, by whom one can get nothing'. Even his resentment against Macheath is somewhat lessened by recalling 'how much we have already got by him' (I. xi). The effect of this satiric commodification is well illustrated by Gay's use of the word 'account'. Repeated throughout the opera, it refers primarily to the trading accounts of the gang which we see Peachum consulting in the very first scene; and, even when used in an ostensibly abstract sense, the word never loses its commercial currency. In scene iv Mrs Peachum regrets Macheath's lack of discretion 'upon Polly's account', a phrase which so puzzles her husband that he repeats it: 'upon Polly's account! What a plague does the woman mean? Upon Polly's account!' (I. iv). The ostensible reason for his bafflement is his ignorance of Polly's attachment to Macheath; yet the force of his remonstrance is provoked by his wife's abstract use of the term 'account'. Since Polly's name is not set down in his account-book, he has some initial difficulty in accounting for a sense of loss which has no direct cash

[106] Pat Rogers, 'Merchants and Ministers', in *Eighteenth Century Encounters* (Brighton, 1985), 100–2.

equivalent. Towards the end of the opera Polly herself uses the term, disingenuously professing to Lucy that 'I suffer too upon your account'. Here again, though the word has prima facie an abstract meaning, we can detect an ironic inflexion, as though Polly's suffering could be quantified and set down as a credit in her account with Lucy. The full effect of this commercialization of the sensibility is seen in the dialogue of Lucy and Macheath. 'You see, Lucy,' declares Macheath, 'in the account of love you are in my debt' (II. xv); to which she replies, 'Come then, my dear husband – owe thy life to me.' These characters have no other vocabulary for their emotions than that of the balance-sheet.

The word 'credit' operates in just the same way. In Act I Peachum describes Harry Padington as a 'poor petty-larceny rascal' who 'will never come to the gallows with any credit' (I. iii). Later, Macheath tells Lucy that Polly 'would fain the credit of being thought my widow' (II. xiii). The opposite of credit for a tradesman is bankruptcy or ruin, and the word 'ruin' is often used to reinforce the opera's ironic market-place morality. ''Tis your duty, my dear, to warn the girl against her ruin,' remarks Peachum to his wife (I. iv) when he hears the rumour that Polly may have married Macheath. A few scenes later he asks Polly directly, 'Tell me, hussy, are you ruined or not?' (I. viii). Of course there is a more obvious joke here, as Peachum cynically reverses the word's customary use as a euphemism for loss of virginity. 'Ruin' would normally signify a female non-virgin's damaged status as second-hand goods in the marriage-market; but for Peachum marriage itself is ruin, since it places an embargo on free sexual trade. Unless, of course, it is contracted in a spirit of speculative investment.

PEACHUM. And had not you the common views of a gentlewoman in your marriage, Polly?
POLLY. I don't know what you mean, sir.
PEACHUM. Of a jointure, and of being a widow. (I. x)

Gay takes a word already shop-soiled into euphemism and gives it a new ironic gloss by reassessing its market value. When Macheath complains that his confinement is made worse by 'the reproaches of a wench who lays her ruin to my door' (II. viii), or when he tells Lucy that Polly claims to be married to him 'only to vex thee, and to ruin me in thy good opinion', we constantly feel that the stock-market index, rather than the Ten Commandments, offers the truer guide to the nature of the ruin involved. 'Redeem' is another word which combines moral, religious, and commercial connotations. Mrs Trapes hopes that Mrs Coaxer, 'for her own sake and mine . . . will persuade the captain to redeem her'. The meaning here suggests far less the saving of a soul than the reclaiming of a pledge from a pawn-shop.[107] For Lucy, virtue is not a moral abstraction but a trading asset: 'Am I then bilk'd of my virtue?' she protests. For Macheath, death, like love, is only conceivable in commercial terms. 'For death is a debt. A debt on demand. So take what I owe,' he sings in the final act; though, as we know, his debt is cancelled and his pledge redeemed.

Only one word, 'honour', is used with any frequency in opposition to these commodifying terms; but the ostensible antithesis between bourgeois trade and aristocratic honour is in fact more apparent than real. Superficially one might expect 'honour' to distinguish the cavalier Macheath from the shopkeeper Peachum; and it is true that Macheath does use the word frequently. But so do many of the other characters, including devious subtraders like Lockit, Filch, Jenny, and Matt of the Mint. It quickly emerges that honour is less a moral absolute than a protectionist code. Macheath declares his confidence in his gang: 'as men of honour, and as such I value and respect you' (II. ii). Lockit is also very much on his dignity as a man of honour. 'This is the first time my honour was ever called in question,' he protests to Peachum in a key scene (II. x), and later promises that 'we will deal like men of honour,' (III. vi). Macheath talks much of his honour in a central scene with Lucy (II. ix): 'From a man of honour, his word is as good as his bond,' he loftily declares, where the proverbial phrase gains ironic force from the pervasive context of insider-dealing. A few lines later he repeats: 'I am ready, my dear Lucy, to give you satisfaction—if you think there is any in marriage—what can a man of honour say more?' Yet in his preceding soliloquy he has already explained just what this honourable declaration amounts to: 'I promised the wench marriage—what signifies a promise to a woman? Does not a man in marriage itself promise a hundred things that he never means to perform?' (II. viii).

[107] Some critics have detected Christ-like echoes in Macheath, who is betrayed by a kiss. See Maynard Mack's essay 'The Augustans' (1950), part of which is reprinted in Yvonne Noble (ed.), *Twentieth Century Interpretations of 'The Beggar's Opera'* (Englewood Cliffs, NJ, 1975), 43. Barabbas, though, might make a better parallel since he, like Macheath, was saved.

In the same way, when Peachum and Lockit proclaim their honour, they do so with a clear view of its market value. 'He that attacks my honour', Lockit insists, 'attacks my livelihood.' Honour is a concept of strictly limited liability; like a back-street trader's guarantee, it is not the antithesis to self-interest but a euphemism for it. No character, not even Polly, is immune from this corrupt and devalued meaning of the word. When she protests in Act I that she did not marry Macheath '(as 'tis the fashion) coolly and deliberately for honour and money' the conjunction of the two terms 'honour' and 'money' suggests that she too recognizes 'honour' as the protectionist jargon of the united company of wives.

Gay's choice of mercantile metaphors was no doubt partly inspired by the speculative rash of shady joint-stock companies associated with the South Sea Bubble; the word 'bubbled'—meaning cheated or deceived—occurs twice in the opera. But his chief model for Peachum was Jonathan Wild, the man who turned crime into a respectable business. Almost certainly some details of Peachum's business methods were taken from Defoe's *True and Genuine Account of . . . Jonathan Wild* (1725), and Gay may have borrowed further hints from Defoe's *Complete English Tradesman*, published the same year.[108] Defoe constantly urged the importance of strict accounting: 'Upon his regular keeping, and fully acquainting himself with his books, depends at least the comfort of his trade, if not the very trade itself.' In this, as in much else, Peachum shows himself as a graduate of the Defoe school of business. The influence of Mandeville's *Fable of the Bees* is also evident in the opera. Bearing the motto 'Private Vices, Public Benefits', Mandeville's poem provoked howls of moralistic indignation with its cynical analysis of the social benefits of vice. Dennis's reaction was typical: 'Vice and luxury have found a champion and a defender which they never did before,' he declared.[109] Mandeville's thesis was simple: vice is the essential dynamo of a thriving, capitalist society. Throughout society he, like

[108] Charles Lamb was so disgusted by Defoe's 'studied analysis of every little mean art, every sneaking address, every trick and subterfuge (short of larceny) that is necessary to the tradesman's occupation', that he enquired ironically whether the *Complete English Tradesman* was actually intended as satire. See his letter of 1822 included in Pat Rogers (ed.), *Defoe: The Critical Heritage* (London, 1972), 86.

[109] First published in 1705, Mandeville's poem had, in the course of two decades, been publicly denounced (twice) by the Grand Jury of Middlesex and attacked by a host of moralists and clergymen, including William Law, Francis Hutcheson, Archibald Campbell, Isaac Watts, and John Dennis.

Peachum, detected one invariable rule:

> All trades and places knew some cheat
> No calling was without deceit;
> Thus every part was full of vice,
> Yet the whole mass a paradise.[110]

In his explanatory remarks added to this last couplet, Mandeville offered this illustrative example:

A highwayman, having met with a considerable booty, gives a poor common harlot he fancies, ten pounds to new rig her from top to toe; is there a spruce mercer so conscientious that he will refuse to sell her a thread satin, tho' he knew who she was? She must have shoes and stockings, gloves, the stay and manto-maker, the sempstress, the linen-draper, all must get something by her and a hundred different tradesmen dependent on those she laid her money out with, may touch part of it before a month is at an end.[111]

According to this argument, Macheath the privateer is transformed into Macheath the public benefactor. Mandeville's real target was the kind of pious idealism which professed to combine Christian morality and Roman virtue with a life of luxury and wealth. Or, as he explains in the 'Moral' to his poem:

> Bare virtue can't make nations live
> In splendour; they, that would revive
> A Golden Age, must be as free
> For acorns as for honesty.

For a man like Gay, who had made 'honesty' into his own trading-card, Mandeville's thesis, with its exposure of high-minded political cant, had an irresistible appeal.

However, Gay's most intimate understanding of the world of trade and commerce came not from books but from his own experience. For years he had operated a form of mental apartheid; banishing, as far as possible, all memory of the crude commercial values of Barnstaple and Willet's shop in favour of the urbane idioms and classical aspirations of Burlington House and the court. Yet increasingly he was aware not of the differences of surface style

---

[110] Compare this with the sentiments expressed in Peachum's first song, 'Through all the employments of life'.

[111] Bernard de Mandeville, *The Fable of the Bees*, ed. F. B. Kaye (2 vols., Oxford, 1924), i. 88.

that separated these two worlds, but of the essential affinities between them. Writers were merchants of words; politicians traded in bankrupt policies; courtiers speculated in false promises, while ministers rigged the market. In *The Beggar's Opera* Gay acknowledges that the commercial world he had left behind was no different in kind from the courtly world he had striven so long to enter. Not yet prepared to argue that trade was the only true basis of honour, he was at least convinced that honour was nothing but a trade. Viewed in the context of such pervasive commercial values, the opera's final irony, its happy ending, fits neatly into Gay's satiric strategy. 'All this we must do', says the Player, referring to Macheath's reprieve, 'to comply with the taste of the town.' This is the perfect businessman's conclusion, giving the public what they want and sending them home with a song on their lips. And the joke is that it worked, brilliantly, far beyond Gay's expectations. The opera was a triumphant business success and, in the phrase of the time, 'made Gay rich and Rich gay'.

Inevitably, the phenomenal success of *The Beggar's Opera* attracted not only imitators and admirers, but considerable envy and hostility. Ostensibly at least, the principal attacks on it were not designed to defend Italian opera, or Robert Walpole's ministry. Opera lovers were on the defensive, and Walpole chose the covert power of censorship, rather than the open forum of debate, to retaliate against this latest literary ambush. Instead, Gay's antagonists disguised their political objections in moralistic tones, accusing him of glamorizing vice in his affectionate depiction of highwaymen and whores. Official displeasure was registered in March when Dr Thomas Herring, the King's chaplain and later Archbishop of Canterbury, delivered a sanctimonious sermon in Lincoln's Inn Chapel denouncing Gay as the criminals' friend. Gay was unabashed. 'I have had the honour to have had a sermon preached against my works by a court chaplain,' he gleefully reported to Swift, 'which I look upon as no small addition to my fame.'[112] More of the same quickly followed. In the preface to a posthumous edition of Herring's sermons William Duncomb solemnly opined that the late Archbishop was 'not singular' in his denunciation of Gay's work:

---

[112] *Letters*, 75. Swift took the same line. *The Beggar's Opera*, he wrote, 'will probably do more good than a thousand sermons of so stupid, so injudicious and so prostitute a divine'. *Intelligencer*, 3 (25 May 1728); *Prose Works*, xii. 36.

and experience afterwards confirmed the truth of his observations, since several thieves and street-robbers confessed in Newgate that they raised their courage at the playhouse by the songs of their hero Macheath, before they sallied forth on their desperate nocturnal exploits.[113]

This theme was taken up by several other pro-government journalists. Writing under the name 'Philopropos', Duncombe himself protested in the *London Journal* at Gay's light-hearted portrayal of 'a gang of highwaymen and pick-pockets, triumphing in their successful villainies'.[114] John Dennis eagerly denounced this 'low and licentious piece, designed for the encouragement of gentlemen on the highway, and their female associates in Drury-Lane'.[115] Another pamphleteer declared ominously that 'Thieving and the highway are edged-tools to play with, and they ought by no means to be set in a gay or ridiculous light to the mob.'[116] Perhaps the most unlikely voice in this moralistic chorus was that of Daniel Defoe, who complained that *The Beggar's Opera* had presented thieves in 'so amiable a light . . . that it has taught them to value themselves on their profession, rather than be ashamed of it'. Defoe traced a direct link between the popularity of *The Beggar's Opera* and the recent increase in street crime: 'Every idle fellow, weary of honest labour, need but fancy himself a Macheath or a Sheppard, and there's a rogue made at once.'[117] This is pretty rich from the author of *Moll Flanders*.

In response to such outbursts Swift devoted one whole issue of his newly launched Dublin weekly, the *Intelligencer*, to a defence of Gay's work. *The Beggar's Opera*, he argued, had

placed vices of all kinds in the strongest and most odious light; and thereby done eminent service both to religion and morality . . . It discovers the whole system of that common-wealth, or that *imperium in imperio* of iniquity, established among us, by which neither our lives nor our properties are secure, either in the highways, or in public assemblies, or even in our own houses. It shows the miserable lives and the constant fate of those abandoned wretches: for how little they sell their lives and souls; betrayed by their whores, their comrades, and the receivers and purchasers of those

[113] *Seven Sermons on Public Occasions* (1763).

[114] *London Journal*, 30 May 1728.

[115] *Remarks upon Several Passages in the Preliminaries to the Dunciad* (1729), 48.

[116] *A View of the Town; or, Memoirs of London* (2nd edn., 1731), 48.

[117] *Augusta Triumphans* (1728), 48; *Second Thoughts are Best* (1729), 2–4; in fact Defoe had done more than anyone else to turn Jack Sheppard into a folk hero with his animated accounts of Sheppard's daring escapes in *Applebee's Journal*.

thefts and robberies. This comedy contains likewise a satire, which, without enquiring whether it affects the present age, may possibly be useful in times to come. I mean, where the author takes the occasion of comparing those common robbers of the public, and their several stratagems of betraying, undermining and hanging each other, to the several arts of politicians in times of corruption.[118]

In this partisan account it is clear that Swift's own instinct, and hence his reading of Gay's satiric intention, is to view Newgate as a Gulliverian metaphor. Hazlitt's comment was more succinct: 'The moral of the piece was to show the *vulgarity* of vice.'[119]

[118] *Intelligencer*, 3 (25 May 1728); *Prose Works*, xii. 35–6.
[119] 'On the Beggar's Opera', in *Works*, ed. P. P. Howe (London, 1930–4), iv. 65–6.

FOURTEEN

The Terror of Ministers

The inoffensive John Gay is now become . . . the terror of ministers . . .

(Arbuthnot to Swift, Mar. 1729)

The Beggar's Opera's success not only brought Gay fame and fortune; it also helped to redefine relations with several of his oldest friends. With Swift it brought a new sense of intimacy. Stella's death, on the night before the opening of *The Beggar's Opera*, left Swift more desolate than ever. Pope offered solemn elegiac phrases of condolence but Swift found greater consolation in the artless enthusiasm of Gay's confidences. 'I would not have talked so much upon this subject, or upon anything that regards myself but to you,' Gay wrote in March; 'but as I know you interest yourself sincerely in everything that concerns me, I believe you would have blamed me if I had said less.'[1] Eagerly anticipating Swift's next visit to London, he promised to make him as comfortable as possible in his Whitehall lodgings.

I have bought two pair of sheets against your coming to town, so that we need not send anymore to Jervas upon that account. I really miss you every day, and I would be content that you should have one whole window to yourself, & half another to have you again.[2]

For his part, Swift was unstinting in his delight at Gay's triumph. 'Get me . . . Polly's mezzo-tinto,' he demanded. 'Lord, how the schoolboys at Westminster, and university lads adore you at this juncture. Have you made as many men laugh as ministers can make

---

[1] 20 Mar. 1728; *Letters*, 73.
[2] Ibid 73.

weep?' He sent enthusiastic reports of the opera's reception in Dublin.

We have your opera for 6d and we are as full of it *pro modulo nostro* as London can be—continual acting, and house crammed, and the Lord Lieutenant several times there, laughing his heart out.[3]

He offered hints for sharpening the satire, as well as sober financial advice.

Ever preserve some spice of the alderman and prepare against age and dulness and sickness and coldness or death of friends. A whore has resources left that she can turn bawd; but an old decayed poet is a creature abandoned and at mercy when he can find none.[4]

Pope's reactions were more guarded. There is a tinge of jealousy in the arch way he ironically compares the new self-importance of the 'courtier' Gay with the upstart dignity of a royal boatman.

The only courtiers I know, or have the honour to call my friends, are John Gay and Mr Bowry; the former is at present so employed in the elevated airs of his own opera, and the latter in the exaltation of his high dignity (that of her majesty's waterman) that I can scarce obtain a categorical answer from either to anything I say to 'em.[5]

In March Gay told Swift 'I have not seen Mr Pope lately, but have heard that both he & Mrs Pope are very well.'[6] Even in Dublin, Swift could detect the signs of a growing estrangement between the two men. 'Mr Pope talks of you as a perfect stranger,' he told Gay in early 1730.[7] Burlington was another former friend who was evidently displeased by Gay's operatic parodies, but his place was quickly supplied by the Duke and Duchess of Queensberry, who henceforward became Gay's staunchest supporters. Arbuthnot, Pulteney, and Lewis were all sincerely delighted at Gay's triumph and greatly amused by his new status as a political heavyweight, and Lord Bathurst was among those anxious to cultivate closer ties with this new star in the literary firmament.

In March Gay spent some time with Pulteney at the the Earl of

---

[3] Swift, *Corr.* iii. 276.
[4] Ibid. 276–7.
[5] Pope, *Corr.* ii. 473.
[6] Letters, 73. Mrs Pope is Pope's mother.
[7] Swift, *Corr.* iii. 380.

Essex's estate, Cassiobury Park, and visited Bathurst and Boling-broke. He remained on intimate terms with Mrs Howard, who was in a mood to share his sense of liberation. 'She is happier than I have ever seen her,' Gay told Swift, 'for she is free as to her conjugal affairs by articles of agreement.'[8] Together the two of them drank Swift's health in Goodridge cider. Gay entered without hesitation into the Countess's new feelings of emancipation, having been a party to the protracted and acrimonious negotiations which preceded it. Just a few weeks before the opening of *The Beggar's Opera* he and Dr Arbuthnot were present to overhear a heated argument between her and one of her husband's emissaries:

He talked of settling the interest of four thousand pounds on her son; this she absolutely refused by saying she had starved with Mr H, and would not put herself in a circumstance to starve without him. She said she wondered at Mr H's persisting in such unreasonable proposals when he had made the matter so public, as to have advised with lawyers belonging to all the courts, and that in case of a lawsuit she had reason and justice to make demands upon him.[9]

Less happy news came from Wiltshire, where the Duchess of Queensberry suffered a sudden bout of smallpox. Since she had recently 'signalized her friendship to me . . . in such a conspicuous manner', Gay was understandably anxious about her condition. However, he was soon pleased to confirm it was only a mild, or in his term 'favourable', attack; 'she had not above seven or eight in her face; she is now perfectly recovered.'[10] 'I am glad your goddess-duchess hath preserved her face,' Swift wrote back, promising Gay '20 dozen of Goodrich cider . . . if you will just cross the water hither from the Bath I will give you a bottle of it every day.'[11] Gay arrived in Bath the first week of May and was soon writing to assure Swift that he was not, as Swift had feared, losing all his newly gained wealth at the gaming-tables. 'I have played at no game but once, and that at back-gammon with Mr Lewis.'[12] Lewis was at

---

[8] *Letters*, 70–2.

[9] BL Add. MSS 22626, fo. 33. Quoted in *Letters*, 133–4. Burgess omits to print the final section of this memorandum, which appears on a separate sheet of the manuscript (fo. 34). It is included in the Appendix below.

[10] *Letters*, 70–2.

[11] Swift, *Corr.* iii. 277.

[12] 16 May 1728; *Letters*, 74.

Bath on account of his wife's ill health and Gay found himself well-supplied with other convalescing companions, including the Boling-brokes and Congreve, who was 'in a very ill state of health, but somewhat better since he came here'. Instead of gambling, Gay spent time supervising a touring company production of *The Beggar's Opera*. In July *Brice's Weekly Journal* reported:

We hear from Bath that Mr Gay, author of the celebrated *Beggar's Opera* has been there these two months drinking the waters for his health, during which time he has taken more than ordinary pains with the comedians of that city, in instructing them in the performance of his said opera, which has so good an effect that they have not only gained a great deal of money by it, but universal applause, insomuch that they played it all last season at Bath and still continue playing it in Bristol at their great booth in Bridewell lane near the corner of St James's Churchyard; and have been sent for by the quality to perform it at their houses, and to the Long Room near the Hot-Well several times.[13]

Writing to Swift, Gay was more reticent about his own involvement in this production. 'The *Beggar's Opera* is acted here', he reported, 'but our Polly here hath got no fame, but the actors have got money'. Meanwhile the 'real' Polly Peachum was the talk of the gossip columns, having run away with her lover, the Duke of Bolton. As requested, Gay sent Swift the recent mezzotints of Polly and Macheath. A few weeks later his own mezzotint portrait, engraved by Francis Kyte after a painting by William Aikman commissioned by Mrs Howard, was published. 'I wish I could contrive to send you one', he told Swift, 'but I fancy I could get a better impression at London.'[14]

Despite his new wealth and fame, Gay still allowed himself to suffer the constraints of a dependent position. 'I don't know how long I shall stay here', he told Swift, 'because I am now, as I have been all my life at the disposal of others.' To Pope he wrote: 'You see I am not free from dependence, tho' I have less attendance than I had formerly.'[15] There is no objective reason why he should have felt himself thus circumscribed in his movements. Pope estimated Gay's current wealth at between £1,000 and £2,000, more than enough to have secured for himself a comfortable independence.[16]

[13] *Brice's Weekly Journal*, 28 July 1728.
[14] *Letters*, 76.
[15] Ibid. 74, 77.
[16] Pope, *Corr.* iii. 480.

Yet he chose instead to place himself in the Duchess of Marlborough's retinue, allowing his movements to be governed not by his own wishes, but by hers. Even now, triumphantly successful and at the height of his fame, Gay still affected the style and tone of a dependant. And, despite Swift's advice, he continued to pin his hopes of advancement on Mrs Howard's dwindling influence, 'for a great deal of my own welfare still depends upon hers'.[17] Gay's consistent representation of himself as a man in the power of others goes some way to explain his friends' exasperated (and ill-founded) belief that he could not be trusted to look after his own affairs. 'Providence never designed him to be above two-and-twenty by his thoughtlessness and cullibility [*sic*],' Swift asserted.[18] But in fact such comments underestimate Gay's resources of self-reliance. His instinct for dependency was part of a psychological survival strategy which allowed Gay not only to preserve his wealth intact, but also to safeguard a private mental territory which found expression in his satires. Gay had internalized the beggars' technique of exploiting the society which he affected to flatter. Where Pope favoured a satiric pose of lofty independence, Gay adopted the more subversive role of a court favourite, biting the hand that fed him.

Gay remained at Bath for most of the summer, spending much of his time with Congreve and keeping up a gossipy correspondence with Mrs Howard. Despite assiduously imbibing the waters, Congreve's health continued to deteriorate and he died the following winter. The Bath regimen proved equally useless to Lady Bolingbroke: 'She went from hence much worse than she came,' said Gay, though in her case a self-prescribed milk diet had 'prodigious good effects' in restoring her appetite and spirits.[19] By midsummer most of Gay's friends had left the city. 'The weather is extremely hot,' he told Swift, 'the place is very empty; I have an inclination to study but the heat makes it impossible.'[20] Instead he made an excursion to Lady Scudamore's place, Holme Lacy on the Wye, where he stayed for much of July. Lady Scudamore was the aunt of Pope's friend Robert Digby, and the rumour was quickly circulating among Pope's acquaintances that Gay still hankered after a court place. Mrs Howard did little to disabuse him of the illusion that she might

[17] *Letters*, 77.
[18] 16 July 1728; Swift, *Corr.* iii. 294.
[19] *Letters*, 75–6.
[20] Ibid. 76.

still have power to advance his claims. On his return to Bath in
August she wrote assuring him, 'I have not had one place to dispose
of, or you should not be without one.'[21] Having recently suffered
illness, she was consulting Arbuthnot about the advisability of
making a trip to Bath herself to take the waters. Meanwhile her tone
makes clear that what she chiefly regretted in Gay's absence was the
lack of a faithful assistant to undertake domestic chores which her
indisposition made irksome to her. 'I have had two letters from
Chesterfield which I have wanted you to answer for me; and I have
had a thousand other things that I have wanted you to do for me.'
Her mock-imperious tone suggests that manipulative style which
Swift so disliked. 'If I should come to the Bath', she declared, 'I
propose being governess to the doctor and you. I know you both to
be so unruly, that nothing less than Lady P[embroke]'s spirit or
mine could keep any authority over you.'[22] In reality, Howard's
influence at court was rapidly declining. In October she wrote to the
King complaining, 'as I am very sensible that I am under your
displeasure, so am I entirely ignorant in what manner I have
incurred it'.[23] Representations by her on behalf of the man whose
Beggar's Opera had infuriated Walpole stood little chance of success.

Throughout August Gay was hopeful that Pope, Arbuthnot, Mrs
Howard, and possibly even Swift himself might join him at Bath.
Arbuthnot was among the season's invalids, suffering a violent fever
at Tunbridge Wells. Meanwhile Pope was in 'a state of persecution'
following the publication in May of the first version of the *Dunciad*.
Strangely, Gay had left London just a few days before the appearance
of his friend's long-planned satiric broadside. He told Swift that he
wished 'to be witness of his [i.e. Pope's] fortitude, but he writes but
seldom'.[24] Swift, who had read a Dublin edition of Pope's poem,
hastened to praise him for it, but encouraged him to make his satire
more explicit: 'I would have the names of those scribblers printed
indexically at the beginning and end of the poem, with an account of
their works for the reader to refer to.'[25] He need not have worried.
Within a fortnight, Curll had rushed out a *Compleat Key to the*

---

[21] *Letters of Henrietta, Countess of Suffolk*, ed. J. W. Croker (2 vols., London, 1824),
312–14.
[22] Ibid.
[23] BL Add. MSS 22627, fo. 4.
[24] *Letters*, 76.
[25] Swift, *Corr.* iii. 293.

Dunciad, offering his own malicious identifications of Pope's victims. Gay wrote to sympathize.

All I could hear of you of late hath been by advertisements in newspapers, by which one would think the race of Curlls was multiplied; and by the indignation such fellows show against you, that you have more merit than anybody alive could have.[26]

Pope eventually arrived at Bath in the first week of September, ill, bad-tempered, and depressed. He told Martha Blount: 'I feel my being forced to this Bath journey as a misfortune', and confessed, 'I set out with a heavy heart.'[27] Despite the hospitality he received *en route* from Lord Cobham at Stowe, Colonel Dormer at Rousham, John Howe at Stowell in Gloucestershire, and Sir William Codrington at Dodington, his journey turned into something of a medical mock-epic. At Dodington he was overwhelmed with patent remedies, as the ladies of the house took turns in acting as his nurse.

My lady Cox, the first night I lay there, mixed my electuary, lady Codrington pounded sulphur, Mrs Bridget Bethel ordered broth. Lady Cox marched first up-stairs with the physic in a gallipot; lady Codrington next, with the vial of oil; Mrs Bridget third, with pills; the fourth sister, with spoons and tea-cups.[28]

Even Pope could see the funny side of this remedial pantomime. 'It would have rejoiced the ghost of Dr Woodward to have beheld this procession,' he told Martha Blount. After such a pharmaceutical cocktail the Bath waters held little dread for Pope. 'By this means I have an opportunity of astonishing Dr Arbuthnot, to see me begin the waters without any physic, and to set him and Mr Gay in an uproar about me and my wilfulness.'[29] Pope remained in Bath for several weeks until the end of October, but in his letters to Lord Oxford, Bathurst, Fortescue, and Swift we find no further mention of Gay. Mrs Lewis, he notes, 'is the youngest and gayest lady here' but otherwise Bath society strikes him as 'full of grave and sad men'.[30]

For some time Gay had been acting with Bathurst as Swift's

---

[26] *Letters*, 77.
[27] Pope, *Corr*. ii. 511.
[28] Ibid. 513–14.
[29] Ibid. 514.
[30] Ibid. 518, 521.

unofficial banker in London, receiving payments on his behalf for
Gulliver's Travels and the *Miscellanies*. The fact that Swift entrusted
him with such a task somewhat belies his protestations at Gay's alleged
fecklessness with money, and Gay was careful to account to him for all
his dealings. Motte, the publisher of the *Miscellanies*, was notoriously
dilatory in making payments, provoking Pope to write to him in angry
terms on his return to London, demanding his share of the money. As
far as Swift's money was concerned, he added this peremptory aside:
'It will be necessary to give Mr Gay a note for the remainder due,
and what patience he pleases he may have, but . . . I will take it upon
myself no further.'[31] The note of asperity here only confirms the
estrangement between himself and Gay. Swift was happy to regard
Pope's *Dunciad* as a companion piece to his own *Gulliver's Travels* and
Gay's *Beggar's Opera*, three consummate satiric expressions of their
joint Scriblerian inheritance: 'You talk of this *Dunciad*, but I am
impatient to have it *volare per ora*—there is now a vacancy for fame:
the *Beggar's Opera* hath done its task.'[32] But Pope, accustomed to
regarding Gay not as his satiric peer but as his protégé and pupil,
could not help seeing *The Beggar's Opera* less as a companion-piece
than as a rival to his own work. Instinctively he felt a certain
resentment at the presumption of an *élève* who had risen to become
a contender for the vacant role of pre-eminent satirist of the age.

Like Pope, Gay was back in London by the start of November, and
soon found that his extended stay at Bath had brought no lasting
improvement to his health. About the middle of the month he suffered
a severe attack of fever which confined him to his room for ten days
under Arbuthnot's care. On 2 December he wrote to Swift assuring
him that his money was 'still in the hands of Lord Bathurst, which I
believe he will keep no longer, but repay upon his coming to town;
when I will endeavour to dispose of it as I do of my own unless I
receive your orders to the contrary'. Despite the warmth of the
summer in Bath, Gay had not entirely neglected his studies there,
and was now ready with *Polly*, the 'second part of the *Beggar's
Opera*'. Within a day or two, he told Swift, he hoped 'to get abroad
about my business', making arrangements with Rich for the performance of this new opera which was 'almost ready for rehearsal'.[33]

[31] Pope, *Corr.* ii. 526.
[32] Swift, *Corr.* iii. 286; *Georgics*, iii. 9.
[33] *Letters*, 78.

Suddenly all these plans were placed in jeopardy. Rich received an ominous message from the Duke of Grafton, the Lord Chamberlain, forbidding him 'to rehearse any new play whatever 'till his grace hath seen it'. The government had received 'information he was rehearsing a play improper to be represented' and Grafton was determined to save Walpole's ministry from any further ridicule on the London stage. Already London was seething with rumours about the political daring of Gay's planned sequel to *The Beggar's Opera*. The *Craftsman* printed a sample of this incriminating gossip.

They spread a report through every part of the town that the sequel to the *Beggar's Opera* was a most insolent and seditious libel; that the character of Macheath was drawn for one of the greatest and most virtuous men in the kingdom [i.e. Walpole]; that this was too plain in the former part; but that in the second, he is transported; turns pirate; becomes Treasurer in a certain island abroad; proves corrupt; and is sacrificed to the resentment of an injured people.[34]

From the start Gay protested his innocence of any subversive political intentions. Now back in regular contact with Mrs Howard, he still hoped, however improbably, to gain court favour and was anxious to play down all hints of seditious sympathies. In his letter to Swift he set out the lines of what was to become a familiar defence.

I am sure I have written nothing that can be legally suppressed, unless the setting vices in general in an odious light, and virtue in an amiable one, may give offence.[35]

Fearing that his letters were being intercepted, Gay may well have intended such professions of political innocence for ministerial eyes. In the preface to *Polly* he repeated similar protestations, while offering his own detailed account of the traumatic events of that first fortnight of December.

After Mr Rich and I were agreed upon terms and conditions for bringing this piece on the stage, and that everything was ready for a rehearsal, the Lord Chamberlain sent an order from the country to prohibit Mr Rich to

[34] Letter from 'Hilarius', *Craftsman*, 135 (1 Feb. 1729).
[35] *Letters*, 78.

suffer any play to be rehearsed upon his stage till it had been first of all supervised by his grace. As soon as Mr Rich came from his grace's secretary (who had sent for him to receive the before-mentioned order) he came to my lodgings and acquainted me with the orders he had received.

Upon the Lord Chamberlain's coming to town, I was confined by sickness, but in four or five days I went abroad on purpose to wait upon his grace with a faithful and genuine copy of this piece ... 'Twas on Saturday morning, December 7th, 1728 that I waited upon the Lord Chamberlain; I desired to have the honour of reading the opera to his grace, but he ordered me to leave it with him, which I did upon expectation of having it returned on the Monday following, but I had it not till Thursday December 12, when I received it from his grace with this answer; that it was not allowed to be acted, but commanded to be suppressed. This was told me in general without any reason assigned, or any charge against me of my having given any particular offence.[36]

In his scrupulous attention to circumstantial detail, (not omitting his own illness) Gay's public narrative of events has the air of a defendant's statement from the dock. As such it is capable of two interpretations. On the one hand this exact recall of names, dates, and places may convey a sense of Gay's complete integrity, as an innocent party with nothing to hide; on the other, this concentration on circumstantial detail may suggest the pseudo-authenticity of an alibi, designed to divert attention from the central charge of political subversion. Portraying himself as a blameless victim, forced to leave his sick-bed to wait on an officious government functionary, Gay makes an unashamed appeal for sympathy. But sickness in itself is no guarantee of innocence, and Gay's portrait of himself as a political martyr is a rhetorical device designed to discredit, rather than answer, the charges against him.

Throughout the preface he maintains the same defensive strategy. Anxious to pre-empt the suspicion that this published version of *Polly* may be a cleaned-up job, purged of the seditious content of the intended stage-version, he offers an exhaustive list of every tiny scribal alteration and emendation to the original copy, read by Grafton. Scrupulously noting where *are* has been changed to *is*, or *compliance* to *complaisance*, he implicitly mocks the code-breaking skills of Walpole's magi.

---

[36] At the end of Nov. it was reported that 'two eminent actors of the said house [i.e. the theatre in Lincoln's Inn Fields] have lately attended his Majesty with a second part of the *Beggar's Opera* in order for his Majesty's approbation'. *Applebee's Original Weekly Journal*, 30 Nov. 1728.

The banning of *Polly* was Walpole's revenge for the success of *The Beggar's Opera*. According to Hervey, Walpole

resolved rather than suffer himself to be produced for thirty nights together upon the stage in the person of a highwayman, to make use of his friend the Duke of Grafton's authority as Lord Chamberlain to put a stop to the representation of it. Accordingly this theatrical *Craftsman* was prohibited at every playhouse.[37]

That last phrase is significant, indicating not only that Walpole suspected Gay's close association with the *Craftsman* group, but that Hervey too shared these suspicions. Throughout the winter the *Craftsman* kept its readers informed of the new opera's progress; on 30 November it reported that it was 'lately carried to court for approbation'; and on 14 December it protested that the opera had been 'suppressed by authority, without any particular reason being alleged'. The fact that this phrase foreshadowed Gay's own assertion that the opera was 'commanded to be suppressed . . . without any reasons assigned' strongly suggests some degree of complicity between them. On 28 December the *Craftsman* printed a ballad attack on Walpole which played with parallels between the prime minister and Macheath.

> If Macheath you should name, in the midst of his gang, fa la,
> They'll say 'tis an hint you would somebody hang; fa la.
> For Macheath is a word of such evil report, fa la,
> Application cries out, 'That's a Bob for the c[our]t, fa la.[38]

There is also some evidence that Pulteney encouraged Gay to write this sequel:

the Duchess told me, that on Gay's being accused of immorality in the end of ye *Beggar's Opera*, some nobleman (I really think Lord Bath but I am not certain) said 'Why Gay you have only *transported* him; pursue him & bring him to punishment—' & see, says she, 'I was punished because Macheath was to be hanged; & Gay's morality vindicated—I told the Lord Chamberlain *I thanked him*—it saved me trouble & courtesies.[39]

---

[37] *Memoirs*, ed. R. Sedgwick (2nd edn., London, 1952), 52.

[38] 'An excellent new ballad, called, A Bob for the C——t'; *Craftsman*, 130 (28 Dec. 1728).

[39] L. W. Conolly, 'Anna Margaretta Larpent, the Duchess of Queensberry and Gay's *Polly* in 1777', *Philological Quarterly*, 51 (1972), 955–7.

But in fact, as published, *Polly* is far less politically *risqué* than *The Beggar's Opera*; its tone, despite some deft social satire, is reassuring rather than provocative, and it requires the single-mindedness of a cryptographer of Laputa, or ministerial magus, to detect in it more than the most glancing of allusions to government ministers.[40] In the opening scene, the complacent philistinism of the colonialist Ducat may perhaps be taken as a veiled caricature of Walpole.

DUCAT. . . . I have a fine library of books that I never read; I have a fine stable of horses that I never ride; I build, I buy plate, jewels, pictures, or anything that is valuable and curious, as your great men do, merely out of ostentation.[41]

Likewise, Mrs Trapes has a song (air v) whose political message is clear: 'In pimps and politicians | The genius is the same . . .' (I. iv. 12–13). But such direct satiric gibes are the exception, rather than the rule. For the most part *Polly* is a relatively innocuous work presenting a sentimental contrast between Old World corruption and New World innocence. Instead of the institutionalized cynicism of Peachum and Lockit, we have a new-found Arcadia of noble savages, full of charming prospects and simple morality. Although retaining his 'Great Man' pretensions, Macheath, disguised as the black slave leader Morano, is less a mock Alexander than an Antony *manqué*, an identification confirmed by the frequent echoes of Dryden's *All for Love*. In choosing to ban such a relatively harmless entertainment Walpole showed a lack of his usual political finesse, and managed to turn a minor theatrical embarrassment into a full-blown political scandal. His nervousness though was understandable. Gay's work had taken on a symbolic importance, and the danger to the government lay less in the specific content of the opera itself, than in the interpretations that might be placed upon it by opposition forces seeking a focus for their anti-ministerial campaign.

[40] Bertrand Goldgar finds several veiled allusions to Walpole in *Polly*; see Bertrand A. Goldgar, *Walpole and the Wits* (Lincoln, Nebr., 1976), 81–3. Calhoun Winton even argues that 'A knowing reader, say Walpole himself, would have found *Polly* considerably more aggressive politically than *The Beggar's Opera*'; see Winton, 136. Yet they provide little textual authority for such assertions, which discount the vast difference in tone between *Polly* and *The Beggar's Opera*.

[41] *Polly*, I. i. 54–7. Goldgar argues that Gay 'can hardly have been ignorant of the similarity between this self-portrait and the ridicule by the opposition press of Walpole's display of rich vulgarity at Houghton'. Goldgar, *Walpole and the Wits*, 82.

In a sense Gay was a victim of his own success. Like any playwright, intoxicated by the sudden celebrity of his first great theatrical triumph, he had become the centre of a media circus, and, thrilled by his instant fame, had done nothing to discourage political interpretations of *The Beggar's Opera* which went far beyond his own more cautious intentions. Indeed, he had allowed himself to take a mischievous delight in such interpretations, the more outrageous and provocative the better. Now though, when forced to pay the price for this political notoriety, he made a bid to disown this dangerous reputation, by invoking a previous literary identity, that of the inoffensive hare. There is a pained sense of injured innocence in his protestations that he himself had never been guilty of the seditious sentiments attributed to him.

Since this prohibition I have been told that I am accused, in general terms, of having written many disaffected libels and seditious pamphlets. As it hath ever been my utmost ambition (if that word may be used upon this occasion) to lead a quiet and inoffensive life, I thought my innocence in this particular would never have required a justification; and as this kind of writing is what I have ever detested and never practised, I am persuaded so groundless a calumny can never be believed but by those who do not know me. But when general aspersions of this sort have been cast upon me, I think myself called upon to declare my principles; and I do with the strictest truth affirm that I am as loyal a subject and as firmly attached to the present happy establishment as any of those who have the greatest places or pensions.[42]

Clearly Gay protests too much. Although in the 'strictest truth' there is no evidence he himself ever wrote seditious *pamphlets*, the idea that he 'detested' the work of those, like Swift and Bolingbroke, who did is simply false. What is at stake here, more than a play, is a question of Gay's own identity; throughout his career he had instinctively led a double life, sheltering his satiric wit under a guise of inoffensive submission. What kindles his best satires into life is the constant friction between the courtier's outward cringe of deference and an inner spark of imaginative rebellion. But in simultaneously running with the hare and hunting with the hounds Gay had been playing a dangerous game. Some of his friends were surprised he had not paid the penalty for such an ambiguous strategy sooner. In March 1715 Pope wrote with comic bravado: 'Yet is there not a

[42] Preface, *Polly* (1729).

proclamation issued forth for the burning of Homer and the Pope by the common hangman; nor is the *What D' Ye Call It* yet silenced by the Lord Chamberlain.'[43]

The glare of publicity surrounding *The Beggar's Opera* threw all Gay's careful self-protective strategies into a new harsh light. This time he was forced to choose, irrevocably, between courtly compliance and imaginative independence. What is fascinating about the preface to *Polly* is the way it seeks, even now, to evade such a psychologically intimidating choice. It protests innocence and loyalty in abject terms of mock-servility that barely disguise a rhetorical sneer of defiance, as when he ironically declares himself 'as firmly attached to the present happy establishment as any of those who have the greatest places or pensions'.

Justifying his decision to print the banned play, Gay presents himself determined to clear his name of all 'false accusations'. In so doing, he solemnly affirms,

I have submitted and given up all present views of profit which might accrue from the stage, which undoubtedly will be some satisfaction to the worthy gentlemen who have treated me with so much candour and humanity, and represented me in such favourable colours.

Here too his protestations of financial hardship are rhetorically self-serving. As might have been predicted, by banning the play Walpole merely increased its subversive appeal. Over 10,000 copies of the opera were printed, more than ten times the usual number. In deciding to undertake such a huge print-run, at his own expense, while the scandal surrounding the opera was still hot news, Gay showed considerably more financial acumen than Swift, who cautioned against such a risky strategy. In early March Swift wrote to Pope: 'I hope he does not intend to print his opera before it is acted; for I defy all your subscriptions to amount to £800. And yet, I believe, he lost as much more for want of human prudence.'[44] In fact, subscriptions to *Polly* earned Gay £1,200, far more than his receipts from *The Beggar's Opera*'s record-breaking run. In financial, as in other, matters Gay was prepared to play the part of the gullible *naif*, while actually demonstrating a business sense far sharper than Swift's. Even after a spate of pirate copies forced him to lower the

---

[43] Pope, *Corr.* i. 287.
[44] Swift, *Corr.* iii. 313.

price of his own edition from six shillings to two shillings, he still made a handsome profit. Cibber later reported the general belief that Gay 'had been a greater gainer, by subscriptions to his copy, than he could have been by a bare theatrical presentation'.[45] Ironically, by banning *Polly*, Walpole not only turned an innocuous drama into a political crisis, but also completely misread Gay's preoccupations. All the evidence suggests that Gay's chief motives were financial rather than political, hoping to cash in on *The Beggar's Opera*'s success with a money-spinning sequel. As he reported to Swift: 'I passed five or six months this year at the Bath with the Duchess of Marlborough, and then, *in view of taking care of myself*, writ this piece'.[46] By 'taking care' of himself Gay clearly signalled his hope of achieving another financial success. But he also implies a desire to mollify critics of *The Beggar's Opera* with a reassuring sequel which might go some way to rehabilitate his reputation at court.

It seems probable that Gay had some sort of sequel in mind even while writing *The Beggar's Opera*. In Act III Macheath, awaiting execution, offers this advice to his rival wives:

My dear Lucy—my dear Polly—whatsoever has passed between us is now at an end. If you are fond of marrying again, the best advice I can give you, is to ship yourselves off for the West Indies, where you'll have a fair chance of getting a husband a-piece; or by good luck, two or three, as you like best. (III. xv. 1–6)

Polly does indeed take us to the West Indies, where the transported Macheath, disguised as the black pirate Morano, now lives with Jenny Diver. When she arrives to search for him Polly is sold, unknowingly, to Ducat by Mrs Trapes as a potential mistress. Escaping, disguised as a boy, she falls in with the pirates. Jenny promptly attempts to seduce her while Macheath alias Morano, plans an assault on the colonial settlement. The colonists, in alliance with the natives, defeat his attack and Macheath is hauled off for execution. Polly is left to marry her idealistic rescuer, the Indian Prince Cawwawkee.

There is much that is both subtle and satisfying in this opera and

---

[45] Colley Cibber, *An Apology for the Life of Colley Cibber*, ed. B. R. S Fone (Ann Arbor, Mich. 1968), 136.
[46] *Letters*, 78; my italics.

Gay again displays his skill in refitting traditional ballads with new ironic lines. The pirates sing a vainglorious version of the popular ballad 'There was a jovial beggar' in which they boast, quite falsely, of their fearlessness: 'The brave, with hope possessed, | Forgetting wounds and death, | Feel conquest in their breast.' This contrasts nicely with the original ballad, which is quite precise about wounds: 'There was a jovial beggar, | He had a wooden leg . . .'[47] Similarly, when Macheath sings 'I'll act like a man of honour' (II. iv. 62) his words are given a hollow ring by the ironic echo of D'Urfey's original use of the same song, in Gay's old favourite, *Wonders in the Sun*.[48] Gay's operatic allusions are equally well chosen. As commander of the colonial forces, Ducat combines pomposity with pusillanimity. 'Sir', he tells the Indian chief, 'fighting is not our business; we pay others for fighting' (III. i. 15–16). Such cowardice is made ridiculous when sung to the heroic tune of the march from Handel's *Scipio*.[49]

Apart from Dryden's *All for Love*, the main literary influence on *Polly* was Southerne's *Oroonoko* (1695), which Gay had already echoed in *The Captives*. Like Southerne's slave prince, Gay's noble savage Cawwawkee is constantly shocked by the European habits of lying, treachery, and deceit. Even as the pirates' captive, his moral stature towers above them. 'You are ashamed of your hearts, you can lie. How can you bear to look into yourselves?' he demands. 'Who that had ever felt the satisfaction of virtue would ever part with it?'[50] With its fondness for such sentimental rhetoric, *Polly* undoubtedly sacrifices much of the subversive bite of *The Beggar's Opera*. The success of that work derived from its novelty and suprise, its joyful and daring clashes of mood, and its teasing refusal to conform to expectations. The pleasures of *Polly*, however, depend

---

[47] The jovial beggar of the ballad is one of Wild's protégés: '. . . seven years I begged | For my old master Wild . . .', and for him a wooden leg is the perfect accessory, ensuring a life of sheer contentment: 'Of all occupations, | A beggar lives the best.'

[48] 'Since all the world's turned upside down' in *Wonders in the Sun*, Act I; see also *Wit and Mirth* (1719), i. 213.

[49] In Handel's opera, first produced in London in Mar. 1726, this march introduces a spectacular heroic scene with the Roman army, followed by slaves and captives, marching through a triumphal arch. Gay's other musical borrowings include the Dead March from Attilio Ariosti's *Coriolanus* (premiered in 1723) and some extracts from minuets in Handel's as yet unpublished *Water Music*, which confirm Gay's intimacy with Handel's work. See Roger Fiske, *English Theatre Music in the Eighteenth Century* (2nd edn., Oxford, 1986), 111.

[50] *Polly*, II. xi. 9–10, 23–4.

precisely upon a certain predictability, and upon the conventional way in which our fantasies of innocence are indulged. The difference is perhaps best indicated by the fact that not only is Morano/ Macheath finally executed, rather than reprieved; but that he is not even allowed a last rousing ironic air. He is ingloriously dispatched out of sight as an unwelcome inconvenience in the culminating celebration of simple domestic virtues—honesty, fidelity, love. Instead of subversion we have affirmation; instead of a satiric exposure of vice, Gay offers a sentimental vision of virtue. In the final song (air 71) the Indian chorus celebrates such moral absolutes as justice, virtue, and truth with no hint of the ways in which such high-sounding terms can be traduced into political euphemisms. Perhaps this is Gay's final irony in this work, paying apparent lip-service to a moral vocabulary and an Arcadian vision which he had consistently shown to be the acceptable face of social exploitation. In the final scene of *The Beggar's Opera* he offered an ironic compliance with 'the taste of the town' by rescuing the rogue Macheath. In doing so he did indeed achieve a huge popular success, but one for which he paid a high political price, denounced from the pulpit and shunned by the court. In *Polly* he complied with another form of popular taste, indulging his audience with sentimental pieties and Arcadian dreams, and hoping that they would not realize he was laughing at them.

One final point is worth mentioning. In creating the 'breeches-role' of Polly herself, Gay was exploiting a familiar theatrical convention. Yet there is an unusual sensuality in the way he uses this androgynous character. First there is the scene where she and Jenny kiss (II. vi), with its hint of lesbian intimacy; but more revealing is the way the 'boy' Polly provokes a genuine sense of sexual confusion in the emotions of his/her idealistic friend Cawwawkee. As these two 'men' embrace in the moment of victory, there is a strong erotic charge in their comradely duet (air 58):

POLLY.   Victory is ours.
CAWWAWKEE.   My fond heart is at rest.
POLLY.   Friendship thus receives its guest.
CAWWAWKEE.   O what transport fills my breast!
POLLY.   Conquest is complete,
CAWWAWKEE.   Now the triumph's great.
POLLY.   In your life is a nation bless'd.

CAWWAWKEE.   In your life I'm of all possess'd.   (III. X. 3–10)

The original words of this song ('Clasp'd in my dear Melinda's arms') make the sexual nature of Cawwawkee's 'transport' quite explicit:

> In the softest moments of love,
> Melting, panting, oh how she moves . . .
> Pray don't trifle, my dearest, forbear,
> I shall die with transports, I fear . . .[51]

Clearly what we have here is a passionate love duet; yet ostensibly what we witness on stage is a passionate embrace between a 'black' man and a white 'man'. Not content with restricting his ballad-opera burlesque to political pantomime or musical parody, Gay here, as in his final play *Achilles*, seems intent on disturbing our sense of gender distinctions.

Walpole's unexpected act of pre-emptive retaliation had a traumatic effect on Gay. Suddenly he was ejected from his Whitehall lodgings and simultaneously suffered the severest attack of illness he had yet experienced. A combination of fever, pleurisy, and asthma racked his body, and he was hurried away by Arbuthnot to a house at Hampstead where 'it was thought I could not live a day'. He told Swift,

> I was several times given up by the physicians and everybody that attended me; and upon my recovery was judged to be in so ill a condition that I should be miserable for the remainder of my life.[52]

Rumours of his death quickly began to circulate, but on 11 January the *Craftsman* announced that 'John Gay Esq, . . . who was reported to be dead, is on the mending hand'. Pope confirmed that Gay was 'in a fair way of recovery, tho' he has been just in the jaws of death; but . . . he was grown so lean that Death thought him not worth swallowing'.[53] By the end of January Gay was well enough to take the air with Lord Oxford's nephew and John Wootton, the painter who had designed most of the plates for his *Fables*. In March he

---

[51] *Wit and Mirth* (1719), vi. 316. 'Die' is the familiar sexual pun for orgasm.
[52] *Letters*, 79.
[53] Letter to Bathurst, Pope, *Corr.* ii. 531.

ered, and have no remainders of the distempers that attacked me'.[54]

Clearly the banning of *Polly* played a large part in provoking this sudden life-threatening illness. Gay's friends all offered comfort and support, especially Pope, who sent almost daily letters of condolence. When Gay was triumphant, Pope had been distant; now that Gay was once again a helpless victim, Pope hastened to overwhelm him with prayers, sympathy, and advice. Pope's mother too was dangerously ill and there is a morbid relish in the way Pope describes himself ministering simultaneously to his dying mother and sick friend.

Dear Gay, No words can tell you the great concern I feel for you; I assure you it was not, and is not lessened, by the immediate apprehension I have now every day lain under of losing my mother. Be assured, no duty less than that should have kept me one day from attending your condition: I would have come and taken a room by you at Hampstead, to be with you daily, were she not still in danger of death. I have constantly had particular accounts of you from the doctor, which have not ceased to alarm me yet. God preserve your life and restore your health. I really beg it for your own sake, for I feel I love you more than I thought, in health, tho' I always loved you a great deal.[55]

Whether Pope's presence hovering officiously by Gay's bedside would have had a salutary effect is debatable. His letters, while urging health and cheerfulness, have a necrophiliac excitement, mingling last rites and obituary sentences. 'Dear Gay, be as cheerful as your sufferings will permit,' he counsels solemnly; 'God is a better friend than a court: Even any honest man is better.' Pious admonitions like these are interspersed with bulletins on his poor mother's diarrhoea and a fantasy scheme for a journey by himself, Gay, and Swift to the sunny climes of southern France which has the other-worldly air of a reunion in paradise.[56] The death of Congreve on 19 January only added to Pope's morbid obsessions, and he sent Gay some funereal verses hardly calculated to raise his friend's spirits. 'Mr Pope tells me that I am dead,' Gay remarked sardonically to Swift.[57]

Gay received more vital encouragement from the regular visits of

[54] Pope, *Corr.* iii. 11; *Letters*, 79.
[55] Pope, *Corr.* iii. 1.
[56] Ibid. 1–3.
[57] Ibid.; *Letters*, 80.

Arbuthnot and Mrs Howard, but most of all from the Duke and Duchess of Queensberry, 'who, if I had been their nearest relation and nearest friend could not have treated me with more constant attendance'. However, the chief contribution the Queensberrys made to Gay's recovery was not in attending at his bedside, but by raising a storm of protest on his behalf at court. It was the Duchess who, despite Swift's advice to the contrary, urged Gay to publish the banned opera, having already (according to legend) supplied occasional rhymes for its songs.[58] Now, in a calculated gesture of defiance, she solicited subscriptions for *Polly* at court, in the presence of the King himself. According to Lord Hervey:

Her solicitations were so universal and so pressing that she came even into the Queen's apartment, went round the drawing-room, and made even the King's servants contribute to the printing of a thing which the King had forbid being recited.[59]

For this act of *lèse-majesté* she was banished from the court by an official letter on 27 February, and the Duke, already alienated from the ministry, followed her into political exile. In the words of a contemporary pamphlet, the Duchess made 'her tender Lord her quarrel join, | And the fair honours of his post resign'.[60] As her farewell gesture of defiance the Duchess sent the King a cheeky note in which she thanked him for giving her 'so agreeable a command as to stay away from court, where she never came for diversion but to bestow a great civility upon the King and Queen'. She added a postscript explaining she had given the Vice-Chamberlain 'this answer in writing to read to his majesty', clearly implying that the 'honest blockhead' German George had trouble with reading English.[61] The banishment of the Queensberrys gave an extra newsworthy twist to the *Polly* scandal. 'You must undoubtedly have heard', Gay wrote to Swift,

that the duchess took up my defence with the king and queen in the cause

[58] For the Duchess's contributions, see Conolly, 'Anna Margaretta Larpent, the Duchess of Queensberry and Gay's *Polly* in 1777', 955–7.

[59] Hervey, *Some Materials towards Memoirs of the Reign of George II*, ed. Romney Sedgwick (London, 1931), 98; see also Mrs Delany's account in *The Autobiography and Correspondence of Mary Granville, Mrs Delany* (London, 1861), i. 193.

[60] *The Female Faction or the Gay Subscribers.*

[61] This letter is quoted in C. F. Burgess, 'John Gay and *Polly* and a Letter to the King', *Philogical Quarterly*, 47 (1968), 596–8. Burgess argues plausibly that Gay may have helped in the composition of the letter.

of my play, and that she hath been forbid the court for interesting herself to increase my fortune for the publication of it without being acted. The duke too hath given up his employment which he would have done, if the duchess had not met this treatment, upon account of ill usage from the ministers; but this hastened him in what he had determined.[62]

Throughout February and March *Polly* enjoyed the status of a *cause célèbre* and the subscription list quickly became a symbolic rallying-point for Walpole's political opponents. Following the Duchess of Marlborough's example, Bathurst, Bolingbroke, Pulteney, Sir William Wyndham, and Lord Oxford all 'contributed very handsomely'. Even Mrs Howard 'declared herself strongly both to the king and queen as my advocate'.[63] Such steadfast demonstrations of support had an immediate effect on Gay's health. In mid-February, Lord Oxford described him as looking well and 'very busy' as he supervised *Polly's* publication. A month later Gay was able to report: 'The play is now almost printed with the music, words and basses engraved on 31 copper plates which, by my friends' assistance hath a probability to turn greatly to my advantage.'[64]

After several weeks spent languishing on his sick-bed, Gay found an invigorating relief in plunging himself into a hectic burst of purposeful activity. He told Swift: 'I am impatient to finish my work, for I want the country air; not that I am ill, but to recover my strength, and I cannot leave my work till it is finished.' By now he had moved from Hampstead and was lodging at the Queensberrys' house in Burlington Gardens, an elegant town mansion which had now taken on the busy air of a campaign headquarters. 'While I am writing this', he told Swift, 'I am in the room next to our dining-room with sheets all round it, and two people from the binder folding sheets.' And, contrary to his protestations of financial self-sacrifice in the preface to *Polly*, he was anxious to convince Swift at least that the decision to rush *Polly* into print was a shrewd economic move.

I print the book at my own expense in quarto, which is to be sold for six shillings with the music. You see I don't want industry, and I hope you will allow that I have not the worst economy ... my fortune (as I hope my virtue will) increases by oppression.[65]

---

[62] *Letters*, 79.   [63] Ibid. 80.
[64] Ibid. 79.   [65] Ibid. 80.

Swift was unpersuaded, and continued to regard Gay as a financial ignoramus and 'bad manager'. In fact, the opposite was true. On 12 March Fenton wrote to Broome:

Honest Gay is printing his contraband play by subscription, by which he will make an ample equivalent for its not being acted, if some few of the quality will follow the junior Duchess of Marlborough's example, who has subscribed £100.[66]

By the summer Gay's receipts from *Polly* had swelled his total wealth to some £3,000, but, as usual, Swift still suspected he would fritter the money away on trivial luxuries. He wrote to Pope: 'I hope Mr Gay will keep his £3,000 and live on the interest without decreasing the principal one penny.' Pope replied: 'Mr Gay assures me his £3,000 is kept entire and sacred.'[67]

Ironically, it was Swift himself who, while never ceasing to lecture his friends on the importance of thrift, proved the most incompetent in money matters. While haranguing Gay on the necessity for prudence, he had been prevailed on to lend £1,000 in a speculative venture which now seemed poised on the brink of disaster. 'Every farthing of any temporal fortune I have is upon the balance to be lost', he lamented. 'I am in danger of losing every groat I have in the world by having put my whole fortune, no less than £1,600 upon ill hands upon the advice of a lawyer and a friend.'[68] In the circumstances it may have been fortunate for Swift that the more prudent Gay was his London banker, though his grudging comments on Gay's handling of his funds indicates no such acknowledgment.

Polly was published on 25 March, less than a fortnight after the appearance of Pope's revised and annotated *Dunciad Variorum*; but the two satires enjoyed very different receptions. Pope's poem was presented by Walpole himself to the King and Queen, who had already expressed approval of the earlier draft.[69] By contrast, Gay's play provoked a minor court revolution, best described in Arbuthnot's facetious account.

[66] Pope, *Corr*. iii. 24–5.
[67] Swift, *Corr*. iii. 342; Pope, *Corr*. iii. 58.
[68] Swift, *Corr*. iii. 374.
[69] See Pope, *Corr*. iii. 26 and Richard Savage, *Collection of Pieces ... Published on Occasion of the Dunciad* (1732), p. vi.

The inoffensive John Gay is now become one of the obstructions to the peace of Europe, the terror of ministers, the chief author of the *Craftsman* and all the seditious pamphlets which have been published against the government. He has got several turned out of their places, the greatest ornament of the court banished from it for his sake [The Duchess of Queensberry], another great lady in danger of being chassé likewise [Mrs Howard], about seven or eight duchesses pushing forward like the ancient Circum Celliones in the church who shall suffer martyrdom upon his account first. He is the darling of the city; if he should travel about the country he would have hecatombs of roasted oxen sacrificed to him. Since he became so conspicuous, Will Pulteney hangs his head to see himself so much outdone in the career of glory. I hope he will get a good deal of money by printing his play, but I really believe he would get more by showing his person. And I can assure you this is the very identical John Gay whom you formerly knew and lodged with in Whitehall two years ago.[70]

It was also Arbuthnot who drew attention to the very different reputations currently enjoyed by Gay and Pope. Far from appearing as 'the terror of ministers' Pope, whose ostensibly daring poem had actually been carefully vetted by the lawyer Fazakerly to eliminate any overt hints of political disaffection, was now something of a court favourite.

Mr Pope is as high in favour as I am afraid the rest are out of it. The king, upon perusal of the last edition of his *Dunciad*, declared he was a very honest man.[71]

Evidently Pope's careful policy of distancing himself from Gay's 'imprudent' satire had paid off. And, while duchesses and court ladies vied with each other to suffer political martyrdom on Gay's behalf, Pope's female admirers merely competed in preparing his pills and potions. There is a degree of ironic exaggeration in Arbuthnot's mock-heroic presentation of Gay as the new demigod of opposition propaganda, but one element in his account is particularly significant. His description of Gay as 'the darling of the city' is echoed in Gay's own report of his supporters:

Most of the courtiers, though otherways my friends, refuse to contribute to

---

[70] Swift, *Corr.* iii. 326. The Circum Celliones were 'A fourth-century sect of African Donatists who rambled from town to town' (ibid. 326 n.).

[71] Ibid. 326.

my undertaking, but the city, and the people of England take my part very warmly, and I am told the best of the citizens will give me proofs of it by their contributions.[72]

Without the subscription list for *Polly*, it is impossible to establish the identities of these 'best of citizens' who supported Gay. Almost certainly they would have included John Barber, Swift's former printer, a man who cheerfully described himself as 'a creature of [Swift's] own making'[73] and who rose through the ranks of city aldermen to be elected sheriff, and finally Lord Mayor of London in 1732. In May 1730 Gay was Barber's guest at a feast of city aldermen, where he enjoyed 'a very fine dinner and a very fine appearance of company'.[74] Clearly Gay, who had once mocked the honours of a 'civic crown', had found a new political constituency for his satires in the City, among the traditional opponents of court power and privilege. Subsequent accounts of the political fall-out from *Polly* have too often presented it as essentially a court affair, a squabble between duchesses and earls. But the impact of the scandal had far wider repercussions, which helped to bring about a change in Gay's own sense of identity and social allegiance. For most of his adult life he had sought to distance himself from the Low Church mercantile values of the City, in favour of an existence on the fringes of the court. The world of city trade recalled all too vividly the poverty of his own Barnstaple background and his early ignominious position as a draper's apprentice, memories which he sought to exorcize in the opulence of Burlington House or Marble Hill. Yet the prevalence of commercial metaphors in *The Beggar's Opera* indicates a growing awareness that the 'modes of the court' were themselves a form of insider-dealing, grubbier and less honest than the business of the City. For Pope, whose *Dunciad* charts the encroachments of the 'Smithfield muses' on the patrician culture of kings, the City remained a symbol of philistine subversiveness. But increasingly for Gay, in his last years, the citizens' language of plain dealing represented a wholesome alternative to the vain pretensions and false promises of a corrupt court. Amid their general acclamation of such high ideals as honesty, truth, and virtue, the noble savages

---

[72] Gay to Swift, 18 Mar. 1729; *Letters*, 80.
[73] Swift, *Corr.* iv. 143.
[74] *Letters*, 90–1.

of *Polly* reserve a special praise for the merits of honest industry. Before dispatching Morano/Macheath to the gallows, the Indian chief Pohetohee interrogates him.

POHETOHEE. Would not your honest industry have been sufficient to have supported you?

MORANO. Honest industry! I have heard talk of it indeed among the common people, but all great geniuses are above it. (III. xi. 37–40)

As he found himself increasingly drawn back to the values of his Barnstaple background, 'industry' was to become one of Gay's most cherished themes. The poet who is chiefly remembered as the creator of mock-Arcadias, mingling court and country modes, achieved a final unlikely dignity as the upholder of city values.

FIFTEEN

Industry and Idleness

You see I don't want industry.

(Gay to Swift, Mar. 1729)

GAY was not the only one to make money out of *Polly*. Within days of its appearance at least two pirate publishers sought to cash in on its notoriety with their own unauthorized reprints. On 10 April, the following paragraph appeared in the *Evening Post*.

Yesterday two illegal, false and spurious editions of *Polly, an Opera; being the Second Part of the Beggar's Opera* were published; the one in octavo without the music, printed for Jeffrey Walker in the Strand, the other in octavo with the music at the end, printed for J. Thomson. This is to advertise all booksellers, printers, publishers, hawkers, etc. not to sell or cause to be sold any of the said editions, the sole property of the said book being, according to Act of Parliament, vested in the author, for whom the book is printed with the music on copper plates in quarto. Prosecutions with the utmost severity will be put in execution against anyone who shall presume to sell any of the aforesaid illegal, spurious editions.

The speed and efficiency with which Gay moved against the pirates is a good indication of his increased confidence and business skills. On 8 May Arbuthnot told Swift that Gay had 'about twenty lawsuits with the booksellers for pirating his book'. A month later, returning from a convalescent trip to Scotland with the Queensberrys, Gay was in time to receive judgement in his favour in his litigation with the pirates.[1] Gay's case was greatly strengthened by

---

[1] Arbuthnot to Swift, 8 May and 9 June 1729; Swift, *Corr.* iii. 332, 337–8. The court decision in Gay's favour was reported in the *Universal Spectator* for 14 June. (See James R. Sutherland, '*Polly* among the Pirates', *Modern Language Review*, 37 (1942), 291–303.)

the courage he had shown not only in financing the edition of *Polly*, but in boldly claiming his own copyright on the title-page. Pope, who had adopted a more cautious strategy, peppering the pages of the *Dunciad Variorum* with pseudonyms, fared less well in the courts. His original injunction in chancery against pirate versions of the *Dunciad* was subsequently dissolved 'because the printer could not prove any property, nor did the author appear'.[2] Pope's only recourse was to lobby his aristocratic supporters, Burlington, Bathurst, and Oxford, to put their signatures to a document assigning property in the *Dunciad* to the publisher Lawton Gilliver. This document was not executed until October, and it was late November before Gilliver entered his authorized edition of the *Dunciad* on the Stationers' Register.

Deprived of his Whitehall lodgings, Gay was now an accepted member of the Queensberrys' household. On his trip with them in May to Edinburgh he met the poet Allan Ramsay, a fellow-writer of songs and ballads who had published a volume of *Fables* five years before Gay's. He returned with the Queensberrys to London in June, busying himself with legal and financial affairs, before accompanying them in August for a three months' stay at their Oxfordshire retreat, Middleton Stoney, near Bicester.

This happy summer in the Oxfordshire countryside provided a much needed period of rest and recuperation. Although the burst of frenetic activity surrounding the publication of *Polly* had been invigorating in its way, it had also been extremely tiring. Even letter-writing was now an exhausting task. When Gay wrote to Swift in March he confessed: 'I have not writ so much together since my sickness.'[3] Now, relaxing with the Duke and Duchess, Gay allowed himself a period of luxurious idleness. Together they read escapist tales like the *Arabian Nights* or the *Mille et un quarts d'heures: contes tartares*; they sent facetious 'cheddar' letters to Mrs Howard; Gay experimented with new country recipes, involving wild mushrooms and white currants; the Duchess tried her hand at landscape painting and accompanied Gay on moonlight walks, while the Duke, entering into the comic spirit, planned ways to reduce his poultry flocks by introducing 'two or three brace of foxes into his garden'.[4]

[2] Arbuthnot to Swift, 9 June 1729.
[3] *Letters*, 81.
[4] Ibid. 84.

Indeed, their hours were so pleasurably occupied that they found no time for more conventional diversions. 'We do not play at cards, and yet the days are too short for us,' Gay told Mrs Howard.

I know that this will scarce be credited, yet it is true. We do not want one another's company, nor are we tired of one another; this too sounds a little incredible, yet it is true.[5]

In their idyllic country retreat the three court exiles abstained from other fashionable vices; the Duchess had 'left off taking snuff' and all three had agreed to give up liquor and drink nothing stronger than water. Their neighbour General Dormer, recently recovered from a fit of gout, was an occasional visitor; Mrs Howard was amused to hear the general had refused to eat a wheatear: 'they call it here a fern-knacker', Gay told her.

Gay's literary friends were less pleased by his retreat into rural isolation. Pope in particular felt snubbed by Gay's long silence and resented the intimacy of his attachment to the Queensberrys, which seemed to exclude former companions. 'I can give you no account of Gay', he told Fortescue in September, 'since he was raffled for, and won back by his duchess, but that he has been in her vortex ever since, immoveable to appearance, yet I believe with his head turning round upon some work or other.'[6] This condescending description of the subscriptions to *Polly* as a 'raffle' indicates a clear sense of irritation. As far as Pope was concerned, Gay's defiant act of political independence had merely reduced him to the status of a rich woman's toy, like a prize in one of his own lotteries. The reasons for Pope's irritation are not difficult to find. Currently, as he told Swift, he himself was being 'civilly treated by Sir R. Walpole',[7] and he clearly found Gay's continuing political notoriety deeply embarrassing. Conscious of Gay's acknowledged difficulty in having 'a will of [his] own', Pope inevitably suspected he would be tempted into acting as the headstrong Duchess's agent in her feud with the court and that any new 'work' would merely pander to her whim for anti-ministerial gestures. Among other friends embarrassed by Gay's political disreputability was Fortescue, elected to parliament in 1727 as a Walpole supporter, and now courting the Prime Minister's

---

[5] *Letters*, 82.
[6] Pope, *Corr.* iii. 52.
[7] Ibid. 81.

influence to gain promotion as a king's counsel and attorney-general to the Prince of Wales. Already Pope noted something of a rift developing between the two former school-friends. He told Fortescue:

I think I should not in friendship conceal from you a fear, or a kind-hearted jealousy he [i.e. Gay] seems to have entertained, from your never having called upon him in town, or corresponded with him since.[8]

Even Swift was critical of Gay's isolation from former friends. In August he told Pope:

I do not like your seldom seeing him: I hope he is grown more disengaged from his intentness on his own affairs, which I ever disliked, and is quite the reverse to you, unless you are a very dextrous disguiser.[9]

Both Pope and Swift had grown so used to regarding Gay as their literary aide-de-camp that they instinctively resented his new independent style. Their suspicions that he had been sucked into the Duchess's 'vortex' were strengthened by the idolatrous tones in which he described her. He told Swift:

To the lady I live with I owe my life and fortune. Think of her with respect; value and esteem her as I do ... She hath so much goodness, virtue and generosity that if you knew her you would have pleasure in obeying her as I do.[10]

There is something of the acolyte's tone of worship in this description of the woman who had converted Gay from a gourmandizing courtier to an ascetic, idealistic teetotaller. 'I continue to drink nothing but water,' he reported to Swift in another letter, 'so that you cannot require any poetry from me.'[11] Throughout the summer of 1729 Gay remained enclosed within his Oxfordshire utopia. 'Gay is sixty miles off, and has been so all this summer,' Pope noted, but temperamentally he was in a different world.

Pope was right to assume Gay was working on a new literary project, but wrong in his suspicions that it would be designed to precipitate fresh political turmoil. Contrary to his friends' fears, Gay had no desire to exacerbate his predicament as a political renegade. Although ejected from his court lodgings at Whitehall, he still

---

[8] Ibid. 52.
[9] Swift, *Corr.* iii. 342.
[10] *Letters*, 87.
[11] Ibid. 88.

retained his office, and salary, as commissioner for lotteries and was disinclined to provoke Walpole into further acts of retaliation. In career terms he faced something of a dilemma. He was clearly anxious to profit from his current popularity by producing some new lucrative work for the next theatrical season. Yet if he persisted in the satiric vein of his ballad-operas he risked not only a new ban, but also the forfeiture of his commissionership and possibly even harsher government retribution. Relaxing at Middleton Stoney he had neither the energy, nor the stomach, for more political controversy. And so, instead of forcing himself to come up with an entirely new work, he fell back upon revamping an old one, *The Wife of Bath*, hoping that his celebrity status would be enough to attract audiences to this creaking reconditioned work. Writing to Swift in November he explained his cautious strategy in offering this bland and reworked comedy as a conscious bid for political and personal rehabilitation.

I have employed my time in new-writing a damned play which I writ several years ago, called *The Wife of Bath*. As 'tis approved or disapproved of by my friends when I come to town, I shall either have it acted or let it alone, if weak brethren do not take offence at it. The ridicule turns upon superstition, and I have avoided the very words bribery and corruption. Folly is indeed a word that I have ventured to make use of, but that is a term that never gave fools offence.[12]

It was well over a year since Gay had last had a letter from Swift, a silence for which he gently chided him. Replying at once, Swift denied receiving 'above 2 letters' from Gay since leaving England (he had in fact received eight). Whenever he wrote to Pope, he argued, his letters were intended for them both, ignoring the fact that, as he well knew, the two men now seldom met. He sympathized with Gay's loss of his Whitehall lodgings which, unlike Pope, he attributed not to Gay's foolhardiness but to Walpole's malice. 'This is a sample of Walpole's magnanimity,' he wrote. 'When princes have a private quarrel with the subjects, they have always the worst of the lay.' He was less encouraging about *The Wife of Bath*, affecting ignorance not only of Gay's original version but of its source.

I have heard of the *Wife of Bath*, I think in Shakespeare; if you wrote one it is out of my head. I had not the cant word 'damned' in my head; but if it

---

were acted and *damned* and printed, I should not be your counsellor to new lick it.[13]

Swift's own advice was that Gay should stick to his new satiric style, rather than falling back on rehashed work. 'I wonder you will doubt of your genius. The world is wider to a poet than to any other man, and new follies and vices will never be wanting any more than new fashions.' He was sceptical too about Gay's extravagant praises for his new patroness. 'I wish for her own sake that I had known the duchess of Q[ueensberry]', he wrote, 'because I should be a more impartial judge than you.' It was, he claimed, the Duchess's own fault that they had never met, 'because she never made me any advances'. This was a familiar pose. In later years Swift always insisted that aristocratic ladies should pay court to *him*, rather than the other way round. His letter ended on a mischief-making note:

God continue to you the felicity of thriving by the displeasure of courts and ministries; and to your goddess, many disgraces that may equally redound to her honour with the last.[14]

While Pope was urging Gay to renounce political controversy, Swift incited him to ever greater acts of defiance. Rehearsals for the *Wife of Bath* began at Lincoln's Inn Fields in mid-December[15] and the play opened on 19 January, a date no doubt chosen to coincide with the events of the plot, which take place on St Agnes's Eve, 20 January. It was not a success and ran for only three nights. 'My old vamped play got me no money, for it had no success,' Gay told Swift in March, confirming his friend's forebodings.[16] In fact the play was not a complete box-office flop, and Gay received £56. 6d. for his author's benefit night.[17] In addition Lintot, who had already paid £25 for the copyright of the original 1713 version, gave Gay another £75 for the rights to the new one, which was published on 3

[13] Swift, *Corr.* iii. 360.

[14] Ibid. 359–62.

[15] 'We hear that a comedy called *The Wife of Bath*, written by Mr Gay, having been revised and altered by him, is now in rehearsal at the Theatre-Royal in Lincoln's Inn Fields, and will be acted in a few days.' *Daily Journal*, 20 Dec. 1729 and 10 Jan. 1730.

[16] *Letters*, 88.

[17] Arthur H. Scouten (ed.), *The London Stage, 1660–1800*, iii: *1729–1747* (2 vols., Carbondale, Ill., 1961), i. 32; *The Wife of Bath* grossed £96 on its opening night, but only £37 on its second night, and £56 on its third. Winton reminds us that, even on their benefit nights, authors had house-charges (of approximately £50) deducted from their profits. He thus concludes: '[Gay] took home . . . about six pounds after Rich had made his deductions.' Winton, 146–7.

February. But after the handsome profits he had reaped from *The Beggar's Opera* and *Polly*, such meagre returns were a desperate disappointment.

Yet such poor receipts were hardly surprising. Everything about this reworked play suggests a powerful desire to regain respectability. *The Wife of Bath* of 1713 was a rambling, episodic play, incoherently plotted but full of racy energy. The revised version is much smoother, with a mechanically efficient plot and characters to match. Chaucer is gentrified into Sir Harry; Myrtilla and Florinda are given a back-history as old school-friends; while many of the original play's theatrical eccentricities are either omitted or toned down to produce a bland comedy of manners. Gone is the scene of mummersetshire clowning in which Antony and William truss up the hapless Doggrell; gone too the pantomimic mirror-scene between Chaucer and Myrtilla with its *Macbeth*-like incantations, and the farce-episode with Merit disguised as a tavern drawer. Gay even removed the play's D'Urfey-esque songs and ballads, like Alison's 'There was a swain full fair', as if determined to purge all hints of plebeian *Beggar's Opera* motifs. But the most drastic evidence of literary gentrification is in the pruned and re-upholstered dialogue. The first version of *The Wife of Bath* was heavily larded with proverbial saws and bawdy asides, in a deliberate, if unconvincing, attempt to capture an authentically Chaucerian atmosphere. The revised version affects an altogether politer style, with disastrous consequences for the character of Alison, the Wife of Bath herself. In 1713 Gay had stuck as closely as possible to Chaucer's original, lifting Alison's salacious and provocative dialogue directly from the lively polemic of *The Wife of Bath's Prologue*. But in the 1730 version all this racy feminist mischief-making has disappeared, replaced by a more conventional merry widow manner.

Financial disappointment was not the worst consequence of Gay's ill-judged decision to stage this revamped play. The disparity between this bland, safe comedy of manners and the daring satire of *The Beggar's Opera* revived suspicions that they were not written by the same hand. On 24 January the *Universal Spectator* reported:

Gay's *Wife of Bath*, altered, a comedy lately acted at Lincoln's Inn playhouse, did not run so much as was expected, therefore people think Mr Gay was not the sole author of *The Beggar's Opera*; and they go so far as to say the first song in that performance was Dr Swift's.[18]

---

[18] *Universal Spectator, and Weekly Journal*, 24 Jan. *1730*.

Gay found himself in an awkward dilemma. The kind of sharp, allusive satire for which his genius was best adapted, and for which audiences clamoured, was precisely the sort of work which would provoke political controversy, with dangerous consequences not only for his reputation at court, but also for his own health and safety. His letters now were regularly intercepted by government snoopers as Walpole kept up the pressure on his most troublesome political opponents. Yet when he tried his hand at a 'safe' social comedy, scrupulously avoiding 'the very words bribery and corruption', the result was a dismal failure. It was an invidious predicament. In the event Walpole won this battle of nerves. Gay had no taste for martyrdom and, bowing to ministerial pressures, he opted for the security of silence. *The Wife of Bath* was the last work he published in his lifetime. For the next three years he continued to write, completing a second, more politically scathing volume of *Fables* and three plays, *Achilles*, *The Distressed Wife*, and *The Rehearsal at Goatham*, all of which contain strong elements of social satire. But he made little serious attempt to have any of these works performed or published in his lifetime. Increasingly the pleasures of retirement bulked larger than the dangerous prize of a controversial fame. In order to remain true to his own literary instincts, Gay chose to write more for his private satisfaction than for the public arena.

Now aged 45 Gay was enjoying a wealthier and more comfortable existence than at any previous time in his life. His letters are increasingly preoccupied with financial matters, not desperately seeking patrons and court favours, but confidently discussing dividends, investments, and receipts in the manner of a man of substance. He returned diligent accounts to Swift itemizing the interest earned on moneys invested on his behalf by Bathurst. 'What I have done for you I did for myself,' he reported, 'which will be always the way of my transacting anything for you.'[19] Swift was less than generous in acknowledging Gay's efforts as his broker, and in one letter even hinted a suspicion that Gay might be tempted to embezzle his cash. 'Pray keep the interest money in a bag, wrapped up and sealed by itself, for fear of your own fingers under your carelessness and necessities.' Gay did his best to laugh off this hurtful insinuation. 'I will not embezzle your interest

[19] *Letters*, 88.

money', he protested, 'though by looking upon accounts I see how money may be embezzled.'[20]

Increasingly one detects in Gay's letters a concern for thrift and an instinct for prudent financial management which recall the balance-sheet preoccupations of his family background in trade. 'I hate to be in debt', he told Swift in early 1730, 'for I cannot bear to pawn five pounds' worth of my liberty to a tailor or a butcher; I grant you this is not having the true spirit of modern nobility, but 'tis hard to cure the prejudices of education.'[21] Such sentiments, as he implies, elevate the bourgeois values of Barnstaple above the fashionable pretensions of Bath or Burlington House. Gay's willingness to champion such middle-class notions of probity, and his explicit acceptance of 'prejudices' which he had for so long affected to despise, reflect an important shift of attitude. 'I will take care of the little fortune I have got' he told Swift in another letter.

You have often twitted me in the teeth with hankering after the court; in that you mistook me, for I know by experience that there is no dependence that can be sure but a dependence upon one's-self.[22]

Swift's gauche remark about the temptations of embezzlement was not intended as an insult, but confirms his habit of regarding Gay in stereotypical terms. As he grew older, Swift's view of Gay was reduced to a few obsessively reiterated motifs, which bore precious little relevance to the reality of Gay's life. He was, in Swift's eyes, Walpole's victim, Mrs Howard's dupe, a financial ignoramus, a gourmandizing *bon vieur* and connoisseur of wine. Among Swift's persistent grumbles in the spring of 1730 was the poor quality of a consignment of 150 bottles of Hermitage wine bought from Dr Arbuthnot's brother; these, 'by the time they got into my cellar cost me £27 and in less that a year all turned sour'.[23] This was a mortifying loss to a man who declared: 'good wine is 90 per cent in living in Ireland.' However, he told Pope, 'I will refer it to our friend Gay.'[24] It was left to Pope to point out the inappropriateness of this last suggestion.

---

[20] *Letters*, 90.
[21] Ibid. 89.
[22] Ibid. 87.
[23] Swift, *Corr.* iii. 381.
[24] Ibid. 375.

You make me smile at appealing to Gay, rather than to me, for pitying any distress in a friend, but particularly this of your bad wine. Do not you know he has wholly abstained from wine almost these two years?[25]

Once again, Swift's comment reflected a fixed image of Gay, un-affected by the evidence in Gay's own recent letters. In his next letter Swift was sardonic on the subject of Gay's new abstemiousness. Still complaining about his sour wine, he wrote: 'But what care you for this, who have left off drinking wine? . . . And by the way, this is an ill encouragement for me to come among you, if my health and business would permit.[26] Gay wrote back immediately to assure you him that 'for all your gibes, . . . I wish you heartily good wine though I can drink none myself'.[27]

As if in conformity with his new sense of himself as a man of substance who had, in his own words, 'grown old enough to wish for retirement',[28] Gay now made gestures towards acquiring those conventional symbols of middle-class respectability, a home and a wife (in that order). The property he set his sights on was the widow Vernon's house by the Thames near Pope at Twickenham which he and Swift had both admired during the Dean's last visit to England. 'Is the widow's house to be disposed of yet?' he asked Pope in August 1728. 'If it was to be parted with, I wish one of us had it. I hope you wish so too, and that Mrs Blount and Mrs Howard wish the same, and for the very same reason that I wish it.'[29] Swift certainly wished it, and urged Gay to buy this 'little villakin' where he could entertain his friends in comfort. 'I hope when you are rich enough', he wrote in March 1730, 'you will have some little oeconomy of your own, either in town or country, and be able to give your friend a pint of port and a bit of mutton; for the domestic season of life will come on'. But he doubted whether the gadfly Gay was ready yet to settle for a life of cosy domesticity: 'You are yet too volatile, and a lady and coach and six horses would carry you to Japan.'[30] Gay hastened to assure him that domesticity was all he dreamt of: 'My ambition at present is levelled to the same point that you direct me to, for I am every day building villakins, and have

[25] Pope, *Corr.* iii. 102.
[26] Swift, *Corr.* iii. 381.
[27] *Letters*, 89.
[28] Ibid. 88.
[29] Ibid. 77.
[30] Swift, *Corr.* iii. 381.

given over that of castles.' However, he protested, even a villakin in Twickenham was still beyond his means. 'If I were to undertake it in my present circumstance, I should in the most thrifty scheme soon be straitened.'[31] He fondly hoped his wealthy friends might help him turn fantasies of domestic bliss into solid reality. Mrs Howard had received a handsome gift of £12,000 from George II to build Marble Hill. Perhaps, he hinted, she might like to do the same for him: 'As soon as you are settled at Marble Hill, I beg you to take the widow's house for me.'[32] The facetiousness of this mock-appeal underlines the essential unreality which Swift rightly detected in Gay's half-hearted quest for a home of his own. Gay's interest in home-ownership was inspired less by a desire for independence than by an ideal of friendship, and a vision of playing host to Pope, Swift, and Mrs Howard. Eighteen months later it was another Thames-side villa near Marble Hill that he claimed to desire. Writing to Swift in November 1731 he promised, 'if you . . . choose to live with me . . . I will purchase the house you and I used to dispute about over-against Ham walks on purpose to entertain you. Name your day and it shall be done.'[33] This property, however, which belonged to Mrs Howard, was for that reason alone repugnant to Swift. 'I will have nothing to do with the house over against Ham walks, or with the owner of it,' he wrote back. 'I have long hated her on your account, and the more because you are so forgiving as not to hate her.'[34]

In the event Gay purchased neither property, and his aspirations to home-ownership remained as pipe-dreams. His situation as a permanent and pampered house-guest of the Queensberrys, whether in their London home in Burlington Gardens or their Wiltshire estate at Amesbury, was too comfortable and convenient to relinquish; and, for variety, Mrs Howard kept an apartment for his use at Marble Hill. To have set up a domestic ménage of his own would merely have involved Gay in considerable expense with no corresponding increase in his personal comfort. Despite claiming that experience had taught him 'there is no dependence that can be sure but a dependence upon one's-self', Gay's habit of dependence was too deep-rooted to be changed. After an initial flurry of enthusiasm, he soon lost interest in the idea. For him liberty and property were

[31] *Letters*, 89.
[32] Ibid. 92.
[33] Ibid. 114.
[34] Swift, *Corr.* iii. 506.

not synonymous ideals, and he found all the freedom he needed without the legal endorsement of a freeholder's status.

One reason why Gay might have sought an independent establishment would have been if he was serious about taking a wife. But his overtures in this direction were even more perfunctory than his house-hunting. The woman his thoughts turned to was Miss Drelincourt, daughter of the Dean of Armagh, to whom Swift had introduced him on his last visit to England. And, as with his interest in the widow's house at Twickenham, it is difficult to resist the suspicion that his choice was influenced as much by Swift's encouragement as by his own inclination. Miss Drelincourt lived in Greek Street, Soho, and it was there, in early 1730, that Gay paid court to her, but with none of the sexual excitement he was able to conjure up on behalf of such fantasy sweethearts as Nelly Bennet or Molly Mog. Confronted with a real-life woman, Gay's wooing was of the most formulaic and lack-lustre kind and there is more than a hint of relief in the way he describes to Swift the lady's unenthusiastic response to his overtures.

I took your advice and some time ago took to love, and made some advances to the lady you sent me to in Soho, but I met no return, so I have given up all thoughts of it, and have now no pursuit or amusement.[35]

Gay manages to make the business of wooing sound more like a chore than a pleasure and his laconic designation of Miss Drelincourt as 'the lady you sent me to' suggests a dutiful visit to a dentist rather than the passion of a lover. In one of his *Fables* he seems to reflect upon his dilemma. This depicts a one-time rake now suffering the dreadful consequences of his youthful debaucheries.

> A rake, by ev'ry passion rul'd,
> With ev'ry vice his youth had cool'd;
> Disease his tainted blood assails,
> His spirits droop, his vigour fails,
> With secret ills at home he pines,
> And, like infirm old-age, declines.
> (fable XXXI, ll. 1–6)

Warned by the phantom Care to look after his health, the rake, like Gay at Amesbury, resolves upon a life of wholesome abstinence.

---

[35] *Letters*, 93.

> He now from all excess abstains,
> With physic purifies his veins;   (ll. 19–20)

Quitting the envy and malice of the court, he seeks 'the peace of rural air';

> And to procure a sober life
> Resolves to venture on a wife.   (ll. 21–2)

But no sooner has he made this resolution than he begins to fear the downside of domesticity.

> His household charge, his annual rents,
> Increasing debts, perplexing duns,
> And nothing for his younger sons.   (ll. 30–2)

It is a revealing insight into the psychology of this younger son that he should depict matrimony not in terms of emotional and sexual fulfilment, but in terms of debts, duns, and entailed impoverishment. It was more than a year before Gay renewed his suit to Miss Drelincourt, but still in the same half-hearted manner. Writing from Amesbury in April 1731 he told Swift:

When I was in town (after a bashful fit for having writ something like a love letter, and in two years not making one visit) I writ to Mrs Drelincourt to apologise for my behaviour, and received a civil answer but had not time to see her. They are naturally very civil so that I am not so sanguine as to interpret this as any encouragement.[36]

Even the most bashful lover might be expected to summon up more enthusiasm than this. Swift wrote back in exasperation.

You are the silliest lover in Christendom. If you like Mrs [Drelincourt] why do you not command her to take you? If she does not, she is not worth pursuing. You do her too much honour; she hath neither sense nor taste if she dares to refuse you, though she had ten thousand pounds.[37]

This impatient reply tells us much about Swift's attitudes to women, but such peremptory behaviour was totally out of character for Gay, whose deferential manner never aspired to command anyone. Gay's intimacy with women was always based on a modest and endearing

---

[36] *Letters*, 109. 'Mrs' was the usual title for ladies of a certain age and status, whether married or not.
[37] Swift, *Corr.* iii. 471.

self-deprecation, a pose of helplessness which invited court ladies to treat him as their confidant and pet. In letters throughout the summer Mrs Howard and the Duchess vie with each other in fussing over their loyal swain while he responds in character with flattering attentions. 'I think the lady I live with is my friend', he told Swift, 'so that I am [at] the height of my ambition.'[38] A man habituated to treating women with the mock-worship of a social inferior was not capable of commanding a wife with the kind of imperious tone which Swift deemed appropriate to marital affairs. Gay's intimate observation of the traumas of Mrs Howard's marriage might have given him further cause for hesitation. As Sir Thomas Willit remarks in Gay's play *The Distressed Wife*: 'If family disputes were to be made public, of all states, the state of matrimony must be the most ridiculous.'[39]

In both sexual and financial matters Gay's friends, misled by his affected 'hail-fellow' manner, frequently misjudged him. In April 1731 Bathurst wrote mockingly to Swift: 'Could any man but you think of trusting John Gay with his money? None of his friends would ever trust him with his own whenever they could avoid it.' Gay, he insisted, 'is much better qualified to bring increase from a woman than from a sum of money'.[40] In fact these bluff comments are entirely wrong in their reading of Gay's character. Under the Duchess's guidance Gay was becoming increasingly thrifty, not to say miserly, in financial matters. In December 1730 he told Swift:

the Duchess is a more severe check upon my finances than even you were and I submit, as I did to you, to comply to my own good. I was a long time before I could prevail with her to let me allow myself a pair of shoes with two heels, for I had lost one, and the shoes were so decayed that they were not worth mending.

Following Swift's own example, Gay had even learnt to begrudge a shilling spent on coach-hire in inclement weather: 'I persuade myself it is shilling weather as seldom as possible and have found out there are few court visits that are worth a shilling.' A few months later he boasted to Swift of his instinct for lucrative investments: 'I am grown so much a man of business, that is to say so

---

[38] *Letters*, 93.
[39] *The Distressed Wife* (1743), I. i. 20–2.
[40] Swift, *Corr.* iii. 453–5.

covetous, that I cannot bear to let a sum of money lie idle.'[41] By
contrast his attitude to women remained tentative, deferential, and
impotent, just the opposite of Bathurst's assertion. Despite his
pretences to the contrary, there is no evidence that Gay was ever
sexually involved with any women at all.

By the summer of 1730 Gay's brief fantasy of domesticity, with a
home and wife of his own, was over. In a confidential letter to Swift
he did his best to explain the ambivalence of his feelings.

You have often told me, there is a time of life that everyone wishes for
some settlement of his own; I have frequently that feeling about me; but I
fancy it will hardly ever be my lot; so that I will endeavour to pass away life
as agreeably as I can in the way I am.[42]

Nothing better represents the psychological disparity between Gay
and Swift than their antithetical notions of personal independence.
What for Gay was freedom, was for Swift a humiliating form of
domestic subordination, and he continued to urge his friend towards
greater self-reliance.

I call the family where you live, and the foot you are upon, a settlement till
you increase your fortune to what will support you with ease and plenty, a
good horse and a garden. The want of this I much dread in you. For I have
often known a she-cousin of a good family and small fortune passing
months among all her relations, living in plenty, and taking her circles, till
she grew an old maid, and everybody weary of her.[43]

Unlike Gay, Swift himself was a notoriously cantankerous house-
guest, who frequently wore out the welcome of the most kindly
hosts. However patiently such genial friends as the Achesons at
Market Hill, or Sheridan at Quilca, sought to appease his demands
for domestic dominance, they always finally despaired of his imperious manner, which relegated them to the role of retainers in their
own home. Gay's instincts were just the opposite; nothing suited
him better than the role of household favourite, happily submitting
to a domestic management which provided for his needs, while
absolving him of all responsibility. 'In short,' he told Swift, 'I am

[41] *Letters*, 100, 104–5, 112.
[42] *Letters*, 93–4.
[43] Swift, *Corr.* iii. 417.

very happy in my present independency, I envy no man, but have the due contempt for the voluntary slaves of birth and fortune.'[44] The two men still also differed in their attitudes to Mrs Howard, soon to be ennobled as the Countess of Suffolk. Swift would never submit to her self-important courtier's manner, and violently berated Gay for behaving as her 'dupe'. Gay good-humouredly resisted the charge. 'I am still so much a dupe that I think you mistake her,' he wrote. 'Come to Amesbury and you and I will dispute this matter and the duchess shall be judge . . . I'll be a dupe for you at any time, therefore I beg it of you that you would let me be a dupe in quiet.'[45]

Throughout the summer Mrs Howard kept up a regular correspondence, entering into a friendly rivalry with the Duchess for the role of Gay's principal female champion. In her country retirement at Amesbury the Duchess amused herself embroidering a chair in floral needle-point and playing at dairymaid by milking her own cows; 'and those two things', Gay told Mrs Howard in his best courtly manner, 'are of more consequence, I verily believe, than hath been done by anybody else'.[46] Mrs Howard's Windsor recreations were more boisterous. 'We hunt with great noise and violence and have every day a very tolerable chance to have a neck broke.' If she were to join them at Amesbury, she boasted, she would have 'a thousand other things to tell that would have no relation to tent-stitch, milking cows, nor drawing pictures'. Moreover, if she were ever to join the Duchess in sketching landscapes, she was sure 'they would be more modern than hers'.[47] Undismayed by such remarks, the Duchess allowed Gay to renew an invitation to Mrs Howard to visit them in Wiltshire and view the chairs for herself. 'For you will be in a more poetical situation sitting upon a group of flowers than hoydening a horse in a crowd.'[48] Despite his reputation as a troublesome house-guest, Swift also received repeated invitations to Amesbury. 'I wish you were here', Gay told him in July: 'You might ride upon the downs and write conjectures upon Stonehenge.'[49] Four months later he wrote again.

[44] *Letters*, 105.
[45] Ibid. 112.
[46] Ibid. 91.
[47] *Letters of Henrietta, Countess of Suffolk*, ed. J. W. Croker (2 vols., London, 1824), ii. 375–7.
[48] *Letters*, 95.
[49] Ibid. 93.

Pray do come to England this year . . . I wish you would and so does the Duchess of Queensberry. What would you have more to induce you? Your money cries 'come spend me' and your friends cry 'come see me.'[50]

The Duchess herself was more guarded in her welcome, adding this postscript to Gay's letter.

I would fain have you come; I cannot say you'll be welcome, for I don't know you, and perhaps I shall not like you; but if I do not—(unless you are a very vain person)—you shall know my thoughts as soon as I do myself.

Such candour was best calculated to whet Swift's curiosity and he wrote back immediately, presenting his most humble acknowledgements to the Duchess and telling Gay of his 'strong inclination to spend a summer near Salisbury downs, having rode over them more than once . . . and reckoned twice the stones at Stonehenge, which are either 92 or 93'.[51] However, the prospect that Swift might indeed venture a visit to Amesbury caused Gay a certain apprehension. Hitherto his flattering invitations had been another example of his instinctive professions of friendship. But in reality he was well aware that Swift's gruff manner might have a destabilizing effect on the tranquillity of the Queensberry household, and thereby jeopardize his own position there. He wrote back in a vein of facetious frankness which barely conceals his own anxieties.

the lady here likes to have her own way as well as you which may sometimes occasion disputes, and I tell you beforehand that I cannot take your part; I think her so often in the right that you will have great difficulty to persuade me she is in the wrong. Then there is another thing I ought to tell you to deter you from this place, which is that the lady of the house is not given to show civility to those she does not like; she speaks her mind and loves truth; for the uncommonness of the thing I fancy your curiosity will prevail over your fear and you will like to see such a woman. But I say no more . . .[52]

Swift took the hint, and did not visit Amesbury. However, Gay's panicky reaction only confirmed his friends' suspicions that he was now so much within the Duchess's 'vortex' as to be virtually inaccessible to lesser mortals. Pope, swirling within his own Grub Street vortex of 'lies and censures', wrote ironically in September,

[50] *Letters*, 99.
[51] Swift, *Corr.* iii. 416–17.
[52] *Letters*, 101.

affecting to admire Gay's spiritual ascent to his Wiltshire paradise. He himself, he confessed was

> not altogether so divested of terrene matters, nor altogether so spiritualized as to be worthy admission to your depths of retirement and contentment. I am tugged back to the world and its regards too often; and no wonder, when my retreat is but ten miles from the capital. I am within ear-shot of reports, within the vortex of lies and censures. I hear sometimes of the lampooners of beauty, the calumniators of virtue, the jokers at reason and religion. I presume these are creatures and things unknown to you, as we of this dirty orb are to the inhabitants of the planet Jupiter.[53]

A month later he wrote again, his tone no longer playful but pathetic. 'Are we never to live together more, as we once did?' he asked, declaring that his whole life had been shaped by one predominant, and now frustrated, desire: 'That desire was to fix and preserve a few lasting, dependable friendships: and the accidents which have disappointed me in it, have put a period to all my aims.'[54] 'Mr Pope complains of seldom seeing you,' Swift told Gay in November, noting Pope's impression that Gay had now assumed the role of 'principal manager' of the Duke of Queensberry's affairs. If this was true, he added, Gay should not scruple to turn it to his own advantage.

> You will have opportunity of saving every groat of the interest you receive, and so, by the time he and you grow weary of each other, you will be able to pass the rest of your wine-less life in ease and plenty.[55]

The cynical opportunism of this advice was nicely countered when the Duchess herself affected to endorse it, recommending that Gay should 'grow rich in the manner of Sir John Cutler', a notorious miser satirized in Pope's *Epistle to Bathurst*.[56] Accordingly, Gay presented himself to Swift as making great strides in niggardliness. 'All the money I get is by saving, so that by habit there may be some hopes (if I grow richer) of my becoming a miser.'[57] Behind such teasing comments one can sense the Duchess's influence, encouraging Gay to mock his friends' proprietorial advice.

---

[53] Pope, *Corr.* iii. 131.
[54] Ibid. 138; the date of the letter is uncertain. See Sherburn's note, ibid.
[55] Swift, *Corr.* iii. 417–18.
[56] *Epistle to Bathurst* (1733), ll. 323–8.
[57] *Letters*, 116.

News from London reached Amesbury as a distant echo, barely troubling the rural tranquillity with its faint rumble of modish concerns. Colley Cibber had succeeded Eusden as Poet Laureate, while at court a new pastoral swain, the 'thresher poet' Stephen Duck, was charming society ladies with his quaint and naïve verses. 'The whole age seems resolved to justify the *Dunciad*,' commented Pope at this elevation of a 'drunken sot' and an 'honest, industrious' farm-labourer as the latest leaders of fashionable poetic taste.[58] Gay, who saw in Duck's sudden rise to fame a parody of his own former role as purveyor of court pastorals, was pleased to be free of all such pseudo-bucolic affectations. 'I do not envy either Sir Robert [Walpole], or Stephen Duck, who is the favourite poet of the court,' he told Swift in November. 'Were I to live here never so long I believe I should never think of London.'[59] In the indolent, self-indulgent atmosphere of Amesbury the current favourite poet was Prior and the Duchess declared herself a great admirer of his two characters 'sauntering Jack and idle Joan', who 'just did nothing all the day'.[60] Another much-loved Prior poem, naturally enough, was *The Female Phaeton*, addressed to the Duchess herself in her more energetic youth ('wild as colt untamed').[61] By now though the Duchess's days of taking a chariot to 'set the world on fire' were over. In a letter to Mrs Howard she complained of a violent earache 'got . . . by taking care of myself (as they call it) in a phaeton'. Even reading was a somewhat strenuous occupation. As Gay told Mrs Howard, the Duchess was 'looking upon a book which she seems to be reading, but I believe the same page hath lain open before her ever since I began this letter'.[62]

Gay's own attitude to this self-indulgent atmosphere of wilful indolence was ambivalent. Accustomed to making efforts at social and literary self-advancement, he experienced a certain guilty unease at his new life of leisure. 'A state of indolence is what I don't like,' he told Swift; ''tis what I would not choose.'[63] Yet he did choose it, remaining in his rural exile with the Queensberrys throughout the autumn and winter. Swift wrote again in November, surprised that

[58] Pope, *Corr.* iii. 142–3.
[59] *Letters*, 99.
[60] *An Epitaph* (1718), ll. 2, 12.
[61] This was the poem that Robert Luck, Gay's former school master, mysteriously claimed as his own composition.
[62] *Letters*, 92, 94.
[63] Ibid. 93.

Gay was still at Amesbury 'so late in the year, at which season I take the country to be only a scene for those who have been ill used by a court on account of their virtues'.[64] This comment has a certain truth. Although the Queensberrys sought to present their bucolic seclusion as a form of Arcadian idyll, they were in effect making a virtue of necessity. Still very much *persona non grata* at court, the Duchess feared a return to town which would only occasion snubs and embarrassment. Gay's own indolence was only partly convalescence; more pertinently it was the necessary silence of a man whose letters were routinely intercepted by government spies and who feared that any new publication would entail a fresh outbreak of damaging political controversy. 'I am determined to write to you', he told Swift, 'though those dirty fellows of the Post Office do read my letters'; but this was as far as his bravado went. Though he professed to believe that 'in their hearts' the ministers who persecuted him 'think me an honest man', he was understandably reluctant to put this belief to the test.[65] Pope safeguarded his own position by striving to remain on good terms with Walpole; Gay's policy was more drastic, publicly forsaking literary ambitions in favour of rural sports. 'I have killed five brace of partridges and four brace and a half of quails,' he told Swift in November. No longer the compliant hare, he did his best to affect the independent air of the hunter.

In private, though, Gay relieved his feelings of frustration by taking his literary revenge in satiric diversions intended to entertain his like-minded Amesbury hosts. Cibber's elevation to Poet Laureate in November 1730 revived suspicions, first mooted in the *Craftsman* eighteen months earlier, that he had ingratiated himself with the ministry by playing a part in the suppression of *Polly*. In a brief one-act comedy *The Rehearsal at Goatham* (not published until 1754), Gay explored this theme, with a lively cartoon-style political allegory. This play, which may have been inspired by seeing Fielding's theatrical attack on Cibber in *The Author's Farce* earlier that spring, is based on the story of Master Peter's puppet-show in *Don Quixote*. But, as so often, Gay's immediate source was D'Urfey, whose *Comical History of Don Quixote* had been republished the previous year.[66] In Gay's version this comic episode becomes a

---

[64] Swift, *Corr.* iii. 420.
[65] *Letters*, 94.
[66] *The Author's Farce*, in which Cibber is satirized as Sir Farcical Comick and Mr

metaphor for asinine political paranoia. The aldermen of Goatham (the Whig government) suspect Peter (i.e. Gay) of being a secret emissary sent from the rival corporation of Assborough (the Tory opposition) to expose their corrupt practices. But in their mule-headed reactions to the puppet-show's innocuous lines, they merely succeed in exposing themselves. The chief alderman, Sir Headstrong Bustle (a clear caricature of Walpole), exclaims: 'To what end hath a man riches and power if he cannot crush the wretches who have the insolence to expose the ways by which he got them!' (ix. 14). In suggesting reasons for the corporation's extravagant suspicions of Peter, Gay clearly indicates his belief that the banning of *Polly* had been the result of a deliberate conspiracy. The aldermen have been fed on malicious rumours by Jack Oaf, a writer, and his friend Will Gosling, whose uncle Cackle keeps the Swan Inn at Goatham. Peter's puppet-show is intended to be performed at the rival Dragon Inn, kept by Cackle's neighbour Broach; Cackle fears the popularity of the show will do him out of business and hence does his best to suppress it.

Here we have an obvious reference to the two main theatres in London at the time, Drury Lane and Lincoln's Inn Fields. Indeed, Broach is easily identifiable as John Rich, the licensee of Lincoln's Inn Fields, who did so well out of *The Beggar's Opera*. Broach is significantly said to be already in a 'good thriving way of business' at the beginning of the play.[67]

Oaf, described as one of 'the favourite wits of our top men', is equally identifiable as Cibber; 'so comically profane upon all occasions, that he makes them all titter and laugh "till they are ready to burst"' (ii. 10). Oaf's speech is peppered with drawling ejaculations, 'rot me', 'pox take me', parodying Cibber's fondness for foppish roles, while his hostility to rivals is designed to reflect upon Cibber's exclusive prejudices as a theatre manager. 'To suffer Peter to come into the town at all was not usage that I expected from the corporation', he complains. 'After the theatrical entertainments I

Keyber, opened at the Little Haymarket on 30 Mar. and ran for forty-one performances in its first season, the longest run of any play since *The Beggar's Opera*. In the advertisement to the printed version of the play, Gay states that he took his plot from the episode of Master Peter and his puppet-show in *Don Quixote*, pt. ii, chs. 25–7. D'Urfey's *The Comical History of Don Quixote* (in three parts, 1694–6) was reprinted in 1729. But in addition, pt. ii of D'Urfey's *Don Quixote* (without the puppet-show episode) had been occasionally revived at Lincoln's Inn Fields. In Apr. 1728 it was performed with Lavinia Fenton and the *Beggar's Opera* cast, 'grossing a very respectable £167 for the single performance' (Winton, 149–50).

   [67] Fuller, i. 69.

have writ, and I may say without vanity, writ up to their tastes — I think the town owed me so much as not to suffer any interlopers in a dramatic way' (i. 75–8). Taking upon him to defend 'the credit of our town', Oaf dismisses Peter's puppet-show as 'a low, dull, vulgar, spiteful, bitter, satirical thing . . . I own, it would be a mighty mortifying thing to me to see this fellow draw an audience' (i. 82–7). In the ensuing dialogue between Oaf, Gosling, and Broach, Gay gives his clearest account of the covert manœuvres which, he believed, led to the suppression of *Polly*. Gosling warns Broach: 'This puppet-show, Mr Broach, I'm afraid will break you . . . You are a madman if you suffer it to be played in your house.' To this Broach calmly replies that 'the magistrates seemed fond of it'. Oaf now plays his strongest card, accusing the puppet-show of treason. But Broach, still undismayed, trumps him.

BROACH. I know there are idle reports about Master Peter and his show. But have you seen it, Mr Oaf? Have you read it, Mr Gosling?
OAF. I cannot say that.
GOSLING. But we know enough of the thing in general.
OAF. There are things quoted.
GOSLING. Passages, very obnoxious passages.   (ii. 53–9)

The dialogue here closely follows the substance of a letter to the *Craftsman* which also identified Cibber as one of those responsible for spreading malicious rumours about *Polly*.

They spread a report through every part of the town that the sequel to *The Beggar's Opera* was a most insolent and seditious libel . . . Happening to step into a coffee-house near St James's some time ago, I found a certain gentleman, famous for his Corinthian face, who was giving the company an account to this purpose.[68]

No matter how much Peter, like Gay, pleads his innocence, the men of Goatham are determined to find political innuendoes in his every phrase. 'All I ask', Peter protests, like Gay in the preface to *Polly*,' is

---

[68] Letter of 'Hilarius', *Craftsman*, 135 (1 Feb. 1729). Cibber had recently appeared on stage as Philautus, 'a conceited Corinthian courtier', in *Love in a Riddle*, making obvious the identification of him as Gay's principal antagonist. Significantly, the *Craftsman* carried simultaneous reports on the banning of Gay's *Polly* and the success of Cibber's *Love in a Riddle* in its issues for 14 Dec. 1728 and 11 Jan. 1729, further underlining the disparity between the two men's political fortunes.

to show and prove myself inoffensive.' But his most innocuous sentences are decoded by Sir Headstrong and his friends as damaging innuendoes. The simple but satisfying satire of the piece lies in the way the very act of censorship becomes a form of self-incrimination. Thus the mere mention of Paris provokes a flurry of self-accusation.

SIR HEADSTRONG. Paris? That now is at me.
BRAYWELL. No. 'Tis at me.
SIR HEADSTRONG. I won't have Paris mentioned.
BRAYWELL. All the world must apply it to me.   (x. 168–71)

This comic mechanism of blurted self-incrimination again repeats a formula used in the *Craftsman* letter, which tells us that Gay

upon reading his play to a certain gentleman, when he came to that part where one of the crew offers, upon some occasion, to wager a gallon—He was happily interrupted with the rebuke. 'Hold, sir; no reflections I beg of you, upon Sir Charles Wager and the galleons.'[69]

Similarly, the mention of a Moorish monarch provokes Sir Head-strong to exclaim: 'Beyond all dispute, I am the Moor.' This is a sly touch. If Walpole, by his ban, chose to acknowledge a parallel between himself and Macheath (alias the 'Negro villain' Morano), so be it. As Peter observes:

The guilty person can frequently make applications that nobody can make but himself. Upon my word, gentlemen, I am perfectly astonished at your observations. I hate private slander. As for general satire; the satirist is not to be accused of calumny; he that takes it to himself is the proclaimer and publisher of his own folly and guilt. (x. 213–18)

The readiness with which Gay, contrary to 'Peter's' solemn declara-tions, is prepared to include 'private slanders' against identifiable figures in this play is evidence that he had little intention of offering it for public performance. As Winton notes, for a brief one-act afterpiece *The Rehearsal* simply has too many characters (twenty-nine speaking parts) for a professional production.[70] Like *The Mohocks* this is a private joke, designed to relieve his own feelings of frustration, and no doubt to provide some entertainment for his

---

[69] Letter of 'Hilarius', *Craftsman*, 135.
[70] 'as in *The Mohocks* doubling is impossible; all of the characters are on stage in the final scene.' Winton, 154.

Amesbury hosts. When Peter enquires who his enemies are, Broach replies: 'Those who are afraid you have merit; and if ever you make it appear, you at once make all fools your enemies. It hath ever been so in all times and all countries,' (iv. 52–4). This is a reworking of Swift's cynical 'Thought': 'when a true genius appears in the world, you may know him by this infallible sign, that the dunces are all in a confederacy against him.'[71] Peter's final words indicate a retreat from a town whose tastes are increasingly determined by Cibberian prejudices.

PETER. There is nothing to be done here. They have the power and
  we must submit. So tomorrow we'll leave the town.

For Gay the 'main end' of a good play; 'exposing knaves and fools' was now an in camera activity. His prolonged seclusion at Amesbury was a necessary submission to the powers that ruled both stage and state, relieved only by such private acts of rebellion.

Gay returned to London with the Queensberrys in the first week of the new year. Their visit was intended as a brief business trip and they hoped to return to Amesbury within a fortnight; but, since their business 'depended upon others', it was not possible to conclude it before March. Gay divided his time between the Queenberrys' house in Burlington Gardens and Twickenham, where Pope, temporarily disabled by severe rheumatic pains, successfully inveigled him into reassuming his former role as amanuensis. On the advice of his physicians Gay was now 'a moderate wine-drinker' after two years of total abstinence and consequently regarded himself as 'qualified for society' once more.[72] In reality though he took little pleasure now in grand social occasions and restricted himself to small gatherings. In March he joined Pope, Lord Oxford, and Lord Bathurst in a convivial evening as Jacob Tonson's guests at Barnes. At Swift's prompting he also called on Mary Barber, the Dublin poetess, who was in London seeking subscriptions for her forthcoming volume of *Poems on Several Occasions*. But he made little effort to revive his quest for a wife. Miss Drelincourt had to be content with an apologetic letter since Gay claimed he 'had not time to see her'.[73]

---

[71] 'Thoughts on Various Subjects', in *Prose Works*, i. 242.
[72] *Letters*, 103–4.
[73] Ibid. 109.

On the whole his London visit was largely uneventful. There is no word of political meetings with Bolingbroke or Pulteney and no mention of new literary projects. It seems likely that he did find time to visit Mrs Howard, who was indiscreet enough to tell him that she 'hated' the Duchess of Queensberry. Such a declaration was an unwelcome reminder of the bitter feuds which now divided so many of his closest friends. Swift despised Mrs Howard, Mrs Howard hated the Duchess of Queensberry, and the Duchess was 'obnoxious' to the court. Swift also hated Walpole, whom Fortescue supported and with whom Pope strove to maintain a diplomatic truce. Moreover, from his apartment in Piccadilly Gay could look across at Burlington House, whose doors were now permanently closed against him, but where Pope remained a welcome guest. Beneath its civilized surface the social world of London was a minefield of half-buried jealousies and resentments; hardly surprising then that Gay was keen to return as soon as possible to the tranquillity of Amesbury.

Gay's own business in town was largely concerned with arrangements for the latest draw of the state lottery. He did his best to persuade Swift to take advantage of this money-making opportunity, proposing to partner him in buying tickets, and sharing the windfall profits; 'you and I will go halves in the ten thousand pounds', he confidently predicted. Anticipating Swift's objections, Gay hastened to assure him there was no taint of court intrigue in this scheme. 'I solicit for no court favours so that I propose to buy the tickets at the market price when they come out.' Even this reassurance was unavailing. The only effect of Gay's proposal was to strengthen Swift's suspicions of his financial irresponsibility. He wrote angrily to Bathurst, rebuking him for entrusting his money to Gay's wayward stewardship.

As to my £200, I know not by what authority your lordship paid it to Mr Gay ... You know Mr Gay very well, for his first offer to me was to throw off the interest at hazard with the government, till I entreated him he would employ it in paying a debt.[74]

Back at Amesbury in April Gay took stock of his position. His current wealth, all debts paid, he estimated at 'above three thousand four hundred pounds', more than enough, he reckoned, to qualify

[74] Swift, *Corr.* iii. 473.

him as 'a happy, that is to say, an independent creature'.[75] Nevertheless, he assured Swift, he continued to devote himself to two twin
objectives, 'getting health and saving money'. And, for the first time
in nearly two years, he also acknowledged an itch to be writing
again. His long period of abstinence, from both alcohol and satire,
was over and 'if I can persuade myself that I have any wit' he
determined to show it, and brave the consequences.

Ten to one but I shall have a propensity to write against vice, and who can
tell how far that may offend? But an author should consult his genius rather
than his interest, if he cannot reconcile 'em.[76]

His words are echoed by Barter, a character in his latest satiric
comedy of manners *The Distressed Wife*. Advised by the worldly
Lady Frankair to pursue his interest at court, Barter replies: ''tis a
life that I am unqualified for. I have the narrow stinted genius of
honesty and independence' (IV. xv).

The Distressed Wife offers clear evidence that Gay spent much of
his time at Amesbury in bitter retrospective contemplation of the
futilities and frustrations of his own earlier career as an assembly-
haunter. Unperformed until May 1734, eighteen months after Gay's
death, this play met with an unenthusiastic reception and had only
four performances. Nine years later the poet James Thomson confessed that reading it gave him 'more disgust than pleasure, it
presents so vile and perhaps so natural a picture of a town life'.
Though he considered 'the design of the play is very good, to
satirize this life so unworthy of a reasonable creature', Thomson felt
obliged to add: 'I don't think it is well executed.' In stigmatizing the
'limbo of vanity' of those who idled their lives away in cards and
gossip, seduction and intrigue, Gay had created a theatrical lampoon
more impressive for its moral indignation than its dramatic subtlety.
Commenting on the play's principal characters, Thomson found the
affectations of Lady Willit 'are drawn so monstrous, they are not the
affectations of a woman of sense and wit but of a fool'.[77] Or, as a
modern critic puts it, she 'produces virtuoso exhibitions of dithering
for dithering's sake'.[78]

---

[75] *Letters*, 105.
[76] Ibid. 106.
[77] Thomson to Elizabeth Young, 28 Sept. 1743; quoted by Douglas Grant in *James
Thomson: Poet of 'The Seasons'* (London, 1951), 292.
[78] Lewis and Wood, 172–3.

Sadly, most of these criticisms are true. As a dramatic entertainment *The Distressed Wife* lacks inventiveness and charm. Obsessed with exposing the vanities of town life, Gay's satire runs all on one note, producing a remorseless repetition of banalities which itself becomes banal. Yet from a biographical perspective it is a highly revealing work, whose very monotony indicates the unusual intensity of Gay's feelings of disillusionment. Unrelieved by any of his customary crowd-pleasing devices, devoid of comic songs or seductive moments of pathos to sweeten the satiric pill, the play presents an uncomfortable parade of predictable motifs as empty and mechanical as the rituals of the life it describes.

The play's central theme concerns the efforts of Sir Thomas Willit to reclaim his spendthrift wife from a life of ruinous triviality in London and persuade her to return with him to their country estate. Lady Willit's contrary ambition is to secure a permanent establishment in London by obtaining for her husband a place at court. Their name, Willit, clearly belongs to the familiar Restoration roll-call of Witwouds and Wishforts, but for Gay the name also had a more personal significance. Willet was the name of the draper to whom he had been apprenticed, and from whose shop he had escaped to make his first entrance into the social world he now viewed with such distaste. In drawing the character of Sir Thomas Willit Gay acts the part of the penitent sinner and offers a gesture of atonement for this youthful act of vanity. Willit is made to embody the highest ideals of mercantile and country values, combining the independence of the landed gentry with the integrity of trade. Willit's uncle Barter is an honest, plain-speaking merchant, whose sober expressions of contempt for the idle vices of fashionable life represent the play's moral touchstone. Detached from the entanglements of the plot, Barter functions as a kind of chorus, dramatically inert, but morally the conscience of the work. He is constantly teased by the two court *habitués*, Lady Frankair and Lord Courtlove, to quit the narrow path of mercantile righteousness for the more fashionable transactions of what Lady Frankair calls 'the Exchange of love and gallantry'.

LADY FRANKAIR. We all know you City people get a prodigious deal of money. But still—a merchant! There's something in that word that gives one an idea of—of—of I don't know what. In short, we ladies have an unaccountable prejudice against you.

Barter responds with a credo which underlines Gay's penitent return to Barnstaple values.

BARTER. Is the name then a term of reproach? Where is the profession that is so honourable? What is it that supports every individual of our country? 'Tis commerce. On what depends the glory, the credit, the power of the nation? On commerce. To what does the crown itself owe its splendour and dignity? To commerce. To what owe you the revenue of your own half-ruined estates? To commerce. And are you so ungrateful then to treat the profession with contempt by which you are maintained? (IV. xvi. 18–31)

Though it is impossible to say with certainty when Gay wrote *The Distressed Wife*, Barter's eloquent defence of the dignity of trade suggests the influence of George Lillo's play *The London Merchant*, which enjoyed a successful run at Drury Lane in 1731. In Lillo's play the moralistically named Thorowgood voices similar sentiments when encouraging Trueman to 'learn the method of merchandise'.

THOROWGOOD. 'Twill be well worth your pains to study it as a science. See how it is founded in reason, and the nature of things; how it has promoted humanity, as it has opened and yet keeps up an intercourse between nations, far remote from one another in situation, customs and religion; promoting arts, industry, peace and plenty; by mutual benefits diffusing mutual love from pole to pole.[79]

For Gay, like Lillo, the integrity of trade comes to represent the highest expression of human endeavour. Like Newton discovering the laws of gravity, Gay seizes on the 'science' of commerce as the symbol of a rational and universal morality far superior to the trivial and selfish tribal customs of courtiers and dilettantes. Predictably, Lady Frankair is unimpressed by such grubby notions. Though Barter may be content with this narrow perspective, 'is it not monstrously absurd', she demands, for his nephew Willit 'to set himself against his own interest? To abandon a preferment that is thrown in his way? How are families to be raised?' Barter's reply is succinct. 'They ought to be raised, madam, by industry and honour' (IV. xv. 57–60).

Words like 'industry', 'honesty', and 'commerce' run like a moral

---

[79] *The London Merchant*, III. i.

refrain throughout *The Distressed Wife*. Even the servant Humphrey has caught the subversive mood. 'What though it be the fashion', he remarks, 'to my thinking, there is no such mighty matter of greatness in being bubbled by knaves and sponging upon industry' (I. vi. 17–19). This echoes Peter's final complaint in *The Rehearsal at Goatham*: 'Because knaves and fools are a captious set of people, I am to be denied the common privileges of industry.'

Acutely aware that his own literary industry was most unlikely to be accorded the 'common privilege' of a public performance, Gay sought instead the private satisfaction of honesty in the expression of his contraband opinions. The term 'honesty' itself, Gay's long-standing trade-mark, is the play's most highly taxed commodity. At one point Gay adapts Falstaff's catechism on honour to suit his own concerns.

SIR THOMAS. Where shall one look for honesty? Who hath it? Or of what use is it to the owner? 'Tis a restraint upon a man's fortune; 'tis a curb upon opportunity, and makes either a public or a private trust worth nothing. What's its reward? Poverty. Is it among the rich? No. For it never keeps company with avarice, luxury and extravagance. Is it among the vulgar? No. For they act by imitation. Who can one trust? If I trust my servant I tempt him. If I trust my friend, I lose him. If I trust my wife for the quiet of the family, she looks upon it as her duty to deceive me. (I. ix. 1–11)

An even stronger note of personal bitterness is evident in the play's treatment of court promises. Against his better judgement Willit has been persuaded to remain in London by the entreaties of his wife, seconded by the repeated promises of Courtlove and Lady Frankair that he will soon be granted a place at court. Like Gay, Willit appears at first as a man without a will of his own, torn between the sober advice of Barter and the seductive blandishments of Courtlove. For Barter the nominal honours of the court are really a form of humiliation.

BARTER. You were born to freedom, and would you seek to make yourself a slave? You were born to fortune, and would you stoop to make yourself a beggar? For of all beggars I look upon a minister's follower to be the meanest. (I. v. 3–8)

Willit does his best to sound equally determined in resisting the specious honours of the court. Early in the play he tells his wife:

The wild-goose chase is over. Let the necessitous and sycophants haunt levees and seek to sponge upon the public. 'Tis a pursuit beneath a free-born country gentleman. (I. ii. 41–4)

But, as Gay well knew, a fatal chasm of hesitation yawned between the articulation of such sentiments and the acceptance of them. It was many years since he had declared 'all my expectations are vanished';[80] but even now Lady Suffolk still played the Lady Frankair role, tantalizing him with vain hopes of that elusive court appointment. Indeed it is difficult to resist the suspicion that Lady Frankair represents Gay's unacknowledged resentment against his court 'steward', that 'unconscionable dealer' Lady Suffolk. Her cynical advice to Lady Willit on managing her husband's moods describes techniques that Gay himself had long endured.

LADY FRANKAIR. 'Tis not, child that he hath any objections to an employment. 'Tis the expectation, 'tis the delay that hath disgusted him. A promise hath disobliged many a country gentleman, but the employment never fails to reconcile 'em again.

(II. vii. 25–9)

Throughout the play Willit stands on the brink of moral and financial ruin. His principles are compromised, his estate plunged in debt, while his place at court depends upon trading his niece, Miss Sprightly, in marriage to the ageing rake Courtlove. The cynicism of this intended transaction is presented starkly when Courtlove attempts to persuade Miss Sprightly's upright friend, Miss Friendless, to assist his suit.

COURTLOVE. Might I hope for your good offices you should not find me ungrateful.
FRIENDLESS. What do you mean, my lord?
COURTLOVE. Mean, madam! I said I would not be ungrateful.
FRIENDLESS. Have I ever called your gratitude in question, my lord?
COURTLOVE. I thought the courtly phrase of transacting business had been better understood.
FRIENDLESS. But why are you so mysterious?
COURTLOVE. I mean then, madam, (you must pardon me) that the thing shall turn out to your own interest too.

[80] *Letters*, 68.

FRIENDLESS. To my interest!

COURTLOVE. A thousand guineas, or a diamond ring of that value.

FRIENDLESS. For what? To sell my friend! Were I a man you would
not have had the courage to have offered me this affront.

COURTLOVE. Excuse me, madam; 'tis an affront that men of the
greatest distinction pocket up without the least scruple.

(IV. viii. 25–45)

As Gay observes in the second volume of *Fables*, 'marriage (as of
late professed) | Is but a money job at best'.[81] In the event Miss
Sprightly saves herself from being sold off in matrimony by revealing
that she is married already. Ironically it is Friendless who consents
to sell herself to Courtlove in a chilling matrimonial sacrifice as
unsentimental as Charlotte Lucas's submission to Mr Collins. This
conclusion was too much for James Thomson.

Poor Miss Friendless! How came the author to be so little her friend as to
make her a matrimonial prostitute to the most foolish of all foolish lords. I
expected, from her sensible and serious turn, that she would have disdained
the proposal and rather lived in a cottage with some person she loved.[82]

But by this time Gay was losing faith in the Arcadian bliss of love in
a cottage. The play's ending, though hasty, is not weak, but deliberately uncomfortable. The brainless Lady Willit escapes scot-free
from the consequences of her selfish intrigues, and is hauled off to
the country as vainly imperious as ever. It is only those with the
sensitivity to appreciate dishonour who are made to suffer its
penalties. Friendless's final hope that in being 'taken off from my
present dependence' she may be 'less unhappy' reduces all human
hopes to the mechanisms of the market-place. 'In every debt',
comments Barter in his summing up, 'some liberty is lost' (V. xiii.
60).

The signs of a reawakened self-confidence are evident in a sudden
flurry of activity. At the end of April Gay made a brisk four-day
visit to London in which he busied himself with re-establishing
more influential contacts than during the whole of his three months
there in the winter. He dined with Pope at Lord Oxford's, revisited
such dangerous political allies as Pulteney and Sir William Wynd-

---

[81] *Fables* (1738), XII. 121–2.
[82] Thomson, letter to Elizabeth Young, 28 Sept. 1743.

ham, called on Arbuthnot, and breakfasted more than once with Patty Blount and Mrs. Howard, who was seething over a recent abusive letter from Swift. He also found time to invest Swift's money in South Sea and East India Company bonds 'which carry four per cent and are as easily turned into ready money as bank bills'. Three weeks later he was back in London again, acting upon the encouragement of Mary Barber and a 'civil' letter from Miss Drelincourt to renew his lukewarm courtship, though with his usual lack of enthusiasm. 'They are naturally very civil', he told Swift, 'so that I am not so sanguine as to interpret this as any encouragement.'[83]

He continued to press Swift to join him in his Wiltshire haven. 'I look upon you as my best friend and counsellor. I long for the time when we shall meet and converse together.' The Duchess too, he insisted, was 'more and more impatient' to see him. But Swift, increasingly prone to debilitating bouts of deafness and vertigo, was unwilling to risk a visit. He urged Pope, himself confined to a sick-room and a diet of ass's milk, to accept the invitation in his place: 'Go down to Amesbury, and forget yourself for a fortnight with our friend Gay and the duchess. Sweeten your milk with mirth and motion.' But to the Duchess his only reply was to offer a sample of his peremptory demands.

Pray, madam, have you a clear voice, and will you let me sit at your left hand, at least within three of you; for of two bad ears, my right is the best. My groom tells me he likes your park, but your house is too little. Can the parson of the parish play at backgammon and hold his tongue? Is any one of your women a good nurse, if I should fancy myself sick for four and twenty hours? How many days will you maintain me and my equipage?[84]

The Duchess gamely rose to the challenge, calling Swift's bluff, point by point. She herself was 'a very good nurse', she told him, 'when people do not *fancy* themselves sick'; Gay played a competent game of backgammon, and Swift's groom was quite wrong about the Amesbury estate: 'the house is big enough, but the park is too little.' But as fast as she complied with Swift's conditions, so he amused himself by dreaming up more.

[83] *Letters*, 108–9.
[84] Swift, *Corr.* iii. 457–8, 445.

I must have horses to ride, I must go to bed and rise when I please, and live where all mortals are subservient to me. I must talk nonsense when I please; and all who are present must commend it.[85]

Increasingly the proposed visit became like an epistolary game of backgammon, as each side raised the stakes with ever more extravagant promises and demands.

Throughout the summer Gay occupied himself with preparing a new volume of *Fables*. 'I have not been entirely idle,' he told Swift in December, 'though I cannot say that I have yet perfected anything.'[86] Most of these new *Fables*, he admitted, 'are of the political kind; which makes 'em run into a greater length than those I have already published'. By May the following year he had completed about fifteen or sixteen; 'four or five more', he thought, 'would make a volume of the same size as [the] first'. This renewed interest in politics was no doubt triggered by his recent meetings with Pulteney, Wyndham, and the *Craftsman* group. Relations between Pulteney and Walpole's administration reached a new low in the early months of 1731, with a hectic exchange of increasingly vitriolic pamphlets leading to a bloodless duel between Pulteney and Hervey at the end of January. Throughout the spring the *Craftsman* kept up its anti-government campaign until in June Walpole's patience finally snapped. The printer of Pulteney's latest polemic was arrested and Pulteney himself was struck off the list of Privy Councillors. 'You will read in the *Gazette* of a friend of yours who hath lately had the dignity of being disgraced', Gay told Swift in July; 'for he and everybody (except five or six) look upon it in the same light.'[87] Away in Dublin Swift professed to be baffled by all these latest twists and turns of political caballing.

I am told that *The Craftsman* in one of his papers is offended with the publishers of (I suppose) the last edition of the *Dunciad*, and I was asked whether you and Mr Pope were as good friends to the new disgraced person as formerly. This I know nothing of, but suppose it the consequence of some Irish mistake.[88]

Such professions of political puzzlement were usually intended to deceive post office spies. 'If I don't write intelligibly to you', Gay later remarked, '['tis] because I would not have the clerks of the post

---

[85] Swift, *Corr.* iii. 451–2, 471.
[86] *Letters*, 116.
[87] Ibid. 113.
[88] Swift, *Corr.* iii. 495.

office know everything I am doing.'[89] Now Pulteney's letters too, like Swift's and Gay's, were subject to government surveillance. In one intercepted letter Walpole was amused to read these words: 'I will be extremely careful what I say, not to give offence and bring you into disgrace for continuing your friendship with such a Jacobite as I am.'[90] The only hint of his own political sympathies that Gay was prepared to commit to paper was a casual remark in November that Sir William Wyndham was a fellow guest at Amesbury.[91]

Gay found the work hard going on his new volume of *Fables*. 'Though this is a kind of writing that appears very easy', he told Swift in May, 'I find it the most difficult of any that I ever undertook; after I have invented one fable, and finished it, I despair of finding out another. But I have a moral or two more which I wish to write upon.' Two months later he was still complaining of difficulties, and his anxieties were increased by a suspicion that Swift himself was unenthusiastic about this new enterprise. 'You seemed not to approve of my writing more fables.'[92] But Swift hastened to reassure him that this was not the case.

There is no writing I esteem more than fables, nor anything so difficult to succeed in, which, however, you have done excellently well, and I have often admired your happiness in such a kind of performance, which I have frequently endeavoured in vain. I remember I acted as you seem to hint; I found a moral first, and then studied for a fable, but could do nothing that pleased me, and so left off that scheme for ever. I remember one, which was to represent what scoundrels rise in armies by a long war, wherein I supposed the lion was engaged; and having lost all his animals of worth, at last Sergeant Hog came to be a brigadier, and Corporal Ass a colonel, etc.[93]

Gay's second volume of *Fables*, not published till 1738, is a frankly political work. Instead of the ironic exposure of courtiers and false friends, it presents an unrelenting attack on ministerial corruption, and, in particular, on Walpole. Each fable is introduced by a kind of political homily, or, as Gay termed it, 'a prefatory discourse . . . by way of epistle', in which bribery, corruption, and government duplicity are emphatically condemned. Abandoning his usual pose of inoffensiveness, Gay assumes a determinedly judgemental voice;

[89] *Letters*, 127.
[90] BL Add. MSS 17 915, fos. 6–7.
[91] *Letters*, 115.
[92] Ibid. 122, 125.
[93] Swift, *Corr.* iv. 38–9.

in place of the deft, self-mocking ironies and aphoristic wit of the earlier *Fables*, he sounds a note of righteous moral indignation. His only gesture towards ironic self-defence is a repetition of *The Rehearsal at Goatham* ploy; that is, a pretence that it is not he who names the guilty men, but they who incriminate themselves by acknowledging their satiric portraits. 'Is't I or you then fix the satire?' he demands in fable I.

> If I lash vice in gen'ral fiction,
> Is't I apply or self-conviction?
> Brutes are my theme. Am I to blame,
> If men in morals are the same?
> I no man call or ape or ass;
> 'Tis his own conscience holds the glass. (ll. 49–54)

Though he still professes to write 'without offence', the self-censoring instinct for political compliancy and personal submission, so painfully evident in the first volume of *Fables*, is here all but banished. The emphatic repetition of the first-person pronoun 'I' in the couplets above signals Gay's determined attempt to speak in his own voice. This determination is even more evident in fable IV, 'The Ant in Office', a direct attack on Walpole, where the word 'I' appears twenty-six times in the eighty lines of the prefatory epistle. Addressed to 'a friend' (probably Fortescue), this fable adopts the Horatian gambit (later perfected by Pope) of rejecting the friend's counsel of caution to issue a fearless personal declaration of principle.

> You tell me that you apprehend
> My verse may touchy folk offend.
> In prudence too you think my rhymes
> Should never squint at courtiers' crimes;
> For though nor this, nor that is meant,
> Can we another's thoughts prevent? (ll. 1–6)

Such prudent advice provides the cue for a bold personal credo. '"Tis my ambition *not* to rise,' Gay now asserts, rhetorically rejecting the servile means to profitable ends.

> If I must prostitute the muse,
> The base conditions I refuse.
> I neither flatter or defame;

Yet own I would bring guilt to shame.
If I corruption's hand expose,
I make corrupted men my foes.
What then? I hate the paltry tribe.
Be virtue mine: Be theirs the bribe. (ll. 15–22)

Significantly, in almost all these new fables the corrupt minister, surrounded by his sycophantic tribe of pimps, spies, and placemen, is finally exposed and defeated by the valiant voice of honesty and virtue. In *The Beggar's Opera* Gay had granted Macheath a reprieve, in ironic compliance with the 'taste of the town'; but in these last *Fables* he adopts a more didactic role, determined to undeceive the town in the interests of the 'public good'. In the *Epilogue to the Satires* (1738) Pope invested satire with an awesome moral power.

O sacred weapon! left for truth's defence,
Sole dread of folly, vice and insolence! . . .
Rev'rent I touch thee! but with honest zeal;
To rouse the watchmen of the public weal . . .[94]

Similar sentiments are evident in these last *Fables*, also published in 1738 under Pope's direction. In fable IV the corrupt machinations of the arrogant ant are finally defeated by 'An honest pismire, warm with zeal, | In justice to the public weal' (ll. 105–6). In fable IX the 'secret frauds' of a corrupt ministerial jackal are exposed by an honest leopard, inspired by his love for the 'public good'. In fable V a dictator bear, feared and admired for his Machiavellian guile, is revealed as a greedy bungler when his boat runs aground on the rocks. In fable III the peculations of a strutting prime-ministerial baboon are exposed when his tame poultry subjects demand an account of their depleted grain-stocks:

The facts were prov'd beyond dispute:
Pug must refund his hoards of fruit;
And though then minister in chief,
Was branded as a public thief.
Disgrac'd, despis'd, confin'd to chains,
He nothing but his pride retains. (ll. 103–8)

Though Gay never mentions Walpole by name, the exposure of this

---

[94] Dialogue ii. 213, 216–17.

corrupt 'minister in chief' makes little secret of the identity of his target. Other coded clues, like the use of the words 'screen' and 'bubble', are liberally distributed throughout the volume, as are references to the ministerial 'secret service' of 'informers, sycophants and spies'.[95]

Much of the political iconography of the *Fables* suggests the influence of Bolingbroke. Though it was still some years before the opposition group of 'Young Patriots' would form themselves into a coherent political force, their ideas were already foreshadowed in Gay's verses. In *The Idea of a Patriot King* (1738), Bolingbroke argued:

> The true image of a free people, governed by a Patriot King, is that of a patriarchal family, where the head and all the members are united by one common interest, and animated by one common spirit ... Parties, even before they degenerate into absolute factions, are still numbers of men associated together for certain purposes, and certain interests, which are not, or which are not allowed to be, those of the community by others. A more private or personal interest comes but too soon and too often, to be superadded, and to grow predominant in them.[96]

Throughout the *Fables* Gay similarly contrasts the image of a benign and patriotic monarch, dedicated to the common good of the whole nation, with that of a greedy minister serving only his own private interest. In his 'prefatory discourse' to fable VI Gay writes:

> Happy were kings, could they disclose
> Their real friends and real foes!
> Were both themselves and subjects known,
> A monarch's will might be his own:
> Had he the use of ears and eyes,
> Knaves would no more be counted wise.
> But then a minister might lose
> (Hard case!) his own ambitious views ...
> Expos'd, their train of fraud is seen.
> Truth will at last remove the screen. (ll. 99–106, 111–12)

Even where the corrupt Walpole-figure is not finally removed at the end of a fable, there is clear identification of an opposition group of virtuous and public-spirited individuals, maintaining the claims of

[95] See fable II, l. 68; fable VI, ll. 3, 112; fable IV, ll. 38, 138, 149.
[96] Henry Bolingbroke, *Works* (4 vols., London, 1844; 1967 reprint), ii, 401–2.

truth and justice against ministerial depravity. Fable x, dedicated to Swift, describes the rule of a cunning bee, 'Rapacious, arrogant and vain, | Greedy of pow'r, but more of gain'. This sybaritic apian who loves luxury and scorns industry is opposed by a fellow bee, 'with honest indignation warm', who speaks up on behalf of 'native rights' and 'honest toil'. 'Be virtuous', he warns the hive:

> Know that in selfish ends pursuing,
> You scramble for the public ruin. (ll. 81–2)

This time, however, the warning goes unheeded.

> He spoke; and, from his cell dismiss'd,
> Was insolently scoff'd and hiss'd.
> With him a friend or two resign'd,
> Disdaining the degen'rate kind. (ll. 83–6)

The allusion, clearly, is to Pulteney, who had 'the dignity of being disgraced' by his removal from the list of Privy Councillors the previous summer.

> Disgrac'd by this corrupted crew,
> We're honour'd by the virtuous few. (ll. 93–4)

Equally clearly this bee-fable, with its emblematic antithesis between 'luxury' and 'honesty', was intended as a reply to Mandeville's *The Fable of the Bees* with its cynical celebration of luxury and vice as the dynamic forces of a modern society. If Mandeville was content to appear as the laureate of institutionalized corruption, Gay was proud to inscribe himself among the 'virtuous few' prepared, if necessary, to be 'as free | For acorns as for honesty'. At the end of fable II an honest sparrow chirps:

> I court no favour, ask no place:
> From such, preferment is disgrace:
> Within my thatch'd retreat I find
> (What these ne'er feel) true peace of mind. (ll. 111–14)

Similar ascetic principles are frequently repeated. In fable VII, dedicated 'To Myself', Gay affects to soliloquize on the theme that virtue is its own reward.

> Think, Gay, (what ne'er may be the case)
> Should Fortune take you into grace,

Would that your happiness augment?
What can she give beyond content.   (ll. 27–30)

Yet there is something unconvincing about such formulaic disclaimers of personal wealth and ambition. As an exercise in self-interrogation this fable lacks the very integrity that it claims, offering not a rigorous self-analysis but a complacent piece of self-congratulation. Thus Gay tells himself:

'Tis not so strange that fortune's frown
Still perseveres to keep you down.
Look round, and see what others do.
Would you be rich and honest too?
Have you (like those she rais'd to place)
Been opportunely mean and base?
Have you (as times requir'd) resign'd
Truth, honour, virtue, peace of mind?
If these are scruples, give her o'er;
Write, practise morals, and be poor.   (ll. 11–20)

Much of Gay's life had indeed been 'opportunely mean and base', and the distaste which he now expressed for such a life was produced less by moral scruples than by personal disillusionment. 'Be poor', he tells himself; yet in letters to Swift he still confessed his hopes of 'growing richer' and 'raising his finances'.[97] The fable alludes facetiously to one of Gay's most enduring fantasies. What if, instead of being born a penniless younger son, he had inherited the birthright to a grand ancestral estate?

Suppose yourself a wealthy heir,
With a vast annual income clear . . .   (ll. 31–2)

Gay quickly banishes this beguiling dream with an abbreviated variation on the nemesis theme of *The Birth of the Squire*. Actually, he tells himself, he is far happier as he is; had he been born to riches he might have been tempted into vice. But, psychologically, the renewal of this fantasy of noble birth is more eloquent than Gay's hurried attempt to disown it. The very triteness of his self-consoling argument that wealth entails its own woes ('In all the affluence you possess | You might not feel one care the less' (ll. 33–4) suggests the

---

[97] *Letters*, 116, 122.

sublimation of an acute sense of social disadvantage into a pious hope of moral egalitarianism. 'O keep me in my humble state!' proclaims the honest peasant (l. 98), shocked by the sight of privileged debauchery and vice. This boast of virtuous poverty is no doubt intended seriously; yet it is impossible to forget Gay's earlier ridicule of such pious literary affectations in *The What D'Ye Call It*, where Peascod exclaims: 'O that I had by charity been bred!' Gay had already parodied, brilliantly, the very pose of stoical humility which he now affected to adopt. And it is difficult to resist the impression that the virtue so strenuously and repeatedly asserted throughout these *Fables* is a virtue fashioned from necessity.

'Industry', like 'honesty', is another favourite watchword. As in *The Distressed Wife*, Gay constantly contrasts the moral integrity of the industrious tradesmen with the corruption of the court. ''Tis industry our state maintains,' proclaims the virtuous bee of fable x. Fable VIII, a paean of praise to British trade and industry, reads like a version of John of Gaunt's speech from *Richard II* redrafted by the Barnstaple Chamber of Commerce.

> Hail happy land, whose fertile grounds
> The liquid fence of Neptune bounds;
> By bounteous nature set apart,
> The seat of industry and art.
> O Britain, chosen port of trade,
> May lux'ry ne'er thy sons invade;
> May never minister (intent
> His private treasures to augment)
> Corrupt thy state. If jealous foes
> Thy rights of commerce dare oppose,
> Shall not thy fleets their rapine awe?
> Who is't prescribes the ocean law?   (ll. 1–12)

'On trade alone thy glory stands', Gay declares, emphatically reiterating the proud credo of Barter and Willit: ''Tis industry supports us all.'

> Be commerce then thy sole design:
> Keep that, and all the world is thine.   (ll. 23–4)

Yet, however sincerely intended, these celebrations of honest toil are tinged with unacknowledged irony. Amesbury itself was hardly a centre of trade and industry, and Gay's clarion call to a national spirit of business enterprise was uttered from a country-house refuge of leisurely retirement. Although claiming that 'I daily reproach myself for my idleness',[98] he nevertheless acknowledged a dispiriting lack of resolve to rid himself of the acquired patrician habit of indolence. He adopted the rhetoric of the industrious bee, but he lived the life of an idle drone.

Similar ironies affect the whole volume. Throughout the first four fables Gay repeatedly asserts his fearless determination to expose ministerial corruption and defend the public good, regardless of the consequences.

> I care not tho' 'tis understood;
> I only mean my country's good:
> And (let who will my freedom blame)
> I wish all courtiers did the same . . .
> I strike at vice, be't where it will;
> And what if great fools take it ill?   (ll. 47–50, 57–8)

Yet such outspoken defiance only has effect if the poems in which it is expressed are published. By May 1732 Gay had completed the sixteen fables which we now have, and told Swift that 'four or five more' would make a satisfactory volume.[99] Yet, instead of applying himself to finish these last few fables, he promptly switched his attention to his stage play *Achilles*. In July Swift encouraged him to persist with the *Fables*, but still Gay delayed. 'I have almost done everything I proposed in the way of fables', he wrote back, 'but not set the last hand to them.' Clearly, he was already fearful of the predictable political repercussions. 'I have determined to go through with it,' he promised, but added, 'after this, I believe I shall never have courage enough to think any more in this way.'[100] By the autumn Gay was already hinting at a prudent policy of self-censorship. 'I find I have a natural propensity to write against vice', he wrote; 'so that I don't expect much encouragement, though I really think in justice I ought to be paid for stifling my inclinations.'[101] This is a rather different tone from the proud declarations of fable IV.

---

[98] *Letters*, 113.
[99] Ibid. 122.
[100] Ibid. 125.
[101] Ibid. 132.

I neither flatter or defame;
Yet own I would bring guilt to shame.
If I corruption's hand expose,
I make corrupted men my foes.
What then? I hate the paltry tribe.
Be virtue mine: Be theirs the bribe.   (ll. 17–22)

Though Gay was undoubtedly indulging in a characteristic form of self-mockery in suggesting that he might accept a bribe to stifle his satires, it was a jest which enshrined a certain truth. Honesty and virtue were still commodities to be traded and these defiant *Fables* were not published till 1738, six years after his death.

The end of 1731 initiated a fresh round in the elaborate game of invitations to Swift which, like the rituals of courtship, sought ever more seductive inducements to woo the coy Dean from his Dublin isolation. Gay offered to meet Swift at Bristol docks and escort him safely to Amesbury. The Duchess promised her abject submission to all his conditions and, as a further mark of humility, declared she was 'ready and glad to ask your pardon upon my knees as soon as ever you come'.[102] But still Swift had new conditions to raise, challenging not only Gay and the Duchess, but also the Duke of Queensberry too to swear willing subservience. Even this impertinent gambit was received in good part. In November the Duke responded with a mock-legalistic welcome: 'I do now formally ratify all the preliminary articles and conditions agreed to on the part of my wife and will undertake for the due observance of them.[103] If, after all this, Amesbury was still not suitable to Swift's exacting demands, Pope and Gay promised him the pick of the stately homes of England; he could stay with Bolingbroke at Dawley, with Bathurst at Riskins, or with Pope at Twickenham, in all of which 'you may make your own conditions'. 'We are infinitely richer than you imagine,' Pope assured him. 'John Gay shall help me to entertain you, though you come like King Lear with fifty knights.' Failing all of these, Gay himself would buy a house, on purpose to accommodate his honoured guest. 'Name your day and it shall be done.'[104] However, all thoughts of travels were dashed in February when

[102] Ibid. 113.
[103] Ibid. 115.
[104] Pope, *Corr.* iii. 249; *Letters*, 114.

Swift strained a leg in a fall downstairs. The pain and isolation of this injury plunged him into deep depression. Gay tried to cheer him up, assuring him that the Queensberrys' estate at Amesbury Downs was 'so smooth that neither horse nor man can hardly make a wrong step'. But Swift, whose lameness persisted for several months, was in no mood to be humoured, even by Gay.

I am not in a condition to make a true step, even on Amesbury Downs . . . to talk of riding and walking is insulting to me, for I can as soon fly as do either.[105]

In his miserable state he particularly resented Gay's advice on the remedial qualities of exercise. 'You pretend to preach up riding and walking to the duchess', he retorted,

yet from my knowledge of you after twenty years, you always joined a violent desire of perpetually shifting places and company, with a rooted laziness, and an utter impatience of fatigue. A coach and horses is the utmost exercise you can bear, and this only when you can fill it with such company as is best suited to your taste; and how glad you would be if it could waft you in the air to avoid jolting.[106]

In this Swift was less than generous. Partly to please the Duchess, and partly too in his desire to emulate Swift himself, Gay had recently subjected himself to a punishing regime of physical exercise in an increasingly desperate pursuit of better health. 'I ride and walk every day,' he told Swift; 'to such excess that I am afraid I shall take a surfeit of it; I am sure, if I am not better in health after it, 'tis not worth the pains. I say this though, I have this season shot 19 brace of partridges.'[107] The Duchess feared Gay's own life was in as much danger from this late conversion to rural sports as those of the creatures he pursued. 'When he began to be a sportsman he had like to have killed a dog and now every day I expect he will kill himself.'[108] Lady Suffolk, herself a late convert to remedial exercise, urged him not to attempt anything too energetic. 'Exercise agrees so well with me that I cannot advise you not to use it; but if her grace

---

[105] *Letters*, 120; Swift, *Corr.* iv. 14.
[106] Swift, *Corr.* iv. 15.
[107] *Letters*, 127.
[108] Ibid. 128.

feeds you moderately, I should think your exercise ought to be so. God bless you.'[109] Sadly, this was advice he failed to heed.

Long sections of Gay's later letters to Swift read like extracts from the city pages of some investor's weekly, with their obsessive details of stocks and bonds, interest rates and company profits. In this, as in his belated and ill-fated conversion to physical exercise, one can sense Gay's increasingly desperate attempt to live down Swift's caricature of him as an indolent wastrel. Time and again he lays claim to the title of a miser. 'Not withstanding your reproaches of laziness', he told Swift in May 1732, 'I was four or five hours about business and did not spend a shilling in a coach or chair.'[110] All such protests were in vain. No amount of thrift or financial circumspection on Gay's part could ever shift Swift's settled view of him. No matter how scrupulously Gay now managed Swift's investments, analysing in detail the premiums and percentages offered by South Sea or East India Company bonds, such efforts could never erase the impression of continuing recklessness confirmed by his suggestion of risking part of Swift's funds in the lottery. 'I have lately heard from Mr [Gay]', Swift told Pope in June 1732;

who promiseth to be less lazy in order to mend his fortune. But women who live by their beauty, and men by their wit, are seldom provident enough to consider that both wit and beauty will go off with years and there is no living upon the credit of what is past.[111]

Despite such comments, Swift still saw himself in the role of Gay's mentor and protector. A year earlier, recalling his last visit to England, he told Pope:

The first time I saw the Queen, I took occasion upon the subject of Mr Gay to complain of that very treatment which innocent persons often receive from princes and great ministers, that they too easily receive bad impressions; yet they will never shake them off. This I said upon Sir R[obert] W[alpole]'s treatment of Mr Gay about a libel, and the Queen fell entirely in with me; yet now she falls into the same error.[112]

Meanwhile, Mrs Howard, now Countess of Suffolk, continued to dangle before Gay's eyes the prospect of a reconciliation with the

[109] 5 Sept. 1731; *Letters of the Countess of Suffolk*, ii. 22.
[110] *Letters*, 122.
[111] Swift, *Corr.* iv. 32.
[112] Ibid. iii. 480–1.

court. 'I have taken care of what you desired me', she told Gay in June 1731: 'I have done my best: I hope for my sake, it will succeed well; for I shall be more concerned, I dare say, if it should not than you would be.'[113] She herself was currently embroiled in a protracted lawsuit with her husband over the Earl of Suffolk's will. 'Poor Lord Suffolk took so much care in the will he made', she told Gay, 'that the best lawyers say it must stand good. I am persuaded it will be tried to the utmost.'[114] Replying, Gay told her: 'I don't like lawsuits; I wish you could have your right without 'em, for I fancy there never was one since the world began, that besides the cost was not attended with anxiety and vexation.'[115] He wrote this feelingly as he himself was still involved in legal proceedings against the pirate publishers of *Polly*. Some months later he told Swift:

I have had an injunction for me against pirating-booksellers, which I am sure to get nothing by, and will, I fear, in the end drain me of some money. When I begun this prosecution, I fancied there would be some end of it, but the law still goes on, and 'tis probable I shall some time or other see an attorney's bill as long as the book.[116]

However, since the Countess herself was 'descended from lawyers', Gay guessed that 'what might be my plague perhaps may be only your amusement'.[117] Indeed, despite the vexations of the law-suit, the Countess found much to amuse her in her new aristocratic status, dividing her time pleasantly enough between Hampton Court and Marble Hill. Prohibited by protocol from remaining as a lady of the bedchamber she contrived to obtain a more elevated court position as Mistress of the Robes, a post which she found 'so much more agreeable to me ... and everything as yet promises more happiness for the latter part of my life than I have yet had a prospect of'.[118] The one vexation which threatened to alloy these happy prospects was her continuing rift with Gay's patroness. Adopting her most courtly manner she did her best to disclaim her earlier more candid outburst. 'I told a lie when I said I hated her', she wrote; 'for nothing is more true than that I love her most

---

[113] *Letters of the Countess of Suffolk*, ii. 3.
[114] Lady Suffolk to Gay, 29 June, 1731; ibid. ii. 2.
[115] *Letters*, 110.
[116] Ibid. 117.
[117] Ibid. 110.
[118] *Letters of the Countess of Suffolk*, ii. 1.

sincerely.' She urged Gay to use his best endeavours as a peace-maker since the Duchess herself showed little inclination to make the first move towards a reconciliation. 'She has a most extra-ordinary way of making her peace,' she complained, leaving it to Gay to negotiate whatever kind of truce he could. 'I put it into your hands to tell her what you think proper.'[119] Not for the first time Gay found himself pulled in opposite directions by the wishes of his friends. While Pope and the Countess urged a recon-ciliation with the court, Swift and the Duchess insisted he should have no truck with such devices. And, just as Gay's letters to Swift were designed to deceive Walpole's post office spies, so his correspondence with the Countess has a contraband character, cryp-tically worded to escape the domestic surveillance at Amesbury. Typically, Gay's own views are equally difficult to decipher. While still loudly proclaiming his contempt for court promises, it is clear that he retained some hopes of a *rapprochement*. In personal terms he did his best to bring about a partial *détente* between his two rival patronesses with a proposed meeting on neutral territory at Highclere, the Hampshire estate of their mutual friend Mr Herbert some twenty miles from Amesbury. 'I shall certainly see Highclere this summer,' the Countess declared in June 1731; 'and shall expect *some people* to meet me there ... If you find her inclined to think me wrong in any particular, desire her to suspend her judgment till then.'[120] Swift felt under no such compulsion to suspend judgement on Lady Suffolk's conduct, sending her an angry letter in July and boasting of its contents to Gay and the Duchess. The lines of opposition were clearly drawn and, though Gay assured the Countess that 'the duchess will meet you at Highclere',[121] he made his own arrangements to avoid attending such an awkward encounter. In September the Countess chided him ironically for this diplomatic withdrawal.

The duchess did not tell me the reason why I did not see you at Highclere, but I do believe it was a good one; because she knows bringing you there would have pleased us both.[122]

---

[119] Ibid. 2.
[120] Ibid. ii. 3.
[121] *Letters*, 110.
[122] *Letters of the Countess of Suffolk*, ii.

Like Macheath, beset by his rival 'wives', Gay opted for the neutrality of silence.

> How happy could I be with either,
> Were t'other dear charmer away!
> But while you thus tease me together,
> To neither a word will I say.[123]

In *Achilles* Thetis asks her son: 'For what do you think women keep company with one another?' To which Achilles replies: 'Because they hate one another, despise one another, and seek to have the pleasure of seeing and exposing one another's faults and follies.'[124] Little wonder that Gay avoided taking sides in such a fraught confrontation.

Instead Gay spent the latter part of the summer 'rambling' from place to place, staying with Bolingbroke at Dawley in August and with Pope at Twickenham in September. Memories of his Barnstaple school-days were revived with Fortescue, at whose chambers in Bell Yard he and Pope spent several agreeable autumn evenings. Meanwhile Pope worked at patching up a quarrel with Aaron Hill. In December Gay was one of a party, including Pope, Burlington, Bathurst, and Wyndham, attending the opening night of Hill's play *Athelwold*, a performance at which 'several ladies were moved to tears'.[125] Burlington however, was less moved, and this chance meeting with his former protégé brought no reconciliation between them. A month later Gay was still unwelcome at Burlington House, where Pope was a regular visitor. 'I seek no new acquaintance, and court no favours,' Gay told Swift, adding, 'I spend no shillings in coaches or chairs to levees or great visits.'[126] In the spring he resumed his rambles, spending a week in March with Pope at Twickenham, where his aversion to physical exercise again came in for criticism. 'He is the reverse of you', Pope told Fortescue, 'and hates exercise—nay, I can't so much as get him into the garden.'[127] From Twickenham he set out with General Dormer and Sir Clement Cottrell to spend a fortnight with them at Rousham, their Oxfordshire estate, thence travelling on to Dawley and back to London, where he divided his time between business calls on bankers and

---

[123] *Beggar's Opera*, air 35.
[124] *Archilles*, I. ii. 25–9.
[125] Pope, *Corr*, iii. 253.
[126] *Letters*, 116.
[127] Pope, *Corr*. iii. 271.

visits to old friends. In May he wrote to Swift passing on the compliments not only of the Duke and Duchess but also of 'Lord Bolingbroke, Bathurst, Sir W. Wyndham, Mr Pulteney, Dr Arbuthnot, Mr Lewis etc.'[128] These names read like a roll-call of the opposition and, although Gay gives no hint of the subjects of their conversations, there is an unmistakable urgency in their desire to welcome Swift himself back to England. 'Every one of 'em is disappointed in your not coming among us.'[129] Gay pictured the pair of them like rural sportsmen: 'Why can't you come, and saunter about upon the Downs a horseback in the autumn to mark the partridges for me to shoot for your dinner?'[130] But even this suggestion is capable of more than one interpretation. In a celebrated letter to Pope, Swift had declared: 'I am not more angry with [Walpole] than I was with the kite that last week flew away with one of my chickens and yet I was pleased when one of my servants shot him two days after.'[131] These were rural sports with a special political appeal.

The injury to Swift's leg meant a further postponement to his long-promised summer visit to Amesbury. He was just about able to ride with the aid of cumbersome wooden leggings called gambadoes, 'but I can no more stand tip-toe on my left leg than I can dance the rope, nor know when I shall'.[132] Meanwhile his friends' discreet lobbying on his behalf had finally yielded dividends. In July Bolingbroke wrote offering Swift the opportunity to exchange his lonely Deanery in Dublin for a comfortable Berkshire living at Burghfield near Reading. The living was worth £400 a year 'over and above a curate paid'.[133] But Swift was characteristically suspicious of what he regarded as a court manœuvre to buy his political acquiescence. It would take more than a country vicarage to tempt him back to England, he told Gay: 'I want to be minister of Amesbury, Dawley, Twickenham, Riskins and Prebendary of Westminster, else I will not stir a step.'[134] At the very least he would require an extra £300 a year to make him consider the move. His income from tithes had 'sunk almost to nothing' and his lawsuit dragged on, placing his

[128] *Letters*, 123.
[129] Ibid. 123.
[130] Ibid. 122.
[131] Swift, *Corr.* iii. 118.
[132] Ibid. iv. 38–42.
[133] Ibid. 44.
[134] Ibid. 58.

fortune in 'the utmost confusion'. Yet, even in these straitened circumstances, Burghfield 'would not answer': 'The dignity of my present station damps the pertness of inferior puppies and squires, which without plenty and ease on your side the channel, would break my heart in a month.' He concluded, 'I would rather be a freeman among slaves, than a slave among freemen.' Swift's letters constantly stress the political independence that was his only recompense for the miseries of living in Ireland. When Gay boasted of his contempt for the government spies who routinely intercepted their correspondence, Swift seems to have resented the implication that it was because the letters were *from Gay* rather than *to Swift*, that they were liable to surveillance. 'I am ten times more out of favour than you,' he insisted.[135]

Meanwhile Swift continued to chide Gay's indolence in not exploiting his satiric talents to the full. 'You mortally hate writing', he rebuked him in May 1732,

only because it is the thing you chiefly ought to do as well to keep up the vogue you have in the world as to make you easy in your fortune; you are merciful to everything but money, your best friend, whom you treat with inhumanity.

He left him with this warning: 'Be assured, I will hire people to watch all your motions, and to return me a faithful account.'[136] Gay's response to this mock-censure was characteristically ambivalent. On the one hand he is given to assert that 'indolence and idleness are the most tiresome things in the world', or that 'I daily reproach myself for my idleness.' But then, in the same breath, he will find excuses for his inactivity: 'You know, one cannot write when one will.'[137] Like an idle schoolboy seeking to appease a stern schoolmaster, he sends dutiful reports of work in progress. In May 1732 he not only promised Swift that he had already written 'about fifteen or sixteen' new fables, but added, 'I have also a sort of scheme to raise my finances by doing something for the stage.' But there is a lack of urgency about both these projects. 'I think and I reject; one day or other perhaps I may think on something that may engage me to write.'[138] A combination of ill health, lassitude, and

---

[135] Ibid. 63–4.
[136] Ibid. 15.
[137] *Letters*, 121, 113.
[138] Ibid. 122, 113.

political inhibitions held him back. 'I am often troubled with the colic,' he told Swift; 'I have as much inattention, and have, I think lower spirits than usual, which I impute to my having no one pursuit in life.'[139] Similarly, while on the one hand claiming that he hated 'to write upon other folks' hints', he was candid enough to acknowledge that he would hardly write at all without the constant goading of his friends. In this respect at least he conceded the appropriateness of Swift's mock-threat of hiring spies to report on his progress. 'If you would advise the duchess to confine me four hours a day to my own room while I am in the country, I will write; for I cannot confine myself as I ought.'[140] In the lazy atmosphere of Amesbury Gay saw himself once more as a man without a will of his own.

By this stage in his career, though, such ritualized confessions of irresolution were somewhat exaggerated, and part of an elaborate persona of self-deprecation. In fact, although wary of rushing into print, Gay was making steady progress throughout 1731 and 1732 with his new volume of *Fables* and his plays *The Distressed Wife* and *Achilles*. Swift was particularly enthusiastic about Gay's plans for a new stage play. Another popular theatrical hit, he reckoned, would bring in 'the best crop for poetry in England'.[141] In order to maximize his profits, he advised Gay to 'take some new scheme, quite different from anything you have already touched'. This was wise advice. Swift was the first to recognize that Gay's theatrical success relied heavily upon novelty, but there was another reason for suggesting a change of tack. Throughout the 1720s theatre managers, with the commendable exception of Rich, had grown increasingly wary of causing political offence, and become correspondingly conservative in their choice of repertoire. Of the sixty-five plays performed at Drury Lane during the 1726–7 season only one, James Moore Smythe's old-fashioned love-chase comedy *The Rival Modes*, was new. It was the same story at Lincoln's Inn Fields, where, that same season, all but four of the fifty plays performed were revivals.[142] The death of Wilks, one of the joint managers of Drury Lane, in September further concentrated control of the London stage, leaving Cibber, in Pope's words, 'absolute and perpetual dictator of the stage'.[143]

[139] Ibid. 123.
[140] Ibid. 121.
[141] Swift, *Corr.* iv. 39.
[142] See Hume, 15–17.
[143] Pope, *Corr.* iii. 318.

Throughout the summer Swift grumbled at Gay's delays and offered terse remedial advice. 'Your colic', he pronounced, 'is owing to intemperance of the philosophic kind. You eat without care and, if you drink less than I, you drink too little.' He attributed Gay's besetting indolence to the usual pernicious distractions: 'Your *inattention* I cannot pardon', he told him in July, 'because I imagined the cause was removed, for I thought it lay in your forty millions of schemes by court hopes and court fears.'[144] However, such court diversions now played little part in Gay's procrastination. And he had at last acquired a sufficiently confident sense of his own literary standards not to be tempted into the kind of panegyric exercise for which he was temperamentally unsuited. Among the 'other folks' offering him literary hints was Pope, who in October suggested Gay might try his hand at some verses on the Queen's Hermitage, a new subterranean construction in the Royal Gardens at Windsor. According to Pope 'every man and every boy' was seizing this occasion to flatter the Queen with verses, and she was 'at a loss which to prefer'. Ever the literary broker, Pope viewed this as a perfect opportunity for Gay to heal his rift with the court, and used every persuasion to urge him to undertake the task.

You would oblige my lady Suffolk if you tried your muse on this occasion . . . Several of your friends assure me it is expected from you: one should not bear in mind all one's life, any little indignity one receives from a court; and therefore I'm in hopes neither her Grace will hinder you, nor you decline it.[145]

Pope's description of the banning of *Polly* as a 'little indignity' shows surprisingly little understanding of the anguish that that episode had caused Gay. On this occasion, though, even the prospect of obliging Lady Suffolk was not enough to tempt Gay to compromise his hard-won principles. He had received too many snubs from the court, over too long a period, to want to join the throng of 'every man and every boy' racking their brains for opportunist rhymes. He wrote back in unusually formal tones, his gentle irony masking a deep sense of irritation.

As to your advice about writing a panegyric, 'tis what I have not frequently done. I have indeed done it sometimes against my judgment and inclination,

---

[144] Swift, *Corr.* iv. 40.
[145] Pope, *Corr.* iii. 318.

and I heartily repent of it. And at present, as I have no desire of reward, and see no just reason of praise, I think I had better leave it alone. There are flatterers good enough to be found, and I would not interfere in any gentleman's profession. I have seen no verses upon these sublime occasions, so that I have no emulation. Let the patrons enjoy the authors and the authors their patrons, for I know myself unworthy.[146]

This was Gay's last letter to Pope, written just two months before he died, and in it he finally declares his own poetic independence. Although the Duchess may have played her part in discouraging him from attempting this *rapprochement* with the court, Gay had at last determined to be like Swift, a free man among slaves, rather than a slave among free men.

By September Swift had changed his tune and now cautioned Gay against finishing his play 'in haste'. 'You are young enough to get some lucky hint, which must come by chance and it shall be a thing of importance ... diverting and usefully satirical.'[147] Sadly though for Gay, time was already running out. His ill health was now a permanently debilitating condition, though he struggled against it with all the resilience and good humour at his command. Forcing himself to adopt the regimen of punishing physical exercise which Swift so constantly recommended, he assured him, 'I am endeavouring to lay in a stock of health to squander in town.'[148]

Swift was still unimpressed. In October he told the Duchess: 'You need not be in pains about Mr Gay's stock of health, I promise you he will spend it all upon laziness, and run deep in debt by a winter in town.' He entreated her to order Gay 'to move his chaps less and his legs more for the six cold months, else he will spend all his money in physic and coach-hire'. He boasted that, although so much older than Gay, he could, until this latest injury, 'ride 500 miles on a trotting horse'.[149] Goaded by such constant teasing, Gay determined to disprove this charge of 'rooted laziness' by embarking, at the end of the summer, on an expedition to Sir William Wyndham's Somerset estate, riding all the way there and back on horseback. Writing to Pope in October he described the countryside abounding in 'beautiful prospects' and sea-views.

---

[146] *Letters*, 131.
[147] Swift, *Corr.* iv. 58.
[148] *Letters*, 125.
[149] Swift, *Corr.* iv. 73, 15.

I was mightily pleased with Dunster castle near Minehead. It stands upon a great eminence, and hath a prospect of that town, with an extensive view of the Bristol channel; in which are seen two small islands, called the steep Holms and flat Holms, and on t'other side we could plainly distinguish the division of fields on the Welsh coast.[150]

There is a kind of desperate cheerfulness about these comments for, however pleasing the scenery, Gay's expedition had sadly failed in its principal objective, as a remedial exercise. Back at Amesbury he complained: 'since my return I cannot so much boast of my health as before I went, for I am frequently out of order with my colical complaints, so as to make me uneasy and dispirited.'[151] After three months of rigorous and unaccustomed exertion he confessed himself profoundly disappointed with the results, 'and really think I am as well without it, so that I begin to fear the illness I have so long and so often complained of is inherent in my constitution, and that I have nothing for it but patience'.[152] He wrote this in October 1732, just two months before he died and it is difficult to resist the suspicion that his sudden fad for physical exercise may have had exactly the opposite effect from that intended. After a lifetime of relative self-indulgence and indolence, this frenetic bout of violent physical exertion may have proved too much of a shock to his system. Instead of increasing his stock of health, it seems to have overdrawn his account, leaving him dispirited and exhausted. Weak as he was, Gay made a last journey to London in early November to deliver the manuscript of *Achilles* to the Covent Garden playhouse. On the 16th he wrote informing Swift that he was back in town 'to follow my own inventions', though he expected to be joined there by the Queensberrys before the end of the month. As usual, he busied himself as much with Swift's financial affairs as his own literary ones, rendering him a meticulous account correct to the last penny: 'I find I have now remaining of yours two hundred and eleven pounds fifteen shillings and sixpence.'[153]

Gay was characteristically pessimistic about his new play's prospects of success. With his natural 'propensity to write against vice', he confessed, 'I don't expect much encouragement.' Still fretting under the official disapproval occasioned by *Polly* he feared another

[150] *Letters*, 130.
[151] Ibid.
[152] Ibid.
[153] Ibid. 131.

bruising involvement in political controversy, with its potentially damaging consequences for his prospects of rehabilitation and his precarious state of health. Seeking ease rather than notoriety, Gay drew up a mental balance-sheet in which the credit of potential financial gain was set against the debit of renewed political ostracism. Too proud to set his hand to the kind of ingratiating panegyric flummery that Pope recommended, he was still prepared to mend fences with the court by maintaining a diplomatic silence. Moreover, as far as money went, he had little need of more. 'Mr Gay is a very rich man,' the Duchess told Swift in August; 'I really think he does not wish to be richer.'[154] With an accumulated fortune of £6,000, and his comfortable position in the Queensberry household, Gay was now at last free of the need to write for profit. Either way, whether he kept silent, or spoke his mind, he anticipated little for his pains but courtly spite and condescension. 'The Great', he concluded wearily, 'are ungrateful.'[155]

In the end it was a desire to express his hard-won sense of self-respect, rather than the lure of financial gain, which prompted Gay to offer *Achilles* to the stage. Whatever the costs to himself, he finally refused to be cowed into a role of apathetic idleness. Inevitably the play is spattered with political gibes and allusions, but there is no sustained attempt to develop a coherent political scheme. Even 'Atex Burnet', determined to discredit the play in his pamphlet *Achilles Dissected*, could find nothing subversive in it save the presentation of 'a monarch engrossed by his Prime Minister'. He probably had in mind the scene where the disguised Achilles, arrested on a ludicrous charge of attempted murder, rebukes the king's ministerial 'screen' Diphilus: 'it may be necessary for him to trump up a horrid conspiracy to screen his own infamous practices' (II. vi. 2–4). But, as the *Daily Courant* observed, it was impossible to deduce a coherent 'secret history' from such scattered satiric asides. In these final plays Gay is less concerned with politics than with establishing his own moral agenda. Neither *Achilles* nor *The Distressed Wife* is a political satire like *The Beggar's Opera*; but what they have in common is a working-out in public of suppressed private preoccupations. In *The Distressed Wife* Gay stood up for Barnstaple values against the affectations of the court; in *Achilles*

---

[154] Ibid. 128.
[155] Ibid. 132.

he finally confronted, albeit obliquely, the issue of his own sexuality.

For this final ballad-opera, Gay did, as Swift advised, 'take some new scheme', though the result was quite unlike anything that Swift had envisaged. In many ways *Achilles* is among the most personal of Gay's works; although there is none of the rhetorical first-person posturing that one finds in the *Fables*, the central preoccupation, concerning gender and sexual identity, has an autobiographical intensity that is singularly lacking in his efforts at verse soliloquy. Gay does not present Achilles the heroic warrior of the *Iliad*, but Achilles the feminized adolescent, a confused transvestite youth, dressed in female petticoats and unable to acknowledge or express his true sexual identity. The play is based on an episode, described in the writings of Statius, Ovid, and Bion, in which Achilles, disguised as a girl, is concealed on the island of Scyros among the daughters of King Lycomedes. His mother, the sea-goddess Thetis, has learned from a prophecy that her son can either have a long life of modest obscurity, or a short, glorious life fighting in the Trojan War. Opting for discretion rather than valour, she forces him to conceal his identity by dressing in women's clothes and assuming the girl's name Pyrrha. But the Greeks, discovering that they cannot win the war without Achilles, mount an expedition to find him. Disguised as a merchant, Ulysses arrives on the island with a consignment of female goods, among which he conceals a sword and armour. When Ulysses displays his wares to the maidens of Scyros, Achilles is tricked into revealing himself.

This story had long exercised a fascination over Gay's imagination. Horace alludes to it in his ode 1.8, 'Ad Lydiam', provoking one of Gay's more interesting marginal annotations: 'The design of this ode', he notes, 'is to reproach Lydia that she suffers Sybaris to be near her in [~~women's apparel~~] actions of effeminacy.'[156] One of Gay's epigraphs to the play, taken from book 13 of Ovid's *Metamorphoses*, asserts that all the Greeks, especially Ajax, were deceived by Achilles' female disguise. This was a passage Gay knew well; it was

---

[156] 'quid latet, ut marinae | filium dicunt Thetidis sub lacrimosa Troiae | funera, ne virilis | cultus in caedet et Lycias proriperet catervas?' (ll. 13–16), ('Why does he skulk, as they say the son of sea-born Thetis did, when the time of Troy's tearful destruction drew near, for fear that the garb of men should hurry him to slaughter and the Lycian bands?') *Horace: The Odes and Epodes* (Loeb edn., London, 1914; repr. 1964), 27. Translation by C. E. Bennett.

translated by Aaron Hill in 1708 and by Gay's pseudonymous namesake and tormentor 'Joseph Gay' (alias J. D. Breval) in 1719; it was also included in Garth's edition of the *Metamorphoses Englished* (1717) to which Gay himself contributed. It seems likely that Gay also knew Bion's fragmentary *Epithalamius of Achilles and Deidameia*, which describes an uneasy adolescent seeking to come to terms with his own sexual identity as he struggles to repress male desire within an ostensibly feminine persona.[157]

Achilles alone hid among the girls, the daughters of Lycomedes, and he learned woolworking instead of arms, and with white arm he sustained a maiden's task, and he appeared like a girl; for he actually became girlish like them, and just such a blossom blushed on his snowy cheeks, and he walked with the walk of a girl, and he covered his hair with a veil. But still he had the heart of a man, and from dawn to night he sat beside Deidamia, and sometimes he kissed her hand, and many a time he raised up her fair weaving and he praised her patterned web; and he did not eat with any other companion, and he did everything in his eagerness to share her bed; and he even spoke a word to her: 'The other sisters sleep with one another, but I sleep alone, and you sleep alone, we two maiden companions, we two fair; but we sleep alone in our separate beds.'[158]

It is tempting to draw a parallel here with Gay's own youthful experience. He too had spent early years not, like his brother, on the battlefields of Europe, but lost in 'a maze of fashions', mastering the mysteries of 'th'inconstant equipage of female dress' amid the hermaphrodite 'he-strumpets' of the New Exchange. As Achilles ruefully comments in his first speech: 'On the first step of a young fellow depends his character in life.' Statius offers a graphic physiological account of the adolescent boy's struggle to contain the guilty sensation of male arousal within the confines of an appropriately submissive feminine demeanour. His scalp tightens and his skin flushes; seeking to check his impulsive masculine movements he becomes awkward, bashful, and clumsy. These were details which Gay copied for comic effect, having his Achilles shuffle

---

[157] No English translation of this work, whose attribution to Bion is contested, is known until long after Gay's death. But Yvonne Noble argues persuasively, from the evidence of *The Shepherd's Week*, *Acis and Galatea*, and *Achilles*, that Gay was familiar with a wide range of Bion's idylls. See Yvonne Noble, 'Sex and Gender in Gay's *Achilles*', in Lewis and Wood, 184–215; I am indebted to Yvonne Noble for several valuable suggestions in this analysis of *Achilles*.

[158] I reproduce the literal translation of this passage provided by Professor Peter Westervelt for Yvonne Noble's essay (Lewis and Wood, 187–8).

awkwardly round the stage in skirts. 'But dear Pyrrha,' Deidamia exclaims at one point, 'for my sake, for your own, have a particular regard to your behaviour . . . You now and then take such, intolerable strides, that I vow you have set me blushing (II. x). Possibly Gay's own 'clumsy tread' was the product of a similar uncertainty; torn between the satirist's assertive stride, and the courtier's instinct for crawling, he assumed an awkward, crab-wise posture, half-bowing and half-roused. Statius presents the climactic disclosure of Achilles' true male identity as an irresistible assertion of masculine nature over feminine art. 'Standing motionless amid the panic, Achilles simply grows huge and dominant: as his womanly garments fall away, *he* (his whole body) erects.'[159]

> illius intactae cecidere a pectore vestes,
> iam clipeus breviorque manu consumitur hasta,
> —mira fides!—Ithacumque umeris excedere visus
> Aetolumque ducem: . . .
> immanisque gradu, ceu protinus Hectora poscens,
> stat medius trepidante domo: Peleaque virgo
> quaeritur. (1. 878–81, 883–5)

(From his breast the garments fall away untouched, now the shield and puny spear are swallowed up by his hands—marvellous to believe!—his head and shoulders loom up above those of Ulysses and Diomede: . . . Mighty of limb, in combat stance, as if he could summon Hector, he stands amid the panic-stricken house: and the girl-that-was for whom they search [they will never find].)[160]

Such an image enacts a powerful fantasy of male dominance and for Gay the attractions of such a vigorous transformation must have been strongly felt. Perhaps at last he might throw off the submissive female posture of deference and express himself as a real man; no longer the compliant hare, he might become a hero of literary combat. The rhetorical bravado of his second volume of *Fables*, with their militant assertions of resolute and heroic resistance, seem to imply just such a willed change of public persona. But, as always, the fantasy of self-assertion remained just that—a fantasy. The rebellious *Fables* remained unpublished and, typically, in Gay's version of the story, the disclosure of Achilles' masculinity is ren-

---

[159] Ibid. 189.
[160] Translation by Yvonne Noble, ibid. 189.

dered not as an exultant thrill of physical self-fulfilment, but as the resigned acceptance of a social duty.

ACHILLES. But what are you, friend, who thus presumes to know me?

ULYSSES. You cannot be a stranger, sir, to the name of Ulysses.

ACHILLES. As I have long honoured, I shall now endeavour, sir, to emulate your fame.

This is not an Achilles who rises up, inspired, to tower over his Greek discoverers, but one who instinctively adopts the courtier's tones of deference and flattery.

The best known classical source of the 'Achilles in Scyros' episode is Ovid's *Ars amatoria*, where it is used, paradoxically, in a celebration of rampant masculinity. Here, Achilles' female disguise becomes a sexual ploy, enabling him to insinuate himself into Deidamia's confidence before raping her. In Ovid's lines, as Yvonne Noble notes, the deliberate verbal assonance linking disclosure of gender (*vir, viri*) with use of force (*vis, vim, vires*) turns sexual violence into an inherent proof of manliness.

> haec illum stupro comperit esse virum
> viribus illa quidem victa est, ita credere oportet:
> sed voluit vinca viribus illa tamen. (1. 698–700)

In Fielding's version this becomes:

> He ravished her, that is the truth on't; that a gentleman ought to believe, in favour of the lady: but he may believe the lady was willing enough to be ravished at the same time.[161]

But Gay's perspective is very different, and distinctly feminine. Instead of dramatizing the rape of Deidamia, he shows us only its consequences – from a specifically female point of view – in her sense of shame and morning sickness. And instead of depicting Achilles as a rapist, he cross-casts him as the potential 'female' victim of rape. For the most original aspect of the play, not found in any of Gay's sources, is the subplot in which 'Pyrrha' becomes the object of King Lycomedes' obsessive lust. First he flatters 'her';

---

[161] Fielding, *Ovid's Art of Love Paraphrased, and Adapted to the Present Time: With Notes and a Most Correct Edition of the Original*, Bk. i (London, 1747), 79. See also Noble, in Lewis and Wood, 207.

then he tries to bribe 'her' with presents; finally, he is encouraged
by his minister, Diphilus, to attempt force.

DIPHILUS. . . . To save the appearances of virtue, the most easy
woman expects a little gentle compulsion, and to be allowed the
decency of a little feeble resistance.   (II. iii. 35–6)

There is some glorious burlesque comedy in the ensuing scene as
the lecherous monarch, confident of overpowering this innocent girl,
finds himself unceremoniously hurled to the ground. 'By a woman!'
he protests, incredulously. Gay creates a constant sense of comic
travesty with his depiction of the sulky Achilles (alias Pyrrha)
compelled into the stereotypical role of the innocent maiden; sitting
amid the sewing-circle, sharing awkwardly in their girl-talk; pursued
by predatory males and shunned by their jealous wives. 'That
Pyrrha, sir, was a most delicious piece,' remarks Diphilus to the
king, assuring him that ravishment is what the little piece 'longs
for'. Ajax too (a wonderfully comic set piece, all bluster and repetition) is smitten, peremptorily threatening to fight duels for Pyrrha's
favours. 'When shall I appear as I am?' Achilles protests at one
point, maddened by these constant male attentions: 'I have no
sooner escaped being ravished but am immediately to be made a
wife' (II. x. 65–8). The theatrical vogue for such travesty roles was
well established and much of this gender-bending comedy is conventional enough. There are a number of predictable *double entendres*,
alluding coyly to Pyrrha's hidden male organ, most notably when
Lycomedes' guards begin to search 'her' for a 'dagger . . . you will
find . . . somewhere or other concealed' (II. v). As Mandeville
observed, the stage had long assumed a licence for flouting the
conventional rules of sexual decorum.

If a woman at a merry-making dresses in man's clothes, it is reckoned a
frolic among friends, and he that finds too much fault with it is counted
censorious. Upon the stage it is done without reproach, and the most
virtuous ladies will dispense with it in an actress, though everybody has a
full view of her legs and thighs; but if the same woman, as soon as she has
petticoats on again, should show her leg to a man as high as her knee, it
would be a very immodest action, and everybody will call her impudent for
it.[162]

---

[162] *The Fable of the Bees* (1714, 1723), 'Remarks (P)'.

Yet, even within this atmosphere of relative sexual licence, Gay's role-reversal theme, subjecting his Homeric hero to the status of a powerless female, has a dangerously anarchic force. And it is significant that, when Handel chose the same story for his last opera, *Deidamia* (1741), his librettist, Rolli, adopted an altogether more heroic and more masculine perspective. In Rolli's version men are the prime movers. King Lycomedes is privy to the secret of Achilles' true identity from the start, having agreed to the deception with Achilles' father Peleus.

We might notice that the goddess Thetis, whom antique plots were able to tolerate, if only to thwart, is obliterated in Rolli's heroic plot in favour of her mortal, but male spouse: Lycomedes can be bound, against the claims of Ulysses, by an oath to Peleus, as he cannot by a promise to a female, a mother.[163]

Rolli's theme is manliness and his *primo uomo* is Ulysses, who discerns, beneath Achilles' female disguise, the lineaments of a fellow warrior. But Gay, by refusing to admit any of the male characters into the secret of Achilles' disguise, and by delaying until the last possible moment—the tenth scene of the final act—the disclosure of his 'true' sexual identity, makes his play not an affirmation of heroic virility, but an exploration of gender itself. Superficially the play is full of anti-female remarks; one critic complains that it is 'studded' with 'sharp and even misogynistic comments.'[164] But in the context of the play's ambiguous sexuality such remarks take on an ironic force. Characters constantly express confident opinions on the distinctive traits of maleness and femaleness which imply an inherently gendered view of social reality. For Achilles, manliness is synonymous with honour, character, fame, and martial glory; it is an essential and immutable inner quality, residing in 'the heart of a man' (I. i. 14–15). 'But my character! my honour! Would you have your son live with infamy?' he protests in his first speech, resisting his mother's plan. As 'Pyrrha' he is equally clear about gender distinctions: 'The spleen, madam', he/she declares to Artemona, as they sit together sewing, 'is a female frailty that I have no pretensions to' (I. ii. 52). Other characters are equally clear-cut in making their gendered distinctions. 'The tongue is a woman's

163 Noble, in Lewis and Wood, 193.
164 Sven M. Armens, *John Gay: Social Critic* (New York, 1954), 142–6.

weapon,' declares Ajax, who naturally prefers the sword (III. i. 18); 'She is a woman, madam', remarks Philoe of Deidamia (III. vii. 50), encompassing in that single term an infinite variety of coquettish deceits. 'Think of dress in ev'ry light; | 'Tis woman's chiefest duty,' trills Artemona (III. vii. 7–8), convinced that fashionable clothes not only attract male approval but also bring 'inward satisfaction'. 'Have you only a womanish fondness?' Achilles demands of Deidamia, adding: 'you cannot truly love and esteem, if in every circumstance of life you have not a just regard for my honour' (II. x. 105–8). 'Honour' is the inner proof of masculinity, just as a 'womanish fondness' is the inherent quality of femaleness. Yet the play's satiric strategy constantly undermines these confident distinctions. Deprived of its outward symbol the sword, masculine 'honour' becomes a far more uncertain thing. Ironically, Gay makes the establishment of an individual's sexual identity dependent not upon inner conviction but upon outward recognition. Subjectively, Achilles may believe that maleness is an inherent quality in 'the heart of a man'; but dressed in woman's petticoats he becomes a symbol of the anarchic force of the sub-conscious to generate its own sexual reality. Characters see in him/her exactly what their desires and fears dictate. Deidamia fears that his disguise will fail to deceive the other women because 'whenever I look upon you, I have always the image of a man before my eyes' (II. x. 97–8). Lycomedes sees a nubile girl, a 'most delicious piece'; Theaspe, the jealous wife, declares: 'I see her as a woman sees a woman' (I. vi. 15–16), that is, as a sexual rival. 'Pyrrha' is a human *What D'Ye Call It*, an amorphous hermaphrodite whose dangerous allure hints at the protean nature of desire. Just as Gay had parodied the generic rules that divided tragedy from comedy to produce his own satiric hybrids, he now deconstructs the gendered boundaries of male and female to create his own subversive travesty. ''Tis to the armour we owe Achilles', comments Ulysses (III. xii. 79), inadvertently confirming that maleness is a matter of costume rather than character.

But Achilles/Pyrrha is not the only one whose sexual identity is compromised. Similar hints of cross-gender satire affect other characters too. The men feel each other's fluttering hearts with a kind of girlish excitement. 'Diphilus, lay your hand upon my heart,' says Lycomedes. 'Feel how my heart flutters' (II. iii, 44–5). Ulysses is reduced to a travelling salesman in ladies' wear and fancy goods with a patter that recalls Gay's days on the New Exchange: 'I would not offer you these pearls, ladies, if the world could produce such another pair' (III. x. 45–6). It is the women, notably Thetis and Theaspe, who are revealed as the most ruthlessly 'masculine' politicians. In his prologue Gay draws attention to the mock-heroic implications of treating his Homeric characters in this comic way.

His scene now shows the heroes of old Greece;
But how? 'tis monstrous! In a comic piece?
To buskins, plumes and helmets what pretence,
If mighty chiefs must speak but common sense?
Shall no bold diction, no poetic rage,
Foam at our mouths and thunder on the stage?
No—'Tis Achilles, as he came from Chiron,
Just taught to sing as well as wield cold iron;
And whatsoever critics may suppose,
Our author holds, that what he spoke was prose. (ll. 15–24)

Armed with the buskins, plumes, and helmet of his restored masculinity, Achilles is still unmanned, compelled to express himself not with the bold diction and cold iron of heroic verse but in a feminized prose. 'In a tongue-combat woman is invincible,' comments Periphas; 'and the husband must come off with shame and infamy.' Even the final disclosure of Achilles' 'real' identity is reduced to a mock-heroic motif. The words of Ulysses' final air, sung to the music of Corelli's saraband and minuet, comically undermine this climactic moment of male self-assertion.

ULYSSES. Thus when the cat had once all woman's graces;
    Courtship, marriage won her embraces:
Forth leapt a mouse; she, forgetting enjoyment,
    Quits her fond spouse for her former
        employment.

CHORUS
Nature breaks forth at the moment unguarded;
    Through all disguise she herself must
        betray
Heav'n with success hath our labours rewarded;
    Let's with Achilles our genius obey.

The irresistible force of nature 'breaking forth' is reduced to this comic image of a cat chasing mice. And it is specifically a *female* cat, whose switch from 'enjoyment' to 'employment' demonstrates not instinctive resolution, but feline fickleness. By drawing this analogy between Achilles' heroic 'genius' and the playful instincts of a female domestic pet, Gay hardly affirms the honour and courage of natural masculinity. Perhaps there was not such a vast distance between the conqueror of Hector and the poet who presented himself in the feminine disguise of a compliant hare.

In the event it seems that the effort, both physical and psychological, of such self-disclosure was too much for Gay to bear. On 1 December, less than a fortnight after delivering *Achilles* to the theatre, he fell victim to a sudden fever. Three days later he was dead.

In his final letter to Swift, written just three weeks before his death, Gay hinted at some enduring preoccupations. Swift loved to caricature Gay as an idle social butterfly; a man who wrote about walking, but whose most strenuous exertion was lolling in a coach-and-six; a man who railed against courts yet dissipated his literary talents by hankering after court preferments. Repudiating these familiar charges, Gay insisted:

I have not been [idle] while I was in the country, and I know your wishes in general and in particular that industry may always find its account.[165]

Gay's contrast of industry and idleness here has the same emblematic quality that Hogarth was later to represent in a series of moralistic prints. The counter-jumper who, twenty-five years earlier, had forsaken the life of trade for the lure of poetry and patrons here reclaims the role of the industrious, not the idle, apprentice. In these, the final words he ever wrote, Gay makes atonement to the despised values of Barnstaple, placing native industry above the temptations of idleness and ease.

[165] *Letters*, 132.

Epilogue

KNOWING Swift's instinctive dread of the emotional entanglements of bereavement, Arbuthnot conveyed the news of Gay's death in brief factual terms.

Poor Mr Gay died of an inflammation, and I believe at last a mortification of the bowels; it was the most precipitate case I ever knew, having cut him off in three days. He was attended by two physicians besides myself. I believed the distemper mortal from the beginning.[1]

Pope, typically, offered a more pathetic account of Gay's final hours. He told Swift that 'he asked of you a few hours before [his death], when in acute torment by the inflammation in his bowels and breast . . . Good God! how often are we to die before we go off this stage? In every friend we lose a part of ourselves.'[2] In a subsequent letter to Caryll, Pope left it ambiguous whether it was he or Martha Blount who was at Gay's bedside when he died.

Your god-daughter has been very ill. I no sooner saw the death of my old friend Mr Gay, whom I attended in his last sickness (it was but three days), but she fell very ill, partly occasioned by the shock his death gave her.

Sherburn comments:

one must feel that Pope does not here intend to say that he was at Gay's bedside when he died. Possibly Miss Blount was. The sentence would be more naturally coherent if Pope had written, '*She* no sooner saw the death . . . but she fell very ill.'[3]

The ambiguity is highly characteristic. Pope, who, throughout Gay's

[1] Swift, *Corr.* iv. 88.
[2] Pope, *Corr.* iii. 335.
[3] Ibid. 337 and note.

life, had liked to present himself as Gay's indispensable mentor and
guide, here claims the role of death-bed friend and counsellor,
sharing the intimacy of Gay's last hours. Who else but he should
have the privilege of hearing Gay's last words, and offering final
unction? For much of his life Gay had striven to escape the shadow
of Pope's well-meaning literary supervision. In death he could no
longer resist being accommodated as a symbolic innocent into the
mythopoeic landscape of his friend's literary world.

The symbolism began with Gay's funeral. Stage-managed by his
aristocratic friends, the funeral was a pompous demonstration of
those honours so constantly denied to him in life. First his body was
ceremoniously carried by the Company of Upholders from the Duke
of Queensberry's house to lie in state at Exeter Exchange in the
Strand, near where Gay had been a bound apprentice thirty years
before. Thence, late at night on 23 December, it was 'drawn in a
hearse, trimmed with plumes of black and white feathers, attended
with three mourning coaches and six horses to Westminster Abbey'.[4]
The *Weekly Miscellany* gives this account of the funeral rites.

On Saturday night last, about 11 o'clock, the corpse of John Gay, Esq.,
author of *The Beggar's Opera* and several other fine poetical pieces, was
(after lying in state in Exeter Exchange) carried to Westminster Abbey, and
there interred with great pomp and solemnity. The pall was supported by
the Right Hon. the Earl of Chesterfield, the Lord Cornbury, the Hon.
George Berkeley, the Hon. Levison Gower, Esq; General Dormer, and
Alexander Pope, Esq., and the funeral was attended by several persons of
distinction.[5]

As Arbuthnot remarked sardonically to Swift, Gay was buried 'as if
he had been a peer of the realm . . . These are little affronts put
upon vice and injustice and is all that remains in our power.'[6] The
solemn farce of such posthumous honours seemed almost calculated
to endorse Gay's ironic epitaph for himself:

> Life is a jest; and all things show it,
> I thought so once; but now I know it.

Belated elegiac tributes continued with the production of *Achilles*,
which opened at the Covent Garden theatre on 10 February 1733,

---

[4] Edmund Curll, *The Life of John Gay* (London, 1733), 72.
[5] *Weekly Miscellany*, 30 Dec. 1732.
[6] Swift, *Corr.* iv. 101.

just seven weeks after Gay's funeral. The Prince of Wales attended on the second night, and the play enjoyed a considerable success, with nineteen performances in its first season. But already the tradition of 'honouring' Gay by denying him the authorship of his own works was well established. Since Pope, together with the Duke of Queensberry, undertook the 'management' of *Achilles* in rehearsal, the play was barely acknowledged to be Gay's work at all. The *Daily Courant* assured its readers that *Achilles* had been left unfinished at Gay's death. 'Mr Gay', it confidently pronounced, 'could not deviate into so much dulness. He had the plan given him, but unhappily died, the play unfinished, and the songs not wrote.' In what was clearly an exercise in political point-scoring, the paper then proceeded to identify the handiwork of all the leading opposition figures, including Bolingbroke, Wyndham, Pulteney, Queensberry, Arbuthnot, and Pope. Gay's cat was ascribed to Arbuthnot ('The Scot insists on eternizing the memory of his cat'), no doubt in tribute to Nelly Bennet's puss; while Pope was credited with finishing the piece ('the little satirist tags the verse, and points the song'). Ten days later another critic, 'Atex Burnet', repeated these assertions, claiming, in particular, that the prologue 'was written by Mr Pope'.[7] The fact that, in the printed version of the play, published on 1 March 1733, the prologue is clearly headed 'Written by Mr GAY' has not prevented modern scholars from endorsing Burnet's claim.[8] In this way the habit of literary expropriation, begun in political mischief-making and confirmed by well-meaning myths, achieves the final authority of scholarly canon law. Yet *Achilles* is an intensely personal play encoding, in its comic motifs, several of Gay's most enduring preoccupations; and every detail of the work, from its title-page mottoes to its final chorus, bears Gay's own distinctive hallmark. The prologue is no exception:

> I wonder not our author doubts success,
> One in his circumstances can do no less . . .
> I own I dread his ticklish situation,
> Critics detest poetic innovation.

---

[7] *Achilles Dissected: Being a Compleat Key of the Political Characters . . . With Remarks on the Whole: By Mr Burnet* (1733), 2.

[8] 'Unquestionably', writes Norman Ault, 'the Prologue reads like Pope.' For Ault, the very publication of the claim that the prologue was 'Written by Mr GAY' tends to prove the opposite. 'For, unquestionably . . . that is a quite abnormal and uncalled-for caption

These lines clearly derive from the exchange between Swift and Gay the previous July. At that time Swift warned: 'The present humour of the players, who hardly ... regard any new play, and your present situation at the court, are the difficulties to be overcome, but those circumstances may have altered.'[9] To this, Gay replied: 'I look upon the success in every respect to be precarious. You judge very rightly of my present situation.'[10] These are the sentiments, and even the vocabulary, repeated in the prologue, and they defy the suggestion that anyone but Gay wrote it.

In itself this is a relatively trivial matter, yet it brings us squarely back to the issue we began with; namely, the persistent tendency to deny Gay's full responsibility for the works which bear his name. Long delayed, deeply considered, and barely mentioned to even his closest friends, Gay's last plays, owning and acknowledging experiences and values which he had spent a lifetime denying, are personal statements which Gay found it almost impossible to offer for public scrutiny. And it is peculiarly appropriate that they should have been produced posthumously, just at a time when his friends were already doing all in their power to authorize their own official, sanitized version of Gay's career. Pope had read *Achilles*, and pronounced it 'of his very best manner, a true original'. But Swift, who seems to have detected in the play the hint of a damaging

---

[and] difficult to explain ... except on the hypothesis that it was a last-minute insertion by Pope to circumvent 'Burnet's' unauthorized attribution of the piece to him, and so preserve his threatened anonymity' ('Help for Gay', in Ault, 219). In fact Ault's hypothesis is both unnecessary and misconceived. It was common practice for prologues to serve as a kind of introductory compliment, supplied at the last minute (to allow for topical asides) by a playwright's friend. Since Gay had been dead for two months by the time of *Achilles*' first performance, Burnet's ascription of the prologue to Pope would have seemed entirely consistent with convention. And, since the piece itself is utterly uncontroversial in its sentiments, there is no reason why Pope, if he had written it, should have shrunk from acknowledging this posthumous courtesy to his friend. It is precisely *because* the attribution of the piece to Pope would have seemed so natural that the printed insistence that it was in fact written by Gay himself is neither 'curious' nor 'supererogatory' (Ault calls it 'curious', p. 219; Fuller calls it 'supererogatory', ii. 390). Ault goes on to find 'internal evidence' of verbal parallels between the prologue and phrases used in Pope's *Imitations of Horace* published just 'five days after the performance of *Achilles*' (p. 219). But again, there is no reason to assume that Pope was here echoing phrases that he had recently *written* rather than phrases he had recently *read*. Moreover, since the closest verbal parallels allude ironically to the subliterary 'fire and force' of Gay's former rival Eustace Budgell, one may even suspect a vicarious act of literary retribution on Pope's part; borrowing a phrase of Gay's to satirize a mutual foe.

[9] Swift to Gay, 10 July 1732; Swift, *Corr.* iv. 39.
[10] Gay to Swift, 24 July 1732; *Letters*, 124.

exposure, took a very different view. He wrote angrily to Pope:

I heartily wish his Grace had entirely stifled that comedy if it were possible, than do an injury to our friend's reputation only to get a hundred or two pounds to a couple of (perhaps) insignificant women. It hath been printed here, and I am grieved to say, it is a very poor performance ... I think it is incumbent upon you to see that nothing more be published of his that will lessen his reputation, for the sake of adding a few pence to his sisters, who have already got so much by his death. If the case were mine, my ashes would rise in judgment against you.[11]

Gay's ashes did not rise in judgement, but were entombed beneath a pompous momument in Westminster Abbey, surmounted by a handsome bust by Rysbrack. On this monument, Gay's own wry self-mocking epitaph was relegated to an inferior position in favour of Pope's formal inscription, which inaugurated the process of transforming the man into a myth.

> Of manners gentle, of affections mild;
> In wit, a man; simplicity, a child;
> With native humour temp'ring virtuous rage,
> Form'd to delight at once and lash the age;
> Above temptation, in a low estate,
> And uncorrupted, ev'n among the great;
> A safe companion, and an easy friend,
> Unblam'd through life, lamented in thy end.
> These are thy honours! not that here thy bust
> Is mix'd with heroes, or with kings thy dust;
> But that the worthy and the good shall say,
> Striking their pensive bosoms—here lies GAY.

The motives which led Pope and the Duke and Duchess of Queensberry to superimpose this frozen tribute to a childlike paragon over Gay's own terse epigram are well illustrated by Johnson's hostile reaction to Gay's couplet. 'I have been often offended', he reported, 'with the trifling distich upon Mr Gay's monument in Westminster Abbey.' This he conjectures to have been

a drunken sally, which was perhaps, after midnight, applauded as a lively epigram, and might have preserved its reputation had it, instead of being engraved on a monument in Westminster, been scribbled in its proper place, the window of a brothel. There are very different species of wit appropriated to particular persons and places; the smartness of a shoeboy would not be extremely agreeable in a chancellor, and a tavern joke sounds but ill in a church.[12]

In elevating Gay to the symbolic status of an innocent child of nature, Pope contrived to purge away the taint of social gaucherie that often marked Gay's larkish shoe-boy wit. But such snobbish endeavours at posthumous propriety represent a denial of Gay's essential character. Throughout his life Gay had broken the rules of literary decorum, determined to demonstrate that 'the sentiments of princes and clowns have not in reality that difference which they seem to have'. The man who mingled street-ballads with grand opera, and who found in Newgate prison the perfect model for the modes of the court, saw no great distinction between tavern jokes and the solemn riddle of death.

Pope's efforts had their desired effect. His solemnizing lines on Gay's 'neglected genius' perpetuated the myth of a blameless innocent, martyred by a cruel world.[13] Simultaneously, the poetess Mary Barber, no stranger herself to struggles for patronage, revived the image of Gay as the poor neglected hare in her nursery poem *A True Tale*. In this poem, a mother gives her infant son Gay's *Fables* to read, but the boy is so shocked by the story of Gay's sad plight that she feels obliged to offer this comforting reassurance.

> This has been yet Gay's case, I own,
> But now his merit's amply known:
> Content that tender heart of thine,
> He'll be the care of Caroline.
> Who thus instructs the royal race,
> Must have a pension, or a place.
> —Mamma, if you were Queen, says he,
> And such a book were wrote for me,
> I find, 'tis so much to your taste,
> That Gay would keep his coach at least.
> . . . What I'd bestow, says she, my dear?
> At least, a thousand pounds a year.[14]

---

[12] 'On Gay's Epitaph', in a Letter from 'Pamphilus' in the *Gentleman's Magazine*, Oct. 1738. Many years later Johnson was almost equally disparaging about Pope's epitaph for Gay; see his 'Life of Pope'.

[13] *Epistle to Dr Arbuthnot*, ll. 255–60.

[14] *Poems on Several Occasions* (1734), 11–12.

As a child-like martyr Gay's posthumous reputation soon acquired the trappings of sainthood. Holy relics from his infancy were proudly displayed. There was his name, carved on the pew in Barnstaple church. And in 1819 a 'curiously formed chair', once allegedly Gay's own possession, was discovered by a Barnstaple cabinet-maker, with a secret drawer containing a hoard of Gay's unpublished manuscripts. The fact that these manuscripts were actually elaborate forgeries only confirms the iconic status that this local hero had attained.[15]

Visitors to Westminster Abbey, hoping to strike their pensive bosoms before Gay's monument, are in for a disappointment. In 1939 some medieval wall paintings were discovered behind the south wall of Poet's Corner and Gay's monument was removed to an obscure and inaccessible safekeeping in the triforium, where it is not available for view. In recent years, admirers of Gay have campaigned gallantly for a restoration of his monument to some more prominent position where 'the stones [might] speak again'.[16] Yet, although their motives are impeccable, their enthusiasm may be misplaced. In fact, it seems oddly appropriate that a poet whose life was spent in self-effacing gestures should, even in death, vacate his place of honour to some more stately rival in the temple of fame. Almost certainly Gay would have relished the irony that his monument should stand, not amid the ostentatious tombs of kings, courtiers, and statesmen, but forgotten and unseen in a dusty attic store-room.

Gay is best remembered not through relics and monuments, nor even through the rhetorical tributes of his more celebrated friends, but through the living force of his work. With his instinct for breaking the literary rules, he was in many ways a man ahead of his time. 'Film might have been his salvation,' writes one critic, noting that *The Mohocks*, a play about street gangs, with music, was two-and-a-half centuries ahead of *West Side Story*.[17] Nowadays it tends to be Brecht, with his *Threepenny Opera*, rather than Pope or Swift, who steals the limelight away. But, as the recent triumphant RSC production of *The Beggar's Opera* proved, Gay's work loses nothing, either in theatrical power, or political subtlety, by comparison with

[15] The best discussion of the 'Poems from Gay's Chair' is by G. C. Faber in his edition of *The Poetical Works of John Gay* (Oxford, 1926), appendix v, pp. 671–89.
[16] See Yvonne Noble, 'John Gay's Monument', in Lewis and Wood, 216–18.
[17] Winton, 169.

his twentieth-century imitator. Even as I write, Vaclav Havel's version of *The Beggar's Opera* is being filmed in Prague, a work which the President of the Czech Republic composed during his own experience of political prison. Sadly, the parallel between politicians and mobsters has lost none of its pertinency over the centuries. Which minister now would be brave enough to stand up and call for an encore of Gay's celebrated song?

> When you censure the age,
> Be cautious and sage,
> Lest the courtiers offended should be:
> If you mention vice or bribe,
> 'Tis so pat to all the tribe;
> Each cries—that was levell'd at me.

APPENDIX

Unpublished and Uncollected Letters

1. Letters transcribed by Gay as official secretary to Lord Clarendon, Envoy Extraordinary to the Elector of Hanover, 1714

(*a*) 7 August 1714

This letter (BL Stowe MSS 242, fos. 61–2) from Lord Clarendon in Hanover to Secretary Bromley in London is written entirely in Gay's hand. Britain still retained the 'Old Style' Julian calendar, but Gay's letters from Hanover are dated according to the 'New Style' Gregorian calendar, which was eleven days ahead of 'Old Style'. This letter, dated 7 August (New Style), was actually sent four days before Queen Anne's death, though the continued assertions of her excellent health, and Princess Caroline's hope that 'she would enjoy good health many years', indicate the political sensitivity of this subject.

Hanover August 7th N.S. 1714

Sr

On Saturday last I had my first Audience of the Elector at Noon at Herrenhausen. He received me in a Room where he was alone, a Gentleman of the Court came to my Lodgings here with two of the Electors Coaches and carried me to Herrenhausen. I was met at my alighting out of the Coach by Mr D'Harenberg Marshall of the Court and at the top of the Stairs by Chevalier Reden, second Chamberlain, the Count de Plaaten, Great Chamberlain being sick. He conducted me through three rooms to the room where the Elector was, who met [me] at the door of that room & being returned three or four steps into that room he stopped and the door was shut. I then delivered my Credentials to him, and made him a Compliment from the Queen, to which he answered, that he had always had the greatest Veneration imaginable for the Queen, that he was always ready to acknowledge the great Obligations he, and his Family have to her Majesty, and that he desired nothing more earnestly than to entertain a good correspondence with her. He asked me whether I left the Queen in good Health, that he wished her Health very heartily. I told him that when I had the Honour to take leave of the Queen, I left her in very good health, that I had received letters from England since my Arrival here, by which I was informed that the Queen continued to enjoy her Health. I told him I was very glad to find his Highness so well inclined, and that I desired I might have a private Audience as soon as possible, that I might have an opportunity of acquainting him fully with what I had received in Command from the Queen. To this he answered, that he was very sorry that the king of Prussia's coming had hindered him so long from seeing me, that he did not desire to delay one Minute longer the receiving her Majesty's Commands, and that I was at liberty to say then, all that I had in Command from her. I then delivered to him the Queen's Answer to his Memorial, and the other Letter, and I spoke upon all the Heads contained in my Instructions, and in your letter of the 22d of June O.S. when I told him that as the Queen had already done all that could be done to secure the Succession to her Crown to his Family, so she expected that if he has any reason to suspect Designs are carrying on to disapoint it, he should speak plainly upon that Subject. He interrupted me, and said these words; Je n'ay jamais cru que la Reine eust aucuns desseins contre les Intérêts de ma Famille, et je ne seache pas d'avoir donné aucun sujet de croire, que je voulusse rien entreprendre contre les Intérêts de sa Majesté, ou que pust luy déplaire, c'est ce que je ne feray jamais. La Reine m'a fait l'honneur de m'escrire pour scavoir ce que [je] souhaitais que l'on fist pour asseurer d'avantage la Succession, surquoy nous avons donné un Mémoire par Escrit à Monsieur Harley, à laquelle il n'y a point encore eu de response. I told him I had just then had the Honour to deliver to him an Answer to that Memorial, and that if when he had perused that Answer, he desired to have any part of that Answer explained, I did believe I should be able to do it to his Satisfaction. Then I proceeded to speak upon the other Points, and when I came to mention Schutz demanding the Writ for the Duke of Cambridge, he said these words; J'espère que la Reine n'a pas cru que cela c'est fait par mon ordre. Je vous asseure que cela a esté fait à mon Insceu, la défunte Électrice avait escrit à Schutz, sans que j'aye sceu, pour s'informer pourquoy le Prince n'avoit pas eu son writ, puisqu'elle croyait qu'on les envoyait à tous ceux qui estoit Pairs, et luy au lieu de cela, alla demander le writ, mesme sans l'ordre de L'Électrice. Je ne feray rien qui puisse en aucune façon choquer la Reine, à qui nous avons tant d'obligations. My speaking to him and the answers he made me, took up something above an hour, then I had audience of the Electoral Prince and Duke Ernest the Elector's Brother in the same Room, then of the Electoral Princess. After that I had the Honour to dine with them all, and after Dinner, here in Town had audience of the Electoral Prince's son and two Daughters. At Dinner the Elector seemed to be in very good humour, talked to me several times, asked several Questions about England, and seemed very willing to be informed. It is very plane to me, he knows very little of our Constitution, and seems to be sensible that he has been imposed upon. The Electoral Prince told me he thought himself very happy, that the Queen had him in her thoughts, that he should be very glad it were in his Power to convince the Queen how gratefull a sense he had of all her favours. Duke Ernest said the Queen did him a great deal of honour to remember him, that he most heartily wished the continuance of her Majesty's health, and hope no one of his Family would ever be so ungratefull as to forget the very great Obligations they all had to her. The Electoral Princess said she was very glad to hear the Queen was well, she hoped she would enjoy good health many years, that her Kindness to this Family was so great, that they could never make sufficient acknowledgements for it. Thus I have acquainted you with all that passed at the first Audience, I have been at Court here every night since, for the time of making ones court here is from six to Nine in the Evening. To morrow I intend to desire a private Audience in order to discourse more fully upon what I have said to him, and to see how he takes the Queen's Answer to his Memorial. All the Ministers here (except Mr Buleau who is not in town) have been in with me, and make great Professions of Respect for the Queen. I have returned all their Visits, and have dealt so plainly with them, as to tell them, that I am very glad to find them in so good a disposition, and rather because they will now have an opportunity to prove their faith by their Works. The Muscovite Envoy and the Polish Envoy have sent to me, hearing I had sent to notifie my Arrival to them. They are just come to town, and I suppose I shall see them to morrow. I believe by this time I have pretty well tired you, so I shall conclude in intreating the favour of you to give my most humble Duty to the Queen, whom I pray God long to preserve.

I am, Sir, Your most faithfull Humble Sert,
Clarendon.

(*b*) BL Stowe MSS 242, fo. 163
Letter dated 15 August NS 1714, from Envoy
Extraordinary Clarendon in Hanover to Secretary Bromley in London; written in Gay's hand. News of the Queen's death, four days earlier, has still not reached the Hanoverian court.

Hanover August 15 n.s. 1714

Sr

I trouble you with this letter by Mr Barlow. I gave you in my letter of the 7th Instant n.s. an Account of the Answers the Elector made to me at my first Audience, I did not then send you an Account of what I said to him, in pursuance of the Queen's Instructions to me, and the Letter I received from you afterwards. I now send it to you in the same words I spoke to him for the Answers you will give me leave to refer you to my

Letter of the 7th Instant. I hope and I think I have not omitted any thing that I was to speak to, if I have not done it in so good language as abler People would have done, I hope I shall be pardoned that. I thought upon this occasion the plainest language was the best, so that if I had been able to do better, I should have been guilty of the same I have done, that it might not be pretended they could not understand me. Mr Berensdorff is govern'd by Robethon who is as bad as bad can be, I have been twice with Mr Berensdorff since my second Audience, he has promised me I shall have an Answer in Writing to what I said to the Elector, when I see that I shall be able to say more. The Elector continues still to say, every time I speak to him that he is ready on his Part to do any Thing to preserve a good Correspondence with the Queen, that he has nor will have no dependence upon any body but the Queen. I told him I hoped he would give these Assurances to her Majesty in the best and fullest Manner, he seems to be a Man of very good temper, the People here generally speak with great Value of him, and his Brother Duke Ernest. It is certain the Elector has never yet spoken to Shutz since he came home, he comes to court in the Evening, but as soon as the Elector appears he goes away, and indeed no body here looks upon him, except the Electoral Prince, and that is in private. Mr Guerts who is President des Finances is a very good Man and always in opposition to Berensdorff, the Count de Blaaten who is great Chamberlain is a fine Gentleman but never meddles with business, Mr Delse and Mr Busch who are two others of ye Council, are men that meddle no farther than they are called upon by the Elector, there are no other Counsellors now here; by what I can he[a]r, I find that the King of Prussia's Journey here was to endeavour to engage this Court in the Project I took the Liberty to mention to you in a Letter from the Hague for dividing the King of Prussia's Territorys in Germany, but I don't find he has succeeded here. The Elector talks of going in three Weeks time, to a place called Vinhousen, and from thence to Guevre, a place where he goes every year to hunt the stag, and stays all the fall of the Year, so that if I am not dispatcht before he goes out of town, I must either follow him to those Places which will be very chargeable to me, or I must stay here till Winter, which I hope the Queen does not intend. I entreat the favour of you, that Mr Barlow may be sent back to me as soon as possible with such farther Commands as the Queen has for me here if any. I suppose in a few days I shall have the Elector's Answer in writing, which I hope will be to the Queen's satisfaction, if so, I suppose I have no more to do here, however I beg the favour of you that I may know the Queen's Commands as soon as possible. This Moon I believe will put an end to whatever might be called Summer in this Country, so it will not be long good travelling in this part of the World. I entreat the favour of you to give [my] most humble Duty to the Queen whom I pray God long to preserve. I have had no Letters nor News from England these two last Posts. I am with great respect, Sr,

Your most obedient humble servant,

Clarendon.

2. Letter from Gay to the Blount sisters at Mapledurham, written in the persona of a 'horse' (1715/17)

My two fair and honoured Ladys.

Though you may at first be in some Surprise at my Hand, yet your wonder will soon cease when I tell you that I am your Horse of Mapledurham, who had the Misfortune to be sent into Devonshire with a Poet on my Back; I have thought fit as in Duty bound not only to acquaint you with my present Wellfare, but also to give you some Account of my Adventures in this long and perilous Journey. in the first place, upon his mounting me, I took a survey of my Rider, and as I found him a somewhat fat and corpulent Person, I, out of my great Civility, took a special Care, to jog on a good hard Trot the better to reduce him into Shape at his Return to London. I concluded him to be a good Catholic for two Reasons; for his frequent mentioning the Word, Pope, and his making many Crosses upon my Sides with his Whip. I travell'd on for the two first Days very melancholy, for what Horse could do otherways, when as he saw such delicate Cocks of Hay lye spoiling on ev'ry Side of him? The last Day I travell'd in Company with a very beautifull dappled Mare, which made me more than ever regret the melancholy Circumstances of a Gentleman that I often heard you talk off, (I think they call him Nicolini) and myself. I could tell you of Stony Roads, dreadfull Precipices, and such like things; but what are all those to fine Ladys? Yet I cannot forbear acquainting you that I pass'd through all those Difficultys, jst as your Ladyships walk among the Temptations of this World, without making the least false Step. As we pass'd through a certain Town I overheard my Master say to his Friend that he should have thought the Ladys there the prettiest he ever saw, had he never been at Maple-durham. One day he lighted from me to kiss a Damsell by the Wayside, her lips were like a scarlet Poppy, her Complexion was fair as the Daisy, her Eyes black as the Sloe, and her Cheeks shining like the brass Bosses of a new Bridle, her Breath was as sweet as a Cows, for you must know that I once kiss'd one by Mistake in the Dark. In the Struggle her straw Hat fell off, which, being at that time very hungry, and having nothing else to do I happen'd unluckily to eat up.. I saw my Master give Her a half Guinea which I suppose was to make her Amends. Upon my settling in the Country, I was put into a large common Field, among several other Horses of Note; where, the better to discover the Secrets of the Parish I struck up an intimate Acquaintance with the Parson's Mare, who made great Complaint to me of his being tyd to An Ale house door on Sundays, & of his carrying double ev'ry Market Day. I have seen several young Men and young Maids together under the Hedges and heard Words not fit to be repeated to Ladys; but I have not as yet seen my Master here, perhaps because he knows that I am acquainted with you, and that all Women are fond of a Secret. I am in great Hopes of meeting my old Master's Hunter at the Bath, because I heard my new One talk of seeing Mr Blount there and I should no less rejoice to see our Coach Horses whom I envy the honour of drawing your Ladyships. Believe me, Ladys, there is no two leg'd Animal half so much as I am

Your most faithfull Humble Servt.
Horse.

First printed, though with some transcription errors, by Maynard Mack in *Scriblerian*, II/I (Autumn 1978), 1–3.

3. Letter from Gay at Bath to Lord Burlington, 3 October 1722 (Chatsworth MSS 173.O)

I have every post day thought I neglected a duty in not writing to your Lordship, though whatever I might say or do can never sufficiently acknowledge my obligations; I believe I need to say this for I hope your Lordship knows me; if you do, you must know that I love you. I have now drank the waters six weeks, but have still my daily complaint, I have left them off for a few days and then shall begin them again, & continue to drink them till the Dutchess leaves this place which I guess will not be till about three weeks hence. Mr Pulteney & Mrs Pulteney Mr Berkeley Dr Arbuthnot left the Bath this morning and the company diminishes every day, but this is not of much importance to me for I live mostly at home. Mr Congreve has had a severe fit of the gout, but is now upon the recovery. If you knew how often I think upon your Lordship you would now then think of me [*sic*] I hope you will not forget me, for I know my heart so well that it will be always sensible of your favours, though I must own I love you more for what I see in yourself than for what you have done for me, wch is much more than I can ever deserve. I am, my Lord, your lordships & Lady Burlington's most obedient most faithful servant   J G

ps I beg my compliments to Lady Jane and Lady Harriet and Mr Bataillier . . . [*passage erased*] I writ to him last post as if we had held a correspondence ever since I came here.

The Dutchess & Mrs Bellenden desire me to make their compliments to your Lordship & Lady Burlington.

(My attention was drawn to this letter by Professor W. A. Speck of Leeds University.)

4. Memorandum of Mr Gay relative to the differences existing between Mrs Howard and Mr Howard (Saturday, 16 December 1727) (BL Add. MSS 22626, fos. 33–4)

Burgess prints the bulk of this memorandum, taken from fo. 33 of the Suffolk letter-book, in his edition of Gay's *Letters* (pp. 133–4). However, he neglected to include this final sentence, which appears on the following page (fo. 34).

He mention'd Mr. Howard's having not above four hundred a year, Ld Suffolk's annuity being paid; she answer'd she had not many times, while with him, known where to get four hundred pence.

SELECT BIBLIOGRAPHY

THIS is intended not as a comprehensive bibliography of Gay's life and works, but as a guide to further reading which includes all the most significant twentieth-century works of scholarship, criticism, and commentary on Gay's career.

EDITIONS

John Gay: Dramatic Works, ed. John Fuller (2 vols., Oxford, 1983). The standard modern scholarly edition.

John Gay: Poetry and Prose, ed. V. A. Dearing, with the assistance of C. E. Beckwith (2 vols., Oxford, 1974). The most recent scholarly edition, which adopts a conservative attitude to the canon of Gay's writings.

The Letters of John Gay, ed. C. F. Burgess (Oxford, 1966).

The Poetical Works of John Gay, ed. G. C. Faber (London, 1926). Although largely superseded by the editions of Fuller and Dearing, Faber's edition is valuable for its scholarly introduction, and for its inclusion of the 1713 version of *Rural Sports* and of several 'Poems of Doubtful Authenticity' omitted by Dearing.

The Beggar's Opera, ed. Peter Elfred Lewis (Edinburgh, 1973).

The Beggar's Opera, ed. Bryan Loughrey and T. O. Treadwell (Harmondsworth, 1986).

Three Hours after Marriage, ed. John Harrington Smith (Los Angeles, 1961). This edition reproduces the variant five-act version of the play.

BIBLIOGRAPHIES

KLEIN, JULIE THOMPSON, *John Gay: An Annotated Checklist of Criticism* (New York, 1974).

NOKES, DAVID, and BARRON, JANET, 'John Gay', in *An Annotated Critical Bibliography of Augustan Poetry* (Hemel Hempstead, 1989), 86–91.

BIOGRAPHIES

GAYE, PHOEBE FENWICK, *John Gay* (London, 1938). A gossipy, unscholarly, and unreliable biography which fills in the factual gaps with unreliable surmises.

IRVING, WILLIAM HENRY, *John Gay: Favorite of the Wits* (Durham, NC, 1940). A careful and scholarly examination of Gay's life and works which makes sensible use of the limited documentary material available.

SHERWIN, OSCAR, *Mr Gay: Being a Picture of the Life and Times of the Author of 'The Beggar's Opera'* (New York, 1929). An impressionistic book which attempts the style of a showbiz memoir rather than a literary biography.

SPACKS, PATRICIA MEYER, *John Gay* (New York 1965). A useful biographical introduction which studies Gay's use of literary masks.

FULL-LENGTH STUDIES

ARMENS, SVEN, *John Gay: Social Critic* (New York, 1954). Argues that Gay should be seen not as a miniaturist, pastoralist, or lightweight entertainer, but as a serious and consistent social critic.

FORSGREN, ADINA, *John Gay: Poet 'Of a Lower Order'* (2 vols., Stockholm, 1964–71). A scholarly and perceptive study of Gay's pastoral styles.

IRVING, WILLIAM HENRY, *John Gay's London* (Cambridge, Mass., 1928; repr. 1968). Using extensive quotations from Gay and his contemporaries, Irving discusses the literary presentation of urban scenes and topical issues.

LEWIS, PETER, and WOOD, NIGEL (eds.), *John Gay and the Scriblerians* (London, 1988). Undoubtedly the most important collection of recent critical essays on John Gay.

NOBLE, YVONNE, (ed.), *Twentieth Century Interpretations of The Beggar's Opera* (Englewood Cliffs, NJ, 1975). A useful collection of critical essays.

SCHULTZ, WILLIAM EBEN, *Gay's 'Beggar's Opera': Its Content, History and Influence* (New Haven, Conn., 1923). Although many of Schultz's assumptions have subsequently been questioned, this remains a useful scholarly study of all aspects of the opera.

WINTON, CALHOUN, *John Gay and the London Theatre* (Lexington, Ky., 1993). A brisk, sensible account of Gay's theatrical career.

CRITICAL AND SCHOLARLY ESSAYS

AULT, NORMAN, 'Help for Gay', in *New Light on Pope* (London, 1949; repr. 1967), 207–21. Considers the question of attribution of several minor works.

BATTESTIN, MARTIN C., '"Menalcas' Song"': The Meaning of Art and Artifice in Gay's Poetry', *Journal of English and German Philology*, 65 (1966), 662–79. An interesting study of art and nature in Gay's pastoral comedy.

—— *The Providence of Wit* (Oxford, 1974). Contains a useful chapter of Gay's metaphorical vocabulary.

BRONSON, BERTRAND, '*The Beggar's Opera*: Studies in the Comic', *University of California Publications in English*, 8/2 (Berkeley, Calif., 1941), 197–231. Examines the operatic sources for Gay's musical satire.

BROWN, WALLACE CABLE, 'Gay, Pope's Alter-Ego', in *Triumph of Form: A Study of the Later Masters of the Heroic Couplet* (Chapel Hill, NC, 1948), 45–66. Compares the couplet usage of Pope and Gay.

CROFT, P. J., (ed.), *Autograph Poetry in the English Language* (2 vols., London, 1973). Contains the first publication of Gay's lines on Heidegger (pp. 64–7).

EMPSON, WILLIAM, '*The Beggar's Opera*: Mock-Pastoral as the Cult of Independence', in *Some Versions of Pastoral* (London, 1935). A persuasive and influential essay which argues that Gay's opera celebrates an ironic collaboration between aristocrats and swains at the expense of the bourgeoisie.

KERNAN, ALVIN B., *The Plot of Satire* (New Haven, Conn., 1965). Contains an interesting chapter on Gay's *Trivia*.

KRAMNICK, ISAAC, 'John Gay—Beggars, Gentry and Society', in *Bolingbroke and his Circle* (Cambridge, Mass., 1968), 223–30. Considers Gay's satiric attacks on commercial values as part of a sustained nostalgic humanist critique of an emerging capitalist society.

NOKES, DAVID, 'Shepherds and Chimeras' and 'Businessman, Beggar-Man, Thief', in *Raillery and Rage: A Study of Eighteenth-Century Satire* (Brighton, 1987), 122–49. A detailed study of Gay's ironic vocabulary in *The Shepherd's Week* and *The Beggar's Opera*.

REES, CHRISTINE, 'Gay, Swift, and the Nymphs of Drury-Lane', *Essays in Criticism*, 23/1 (Jan. 1973), 1–21. A witty study of literary parallels with Gay's Newgate 'nymphs'.

SHERBO, ARTHUR, 'John Gay: Lightweight or Heavyweight?', *Scriblerian*, 8/1 (1975), 4–8. Sherbo divides Gay's recent critics into two rival camps; the 'heavyweights', who see him as a serious social critic; and the 'lightweights', who see him as a charming entertainer.

SHERBURN, GEORGE, 'The Fortunes and Misfortunes of *Three Hours after Marriage*', *Modern Philology*, 24 (1926), 91–109. A valiant scholarly attempt to disprove the traditional accounts of this play's 'failure'.

SUTHERLAND, JAMES, '*Polly* among the Pirates', *Modern Language Review*, 37 (1942), 291–303. A bibliographical study of pirate editions of *Polly*.

—— 'John Gay', in *Pope and his Contemporaries: Essays Presented to George Sherburn* (Oxford, 1949), 201–14. An essay, characteristic of its period, which presents Gay as an 'Augustan Peter Pan'.

SWAEN, A. E. H. 'The Airs and Tunes of Gay's *Polly*', *Anglia*, 60 (1936), 403–22. A discussion of Gay's musical sources.

WARNER, OLIVER, *John Gay*, Writers and their Work 171 (London, 1964). A brief and fairly superficial introduction.

WORKS OF RELATED INTEREST

Gay's heterogeneous writings impinge upon so many areas of early eighteenth-century life from Italian opera to the South Sea Bubble, and from the Hanoverian court to Newgate prison, that a complete list of contextual studies would be virtually synonymous with a bibliography of Augustan literature and society. The following books, however, are worthy of particular attention, since they contain illuminating discussions of Gay's relationships with patrons and fellow writers, or provide valuable information about the specific cultural contexts within which he worked.

CHALKER, JOHN, *The English Georgic: A Study in the Development of a Form* (London, 1969).

DEUTSCH, O. E., *Handel: A Documentary Biography* (London, 1955).

EHRENPREIS, IRVIN, *Swift: The Man, his Works and the Age* (3 vols., London, 1962–83).

FOSS, MICHAEL, *The Age of Patronage: The Arts in Society 1660–1750* (London, 1971).

GOLDGAR, BERTRAND, *Walpole and the Wits: The Relation of Politics to Literature, 1722–42* (Lincoln, Nebr., 1976).

HUME, ROBERT D., *Henry Fielding and the London Theatre, 1728–1737* (Oxford, 1988).

LANG, PAUL HENRY, *George Frederic Handel* (New York, 1966).

LEES-MILNE, JAMES, *Earls of Creation* (London, 1962).

MACK, MAYNARD, *Alexander Pope: A Life* (New Haven, Conn., 1985).

NOKES, DAVID, *Jonathan Swift: A Hypocrite Reversed* (Oxford, 1985).

PAULSON, RONALD, *Hogarth* (3 vols., Rutgers University Press, 1991; Cambridge, 1992).

ROGERS, PAT, *Literature and Popular Culture in Eighteenth Century England* (Brighton, 1985).

INDEX

In general, works are listed under the name of the author. Peers are listed under their best-known title.